A Companion to Digital Art

WILEY BLACKWELL COMPANIONS TO ART HISTORY

These invigorating reference volumes chart the influence of key ideas, discourses, and theories on art, and the way that it is taught, thought of, and talked about throughout the English-speaking world. Each volume brings together a team of respected international scholars to debate the state of research within traditional subfields of art history as well as in more innovative, thematic configurations. Representing the best of the scholarship governing the field and pointing toward future trends and across disciplines, the *Blackwell Companions to Art History* series provides a magisterial, state-of-the-art synthesis of art history.

1 *A Companion to Contemporary Art since 1945*
edited by Amelia Jones
2 *A Companion to Medieval Art*
edited by Conrad Rudolph
3 *A Companion to Asian Art and Architecture*
edited by Rebecca M. Brown and Deborah S. Hutton
4 *A Companion to Renaissance and Baroque Art*
edited by Babette Bohn and James M. Saslow
5 *A Companion to British Art: 1600 to the Present*
edited by Dana Arnold and David Peters Corbett
6 *A Companion to Modern African Art*
edited by Gitti Salami and Monica Blackmun Visonà
7 *A Companion to Chinese Art*
edited by Martin J. Powers and Katherine R. Tsiang
8 *A Companion to American Art*
edited by John Davis, Jennifer A. Greenhill and Jason D. LaFountain
9 *A Companion to Digital Art*
edited by Christiane Paul
10 *A Companion to Public Art*
edited by Cher Krause Knight and Harriet F. Senie

A Companion to Digital Art

Edited by

Christiane Paul

WILEY Blackwell

This edition first published 2016

Registered Office
John Wiley & Sons, Ltd, The Atrium, Southern Gate, Chichester, West Sussex, PO19 8SQ, UK

Editorial Offices
350 Main Street, Malden, MA 02148-5020, USA
9600 Garsington Road, Oxford, OX4 2DQ, UK
The Atrium, Southern Gate, Chichester, West Sussex, PO19 8SQ, UK

For details of our global editorial offices, for customer services, and for information about how to apply for permission to reuse the copyright material in this book please see our website at www.wiley.com/wiley-blackwell.

Library of Congress Cataloging-in-Publication Data

Names: Paul, Christiane, editor.
Title: A companion to digital art / Edited by Christiane Paul.
Description: Hoboken : John Wiley & Sons Inc., 2016. | Includes bibliographical references and index.
Identifiers: LCCN 2015039613 (print) | LCCN 2015040809 (ebook) | ISBN 9781118475201 (cloth) | ISBN 9781118475188 (Adobe PDF) | ISBN 9781118475218 (ePub)
Subjects: LCSH: Computer art.
Classification: LCC N7433.8 .C615 2016 (print) | LCC N7433.8 (ebook) | DDC 776–dc23
LC record available at http://lccn.loc.gov/2015039613

A catalogue record for this book is available from the British Library.

Cover image: Scott Snibbe, *Deep Walls*, interactive video installation, San Francisco Museum of Modern Art, 2002. Reproduced by permission of Scott Snibbe.

Set in 10/12pt Galliard by SPi Global, Pondicherry, India

1 2016

Contents

List of Figures

Notes on Contributors

Anne Balsamo serves as the Dean of the School of Media Studies at The New School in New York City. Previously she was a faculty member at the University of Southern California in the Annenberg School of Communication and the Interactive Media Division of the School of Cinematic Arts. In 2002 she co-founded Onomy Labs, Inc., a Silicon Valley technology design and fabrication company that builds cultural technologies. From 1999 to 2002 she was a member of RED (Research on Experimental Documents), a collaborative research/design group at Xerox PARC that created experimental reading devices and new media genres. Her book *Designing Culture: The Technological Imagination at Work* (2011) offers a manifesto for rethinking the role of culture in the process of technological innovation in the 21st century. Her first book, *Technologies of the Gendered Body: Reading Cyborg Women* (1996), investigated the social and cultural implications of emergent biotechnologies.

Konrad Becker is a researcher, artist, and organizer. He is director of the Institute for New Culture Technologies/t0 and World-Information.Org, a cultural intelligence provider. As co-founder of the Public Netbase project in Vienna (1994–2006) he initiated numerous pioneering media projects in various domains, including electronic music. He has conceptualized and produced international conferences, as well as exhibitions and cultural interventions, and his work has been characterized by extensive cooperation with collectives and protagonists of new artistic practices. As an interdisciplinary researcher he investigates cultural and social implications of technology in information societies. His publications include texts on the politics of the infosphere that have been translated into several languages. His latest books in English include *Dictionary of Operations* (2012), *Strategic Reality Dictionary* (2009), *Critical Strategies in Art and Media*, co-edited with Jim Fleming (2010), *Deep Search: The Politics of Search beyond Google*, co-edited with Felix Stalder (2009). http://www.world-information.net.

Max Bense (1910–1990) was a German writer and philosopher of science, logic, aesthetics, and semiotics. Bense studied mathematics, physics, and philosophy in Bonn, Cologne (Germany), and Basle (Switzerland). From 1949 onward he was a professor of the philosophy of technology, scientific theory, and mathematical logic at the Technical

University of Stuttgart where he taught until 1976. In the late 1950s and the 1960s he was the key figure of the Stuttgart School, thought of as an experimental testing ground for rational aesthetics. Influenced by cybernetics and computer art, Bense devoted himself to creating a foundation for aesthetics based in information theory. He coined the term "information aesthetics" and tried to develop a scientifically sound and quantifiable aesthetic. Among his publications are *Aesthetic Information* (1957), *Mathematics and Beauty* (1960), *Aesthetica: An Introduction to New Aesthetics* (1965), *An Introduction to Information Theoretical Aesthetics* (1969), and *The Representation and Grounding of Realities: The Sum of Semiotic Perspectives* (1986).

Kyle Chayka is a writer and curator living in Brooklyn. He has contributed to publications including *The New Yorker*, *The New Republic*, *ARTnews*, and *Modern Painters*, covering art's intersection with technology and the rise of artists working on the Internet. His writing can be found in *Reading Pop Culture: A Portable Anthology* (2013) and he is the author of *The Printed Gun: How 3D Printing Is Challenging Gun Control* (2013). Chayka is the curator of *Dying on Stage: New Painting in New York* at Garis & Hahn Gallery and co-curator of *Shortest Video Art Ever Sold* and *National Selfie Portrait Gallery* at Moving Image art fair in New York and London.

Sarah Cook is a curator of contemporary art, writer, and new media art historian. She is the author (with Beryl Graham) of *Rethinking Curating: Art After New Media* (2010) and co-editor (with Sara Diamond) of *Euphoria & Dystopia* (2011), an anthology of texts about art and technology drawn from over a decade's research at the world-renowned Banff New Media Institute. Sarah Cook received her PhD in curating new media art from the University of Sunderland (2004) where she co-founded the online resource for curators CRUMB (http://www.crumbweb.org). She lectures and publishes widely and has curated exhibitions in Canada, the USA, New Zealand, Mexico City, across Europe, and online, which have been reviewed in publications including *Art Monthly*, *ArtForum*, *Mute*, *Rhizome*, and *we-make-money-not-art*. She has been invited an speaker at museums and galleries worldwide including Stedelijk Museum (Amsterdam), Tate (London), Centro Nacional de las Artes (Mexico), National Gallery of Canada (Ottawa), Istanbul Modern (Istanbul), and Fundacion Telefonica (Buenos Aires).

Sean Cubitt is Professor of Film and Television at Goldsmiths, University of London, Professorial Fellow of the University of Melbourne, and Honorary Professor of the University of Dundee. His publications include *Timeshift: On Video Culture* (1991), *Videography: Video Media as Art and Culture* (1993), *Digital Aesthetics* (1998), *Simulation and Social Theory* (2001), *The Cinema Effect* (2005), and *EcoMedia* (2005). He is the series editor for Leonardo Books at MIT Press. His current research focuses on the history and philosophy of visual technologies, media art history, as well as ecocriticism and mediation.

Annet Dekker is an independent researcher, curator, and writer and core tutor at Piet Zwart Institute, Rotterdam. In 2009 she initiated the online platform http://aaaan.net with Annette Wolfsberger; they coordinate artists-in-residences and set up strategic and sustainable collaborations with (inter)national arts organizations. Previously Annet worked as web curator for SKOR (2010–2012), was program manager at Virtueel Platform (2008–2010), head of exhibitions, education, and artists-in-residence at the Netherlands Media Art Institute (1999–2008), and editor of several publications on digital art and issues of preservation. In 2008 she began PhD research into strategies for documenting net art at the Centre for Cultural Studies, Goldsmiths University, London.

M. Beatrice Fazi is Research Fellow in Digital Humanities & Computational Culture at the Sussex Humanities Lab (University of Sussex, UK). Her research explores questions at the intersection of philosophy, science, and technology. Her current work investigates the limits of formal reasoning in relation to computation, and addresses the ways in which these limits shape the ontology of computational aesthetics. Through doing so, she aims to offer a reconceptualization of contingency within formal axiomatic systems, *vis-à-vis* technoscientific notions of incompleteness and incomputability.

Ben Fino-Radin is a New York-based media archaeologist specializing in the preservation of digital contemporary art and culture. Fino-Radin serves as Digital Repository Manager at the Museum of Modern Art's department of conservation, and as Adjunct Professor in NYU's Moving Image Archiving and Preservation program. In private practice Fino-Radin has advised museums and artists, including the Whitney Museum of American Art, artist Cory Arcangel, and the art collective JODI. Fino-Radin holds an MS and MFA in Library and Information Science and Digital Art, respectively, from Pratt Institute and is an alumnus of Rhizome at the New Museum where he formerly served as Digital Conservator.

Mary Flanagan pushes the boundaries of medium and genre across writing, visual arts, and design to innovate in these fields with a critical play-centered approach. As an artist she has created over twenty major works ranging from game-inspired systems to computer viruses and embodied interfaces to interactive texts,which are exhibited internationally. As a scholar interested in how human values are in play across technologies and systems, Flanagan has written more than twenty critical essays and chapters on games, empathy, gender and digital representation, art and technology, and responsible design. Her recent books include *Critical Play* (2009) and *Values at Play in Digital Games*, with Helen Nissenbaum (2014). Flanagan's work has been supported by grants and commissions from organizations including the British Arts Council, the National Endowment for the Humanities, the ACLS, and the National Science Foundation. Flanagan is the Sherman Fairchild Distinguished Professor in Digital Humanities at Dartmouth College, Massachusetts.

Rudolf Frieling graduated from the Free University in Berlin and received a PhD from the University of Hildesheim, Germany. As a curator, he worked at the International VideoFest Berlin (1988–1994) and at the ZKM Center for Art and Media in Karlsruhe (1994–2006). During that period he directed and co-edited the multimedia and publishing projects *Media Art Action* (1997), *Media Art Interaction* (2000), *Media Art Net 1/2* (2004/2005), and *40yearvideoart.de-part 1* (2006). Since 2006 he has been Curator of Media Arts at SFMOMA where he has curated the survey shows *In Collaboration: Early Works from the Media Arts Collection* (2008), *The Art of Participation: 1950 to Now* (2008/2009), and *Stage Presence: Theatricality in Art and Media* (2012). He also collaborated on the SFMOMA presentation of *Exposed: Voyeurism, Surveillance and the Camera* (2010). Frieling's recent commissions for SFMOMA's public spaces include *Bill Fontana: Sonic Shadows* (2010) and *Jim Campbell: Exploded Views* (2011/2012). He also is Adjunct Professor at the California College of Art in San Francisco and the San Francisco Art Institute.

Darko Fritz is an artist and independent curator. He studied architecture in Zagreb and fine art at the Rijksakademie in Amsterdam. Since 2000 his research on histories of international media art has resulted in several publications and exhibitions. In 2000 he curated the first retrospective exhibition of international, historical digital art, titled *I am Still Alive* (early computer-generated art and recent low-tech and Internet art) in Zagreb. He also curated the exibition *CLUB.NL—Contemporary Art and Art Networks from the Netherlands* (Dubrovnik, 2000); *Bit International—Computers and Visual Research, [New] Tendencies, Zagreb 1961–1973* (Neue Galerie, Graz, 2007 and ZKM, Karlsruhe, 2008); *Reconstruction: private=public=private=public=* (Belgrade, 2009); and co-curated *Biennale Quadrilaterale 3: Angles and Intersections* (Museum of Modern and Contemporary Art, Rijeka, 2009). In 2002 he published *A Brief Overview of Media Art in Croatia (Since the 1960s)* and edited the related database at the portal Culturenet. Supported by a grant from the Mondriaan Foundation, Amsterdam, he started the research project *The Beginning of Digital Arts in the Netherlands (1955–1980)* in 2010. Fritz is founder and program coordinator of the *grey) (area – space for contemporary and media art* (since 2006).

Matthew Fuller is the author of various books including *Media Ecologies, Materialist Energies in Art and Technoculture* (2007), *Behind the Blip, Essays on the Culture of Software* (2003), and *Elephant & Castle* (2011). He co-authored *Urban Versioning System v1.0* (2008) with Usman Haque and *Evil Media* (2012) with Andrew Goffey. Fuller is the editor of *Software Studies, a Lexicon* (2008) and co-editor of the journal *Computational Culture.* He is involved in a number of projects in art, media, and software and works at the Centre for Cultural Studies, Goldsmiths, University of London.

Philip Galanter is an artist, theorist, and curator. As assistant professor at Texas A&M University he conducts graduate studios in generative art and physical computing. Galanter creates generative hardware systems, video and sound art installations, digital fine art prints, and light-box transparencies, which have been shown in the United States, Canada, the Netherlands, Peru, Italy, and Tunisia. His research includes the artistic exploration of complex systems and the development of art theory bridging the cultures of science and the humanities. Galanter's writing has appeared in both art and science publications, and more recent publications have focused on computational aesthetic evaluation and neuroaesthetics. As a curator he collaborated with Douglas Repetto on the first *ArtBots* exhibits (2002 and 2003)—covered by CNN, NBC, NPR, *New York Times*, *Wired*, and *Nature*—and with Ellen Levy on *COMPLEXITY*, the first traveling fine art museum exhibition focused on complex systems and emergence.

Charlie Gere is Professor of Media Theory and History in the Lancaster Institute for Contemporary Arts, Lancaster University. He is the author of *Digital Culture* (2000/2008), *Art, Time and Technology* (2006), and *Community without Community in Digital Culture* (2012), co-editor of *White Heat Cold Logic: British Computer Art 1960–1980* (2009) and *Art Practice in a Digital Culture* (2010), as well as having written many chapters and papers on technology, art, and culture. In 2007, along with Jemima Rellie and Christiane Paul, he co-curated *Feedback*, an exhibition of art responsive to instructions, input, or its environment, at the LABoral Center in Gijon, Spain.

Olga Goriunova is an assistant professor at the Centre for Interdisciplinary Methodologies, University of Warwick. She is the author of *Art Platforms and Cultural Production of the Internet* (2012) and editor of *Fun and Software: Exploring Pleasure, Pain and Paradox in Computing* (2014). She curated the *Fun and Software* exhibitions in 2010–2011 (Arnolfini, Bristol, UK, and MU, Eindhoven, The Netherlands) and was previously involved in running the Runme.org software art repository and organizing the *Readme* software art festivals (2002–2006).

Beryl Graham is Professor of New Media Art at the School of Arts, Design and Media at the University of Sunderland and co-editor of CRUMB. She curated the international exhibition *Serious Games* for the Laing and Barbican art galleries, and has also worked with The Exploratorium, San Francisco, and San Francisco Camerawork. Her books include *Digital Media Art* (2003) and the edited anthology *New Collecting: Exhibiting and Audiences after New Media Art* (2014), and she co-authored, with Sarah Cook, *Rethinking Curating: Art After New Media* (2010). She has published chapters in many books including *New Media in the White Cube and Beyond* (2008), *Theorizing Digital Cultural Heritage* (2010), and *The 'Do-It-Yourself' Artwork* (2010). Dr. Graham has presented papers at conferences including "Navigating Intelligence" (Banff), "Museums and the Web" (Vancouver), and "Decoding the Digital" (Victoria and Albert Museum). Her PhD concerned audience relationships with interactive art in gallery settings and she has written widely on the subject for books and periodicals including *Leonardo*, *Convergence*, and *Art Monthly*. http://www.berylgraham.com.

Oliver Grau was appointed first Chair Professor for Image Science in the German-speaking countries at the Department for Image Science at Danube University in 2005. He has received several awards and his publications have been translated into thirteen languages. His main research areas are the history of media art, immersive images, emotion and immersion, the history of telepresence and artificial life, as well as digital humanities. His publications include *Virtual Art* (2003), *Mediale Emotionen* (2005), *MediaArtHistories* (2007), and *Imagery in the 21st Century* (2011). Grau has given keynotes at conferences and events worldwide, including the Olympic Games and the G20 Summit, and was founding director of the MediaArtHistories Conference Series. He conceived new scientific tools for image science, among others the first international archive for digital art (ADA, https://www.digitalartarchive.at/, since 1999). Since 2005 Grau has also been head of the Goettweig's Graphic Print archive (http://www.gssg.at). He serves as editorial board member of several international journals and was among the first elected members of the Berlin-Brandenburg Academy of Science.

Erkki Huhtamo is Professor of Media History and Theory in the Departments of Design Media Arts and Film, Television, and Digital Media at at the University of California Los Angeles. He is considered one of the founders of the discipline of media archaeology. His publications include *Media Archaeology, Approaches, Applications, and Implications*, co-edited with Jussi Parikka (2011), *Illusions in Motion: Media Archaeology of The Moving Panorama and Related Spectacles* (2013). He has curated numerous exhibitions and events, among them the major international exhibition *Alien Intelligence* (KIASMA Museum of Contemporary Art, Helsinki, 2000).

Jon Ippolito is a new media artist, writer, and curator and recipient of Tiffany, Lannan, and American Foundation awards. At the Guggenheim he curated *Virtual Reality: An Emerging Medium* (1993), the first art museum exhibition of virtual reality, and the 2000 Nam June Paik retrospective with John G. Hanhardt. As Associate Professor of New Media at the University of Maine, Ippolito founded a peer-to-peer digital badges initiative and a graduate Digital Curation program. At the Still Water lab, co-founded with Joline Blais, he helped build social software such as the Variable Media Questionnaire, The Pool, ThoughtMesh, and the Cross-Cultural Partnership. In over a hundred presentations, Ippolito has spoken out on copyright maximalism, academic insularity, and technological obsolescence. He has published articles in periodicals ranging from the *Art Journal* to the

Washington Post and chapters in over twenty books. Ippolito co-authored the book *At the Edge of Art* (2006) with Joline Blais and *Re-collection: Art, New Media, and Social Memory* (2014) with Richard Rinehart.

Aneta Krzemień Barkley is a researcher and curator who completed a collaborative PhD at the Centre for Architecture and Visual Arts (CAVA), University of Liverpool and FACT (Foundation for Art and Creative Technology) in Liverpool, UK. As part of her research—funded by the Arts and Humanities Research Council, UK—she co-curated *Turning FACT Inside Out* (2013), FACT's ten-year anniversary exhibition. Previously Aneta was Research Assistant at the Electronic and Digital Art Unit (EDAU) at the University of Central Lancashire (UClan) where she co-organized and co-curated a series of exhibitions and conferences (*Digital Aesthetic* 2007, 2012) and lectured in the School of Art, Design and Performance.

Machiko Kusahara started writing and curating in the field of digital art in the early 1980s. Since then she has written, lectured, curated, and served as a jury member internationally in the field of media art. Her research is focused in two related fields: media art in Japan today, including device art, and its relation to Japanese postwar avant-garde art; and media-archaeological research on early Japanese visual entertainment from the Edo-era magic lantern show and late 19th-century panorama to prewar optical toys. Kusahara is Professor of Media Art and Media Studies at Waseda University's School of Culture, Media, and Society in Tokyo. She holds a PhD from the University of Tokyo with a research focus on correlations between art, technology, and culture.

Lev Manovich is the author of *Software Takes Command* (2013), *Soft Cinema: Navigating the Database* (2005), and *The Language of New Media* (2001), as well as 120 articles on the history and theory of media, software culture, and digital art. Manovich is a professor at The Graduate Center, CUNY, and a Director of the Software Studies Initiative that works on the analysis and visualization of big cultural data. Manovich was born in Moscow where he studied fine arts, architecture, and computer programming. He moved to New York in 1981, receiving an MA in Experimental Psychology from New York University (1988) and a PhD in Visual and Cultural Studies from the University of Rochester (1993). Manovich has been working with computer media as an artist, computer animator, designer, and programmer since 1984. His art projects have been presented by venues such as Chelsea Art Museum (New York), ZKM (Karlsruhe), The Walker Art Center (Minneapolis), KIASMA (Helsinki), Centre Pompidou (Paris), ICA (London), and the Graphic Design Museum (Breda, NL).

Armin Medosch is a curator, writer, and artist working on topics such as media art, political avant-gardes, network culture, and interdisciplinary social and political theory. He was the founding editor of the award-winning international online magazine *Telepolis* (1996–2002) and has a track record as cultural producer, ranging from the curation of large exhibitions such as *Waves* (Riga, 2006 and Dortmund, 2008) to collaborative curatorial projects such as *Kingdom-of-Piracy* (2001–2006), co-curated with Shu Lea Cheang and Yukiko Shikata; and the organization of conferences such as *Good Bye Privacy!*, Ars Electronica's 2007 theme conference, and *Networks and Sustainability* (Riga, 2010). He earned a PhD in Arts and Computational Technology (ACT) from Goldsmiths, University of London in 2012 for his work on the international art movement New Tendencies. Current work includes the exhibition *Fields* as part of Riga Culture Capital 2014 and research on a new book on political art in the digital field.

Christiane Paul is Associate Professor at the School of Media Studies, The New School, and Adjunct Curator of New Media Arts at the Whitney Museum of American Art. Her recent books are *Context Providers—Conditions of Meaning in Media Arts* (Intellect, 2011; Chinese edition, 2012), co-edited with Margot Lovejoy and Victoria Vesna; *New Media in the White Cube and Beyond* (University of California Press, 2008); and *Digital Art* (Thames & Hudson, 2003 / 2008 / 2015). At the Whitney Museum she curated exhibitions including *Cory Arcangel: Pro Tools* (2011), *Profiling* (2007), *Data Dynamics* (2001), and the Net art selection for the 2002 Whitney Biennial, and is responsible for *artport*, the Whitney Museum's web site devoted to Internet art. Other curatorial work includes *The Public Private* (Kellen Gallery, The New School, 2013), *Eduardo Kac: Biotopes, Lagoglyphs and Transgenic Works* (Rio de Janeiro, Brazil, 2010); *Biennale Quadrilaterale 3* (Rijeka, Croatia, 2009–10); and *Feedforward—The Angel of History* (co-curated with Steve Dietz; LABoral, Gijon, Spain, October 2009).

Richard Rinehart is Director and chief curator of the Samek Art Gallery at Bucknell University. He has served as Digital Media Director and Adjunct Curator at the UC Berkeley Art Museum and as curator at New Langton Arts and for the San Jose Arts Commission. He juried for the Rockefeller Foundation, Rhizome.org, and other organizations. Rinehart has taught courses on art and new media at various institutions, among them UC Berkeley, UC Santa Cruz, and the San Francisco Art Institute. He served on the boards of the Berkeley Center for New Media, New Langton Arts, and the Museum Computer Network. He led the NEA-funded project "Archiving the Avant-Garde" to preserve digital art, and co-authored, with Jon Ippolito, *Re-collection: Art, New Media, and Social Memory* (2014). Rinehart's papers, projects, and more can be found at http://www.coyoteyip.com.

Edward A. Shanken writes and teaches about the entwinement of art, science, and technology with a focus on interdisciplinary practices involving new media. Recent academic posts include Visiting Associate Professor, DXARTS, University of Washington; Faculty of Media Art Histories, Donau University Krems; Hohenberg Chair of Excellence in Art History, University of Memphis; and Universitair Docent, New Media at University of Amsterdam. He edited and wrote the introduction to a collection of essays by Roy Ascott, *Telematic Embrace: Visionary Theories of Art, Technology and Consciousness* (2003). His critically praised survey *Art and Electronic Media* (2009) has been expanded with an extensive, multimedia Online Companion at www.artelectronicmedia.com. His most recent book, *Inventing the Future: Art—Electricity—New Media*, was published in Spanish in 2013 and is forthcoming in Portuguese and Chinese. Many of his essays are available on his web site, www.artexetra.com.

Nathaniel Stern is an artist, writer, and teacher. He is an associate professor of Art and Design in the Peck School of the Arts at the University of Wisconsin–Milwaukee; a research associate at the Research Centre, Faculty of Art, Design and Architecture, University of Johannesburg; and author of *Interactive Art and Embodiment: The Implicit Body as Performance* (2013).

McKenzie Wark is the author of *A Hacker Manifesto* (2004), *Gamer Theory* (2007), *The Beach Beneath the Street* (2011), *Telesthesia: Communication, Culture & Class* (2012), *The Spectacle of Disintegration* (2013), and various other publications. He teaches at the The New School in New York City.

Jennifer Way is an Associate Professor of Art History at the University of North Texas. Her recent publications about art and technology include "Back to the Future: Women Art Technology" in *Cyberfeminism 2.0* (2012); "Women Art Technology" in *Media N: Journal of the New Media Caucus Association* 2 (2012); and, with Morehshin Allahyari, "Digital/New Media Art and Contemporary Iran: Questions of Gender" in *Media N* (2013); as well as "Romantic Self-Exiles" in *Anglistica, An Interdisciplinary Journal* (2013). She serves on the editorial board for *Moebius, Journal of Critical Approaches to Culture and Technology*. "Women Art Technology," her ongoing research project, trains students to create an expanding digital database of oral history interviews with women who use digital technology in any capacity in the artworld.

Acknowledgments

First and foremost I would like to thank the authors who have contributed to this volume for sharing their insights and expertise and patiently working with me. All of them have played a role in shaping the field of digital art through their books and essays, artworks and exhibitions, conferences, initiatives, and organizations, and this *Companion* would not exist without their groundbreaking work over the course of many years or even decades.

My thanks also go to Jayne Fargnoli, the Executive Art History Editor at Wiley-Blackwell Publishing, for her trust and support of this project, and the project editor, Julia Kirk, for her guidance and patience throughout the editorial process.

I am deeply grateful to the Brown Foundation Fellows Program run by the the Museum of Fine Arts, Houston, and its director Katherine Howe for awarding me a residency at the Dora Maar House in Menerbes, France, which enabled me to work on this book in the most beautiful and inspiring environment. Special thanks to Gwen Strauss, the assistant director of the Brown Foundation Fellows Program, whose amazing hospitality and generosity made my stay in Menerbes so enjoyable. Big thanks also go to my co-fellows at the Dora Maar House, Kathy Grove and Greg Pierotti, for poetic journeys and inhouse nuits blanches, and to Marie Ducaté and Gwendolyn Owens for colorful art and conversations.

I am indebted to all the artists, scientists, inventors, programmers, and theorists whose work over more than half a century has created the history that made this book both possible and necessary.

Introduction

From Digital to Post-Digital—Evolutions of an Art Form

Christiane Paul

Compiling a companion to the vast territory of digital art is both an interesting challenge and an impossibility. It is inconceivable to cover all the histories, expressions, and implications of digital art in one volume, and almost all of the articles assembled here could each be expanded into a book of its own. Accepting its own impossibilities, this anthology strives to give a survey of the histories of digital art practice; the aesthetics of the art; the politics of digital media and network cultures and artistic activism; as well as the issues that digital art raises for the institution in terms of its presentation, collection, and preservation.

The challenge of creating a companion to digital art begins with defining the art form and delineating its territory. The terminology for technological art forms has always been extremely fluid and what is now known as digital art has undergone several name changes since it first emerged. Originally referred to as computer art, then multimedia art and cyberarts (1960s–1990s), art forms using digital technologies became digital art or so-called new media art at the end of the 20th century. The term "new media art" co-opted the label that, at the time, was used mostly for film/video, sound art, and various hybrid forms, and had been used throughout the 20th century for media that were emerging at any given time. The problematic qualifier of the "new" always implies its own integration, datedness, and obsolescence and, at best, leaves room for accommodating the latest emerging technologies. Some of the concepts explored in "new" media art date back almost a century—and others even several centuries, as a couple of chapters in this volume show—and have previously been addressed in various other traditional arts. The terms "digital art" and "new media art" are sometimes used interchangeably, but new media art is also often understood as a subcategory of a larger field of digital art that comprises all art using digital technologies at some point in the process of its creation, storage, or distribution. It is highly problematic to classify all art that makes use of digital technologies somewhere

A Companion to Digital Art, First Edition. Edited by Christiane Paul.

in its production and dissemination process as digital art, since it makes it almost impossible to arrive at any unifying statement about the art form.

Walking into any gallery or museum today, one will presumably encounter work that involved digital technologies at some point in its production: photographs that are digital chromogenic prints; videos that were filmed and edited using digital technologies; sculptures that were designed using computer-aided design (CAD) or produced using digital manufacturing processes, and so on. At the same time, these works present themselves in the form of finite objects or sequences of images as they would have done decades or even centuries ago when they were produced by means of various analog technologies. Most importantly, works that involve digital technologies as a production tool do not necessarily reflect on these technologies. The materiality and aesthetics of these digitally produced works are still radically different from those of an interactive web site that could be presented as an installation or projection, or experienced on a screen; or a sensor-based interactive installation that needs to be "performed" by the audience; or a work that takes a material form but involved and critically addresses digital technologies. One needs to distinguish between art that uses digital technologies as a tool for the production of a more traditional art object—such as a photograph, print, or sculpture; and the digital-born art that employs these technologies as a tool for the creation of a less material, software-based form that utilizes the digital medium's inherent characteristics, such as its participatory and generative features.

In this volume, digital art is predominantly understood as digital-born, computable art that is created, stored, and distributed via digital technologies and uses the features of these technologies as a medium. The digital artworks discussed in this book are computational; process-oriented, time-based, dynamic, and real time; participatory, collaborative, and performative; modular, variable, generative, and customizable, among other things. While these characteristics are not exclusive to digital art (some of them apply to different types of performative events or even video and installation art), they are not intrinsic to objects such as digital photographs or prints.

Digital art defined as born digital, and created, stored, and distributed via digital technologies, still is far from a unified category but can take numerous forms: (interactive and/or networked) installations; software or Internet art without any defined physical manifestation; virtual reality or augmented reality; locative media art distributed via mobile devices, such as smartphones, or using location-based technologies ranging from the global positioning system (GPS) to radio frequency identification (RFID). All of these manifestations of digital art projects will surface and be discussed in the following chapters.

As digital technologies have "infiltrated" almost all aspects of art making, many artists, curators, and theorists have already pronounced an age of the "post-digital" and "post-Internet" that finds its artistic expression in works both deeply informed by digital technologies and networks, yet crossing boundaries between media in their final form. The terms "post-digital" and "post-Internet" attempt to describe a condition of artworks and "objects" that are conceptually and practically shaped by the Internet and digital processes—taking their language for granted—yet often manifest in the material form of objects such as paintings, sculptures, or photographs. Post-digital and post-Internet capture a condition of our time and form of artistic practice and are closely related to the notion of a "New Aesthetic," a concept originally outlined by James Bridle at SXSW[1] and on his Tumblr (Bridle 2011). The condition described by the "post-" label is a new, important one: a post-medium condition in which media in their originally defined format (e.g., video as a linear electronic image) cease to exist and new forms of materiality emerge. However, the label itself is highly problematic in that it suggests a temporal condition while we are by no means *after* the Internet or the digital. Internet art and digital art, like good old-fashioned painting, are not obsolete and will continue to thrive.

Whether one believes in the theoretical and art-historical value of the post-digital, post-Internet, and New Aesthetic concepts or not, their rapid spread throughout art networks testifies to a need for terminologies that capture a certain condition of cultural and artistic practice in the early 21st century. At its core seems to lie a twofold operation: first, the confluence and convergence of digital technologies in various materialities; and second, the ways in which this merger has changed our relationship with these materialities and our representation as subjects. The post-digital and New Aesthetic capture the embeddedness of the digital in the objects, images, and structures we encounter on a daily basis and the way we understand ourselves in relation to them. The New Aesthetic, in particular, captures the process of seeing like and being seen through digital devices. The post-digital and New Aesthetic provide us with a blurry picture or perhaps the equivalent of a "poor image," as Hito Steyerl would understand it, a "copy in motion" with substandard resolution, a "ghost of an image" and "a visual idea in its very becoming," yet an image that is of value because it is all about "its own real conditions of existence" (Steyerl 2009). Both Kyle Chayka's essay on the impact of commercial social media on online artistic practice and Edward Shanken's text on the relationship between contemporary art and new media in this book engage with aspects of the post-digital and post-Internet culture.

The merger and hybridity of forms that has brought about the need for the current post-digital culture raises profound questions about medium-specificity and its usefulness in general. While we certainly live in a "convergence culture" (Jenkins 2006) in which content flows across multiple media platforms, it seems dangerous to abandon medium-specificity at a point where the intrinsics and aesthetics of the digital medium are far from understood or integrated into the artworld at large. The essays in Part IV of this volume, in particular, illustrate the challenges posed by the relationship between digital art and the institution. Overall, the texts assembled here make a contribution to an understanding of the specifics of the digital medium rather than abandoning these very specifics.

The four parts of this book—Histories of Digital Art; Aesthetics of Digital Art; Network Cultures: The Politics of Digital Art; Digital Art and the Institution—will each address specific topographical characteristics and challenges of the territory of digital art. At the same time, the essays in these sections build on similar ideas and are interlinked. It is not coincidental that certain motifs weave through the book and its different sections, emerging in completely different contexts.

One typically would not associate digital art with phantoms and ghosts, but "ghost stories" surface in various texts in this volume, testifying to the unstable relationship that media and "communication arts" of any kind have with the representation of the world. In his essay, Sean Cubitt talks about the iconography of the phantom in a history of failed or failing communication. Charlie Gere explores the hauntology of the digital image, using Jacques Derrida's term—a combination of the verb "haunt" and the suffix "-ology" that, in its French pronunciation, is almost indistinguishable from the word "ontology"—to argue that digital imagery breaks with the idea of the image as re-presentational and making present what it depicts. Konrad Becker references the anxieties about representations of reality that technological set-ups from the daguerrotype and phantasmagoria to the telegraph have produced. As Becker puts it, the history of communication machines is a ghost story. Another frequently emerging thread in this volume is that of the social as a core element of digital media and digital art. The essays by Sean Cubitt, Beatrice Fazi and Matthew Fuller, and Annet Dekker more or less explicitly underline that digital media create modes of existence, and that digital art is therefore not produced by the social but *is* social.

Histories of Digital Art

Artists have always quickly adopted and reflected on the culture and technologies of their time, and began to experiment with the digital medium decades before the "digital revolution" was officially proclaimed in the 1990s.

The years from 1945 onwards were formative forces in the evolution of digital media, marked by major technological and theoretical developments: digital computing and radar; cybernetics, formalized 1948 by Norbert Wiener; information theory and general systems theory; as well as the creation of ARPANET, the first manifestation of the Internet, in 1969. In the 1940s Norbert Wiener pointed out that the digital computer raised the question of the relationship between the human and the machine and coined the term "cybernetics" (from the Greek term *kybernetes* meaning "governor" or "steersman") to designate the important role that feedback plays in a communication system. In *Cybernetics: or, Control and Communication in the Animal and the Machine* (1948), Wiener defined three central concepts which he maintains were crucial in any organism or system—communication, control, and feedback—and postulated that the guiding principle behind life and organization is information, the information contained in messages.

The 1950s and 1960s saw a surge of participatory and/or technological art, created by artists such as Ben Laposky, John Whitney Sr., and Max Mathews at Bell Labs; John Cage, Alan Kaprow, and the Fluxus movement; or groups such as Independent Group/IG (1952/1954: Eduardo Paolozzi, Richard Hamilton, William Turnball et al.), Le Mouvement (Galerie Denise Rene in Paris 1955); ZERO (1957/1959: Otto Piene, Heinz Mack et al.); GRAV/Groupe de Recherche d'Art Visuel (1960–1968: Francois Morellet, Julio le Parc et al.); New Tendencies (1961–1973); The Systems Group (1969: Jeffrey Steele, Peter Lowe et al.). The fact that the relationship between art and computer technology at the time was often more conceptual was largely due to the inaccessibility of technology (some artists were able to get access to or use discarded military computers). Both Charlie Gere and Darko Fritz, in their respective essays, discuss these early groups, networks, and movements in their historical contexts.

While computers and digital technologies were by no means ubiquitous in the 1960s and 1970s, there was a sense that they would change society. It is not surprising that systems theory—as a transdisciplinary and multiperspectival domain comprising ideas from fields as diverse as the philosophy of science, biology, and engineering—became increasingly important during these decades. In an art context it is interesting to revisit the essays "Systems Esthetic" (1968) and "Real Time Systems" (1969) by Jack Burnham, who was contributing editor of *Artforum* from 1971 to 1973 and whose first book, *Beyond Modern Sculpture: The Effects of Science and Technology on the Sculpture of Our Time* (1968) established him as a leading advocate of art and technology. Burnham used (technologically driven) systems as a metaphor for cultural and art production, pointing to the "transition from an object-oriented to a systems-oriented culture. Here change emanates not from things but from the way things are done" (Burnham 1968). The systems approach during the late 1960s and the 1970s was broad in scope and addressed issues ranging from notions of the art object to social conditions, but was deeply inspired by technological systems. The notion of communication networks as open systems also formed the foundation of telematics—a term coined by Simon Nora and Alain Minc for a combination of computers and telecommunications in their 1978 report to French president Giscard d'Estaing (published in English as *The Computerization of Society*). During the 1970s artists started using "new technology" such as video and satellites to experiment with "live performances" and networks that anticipated the interactions that would later take place on the World Wide Web.

What is now understood as digital art has extremely complex and multifaceted histories that interweave several strands of artistic practice. One of these art-historical lineages can be traced from early instruction-based conceptual art to "algorithmic" art and art forms that set up open technological systems. Another lineage links concepts of light and the moving image from early kinetic and op art to new cinematic forms and interactive notions of television and cinema. Embedded in the latter is the evolution of different types of optical environments from illusion to immersion. These lineages are not distinct strands but interconnected narratives that intersect at certain points. Several of the contributors to this volume have written books that have made crucial contributions to an understanding of these histories. In *The Language of New Media* (2001), Lev Manovich has discussed new media and digital art within the histories of visual cultures throughout the last centuries, from cinematic devices and the language of film to the database as a new symbolic form. Oliver Grau has written a history of virtual art entitled *Virtual Art: From Illusion to Immersion* (2003), and Erkki Huhtamo, in *Illusions in Motion—Media Archaeology of the Moving Panorama and Related Spectacles* (2013), has analyzed the panorama as the origin of new modes of vision.

Instruction- and rule-based practice, as one of the historical lineages of digital art, features prominently in art movements such as Dada (which peaked from 1916 to 1920), Fluxus (named and loosely organized in 1962), and conceptual art (1960s and 1970s), which all incorporated variations of formal instructions as well as a focus on concept, event, and audience participation as opposed to art as a unified object. This emphasis on instructions connects to the algorithms that form the basis of any software and computer operation—a procedure of formal instructions that accomplish a "result" in a finite number of steps. Among the early pioneers of digital algorithmic art were Charles Csuri, Manfred Mohr, Vera Molnar, and Frieder Nake, who started using mathematical functions to create "digital drawings" on paper in the 1960s. The first two exhibitions of computer art were held in 1965: *Computer-Generated Pictures*, featuring work by Bela Julesz and A. Michael Noll at the Howard Wise Gallery in New York in April 1965; and *Generative Computergrafik*, showing work by Georg Nees, at the Technische Hochschule in Stuttgart, Germany, in February 1965. A close reading of instruction-based work is undertaken in Philip Galanter's essay for this book, which outlines a history of generative art and generative systems from ancient forms to the digital works that explore generative computer code in relationship to artificial life and intelligence as well as biological processes, such as Harold Cohen's *AARON* (1973–present) and Christa Sommerer and Laurent Mignonneau's *Life Writer* (2005).

The historical lineage connecting digital art to kinetic and op art artworks—which employ motion, light, optics, and interaction for the creation of abstract moving images—also resurfaces in various texts in this book. In scientific terms, kinetic energy is the energy possessed by a body by virtue of its motion, and kinetic art, which peaked from the mid-1960s to the mid-1970s, often produced movement through machines activated by the viewer. Kinetic art overlaps with the optical art or op art of the 1960s, in which artists used patterns to create optical illusions of movement, vibration, and warping. As Charlie Gere highlights in his essay, there was a direct connection between op art and the work of the Groupe de Recherche d'Art Visuel (GRAV). Inspired by op artist Victor Vasarely and founded in 1960 by Julio Le Parc, Vera Molnar, and Vasarely's son Yvaral, GRAV created scientific and technological forms of art by means of industrial materials, as well as kinetic works and even interactive displays. The term "op art" first appeared in print in *Time* magazine in October 1964, but works falling into the op art category had been produced much earlier. Duchamp's *Rotary Glass Plates (Precision Optics)*, for example, which was created in 1920 with Man Ray, consisted of an optical machine and invited users to turn on the apparatus and stand at a certain distance from it in order to see the effect unfold. The influence of these pieces, such as Laszlo Moholy-Nagy's kinetic light sculptures and his concept of virtual volumes as an outline or trajectory presented by an object in motion can be traced in quite a few digital art installations.

From the 1990s up to today, the rapidly evolving field of digital art again went through significant changes. In the early 1990s digital interactive art still was a fairly new field within the artworld at large, and many artists developed their own hardware and software interfaces to produce their work. In the new millennium, off-the-shelf systems increasingly began to appear and they broadened the base for the creation of digital art. In addition, digital media programs, departments, and curricula were formed and implemented around the world, often spearheaded by leading artists in the field. Since digital art did not play a major role on the art market and artists were not able to support themselves through gallery sales, many of them started working within academic environments. The proximity to academic research centers and laboratories provided an ideal context for many of these artists. From 2005 onwards, so-called "social media" platforms gained momentum and exploded and, at the same time, the "do it yourself" (DIY) and "do it with others" (DIWO) movements, supported by access to cheap hardware and software interfaces, became increasingly important forces.

The articles in this section construct a "higher resolution" picture of very different aspects of the histories of digital art, ranging from archiving to the history of digital networks and from histories of feminist digital art and generative art to the history of the presentation of digital artwork. Oliver Grau outlines the range of complex topics that digital art has explored over time—ranging from globalization and ecological and economic crises (virtual economy) to media and image revolutions—and argues that digital art is uniquely equipped to reflect on the most pressing issues of our time. Grau surveys the evolution of "image worlds" and their integration into image history and the problems of documentation of media art today. He argues for collective strategies in creating archives of digital art in order to create new structures and tools for media art research and the humanities.

Darko Fritz tells the story of the international networks of early digital arts, groups of people around the world who engaged with the creative use of computers in an art context and shaped the frameworks in which we encounter and understand digital art today. Looking back to the Institute of Electrical and Electronics Engineers (IEEE) and its Computer Society, which had its roots in the late 19th century, and the Association for Computing Machinery (ACM), established in 1947 and organizing an annual Computer Arts Festival since 1968, Fritz shows how science- and technology-based alliances gradually arrived at a broader understanding of culture. Fritz follows the evolution of several initiatives that began to explore the relationship between art, science, and technology in the 1960s, such as New Tendencies (1961–1973) and Experiments in Art and Technology (E.A.T.), conceived in 1966. Starting out in Zagreb in 1961 as an international exhibition presenting instruction-based, algorithmic, and generative art, New Tendencies became an international movement and network that provided an umbrella for a certain type of art and ultimately struggled with delineating its many forms. Other groups discussed include the Computer Arts Society (CAS), founded in 1968 by Alan Sutcliffe, George Mallen, and John Lansdown; and its American branch CAS US; as well as the Research Center Art Technology and Society, established in Amsterdam in 1967 by Robert Hartzema and Tjebbe van Tijen who co-wrote a critical manifesto calling for a debate about the role of artists and designers in world fairs. Fritz also surveys the emergence of significant magazines on electronic and digital arts in the late 1960s and throughout the 1970s and follows their legacy to current organizations and networks such Ars Electronica and ISEA International. His narrative perfectly illustrates how very similar identity struggles between arts, technology, and industry, and their respective agendas, surface in different constellations throughout history.

A different approach to telling a history of digital art, rooted in media archaeology, is provided in Erkki Huhtamo's contribution to this volume. As a discipline, media archaeology questions technological determinism and focuses on the range of factors that influence the formation of media culture. Huhtamo discusses the relationship between art and technology in the 1950s and 1960s, as well as archaeologies of projection and traces the history of media-archaeological art—art that in its form and content engages with the evolution of technologies and their related concepts. The works of artists Toshio Iwai and Paul DeMarinis are used as examples of creating alternative archaeologies of moving images and sounds. Histories of digital art tend to be Euro- or US-centric, ignoring the fact that artists around the world have been exploring technological and digital art forms. Japan and South America, in particular, have a rich history of artistic experimentation with technological art forms that cannot be comprehensively addressed in this book. In her contribution to this volume Machiko Kusahara takes a look at postwar Japanese avant-garde art of the 1950s and 1960s—and its social and political context—as a proto-media art. Not coincidentally, Japanese art groups and their activities have received renewed attention in the past decade, with several major exhibitions devoted to them—among them *Gutai: Splendid Playground* (Guggenheim, New York, 2013) and *Tokyo 1955–1970: A New Avant-Garde* (MoMA, New York, 2012–2013).

Philip Galanter uses one of the key characteristics of the digital medium—its potential for being generative—as a lens through which to tell a history of the art form. In his comprehensive survey of generative art theory, Galanter develops a specific definition of generative art and uses concepts from complexity science to both trace common features among different types of generative art throughout history and discuss specifics of digital generative art. As Galanter defines it, the term "generative art" describes any art practice in which the artist hands over control to a system with functional autonomy that then contributes to or creates a work of art. The essay provides a survey of the many forms this system can take, from natural language instructions and mathematical operations to computer programs and biological systems. Galanter's understanding of digital generative art strives to provide an umbrella that covers the whole spectrum of generative art communities in the field, including computerized music, computer graphics and animation, VJ culture, glitch art, open source tools, and others. His essay chronicles the lineage of generative art from Islamic art and architecture and ancient tilings, through LeWitt's wall drawings and Carl Andre's sculptures, to the chance operations of John Cage and William Burroughs and the generative artificial life works of Christa Sommerer and Laurent Mignonneau.

Both Erkki Huhtamo and Jennifer Way discuss the work of female artists working in the field of digital media, and Way more comprehensively explores feminist approaches to engaging with digital technologies. She examines how women's identities, needs and priorities intersect with digital technologies; how feminist artists created alternatives to the mainstream representations of women in digital culture; and how female artists approached networked feminism, DIY feminism, technofeminism, hacktivist pedagogy, and fabriculture.

Charlie Gere's text provides a historical and philosophical foundation for the examination of digital aesthetics that is undertaken in the second section of this book. Using images from the early history of digital art as a starting point, he examines the idea of the digital image as a form of writing, in the sense articulated by Jacques Derrida who in turn built on the writings of James Joyce. The title of Gere's essay, "The Hauntology of the Digital Image," conflates the title of André Bazin's famous 1958 article "The Ontology of the Photographic Image" with Derrida's notion of "hauntology," which describes a spectralizing force that is neither living nor dead, present nor absent. While Derrida sees the hauntological at play in the media themselves, Gere argues that the digital image is particularly hauntological: encoded and constructed in binaries—ones and zeroes, on and off states—it constitutes a more pronounced disconnect between a representation and the subject/object it represents. Gere uses Leon Harmon and Ken Knowlton's famous series *Studies in Perception*, created at Bell Labs in the 1960s, and their 12-foot-long computer-generated mural of a nude consisting of bitmapped fragments, as a point of departure for understanding the digital image as encryption, glyph, and written mark, as a form of writing. His essay establishes a range of artistic and literary connections, between the work done at Bell Labs, and post-structuralist French theory (in their privileging of writing), as well as avant-garde art of the 1960s. Drawing on Derrida's reading of James Joyce's work for understanding the emerging world of new information and communications technologies, Gere also establishes links between bitmapping, hypertext, "word processing," and early personal computing.

By examining the histories and experiences of presenting participatory artworks Rudolf Frieling both picks up on some of the issues of documentation outlined by Oliver Grau in the first chapter in this section and lays the groundwork for Beryl Graham's analysis of the need for documenting exhibitions in the final chapter in this book. Frieling's text underscores one of the most crucial elements in telling digital art's history: the fact that digital artworks seldom are static objects but evolve over time, are presented in very different ways over the years, and adapt to changing technological environments.

Aesthetics of Digital Art

Aesthetics is a complex philosophical territory in the first place, and the hybridity of the digital medium makes it particularly challenging to develop a more or less unified aesthetic theory. Each of the distinguishing aesthetic characteristics of the digital medium—which do not necessarily all surface in one work and occur in varying combinations—poses its own set of challenges for the development of a cohesive theoretical framework. As mentioned before, digital artworks are computational and can be time-based and dynamic, interactive and participatory, generative, customizable, and variable. The time-based nature of digital art tends to be more difficult to grasp than that of traditional film or video, which ultimately still present themselves as linear, finished works. Digital art, however, is potentially time-based, dynamic, and non-linear: even if a project is not interactive in the sense that it requires direct engagement, the viewer may look at a visualization driven by real-time data flow from the Internet that will never repeat itself, or a database-driven project that continuously reconfigures itself over time. A viewer who spends only a minute or two with a digital artwork might see only one configuration of an essentially non-linear project. The context and logic of a particular sequence may remain unclear. Every art project is embedded in a context, but audiences of digital art might require layers of contextual information, both relating to the materiality of the work and the logic behind its process, and transcending the work itself. The characteristics of digital art require an understanding of computational processes that cannot be taken for granted among an art audience at large.

In her writings on digital aesthetics, Claudia Giannetti (2004) has pointed out that a digital aesthetics requires models that are largely process-based, contextual, and interrelational, and has analyzed digital aesthetics in its embeddedness in the larger context of art, science, and technology, as well as cybernetics and communication. Katja Kwastek, in her book *Aesthetics of Interaction in Digital Art* (2013), uses theories of aesthetics based on process, play, and performance as a starting point for developing a model around real and data space, temporal structures, and relationships between materiality and interpretability.

The development of an aesthetics of the digital is commonly approached by examining the above-mentioned characteristics of the medium, as well as modes of digital mediation. The challenges of this endeavor are nicely illustrated in Philip Galanter's text on theories of generative art in the historical section of this volume. Galanter outlines the complexities of understanding just a single feature of the digital—in this case generativity—in its intersection with non-digital art forms.

The texts brought together in Part II of this volume offer an array of approaches to defining an aesthetics of the digital, ranging from the attempt to develop a medium-independent vocabulary that still highlights specificities of the digital to an analysis of characteristics such as interactivity and the computational. The section opens with the only text that was not written for this volume, "Small Abstract Aesthetics" (1969) by philosopher and writer Max Bense (1910–1990) who started teaching at the University of Stuttgart in 1949 and became the leader of the "Stuttgart school," which focused on semiotics and concrete poetry. Bense's work in the philosophy of science and information aesthetics—a discipline he founded along with Abraham A. Moles, who took a slightly different approach to the field—proved to be influential for digital art in that it outlined a computational aesthetics. While Bense approached computational aesthetics in a quite literal sense—as the possibilities of mathematically calculating aesthetics—his theories nevertheless opened up new ways of thinking about the aesthetics of art forms that are coded and written as algorithms. Bense based his investigations of mathematical principles in the history of art on the investigations of the American mathematician George David Birkhoff (1884–1944) who made the first attempts at formalizing enjoyment of art as an unconscious calculation of proportions and introduced the concept of the Esthetic Measure, defined as the ratio between order and complexity. Bense developed a model of aesthetic judgments similar to Birkhoff's, using his formula of the interplay of complexity, but introducing mathematician Claude Shannon's (1916–2001) notion of input and output of information. Philip Galanter references Bense's contributions to generative aesthetics in his discussion of the relationship between order and complexity in generative art.

Sean Cubitt's essay on digital aesthetics takes a much more general approach by focusing on three qualities that could be seen as part of all aesthetic experience—the non-identical, ephemeral, and unknowable—and shows how these qualities have specific valences in digital art, distinguishing it from other art forms. Cubitt strives to develop a meta-vocabulary that both does justice to the specificity of digital aesthetics and connects it to other artistic practices, acknowledging that digital art covers a spectrum from the deeply conceptual to "retinal art" that stands in the tradition of visual pleasure. Referencing Žižek's notion of "unknown knowns" as the unconscious of our time, Cubitt analyzes aspects of the digital as unknown knowledge, an approach that becomes a starting point for Beatrice Fazi and Matthew Fuller's proposal for a computational aesthetics that discovers and invents the unfamiliar and nameless, and that which is yet to be known. As Fazi and Fuller put it, computational aesthetics must construct its own concepts. Fazi and Fuller focus on the essential characteristic that both precedes and grounds the digital: computation as a method and force of organization, quantification, and rationalization of reality. Showing how digital art is inherently interwoven with features of digital structures, Fazi and Fuller examine ten aspects of computational aesthetics, among them abstraction and concreteness, discreteness, axiomatics, speed, and scale. As they make clear, computation is not simply a technical strategy of automation and distribution, but has its social and cultural manifestations. Scalability as one aspect of the computational, for example, is deeply linked to the development of platforms for cultural expression, affecting the expression of individual histories, as well as social and cultural forces.

For Cubitt, one of the conditions of the social in the digital era is alienation from the natural, technical, and data environments, which thereby become unknown knowns of the present. Fazi and Fuller strive to capture the unknown as an "unnameable familiarity" of certain patterns that reverberate through art installations, office work, and social forms. They argue that—to the extent that computation produces modes of existence—computational aesthetics is not produced by the social but *is* social, a notion that resonates throughout this volume. In her contribution Olga Goriunova understands digital art as processes of emergence and focuses on how the art "becomes" and how its modes of becoming evolved over the past two decades. She explores forms of mediation such as relationality, collaboration, and technicity as aspects of live processes and thereby of digital art's emergence. Goriunova treats art platforms as an environment for work that, while existing within an aesthetic register, has not yet become art but promises new forms and aesthetic concepts, and approaches digital aesthetics as a perceptual and affective register of life.

The propositions made by Cubitt, Fazi and Fuller, as well as Goriunova, are complemented by Nathaniel Stern's examination of interactive artworks as interventions in and into process. Stern argues that these works create situations that enhance, disrupt, and alter experience and action by staging embodiment as moving-thinking-feeling—as the body's potential to vary and its articulation of both the actual and virtual. In his analysis he draws upon Mark B.N. Hansen's reading of Maurice Merleau-Ponty's phenomenology and differentiation between the "body-image" and the "body-schema," as well as N. Katherine Hayles's distinction between the culturally constructed body and contextual experiences of embodiment that are embedded in the specifics of place, time, and physiology. Through a close reading of works by Rafael Lozano-Hemmer, Camille Utterback, and Scott Snibbe, Stern addresses the mutual emergence of bodies and space, as well as the ways in which signs and bodies require one another to materialize, and bodies form expressive communities.

Interaction and the public in turn are the cornerstones of Anne Balsamo's investigation of so-called "public interactives," interactive experiences in public settings. Balsamo proposes three broad definitions of public interactives: as an art form evoking new perceptions; as devices shaping new technological literacies; and as a form of public communication for the purposes of exchange, education, entertainment, and cultural memory. Her aesthetic exploration focuses on the dynamics of cultural reproduction, the cultural values and experiences that are replicated in the development of public interactives and the ones that are newly created as technologies are developed for commercial purposes.

Network Cultures: The Politics of Digital Art

The history and aesthetics of digital art obviously cannot be separated from its social and political context. The technological history of digital art is inextricably linked to the military-industrial complex and research centers, as well as consumer culture and its associated technologies. From simulation technologies and virtual reality to the Internet (and consequently the World Wide Web), digital technologies were developed and advanced within a military context. In 1957, the USSR's launch of Sputnik at the height of the Cold War had prompted the United States to create the Advanced Research Projects Agency (ARPA) within the Department of Defense (DOD) in order to maintain a leading position in technology. In 1964, the RAND corporation, the foremost Cold War think-tank, developed a proposal for ARPA that conceptualized the Internet as a communication network without central authority. By 1969, the infant network was formed by four of the "supercomputers" of the time—at the University of California at Los Angeles, the University of California at Santa Barbara, the Stanford Research Institute, and the University of Utah. Named after its Pentagon sponsor, ARPANET came into existence in the same year Apollo landed on the moon.

John Whitney—whose work gained him the reputation of being the father of computer graphics—used tools that perfectly capture the digital medium's roots in the military-industrial complex. He employed an M-5 anti-aircraft gun director as the basic machinery for his first mechanical, analog computer in the late 1950s. Whitney would later use the more sophisticated M-7 to hybridize both machines into a 12-foot-high device, which he used for his experiments in motion graphics. The machine consists of multiple rotating tables, camera systems, and facilitated the pre-programming of image and motion sequences in a multiple-axis environment (Youngblood 1970, 208–210).

Given the deep connections between the digital medium and the military-industrial-entertainment complex, as well as the multiple ways in which digital technologies are shaping the social fabric of our societies—to a point where political action is named after the social media platform supporting it, as in "Twitter Revolution"—it does not come as a surprise that many digital artworks critically engage with their roots, and digital (art) activism has been an important field of engagement. In his essay on "Shockwaves in the New World Order of Information and Communication," Armin Medosch weaves a comprehensive narrative of political digital art practices as they have changed over time along with advances in technology and developments in the political economy. As Medosch points out, artists/activists early on realized that the form of media itself was political. On the background of the theories of emancipatory media production developed by Hans Magnus Enzensberger and Jean Baudrillard in the 1970s, Medosch explores the forces and concrete modalities of technological and economic change in order to assess how artists unlocked the emancipatory potential of media. Starting from TV art projects from the 1980s and 1990s, and the "camcorder revolution," his text traces radical art practices and strategies from tactical media (interventions into the media based on an immediacy of action) and "hacktivism" (the blend of hacking and activism) to electronic civil disobedience. Medosch also outlines how activist engagement shifted from tactical media to the notion of the commons in the 2000s, both due to the rising importance of intellectual property that needed protection in the digital domain and artists' realization that free and open source software (FOSS) was crucial in achieving sustainability. The essay examines these developments across a wide geographical range, from Eastern and Central Europe to the United States, Brazil, and India, providing an account of the ways in which digital activist/art practices created shockwaves in the new world order of information and communication.

Konrad Becker's essay builds on and complements Medosch's narrative by exploring how digital art practice can function as critical intelligence, doing more than simply propagating technical progress and addressing the challenges of a networked digital universe. Becker takes today's "creative imperative"—the diffusion of art into business practice and the realm of the creative industries earlier discussed by Medosch—as a starting point for unraveling the historical and conceptual complexities of today's digital environment. Delineating qualities of digital communication and interactive media, Becker shows how the information society and distribution of wealth have become increasingly reliant on the "intangible materials" of intellectual property and licensing rights. This intangibility in turn is tied to an asymmetric invisibility in which classification and analysis of data are not visible or accessible to society at large and create a non-information society for the majority. Becker's asymmetric invisibility mirrors Cubitt's concept of the unknown knowledge produced by the alienation of the data environment. Becker discusses the evolution of both the "creative empire" from the 19th century onwards and the anxieties about representations of reality that technological set-ups from the daguerrotype and phantasmagoria to the telegraph have produced. As Becker puts it, the history of communication machines is a ghost story. Sensors and software systems—supporting anything from biometrical passports to airline profiling and homing guidance systems—produce today's phantoms in the city and require that cultural intelligence address psycho-geographical analysis and representation of multidimensional spaces.

McKenzie Wark's contribution to the politics section exemplifies many of the concepts outlined by Armin Medosch and Konrad Becker, in using the mailing list Nettime, founded by Pit Schulz and Geert Lovink, as a case study for analyzing the artistic avant-garde of the 1990s. Nettime provided the platform on which many of artists, writers, and activists mentioned in Medosch's text engaged in "discursive interactions," as Wark puts it. Transnational in terms of its constituents, Nettime was an environment populated by people working at the intersection of digital media art, theory, and activism and largely critical of the dominant media theory at the time. Wark argues that Nettime was a convergence of three things characteristic of any avant-garde—thought, art, and action—and, as the historic avant-gardes before it, engaged in critical experiments with forms of organization. He interprets Nettime as an attempt to reject the theory of media that caters to the culture industry and spectacle and engages in the celebration of the type of "creativity" that Becker extensively critiques in his text. Wark's reading of Nettime perfectly captures the spirit of the digital art practice of the 1990s, a silver (not quite golden) age of an early social media environment that stands in stark contrast to the world of Web 2.0, which is addressed in Kyle Chayka's examination of art making on social media platforms. Considering prominent artworks of the Web 2.0 era—*Hyper Geography* (2011–) and *The Jogging* (2009–) among them—Chayka analyzes the platforms on which they have been created, such as Tumblr, and illustrates how these platforms problematize artistic work and change the status of both the image and author as the artwork perpetuates itself, losing fidelity and the ties to its creator.

Lev Manovich analyzes another important aspect of network culture that evolved along with Web 2.0: the rise of "big data"—the massive data sets that cannot be easily understood by using previous approaches to data analysis—and developments in data visualization as artistic practice. As Manovich points out, data visualization had not been part of the vernacular visual culture before the end of the 1990s, although it already emerged as a strong artistic practice in the 1990s. Using examples he surveys the work of artists who have challenged fundamental principles of the data visualization field by pioneering what Manovich defines as "media visualization," representations using visual media objects such as images and video instead rather than lines and graphs.

A discussion of network culture and its political aspects also requires the consideration of computer games, which have emerged as a dominant cultural form and area of artistic practice over the past couple of decades. Mary Flanagan's text addresses the concept of "critical play" as a productive paradox, posing the questions of how artists and creative practitioners can reflect upon the cultural beliefs, norms, and human values embedded in computer games, and how these games can be most effectively used to bring about political and social change. Flanagan makes three propositions—regarding the examination of dominant values, the notion of goals, and the creation of extreme and unfamiliar kinds of play—to illustrate how games can become a site of investigation for gender, politics, and culture, and how artists can design from a "critical play" perspective. Coming from very different perspectives, the chapters in this section strive to provide a framework for approaching the sociopolitical context of digital art and its history.

Digital Art and the Institution

For decades, the relationship between digital art and the mainstream artworld and institutions has been notoriously uneasy. When it comes to an in-depth analysis of the complexities of this relationship, a lot of groundwork remains to be done. Key factors in this endeavor are investigations of art-historical developments relating to technological and participatory art forms and their exhibition histories; as well as continuous assessment of the challenges that digital media art poses to institutions and the art market in terms of presentation, collection, and preservation. The essays in this section address these issues from various perspectives.

In the 21st century, contemporary art has increasingly been shaped by concepts of participation, collaboration, social connectivity, and performativity, as seen in the works of Tino Seghal, Rirkrit Tiravanija, Carsten Höller, and many others. Nicolas Bourriaud has described these artists' practice with the term "relational aesthetics," which he first used in 1996—in the catalogue for his exhibition *Traffic* at CAPC musée d'art contemporain de Bordeaux—and further discussed in his 1998 essay and 2002 book of the same name. He defines the relational aesthetics approach as "a set of artistic practices which take as their theoretical and practical point of departure the whole of human relations and their social context, rather than an independent and private space" (Bourriaud 2006, 163). Obviously, this set of artistic practices also is key to most of new media art in the age of the World Wide Web. Yet the prominent practitioners of new media art remain absent from the list of artists frequently cited by Bourriaud—despite the fact that he uses the new media terminology such as "user-friendliness," "interactivity," and "DIY" (Bishop 2004).

One could argue that the participatory, "socially networked" art projects of the 21st century, which have received considerable attention from art institutions, all respond to contemporary culture, which is shaped by networked digital technologies and "social media"—from the World Wide Web to locative media, Facebook, and YouTube—and the changes they have brought about. However, art that uses these technologies as a medium still remains largely absent from major exhibitions in the mainstream artworld. While art institutions and organizations now commonly use digital technologies in their infrastructure—"connecting" and distributing through their web sites, Facebook pages, YouTube channels, and Twitter tours—they still place emphasis on exhibiting more traditional art forms that reference technological culture or adopt its strategies in a non-technological way. Richard Rinehart's essay in this section takes a close look at the attention that digital art began to receive from mainstream art institutions around the turn of the millennium and the problems that surrounded the attempt to integrate it.

From an art-historical perspective, it seems difficult or dubious not to acknowledge that the participatory art of the 1960s and 1970s and the 1990s and 2000s were responses to cultural and technological developments—computer technologies, cybernetics, systems theory, and the original Internet/ARPANET from the mid-1940s onwards; and the World Wide Web, ubiquitous computing, databasing/data-mining, and social media from the 1990s onwards. While different in their scope and strategies, the new media arts of the 1960s and 1970s and today faced similar resistances and challenges that led to their separation from the mainstream artworld, respectively. Charlie Gere has argued that the idealism and techno-futurism of early computer arts at some point were replaced with the irony and critique of conceptual art

(Gere 2008), and Darko Fritz's discussion of the New Tendencies exhibitions and networks in this volume also shows the tension between digital and conceptual art.

Apart from historical baggage, the reasons for the continuing disconnect between new media art and the mainstream artworld lie in the challenges that the medium poses when it comes to the understanding of its aesthetics; its presentation and reception by audiences; as well as its preservation. Edward Shanken has researched this disconnect for many years, and his contribution to this book proposes that new media art has both tried to situate its practices within the theoretical and exhibition contexts of mainstream contemporary art and, at the same time, has developed its own theoretical language and institutional contexts. Shanken argues that the former attempts remained largely fruitless while the latter became so successful that an autonomous, but also isolated, new media artworld emerged. His essay outlines aspects of convergence and divergence between the two artworlds, as well as the changes that new means of production and dissemination have brought about for the roles of the artist, curator, and museum. Most importantly, Shanken examines what new media art and mainstream contemporary art have to offer each other in the process of generating critical discourse around the social impact of emerging technological media and cultural practices. He probes the possibilities of constructing a hybrid discourse that gives insights into mainstream contemporary art and new media art, respectively, while creating a basis for a productive mixing of their practices.

Using the metaphor of a marriage, Richard Rinehart explores the coupling of new media art and art institutions and the troubles and ups and downs in their relationship. His text focuses on the period from the late 1990s to the present, examining the shifts in the status of new media art that occurred with the advent of the World Wide Web and the hi-tech bubble of that period. Rinehart addresses the practical consequences of the conflation of the hi-tech industry and new media art on the operational and logistical level—a fusion previously critiqued in the essays by Armin Medosch and Konrad Becker—and shows how techno-positivist hyperbole affected the relationship between new media and the contemporary artworld. His text provides a close analysis of the watershed moment for new media art exhibitions in the United States that occurred when major museums mounted digital art shows in the early 2000s. Rinehart also raises the question why, even today, new media art is not collected by museums and private collectors on the scale at which it is exhibited and talked about. He ponders how the partnership between new media art and art institutions helps or hinders collection and preservation, and whether art museums are indeed the best places for these operations. In the process, Rinehart draws attention to the essential adjustment of perspective that new media art preservation requires: finding a common ground between the museological view that sees unique and original materiality as essential and the technological view that all computational activity is enacted at many layers that function as abstractions from physical materiality, making the latter replaceable.

Successful curation lies at the heart of presenting new media to a wide range of audiences and integrating it into the mainstream artworld. Many of the challenges surrounding the curation and preservation of new media art are related to its fusion of materiality and immateriality. Probably more than any other medium of art, the digital is embedded in various layers of commercial systems and technological industry that continuously define standards for the materialities of any kind of hardware components. The curation of new media works in the gallery environment requires a process of interfacing the digital. This process relates not only to delivery mechanisms but also to exchanges between the curator, artwork, and audience. The white cube creates a "sacred" space and a blank slate for contemplating objects. Most new media art is inherently performative and contextual —networked and connected to the "outside"—and often feels decontextualized in a white space. Curators have to accommodate the specific requirements of the different forms of new media art, ranging from (networked) installations and software art, virtual reality and augmented reality, to net art and locative media art distributed via smartphones, tablets, and other mechanisms. The variability and modularity of new media works implies that there usually are various possible presentation scenarios: artworks are often reconfigured for the specific space and presented in very different ways from venue to venue.

The challenges outlined above require new curatorial models and approaches. In new media art, the traditional roles of curators are redefined and shift to new collaborative models of production and presentation. The changes in the curatorial role tend to become most obvious in online curation, which by nature unfolds in a hyperlinked contextual network. As an art form that exists within a (virtual) public space and has been created to be seen by anyone, anywhere, at any time (provided one has access to the network), net art can be presented to the public independently of the institutional artworld and its structures of validation and commodification. Models for online curatorial practice range from the more traditional model of a single curatorial "filter" to multiple curatorial perspectives and forms of automated curating that integrate technology in the curatorial process.

In the mid-1990s an online artworld—consisting of artists, critics, curators, theorists, and other practitioners—developed in tandem with net art and outside of the institutional artworld. In the late 1990s, curatorial practice in the online world began to unfold not only independently of institutions —through projects by independent curators or organizations such as Rhizome and Turbulence—but also in an institutional context—through web sites affiliated with museums, such as the Walker Art Center's "Gallery 9," SF MOMA's "e-space" and the Whitney Museum's "artport." These different curatorial projects differ substantially in their respective interpretation of selection, filtering, and "gatekeeping" as fundamental aspects of the curatorial process.

Curators of digital art often function in distributed and multiple contexts, from online and experimental media spaces to traditional art institutions and gallery spaces within universities. Because new media art is deeply interwoven into our information society—the network structures that are creating new forms of cultural production—it will always transcend the boundaries of the museum and gallery and create new spaces for art. The process of curating new media both addresses and shapes the cultural implications of new media practice itself and its creation of spaces for production, dissemination, and reception.

These fundamental issues are tackled in Sarah Cook's and Aneta Krzemień Barkley's essay on the digital arts inside and outside of the institution. Exploring formats for exhibiting digital art that have emerged over time, the authors use the questions *who*, *when*, *what*, *where*, *how*, and *why* as a structure for approaching the curating of digital arts. As they point out, the new media landscape has been forming for over fifty years, and the critical study of curatorial practice is an even younger field that came into being only in the past three decades and long after art history or museology. While many contributions have been made over the last decade, the analysis of curatorial practice in the field of digital arts still is largely uncharted territory. Cook and Krzemień Barkley both sketch out an overview of curatorial approaches and use selective examples to illustrate curatorial models within institutions and on the "peripheries" of institutional practice. They also address the social contexts in which digital art has emerged—the grass-roots, ad-hoc, and temporary get-togethers and initiatives that developed along with or even tried to counter the commercial digital landscape.

One of the biggest challenges of integrating digital art into the mainstream artworld and nurturing its collectability has been the preservation of this art form. Digital art is engaged in a continuous struggle with an accelerating technological obsolescence that serves the profit-generating strategies of the tech industry. Over the past fifteen years numerous initiatives, institutions, and consortia have been hard at work to establish best practices for the preservation of digital art. While it is beyond the scope of this book to give an in-depth survey of this work, a couple of the texts in the final section of this volume specifically engage with the preservation of digital art. Ben Fino-Radin's chapter on tools, methods, and strategies of digital conservation gives an introduction to the nuts and bolts of this emerging field of practice. Grounded in the theory and ethics of conservation, his text provides hands-on technical guidance and uses case studies to illustrate how tools and methods can be applied. He surveys the process of "learning the work" through the initial conservation assessment and artist interview; the capture and storage of the piece; and the role of emulation, virtualization, as well as recreation, reinterpretation, and replacement as preservation strategies.

Jon Ippolito's "Trusting Amateurs with Our Future" shifts the focus of preservation to practices outside of the institution. He addresses "unofficial" preservation practices and illustrates why they can sometimes be more effective than professional endeavors. As Ippolito points out, only a tiny portion of new media artworks created since 1980 has been preserved, while a massive portion of video games has been restored and kept alive by a global community of dispersed amateurs. Ippolito proposes to keep multilayered technological culture alive through "proliferative preservation" that writes new versions of a work into the "cultural niche" formerly occupied by a single version and employs the benefits of crowdsourcing to offset the range of quality that amateur contributions yield. He also engages with the problematic aspects of amateur preservation, such as the loss of artistic integrity that might result from deviations from a work's original intent, and the loss of material context, such as the detachment of a work from its original hardware, which easily occurs once amateurs reinterpret new media projects. Ippolito's text shows how a symbiotic arrangement between amateurs and professionals might provide an injection of creativity and vitality to traditional preservation.

In her essay, Annet Dekker uses work by the artist duo JODI as a case study for rethinking the relationship between preservation and documentation. Over a period of roughly a decade, JODI created a series of projects based on the computer game *Jet Set Willy*—*Jet Set Willy ©1984*, *Jet Set Willy Variations*, and *Jet Set Willy FOREVER*—that incorporated documentation of its own process in interesting ways. Analyzing JODI's work, Dekker distinguishes three different types of documentation: documentation as process (documentation being used as a tool in making decisions about the development of the work); documentation as presentation (creating audiovisual material about the work); and documentation for recreation of the work at a future point. Building on these distinctions, Dekker proposes the use of documentation as a main strategy for identifying authenticity, a determining factor in the decisions made in the conservation process. By means of concrete examples Dekker shows how the traditional signifiers of authenticity—material, authorship, and date—become fluid entities when applied to immaterial, multi-authored, process-oriented new media work and proposes the more speculative notion of authentic alliances, made up of very different constituents that nevertheless form a whole. The title of Dekker's text, "How to Survive FOREVER," could be read both as a strategy for achieving eternal life for artworks and a guideline for "surviving" a state of eternal existence created by ongoing documentation.

In the final chapter of this book, Beryl Graham both continues the discussion of documentation and picks up on Rudolf Frieling's exploration of the histories of the display of artworks over time. Graham proposes that the histories of exhibitions are of particular importance to new media art. She argues that it is not only the installation-based and interactive nature of much of new media art that makes these exhibition histories crucial but that the interconnected threads between art practice, criticism, collection, exhibition, and future historicization can be easily broken. A deep understanding of the systems and processes of digital art production and distribution are necessary for keeping these threads connected and ensuring the collection, exhibition, and historicization of digital art. Graham addresses the "behaviors" of artworks—live, social, participative—as well as the necessity of expanding the documentation of exhibitions to the documentation of its audiences.

Together, the texts in this volume provide a survey of key perspectives and discussions that have emerged since the advent of digital art more than fifty years ago. They give insight into the histories, aesthetics, politics, and social context of digital art as well as its relationship to institutions and its historicization, which is enabled by presentation, collection and preservation. Most importantly, the *Companion to Digital Art* points to the future of digital art, illustrating where it has been, where it might go, and what needs to be accomplished to support the art practice that plays the most vital role in opening up new perspectives—from critical to poetic—on today's technologically mediated environment.

Note

1 *The New Aesthetic: Seeing Like Digital Devices*, SXSW, March 12, 2012. http://schedule.sxsw.com/2012/events/event_IAP11102 (accessed September 24, 2015).

References

Bishop, Claire. 2004. "Antagonism and Relational Aesthetics." *October* 110: 51–79.

Bourriaud, Nicolas. 2002. *Relational Aesthetics.* Dijon: Les presses du réel.

Bourriaud, Nicolas. 2006. "Relational Aesthetics." In Claire Bishop, *Participation.* Cambridge, MA: Whitechapel Gallery, The MIT Press.

Bridle, James. 2011. "The New Aesthetic." Date accessed January 5, 2015. http://new-aesthetic.tumblr.com/ (accessed September 24, 2015).

Burnham, Jack. 1968a. *Beyond Modern Sculpture: The Effects of Science and Technology on the Sculpture of This Century.* New York: George Braziller.

Burnham, Jack. 1968b. "Systems Esthetic." *Artforum.*

Burnham, Jack. 1969. "Real Time Systems." *Artforum.*

Giannetti, Claudia. 2014. *Ästhetik des Digitalen: Ein intermediärer Beitrag zu Wissenschaft, Medien- und Kunstsystem.* Vienna, New York: Springer.

Gere, Charlie. 2008. "New Media Art and the Gallery in the Digital Age." In *New Media in the White Cube and Beyond*, edited by Christiane Paul. Berkeley, CA: University of California Press.

Grau, Oliver. 2003. *Virtual Art: From Illusion to Immersion.* The MIT Press.

Huhtamo, Erkki. 2013. *Illusions in Motion—Media Archaeology of the Moving Panorama and Related Spectacles.* Cambridge, MA: The MIT Press.

Jenkins, Henry. 2006. *Convergence Culture: Where Old and New Media Collide.* Cambridge, MA: The MIT Press.

Kwastek, Katja. 2013. *Aesthetics of Interaction in Digital Art.* Cambridge, MA: The MIT Press.

Manovich, Lev. 2001. *The Language of New Media.* Cambridge, MA: The MIT Press.

Steyerl, Hito. 2009. "In Defense of the Poor Image." *e-flux journal* #10. http://www.e-flux.com/journal/in-defense-of-the-poor-image/ (accessed September 24, 2015).

Youngblood, Gene. 1970. *Expanded Cinema.* Toronto and Vancouver: Clarke, Irwin & Company.

Part I

Histories of Digital Art

1

The Complex and Multifarious Expressions of Digital Art and Its Impact on Archives and Humanities

Oliver Grau

Introduction

Compared to traditional art forms—such as painting or sculpture—media art has more multifarious potential for expression and visualization; although underrepresented on the art market, which is driven by economic interests, it has become "the art of our time," thematizing complex challenges for our life and societies, like genetic engineering (Anker and Nelkin 2003; Reichle 2005; Hauser 2008; Kac 2007), the rise of post-human bodies (Hershman-Leeson 2007), ecological crises[1] (Cubitt 2005; Himmelsbach and Volkart 2007; Demos 2009; Borries 2011), the image and media revolution (Grau 2011; Mitchell 2011) and with it the explosion of human knowledge (Vesna 2007; Manovich 2011), the move toward virtual financial economies,[2] and the processes of globalization[3] and surveillance, to name just a few. Visually powerful, interactive media art, often supported by databases or the World Wide Web, is offering more and more freedom for creative expression and evidently is much better equipped to directly address the challenges of our complex times within the very medium that shapes them. Although it has been around for decades and has even quantitatively dominated many art schools, digital media art has not fully arrived in the core collecting institutions of our societies. Due to the lack of institutional support and rapid changes in storage and presentation media, works that originated approximately ten years ago can often not be shown anymore. It is no exaggeration to state that we are facing the "total loss of an art form" created in the early years of our post-industrial digital societies. Over the last fifty years digital media art has evolved into a vivid contemporary form. Although there are well-attended festivals worldwide,[4] funded collaborative projects, discussion forums, publications (Grau 2003a, 2011; Dixon 2007; Popper 2007; Sommerer and Mignonneau 2008; Vesna 2007; Shanken 2009; Da Costa and Kavita 2010; Gardiner and Gere 2010; Wilson 2010), and database documentation projects,[5]

A Companion to Digital Art, First Edition. Edited by Christiane Paul.

digital media art is still rarely collected by museums, barely supported within the mainframe of art history, and has relatively low accessibility for the general public and scholars.

Media Art's Revolution?

Media art is the art form using the technologies that fundamentally change our societies. Globalization, the information society, social networks, and Web 2.0—the list could be far longer—are enabled by digital technologies. Although not all digital media art comments on social, cultural, and political conditions, it is nevertheless the art form with the most comprehensive potential for cultural urgency. We know that digital art today is taking highly disparate forms, like time-based installation art, telepresence art, genetic and bio art, robotics, net art, and space art; this "art of our times" is experimenting with nanotechnology, artificial or A-life art; and creating virtual agents and avatars, mixed realities, and database-supported art. Through its expressive potential—visually, aurally, and beyond—all senses can be addressed, an ability which exceeds technically that of traditional art media from earlier centuries such as painting and sculpture; thus digital media art attains a key role in the reflection of our information societies. The artworks both represent and reflect on the revolutionary development that the image has undergone over the years—even as visionary demonstration of new instruments for visual analysis and tools for playful or scientific comparison of large amounts of images.[6]

Contemporary media art installations can include digital stills and video, 3D objects and animation, digital texts and music, sound objects, noises and textures, whereby different meanings may be inscribed and combined with each other. Meaning can develop by chance, experiment, and well-directed strategy. Active, "combining" users become the source for generating art and meaning if the artist leaves enough degrees of freedom to them to engage. They are dynamically involved in navigation, interpretation, transfer, contextualization, or production of images and sounds which may be generated by their participation. Memory, thoughts, and experiments—along with chance—may create fertile connections. The art system increasingly transforms itself into a type of organism comprising slices that organize themselves while the user has an opportunity to experience and produce combinatory meaning.

Media Art's Multifarious Potential for Complex Expression

Thousands of artworks make use of and express the multifarious potential of media art. In the installations *Osmose* (1995) and *Éphémère* (1998) Charlotte Davies transports us into a visually powerful 3D simulation of a lush mineral-vegetable sphere, which we can explore via a bodily interface consisting of a vest that monitors breathing; both works are classics of digital media art that generated more than 100 scientific and art-historical articles but were ignored by museum collections (Davis 2003; Davis and Harrison 1996).

Open-ended questions about the complicated ethical issues involved in the manipulation of DNA are raised in Eduardo Kac's installation *Genesis* (1999) (Kac 2005, 2007, 2011; Kac and Ronell 2007). For *UNMAKEABLELOVE* (2007), inspired by

Samuel Beckett's *The Lost Ones* (1971/1972), Jeffrey Shaw and Sarah Kenderdine used their cybernetic theatrical environment *Re-Actor* to create a real-time augmented world of thirty simulated humans. The dark space or "prison camp" formed by a hexagon of six rear-projected silver screens results in a powerful reappearance of the phantasmagoria. Shaw got inspiration from media arts history:

> The history of the cinematic experience is a rich chronicle of viewing and projection machines. Before Hollywood imposed its set of ubiquitous formats, there were a myriad of extraordinary devices, like the Lumiere Brothers Photodrama, the Cyclorama, Cosmorama, Kineorama, Neorama, Uranorama and many more. The Kaiserpanorama—a stereoscopic cylindrical panoptic peepshow—is an especially relevant forerunner of a newly configured display system, *Re-Actor*. (Kenderdine and Shaw 2009)

William Kentridge, one of the best known artists of our time, also has been working on the subject of a history of vision for years. Even historic image media like the mirror anamorphosis[7] have made their way into his contemporary media art. In 2007 he created a hybrid previously nonexistent in the media history of seeing: for his eight-minute *What Will Come (Has Already Come)* he combines a hand-drawn animation film with cylindrical mirror anamorphosis, connecting it for the first time to moving images and thereby helping us to put the latest image revolution into historical perspective.

Victoria Vesna's *Bodies@Incorporated* (1993) allowed visitors to construct their own avatars. Using a variety of web tools, users could create a 3D representation of their body. Throughout the site, references are made to identity politics and other concepts used to separate and identify bodies (Vesna 1998; Gonzales 2010).

The Golden Nica winner *Murmuring Fields* (1998–2000) by Fleischmann and Strauss is yet another example of a work largely ignored by museums. Here, interacting users maneuver through a virtual space of media philosophy in which statements by Flusser, Virilio, Minsky, and Weizenbaum can be heard—a new type of *Denkraum*, or sphere of thought (Fleischmann and Strauss 2000, 2008), and an early prefiguration of web-based knowledge exchange.

Johanna and Florian Dombois' *Fidelio, 21st Century* (2004), named after Beethoven's *Fidelio*, was the first classical opera directed as an interactive virtual 3D experience. Protagonists embody music, follow the dramaturgic direction and react to the interventions of the audience (Dombois and Dombois 2001; Dombois 2009). All these examples demonstrate that digital media art can deal with questions and challenges of our time in an experimental and participatory way, where traditional art media could simply offer metaphorical approaches. In the best humanistic tradition, digital media art takes on the big contemporary questions, dangers, and proposed transformations, yet it is not adequately collected, documented, and preserved by traditional museums and art institutions. A techno-cultural society that does not understand the challenges it is facing and is not equally open to the art of its time is in trouble.

Today we know that the virtualization and increasing complexity of financial products is partly responsible for the crisis that cost us trillions of euros and dollars in the crash of 2008. More than a decade ago the architecture and art studio Asymptote proposed a 3D info-scape for the New York Stock Exchange (NYSE) to manage financial data within a real-time virtual environment, providing a better, more transparent image and thereby a better idea of transactions—before we get driven into the next mega-crash.[8]

The NYSE did not want further development of a visualization of their "financial products"—and following Lehman Brothers' bankruptcy in 2008 we know why.

Ingo Günther's obsessive cartographic work *Worldprocessor*—an artwork that implicitly conveys the explosion, ubiquity, and the availability of data by the introduction and consolidation of digital media on illuminated globes—multiplies more and more and appears as a clairvoyant prefiguration of the attempts of the growing visualization industries to make our complex time understood. Between the late 1980s until now he destroyed more than 10.000 globes in his creative process and the attempt to create a more realistic image of economy, power, and all kinds of meaningful parameters (Günther 2007).[9]

At least since the time of Edward Snowden's release of documents we have known that Facebook also is systematically used for US National Security Agency surveillance, but many artists, like Seiko Mikami in her robotic installation *Desire of Codes, 2011*, were already dealing with this big issue of our time before the worldwide espionage became generally known[10] (also see Levin 2002; Ozog 2008). Paolo Cirio and Alessandro Ludovico's *Face to Facebook* (2011) also addressed the issue in the form of a "media hack performance" as social experiment: the artists stole one million Facebook profiles, filtered them with face recognition software and then posted them on a custom-made dating web site, searchable by gender and characteristics identified on the basis of their facial expression. Cirio and Ludovico's mission was to give all these virtual identities a new shared place to expose themselves freely, breaking Facebook's constraints and boring social rules. The project is a form of artistic activism that also is meant to explore the contested space of ownership rights to personal data from multiple perspectives, crossing boundaries between personal and corporate spaces and opening them up for controversy and dispute, and exposing the simplifying aspects of face recognition. The performative intervention generated approximately a thousand items of media coverage around the world, eleven lawsuit threats, five death threats, and an exchange of letters between the artists' and Facebook's lawyers.[11]

In addition to shaping highly disparate areas of culture, digital media art also questions notions of the "original" work of art. As we know, the interconnection "artist—original," which was still apparent in the age of craftsmanship, became complicated through machinization and multiplication in the post-industrial era. Today, the software supporting digital artwork by definition exists in a multiplied state. Intensifying this condition are the complicated iterations generated by the interactive interventions of users within the framework of a piece enabled by the degrees of freedom that the artist offers—a multiplication of the expressions of the work.

The more open the system of the artwork is, the more the creative dimension of the work moves toward the normally passive beholders who transform into players and can select from a multitude of information and aesthetic expressions. They can recombine, reinforce, or weaken; can interpret and even partly create. The previously critically distanced relationship toward the object—the precondition of the aesthetic experience and scientific insight in general, as described by Cassirer (1954, 1963), Adorno (1973), or Serres (1981, 152)—now changes to become a field of participatory experience.

Media Art and the Humanities

It is essential to create an understanding of the fact that the present "image revolution," which uses new technologies and has also developed a large number of so far unknown visual expressions, cannot be conceptualized without our image history. Art history and media studies help understand the function of today's image worlds in their importance for building and forming societies. By telling the history of illusion and immersion, the history of artificial life or the tradition of telepresence, art history offers sub-histories of the present image revolution. Art history might be considered a reservoir in which contemporary processes are embedded—an anthropologic narration, on the one hand, and the political battleground where the clash of images is analyzed, on the other. Furthermore, art-historical methods may strengthen our political-aesthetic analysis of the present through image analyses. Last but not least, the development and significance of new media should be illuminated, since the first utopian expressions of a new medium often take place in artworks.

The evolution of media art has a long history and by now a new technological variety has appeared. Today's media art cannot be fully understood without its history. In 2005, the Database for Virtual Art, the Banff New Media Institute, and Leonardo produced the first international MediaArtHistories conference. Held at the Banff Centre in Canada, *Re:fresh!* represented and addressed the wide array of nineteen disciplines involved in the emerging field of media art.[12] Through the success of the following conferences—at House of World Cultures in Berlin in 2007 (following a brainstorming conference in Göttweig in 2006 hosted by the Department for Image Science at the Danube University, Austria), Melbourne in 2009, Liverpool in 2011, Riga in 2013, and Montreal in 2015—an established conference series was produced.[13] It was not planned to create a new canon, but rather to build a platform for the many-voiced chorus of the approaches involved. The subtitle HistorIES opened up the thinking space to include approaches from other disciplines beside "art history."

All the conferences around the world were organized via the MediaArtHistory.org platform, which is developing into a scholarly archive for this multifaceted field, ranging from art history to media, film, cultural studies, computer science, psychology, and so on. A couple of thousand peer-reviewed applications have been coordinated on MediaArtHistory.org.[14] With the nineteen disciplines represented at *Re:fresh!* serving as its base, MAH.org is evolving with future conferences under the guidance of an advisory board including Sean Cubitt, Douglas Kahn, Martin Kemp, Timothy Lenoir, Machiko Kusahara, and Paul Thomas.

Image Science: From the Image Atlas to the Virtual Museum

The integration of a "new" image form into image history does not constitute a new method; there have been different historic forerunners. Inspired by Darwin's work *The Expression of the Emotions* (1872), Aby Warburg began a project outlining an art-historical psychology of human expression. His famous *Mnemosyne* image atlas from 1929 tracks image citations of individual poses and forms across media—most significantly, independent of the level of art nouveau or genre. He redefined art history as medial bridge building, for example by including many forms of images. Warburg argued that art history could fulfill its responsibility only by including most forms of images including the most recent in time. The atlas, which has survived only as "photographed clusters," fundamentally is an attempt to combine the philosophical with the image-historical approach. Warburg arranged his visual material by thematic areas. He considered himself an image scientist and reflected upon the image propaganda of World War I through examination of the image wars during the Reformation.

Warburg intended to develop art history into a "laboratory of the cultural studies of image history" that would widen its field to "images … in the broadest sense" [*Bilder … im weitesten Sinn*] (Warburg 1922, 261).[15] Therefore every reflection on the complexity of digital imagery and its multifarious potential could start with Warburg's research.

We all know about the fundamental historical importance of archives to both scholarship and the creation of new knowledge. Let us remember, too, that the discipline of film studies was started by art historians. An initiative by Alfred Barr and Erwin Panofsky founded the enormous Film Library at New York's MoMA (Museum of Modern Art), called the "Vatican of Film" by their contemporaries. Thus film research in the 1930s already incorporated a dominant image science approach and further cultivated it. The initiative allowed for the large-scale comparison of films for the first time. The same spirit, committed to new investments for infrastructures to provide for and analyze the media art of our time, is needed in the digital humanities.

Art History—Visual Studies—Image Science

With strong representation from art history (Belting 2007; Bredekamp 2010; Grau 2011; Kemp 2011; Mitchell 2011), image science[16] (and its sister discipline of visual studies/visual culture in the Anglo-Saxon tradition) encourages interdisciplinary connections with history of science, neuroscience, psychology, philosophy, communication studies, emotions research, and other disciplines (Bredekamp, Bruhn, and Werner 2003; Müller 2003; Grau and Keil 2005; Sachs-Hombach 2005; Jakesch and Leder 2009; Zeki 2011).[17]

Preconditions

In contrast to other disciplines concerned with images, ones that frequently try to explain images as isolated phenomena originating in and of themselves, art history has the critical potential to define images in their historical dimension, which is the discipline's primary strength. Precisely because art history emphasizes a rigorous historicization and the practice of a critical power of reflection it can make the most natural possible contributions to the discussion around images. No image can be "read" if one has not read other images before.

Scientific work with images is based on three preconditions: (1) definition of the object; (2) building of an image archive; and (3) familiarity with a large quantity of images. This enables and defines the understanding that images follow a diachronic logic; without this historic base, image science remains superfluous and cannot realize its full potential.

All of these approaches to comparison are based on the insight that images act diachronically, within a historical evolution, and never function simply as an act without reference. This diachronic dynamic of image generation is increasingly interwoven with an understanding of images alongside those of their time, the synchronic approach. This dynamic process of change has fueled the interdisciplinary debate about the status of the image, a debate with protagonists such as Mitchell, Belting, Elkins, Stafford, and Manovich (Freedberg 1989; Crary 1990; Mitchell 1995; Elkins 1999; Manovich 2001; Stafford 2001; Gunning 2003; Huhtamo 2004). Image science, or *Bildwissenschaft*, now allows us to consider media from peep-show to panorama, anamorphosis, stereoscope, magic lantern, phantasmagoria, films with odors and colors, cinéorama, IMAX, and the virtual image spaces of computers (Grau 2003a).

Since the academic institutionalization of art history at around 1800, different discourses emerged that dealt with the autonomy of art as well as with questions of the complexity of the image (Wind 1994): that is, art as a (rationalized) expression of diverse cultural expressions; questions of art history in the means of a history of style; the style of a certain epoch as a manifestation of the "Kunstwollen" (Alois Riegl)—an appropriate translation would be "artistic will"—that fades away the differentiation of high and low artistic expressions by emphasizing the (hedonist) will to create art.

Contrary to the emphasis of the form as a means of classification of art and image making—as, for example, in the perspective of formal aesthetics most prominently developed by Heinrich Wölfflin (Wimböck 2009)—Aby Warburg opened up a viewpoint that analyzes images in a complex cultural setting. His aim was to reveal the authentic position of an artwork and its visual complexity in order to understand images (Hofmann, Syamken, and Warnke 1980, 58) not only in the context of artistic mastery, but in their contemporary meaning which is informed by the "afterlife" of certain visual traditions (Didi-Huberman 2010). Even though this technique, which led to the iconological method of Erwin Panofsky,[18] pointed out that the complexity of a visual work can only be understood by unfolding its intrinsic discourses, it led to profound criticism; Ernst Gombrich claimed that Warburg's notion of the image and the solution of a "visual puzzle"—that is, the decoding of a complex religious depiction in its contemporary contexts—was too rational. In his groundbreaking essay "Icones Symbolicae" Gombrich (1986) demonstrates that the complexity of images in art history is solved not only by "decoding" the meaning of a certain symbol or allegory but also by considering its aesthetics and expressions (Gombrich 1986, 153). Following the concept of imagery in Neoplatonic thought,[19] Gombrich states that the complexity of images is not revealed in its entirety by solving what is rationally explicable.

However, images do not reveal their meaning only in terms of hermeneutic and semiotic analyses either. Again it was Warburg who introduced the term "Schlagbild" (pictorial slogan) (Diers 1997) to the discourse on the complexity of images to point out that (political) images have to deliver certain meanings in an immediate and effective manner. The idea of the "Schlagbild"—but without its political connotations—emerges again in Roland Barthes' notion of the "punctum" (Barthes 1980) as well as the "starke Bild" (strong image) (Boehm 1994); The image turns out to be a medium that is able to communicate higher emotional values than the written word.

Older definitions of the image, such as those by Gottfried Böhm, Klaus Sachs-Hombach, or W.J.T. Mitchell, became problematic in the context of the digital age. Beside earlier definitions of interactive, immersive, telematics, and generative digital images (Grau 2000) this carefully crafted definition by Thomas Hensel is a good start for outlining the problems:

> IMAGES are not reducible to a particular technology (like graphic prints or neutron autoradiography), not to certain devices or tools (paint brushes or telescope), not to symbolic forms (perspective), not to genres in the broadest sense (still life or summation image), not to an institution (museum or lab), not to a social function (construction or diagnostics), not to practices/media (painting or Morse Code), materials (canvas or photographic paper) or certain symbolism (Christian iconography or alphanumeric code)—but they are virulent in all of them. (Hensel 2008, 39)

Complex Imagery

We find complex and detailed images of the past, rich in information, in the special light atmospheres produced by medieval church windows or illuminated book narratives (Pächt 1962; Kemp 1994, 67). Before 1500 the medieval image system (Kemp 1989) was characterized by a multiplicity of "image frames" ("Bildfelder"). Therefore, medieval visual works were "complex image systems" (Kemp 1989, 123) that were systematically organized by a narrative, thematic, or figurative structure. Even though the visual artworks were not coherent in an illusionary way, they were aggregate spaces (Erwin Panofsky) that combined a multitude of materials, perspectives, and themes. A look at medieval triptychs, paintings, ceilings etc. would underscore this hypothesis, but it is also instructive to examine artworks that are situated in times of transition, as is the case with the ceiling of the Sistine Chapel by Michelangelo—a Renaissance masterpiece that illustrates the complexity of visual artworks.[20] In terms of complexity, Renaissance and baroque ceiling panoramas sometimes demonstrated a real cosmos of religious or pagan knowledge. We discover complexity in graphic prints—perhaps the most detailed image medium of the past—with their attempts to circulate encyclopedic visual knowledge, and we find it in 19th-century panoramas, the dinosaur of image history, showing scientifically and visually complex landscapes too far away to reach or thousands of humans engaged in bloody battles.

Complex images are also at the core of media arts' potential and gain their distinctiveness from their undistinctiveness: media arts' complexity nowadays is produced through interaction and variability, simultaneity, sequentiality, and narration. In media arts, connected polydimensional visual spaces of experience and immersion can be created, image spaces open for unfolding and compression, development or evolution, theoretically resembling fractals of unlimited resolution—to use some keywords. They are produced through endless creations of interfaces through ever new display innovations (Grau 2003a).

In today's social media-based image world definitions have become even more difficult: images, along with the cultures from which they originated, are on the move; myriads of images, with extreme mobility, flow around the globe as messages of transnational and transcultural communication in fractions of a second. Images from formerly separate contexts are occupied, interpreted, amalgamated, and given new meanings. What we are witnessing at the moment is a shift in our image cultures, which are connected to international media, toward a single image culture that increasingly operates transculturally. Formerly passive recipients, who reflected on discrete works of art in a distanced yet intellectually active manner, have now become interactive users with considerable degrees of freedom in their processing of images. Moreover they have become active mediators and facilitators of image worlds, as well as their producers, in that they increasingly collect, modify, distribute, and position images selectively and strategically. New visual information often arises through dialogue in which one or more networks are involved.

The *mise en scène* of the images, individually or in clusters, their metamorphoses and their dissemination, are significantly determined by the users of social networks. Vibrant subcultures develop unbeknownst with a speed of image turnover hitherto unimaginable. Something completely new, image and meaning, often arises from the contradictions, tensions, and differences which manifest visually. This process is nothing new in terms of theories of interculturalism: the fruitful fusion of Roman and

Greek cultures, for example, or of Christian and Islamic cultures in medieval Spain, demonstrated this procedure over long periods of time.

In addition to global icons—seemingly banal but, as we know, actually highly complex—there also are myriads of image clouds arranged in clusters that lie over the globe like a second visual sphere. This is where different ways of seeing the world encounter each other and are actively negotiated; this is where the rudiments of a new culture form. If one wants to understand an image, at least partly, it has to be considered in context. And contexts are becoming more and more complicated due to the many different visual media surrounding them: what is new here is that there apparently is no limit to the acceleration of visual exchange processes, which, because of their multifaceted branching and connections, cannot be captured or analyzed by the instruments employed by the humanities in the 19th and 20th centuries.

If ever the theory of a homogeneous or "pure" culture—ideologically elevated and repeatedly misused—had any validity, this idea is now virtually obsolete. A cultural theory that is playful and favors egalitarian exchange may be desirable, but is rather naïve if one considers the power of commercial global players to create global icons, the inroads of political control over the networks, language barriers, inadequate knowledge of digital cultural techniques, and the power of certain media conglomerates that are coming together to form economic cartels.

Collective Strategies: New Tools for the Humanities

In the first generation of digital humanities,[21] data was everything. In the 1990s massive amounts of data were archived and searched, and databases combined for interoperable searches, yielding a complexity and realization of data at a previously inconceivable rate. Yet the amount of material to be digitized is so vast that, in reality, we are only at the tip of the data iceberg. In non-textual fields, such as the visual arts, music, performance, and media studies, we are only "at the tip of the tip." Let us remember that digital art has still not "arrived" in our societies, no matter how well attended digital art festivals are or how many art-historical and scientific articles the artists have published. Due to the fact that this art depends entirely on digital storage methods, which are in a constant state of change and development, it is severely at risk. Many artworks that are not even ten years old can no longer be shown, and it is no exaggeration to say that half a century of art of our time is threatened to be lost for the next generations.

If we look beyond the humanities we can conclude that, during the last decades, the natural sciences started to pursue new research goals through large collective projects: in astronomy, for example, the Virtual Observatory compiles centuries worth of celestial observations[22]; global warming is better understood with projects like the Millennium Ecosystem Assignment, which, at a detail never before calculable, is evaluating twenty-four separate life systems and the global change of which they are part.[23] The rapid expansion of computational power has also affected biology, and the Human Genome Project has already become legendary.[24] So far, unknown collective structures give answers to complex problems. For the field of media art research and the digital humanities in general, an appropriate approach is needed to achieve equivalent goals.

Comparable with the developments in the natural sciences, digital media and new opportunities for networked research catapult the cultural sciences within reach of new and essential research, such as appropriate documentation and preservation of media art or, even better, an entire history of visual media and human cognition by means of thousands of sources. These topics express current key questions with regard to image revolution. In order to push the development of humanities and cultural sciences, it is necessary to use the new technologies globally. Timelines and new methods of visualization are part of the history of the invention of visual techniques, image content, and especially their reception in the form of oral history in the popular and high culture of Western as well as non-Western cultures. We live in an exciting time for both image science and the humanities. The credo is to not give up the established individual research, but to complete it in a new way through collective, Net-based working methods that allow us to deal with explosive questions in the field of humanities and cultural sciences.

The Archive of Digital Art (formerly Database of Virtual Art)

As a counterpart to the systematic analysis of the triad of artist, artwork, and beholder in the context of digital or virtual art, we originated the first documentation project in digital art, the Archive of Digital Art (ADA; formerly Database of Virtual Art),[25] which celebrated its tenth anniversary in 2010 (Grau 2000) (see Figure 1.1). As a pioneering effort supported by the German Research Foundation and Austrian Science Fund, it

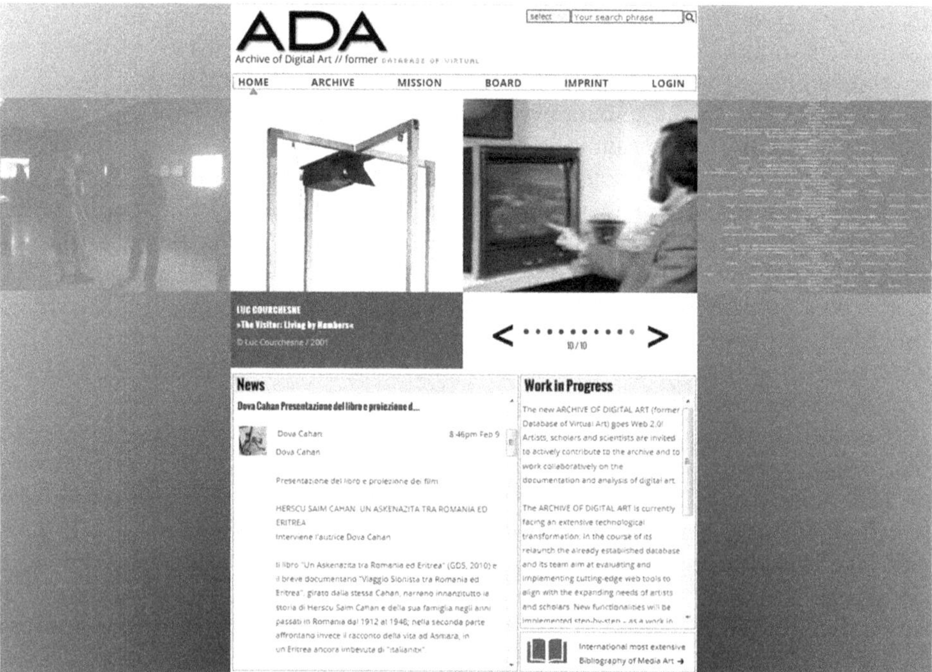

FIGURE 1.1 Archive of Digital Art (ADA). Screenshot. Source: Oliver Grau, Danube-University Krems, Austria.

has been documenting the last decades of digital installation art as a collective project done in cooperation with renowned media artists, researchers, and institutions. We know that today's digital artworks are "processual," ephemeral, interactive, multimedia-based, and fundamentally context-dependent. Because of their completely different structure and nature they require a modified or, as it was termed a few years ago, an "expanded concept of documentation" (Grau 2003b).

As probably the most complex resource available online—hundreds of leading artists are represented with several thousand documents including technical data, and more than 3500 articles and a survey of 750 institutions of media art are listed—the database became a platform for information and communication. The database runs completely on open-source technology and, since the artists are members, it avoids copyright problems. Besides the artists, there also are more than 250 theorists and media art historians involved in making ADA a collective project.

The system allows artists and specialists to upload their information, and the ADA relies on its advisory board for making selections. Besides that, the criterion for determining whether artists are qualified to become members is the number of their exhibitions, publications, awards, and public presentations; high importance also is ascribed to artistic inventions like innovative interfaces, displays, or software. The system offers a tool for artists and specialists to individually upload information about works, people, literature, exhibits, technologies, and inventions.[26] Over the last ten years about 5000 artists have been evaluated, of which 500 fulfilled the criteria to become a member of the ADA. From the beginning, the long-term goal of the project was not simply the documentation of festivals, awards, or similar events, but a scientific overview with the corresponding standards of quality. Members have to qualify with at least five exhibitions or articles about their work, or, alternatively, may be suggested by the board.

Bridging the Gap: New Developments in Thesaurus Research

Now coexisting with one of the probably most important yet little-known art collections, the Göttweig print collection—representing 30,000 prints with an emphasis on Renaissance and baroque works[27] and a library of 150,000 volumes going back to the 9th century, among them the Sankt Gallen Codex—the Archive of Digital Art strives to achieve the goal of providing a deeper media art-historical cross-examination. Just as the MediaArtHistories conference series aims to bridge a gap, the combination of the Göttweig collection and ADA and other databases seeks to enable further historic references and impulses. The Göttweig collection also comprises proofs of the history of optical image media, intercultural concepts, caricatures, and landscapes in panoramic illustrations. This range will provide resources for a broader analysis of media art in the future (Figure 1.2).

It is important to note that keywording is bridge building! The hierarchical thesaurus of the ADA constitutes a new approach to systematizing the field of digital art. It was built on art-historical thesauri from institutions such as the Getty and the Warburg Institute as well as categorizations developed by festivals and discussions with artists in order to support historical comparisons. On the one side, keywords that have relevance in media art were selected from the Getty Art & Architecture Thesaurus, in the subject catalogue of the Warburg Library in London. On the other, new keywords

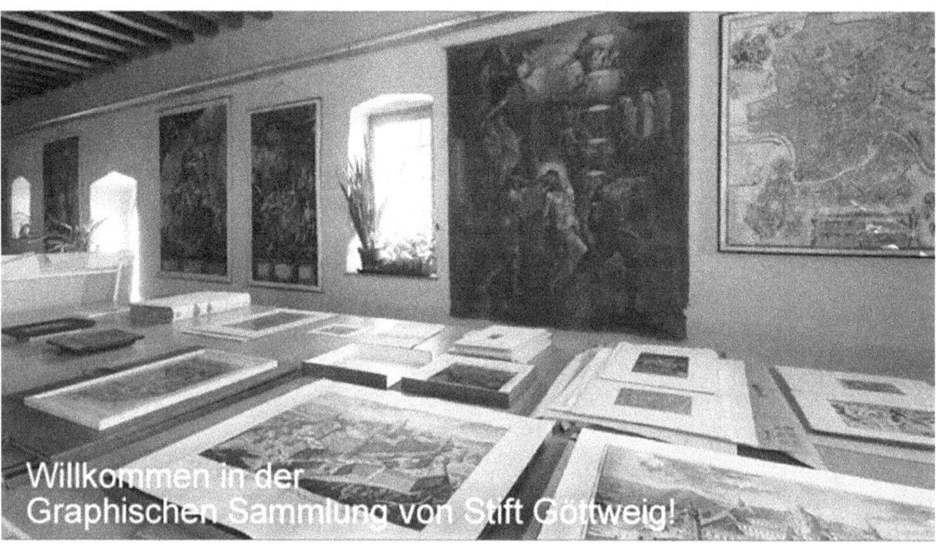

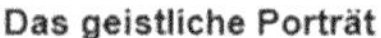

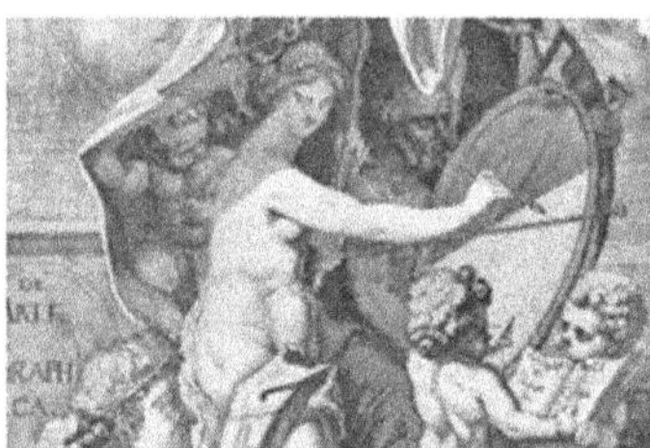

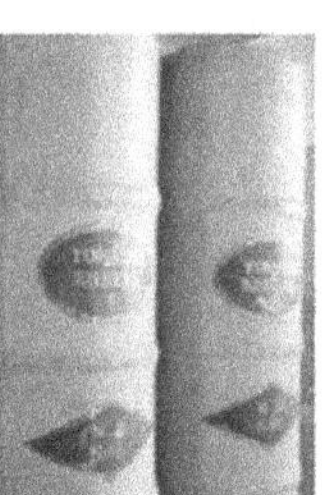

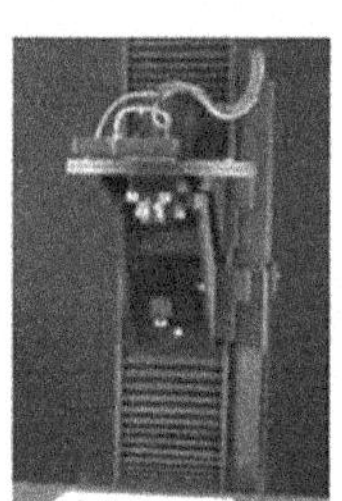

FIGURE 1.2 Göttweig Print Collection Online. Screenshot. Source: Oliver Grau, Danube-University Krems, Austria.

were selected from the terms most commonly used by media festivals such as Ars Electronica, DEAF, and Transmediale. Important innovations such as “interface” or “genetic art” are considered along with keywords that play a role in traditional arts—such as “body” or “landscape”—and thus have a bridge-building function. It was important to limit the number of keywords to a few hundred words so that members of the ADA can assign terms and tag their works without lengthy study of the index.

The range of categories leads to a natural overlap, so that the hybrid quality of the artworks can be captured through clustering. The thematic usability of the categories for the humanities was important —to avoid developing only new terminology, separated from our cultural history. It was crucial to compile a thesaurus that connects cultural history with media art and does not isolate them from one another. As to be expected, the material has also produced a multitude of fractures and discontinuities, which are made visible in the terminology of the database.

One of the goals for the future is to both document works within a context of complex information and, at the same time, allow users to find individual details quickly. In addition to statistically quantifiable analyses and technical documentation, databases should also present personal connections and affiliations, as well as funding information, with the goal to reveal interests and dependences. Going beyond searches of themes, media art documentation should also consider questions of gender, track the movement of technical staff from lab to lab and technical inventions pertaining to art, as well as public and private funds allocated to research, and, through the thematic index, show virtual and immersive art's reminiscences of its predecessors, for example, panorama or laterna magica. Media art documentation becomes a resource that facilitates research on the artists and their work for students and academics. By these means, documentation changes from a one-way archiving of key data to a proactive process of knowledge transfer.

Media Art Education

The future of media art within the digital humanities requires further establishment of new curricula, like the one we developed for the first international Master of Arts in MediaArtHistories with renowned faculty members from around the world—a program that also addresses the practice of and expertise in curating, collecting, preserving, and archiving media arts. The necessity for an international program capable of accommodating future scholars coming from diverse backgrounds and all continents was met by a low-residency model allowing professionals to participate in the advanced program of study parallel to ongoing employment and activities. Students and specialists are brought together for concentrated blocks of time in an intensely creative atmosphere focusing on the histories of media art and its kindred arenas.

The needs of the field made it necessary to create a program specific to MediaArtHistories—with a faculty of experts that universities typically would not be able to gather in one institution—in order to pave the way for the development of innovative future educational strategies in media arts. Offering both an overview of relevant approaches and the possibility for specialization through focused projects and master's theses, the Masters of Arts program provides an introduction for students new to this emergent field and depth for experienced students. The integration and continuing evolution of the aforementioned projects—the ADA, the Göttweig Graphic Collection online, and the platform MediaArtHistory.org with the MediaArtHistories Archive—creates synergies with the development of courses for the program in order to support curators and archivists in their professional needs. The ultimate goal is to set a standard for administrators and policy makers so that we can work toward joining up common methods, histories, and research in the spaces shared by art history and media studies.

The Problem of Media Art Documentation Today—Future Needs

After the foundation of the original Database of Virtual Art, a number of online archives for documentation were established: the Langlois Foundation in Montreal (2000–2008), Netzspannung at the Fraunhofer Institut (2001–2005), and MedienKunstNetz at ZKM (2004–2006). Although they continue to exist as online archives, all these projects were eventually terminated, or their funding expired, or they lost key researchers like V2 in Rotterdam, Netherlands.[28] The Boltzmann Institute for Media Art Research in Linz (2005–2009) was also closed. Thus the original archives that often represent the only remaining image source for some works do not only, step by step, lose their significance for research and preservation, but also partly disappear from the Web. Not only the media art itself but also its documentation fades and is partly lost, so that future generations will not be able to get an idea of the past. What we need is a concentrated and compact expansion of the ability to sustain it. Although a number of preservation projects[29] have been supported over time, a concerted and sustainable strategy, neither institutional nor governmental, so far does not exist. There still seems to be a tendency toward particularization in preservation, instead of a focus on concentrating forces, which is an essential strategy in most other fields.

A New Structure for Media Art Research

University-based research projects, in particular, and also some of those linked to museums have developed expertise that needs to be included in cultural circulation, not only in order to pass it on to future generations of scientists and archivists but also to give it a chance to flow into future university curricula in the fields of art, engineering, and media history. Clearly, the goal also must be to develop policies and strategies for collecting the art of our recent history under the umbrella of a strong, Library of Congress-type of institution. Ultimately, however, this effort can only be organized with the help of a network of artists, computer and science centers, galleries, technology producers, and museums. The projects that collected culturally important documents in the past and often expired or were not further supported or lost their base must be supported and reanimated. They should be organized like a corona around an institution that takes on the duty of documentation and maybe even collection of contemporary media art. Interestingly, libraries show increasing interest in archiving multimedia works and their documentation. However, the usually complex cultural and technical knowhow needed to preserve principal works of the most important media art genres of the last decades is often lacking.

Not only can the international status of media art, its international themes and international protagonists be a hindrance in creating common projects, but the funding infrastructure of media art so far has typically promoted national projects for only two, three, or a limited number of years, neglecting sustainability. A structure that updates, extends, and contextualizes research—whether in historical or contemporary contexts—is badly needed. The funding and support infrastructures that have been built toward the end of the last century are not suitable for the scientific and cultural tasks in the humanities of the 21st century.

The European Commission expressed the goal to double funds for pilot projects in interdisciplinary foundational research.[30] But this is not enough: for up-to-date digital humanities, the funding structures must be internationalized in ways similar to those enabling modern astronomy, genomics, and climatology. In order to create enough momentum and the necessary sustainability, responsible sponsors like the NSF, DFG, EU and so on have to ensure long-term and sustainable international structures. Only if we develop systematic and concentrated strategies for collection, preservation, and research will we be able to fulfill the demands of digital culture in the 21st century.

But even the best documentation and archiving cannot replace the preservation of digital-born projects, which started to be researched in a range of international projects such as DOCAM[31] in Canada, the Variable Media Network[32] or the Capturing Unstable Media[33] project carried out by V2. We should welcome the fact that further basic means for promoting the reception of media art are provided, even though much larger efforts still must be undertaken on a national and international level. We need proper and sustainable international collection and research funding policies, similar to the ones that facilitated the success of the natural sciences or collections in museums, which in many countries are forced by law to collect and preserve contemporary art also.[34] As recently expressed in an international declaration,[35] signed by more than 450 scholars and leading artists from forty countries as of 2014, there is an urgent need to create a stable international platform of interoperable archives, of expertise and support for important regional histories, and to internationalize research, modes of interpretation, and shared resources. The signees of the declaration intend to establish an appropriate scientific structure for documenting and preserving, for promoting study and appreciation; to create a permanent resource for future scholars, artists, curators, and creative engineers; and to make major interventions in the understanding of media as a basic framework of society. In astronomy, the funding agencies developed and modernized their systems toward sustainability, which is needed in the humanities as well. The Virtual Observatory infrastructure is funded on an ongoing basis, and there is international coordination between a dozen or so countries that produce astronomical data. Considering the current upheavals and innovations in the media sector, where the societal impact and consequences cannot yet be predicted, the problem is pressing.

We are experiencing exciting developments in Web 2.0, experimenting with new strategies for collective documentation and content management that exceed the work of expert networks. But one needs to keep in mind that amateurs cannot replace the work of professionals who have been educated in their field over many years—a process common in other dissemination systems. Nevertheless, amateurs can play a very important role in facing the enormous challenge of negotiating and traversing through a network of helpful exchanges and efficient guidance. Moreover, a long-term commitment to the profession by the best experts in the field is needed. An enormous and sustaining infrastructure has been developed and established for traditional artistic media such as painting, sculpture, architecture, even film, photography and their corresponding archives over the course of the past century. Publicly financed archives, museums, and educational institutions may be obliged to collect and preserve the art of our time, but the archival systems of our society were caught off guard by the shorter lifespan of digital storage media. What is urgently needed is the establishment of an appropriate structure to preserve at least the usual 1–6% of present media art production. This important step is still missing for the first two generations of media art. If we compare the available budget for traditional art forms worldwide with the one for digital culture, we understand how inadequate the support for our present digital culture is—so low it is almost statistically immeasurable. The faster this essential modification to our cultural heritage record can be carried out, the smaller the gap in the cultural memory will be and the more light will be shed on "the dark years," which started about 1960 and last until now.[36] We need to take into account the hybrid character of media art, which requires a paradigm shift toward process and context recording, which increasingly includes the capture of the audience experience (Grau 2003b; Muller 2008).

The hope for the future is to bring together the expertise of the most important institutions in order to create an up-to-date overview of the whole field; to provide the necessary information for new preservation programs within the museum field; new university programs for better training of the next generation of historians, curators, restorers, engineers, and others involved in preservation; and new forms of open access to media art. Just as research in the natural sciences has long recognized team efforts, a similar emphasis on collaborative research should govern the thinking of the humanities.

Notes

1 The topic of the Transmediale Berlin in 2009: "Deep North;" Ars Electronica festival in 2009: "Human Nature." See also the (educational) art project "Media Art Ecologies Program" by furtherfield.org.
2 See the dissertation of Daniela Plewe, Paris, Sorbonne, 2011. http://www.transactional-arts.com/summary.html (accessed January 4, 2015).
3 Ars Electronica's festival theme in 2002: "Unplugged. Art as the scene of global conflicts." Also see art projects such as Ken Goldberg's *Telegarden* (1995–1996), Nam June Paik's *Global Groove* (1973), Viktoria Binschtok's *Globen/Globes* (2002), etoy's *The Digital Hijack* (1996), Marko Peljihan's *UCOG-144: Urban Colonization and Orientation Gear-144* (1996), Ga Zhang's *Peoples' Portrait* (2004).
4 For example: Ars Electronica, Austria; Transmediale, Germany; Intersociety of Electronic Arts (ISEA) Conference; Dutch Electronic Art Festival; European Media Art Festival, Germany; FILE, Brazil; Microwave Festival Hong Kong; Korean Media Art Festival; Siggraph and others.
5 For example, Archive of Digital Art: https://www.digitalartarchive.at/; Netzspannung.org: http://netzspannung.org/archive/; V2_Archive: http://framework.v2.nl; Docam: http://www.docam.ca; Daniel Langlois Fondation: http://www.fondation-langlois.org; Variable Media Initiative: http://variablemedia.net (accessed January 4, 2015).
6 Accessed January 4, 2015. For an overview: http://digitalartarchive.at.
7 The anamorphosis is an imaging technique that was invented in the Renaissance, most prominently developed by Leonardo da Vinci. From a technical standpoint, anamorphic images are "distorted" images that are reconstituted either by a mirror or by the particular position of the beholder. Besides its lesser known importance in early cartography and other scientific imaging techniques, it is a technique that made an appearance most prominently in Hans Holbein's *The Ambassadors*. The anamorphosis was also of great importance for baroque church ceilings to create certain illusionary effects.
8 Asymptote, *NYSE 3D Trading Floor* (1998). http://www.asymptote.net (accessed January 4, 2015).
9 Also see Rafael Lozano-Hemmer, *Zero Noon* (2013), and George LeGrady, *Data Flow* (2008).
10 Also see art projects such as Timo Toots's *Memopol* (2012), Mediengruppe Bitnik's *Surveillance Chess* (2012), and Dragan Espenschied and Alvar Freude's *Insert Coin* (2001).

11 http://www.lovely-faces.com (accessed January 4, 2015).

12 Some of the conference results can be found in the anthology *MediaArtHistories* (Grau 2007) and Broeckmann and Nadarajan (2009).

13 http://www.mediaarthistory.org (accessed January 4, 2015).

14 The content development of *Re:fresh!* was a highly collective process. It involved three producing partners, a large advisory board, two chairs for each session, call and review for papers, a planning meeting in 2004, keynotes, poster session, and the development of application content over the time of two and a half years.
The conference brought together colleagues from the following fields: invited speakers (based on self-description from biographical material) HISTORIES: Art History = 20; Media Science = 17; History of Science = 7, History of Ideas = 1; History of Technology = 1; ARTISTS/CURATORS: Artists/Research = 25; Curators = 10; SOCIAL SCIENCES: Communication/Semiotics = 6; Aesthetics/Philosophy = 5, Social History = 2; Political Science = 2; Woman Studies = 2, Theological Studies = 1; OTHER CULTURAL STUDIES: Film Studies = 3; Literature Studies = 3; Sound Studies = 3, Theatre Studies = 2; Performance Studies = 1; Architecture Studies = 1, Computer Science = 2; Astronomy 1.

15 We know that National Socialism put a sudden end to this work and although its emigrants could create important impulses in the United States and England, the image science approach did not return until the 1970s with the Hamburg School. Also see Wedepohl (2005).

16 Image science has been established as the common translation of the German *Bildwissenschaft(en)*, and is used at the *Wissenschaftskolleg*, Berlin, the *Journal on Interdisciplinary Image Science*, the Center for Image Science, Danube University, and by American colleagues like W.J.T. Mitchell and Barbara Stafford. Earlier translations such as "visual science," "image history," or "picture studies" are no longer in use.

17 Albeit concentrated on the gravitational field of art history, the programs in image science at Danube University are interdisciplinarily aligned. http://www.donau-uni.ac.at/dis (accessed January 4, 2015.

18 "Ikonologie"—the English term "iconology" conveys a different approach to images (see Mitchell 1989)—is a method of analyzing artworks that was highly influenced by the philosophy of the symbolic form of Ernst Cassirer. Warburg introduced "Ikonologie" to art history, whereas Erwin Panofsky "institutionalized" the methodology of emphasizing the meaning of an artwork instead of its form.

19 By combining the philosophy of Plato with Jewish and Egyptian traditions, the Neoplatonic philosophy introduces—in short—a mystical system of thought that emphasizes irrational aspects in the creation of (a higher) knowledge.

20 Hofmann states that Michelangelo evokes an effect that is distinct from the concept of the central perspective (1998). The combination of multiple frames on an area of 13 × 36 meters is characterized by its polyfocal composition: instead of offering a coherent illusion, Michelangelo establishes a complex pattern of different layers that dispenses with the idea of a spatial and temporal fixation. Hofmann as well as Panofsky points out that the dimensions of the bodies are varying and different layers of reality are united. The ceiling establishes a complex reference system in between the different areas. Therefore, the beholder is encouraged to follow certain visual axes to understand the complexity of the painting.

21 For the discussion and development of the field, see the journal *Digital Humanities Quarterly* and also the *Companion to Digital Humanities*. http://www.digitalhumanities.org/companion (accessed January 4, 2015).

22 The International Virtual Observatory Alliance (IVOA) was formed in June 2002 with a mission to "facilitate the international coordination and collaboration necessary for the development and deployment of the tools, systems and organizational structures necessary to enable the international utilization of astronomical archives as an integrated and interoperating virtual observatory." The IVOA now comprises seventeen international VO projects.

23 The Millennium Ecosystem Assessment assessed the consequences of ecosystem change for human well-being. From 2001 to 2005, the MA involved the work of more than 1360 experts worldwide. Their findings provide a state-of-the-art scientific appraisal of the conditions and trends in the world's ecosystems and the services they provide, as well as the scientific basis for action to conserve and use them sustainably.

24 The Human Genome Project was an international scientific research project with the primary goal of determining the sequence of chemical base pairs which make up DNA and identifying and mapping the approximately 20,000–25,000 genes of the human genome from both a physical and functional standpoint. The mega project started 1990 with the collective work of more than 1000 researchers in forty countries; the plan was to achieve the goal in 2010. A working draft of the genome was released in 2000 and a complete one in 2003. See International Human Genome Sequencing Consortium (2004).

25 http://digitalartarchive.at (accessed January 4, 2015).

26 The PostGreSQL Database is open source and the operation system is Linux-based.

27 The digitization of the collection is a project developed by the Department of Image Science at Danube University and conducted in cooperation with the Göttweig Monastery. The collection of prints at Göttweig Monastery, which itself was founded in 1083, is based on acquisitions made by various monks since the 15th century. The first report of graphic art kept in the monastery dates back to 1621, with an archive record that mentions a number of "tablets of copper engraving" ("Täfelein von Kupferstich"). The actual act of founding the collection is attributed to Abbot Gottfried Bessel whose systematic purchases in Austria and from abroad added a remarkable total of 20,000 pieces to the collection in a very short space of time! Reaching to the present day, the print collection at Göttweig Monastery has grown to be the largest private collection of historical graphic art in Austria, with more than 30,000 prints. The Department of Image Science's digitization center at the Göttweig Monastery uses technology to scan paintings and prints from the collection (up to 72 million pixels). http://www.gssg.at (accessed January 4, 2015).

28 Also compare the OASIS (Open Archiving System with Internet Sharing, 2004–2007) or the GAMA project (2008–2009), a gateway and meta-database that is not connected with the Europeana. "The issue of generally accepted machine-readable descriptive languages in these semantic and metadata approaches and the long-term interoperability of databases have led to an emphasis on questions concerning the openness of the sources and the source codes" (Wolfensberger 2009).

29 There are a number of promising case studies archived by TATE, the Guggenheim, or MOMA, as well as individual research projects by colleagues such as Caitlin Jones's "Seeing Double: Emulation in Theory and Practice, The Erl King Case Study." http://206.180.235.133/sg/emg/library/pdf/jones/Jones-EMG2004.pdf (accessed January 4, 2015).

30 http://ec.europa.eu/digital-agenda/en/our-goals (accessed January 4, 2015).

31 DOCAM is a multidisciplinary research endeavor initiated by the Daniel Langlois Foundation in collaboration with numerous national and international partners, such as the Database of Virtual Art, who wrote letters of support, and is funded by the Social Sciences and Humanities Research Council of Canada. http://www.docam.ca/ (accessed January 4, 2015).

32 http://www.variablemedia.net/ (accessed January 4, 2015).

33 http://v2.nl/archive/works/capturing-unstable-media (accessed January 4, 2015).

34 Museum collections and archives—especially when state owned—have the legal obligation to ensure the physical preservation, appropriate documentation, and accessibility of cultural objects to researchers and the public; regulations are stipulated in Austria by the Denkmalschutzgesetz (Landmark Protection Law) or the Bundesmuseengesetz (Federal Museums Law) and in Germany by the Kulturgutgesetz (Cultural Asset Law).

35 MEDIA ART NEEDS GLOBAL NETWORKED ORGANISATION & SUPPORT—International Declaration. http://www.mediaarthistory.org (accessed January 4, 2015).

36 The loss might be even more radical and total than that of the panorama, the mass media of the 19th century. Almost twenty panoramas survived, which is much more than 3% of the 360° image worlds—we should be glad if 3% of the most important exhibited media artworks survived.

References

Adorno, Theodor W. 1973. *Ästhetische Theorien*. Frankfurt am Main: Suhrkamp.

Anker, Suzanne, and Dorothy Nelkin. 2003. *The Molecular Gaze: Art in the Genetic Age*. New York: Cold Spring Harbor Laboratory Press.

Barthes, Roland. 1980. *La Chambre Claire: Note sur la photographie*. Paris: Gallimard.

Belting, Hans, ed. 2007. *Bilderfragen: Die Bildwissenschaften im Aufbruch*. Munich: Fink.

Boehm, Gottfried. 1994. "Die Wiederkehr der Bilder." In *Was ist ein Bild?*, edited by Gottfried Boehm, 11–38. Munich: Fink.

Borries, Friedrich von. 2011. *Klima Kunst Forschung*. Berlin: Merve.

Bredekamp, Horst. 2010. *Theorie des Bildakts*. Frankfurt am Main: Suhrkamp.

Bredekamp, Horst, Matthias Bruhn, and Gabriele Werner, eds. 2003. *Bildwelten des Wissens. Kunsthistorisches Jahrbuch für Bildkritik*. Berlin: Akademie Verlag.

Broeckmann, Andreas, and Gunalan Nadarajan, eds. 2009. *Place Studies in Art, Media, Science and Technology: Historical Investigations on the Sites and the Migration of Knowledge*. Weimar: Verlag und Datenbank für Geisteswissenschaften.

Cassirer, Ernst. 1954. *Philosophie der symbolischen Formen*. Darmstadt: Wissenschaftliche Buchgesellschaft.

Cassirer, Ernst. 1963 [1927]. *Individuum und Kosmos*. Wissenschaftliche Buchgesellschaft: Darmstadt.

Crary, Jonathan. 1990. *Techniques of the Observer: On Vision and Modernity in the Nineteenth Century*. Cambridge, MA: The MIT Press.

Cubitt, Sean. 2005. *Ecomedia*. Amsterdam and New York: Rodopi.

Da Costa, Beatriz, and Philipp Kavita, eds. 2010. *Tactical Biopolitics: Art, Activism, and Technoscience*. Cambridge, MA: The MIT Press.

Davies, Char, and John Harrison. 1996. "Osmose: Towards Broadening the Aesthetics of Virtual Reality." *Computer Graphics (ACM)* 4(30): 25–28.

Davies, Char. 2003. "Landscape, Earth, Body, Being, Space and Time in the Immersive Virtual Environments Osmose and Ephemére." In *Women, Art, and Technology*, edited by Judy Malloy, 322–337. Cambridge, MA: The MIT Press.

Demos, T.J. 2009. "The Politics of Sustainability: Contemporary Art and Ecology." In *Radical Nature: Art and Architecture for a Changing Planet 1969–2009*, edited by Franceso Manacorda, 16–30. London: Barbican Art Gallery.

Didi-Huberman, Georges. 2010. *Das Nachleben der Bilder. Kunstgeschichte und Phantomzeit nach Aby Warburg*. Berlin: Suhrkamp.

Diers, Michael. 1997. *Schlagbilder. Zur politischen Ikonografie der Gegenwart*. Frankfurt am Main: Taschenbuch Verlag.

Dixon, Steve. 2007. *Digital Performance: A History of New Media in Theatre, Dance, Performance Art, and Installation*. Cambridge, MA: The MIT Press.

Dombois, Johanna. 2009. "Master Voices: Opernstimmen im virtuellen Raum. Fidelio, 21. Jahrhundert." In *Stimm-Welten: philosophische, medientheoretische und ästhetische Perspektiven*, edited by Doris Kolesch, 127–142. Bielefeld: Transcript.

Dombois, Johanna, and Florian Dombois. 2001. "op.72. II 1–5, 3D. Beethoven's 'Fidelio' in a Virtual Environment." In *Proceedings of the 5th World Multi-Conference on Systematics, Cybernetics and Informatics*, Volume X, 370–373, Orlando, FL, USA, July 22–25, 2001.

Elkins, James. 1999. *The Domain of Images*. Ithaca, NY: Cornell University Press.

Fleischmann, Monika, and Wolfgang Strauss. 2000. "Extended Performance. Virtuelle Bühne, Selbstrepräsentanz und Interaktion." In *Kaleidoskopien, Theatralität, Performace, Medialität. Körperinformationen* 384, Institut für Theaterwissenschaft, University of Leipzig, 52–57.

Fleischmann, Monika, and Wolfgang Strauss. 2008. "Staging of the Thinking Space. From Immersion to Performative Presence." In *Paradoxes of Interactivity*, edited by Uwe Seifert, Jin Hyon Kim and Anthony Moore, 266–281. Bielefeld: Transcript.

Freedberg, David. 1989. *The Power of the Images: Studies in the History and Theory of Response*. Chicago: University of Chicago Press.

Gardiner, Hazel, and Charlie Gere, eds. 2010. *Art Practice in a Digital Culture*. Farnham, UK: Ashgate Press.

Gombrich, Ernst H. 1948. "Icones Symbolicae: The Visual Image in Neo_Platonic Thought." *Journal of the Warburg and Courtauld Institutes* 11: 163–192.

Gonzales, Jennifer. 2010. "The Appended Subject Hybrid Incorporations: Bodies© INCorporated: Race and Identity as Digital Assemblage." In *Race in Cyberspace*, edited by Beth Kolko, Lisa Nakamura, and Gil Rodman. New York: Routledge.

Grau, Oliver. 2000. "The Database of Virtual Art." *Leonardo* 4(33): 320.

Grau, Oliver. 2003a. *Virtual Art: From Illusion to Immersion*. Cambridge, MA: The MIT Press.

Grau, Oliver. 2003b. "For an Expanded Concept of Documentation: The Database of Virtual Art." *ICHIM*, École du Louvre, Paris 2003, Proceedings: 2–15.

Grau, Oliver. 2011. *Imagery in the 21st Century*. Cambridge, MA: The MIT Press.

Grau, Oliver, and Andreas Keil, eds. 2005. *Mediale Emotionen: Zur Lenkung von Gefühlen durch Bild und Sound*. Frankfurt: Fischer.

Gunning, Thomas. 2003. "Re-Newing Old Technologies: Astonishment, Second Nature, and the Uncanny in Technology from the Previous Turn-of-the-Century." In *Rethinking Media Change, The Aesthetics of Transition*, edited by David Thorburn and Henry Jenkins, 39–59. Cambridge, MA: The MIT Press.

Günther, Ingo. 2007. "Worldprocessor.com." In *ACM SIGGRAPH 2007*, San Diego, Proceedings, New York.

Hauser, Jens, ed. 2008. *Sk-interfaces. Exploding Borders—Creating Membranes in Art, Technology and Society*. Liverpool: Liverpool University Press.
Hensel, Thomas. 2008. "Das Bild im Spannrahmen." *Gegenworte: Hefte für den Disput über Wissen* 20: 35–39.
Hershman-Leeson, Lynn. 2007. "The Raw Data Diet, All-Consuming Bodies, and the Shape of Things to Come." In *Database Aesthetics: Art in the Age of Information Overflow*, edited by Victoria Vesna, 249–252. Minneapolis: University of Minnesota Press.
Hofmann, Werner, Georg Syamken, and Martin Warnke, eds. 1980. *Die Menschenrechte des Auges: über Aby Warburg*. Frankfurt am Main: Europ. Verl.-Anst.
Himmelsbach, Sabine, and Yvonne Volkart. 2007. *Ökomedien. Ökologische Strageien in der Kunst heute*. Basle: Edith-Russ-Haus für Medienkunst.
Hofmann, Werner. 1998. *Die Moderne im Rückspiegel: Hauptwege der Kunstgeschichte*. Munich: Beck.
Huhtamo, Erkki. 2004. "Elements of Screenology: Toward an Archaeology of the Screen" *Iconics, The Japan Society of Image Arts and Sciences* 7: 31–82.
International Human Genome Sequencing Consortium. 2004. "Finishing the Euchromatic Sequence of the Human Genome." *Nature* 431: 931–945.
Jakesch, Martina, and Helmut Leder. 2009. "Finding Meaning in Art. Preferred Levels of Ambiguity in Art Appreciation." *Quarterly Journal of Experimental Psychology* 62.
Kac, Eduardo. 2005. *Telepresence and Bio Art—Networking Humans, Rabbits and Robot*. Ann Arbor: University of Michigan Press.
Kac, Eduardo. 2007. *Bio Art. Signs of Life. Bio Art and beyond*. Cambridge, CA: The MIT Press.
Kac, Eduardo. 2011. *Life, Light & Language/ La vie, la lumière & le langage*. Enghien-les-Bains: Art Center.
Kac, Eduardo, and Avital Ronell. 2007. *Life Extreme: An Illustrated Guide to New Life*. Paris: Dis-Voir.
Kemp, Martin. 2011. *Christ to Coke: How Image Becomes Icon*. Oxford: Oxford University Press.
Kemp, Wolfgang. 1989. "Mittelalterliche Bildsysteme." *Marburger Jahrbuch für Kunstwissenschaft* 22: 121–134.
Kemp, Wolfgang. 1994. "Über Bilderzählungen." In *Erzählen: Eine Anthologie*, edited by Michael Glasmeier, 55–69. Berlin: Akademie der Künste.
Kenderdine, Sarah, and Jeffrey Shaw. 2009. "UNMAKEABLELOVE: Gaming Technologies for the Cybernetic Theatre Re-Actor." In *ACE 09 Proceedings of the International Conference on Advances in Computer Entertainment Technology*, Athens, Greece, October 29–31, 2009.
Levin Thomas Y. 2002. *CTRL [SPACE] Rhetorics of Surveillance. Rhetorics of Surveillance from Bentham to Big Brother*. Cambridge, MA: The MIT Press.
Manovich, Lev. 2001. *The Language of New Media*. Cambridge, MA: The MIT Press.
Manovich, Lev. 2011. "Trending. The Promises and the Challenge of Big Social Data." In *Debates in the Digtial Humanities*, edited by Matthew K. Gold, 460–475. Minneapolis: University of Minnesota Press.
Mitchell, W.J.T. 1989. *Iconology: Image, Text, Ideology*. Chicago: University of Chicago Press.
Mitchell, W.J. T. 1995. *Picture Theory: Essays on Verbal and Visual Representation*. Chicago: University of Chicago Press.
Mitchell, W.J.T. 2011. *Cloning Terror. The War of Images. 9/11 to the Present*. Chicago: University of Chicago Press.

Muller, Lizzie. 2008. *Towards an Oral History of New Media Art*. Montreal: Daniel Langlois Foundation.
Müller, Marion. 2003. *Grundlagen der visuellen Kommunikation*. Konstanz: UVK.
Ozog, Maciej. 2008. "Visions of Surveillance in Media Art." *Art Inquiry* 10: 167–186.
Pächt, Otto. 1962. *The Rise of Pictorial Narrative in Twelfth Century England*. Oxford: Clarendon Press.
Popper, Frank. 2007. *From Technological to Virtual Art*. Cambridge, MA: The MIT Press.
Reichle, Ingeborg. 2005. *Kunst aus dem Labor. Zum Verhältnis von Kunst und Wissenschaft im Zeitalter der Technoscience*. Vienna: Springer.
Sachs-Hombach, Klaus, ed. 2005. *Bildwissenschaft*. Frankfurt am Main: Suhrkamp.
Serres, Michel. 1981. *Carpaccio: Ästhetische Zugänge*. Reinbek: Rowohlt.
Shanken, Edward. 2009. *Art and Electronic Media*. London: Phaidon.
Sommerer, Christa, and Laurent Mignonneau, eds. 2008. *Interface Cultures: Artistic Aspects of Interaction*. Bielefeld: Transcript.
Stafford, Barbara. 2001. *Devices of Wonder: From the World in a Box to Images on a Screen*. Los Angeles: Getty Research Institute.
Vesna, Victoria. 1998. "Under Reconstruction: Architectures of Bodies INCorporated." In *Veiled Histories: The Body, Place and Public Art*, edited by Anna Novakov, 87–117. New York: Critical Press.
Vesna, Victoria. 2007. *Database Aesthetics: Art in the Age of Information Overflow*. Minneapolis: University of Minnesota Press.
Warburg, Aby. 1922. "Heidnisch-antike Weissagung in Wort und Bild *zu* Luthers Zeiten." In *Zeitschrift für Kirchengeschichte* 40: 261–262.
Wedepohl, Claudia. 2005. "Ideengeographie: ein Versuch zu Aby Warburgs 'Wanderstrassen der Kultur.'" In *Ent-grenzte Räume: Kulturelle Transfers um 1900 und in der Gegenwart*, edited by Helga Mitterbauer and Katharina Scherke. Vienna: Passagen.
Wilson, Stephen. 2010. *Art + Science Now: How Scientific Research and Technological Innovation Are Becoming Key to 21st-Century Aesthetics*. London: Thames & Hudson.
Wimböck, Gabriele. 2009. "Im Bilde. Heinrich Wölfflin (1864–1945)." In *Ideengeschichte der Bildwissenschaft*, edited by Jörg Probst und Jost Philipp Klenner, 97–116. Frankfurt am Main: Suhrkamp.
Wind, Edgar. "Warburgs Begriff der Kulturwissenschaft und seine Bedueutng für die Ästhetik." In *Bildende Kunst als Zeichensystem. Vol. 1: Ikonographie und Ikonologie: Theorien, Entwicklung, Probleme*, edited by Ekkehard Kaemmerling, 165–184. Cologne: DuMont, 1987.
Wolfensberger, Rolf. 2009. "On the Couch—Capturing Audience Experience." MA thesis, Danube University.
Zeki, Semir. 2011. "Masking Within and Across Visual Dimensions: Psychophysical Evidence for Perceptual Segregation of Color and Motion." *Visual Neuroscience* 2(5): 445–451.

Further Reading

Dotzler, Bernhard. 2001. "Hamlet\Maschine." In *Trajekte: Newsletter des Zentrums für Literaturforschung Berlin* 3(2): 13–16.
Fleischmann, Monika, Wolfgang Strauss, and Jasminko Novak. 2000. "Murmuring Fields Rehearsals—Building up the Mixed Reality Stage." In *Proceedings of KES International Conference on Knowledge Engineering Systems*, 90–94. Brighton: KES.

Grau, Oliver. 1998. "Into the Belly of the Image." *Leonardo, Journal of the International Society for the Arts, Sciences and Technology* 5(32): 365–371.

Grau, Oliver. 2001. "Virtuelle Kunst" In *Geschichte und Gegenwart: Visuelle Strategien.* Berlin: Reimer.

Grau, Oliver, ed. 2007. *MediaArtHistories.* Cambridge, MA: The MIT Press.

Hamker, Anne. 2003. *Emotion und ästhetische Erfahrung.* Münster: Waxmann.

Latour, Bruno, and Peter Weibel, eds. 2002. *ICONOCLASH: Beyond the Image Wars in Science, Religion and Art.* Karlsruhe: ZKM.

Leidloff, Gabriele, and Wolf Singer. 2008. "Neuroscience and Contemporary Art: An Interview." In *Science Images and Popular Images of the Sciences*, edited by Bernd Hüppauf and Peter Weingart, 227–238. London: Routledge.

Plewe, Daniela. 1998. "Ultima Ratio. Software und Interaktive Installation." In *Ars Electronica 98: Infowar: Information, Macht, Krieg*, edited by Gerfried Stocker and Christine Schöpf, 136–143. Vienna and New York: Springer.

Shikata, Yukiko. 2000. "Art-Criticism-Curating as Connective Process." *Information Design Series: Information Space and Changing Expression* 6: 145.

Sommerer, Christa, and Laurent Mignonneau. 2003. "Modeling Complexity for Interactive Art Works on the Internet." In *Art and Complexity: At the Interface*, edited by John Casti and Anders Karlqvist, 85–107. Amsterdam: Elsevier.

2

International Networks of Early Digital Arts

Darko Fritz

The histories of international networks that transgressed Cold War barriers and were involved with digital arts in the 1960s and early 1970s are, in many respects, an under-researched subject. The following tells a short, fragmented history of networks of digital art—that is, organizations that group together interconnected people who have been involved with the creative use of computers. Criteria used for the inclusion of these networks are both the level of their international activities and the duration of the network, which had to operate for longer than a single event in order to qualify. Educational networks mostly had a local character, despite the fact that some of them involved international subjects or students, and created clusters of global unofficial networks over time.[1]

There are many predecessors to today's international art-science-technology networks, alliances that were primarily science- and technology based but that understood culture in a broader sense. Some of them reshaped world culture regardless of and beyond their primary mission and goals. The brief history and success story of the Institute of Electrical and Electronics Engineers (IEEE) and its Computer Society may function as a case study of a network's continuing growth over a century and a half, a dream come true for a capitalist economy. I will describe IEEE and a few other networks of digital arts, using text excerpts from their original documents, including official homepages, and adding critical comments by others and myself.

The IT Sector as Capitalist Dream of Growth

The Institute of Electrical and Electronics Engineers is a US network that transgresses national borders and became an international community of interest. Its growth and history are a reminder of the rapid evolution of technological innovations over the last century and a half that reshaped first Western and later world

A Companion to Digital Art, First Edition. Edited by Christiane Paul.

culture in many respects. Looking at its history provides a basis and interesting background for an examination of digital art networks.

Back in the 1880s electricity was just beginning to become a major force in society. There was only one major established electrical industry, the telegraph system, which—in the 1840s—began to connect the world through a communications network "faster than the speed of transportation" (IEEE 2013). The American Institute of Electrical Engineers (AIEE) was founded in New York in 1884 as an organization "to support professionals in their nascent field and to aid them in their efforts to apply innovation for the betterment of humanity" (IEEE 2013). Many leaders and pioneers of early technologies and communications systems had been involved in or experimented with telegraphy, such as Western Union's founding President Norvin Green; Thomas Edison, who came to represent the electric power industry; and Alexander Graham Bell, who personified the newer telephone industry. As electric power spread rapidly—enhanced by innovations such as Nikola Tesla's AC induction motor, long-distance alternating current transmission, and large-scale power plants, which were commercialized by industries such as Westinghouse and General Electric—the AIEE became increasingly focused on electrical power.

The Institute of Radio Engineers (IRE), founded in 1912, was modeled on the AIEE but devoted first to radio and then increasingly to electronics. It too furthered its profession by linking its members through publications, the development of standards, and conferences. In 1951 IRE formed its Professional Group on Electronic Computers. The AIEE and IRE merged in 1963 to form the Institute of Electrical and Electronics Engineers, or IEEE. At the time of its formation, the IEEE had 150,000 members, 140,000 from the United States and 10,000 international ones. The respective committees and subgroups of the predecessor organizations AIEE and IRE combined to form the modern IEEE Computer Society.[2]

The Computer Group was the first IEEE subgroup to employ its own staff, which turned out to be a major factor in the growth of the society. Their periodical, *Computer Group News*, was published in Los Angeles and, in 1968, was followed by a monthly publication titled *IEEE Transactions on Computers*. The number of published pages in these periodicals grew to about 640 in the *Computer Group News* and almost 9700 in the *Transactions*. By the end of the 1960s membership in the Computer Group had grown to 16,862, and, in 1971, it became the Computer Society. The *Computer Group News*, renamed *Computer* in 1972, became a monthly publication in 1973, and significantly increased its tutorial-based content. By the end of the 1970s, Computer Society membership had grown to 43,930. The society launched the publications *IEEE Computer Graphics & Applications* in 1981; *IEEE Micro* in 1981; both *IEEE Design & Test* and *IEEE Software* in 1984; and *IEEE Expert* in 1986. *IEEE Transactions on Software Engineering* (introduced in 1989) and *IEEE Transactions on Pattern Analysis & Machine Intelligence* moved from bimonthly to monthly publication in 1985 and 1989, respectively. The society sponsored and cosponsored more than fifty conferences annually, and the number of meetings held outside the United States, many of them sponsored by technical committees, grew significantly over the years. In the 1980s the society sponsored and co-sponsored more than ninety conferences outside the United States. In 1987 CompEuro was initiated, and by the end of the 1980s, 56 standards had been approved and 125 working groups, involving over 5000 people, were under way. In the new political and economic climate after the (un)official end of the Cold War, the Central and Eastern European Initiatives, as well as committees in Latin America and China, were formed (1990s).

As new areas and fields in information processing were developed, the society added new journals to meet the demands for knowledge in these subdisciplines: *Transactions on Parallel & Distributed Systems* (1990); *Transactions on Networking*, jointly launched with the IEEE Communications Society and ACM SIGCOM (1991); *Transactions on Visualization & Computer Graphics* (1995); and *Internet Computing* (1997) and *IT Professional* (1999). By the end of the 1990s IEEE Computer Society was publishing twenty-four journals and periodicals, and the total number of editorial pages published had risen to 70,661 in 1999. The 1990s also were the decade that saw the coming of age of the Internet and digital publications, and the IEEE Computer Society's digital library was first introduced in 1996 in the form of a set of CDs of 1995 periodicals. Soon afterwards, this set was posted on the Web, and, in 1997, the IEEE Computer Society Digital Library (CSDL) was formally launched as a product. Toward the end of the 1990s, the Computer Society had a staff of over 120. In addition to the Washington headquarters and the California publication office, the Society opened offices in Tokyo and Budapest, Moscow and Beijing. The Society's relationship with the IEEE also changed; while it had previously operated fairly independent of the IEEE, it now became more integrated into it. A whole set of new publications was launched: *IT Professional, IEEE Security and Privacy, IEEE Transactions on Mobile Computing, IEEE Pervasive Computing, IEEE Transactions on Affective Computing, IEEE Transactions on Haptics, IEEE Transactions on Learning Technologies, IEEE Transactions on Services Computing, IEEE Transactions on Information Technology in Biology*, and *IEEE Transactions on Nanobiosciences.* In some cases these publications were developed in collaboration with other IEEE societies. In the 2010s, the Computer Society was involved in close to 200 conferences a year, and increasingly became a conference and proceedings service for other IEEE Societies. In the early 21st century, IEEE comprised 38 societies; published 130 journals, transactions, and magazines; organized more 300 conferences annually; and had established 900 active standards. IEEE today is the world's largest technical professional society. The history of IEEE is the realization of a capitalist, market-driven dream of everlasting growth.

The Emergence of Digital Arts and Related Networks

If we examine the histories of the ever-changing currents of modern and contemporary arts' and culture's interests over the last century and a half, we cannot trace such a continuing growth and such massive figures, especially not in the field of digital arts and the related blending of art-science-technology. The streams of rationality and specific methodologies that are embodied, in different ways, in art-science-technology practices, digital arts, and other forms of media art constantly came in and out of focus within the major streams of modern and contemporary art, a trend that is continuing up to the present. Only computer-generated music, under the umbrella of electronic music, has a continuous history of production, institutions, and education that continues without breaks over the decades and is still an active field today. In sound and text-based arts, we can continuously trace the creative use of computers since the 1950s.

Several initiatives that had started exploring the relationship between art, science, and technology in the 1960s shifted their focus toward the use of digital technologies by the end of the decade. In the beginning of the 1960s, a majority of art practitioners (artists, art historians, and theoreticians) shared an approach to "machines" that did not differentiate much between mechanical and information process machines, as will be seen in the following discussion of the practices of both New Tendencies (1961–1973) and Experiments in Art and Technology (E.A.T., since 1967). In the late 1960s digital art became the focus of several art exhibitions and expanded theoretical discourse, which resulted in the creation of new networks dedicated to digital arts.

After a series of smaller solo exhibitions and local gallery presentations starting in the mid-1960s, the first international group exhibition dedicated exclusively to computer-generated art was held at Brno in the Czech Republic in February 1968. That show, as well as a series of international group exhibitions on cybernetics and computer art that took place the following year, were organized by major art institutions and presented across Europe, the United States, and Japan, with some of them traveling around the world.[3] This presence within the structures of cultural institutions fueled both the professional and mainstream imagination and created both an artistic trend and a certain hype surrounding imaginary futures that most radically presented itself at the world fairs of that time. There suddenly seemed to be a necessity for international networks for digital arts that would transgress the exhibition format and fulfill the need for networking on a regular rather than just occasional basis.

Lacking their own networks, digital art practitioners originally participated in information technology ones and their annual conferences. Experiments in Art and Technology (E.A.T.) held presentations at the annual meeting of the IEEE in 1967 (Figure 2.1). Digital art was presented at the International Federation for Information Processing

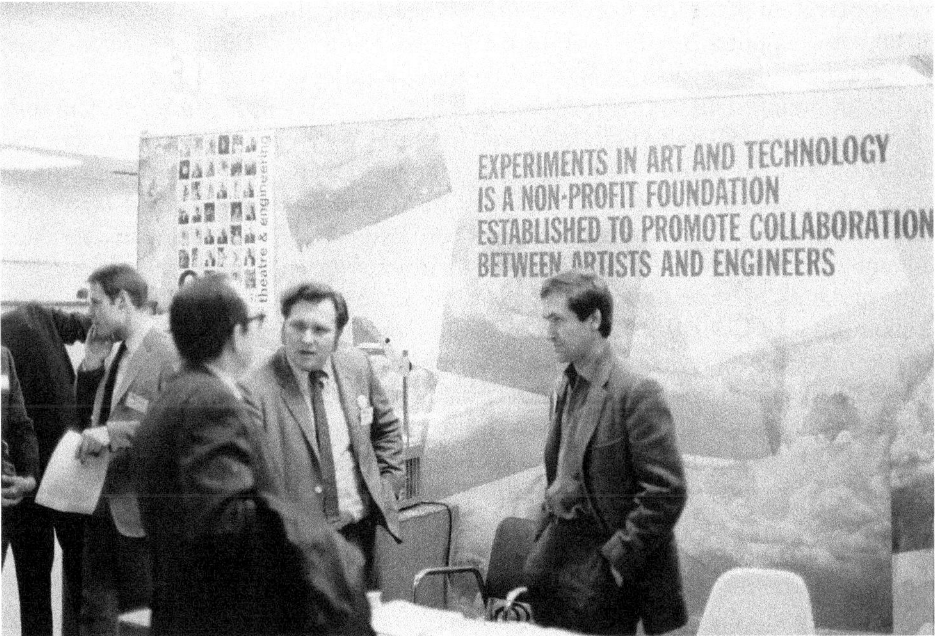

FIGURE 2.1 Experiments in Art and Technology (E.A.T.) at the annual meeting of the Institute of Electrical and Electronics Engineers (IEEE), March 20–24, 1967, Coliseum and Hilton Hotel, New York. Artists Tom Gormley and Hans Haacke are talking to an engineer. Courtesy: Experiments in Art and Technology. Photography: Frank Grant.

(IFIP; since 1960) and the Association for Computing Machinery (ACM) and their Special Interest Group on Graphics and Interactive Techniques (SIGGRAPH; since 1974). Next to their core focus on information technology (IT) industry and business, both IFIP and ACM/SIGGRAPH hold competitions and awards for digital arts that often focus more on technical excellence than artistic and cultural achievements and development of critical discourse. The critique of these mainstream IT industries for their lack of critical discourse and social awareness was common among the practitioners with a background in humanities, art, and culture.

IFIP, an umbrella organization for national societies working in the field of information processing, was established in 1960 under the auspices of UNESCO as a result of the first World Computer Congress held in Paris in 1959. Today the organization represents IT Societies from fifty-six countries or regions, with a total membership of over half a million. IFIP links more than 3500 scientists from academia and industry—organized in more than 101 Working Groups reporting to thirteen Technical Committees—and sponsors 100 conferences yearly, providing coverage of a field ranging from theoretical informatics to the relationship between informatics and society, including hardware and software technologies, as well as networked information systems. In the 1960s IFIP conferences provided space for much needed international networking of the digital arts community. An important meeting and networking point was the 1968 IFIP Congress in Edinburgh, where the art networks Computer Arts Society UK and Netherlands were both initiated and started their collaboration.

ACM, the first association for computing, was established in 1947, the year that saw the creation of the first stored-program digital computer, and has been organizing an annual Computer Arts Festival since 1968. ACM's Special Interest Groups (SIGs) in more than thirty distinct areas of information technology address interests as varied as programming languages, graphics, human–computer interaction, and mobile communications. SIGGRAPH, the Special Interest Group on Graphics and Interactive Techniques, is the annual conference on computer graphics convened by the ACM since 1974. SIGGRAPH conferences have been held across the United States and attended by tens of thousands of computer professionals. The papers delivered there are published in the *SIGGRAPH Conference Proceedings* and, since 2002, in a special issue of the *ACM Transactions on Graphics* journal. ACM SIGGRAPH began their art exhibitions with *Computer Culture Art* in 1981, presenting computer graphics, which developed into a survey of interactive and robotic art titled *Machine Culture* in 1993. SIGGRAPH established several awards programs to recognize contributions to computer graphics, among them the Steven Anson Coons Award for Outstanding Creative Contributions to Computer Graphics that has been awarded bi-annually since 1983 to recognize an individual's lifetime achievement.

At the other end of the spectrum was the art and culture scene established by socially critical art groups around the world that criticized the art market and cultural industry and power structures in general. The different attitudes toward the IT sector represented by the culture and industry positions, respectively, became explicit in the ACM Counter-Conference in Boulder[4] that was held in parallel to the 1971 National Conference of the ACM in Chicago. An anonymous comment in the *PAGE* bulletin of the Computer Arts Society London read: "These two meetings will mark a climax in the campaign for social responsibility in the computer profession. Their repercussions will be felt for years to come" (*PAGE* 1971).

The critique came from the Computer Arts Society (CAS), founded in 1968 by Alan Sutcliffe, George Mallen, and John Lansdown as the first society dedicated to digital arts in order to encourage the use of computers in all art disciplines. Over the next few years CAS became the focus of computer arts activity in Britain, supporting practitioners through a network of meetings, conferences, practical courses, social events, exhibitions and, occasionally, funding. It ran code-writing workshops, held several exhibitions, and produced the news bulletin *PAGE* (1969–1985), edited by Gustav Metzger and focused on recent events and initiatives. Its first exhibition in March 1969, *Event One*, employed computers as tools for enhancing the production of work in many fields, including architecture, theater, music, poetry, and dance (Mason 2008). By 1970 CAS had 377 members in seventeen countries. The spin-off organization Computer Arts Society Holland (CASH) was initiated by Leo Geurts and Lambert Meertens and held its first meeting in Amsterdam in 1970. Ten out of its thirty-four attendants were creatively involved in the arts (visual art, music, design, literature) and nine more from a theoretical or museological perspective (art history, art criticism, musicology, museum). Sixteen of the participants had experience working with computers (Wolk 1970). Recognizing computer literacy as an essential challenge for participants coming from the arts and humanities, CASH organized programming courses at Honeywell Bull venues in Amersfoort and The Hague. The access to computers was made possible as well, by means of time-sharing computer systems, enabling users with backgrounds in humanities and arts to use computers for the first time. Leo Geurts and Lambert Meertens edited two issues of the *PAGE* bulletin that presented new developments in the Dutch scene in 1970 and 1971.

An American branch, CASUS, was formed in 1971. *PAGE* no. 22 from April 1972 was co-edited by Kurt Lauckner of Eastern Michigan University, who was coordinator of CASUS, and Gary William Smith of Cranbrook Academy of Art, who was US chairman of the visual arts. The US chairman of Music Composition was David Steward, coming from the Department of Music of Eastern Michigan University (Ypsilanti, Michigan) where Lauckner was at the Mathematics Department. "Due to both the visual as well the verbal nature" (PAGE 1972), the proceedings of the First National Computer Arts Symposium, held at Florida State University, was made and distributed as eight and a half hours video tape, instead of print.

In 1969 the first meeting of "De werkgroep voor computers en woord, beeld en geluid" (Working group for computers and verbal, visual and sonic research) was held at the Institute of Art History of Utrecht University in the Netherlands. It was primarily a platform for information exchange between those who were pioneering in the use of computers in different fields on both a national and international level. Art historian Johannes van der Wolk, who edited, self-published, and distributed eleven newsletters of the working group written in Dutch, handled the organization of the group all by himself. The working group wasn't a formal organization, and Wolk's private address was used as contact. One hundred and fifty-five articles in total were published in the newsletters. Subscribers were considered members in the group and, by 1972, the mailing list comprised 126 subscribers, 92 from the Netherlands and 34 from abroad. Members participated by providing information for publication, and shaped the newsletter's content via replies to questionnaires. Following the distribution of a questionnaire regarding expressions of interest, an issue presented thirty-eight responses, of which ten were related to arts and creativity (Wolk 1971). Van der Wolk initiated both symposia of the Dutch Working Group for computers and verbal, visual, and sonic research that were held in Deft and Amsterdam in 1970.

In 1967, Robert Hartzema and Tjebbe van Tijen founded the Research Center Art Technology and Society in Amsterdam, which lasted until 1969. The center published two reports, the first on the necessity of improving connections between the categories of artists, designers, and cultural animators, on the one hand, and engineers, technicians, and scientists, on the other; the second on the discrepancy between the economic and cultural development of science and technology versus art, noting a one-sided growth of the science/technology sector with art lagging behind (van Tijen 2011). The first stage of the Research Center was organized out of offices in the Sigma Center, Amsterdam. Later the Stedelijk Museum in Amsterdam housed the project for over a year. In 1968 and 1969 a series of conferences organized by the Research Center was held at the Museum Fodor, Amsterdam. In 1968 the Research Center's co-founder Tjebbe van Tijen, together with Nic Tummers, wrote a manifesto and campaigned against the World Fair Expo '70 in Osaka for over a year, calling for a debate about the function of world fairs and the role of artists, designers, and architects in these undertakings. The manifesto critiqued the inauguration of national pavilions in the world fair after an initial expression of architectural unity, and called for resistance to the overall concept:

> Don't the World's Fairs force themselves upon us as manifestations of the "freedom" to have to produce things for which there is no need and to have to consume what we were forced to produce? Don't artists, designers and architects give the World Fairs a "cultural image" and aren't they being (mis)used to present a sham freedom? (van Tijen and Tummers 1968)

The manifesto was distributed internationally, often inserted in art magazines supportive of its cause. People were asked to start a debate in their own circles and send reactions back to the manifesto's authors. Dutch architect Piet Blom finally refused the invitation to participate in the world fair. Events around the Expo '70 marked a local turning point, dividing the Japanese art scene into pro and contra Expo '70 and influencing developments of media art in Japan that would later be criticized for their supposed non-criticality—Japanese "device art," the art of the electronic gadgets, being an example. Machiko Kusahara puts these developments into historical and local perspective:

> following the 1963 decision to realize Osaka Expo '70, experimental artists and architects were invited to design major pavilions to showcase latest media technologies. However, Expo was criticized as a "festival" to draw public attention away from US–Japan Security Treaty to be renewed in 1970. Avant-garde artists had to make a decision. Some leading artists left Japan and joined FLUXUS in New York. Some joined anti-Expo movement. Others (GUTAI, Katsuhiro Yamaguchi, Arata Isozaki and others) stayed and supported the huge success of Expo. They remained the main stream in Japanese media art. The collaboration system between artists and the industry for Expo became a tradition since then. (Kusahara 2007)

E.A.T. did not join in the criticism, but used Expo '70 as an opportunity to realize some of their ideas about the integration of art and technology through their work on the Pepsi pavilion. E.A.T. was conceived in 1966 and founded as a non-profit organization by engineers Billy Klüver and Fred Waldhauer and artists Robert Rauschenberg and Robert Whitman in New York in 1967. Its focus was on the involvement of industry and technology with the arts and the organization of collaborations between artists and engineers through industrial cooperation and sponsorship. Klüver's vision was that "The artist is a positive force in perceiving how technology can be translated to new environments to serve needs and provide variety and enrichment of life" (Klüver and Rauschenberg 1966). In 1967, the E.A.T. expressed their goal to:

> Maintain a constructive climate for the recognition of the new technology and the arts by a civilized collaboration between groups unrealistically developing in isolation. Eliminate the separation of the individual from technological change and expand and enrich technology to give the individual variety, pleasure and avenues for exploration and involvement in contemporary life. Encourage industrial initiative in generating original forethought, instead of a compromise in aftermath, and precipitate a mutual agreement in order to avoid the waste of a cultural revolution. (Klüver and Rauschenberg 1967)

E.A.T.'s positive, fairly non-critical, and supportive attitude toward corporations and industry becomes evident in their mission statement:

> to assist and catalyze the inevitable active cooperation of industry, labor, technology and the arts. E.A.T. has assumed the responsibility of developing an effective method for collaboration between artists and engineers with industrial sponsorship.
>
> The collaboration of artist and engineer under industrial sanction emerges as a revolutionary contemporary process. Artists and engineers are becoming aware of their crucial role in changing the human environment and the relevant forces shaping our society. Engineers are aware that the artist's insight can influence his direction and give human scale to his work, and the artist recognizes richness, variety and human necessity as qualities of the new technology.
>
> The raison d'être of E.A.T. is the possibility of a work which is not the preconception of either the engineer, the artist or industry, but the result of the exploration of the human interaction between these areas. (Klüver and Rauschenberg 1967)

Gustav Metzger commented on the E.A.T. collaboration with the industry in 1969: "The waves of protest in the States against manufacturers of war materials should lead E.A.T. to refuse to collaborate with firms producing napalm and bombs for Vietnam," and continues, "Forty-five professors at the M.I.T. have announced a one-day 'research stoppage' for March 4 in protest against government misuse of science and technology" (Metzger 1969).

E.A.T. arranged for artist visits to the technical laboratories of Bell, IBM, and RCA Sarnoff, all located in the United States.[5] By 1969 the group had over 2000 artist and 2000 engineer members. They implemented a database "profiling system" to match artists and engineers according to interests and skills. A "Technical Services Program" provided artists with access to new technologies by matching them with engineers or scientists for one-on-one collaborations on the artists' specific projects. E.A.T. was not committed to any one technology or type of equipment per se. The organization tried to enable artists to directly work with engineers in the very industrial environment in which the respective technology was developed. Technical Services were open to all artists, without judgment of the aesthetic value of an artist's project or idea. E.A.T. operated in the United States, Canada, Europe, Japan, and South America, and about twenty local E.A.T. groups were formed around the world.

In 1966 E.A.T. organized a series of interdisciplinary events titled *9 Evenings: Theatre and Engineering* in New York, which involved ten artists, musicians, and dancers; thirty engineers; and an audience of 10,000. Despite the fact that the (mostly analog) technology did not work properly most of the time, which led to bad publicity, these events gained a reputation as milestones in live technology-based arts. In 1968, once again in New York, E.A.T. participated in the organization of a major exhibition on art and science titled *The Machine, as Seen at the End of the Mechanical Age* at the Museum of Modern Art (MoMA), which featured 220 works by artists ranging from Leonardo da Vinci to contemporary ones. E.A.T. proposed a "competition for the best contribution by an engineer to a work of art made in collaboration with an artist" (Vasulka 1998), judged by a panel consisting of engineers only, and organized a related exhibition with the title *Some More Beginnings* at the Brooklyn Museum, New York, the same year.

E.A.T. then went on to organize artist–engineer collaborations working on the design and program of the Pepsi-Cola Pavilion at Expo '70 in Osaka. Twenty artists and fifty engineers and scientists contributed to the design of the pavilion. Digital technologies were used in some of the works resulting from this collaboration. From 1969 to 1972 E.A.T. also realized a series of socially engaged, interdisciplinary projects that made use of user-friendly analogue telecommunication systems in the United States, India, Japan, Sweden, and El Salvador.

In 1980 E.A.T. put together an archive of more than 300 of the documents it had produced: reports, catalogues, newsletters, information bulletins, proposals, lectures, announcements, and press covers. Complete sets of this archive were distributed to libraries in New York, Washington, Paris, Stockholm, Moscow, Ahmadabad, and London, illustrating E.A.T.'s understanding of a globalized cultural network, as well their care in preservation and archiving.[6]

E.A.T. has been an important initiative that, in a constructive and positivist manner, supported collaborations between artists and engineers in the literal sense, by bringing them together. As its value system was not artistic or cultural but quantitative only, some non-critical projects and unequal collaborations took place next to successful ones. E.A.T. considered digital technologies as one of the available technologies at the time, with no particular focus on them. After being criticized for its lack of social responsibilities in its undertakings for Expo '70, E.A.T. changed course and realized a series of socially engaged projects using analogue technologies. Some projects took place in underdeveloped countries, putting E.A.T. ahead of its time in its understanding of a technology-driven globalized world. E.A.T. bridged the industrial and information society of the 1960s and 1970s through different projects that placed the machine at the center of creative impulses, questioning basic notions of life (of humans and machines) and communication amongst humans.

Bridging Analog and Digital Art in New Tendencies

In a different cultural context New Tendencies started out as an international exhibition presenting instruction-based, algorithmic, and generative art in Zagreb in 1961, and then developed into an international movement and network of artists, gallery owners, art critics, art historians, and theoreticians. Adhering to the rationalization of art production and conceiving art as a type of research theoretically framed by people such as Matko Meštrović, Giulio Carlo Argan, Frank Popper, and Umberto Eco, among others (Eco 1962; Meštrović 1963; Argan 1965, Popper 1965), New Tendencies (NT) was open to new fusions of art and science. NT from the very beginning focused on experiments with visual perception that were based on Gestalt theory[7] and different aspects of "rational" art, which involved the viewer in participatory fields of interaction: for example, arte programmata, lumino-kinetic art, gestalt kunst, neo-constructivist and concrete art; all of the aforementioned were later subsumed under the collective name NT or simply *visual research*. From 1962 onward New Tendencies acted as a bottom-up art movement without official headquarters, experimenting with new ways of organization in the form of a decision-making system that involved the collective in different organizational forms, which would change over time. Between 1961 and 1973 the Gallery of Contemporary Art organized five NT exhibitions in Zagreb; in addition, large-scale international exhibitions were held in Paris, Venice, and Leverkusen. The movement was truly international, both transcending Cold War blocs and including South American and, at a later point, Asian artists. This scenario, unique in the Cold War context, was possible due to Zagreb's position in then socialist but non-aligned Yugoslavia. From 1961 to 1965 New Tendencies both stood for a certain kind of art and acted as an umbrella or meta-network for approximately 250 artists, critics, and art groups. The latter included, among others, Groupe de Recherche d'Art Visuel (GRAV) from France; Equipo 57 from Spain; Gruppo di ricerca cibernetica, Gruppo MID, Gruppo N, Gruppo T, Gruppo 63, Operativo R, and Azimuth from Italy; Zero from Germany; Art Research Center (ARC) and Anonima Group from the United States; and Dviženije from the USSR.

Part of the NT aesthetics was quickly adopted, simplified, and commercialized by mainstream cultural industries and became known as op art (optical art) by the mid-1960s, a point in time that could already be seen as the beginning of the end of New Tendencies as an art movement. Having cultivated a positive attitude toward machines from the beginning, New Tendencies adopted computer technology via Abraham Moles's information aesthetic (Moles 1965). Its organizers saw this as both a logical progression of New Tendencies and another chance of keeping the rational approach to art on track while body art, land art, conceptual art, and other new contemporary art forms took center stage in the artworld, and, to a large extent, overshadowed or even excluded the previously developed language of concrete art. The new interest in cybernetics and information aesthetics resulted in a series of international exhibitions and symposia on the subject *computers and visual research*, which now took place under the umbrella of the rebranded *tendencies 4* (*t4*, 1968–1969*) and tendencies 5* (*t5*, 1973) events, after the prefix "new" had been dropped from the name in 1968. Brazilian artist and active NT participant Waldemar Cordeiro's statement that computer art had replaced constructivist art[8] can be traced through the histories of both [New] Tendencies networks themselves.

The years 1968 to 1973 were the heyday of computer-generated arts not just in Zagreb but around the world; computer arts started to be distinguished from other forms of media and electronic arts. As has always been the case in the field of media arts, a technologically deterministic and techno-utopian discourse, on the one hand, and a critically minded and techno-dystopian one, on the other, coexisted.

On May 5, 1969, at the symposium in Zagreb, art critic Jonathan Benthall from London read the Zagreb Manifesto he had coauthored with cybernetician Gordon Hyde and artist Gustav Metzger, and whose opening line was: "We salute the initiative of the organizers of the International Symposium on Computers and Visual Research, and its related exhibition, Zagreb, May 1969." The following line identified the "we" of the opening sentence: "A Computer Arts Society has been formed in London this year,[9] whose aims are 'to promote the creative use of computers in the arts and to encourage the interchange of information in this area'" (Hyde, Benthall, and Metzger 1969).

The manifesto goes on to state that "It is now evident that, where art meets science and technology, the computer and related discipline provide a nexus." The conclusion of the Zagreb Manifesto is pregnant with ideas that circulated at the end of the 1960s and may be reconsidered today as still contemporary issues:

> Artists are increasingly striving to relate their work and that of the technologists to the current unprecedent(ed) crisis in society. Some artists are responding by utilizing their experience of science and technology to try and resolve urgent social problems. Others, researching in cybernetics and the neuro-sciences, are exploring new ideas about the interaction of the human being with the environment. Others again are identifying their work with a concept of ecology which includes the entire technological environment that man imposed on nature. There are creative people in science who feel that the man/machine problem lies at the heart of the computer the servant of man and nature. Such people welcome the insight of the artist in this context, lest we lose sight of humanity and beauty. (Hyde, Benthall, and Metzger 1969)

At the same symposium, Gustav Metzger—co-author of the Zagreb Manifesto and at the time an editor of the *PAGE* bulletin published by the Computer Arts Society from London—took the critical stance a step further while calling for new perspectives on the use of technology in art: "There is little doubt that in computer art, the true *avantgarde* is the military" (Metzger 1970).[10] He later elaborated on one of his own artworks—a self-destructive computer-generated sculpture in public space—for which he presented a proposal at the *tendencies 4—computers and visual research* exhibition that ran in parallel to the symposium of the same title (Figure 2.2). It was one of the rare moments in the 1960s when one socially engaged international network surrounding computer-generated art communicated with another one in a fruitful manner. At the time, the scope of interests of CAS London and [New] Tendencies Zagreb was largely the same.

The aforementioned symposium and exhibition in Zagreb were the concluding events of the ambitious tendencies 4 program that had begun in Zagreb a year earlier, in the summer of 1968, with an international colloquium and exhibition of computer-generated graphics also titled *Computers and Visual Research*. The formal criteria applied in the selection of "digital" works for the exhibition were rigorous; flowcharts and computer programs of digital works were requested, and the artworks by pioneer Herbert Franke, created by means of analog computing, were not included but were presented in a parallel 1969 exhibition titled *nt 4—recent examples of visual research*, which showed analog artworks of previous New Tendencies styles.

In connection with the tendencies 4 and tendencies 5 programs, nine issues of the bilingual magazine *bit international* were published from 1968 to 1972. The editors' objective was "to present information theory, exact aesthetics, design, mass media, visual communication, and related subjects, and to be an instrument of international

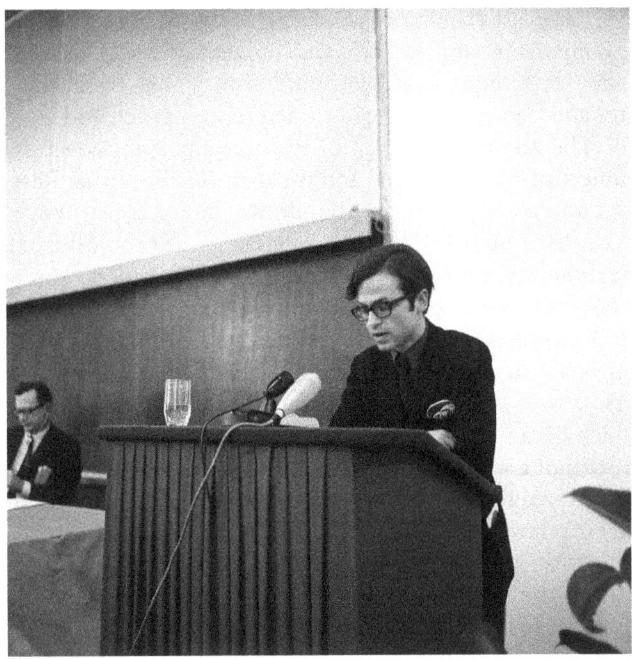

FIGURE 2.2 Jonathan Benthall from the Computer Arts Society, London, at the symposium at tendencies 4, "Computers and Visual Research," RANS Moša Pijade, Zagreb, 1969.

cooperation in a field that is becoming daily less divisible into strict compartments" (Bašičević and Picelj 1968). The magazine's title *bit*, short for binary digit, refers to the basic unit of information storage and communication. The total number of editorial pages published in the nine issues of *bit international* and the related *tendencies 4* and *tendencies 5* exhibition catalogues was over 1400.

Between 1968 and 1973 [New] Tendencies in Zagreb functioned as an international network that once again bridged the Cold War blocs, but this time for a different group of people and organizations: more than 100 digital arts practitioners, among them Marc Adrian, Kurd Alsleben, Vladimir Bonačić, Charles Csuri, Waldemar Cordeiro, Alan Mark France, Herbert Franke, Grace Hertlein, Sture Johannesson, Hiroshi Kawano, Auro Lecci, Robert Mallary, Gustav Metzger, Leslie Mezei, Petar Milojević, Manfred Mohr, Jane Moon, Frieder Nake, Georg Ness, Michael Noll, Lilian Schwartz, Alan Sutcliffe, and Zdenek Sykora; art groups such as ars intermedia from Vienna, Grupo de Arte y Cybernética from Buenos Aires, and Compos 68 from the Netherlands; artists based at universities such as the Computation Center at Madrid University and the Groupe art et Informatique de Vincennes (GAIV), in Paris; science research centers, such as the Institute Ruđer Bošković from Zagreb; theoreticians such as Jonathan Benthall, Max Bense, Herbert Franke, Abraham Moles, and Jiří Valoch, among others; corporate research departments, such as Bell Labs, IBM, MBB Computer Graphics, CalComp, and networks such as the Computer Arts Society (CAS) from London.

In 1973 the curators of the Gallery of Contemporary Art in Zagreb opened up the [New] Tendencies to conceptual art, partly due to a proposal by Jonathan Benthall

(Kelemen 1973).[11] The last exhibition, *tendencies 5*, consisted of three parts: *constructive visual research*, *computer visual research*, and *conceptual art*. This combination made [New] Tendencies the unique example in art history that connected and presented those three forms and frameworks of art—concrete, computer, and conceptual—under the same roof.[12] The audio recordings of the accompanying symposium's proceedings—on the subject of "The Rational and the Irrational in Visual Research Today"—is evidence of a mutual disinterest and blindness among constructive and computer visual research, on the one hand, and conceptual art, on the other. In the *computer visual research* exhibition section of the *tendencies 5* exhibition, a new generation of computer artists presented their works, among them the groups Groupe Art et Informatique de Vincennes (GAIV) from France, and Computation Center at Madrid University from Spain, as well as Centro de Arte y Comunicación from Argentina (CAYC).[13] CAYC would later shift their initial focus on digital arts toward conceptual art practices, which became obvious in the 1971 exhibition *Arte de sitemas*[14] in which both groups of computer and conceptual artists participated. The developments of constructing digital images were out of focus for most of the conceptual art of that time, as its interest relies on non-objective art. Nevertheless, NT organizers tried to bind those practices throughout the notion of the program. Radoslav Putar, director of the Gallery, used the term "data processing" to describe methods of conceptual art, though this possible link was not investigated further (Putar 1973). Frieder Nake (1973) identified a similarity between computer and conceptual art on the level of "separation of head and hand," and discussed that separation as a production structure following the logic of capitalism.

The very process of mounting New Tendencies' international exhibitions at different venues around Europe run by different organizers, as well as the ways of producing publications and gathering in formal and informal meetings, were marked by different types of communication and teamwork and the formation of different committees for particular programs. Due to its popularization and growing importance, New Tendencies passed through numerous disagreements between the organizers and different factions, particularly the participants in the first phase of New Tendencies before 1965, which considered itself as a movement. At specific moments, organizations from Milan, Paris, or Zagreb would lead the actions, while different international committees performed different tasks formed over time. The peak of complexity of the [New] Tendencies organization was reached during the *tendencies 4* exhibition, which, following detailed preparations, was communicated through fourteen circular newsletters *(PI—programme of information)* written in Croatian, English, and French. The output, realized within a year (1968–1969), consisted of a juried competition, six exhibitions, two international symposia (both with multi-channel simultaneous translations into Croatian, English, French, German, and Italian), the initiation and publication of the initial three issues of the magazine *bit international*, and finally the exhibition catalogue *tendencies 4*. These activities demonstrate the energy surrounding digital arts in Zagreb and among the international partners and participants, as well as their agenda to contextualize the practice and theory of digital arts within mainstream contemporary art in the long run.

A spin-off or extension of the [New] Tendencies network of digital arts was active in Jerusalem from 1972 until 1977. The leading figure was Vladimir Bonačić, a scientist-turned-artist thanks to New Tendencies who created interactive computer-generated light objects in both gallery and public spaces. On the basis of an agreement between the Ruđer Bošković Institute from Zagreb and the Israel Academy of Sciences, the Jerusalem Program in Art and Science, a research and training program for post-graduate interdisciplinary studies in art and science, was founded, in 1973, at the Bezalel Academy of Arts and Design in Jerusalem, which Bonačić directed and where he taught computer-based art. For this program he established collaborations with the Hebrew University of Jerusalem and the Israel Museum. In 1974 he organized an international Bat Sheva seminar, "The Interaction of Art and Science," in which several [New] Tendencies protagonists participated, among them Jonathan Benthall, Herbert W. Franke, Frank Joseph Malina, Abraham Moles, A. Michael Noll, and John Whitney. In 1975, Willem Sandberg, a Dutch typographer and director of the Stedelijk Museum, received the Erasmus Prize in Amsterdam. On Sandberg's recommendation, half of the prize was dedicated to the Jerusalem Program in Art and Science. Alongside computer-generated interactive audiovisual art objects, the projects created by Bonačić's *bcd cybernetic art team* included the development of a new design for a computable traffic light system; the first functional digitalization of the Arabic alphabet was also realized within the academy program (Bonačić 1975). From 1978 to 1979 the *bcd cybernetic art team* realized a socially engaged project titled *Palestine Homeland Denied* in the form of thirty-five printed posters, which included the computer-generated alphabet and images of 385 destroyed Palestinian villages.

Computer-generated art's attraction gradually faded from the artworld at large during the 1970s. Computer graphics of the 1970s explored possibilities for figurative visuals and—by delivering animations and special effects for the mainstream film industry—entered the commercial world as well as the military sector, advancing virtual reality techniques that simulated "real life." This development—within the larger context of an increasing dominance of conceptual and non-objective art building on post-Duchampian ideas of art and representation—led to the almost-total exclusion of computer-generated art from the contemporary art scene around the mid-1970s. This process was further fueled by the rising anti-technological sentiment among the majority of a new generation of artists, created by the negative impact of the corporate-military-academic complex's use of science and technology in the Vietnam War and elsewhere and expressed in the previously mentioned statement by Gustav Metzger in 1969, the protest movement by Japanese artists against Expo '70, and similar events, such as the throwing of stones at a computer artist in Los Angeles[15] a year later. The misuse of science and technology in the Vietnam War was described by Richard Barbrook:

> M.I.T. modernization theory would prove its (USA) superiority over the Maoist peasant revolution. [...] Since the information society was the next stage in human development, the convergence of media, telecommunications and computing must be able to provide the technological fix for anti-imperialist nationalism in Vietnam. During the late-1960s and early-1970s, the US military made strenuous efforts to construct an electronic barrier blocking the supply routes between the liberated north and the occupied south. Within minutes of enemy forces being detected by its ADSID sensors, IBM System/360 mainframes calculated their location and dispatched B-52 bombers to destroy them. (Barbrook 2007, 177)

In the mid-1970s major protagonists in the field of digital art, such as Frieder Nake, Gustav Metzger, and Jack Burnham, shifted the tone of discourse on art, science, and technology. In Zagreb the [New] Tendencies movement experienced difficulties: *tendencies 6* started with five-year-long ongoing preparations by a working group that could not find a consensus on how to contextualize and support "computers and visual research" and finally organized only an international conference titled *tendencies 6—Art and Society* in 1978, which again confronted very few computer artists with a majority of conceptual art practitioners. The planned *tendencies 6* exhibition never took place. Instead, the *New Art Practices* exhibition—running in parallel with the last [New] Tendencies event, the "Art and Society" conference— presented the first regional (Yugoslav federation) institutional retrospective of conceptual art practices. While developing the exhibition concept for *tendencies 6*, the organizers from Zagreb actually sent more than 100 calls for works to video activists and community-engaged video collectives around the world, but there were no answers. The video activism of the 1970s also remains an under-researched phenomenon that is often skipped in the narratives of both media art and mainstream contemporary art history, yet provides contents that bridge the gap between socially engaged art and technologies.

Media-oriented conceptual artists of the 1970s started to use mostly analog media such as typewritten text, video, photography, and Xerox, and only a few used digital technologies. It took about twenty years until digital arts returned to the contemporary art scene in the (late) 1980s, but this time infused with the experiences of both social engagement and conceptual art practices. This return after a long disconnect would lead to the creation of many new digital arts networks. The boom of digital art networks since the 1990s has been propelled by the advances in Internet technologies and a cultural climate infused by the fast growth of new media and digital cultures that have gradually become interwoven with the everyday life of the majority of the world's population in the 21st century. Some digital art networks disappeared quickly, but others are long-lasting and still growing; growth diagrams show that their curve almost catches up with that of the IT sector and creative industries.

Digital Art Networks of the 1980s

The 1970s saw the emergence of significant magazines on electronic and digital arts such as *Radical Software* (1970–1974) by the Raindance Collective and *Computer Graphics and Art* (1976–1978). The *Leonardo* journal (1968–) is the only one of the early periodicals that is still published today; it expanded its organizational frame beyond a printed magazine and to the network at a later point, in the 1980s.

Leonardo is a peer-reviewed academic journal founded in 1968 "with the goal of becoming an international channel of communication for artists who use science and developing technologies in their work" (MIT 2013). It was established in Paris by artist and scientist Frank Malina. Roger Malina, who took over operations of the journal upon Frank Malina's death in 1981, moved it to San Francisco. In 1982 the International Society for the Arts, Sciences and Technology (ISAST) was founded to further the goals of Leonardo by providing a venue of communication for artists working in contemporary media. The society also publishes the *Leonardo Music Journal*, the *Leonardo Electronic Almanac*, *Leonardo Reviews*, and the *Leonardo Book Series*. All publications are produced in collaboration with The MIT Press. Other activities of Leonardo include an awards program, as well as participation in annual conferences and symposia such as the Space and the Arts Workshop, and the annual College Art

Association conference. Leonardo has a sister organization in France, the Association Leonardo, that publishes the *Observatoire Leonardo des arts et des technosciences* (OLATS) web site. While encouraging the innovative presentation of technology-based arts, the society also functions as an international meeting place for artists, educators, students, scientists, and others interested in the use of new media in contemporary artistic expression. A major goal of the organization is to create a record of personal and innovative technologies developed by artists, similar to the documentation of the findings of scientists in journal publications. Leonardo has helped to bridge the gap between art and science from the 1960s until today and has shown developments in art and science intersections as a continuum.

Since the late 1980s and in the 1990s, in particular, media arts have come into global focus again, and numerous institutions, magazines, media labs, university departments, online platforms, conferences, and festivals have emerged, not necessarily functioning as organized international networks, but providing a place for personal networking. Practices that were once subsumed under terms such as (new) media art, digital art, art and technology, art and science have become so diversified that no single term can work as a signpost any more. We may trace these developments within single platforms such as *Leonardo*, the longest lasting journal in the field as of today, and the longest lasting festival, Ars Electronica, launched in Linz, Austria, in 1979. Initially it was a biennial event, and has been held annually since 1986, with each festival focused on a specific theme. In its growth phase, two key factors drove the festival's subsequent development: on the one hand, the goal to create a solid regional basis by producing large-scale open-air projects such as the annual multimedia musical event Klangwolke (Sound Cloud); and, on the other hand, to establish an international profile by collaborating with artists, scientists, and experts—for instance, by hosting the first Sky Art Conference held outside the USA. Since 1987 Ars Electronica organizes the Prix Ars Electronica, a yearly competition in several categories that have changed over time. In 1996 the *Ars Electronica Center* opened as a year-round platform for presentation and production that includes the *Ars Electronica Futurelab*, a media art lab originally conceived to produce infrastructure and content for the Center and Festival, but increasingly active in joint ventures with universities and private-sector research and development facilities. In 2009 the Center moved to a new building,

> reoriented with respect to both content and presentation. In going about this, the principle of interaction was expanded into comprehensive participation. In designing exhibits and getting material across, the accent is placed on the shared presence of artistic and scientific pursuits. The substantive focus is on the life sciences. (Ars Electronica 2013)

Media artist and theoretician Armin Medosch (2013), among others, has criticized Ars Electronica for a growing lack of criticality:

> Ars Electronica only continues with a long tradition, by uncritically incorporating a positivistic view of science whilst riding the waves of hype about technological innovations. The point is, that this criticism isn't new either. In 1998, when Ars Electronica chose the topic of "Infowar" media philosopher Frank Hartmann wrote: "Interestingly enough, the word 'culture' has hardly been heard at this conference, which in the end is part of a cultural festival. The social aspects of cyberwar have been excluded. It seems

> to me that one wanted to decorate oneself with a chic topic that reflects the Zeitgeist, while avoiding any real risk by putting the screen of the monitor as a shield between oneself and the real danger zones." These are the words of the same Frank Hartmann who will speak at the Ars Electronica conference as one of the few non-natural scientists this year [2013]. Ars Electronica manages to discuss the Evolution of Memory in an utterly de-politicised manner, and that only months after Edward Snowden exposed the existence of the NSA's gigantic surveillance program that exceeds anything that we have known before. [...] The pseudo-scientific metaphors that Ars Electronica loves so much, usually taken from genetics and biology, and in recent times increasingly from neuro-science, lead to the naturalisation of social and cultural phenomena. Things that are historical, made by humans and therefore changeable, are assumed to be of biological or of other natural causes, thereby preventing to address the real social causes. In addition, such a manoeuvre legitimates the exercising of power. By saying something is scientific, as if "objective," a scientific or technocratic solution is implied. The pseudo-scientification leads to the topic being removed from democratic discussion. [...] Through the way how it has addressed information technologies since 1979 Ars Electronica has concealed their real consequences in a neoliberal information society. For this it has used again and again flowery metaphors which seemingly break down barriers between cultural and scientific domains in a pseudo-progressive way. According to Duckrey, Ars Electronica has in 1996, with their frequent references to a "natural order," "reduced diversity, complexity, noise and resistance, blending out the cultural politics of memory in the age of Memetics." (Medosch 2013)

Facing the challenges of keeping the critical discourse up to date with the latest developments in the field(s) and the large quantity of presented artworks, as well as its own growth over several decades, Ars Electronica still plays an important role in the field of digital arts next to other large-scale festivals that have been organized over the decades, such as DEAF—Dutch Electronic Art Festival in Rotterdam (organized by V2 since 1987) or Transmediale in Berlin (since 1988). Such festivals offer possibilities for presenting and sometimes producing demanding and complex projects. As media (art) cultures are developing rapidly, such festivals have recently attracted wider audiences and necessarily entered the dangerous field of populism, with or without criticality. New kinds of spaces have been developed for personal meetings, work, and presentations, and new institutions with media or hack labs, festivals, temporary workshops, and camps have evolved. Different from the field of contemporary art, insights into context in the process-based new media field are often provided by presentations at conferences and festivals rather than through artworks presented in exhibitions or on online platforms. In the context of international networking, festivals and conferences have been and still are regular gathering places for practitioners.

Is It Possible to Organize a Meta-Network?

At the beginning of the 1990s electronic and digital arts networks rapidly emerged all over the world, and the idea of a meta-network was formed within this new wave of enthusiasm.

Founded in the Netherlands in 1990, ISEA International (formerly Inter-Society for the Electronic Arts) is an international non-profit organization fostering interdisciplinary academic discourse and exchange among culturally diverse organizations and individuals working with art, science, and technology. The main activity of ISEA International is the annual International Symposium on Electronic Art (ISEA) that held its 25th anniversary celebration in 2013, where one of the founders, Wim van der Plas, reflected on its history and goals:

> The first ISEA Symposium was not organised with the goal to make it a series, but with the aim to establish the meta-organisation. The symposium, held in 1988 in Utrecht, The Netherlands, was the reason for creating a gathering where the plan for this association of organisations could be discussed and endorsed. This is exactly what happened and the association, called Inter-Society for the Electronic Arts (ISEA) was founded 2 years later in the city of Groningen (The Netherlands), prior to the Second ISEA symposium, in the same city. The continuation of the symposia, thus making it a series, was another result of the historic meeting in Utrecht. Quite possibly the goal was too ambitious and the founding fathers too much ahead of their times. When a panel meeting was organized on the stage of the second symposium, with representatives of SIGGRAPH, the Computer Music Association, Ars Electronica, ISAST/Leonardo, ANAT, Languages of Design and others, there was quite a civilized discussion on stage, but behind the curtains tempers flared because nobody wanted to lose autonomy.
>
> [...] It was an association and it's members were supposed to be institutes and organisations. However, because we had no funding whatsoever, we decided individuals could become members too. We managed to get about 100, later 200 members, many of them non-paying. Only a few [5–10] of the members were institutions. [...] Over the years, more than 100 newsletters have been produced. The newsletter had an extensive event agenda, job opportunities, calls for participation, etc. [...] Our main job was to coordinate the continued occurrence of the symposia. [...] (van der Plas 2013)

A main goal of the 1999 ISEA International "General Assembly on New Media Art," called Cartographies, was to make progress "toward a definition of new media art" (van der Plas 2013). Present were representatives of the Inter-Society, the Montreal Festival of New Cinema & New Media, Banff, the University of Quebec, McGill University, the Daniel Langlois Foundation (all Canadian organizations), Ars Electronica (Austria), V2 (Netherlands), Art3000 (France), Muu (Finland), Mecad (Spain), DA2 (UK), Walker Art Center (USA), and others. Valérie Lamontagne summarized the conversation by stating that "Certain initiatives did result from this discussion, mainly the desire to form a nation-wide media arts lobbying organization" (Lamontagne 1999).

Since 2008 the University of Brighton has hosted the headquarters of ISEA International, which has moved from an association to a foundation as organizational structure. Van der Plas commented: "The ISEA INTERNATIONAL foundation, contrary to the Inter-Society, has limited its goals to what it is able to reasonably accomplish. The Inter-Society had been too optimistic and too naïve. A volunteer organisation requires professionals to make it work effectively" (van der Plas 2013).

The ISEA symposia still take place annually in cities around the world and have grown to such an extent that the 19th edition in Sydney (2013) featured five parallel sessions over three days, accompanied by exhibitions, performances, public talks, workshops, and other events. Roger Malina, who coined the Inter-Society's name, commented on the problems the organization is facing today: "It is not at all clear to me what the right networking model is to use for an Inter-Society. Clearly we don't want a 19th or 20th century model of 'federation'" (Malina 2013).

With the advent of the World Wide Web in the mid-1990s, new kinds of local, regional, and international networks on different topics were created, mostly organized as specialized Internet mailing lists (moderated or not), free of membership fees and supporting openness in all respects, among them the Thing, Nettime, Rhizome, and Syndicate mailing lists/networks of the 1990s, to name just a few. The English language became a new standard for international communication, and other languages determined the local or regional character of the online network. Some networks were more focused on practice while others concentrated on developing social and theoretical discourse, but most of them merged theory and practice. A new element in networking practice was that many of the participants in the same network would not meet in person. New strategies for face-to-face meetings were developed, such as those hosted by institutions, festivals, and conferences in the field.

Conclusion

The practices of networks such as [New] Tendencies, E.A.T., and the Computer Arts Society supported art that made use of machinic processes of communication and information exchange, and bridged both society's and art's transition from the industrial age to the information society. Their practices reinforced a creative use of digital technologies for actively participating in social contexts. These networks promoted an interdisciplinary approach and led the evolution of digital culture from cybernetics to digital art. They provided a context for digital arts within contemporary art, among other fields, and illustrated how a network of digital arts operated even before the time of Internet. The rapid expansion of institutions and networks of digital arts and cultures since the 1990s has gone hand in hand with negative social trends brought about or controlled through technologies, reminding us of the everlasting necessity of taking a critical stance toward social responsibilities. It is fascinating to see how history repeats itself both in terms of mistakes and advances, and there is much to learn from only half a century of digital arts and its many layers and interpretations.

Notes

1 An example of an internationally oriented education organization may be the Institute of Sonology in the Netherlands, founded in 1967. Their activities in digital music and arts lasted over half a century, and their involvement in electronic art even longer. The Philips Pavilion, an iconic automated immersive audiovisual and multimedia environment by architect Le Corbusier and composers Xenakis and Edgar Varèse made for the 1958 Brussels World's Fair, was produced at the Centre for Electronic Music (CEM), a predecessor of the Institute of Sonology.

2 The Computing Devices Committee merged with the PTGEC to form the IEEE Computer Group in 1964. The name change to IEEE Computer Society happened in 1971.

3 *Computerart* curated by Jiří Valoch, Dům umění města (House of Arts), Brno, February 1968; traveled to Oblastní galerie vysociny, Jihlava, March 1968 and Oblastni galerie vytvarného umění and Gottwaldov, April 1968. *Cybernetic Serendipity* curated by Jasia Reichardt, Institute for Contemporary Arts, London, August 2–October 20, 1968; traveled to Washington, DC and San Francisco, 1969–1970. *tendencies 4*, Galerije Grada Zagreba, Zagreb, 1968–1969. *Computer Art*, Gallery Computer Technique Group, Tokyo, September 5–21, 1968. *The machine as seen at the end of the mechanical age*, organized by K.G. Pontus Hulten, Museum of Modern Art, New York, November 25, 1968–February 9, 1969. *Some more beginnings: Experiments in Art and Technology*, Brooklyn Museum and Museum of Modern Art, New York, November 26, 1968–January 5, 1969. *Computerkunst—On the Eve of Tomorrow*, organized by Käthe Clarissa Schröder, Kubus, Hannover, October 19–November 12, 1969, traveling exhibition. *IMPULSE: Computer-Kunst* rebranded by Goethe-Institut and set up by IBM, traveled to twenty-five cities in Europe and Asia 1970–1973.

4 The ACM Counter-Conference was held August 3–5, 1971 at the Harvest House Hotel, Boulder, Colorado.

5 The Cold War perspective on suspected industrial espionage is illustrated by the fact that, on another occasion, artist Ivan Picelj, who was involved with New Tendencies, for security reasons was not allowed to enter Bell Labs while visiting the United States in the mid-1960s, as he was coming from then socialist Yugoslavia. Interview by Darko Fritz, 2005.

6 Their main projects are captured in films. The most complete archives and research initiatives are in the Getty Research Library in Los Angeles and at the Daniel Langlois Foundation Collection in Montreal.

7 Gestalt ("organized whole") described parts that, identified individually, have different characteristics than the whole that they form. Gestalt theory of visual perception was created by psychologists in Germany in the 1920s to systematically study perceptual organization.

8 "Constructive art belongs to the past, its contents corresponding to the Paleocibernetic Period being those of the Computer Art" (Cordeiro 1973).

9 Other sources indicate that the first meeting of CAS, initiated by Alan Sutcliffe, was held in a room belonging to the University College London, in or near Gower Street, in September 1968. Subsequent meetings were often held at the offices of Lansdown's architectural practice (Sutcliffe 2003).

10 The August 1963 edition of the *Computers and Automation* magazine sponsored the first computer art competition. Ballistic Research Laboratory (BRL), part of the United States Army (programmer unknown), won both the first and second prize with *Slater Patterns* and *Stained Glass Windows*. BRL also won first prize in 1964. Michael Noll's *Computer Composition with Lines* won in 1965 and Frieder Nake's *Composition with Squares* in 1966.

11 It is surprising that conceptual art was not discussed earlier within that framework. Three of the responsible organizers of NT—Matko Meštrović, Radoslav Putar, and Dimitrije Basičević (Mangeleos)—had been part of "Gorgona," a pre-conceptual art group (behavior as art) working in Zagreb between 1959 and 1966.

12 The exhibition *bit international—[New] Tendencies—Computers and Visual Research, Zagreb (1961–1973)* curated by Darko Fritz presented all three major waves of NT, concrete, computer, and conceptual art (unlike previous retrospectives, which focused

on concrete art). The exhibition was held in 2007 at Neue Galerie Graz and 2008–2009 at ZKM, Karlsruhe, and was accompanied by the book *A Little-Known Story about a Movement, a Magazine, and the Computer's Arrival in Art: New Tendencies and Bit International, 1961–1973* (Rosen, Fritz, Gattin, and Weibel 2011).

13 The Art and Communication Centre (Centro de Arte y Comunicación, CAYC) in Buenos Aires was initially established as a multidisciplinary workshop by Víctor Grippo, Jacques Bedel, Luis Fernando Benedit, Alfredo Portillos, Clorindo Testa, Jorge Glusberg, and Jorge González in August 1968. From 1968 until his death in early 2012, Jorge Glusberg was the Director of the Center for Art and Communication. In 1972 the Scuola de Altos Estudios del CAYC was founded.

14 Organized by CAYC and Jorge Glusberg for the Museo de Arte Moderno, Buenos Aires, 1971.

15 The event happened on the occasion of the *Art and Technology* exhibition opening at the Los Angeles County Museum of Art in 1971 (Collins Goodyear 2008).

References

Argan, Giulio Carlo. 1965. "umjetnosti kao istraživanje" [art as research]. In *nova tendencija 3*, exhibition catalogue. Zagreb: Galerije grada Zagreba.

Ars Electronica. 2013. "About Ars Electronica." http://www.aec.at/about/en/geschichte/ (accessed December 5, 2014).

Bašičević, Dimitrije, and Ivan Picelj, eds. 1968. "Zašto izlazi 'bit'" [Why "bit" Appears]. In *bit international 1*: 3–5. Zagreb: Galerije grada Zagreba.

Barbrook, Richard. 2007. *Imaginary Futures.* London: Pluto Press.

Bonačić, Vladimir. 1975. "On the Boundary between Science and Art." *Impact of Science on Society* 25(1): 90–94.

Collins Goodyear, Anne. 2008. "From Technophilia to Technophobia: The Impact of the Vietnam War on the Reception of 'Art and Technology.'" *Leonardo* 41(2): 169–173.

Cordeiro, Waldemar. 1973. "Analogical and/or Digital Art." Paper presented at *The Rational and Irrational in Visual Research Today/Match of Ideas*, Symposium *t5*, June 2, 1973, Zagreb. Abstract published in the symposium reader. Zagreb: Gallery of Contemporary Art.

Eco, Umberto. 1962. "Arte cinetica arte programmata. Opere moltiplicate opera aperte." Milan: Olivetti.

Hyde, Gordon, Jonathan Benthall, and Gustav Metzger. 1969. "Zagreb Manifesto." *bit international 7*, June, edited by Božo Bek: 4. Zagreb and London: Galerije grada/Studio International. Audio recordings, Museum of Contemporary Art archives, Zagreb.

IEEE. 2013. "IEEE—History of IEEEE."http://www.ieee.org/about/ieee_history.html (accessed December 5, 2014).

Kelemen, Boris. 1973. Untitled. In *tendencije 5*, exhibition catalogue. Zagreb: Galerija suvremene umjetnosti.

Klüver, Billy, and Robert Rauschenberg. 1966. "The Mission." *E.A.T. Experiments in Arts and Technology*, October 10.

Klüver, Billy, and Robert Rauschenberg. 1967. *E.A.T. News* 1(2). New York: Experiments in Arts and Technology Inc.

Kusahara, Machiko. 2007/2008. "A Turning Point in Japanese Avant-garde Art: 1964–1970." Paper presented at *re:place 2007*, Second International Conference on the Histories of

Media, Art, Science and Technology, Berlin, November. In *Place Studies in Art, Media, Science and Technology—Historical Investigations on the Sites and the Migration of Knowledge*, edited by Andreas Broeckman and Gunalan Nadarajan. Weimar: VDG, 2008.

Lamontagne, Valérie. 1999. "CARTOGRAPHIES—The General Assembly on New Media Art." *CIAC*. http://magazine.ciac.ca/archives/no_9/en/compterendu02.html (accessed December 5, 2014).

Malina, Roger. 2013. "We don't want a federation." Presented at *The Inter-Society for the Electronic Arts Revived?*, panel at ISEA 2013, Sydney, June 7–16. http://www.isea2013.org/events/the-inter-society-for-the-electronic-arts-revived-panel/(accessed June 21, 2013).

Mason, Catherine. 2008. *A Computer in the Art Room: the Origins of British Computer Arts 1950–80*. Hindringham, UK: JJG Publishing.

Medosch, Armin. 2013. "From Total Recall to Digital Dementia—Ars Electronica 2013." *The Next Layer*. http://www.thenextlayer.org/node/1472 (accessed September 6, 2014).

Meštrović, Matko. 1963. Untitled. In *New Tendencies 2*, exhibition catalogue. Zagreb: Galerije grada Zagreba.

Metzger, Gustav. 1969. "Automata in history." *Studio International* 178: 107–109.

Metzger, Gustav. 1970. "Five Screens with Computer." In *tendencije 4: computers and visual research*, exhibition catalogue. Zagreb: Galerija Suvremene Umjetnosti.

MIT. 2013. "MIT Press Journals—About Leonardo." http://www.mitpressjournals.org/page/about/leon (accessed August 1, 2014).

Moles, Abraham. 1965. "Kibernetika i umjetničko djelo." In *nova tendencija 3*, exhibition catalogue. Zagreb: Galerije grada Zagreba.

Nake, Frieder. 1973. "The Separation of Hand and Head in "Computer Art". In *The Rational and Irrational in Visual Research Today/Match of ideas*, symposium t–5, 2 June 1973, symposium reader, Gallery of Contemporary Art, Zagreb, n.p.

PAGE. 1971. No. 16, 7. London: Computer Arts Society.

van der Plas, Wim. 2013. "The Inter-Society for the Electronic Arts Revived?." Introduction to panel session at ISEA 2013, Sydney, June 7–16. http://www.isea2013.org/events/the-inter-society-for-the-electronic-arts-revived-panel/ (accessed December 5, 2014).

Popper, Frank. 1965. "Kinetička umjetnosti i naša okolina." In *nova tendencija 3*, exhibition catalogue. Zagreb: Galerije grada Zagreba.

Putar, Radoslav, 1973. Untitled. In *tendencije 5*, exhibition catlogue. Zagreb: Galerija suvremene umjetnosti.

Rosen, Margit, Darko Fritz, Marija Gattin, and Peter Weibel, eds. 2011. *A Little-Known Story about a Movement, a Magazine, and the Computer's Arrival in Art: New Tendencies and Bit International, 1961–1973*. Karlsruhe and Cambridge, MA: ZKM/The MIT Press.

Sutcliffe, Alan. 2003. Interview with Catherine Mason, January 17. *CAS*. http://computer-arts-society.com/history (accessed January 15, 2015).

van Tijen, Tjebbe. 2011. "Art Action Academia, Research Center Art Technology and Society." http://imaginarymuseum.org/imp_archive/AAA/index.html (accessed December 5, 2014).

van Tijen, Tjebbe. 2011. "Art Action Academia, Manifesto against World Expo in Osaka." http://imaginarymuseum.org/imp_archive/AAA/index.html (accessed December 5, 2014).

van Tijen, Tjebbe, and Nic Tummers. 1968. "Manifesto against World Expo in Osaka." Distributors FRA Paris, Robho revue and GBR London, Artist Placement Group (APG). http://imaginarymuseum-archive.org/AAA/index.html#A14 (accessed August 1, 2012).

Vasulka, Woody. 1998. "Experiments in Art and Technology. A Brief History and Summary of Major Projects 1966–1998." http://www.vasulka.org/archive/Writings/EAT.pdf (accessed December 5, 2015).

Wolk, Johannes van der, ed. 1970. "# 30." *De werkgroep voor computers en woord, beeld en geluid.* Newsletter no. 5, May 15, Utrecht: 2.

Wolk, Johannes van der, ed. 1971. "# 105." *De werkgroep voor computers en woord, beeld en geluid.* Newsletter no. 9, June 30, Utrecht: 3–5.

Further Reading

Brown, Paul, Charlie Gere, Nicholas Lambert, and Catherine Mason, eds. 2008. *White Heat Cold Logic: British Computer Art 1960–1980.* Cambridge, MA: The MIT Press, Leonardo Book Series.

Denegri, Jerko. 2000/2004 (English translation). *Umjetnost konstruktivnog pristupa. The Constructive Approach to Art: Exat 51 and New Tendencies.* Zagreb: Horetzky.

Fritz, Darko. 2006. "Vladimir Bonačić – Early Works." Zagreb: UHA ČIP 07–08, 50–55.

Fritz, Darko. 2007. "La notion de «programme» dans l'art des années 1960 – art concret, art par ordinateur et art conceptuel" ["Notions of the Program in 1960s Art – Concrete, Computer-generated and Conceptual Art"]. In *Art++*, edited by David-Olivier Lartigaud. Orléans: Editions HYX (Architecture-Art contemporain-Cultures numériques), 26–39.

Fritz, Darko. 2008. "New Tendencies." Zagreb: Arhitekst Oris 54, 176–191.

Fritz, Darko. 2011. "Mapping the Beginning of Computer-generated Art in the Netherlands." Initial release, http://darkofritz.net/text/DARKO_FRITZ_NL_COMP_ART_n.pdf (accessed December 5, 2014).

Meštrović, Matko. "The Ideology of New Tendencies." *Od pojedinačnog općem (From the Particular to the General).* Zagreb: Mladost (1967), DAF (2005).

Rose, Barbara. 1972. "Art as Experience, Environment, Process." In *Pavilion*, edited by Billy Klüver, Julie Martin, and Barbara Rose, 93. New York: E.P. Dutton.

3

Art in the Rear-View Mirror

The Media-Archaeological Tradition in Art

Erkki Huhtamo

We look at the present through a rear-view mirror. We march backwards into the future.

Marshall McLuhan, *The Medium is the Massage* (1967)

Marshall McLuhan's famous saying, quoted above, perfectly characterizes one of the vital trends within contemporary arts: a growing number of artists have been drawn toward the past for inspiration. Devices that have disappeared not only as material artifacts but even from cultural memory have been unearthed, dissected, reinvented, and combined with ideas from other times and places. Such activities may at first seem motivated by a nostalgic quest for a simpler time when gadgets were few and easy to master, and media culture itself less all-embracing than it is today. However, such an interpretation would be misguided, unless one wants to consider all the silly "steampunk" concoctions, created by hobbyists from fleamarket junk, as art (I do not). Intellectually and emotionally challenging works are created by ambitious artists who have done their historical homework. The trend has grown significantly since I first brought it to public attention with my curatorial activities and the essay "Time Machines in the Gallery: An Archeological Approach in Media Art," written in 1994 and published in 1996 (Huhtamo 1996; Hertz and Parikka 2012, 429; Strauven 2013, 65).

I began paying attention to technological art that references the media of the past in the late 1980s. Rather than in the fine arts world, I encountered such works at the Ars Electronica in Linz, Austria, at the annual SIGGRAPH conferences in the United States and at media arts festivals. This may sound paradoxical, because these events were dedicated to showcasing the newest of the new. "Virtual reality" and "interactive media" were buzzwords around 1990. They inspired artists and scholars alike, but amidst all the enthusiasm, it was also dawning on practitioners and theorists that all the fancy head-mounted displays, tactile interfaces, and other manifestations of

A Companion to Digital Art, First Edition. Edited by Christiane Paul.

"cyberculture" were not entirely unprecedented. There had been cultural forms that had anticipated them, sometimes by centuries, raising very similar issues. By exploring forms like panoramas and stereoscopy, artists such as Jeffrey Shaw, Michael Naimark, and Luc Courchesne—although producing works that were contemporary high-tech creations—were also implying that there was a technological past worth exploring. All the claims about a cultural or even an ontological "rupture" that was supposed to be taking place—propagated by utopian virtual reality advocates with almost evangelical fervor—began feeling exaggerated and misleading.

An "archaeological" trend was in the air. I began questioning the discursive construction of contemporary media culture, wondering what may have been hidden behind its dominant utopian and "progressivist" narratives. I was not alone, as I discovered when studying the writings of scholars like Siegfried Zielinski and Friedrich Kittler (Huhtamo and Parikka 2011, 1–21). Like Zielinski, I started calling my research "media archaeology"; Kittler did not, but there were similarities. In idiosyncratic ways everyone was animated by a desire to question the prevailing "grand narratives" about technology, science, and media. They seemed overly selective, one-dimensional, and deterministic. Cross-references between different media forms were rare; linear accounts, written under the aegis of the 18th-century idea of progress, dominated. Historians told stories about successful inventors, entrepreneurs, companies, and institutions. They focused on creations that had "left their mark." The trajectories pointed toward constant betterment of both the gadgets themselves and the lives they were claimed to empower.

The assumed objectivity of the dominant narratives about media culture and its history raised suspicions. Did they really provide truthful accounts of the past(s)? What if something essential had been left by the roadside, cracks filled in, and stains painted over? Media archaeologists turned away from linear histories built around "winning" technologies. Influenced by Michel Foucault's archaeology of knowledge, they began exploring the archives for omissions, undetected or masked ruptures, and dark corners. They were determined to shed light on things that had been deemed as dead-ends and forgotten back alleys, treating these as symptoms to tease out alternative ways of reading the past. Attention was paid to ambitious failures: ideas that might have succeeded had the constellations of cultural circumstances been favorable. By including the excluded, the past could be made to speak with fresh voices that also shed light on the present.

An example of such a significant failure is the Telharmonium, an enormous organ-like electric music instrument designed by the American inventor Thaddeus Cahill (1867–1934) at the beginning of the 20th century. Cahill was not only occupied with the device; he purported to turn the technology into what Raymond Williams called a "cultural form" (Williams 1974/1992). A communications network was built around the Telharmonium, which was permanently located at the "Telharmonic Hall" (39th Street and Broadway, New York City). Live music was sent to subscribers such as hotels and stores via telephone wires; even wireless transmissions were experimented with (in 1907, with the help of Lee De Forest) (Huhtamo 1992a, 11). Cahill's project anticipated the consolidation of industrial background music (Muzak) by decades, but it also belongs to an archaeology of broadcasting.[1] Its complex ramifications and the equally complex reasons for its failure have been explored in exhaustive (but not exhausting) detail by Reynold

Weidenaar (Weidenaar 1995). Although Weidenaar does not call himself a media archaeologist, his interests are media-archaeological:

> Technological development is rarely stilled at detours and dead ends; instead, it is redirected and refocused. Such continuity to success, however, is exactly what we must not seek to impose on technological history, and that is why failures are studied. The view of progress as an autonomous and inevitable march to perfection is of limited use and very often mistaken. The history of technology is more valuable for its illumination of an age, its revelation of sociocultural contexts, than it is for disclosure of successful inventions and processes. (Weidenaar 1995, viii)

Weidenaar speaks against technological determinism, joining a debate that was sparked by Marshall McLuhan's work in the 1960s. Raymond Williams castigated McLuhan for advocating it at the expense of—as Lynn Spigel put it—"the power dynamics of social relationships and institutional practices" (Spigel 1974/1992, xvi). For the supporters of technological determinism, Williams explained,

> progress is the history of inventions which "created the world." The effects of the technologies, whether direct or indirect, foreseen or unforeseen, are as it were the rest of history. The steam engine, the automobile, television, the atomic bomb, have made modern man and the modern condition. (Williams 1974/1992, 7)

Williams did not find it surprising that such arguments had been "welcomed by the 'media-men' of the existing institutions" (Williams 1974/1992, 128). Technological determinism still promises wired/wireless paradises on earth, to be reached by means of ever more powerful and fancy gadgets. Such promises abound in marketing discourses and in the forecasts by techno-utopians like Nicholas Negroponte and Raymond Kurzweil.

Media archaeology questions technological determinism by emphasizing the multiplicity of the factors that affect historical agents at any one moment and contribute to the formation of media culture. It points out that technology can never be "bare," an autonomous force acting by itself. However, the issue is anything but simple (Huhtamo 2013a). McLuhan may or may not have been a technological determinist (the issue is still under debate), but he was definitely a humanist. For him the media were "extensions of man," prostheses that extended the human body and mind, enhancing the human being's capabilities to see, hear, move, and comprehend. The human remained the center of McLuhan's thinking, whereas for Kittler the onslaught of technological devices used for the "inscription" and storage of words, sounds, images, and numerical data pointed toward the posthuman condition, where humans would disappear and history come to an end[2] (Kittler 1990). Consciousness would be uploaded into far smarter machines than the human brain, a condition Kittler seemed to welcome.

Media archaeology has neither developed a rigid set of methodological principles nor built a dedicated institutional framework; it remains a "traveling discipline" (Huhtamo and Parikka 2011, 3). The diversity of approaches among its practitioners (including those who do related work without using the term) reflects this disparity. Although Kittler's initial position was influenced by Derrida's deconstructionism, Lacan's psychoanalysis, and Foucault's archaeology of knowledge, he tended, somewhat paradoxically, to conjure up new grand narratives. Zielinski promulgates a radical heterogeneity of approaches in order to resist Western logocentrism and its stranglehold on self-expression, while I emphasize the ways in which iterative discursive formulas (topoi) travel across time and space, affected by changing circumstances and affecting them in turn. Others excavate areas that have been rarely visited by media scholars, as exemplified by Jussi Parikka's *Insect Media* (Parikka 2010).

Artists and Media Archaeology—Before the Beginnings

"The point is confirmed: history is a story of loss and recovery and comes to us in bits and pieces," wrote the musicologist Glenn Watkins in *The Gesualdo Hex* (2010), an ambitious exploration of Carlo Gesualdo's discursive afterlife and an attempt to break myths surrounding it (Watkins 2010, 14). The ways in which artists put such bits and pieces together differ radically from the ways researchers do it. Artists inhabit a more flexible cultural space without all the restrictions (of method, source criticism, peer pressure) that constrain scholars. They are allowed and expected to dream and fantasize; they enjoy more liberties to compare, conclude, and leap between times and places—or between real and imaginary things—than researchers. Most importantly, the results of the excavations made by artists are expressed by different means. Instead of being translated into the meta-language of words, artworks often re-enact features of the excavated object itself. References to other media, and even to imaginary projections of utopian futures as they have been filtered through the artist's mind, are added to the mix.

Even so, archaeologically oriented artists share things with scholars. Both parties refuse to take the past at face value, acknowledging the impossibility of reaching certainties about things that used to exist "out there," independently of the observer's own stance and judgment. Like artists, media archaeologists travel between temporalities, comparing them, juxtaposing them, and persuading them to illuminate each other. Media-archaeological research is a form of armchair travel, but it cannot be practiced in an anarchic fashion. When an artist jumps into the time machine and grasps the controls, one may expect a wilder ride, taken to the limits of the imagination. Such rides, as well as the ideas behind them and the contexts that inform them, concern us in this chapter. Its aim is to shed light on the peculiar nature of creating a *certain* kind of technological art. To be worth being identified as media-archaeological, an artwork must evoke earlier media in one way or another. Such works can be treated as "metacommentaries" on media culture, its motifs, its structures, and its ideological, social, psychological, and economic implications (Huhtamo 1995b).

As novel as media-archaeological art seemed in the late 1980s, it is now clear that its origins—as well as those of media archaeology itself—must be traced further back in time. Early formative contributions to media archeology were made by scholars like Aby Warburg, Walter Benjamin, Dolf Sternberger, and Ernst Robert Curtius, active in the first half of the 20th century (Huhtamo and Parikka 2011, 3, 6–7, 14). There were parallel developments in the arts, in spite of the prevalence of modernist attitudes that eschewed the past, even advocating its destruction. Le Corbusier, Walter Gropius, Kasimir Malevich, Piet Mondrian, and, in a more aggressive sense, the Futurists, led by Filippo Tommaso Marinetti, purported to free art from the dead hand of the past, calling for a new aesthetics in accordance with the modalities and sensibilities of modern life. Such a rupturist idea of modernism still has some validity, although no longer without qualifications, as, for example, Kirk Varnedoe and Adam Gopnik's exhibition catalogue *High and Low: Modern Art and Popular Culture* (Varnedoe and Gopnik 1990) and J.K. Birksted's research on Le Corbusier's indebtedness to 19th-century occultist trends have demonstrated (Birksted 2009).

It would be difficult to claim that media-archaeological attitudes developed before the 20th century. Although artists have been making references to art making in their works at least since the Renaissance, as Aby Warburg's pioneering research demonstrated, the references mostly concerned styles and motifs—Warburg's "pathos formulas" (Michaud 2004, 7–9 and passim)—rather than tools and conditions of visual illusions. It has been established with relative certainty that artists resorted to the camera obscura since the time of Leonardo da Vinci. The discussion about Vermeer's possible use of it is a well-known episode of recent debates in the arts, involving the artist David Hockney (Hockney 2001). However, except in pedagogical illustrations, such devices relatively rarely emerged as self-conscious subject matter or as discursive issues commented on by the artist (Kofman 1998; Bubb 2010).

Hans Holbein the Younger's *Ambassadors* (1533, National Gallery, London) is an intriguing case, because it contains an anamorphically distorted scull in the same pictorial space as portraits of the personalities who posed for the artist (Kemp 1990, 208–210). Two visual systems, implying different senses of reality, coexist. The distorted skull has been interpreted as a self-conscious demonstration of the artist's skill in techniques of perspective (to which anamorphosis belongs as a kind of inversion of its principles), or as a metaphoric memento mori reference. No apparatus is needed to read it correctly; one only has to view the painting from a certain angle close to its surface (Ades 2000).[3] To find examples of an emerging media-archaeological awareness from earlier centuries, one would probably have to look outside the traditions of academic art and consider the "subsculptural" works of automata makers, fairground artists, and other creators of media spectacles, who may have self-consciously commented on the media they had appropriated for their own creations (Burnham 1968, 185). The same goes for illustrators who depicted such shows in their works. Such research has to be accomplished elsewhere.

Dadaists, surrealists, and related hard-to-classify figures such as Marcel Duchamp and Frederick Kiesler may well have been the first to have developed conversational relationships with technology. Francis Picabia's Dadaist paintings of machines are early examples (Pontus Hultén 1968, 82–95). The surrealists, in particular, plundered the archives of the past, using them as repositories for ideas to s(t)imulate the operations of the unconscious mind. Max Ernst's graphic novels *La femme 100 têtes* (1929) and *Rêve d'une petite fille qui foulut entrer au carmel* (1930) demonstrated how popular illustrations from magazines, encyclopedias, children's books, and other sources could be turned into uncanny collages that penetrated beyond the rational surface of bourgeois normality while preserving traces of their actual referents. Bachelor machines, or *machines célibataires*, are a perfect example of such explorations. Imagined by writers and artists like Alfred Jarry, Raymond Roussel, Franz Kafka, Marcel Duchamp, Francis Picabia, and others, they were discursive engines, psychomechanisms that evoked industrial machinery and engineering applications stripped of rational purpose.[4] They embodied erotic fantasies, language games, nightmares and obsessions, as well as pataphysical humor (Carrouges 1954, Clair and Szeemann 1975).

Among their multitudes of cultural references, Ernst's graphic novels contain media-related illustrations from the popular-scientific magazine *La Nature*, including pictures of Étienne-Jules Marey's famous Station Physiologique (claimed to be the world's first "film studio") and his version of the zoetrope, a familiar optical toy.[5] When it comes to his treatment of the latter, Ernst reversed the customary positions and mutual sizes of the user and the device. He placed a girl inside the spinning drum, whereas in real life the users would gather around it, stroking it, and peeking at an animation through the slits on its side. Instead of a picture strip, Marey's zoetrope contained a sequence of sculptures depicting a bird in flight, modeled after a chronophotographic sequence. In a surrealist spirit, Ernst has made one of the birds come alive and fly out of the zoetrope (using a figure cut from another illustration of Marey's bird sculptures also published in *La Nature*). The zoetrope seems huge, and the human being small. Such transformations defamiliarize the familiar, turning a domestic "proto-interactive" philosophical toy into a nightmarish mindscape—a dizzying environment spinning out of control.

Ernst's treatment of Marey's zoetrope could be interpreted in terms of media-cultural developments. Where the zoetrope, and even the early hand-cranked film projectors, subordinated media imagery to the user's deliberate actions, the media culture of the 1920s and 1930s was dominated by industrial cinema and radio broadcasting that limited the possibility of user interventions (Brecht 1986, 53–55).[6] Images were projected onto the cinema screen or sounds beamed to the home from an elsewhere (the projection booth, radio station). As it was industrialized, media culture was turned into an immersive "phantasmagoric" environment haunting the users' minds. Taking detours through the past, the surrealists punched holes into an increasingly airtight and calculated commercial mediascape. Whereas Ernst resorted to graphic art, others produced versions of old media devices. Joseph Cornell created hand-spun thaumatrope disks (another 19th-century optical toy) as "surrealist toys" (Koch 1998, 162–163).[7] Frederick Kiesler referred to the peepshow box—a centuries-old visual entertainment—in his theatrical and exhibition designs (Béret 1996).

Although Marcel Duchamp was not a "media artist," it could be claimed that few artists have developed a more complex relationship with media than he did. His first *succès de scandale*, the painting *Nude Descending a Staircase* (1912), already harked back to chronophotography. Among Duchamp's manifold interests, optical "research"—conducted by one of his alter egos, the "precision oculist"—occupied him throughout his career (Huhtamo 2003, 54–72). Posing as an optician-scientist, Duchamp bridged the past and the present, combining 3D with 4D. His series of rotating optical disks produced pulsating sensations of relief. The disks were influenced by contemporary theories about the 4th dimension and, as I have suggested elsewhere, also by devices such as Joseph Plateau's Phenakistiscope (1833), a "persistence of vision" device that was turned into a commercial toy soon after it had been introduced in scientific circles (Dalrymple-Henderson 1998; Huhtamo 2003, 64). Whereas the *Large Glass* (1915–1923) can be analyzed as a conceptual bachelor machine, actual hand-cranked or motor-driven machines were constructed for the disk experiments. They led to the film *Anémic Cinéma* (1925) and the *Rotoreliefs* (1935), a boxed set of optical disks to be "played" on a standard gramophone. Although efforts to market the latter for consumers failed, they were media art *avant la lettre* in their attempt to bypass the gallery system.

Duchamp's most complex media-archaeological contribution was his final chef d'oeuvre, *Étant donnés: 1. la chute d'eau, 2. le gaz déclairage* (*Given: 1. The Waterfall 2. The Illuminating Gas*, 1946–1966). Peeping through two small holes drilled into an old wooden door reveals an obscene scene: a reclining nude female mannequin with legs spread, surrounded by physical props such as a "burning" gas torch and a waterfall (an optical trick). *Étant donnés* can be related to the tradition of illusionistic museum dioramas, but it also evokes erotic peepshow cabinets. Stereoscopy is a reference point as well: the pair of peepholes (for only one user at a time) evokes the stereoscope, and so does the deep perspective, which brings to mind the clandestine 19th-century pornographic stereoviews showing women spreading their legs for the viewer.[8] Stereoscopy inspired Duchamp throughout his career, from the "rectified readymade" *Handmade Stereopticon Slide* (1918), which had its origin in a found Victorian stereocard, to his very last work, the *Anaglyphic Chimney* (Huhtamo 2013b, 123–133 English, 129–141 German).

Art, Technology, and the Past in the 1950s and 1960s

The connections between art and technology became more intense during the 1950s and 1960s as part of a general expansion and questioning of the notion of art. Artists moved on from commenting on technology indirectly in paintings and other traditional forms to constructing functioning devices to administer visual and auditory experiences for their audiences. Yet, no consensus about the implications of the human–machine relationship was reached. Schematically speaking, one might suggest that a divide opened up between those who embraced technology as a potential force for improving and enriching modern life, and those who detracted and ridiculed it, demonstrating their mistrust of the technological and corporate information society. The former line had its origins in Russian and Bauhausian constructivism and manifested itself in phenomena like kinetic art and cybernetic art, while the latter aligned itself with the legacy of Dadaism and was epitomized by groups like Fluxus, Lettrisme, Le Nouveau Réalisme, and OuLiPo, although the latter—Lettrisme and OuLiPo in particular—are also important for a genealogy of generative, algorithmic art forms.

Although the situation was never so clearcut, the constructivist line continued the anti-passéist agenda of early 20th-century modernists, as works like Nicolas Schöffer's machine sculptures, responsive cybernetic towers, and writings about technology-saturated urban utopias demonstrate. Collaborations between artists, designers, engineers, and corporations were considered a viable way of inventing the future; the past had little to contribute. It was the neo-Dadaist trend that drew inspiration from the past, making ambiguous and impish references to "obsolete" cultural forms and mixing them with products and ideas from contemporary culture. In an "anything goes" spirit, Fluxus graphics recycled Victorian fonts and stock images, while Fluxus actions mistreated objects that had symbolic value for the dominant social order, such as pianos and television sets. Jean Tinguely's ramshackle-looking machine sculptures harked back to bachelor machines, but their rekindled Dada acts (including self-destruction) gained new significance from the shadow of the nuclear holocaust, replacing the naïve belief in social harmony and eternal peace with sarcastic humor and skepticism[9] (Brougher, Ferguson, and Gamboni 2013, 57–58, 178–181).

Experimental artists of the 1960s did not ignore media history, but it was rarely their major concern. Stan Vanderbeek, who satirized contemporary society with his early collage animations, constructed a "Primitive Projection Wheel," a zoetrope made of a horizontally positioned bicycle wheel to present a short animation[10] (Kranz 1974, 240). However, this was just a minor part of his extensive activities that embraced experimental computer animation and movie "murals" shown in the *Movie-Drome* (1963), a dome-like projection environment. Vanderbeek's real goal was nothing less than the reinvention of the moving image culture. Another pointer that reminds us of the need to avoid overemphasizing the role of the past as an inspiration is Brion Gysin and Ian Sommerville's *Dream Machine* (or *Dreamachine*, 1961).[11] It has often been compared to the zoetrope, and for a good reason: it is a spinning cylinder and, like the zoetrope, springs from the tradition of stroboscopic light research (Geiger 2005, 11–13).[12] Yet, instead of paying attention to the formal similarities only, one should also consider the differences related to function and the context of invention and use.

The circumstances that led to the invention of the Dream Machine were quite specific. Gysin, a bohemian poet and painter, was inspired by "spontaneous hallucinations" he experienced on a bus trip in southern France. They were triggered by a row of trees by the roadside, experienced through closed eyelids in the setting sun. Gysin characterized the sensation with a media-related metaphor as "a multidimensional kaleidoscope whirling out through space" (diary entry, December 21, 1958, quoted in Weiss 2001, 113).[13] This is not unlike the stroboscopic experiences that contributed to the invention of "persistence of vision" demonstration devices like the zoetrope in the 19th century. For example, in 1825 the scientist Peter Mark Roget called attention to "a curious deception which takes place when a carriage wheel, rolling along the ground, is viewed through the intervals of a series of vertical bars, such as those of a palisade, or of a Venetian window-blind" (Carpenter 1868, 432).[14] Although Roget's research goals were different, Gysin did associate his experience with the flickering of silent films he had seen, drawing a connection to the "flicker tradition" from which film had emerged.

Gysin wanted to produce a machine for creating the kinds of sensations he had experienced. The solution was found by Ian Sommerville, a Cambridge mathematics graduate (and boyfriend of Gysin's pal William Burroughs), who placed a slotted cylinder with a light bulb inside on a gramophone, spinning it at the speed of 78 rpm. Gysin added a colorful calligraphic painting strip inside the drum to enhance its effect (Gysin 2001, 114). When the invention was featured in the *Olympia* magazine in January 1962, a do-it-yourself version was included, meant to be cut out and assembled by the reader. It was essentially a zoetrope: the vertical slits were narrow, and the reverse side (forming the inside of the cylinder when the pages would be folded and pasted together) was covered by colorful "calligraphy," reproduced as a color foldout in Laura Hoptman's *Brion Gysin: Dream Machine* (2010, 178–182). Although the word "zoetrope" was not used, it is likely that the instrument had contributed to the design. But the device evolved further: the paintings were left out and the slits widened into different shapes (Gysin and Sommerville 1962).[15] The *Dream Machine* drifted away from the zoetrope, which made sense, because they had very different purposes.

The zoetrope was a moving picture machine, whereas the *Dream Machine* was meant to tease out images assumed to pre-exist in the user's mind. Gysin suggested that the "spectator penetrates inside an immense psychical reserve (his own) that is continuously modified by external impulses" (Fabre 2003, 169).[16] "The whole human program of vision," including archetypes, gestalt formations, and religious symbols, would be reached by the *Dream Machine* (Hoptman 2010, 120–121). In this sense the goals had affinities with shamanistic techniques, Jungian deep psychology, and experiments with chemical substances. Gysin and Sommerville were influenced by W. Grey Walter's book *The Living Brain* (1953), in which he described experiments with an electronic stroboscope. They understood that the mind could be affected by s(t)imulating alpha waves in the brain by means of flickering light. The *Dream Machine* provided a way of making the laboratory experiments by Walter, John R. Smythies, and others available for everybody. It was found to be most effective when the flicker was received through closed eyelids, but could also be used by staring at the cylinder with eyes open. The light bulb had to be outside the direct field of vision (Gysin and Somerville 1962; Hoptman 2010, 178).

Although the *Dream Machine* was first introduced in the artworld in 1962 in exhibitions in Paris and Rome, Gysin saw commercial potential and began efforts to have it mass-produced (Hoptman 2010, 178).[17] He even claimed to have patented it. I have found out that the claim is not true, even though he mentioned the French patent number (P.V. 868.281), the date (July 18, 1961), and even quoted the description (in English in Gysin 1962, 172).[18] What he claims to be the "patent number" is only a filing number (P.V. means *proces-verbal*). He may have handed in his application, possibly on the said day, but whether the application was rejected, whether he was unable to collect enough money for the legal fees, or whether there was some other reason, the patent was never issued.[19] The Dutch Philips Corporation is said to have investigated the possibility of manufacturing the device, but that led nowhere; neither did later efforts to find commercial partners (Geiger 2003a, 66).[20] Philips may well have been contacted, because it had shown interest in experimental arts. It had collaborated with Le Corbusier, Iannis Xenakis, and Edgard Varèse to create its pavilion for the Brussels World's Fair (1958), and would soon produce pioneering technological artworks with Edward Ihnatowicz, whose responsive cybernetic creature *Senster* (1970) was exhibited at its showroom in Eindhoven, and Nicolas Schöffer.

The *Dream Machine* deserves a place in the history of media-archaeological art, because it belongs to a tradition running from the "natural magic" of 17th-century Jesuits to kaleidoscopes, phenakistiscopes, and zoetropes, quack machines for healing with light, and kinetic artworks such as Duchamp's *Rotoreliefs* and Schöffer's *Le Lumino* (1968) and *Varetra* (1975). The latter were motorized light boxes for the home that were in fact manufactured by Philips. Gysin seems to have considered the *Dream Machine* as a potential replacement for the alienating television set, but its fate was much like that of *Rotoreliefs*, which Gysin may have known, because he mentioned Duchamp as "the first to recognize an element of the infinite in the Ready-Made—our industrial objects manufactured in 'infinite' series" (Grysin 1962).[21] Ironically, both *Rotoreliefs* and the *Dream Machine* survived against their creators' wishes as limited fine art editions (Hoptman 2010). [22] The latter became gradually a cult object, used—with or without chemical substances—within various subcultural settings.[23]

Another warning against oversimplifying matters is the work of the unjustly neglected Swiss artist Alfons Schilling (1934–2013). He explored many forms of technology, but creating conversations with the past was hardly his major goal (Schilling et al. 1997).[24] Like Duchamp, Schilling began his career as a painter. His first innovation, perfected in 1961, was a method of creating drip paintings by throwing paint on moving circular canvases spun by motors (the paintings were exhibited either in stasis or motion). It would be tempting to associate these paintings with Duchamp's rotating disks, but there is a difference. Duchamp's disks always produced discrete figures in motion (including their pulsating illusions of depth), whereas Schilling's rotating paintings emphasized the fusion of colors and shapes when spun. Their media-archaeological reference point is not the phenakistiscope or the zoetrope, but rather another demonstration device, the "Newton's Wheel," used by color theorists to explore the spectrum and the fusion of colors. However, Schilling's idea could also be interpreted without such historical reference points "simply" as a machinic extension of abstract expressionism.[25]

There is another intriguing parallel between Duchamp and Schilling: both largely abandoned painting early in their careers to explore other means of expression. Moving first to film and then to three-dimensional imaging, the relationship between time and space became Schilling's central occupation (as it was for Duchamp). He experimented with holography, stereoscopic drawings and paintings, lenticular 3D pictures, random dot stereograms (invented by the scientist Béla Julesz, with whom he communicated), and "autobinary" stereo images.[26] With the video art pioneer Woody Vasulka, he constructed wearable "binocular video spectacles" (1973) that replaced the user's direct vision by scenes from a stereoscopic pair of video cameras. The concoction was one of the earliest examples of an artist-made head-mounted display. Schilling also gave public performances with 3D slide projectors, demonstrating unusual optical effects—known as the "Schilling effect"—by spinning shutter disks in front of the lenses.

From a media-archaeological point of view, Schilling's series of *Vision Machines* (*Sehmachinen*) from the 1970s and 1980s is particularly important. They were wearable prosthetic devices built of wooden rods, mirrors, lenses, rotating shutter blades, and other accessories. Like his video spectacles, they playfully probed the relationship between the observer's mind, eyes, and the world. Instead of simply extending the user's vision in the manner of microscopes and telescopes, they explored the (im)possible. As Max Peintner has shown, Schilling's contraptions were deeply rooted in the history of perspectival imaging, joining the broad tradition of perspective machines, katoptric experiments, and optical prostheses described by Martin Kemp in his book *Science of Art* (Kemp 1990; Schilling 1997). Significantly, Schilling pictured the painter Andrea Mantegna, a Renaissance master of the perspective in one of his drawings, wearing his video spectacles (Schilling 1997, 260). Filippo Brunelleschi's experiments, undertaken with a peep viewer constructed for the purpose, also appealed to Schilling's own efforts to combine real and artificial spaces (Kemp 1990, 11–13; Wein 2010, 261). Schilling's series of vision machines included a wearable tent camera obscura and two models—the wearable version *Kleiner Vogel* (*Little Bird*, 1978) and the permanent installation *Optisches System* (*Optical System*, 1983)—inspired by Charles Wheatstone's mirror stereoscope (1838). Both used angled mirrors to extend the parallax difference between the eyes, thereby radically transforming the observer's impression of the surroundings. Such inventions bridged the past and the present, the inherited and the innovative, in ways that resonate with media-archaeological interests.

An important artist whose interests are worth comparing with those of Schilling was the American Jim Pomeroy (1945–1992). Both were known for their exploration of technology in search of possibilities for art, but their attitudes were very different. Schilling's stance was cool and formal; he called himself an "artist and visual thinker" or "artist and innovator," and rarely paid much attention to thematic social and cultural issues. Pomeroy was colorful and eclectic, a manifestation of a long American tradition of enthusiastic self-taught tinkerers (DeMarinis 1993, 1–15).[27] He impersonated eccentric alter egos stemming from his performances and demonstrated fantastic arrays of homemade inventions, from bricolaged sound machines to 3D slide projections, spiced up with tongue-in-cheek humor and intelligent social satire. Pomeroy's version of the zoetrope, *Newt Ascending Astaire's Face* (1975), presented a lizard-like amphibian endlessly climbing Fred Astaire's motionless face (only the eyeballs moved). The title was a pun à la Raymond Roussel on Duchamp's *Nude Descending a Staircase* (Sheldon and Reynolds 1991, 30, 41).[28]

Besides sound, 3D was a big inspiration for Pomeroy.[29] For *Considerable Situations* (an Artpark outdoors project exhibited in Lewiston, NY, 1987) he installed a series of seven robust stereoscopic viewers around the Niagara Falls. They contained imaginary and impossible artworks "placed" within the real landscapes directly in front of the viewing devices. For a series called *Reading Lessons* (1988) Pomeroy digitally reworked old stereoviews from the Keystone View Company.[30] Pun-like texts inserted into the views persuaded the eyes of the observer to wander from plane to plane. The opening view has the words "Reading Lessons and Eye Exercises" distributed around a reading figure literally pushing the soles of his shoes in the viewer's face. The humoristic and absurd text and image combinations are not just pranks. "We are not seduced by farce, but rather, sharpened," Pomeroy wrote (Pomeroy 1988).[31] As an ambiguous homage to popular stereoscopy, he released his stereoscopic photographs as a boxed set of View-Master reels and viewer.

In the performance *Apollo Jest. An American Mythology* (1978) Pomeroy combined projected stereoscopic slides with a matter-of-fact voiceover narration to "prove" that the moon landing actually *did* take place.[32] As is well known, according to conspiracy theories, the event had been staged in a Hollywood film studio. A female voice presents a series of arguments, while miscellaneous "found" stereoviews prove them right by "incontestable" visual evidence (the Empire State Building serves as a stand-in for a rocket, etc.). With deadpan humor and theoretical insight, Pomeroy attacks naïve beliefs in documentary truth and the ontology of the photograph. Deliberate "matches" between words and images reveal the artificial, semiotic nature of the relationship. As Roland Barthes famously demonstrated, photographs can never be sites of incontestable truth. Their meanings depend on cultural coding and textual "anchoring" that can be (ab)used for ideological purposes (Barthes 1977, 15–31).[33] In a gesture that perfectly matches the character of Pomeroy's art, the stereoviews from *Apollo Jest* were issued as a set of eighty-eight bubblegum cards combined with a cardboard stereo viewer (Pomeroy 1983).

Avant-Garde Cinema, New Film Historicism, and Archaeologies of Projection

In his introduction to a special issue of Afterimage titled "Beginning … and beginning again" (Field 1981, 3):

> It is perhaps that the history of cinema is too important to be left solely to historians; and that the work of radical filmmakers involves a constant return to beginnings, an understanding of the past at work in the present.

Beside texts by revisionist film historians like Noel Burch, the issue contained material about filmmakers such as Klaus Wyborny who had since the late 1960s incorporated references to early cinema into their works. Other names could be added to the list: Ken Jacobs, Hollis Frampton, Malcolm LeGrice, Ernie Gehr, Robert Breer, and Werner Nekes. The latter's experimental feature film *Uliisses* (1980–1982) was packed with media-archaeological references (Nekes 1987).[34] As Tom Gunning has explained, all this was part of a wider change of emphasis within the arts (Gunning 2003, 222–272). Where the experimental cinema of the 1950s and the earlier 1960s had been dominated by personal and (mytho)poetic works, often with echoes of surrealism (epitomized by the work of Stan Brakhage), the late 1960s witnessed a turn toward structural and conceptual forms. The rediscovery and semiotic investigation of early visual culture focused attention on the film language, the materiality of film, and the "cinematic apparatus" (the material-metapsychological context of the filmic experience).

A paradigmatic work is Ken Jacobs's *Tom, Tom the Piper's Son* (1969), a painstaking reworking and dissection of an American Mutoscope and Biograph Co. silent film with the same title from 1905. By re-photographing it at length and in minute detail, the brief film was extended to nearly two hours, forcing it to reveal its barely noticeable secrets as a filmic text. Bart Testa has rightly characterized *Tom, Tom the Piper's Son* as "an archaeological essay in addition to a semiotic genealogy of film language" (Testa 1992, 222–272). "Structural" filmmakers like Jacobs purported to reinvent the medium as a reaction to the calculated and standardized nature of 1960s mainstream cinema. In this sense there were parallels with the work of radical filmmakers working within the commercial production, exhibition, and distribution circuit, such as Jean-Luc Godard and Nagisa Oshima, who submitted film language to semiotic scrutiny, revealing its artificial and illusionistic nature. Godard's *Les Carabiniers* (1963) included a re-enactment of Edison's *Uncle Josh at the Moving Picture Show* (1902), considered by many as a reflection of early, confused reactions to cinema. Complex and layered treatment of cinema history and the cinematic apparatus (*dispositif*) characterized Godard's video series *Histoire(s) du cinéma* (1988–1998), a truly media-archaeological work "written" with images and sounds.

A perfect example of an early form of "primitive" moving image technology that was rediscovered by both filmmakers and experimental artists of the 1960s was the flipbook. Although such simple "thumb movies" became popular during the earliest years of the cinema (adding a tactile dimension to the visual experience), the flipbook had already been invented in the 1860s, and even patented by the Englishman John Barnes Linnett in 1868.[35] Flipbooks were made by experimental filmmakers such as Robert Breer (as early as 1955), Oskar Fischinger (as Mutoscope reels), Stan Vanderbeek, Douglass Crockwell, Andy Warhol, Jack Smith, and Birgit and Wilhelm Hein, as well as by Fluxus artists like George Brecht, Mieko Shiomi and Dick Higgins. In the 1970s, diverse artists such as John Baldessari, Gilbert & George, Eduardo Paolozzi and François Dallegret contributed to the artists' flipbook tradition. It continues to grow, now including works by visual artists like Keith Haring, animation filmmakers like Peter Foldes and Taku Furukawa, and media artists like Gregory Barsamian and Tony Oursler (Gethmann et al. 2005).[36] Robert Breer also created his own versions of Mutoscope viewers and exhibited his flipbooks as murals (Gethmann et al. 2005, 74).

The discovery of early cinema by avant-garde filmmakers became associated with emerging forms of cinema scholarship, such as writings on the cinematic apparatus (*dispositif*) by scholars such as Jean-Louis Comolli and Jean-Louis Baudry and the "new film historicism" represented by Tom Gunning, André Gaudreault, Noel Burch, Charles Musser, Thomas Elsaesser, Miriam Hansen, and others (Testa 1992, 18). The forms and cultural roles of the earliest cinema were reassessed in a process of freeing them from historical explanations that saw them merely as primitive beginnings of something infinitely more advanced (and important). The prevailing narratives were found to be selective, teleological, and ideologically neutralizing or reactionary. Both with regard to its modes of representation and its institutional forms, early cinema was found to have a character of its own, connected with neighboring and preceding cultural forms within intricate webs. Comparisons with future developments were also possible, as Gunning demonstrated by discussing the complex relationships between the successive "new beginnings" introduced by avant-garde cinema and the cinema of the earliest times (Gunning 1983, 355–366).

Eadweard Muybridge's (1830–1904) influence on Hollis Frampton and others was an important step, because it moved the media-archaeological focus further back in time. Muybridge's work had anticipated cinema by bridging serial photography, animation devices like the phenakistiscope, and magic lantern slide projections. As a kind of materialized synthesis, Muybridge's Zoopraxiscope was a magic lantern modified to project brief moving image sequences (based on photographs) from spinning disks. According to Gunning, the (re)discovery of Muybridge was influenced by the re-issuing of Muybridge's chronophotographs as Dover's paperback editions in 1969 (Gunning 2003); "the flurry of articles" inspired by the 1972 centennial of Muybridge's work with Leland Stanford; the appearance of two biographies (by Haas and Hendricks); and Thom Andersen's documentary film *Muybridge: Zoopraxographer* (1975). Hollis Frampton's essay "Eadweard Muybridge: Fragments of a Tesseract" (1973) was symptomatic as well, although references to Muybridge had been made earlier by minimalists and conceptualists like Sol LeWitt (1964) and William Wegman (1969) (Sheldon and Reynolds 1991).[37]

Freezing motion and separating it into discrete moments, as well as the adopting a detached "scientific" approach, were in line with conceptualism; many homages were produced. Frampton contributed the memorable series *Sixteen Studies from Vegetable Locomotion* (with Marion Faller, 1975), which commented on Muybridge's work in an intelligent tongue-in-cheek fashion by substituting vegetables in various states of motion for humans or animals (Frampton 1984).[38] Muybridge may since have become the most common reference point for media-archaeologically inclined artists. I will mention just a few examples. In the interactive CD-ROM *Bio-Morph Encyclopedia* (1994), created by the Japanese multimedia artist Nobuhiro Shibayama, Muybridge's chronophotographic series have been embedded within a simulated book and reanimated by transforming them by means of morphing. The pseudo-scientific nature of Muybridge's images has been compromised by placing them within a fantastic interface that harks back to medieval illuminated manuscripts, adventure games, and Salvador Dali's brand of amorphic surrealism.

Rebecca Cummins's *Shadow Locomotion: 128 Years After Muybridge, The Red Barn, Stanford University, Palo Alto* (2004) could be characterized both as an emulation and as an inversion of Muybridge's process. While the latter froze physical motions, Cummins has discovered a way of animating the frozen, then freezing it again. In a series of photographs, a rider sits motionless on horseback on the same track where Muybridge chronophotographed Leland Stanford's horses in the 1870s. Shot hourly between 11 am and 5 pm, time (and motion) is indicated by the changing position of the shadow cast by the horse and the rider, turned into a sundial (Cummins 2013).[39] The honor for the most eccentric piece of Muybridgiana belongs to Steven Pippin's *Laundromat-Locomotion*, produced by the San Francisco Museum of Modern Art in 1998. Pippin turned a public laundry into a chronophotographic studio and shooting track. Custom-made cameras were produced and attached to a row of washing machines (echoing Muybridge's customized electric shutters). Like Stanford's horses, the subjects triggered the shutters by running across a row of trip wires.[40] The exposed prints were developed by spinning them in the same machines, which gave them an "archaic" look.

Avant-garde filmmakers extended their explorations to other types of projected images as well. Ken Jacobs, whose profuse work with found footage film had raised issues about the shape of film history since the 1950s, played a central role here by moving into experimental live performance. His "paracinema" falls under two subheadings, *The Nervous System* and *The Nervous Magic Lantern*. Both are technological systems that have been utilized in series of performances. In the former Jacobs uses a pair of modified 16 mm film projectors that can project single frames—both forward and backward—and a variable-speed motorized shutter wheel rotating in front of their lenses. By projecting two identical prints of the same film on top of each other with a slight time difference and manipulating the speed of the wheel, Jacobs makes filmic space "elastic" and occasionally very three-dimensional. In the later *Nervous Magic Lantern* events he went further back to the basics. The effects are produced by manipulating light by means of color filters and spinning wheels.[41]

Jacobs got the basic ideas and technological solutions behind his paracinema from Alfons Schilling's inventions and projections, as he admitted in 1981 in connection with his presentation in the Cineprobe series at the Museum of Modern Art in New York:

> A new and at least equally fecund technique for creating 3D imagery has been discovered and brilliantly, poetically utilized by the artist Alfons Schilling. Perhaps you have also been awed by his projections of stereo-slides in which space seems entirely malleable under his touch: an ultimate cinema of two frames, infinitely rich in effect. With his encouragement I approached this new continent of perceptual experience in a further chapter of THE IMPOSSIBLE: HELL BREAKS LOOSE. Staying at the edge of the voluptuous phenomena produced by what may be called the "Schilling Effect" the experience here is more in the nature of animated stereoptican [*sic*] pictures and is aptly referred to as "The Nervous System". But as with the "Schilling Effect" its more occasional depth imagery is available without recourse to viewing devices of any kind and is even perceptible to the cyclops, to one-eyed vision. Recently Alfons nudged me over the edge into working with the "Schilling Effect" and a few weeks ago CHERRIES was presented at The Millennium in—allow me—all its glory. (Schilling 1997, 184)[42]

Schilling's seminal role has either been belittled or ignored by American scholars who have written about Jacobs's work. In *Optic Antics: The Cinema of Ken Jacobs* (2011) Schilling is mentioned just once—performing his "Binocular Works" at the

Collective for Living Cinema in December 1975, "to which Jacobs also contributed" (Pierson, James, and Arthur 2011, 16). Brooke Belisle's recent study, which discusses Jacobs's work in 3D, mentions briefly that *The Nervous Magic Lantern* "relies on precinematic technologies, using a spinning shutter that Alphonse [*sic*] Schilling adapted, in his work with stereoscopic images, from nineteenth-century strategies of magic-lantern projection," but without elaborating on the shutter's role in Schilling's and Jacobs's work (Belisle 2014, 11).[43] The catalogue of Jacobs's 1989 retrospective does not mention Schilling at all, although *The Nervous System* is discussed in Jacobs's program notes, in a long interview with him, and in Tom Gunning's essay (Schwartz 1989).

Such "memory lapses" remind us that media-archaeological excavations should not be limited only to identifying forgotten predecessors and unacknowledged cultural contexts. They must be performed on the terrain of contemporary art as well. In spite of the valiant efforts by the *Leonardo* magazine and chroniclers such as Gene Youngblood, Douglas Davis, and Frank Popper, our overall knowledge of even the recent history of technological arts, which has been largely dismissed by museums, commercial galleries, mainstream critics, and art historians, remains fragmentary. Behind a few household names there are large areas of terra incognita with ambitious bodies of work craving for recognition (Schilling being a perfect example). When it comes to Jacobs, who has been widely celebrated as one of the major figures of American experimental cinema, it would be unfair to claim that he simply copied Schilling's ideas and presented them as his own. By the time he discovered Schilling, Jacobs had already produced a substantial and varied body of films, and issues it had raised and investigated were then transferred to his performance work. However, Schilling clearly provided a stimulus that gave it a direction.

Jacobs has since moved both forward and backward in time. *The Nervous Magic Lantern* retreated to the "primitives" of light, color, and shadows (perhaps echoing the multimedia lightshows of the 1960s), whereas works like *Capitalism* (2006) extended Schilling's discoveries into the realm of the digital. In *Capitalism*, a video, old stereoviews have been digitally manipulated to give them jerky motions and depth, but also to extract ideological readings from them (Belisle 2014, 11). In 2006 Jacobs was granted a patent for "Eternalism," which summarizes his work with a limited number of frames, including provisions for both film-based and digital versions.[44] The patent text itself is of media-archaeological interest. Jacobs describes how his invention "could be used to provide more lively 'snapshots' of familiar things and events" in the form of an electronic wallet containing "a great many (low memory demanding) moving replicas of loved ones in characteristic living gestures." Here he (inadvertently?) activates a topos—the moving portrait—that was often evoked in the early years of cinematography as one of the medium's possible uses (Huhtamo 2011, 27–47). The idea has since been realized on a massive scale by the brief gif files and Instagram movies flowing between social media sites, iPads, and smartphones.

Ken Jacobs is not the only artist whose non-filmic projection works bring up historical precedents. Tony Oursler's *The Influence Machine* was a large-scale outdoor installation shown in New York and London (Oursler 2000). Evoking the history of the magic lantern, in particular the Phantasmagoria (a form of ghost show that appeared in the late 18th century), as well as the relationship between media and spiritism, Oursler projected faces on trees and buildings, transforming the rational urban environment into an uncanny haunt. Christa Sommerer and Laurent Mignonneau, who are well known for their pioneering work with artificial life (a-life) installations, used modified antique magic lanterns and hand-cranked film projectors in a pair of works titled *Excavate* and *Escape* (2012). These were first shown in Salenstein, Switzerland, in a wet and dark cave that served as an air raid shelter during World War II. By operating the devices, visitors activate uncanny projected scenes. Sommerer and Mignonneau have used modified early technology in earlier works as well: an antiquated mechanical typewriter serves as the interactive user interface in *Life Writer* (2006).

A no less imaginative way of revisiting the history of projected images is the installation *Slide Movie—Diafilmprojektor* (2006) by Gebhard Sengmüller, another accomplished practitioner of media-archaeological art.[45] Resurrecting the 35 mm carousel slide projector and redefining it as an artistic medium, he turned a violent eighty-second scene from Sam Peckinpah's *Bring Me the Head of Alfredo Garcia* (1974) into 1920 slides and loaded them into a battery of twenty-four slide projectors, all focused on the same spot. Through careful synchronization, the clicking and clacking automated projectors reanimate the film scene, giving it a curious archaic feel. Perhaps the most complex reimagination of the magic lantern show is *Demi-Pas* (2002) by the French artist Julien Maire. Here again the artist has purported to recreate the experience of film by other means. Maire built a high-tech magic lantern ("Inverted Camera") and invented dozens of complex mechanical lantern slides with tiny motors and other animation devices (Maire 2002).[46] The performance keeps shifting between the familiar and the unfamiliar, the old and the unprecedented, as one effect follows another in a discontinuous continuity.

New Media Art, Media Archaeology, and Female Media Artists

In the 1980s a growing number of artists began creating installations in which digital technology played a central role. They often invited gallery visitors to physically interact with these works, and also evoked virtual reality, which was the "grand narrative" of technoculture around 1990. Such works did not necessarily refer to the past, but a surprising number of them did, which may have reflected the uncertainties about media culture at the time. Cinema as well as television and radio broadcasting were being challenged by cable and satellite television (including on-demand systems), video games, CD-ROM-based multimedia, computer networking, and other interactive forms. These developments coincided with the end of the Cold War and the territorial and cultural transformations that followed, adding further elements to a sense of rupture. A media-archaeological approach represented a search for reference points and continuities, but its goal not to discover "permanent values." Rather, it manifested a need to start dialogues between different media forms, systems, and related ideas. In 1994, I considered the appearance of this approach as a sign of the times, as proof that "media art is gradually reaching maturity, but it also implies a certain anxiety (Huhtamo 1994c)."

I first encountered art informed by media archaeology in the late 1980s at events like Ars Electronica, SIGGRAPH, and the European Media Art Festival (Osnabrück, Germany). My involvement with it got a boost from being a member of the team that organized ISEA '94, the 5th International Symposium of Electronic Arts, which was held in Helsinki, Finland, in 1994. I co-curated its main exhibition and a side event dedicated to the work of Toshio Iwai, one of the leading proponents of media-archaeological art (Huhtamo 1995a).[47] I also gave my first-ever keynote address on media archaeology, and organized with Machiko Kusahara a program dedicated to the archaeology of the simulator ride film genre (Huhtamo 1994a, 1994b). The main exhibition included several works with explicit media-archaeological emphasis: *The Edison Effect* (1989–1996) by Paul DeMarinis, *To Fall Standing* (1993) by Rebecca Cummins, *The Banff Kinetoscope, or Field Recording Studies* (1993–1994) by Michael Naimark, *The Virtual Body* (1994) by Catherine Richards, and *A Dialogue with Hunger* (1993) by Heidi Tikka.[48] Other projects, like Christa Sommerer and Laurent Mignonneau's *Anthroposcope* (1993), George Legrady's *An Anecdoted Archive from the Cold War* (1993), and Christine Tamblyn's *She Loves It, She Loves It Not: Women and Technology* (1993) also referred to media cultural forms of the past.

These works developed what I called meta-discourses on media culture, its history, implications and underpinnings (Huhtamo 1992b, 1995b). In *To Fall Standing* Rebecca Cummins examines parallels between military technology and moving images, an issue discussed by Paul Virilio in *War and Cinema: The Logistics of Perception* (Virilio 1985). The installation is inspired by Étienne-Jules Marey's "chronophotographic gun" (1882), which was designed for capturing chronophotographic sequences of birds in flight, but its weapon-related connotations were obvious. As it happens, Marey's research was funded by the French army. Cummins fitted a miniature surveillance video camera inside the barrel of a 1880s shotgun. When the user points it at another exhibition visitor and pulls the trigger—an ambiguous and disconcerting act—a digital stop-motion image sequence reminiscent of Marey is captured and displayed in a series of monitors. But *To Fall Standing* does not only re-enact Marey's experiments. It also creates associations with other situations in which gun-like interfaces are used, from fairground shooting galleries and toy guns to the missile-mounted cameras of the (then recent) Persian Gulf war.[49]

The reference point behind Naimark's, Richards's, and Tikka's works is the long history of "peep media" (the practice of peeking at hidden images through lenses), but they dealt with it in very different ways (Huhtamo 2006). Naimark's *See Banff!* is a historicist peepshow cabinet, a melange of features from two early viewing devices, The Kinetoscope and the Mutoscope, that had offered many observers their first peeks at cinematography around 1900. The cabinet contains stereoscopic time-lapse sequences of pictures shot with a custom-made pair of 16 mm film cameras mounted in a baby carriage while running along trails in the Canadian wilderness. By turning a hand-crank—installed in the manner of the Mutoscope but secretly connected to the track ball of a Macintosh computer inside the cabinet—the user interactively manipulates the deliberately jerky motion sequences.[50] The work stems from Naimark's interest in mapping locations by means of interactive moving pictures (he was a member of the team that created the *Aspen Movie Map*, the ancestor of *Google Streetview*, at MIT, 1978–1980) and panoramic imaging, but it also recalls the explorations of filmic space by avant-garde filmmakers such as Ken Jacobs.

Catherine Richards's *The Virtual Body* (1994), "at once a scientific instrument, an aesthetic object, and a postmodern magic box," is a column-like viewer with a video simulation of a rococo salon inside.[51] It evokes the 17th-century Dutch "perspective boxes" by artists such as Samuel van Hoogstraten (who also inspired Rafael

Lozano-Hemmer's project *Body Movies*), but evidently also commented on the virtual reality craze of the time. Like virtual reality head-mounted displays, the work "virtualizes" (visually excludes) the peeper's body, only to reintroduce it visually: users are expected to insert their hands into the box through a hole on its side to manipulate the views. This solution evokes the design of 19th-century box camera obscuras (drawing instruments).[52] An intriguing discursive anticipation of Richards's work can be found in an entry in Nathaniel Hawthorne's *American Notebook*, where he describes (in 1838) a presentation by an itinerant peep-showman he had seen. The man displayed

> views of cities and edifices in Europe, of Napoleon's battles and Nelson's sea-fights, in the midst of which would be seen a gigantic, brown, hairy hand (the Hand of Destiny) pointing at the principal points of the conflict, while the old Dutchman explained. (Hawthorne 1896, 179–180)

Heidi Tikka's *A Dialogue with Hunger* (1993) combines media-archaeological concerns with reflections on gender in media spectatorship. Peeping at intimate stereoscopic close-up views of the female body made a projector turn on, flooding the peeper with the very same scene. By combining two basic forms of the moving image apparatus (projection and peeping) and sandwiching the observer between them, Tikka investigated the relationships between private and public experiences as well as issues of desire and shame associated with them.[53] The motif of peeping was clearly in the air, probably inspired by the boost given to peep media by the discourse on virtual reality.[54] An artist-created peepshow installation that thematically resonates with Tikka's work is Lynn Hershman and Sara Roberts's *A Room of One Own* (1993). Peeping into the box and slightly turning its eyepiece lights up dollhouse-like miniature scenes, but also activates videos where a seductive woman directly addresses the peeper. The voyeurism inherent in the situation is challenged, but unlike in Tikka's case, the hidden views are not externalized. The "affair" remains between the peeper and the peeped.

There has been an extraordinary amount of interest in media-archaeological approaches among female artists (although not always explicitly defined as such by the artists themselves). One could argue that this must have something to do with the parallels between media archaeology, feminist theory, and women's history. Much like media archaeologists, feminist theorists and women's historians are engaged in activities aimed at uncovering suppressed phenomena and discourses, combating narratives converted into "truths" in the male-dominated society. Terry Castle's and Rachel P. Maines's writings are exemplary in this respect (Castle 1995; Maines 2001). When it comes to artists, a parallel case is the work of Kara Walker, although she probably would not consider herself a media archaeologist (Berry et al. 2007). Walker appropriates bourgeois cultural forms known as women's and children's pastimes (silhouette cutting, shadow puppetry) and uses them in powerful—subversive yet graceful—ways to reveal silenced aspects of black history (particularly of black women). Walker has also placed similar subject matter within circular panoramas, a cultural form used in the 19th century to promote conservative military and nationalistic agendas.[55]

Heidi Kumao's "cinema machines" (1991–1999), a series of installations modeled on 19th-century optical toys, in particular Émile Reynaud's Praxinoscope, demonstrate how media-archaeological interests can be combined with a critical exposé of women's everyday life. As Kumao explained in an interview, her original inspiration came from a print depicting Reynaud exhibiting his Pantomimes Lumineuses with the Théatre Optique (a mega version of the Projecting Praxinoscope) at the Musée Grevin in Paris.[56] Kumao concocted similar devices (animated by motors) and placed them in boxes or kinds of doll's houses, on stools and so forth. The devices project short video loops related to women's or children's lives.[57] In *Childhood Rituals: Consumption* (1991–1993) a hand keeps spoon-feeding a child, while in *Kept* (1993) a woman sweeps the floor endlessly. Ephemeral moments loaded with ideological importance are captured and exposed in a way that matches the nature of the medium. The fact that zoetropes and praxinoscopes present moving image sequences that are only a few seconds long has been considered a limitation, a "primitive" feature, but Kumao turns obsessive repetition into an asset. It is thought-provoking that very short and often looped Instagram or Vine videos have since became a popular phenomenon, routinely uploaded on the Internet by millions of users.

It would be tempting to interpret the eagerness with which women artists have embraced media archeology as "just" an act of resistance against the appropriation of technology by "boys with their toys," but that reading would be too limiting. The performance and installation artist Ellen Zweig found the camera obscura suitable for the kinds the stories she wanted to tell.[58] *She Traveled for the Landscape* (1986) is a pair of camera obscura-performances, realized as part of the multi-artist project *Ex(centric) Lady Travellers*, dedicated to Victorian woman travelers and their modern counterparts.[59] Zweig was inspired by the life of Marianne North (1830–1890), a globetrotting Victorian adventuress, who painted pictures of landscapes and flowers while touring the world. In *Camera in a Coach*, performed in Houston, Texas in April 1986, Zweig literalized the link between traveling and optics by turning an antique stagecoach into a mobile room camera obscura (accompanied by sound tape). The following June she used the camera obscura ("Giant Camera") at the Cliff House by the Ocean Beach in San Francisco as a theatre for a performance (again, a pre-recorded soundtrack was played).

In the Victorian world the camera obscura was used as an optical aid for producing landscape sketches; whether Marianne North herself used it is unclear, but she certainly was aware of such instruments (North 1893).[60] A particularly popular form was the room camera obscura (like the one at Cliff House), which was a favorite pastime destination at seaside resorts and other scenic locations. The view from the outside was projected inside a small building by a combination of a rotating lens and mirror on its roof. The view was displayed on a tabletop serving as screen. The fascination with this presentation was based on the almost uncanny character of the silent views of trees, waves, humans, and animals one could touch with one's fingers. Besides, they were not static but in full motion. The visitors inside the dark chamber enjoyed their voyeuristic role as unseen observers.[61] Zweig's audience at Cliff House was shown a sequence of tableaux created by actors moving around the camera obscura in Victorian costumes. In one of them, Marianne North was seen painting wildflowers (she had visited the site in 1876). Zweig operated the lens, framing the scenes much like a television camerawoman (as a real-time transmission device the camera obscura belongs to the prehistory of television as well).[62]

Zweig went on to build her own camera obscuras and to combine them with performances in projects like *In a Barrel of Her Own Design*, shown at the Artpark in Lewiston, NY (1988) and *Such Ruins Give the Mind a Sense of Sadness*, installed at the Exploratorium in San Francisco in 1989. The former included a "barrel camera obscura" one could sit on while peeking inside, inspired by another daredevil, Annie Edson Taylor, the first woman to ride the Niagara Fall in a barrel in 1901.[63] Zweig may have been influenced by the Neapolitan "natural magician" Giambattista della Porta, who described in his *Magia naturalis* (1658) "How in a Chamber you may see Hunting, Battles of Enemies, and other delusions."[64] Della Porta's performances were realized with sets that consisted of trees, mountains, rivers, and animals "that are really so, or made by Art, of Wood, or some other matter." In the latter case, little children would be put behind "counterfeit Stags, Bores, Rhinocerets, Elephants, Lions, and what other creatures you please" to carry them around in front of the camera obscura, which had to be located on "some spacious Plain, where the Sun can freely shine" (Porta 1658).

Zweig has continued using optical tricks and devices from the past as inspiration. Her video installation *Hubert's Lure* (1994) was a tribute to Hubert's Museum and Flea Circus, a dime museum that operated in New York City from 1925 to the 1960s. Zweig used the Pepper's Ghost illusion, first introduced by Henry Dircks and John Henry Pepper in London in 1862, to recreate the museum's performances. The latter trick has inspired many others as well, including the French video artist Pierrick Sorin, David Wilson, the founder of the Museum of Jurassic Technology (Los Angeles), and the New York-based film, installation, and performance artist Zoe Beloff. Beloff is a major practitioner of media-archaeological art (Parikka 2011) and has used arrays of antique hand-cranked projectors, stereoscopic slides, 78 rpm phonographs, and optical toys in order to explore media's associations with the unconscious, the pathological, and the esoteric. The result is an idiosyncratic world in which technology is "transfigured." The discursive dimension of media culture is brought (back) to life on multiple levels.

Beloff's interactive installation *The Influencing Machine of Miss Natalija A.* (2001) was influenced by a case study about a woman who thought she was being manipulated by a mysterious electrical apparatus, analyzed by the Viennese psychoanalyst Victor Tausk (Sconce 2011, 70–94).[65] *The Ideoplastic Materializations of Eva C.* (2004) and *Shadow Land or Light From the Other Side* (2000) both evoke the relationship between mediums, spirit materializations, and media, while the 3D film *Charming Augustine* (2006) tells the story of a hysteric patient, who lived at the Salpêtrière mental hospital in Paris in the 1870s. Beloff charts the borderline between material reality and memory, the external and the internal, the rationally mediated and that which is "beyond." To accompany *The Sonnambulists* (2008) Beloff published a media-archaeological compendium of excerpts from writers who had influenced her work, including the psychoanalyst Pierre Janet, authors Raymond Roussel and André Breton, and the engineer Henry Dircks, the original creator of the Pepper's Ghost (Beloff 2008). Beloff has even managed to adapt multimedia into a vehicle for her media-archaeological explorations, as her pioneering interactive CD-ROMs *Beyond* (1996) and *Where Where There There Where* (1998) demonstrate.[66]

Alternative Archaeologies of Moving Images and Sounds: Toshio Iwai and Paul DeMarinis

Media-archaeological references have proliferated in postmodern culture to such an extent that covering extensively is no longer possible (Pepper's Ghost was even used in a musical stage performance to "resurrect" the rapper Tupak Shakur). Yet, it

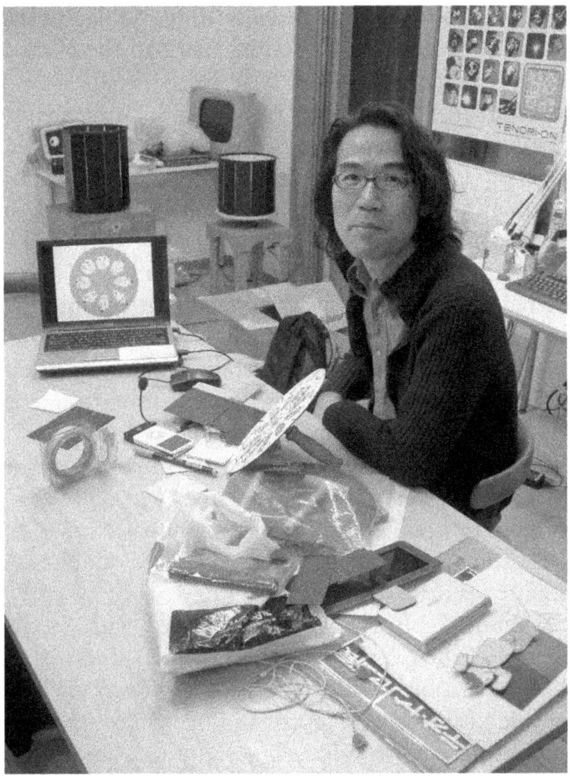

FIGURE 3.1 Toshio Iwai portrait. Photo: Erkki Huhtamo.

makes sense to single out artists who have developed the most consistent bodies of work. The names of Toshio Iwai and Paul DeMarinis stand out. Both have resurrected devices from different eras and linked seemingly incompatible areas and ideas. Iwai has characterized his work as "Another Evolution of the Moving Image."[67] It might be suggested that DeMarinis has created "Another Evolution of Sound Media," but such generalizations would not do either of them justice. Their works cover *both* images *and* sounds, and hardly fit under an "evolutionary" umbrella. Both Iwai's and DeMarinis's oeuvres suggest radically different ways of conceiving media history.

Toshio Iwai (b.1962) graduated from the Plastic Art and Mixed Media master's program of the Tsukuba University, Japan, in 1987 (Figure 3.1).[68] During his years of study he explored different methods of creating animations—from handmade flipbooks to computer programming—and also began applying his ideas in installations that gained public attention almost instantaneously. Iwai himself has traced his origins as a media artist back to his childhood.[69] Rather than buying him toys, his mother gave him a craftbook and tools, encouraging him to create them himself. Iwai filled craftbook after craftbook (all of which he still treasures) with his inventions, and descriptions of those he had seen on television or elsewhere. Iwai's technician father helped him build some of his inventions. Iwai became a ham radio operator and collected sounds and images, which he then imbued with new interpretations. He treasured a tiny hand-cranked music box, which gave him an impulse to create future work with interactive media (Iwai 2000). At primary school he began drawing animations in the margins of his textbooks, turning them into flipbooks. Iwai summarized these experiences in a private conversation by stating that "all the elements of the creative activities in my adult life began back then."

At Tsukuba, Iwai studied the principles of devices such as the phenakistiscope, the zoetrope, and the praxinoscope inside out by constructing replicas. His replica of Émile Reynaud's Praxinoscope Théatre was painstakingly produced from photographs as a class assignment, as there was no access to an original. According to Iwai, the project was worthwhile because it revealed how it functioned. Iwai then began to figure out how to produce animations for these device and to modify their operating principles. He tried anything from copying machines to digital plotter printouts. Studying the history behind moving image technology provided insights as well. Etienne-Jules Marey's zoetrope, which contained three-dimensional bird sculptures, inspired Iwai to create his own version, also with physical objects inside. He found the zoetrope "a superior accomplishment in the early evolution of interactive imagery devices" (Moriyama 1997, 54).[70] As a personal and tactile device, it affected his subsequent work with interactive media. In his early series of installations called *Time Stratum* (1985–1990), Iwai used flickering light produced by regular CRT monitors or projectors to animate images and cut-out figures, while stepper motors allowed him to display phenakistiscope-like animations as wall-mounted pieces without viewing devices.

Influenced by Muybridge, Iwai also experimented with sequential imagery. In *Digital Portrait System* (1986), a video portrait of the subject is gradually distorted, whereas in the public installation *Another Time, Another Space* (1993) images of passers-by are captured by video cameras and morphed into continuous "flows."[71] In the late 1980s Iwai also became interested in video games. The installation *Man-Machine-TV No. 1–8* (1989) playfully demonstrated the beginning merger between his interests. Eight identical TV monitors were provided with custom-made user interfaces, including a hand crank, switches, dials, sound and light sensors, a joystick, and a video camera. Using these interfaces triggered visual responses that were mostly abstract, although the hand crank made a virtual robot march and the physical joystick controlled a virtual joystick.[72]

Iwai's discovery of gaming made interactive sound an integral part of his art, but conventional video games were not for him. As he explained:

> The thing that excited me most about them at that time was how computers were essentially machines to interactively and simultaneously control audio and visuals. [...] Yet video games were all about getting points and competing with others. That wasn't what I was after. I was looking for a more physiological aspect—a device which could offer the pleasure of unifying myself with audio and visuals [...]. (Moriyama 1997, 98)

A key work that fulfilled this goal was *Music Insects* (1990), created during a residency at the Exploratorium in San Francisco.[73] The user interacts with tiny "insects" that traverse the screen, emitting light and sound when they hit colored dots. The terms of the interaction can be manipulated in different ways, resulting in audiovisual compositions. Rather than a game, *Music Insects* is an audiovisual music instrument. As such it anticipated *Electroplankton* (2005), Iwai's software application for the Nintendo DS console, and perhaps his most famous creation, *Tenori-on* (2007), a professional digital instrument developed with Yamaha.[74]

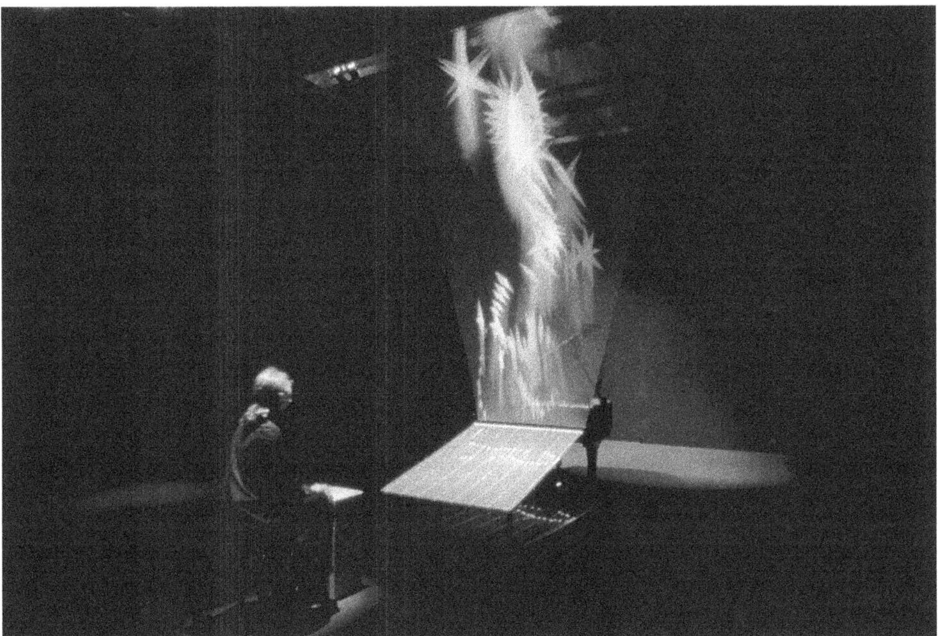

FIGURE 3.2 Toshio Iwai, *Piano – As Image Media*, 1995, installation shot. Photo: Daisuke Akita.

Iwai's overwhelming oeuvre includes much more: the experimental television programs *Einstein TV* (1990–1991) and *UgoUgo Lhuga* (1992–1994); interactive installations such as *Piano ~ as Image Media* (1995) (Figure 3.2) and *Composition on the Table* (1999); the large-scale audiovisual performance *Music plays Images x Images Play Music* (1996), with Ryuichi Sakamoto; and *Sound-Lens* (2001), a portable analog device for reading different varieties of light and turning them into an ever-changing soundscape (it was used both at exhibitions and in performance tours in urban spaces). There is also *Distorted House* (2005), an arcade game-like installation based on "morphovision," a scientific principle Iwai discovered through his experiments and developed into an application with NHK's Science & Technical Research Laboratories (Iwai 2005a).[75] Solid objects placed on a fast-rotating turntable are progressively scanned by different light patterns, which makes the objects magically "bend" or "melt" in front of the viewer's incredulous eyes.

The story of morphovision's development is a good example of Iwai's media-archaeological approach (Iwai, 2005b). He has traced the principle's evolution to several earlier steps. His 1980s zoetropes with three-dimensional "sculptures" inside made him discover how the objects seemed to bend when observed in motion through the slits. *Another Time, Another Space* (1993) digitally distorted bodies in real time, which led Iwai to ponder "the possibility of experiencing a distortion of real space not through pictures but with solid objects" (ibid.). He began experimenting with a cylinder that had slits in spiral form; a rod which was placed inside and shaken manually seemed to bend. He noticed aesthetic parallels with the art of M.C. Escher, calling an early prototype version *M. C. Escher like Space Transformer* (1999) (Iwai 2000).

It was during the development process that Iwai became aware of the curious fact that he had in fact rediscovered a forgotten phenomenon demonstrated in 1829 by Joseph Plateau, the inventor of the Phenakistiscope.[76] Plateau's Anorthoscope did something similar, but in reverse (and without the spatial distortion happening in morphovision): anamorphically distorted views drawn on spinning discs became "corrected" when observed in motion through a shutter disc spinning into the opposite direction.

Iwai's attention has increasingly turned toward visual education, which is not surprising given the beginnings of his own practice. In recent years he has spent much time in his home studio with his daughters, teaching them how to create animations and toys from simple everyday materials, and turning living room furniture, rugs, gloves, and anything possible into fantasy animals. Iwai has made the results public in workshops, exhibitions, and books, becoming a noted educational thinker.[77] The latest stage of his career has transformed him into a successful author of illustrated children's books. The three-volume series "A House of 100 Stories" (2008–2014) has sold well and been translated into several languages.[78] How can we make sense of all this from a media-archaeological point of view? It is clear that Iwai's creations do not always have explicit reference points in the past, even though there are links that may have remained hidden. Iwai once surprised me by stating that *Elektroplankton* was his version of Duchamp's *Boite en Valise* (1941).[79] After some reflection it made sense: the tiny game cartridge indeed contained many aspects of his career as a miniature "museum."

Applying Wittgenstein's idea of family resemblance to Iwai's output, one could suggest that his practice forms a web of interconnected ideas in a state of constant transformation. The ingredients are brought together in unusual places and combinations, but not always all at the same time. Iwai operates within this web as he wishes, pulling some strings together and severing others. The old meets the new, low tech meets high tech. Iwai has made numerous forays into entertainment and design, even designing a raincoat from new super non-absorbent material that makes it possible to play with the raindrops—to enjoy the rain. He has also applied ideas from his art installations to museum displays. Time Stratum (1985–1990) provided a model for the kinetic exhibits he designed for Hayao Miyazaki's Ghibli Museum (Mitaka) featuring characters from Ghibli Studios world-famous anime films. Such disregard for borders could be seen as typically Japanese, but it also characterizes Iwai's apparently total indifference toward categorization (Kusahara 1997). Such a consistently amorphic profile hardly matches the Western criteria for a "museum artist" operating within the fine arts world.

The Japanese curator Masato Shirai has called Iwai's work "astonishment art," explaining:

> Iwai's astonishments, though, come multi-layered [...] astonishment at the effects produced by the visual and auditory stimuli, astonishment at the mechanisms of creation, astonishment that it is all controlled by a computer program [...] these elements of composition are sharpened and refined as technique. (Moriyama and ICC 1997, 16)

The motif of astonishment links Iwai's work to the long tradition of "natural magic," a cultural phenomenon dedicated to demonstrating human ingenuity through technological marvels. Natural magic was one of the formative influences of media culture, and has not disappeared: it is still present in the technological wizardry of theme park rides, special effects films, novelty apps for smartphones—and in artworks like the ones Iwai and other magicians of new media have created. Iwai's work celebrates making and inventing; social and ideological issues emerge mostly as by-products. Yet, Iwai's achievements go further than that, as Shirai has wisely explained:

> Every art form must have about it something of the extraordinary in order to lift us from our daily life. Astonishment is one of the elements in art through which the extraordinary can be triggered. Perhaps it can be said that simply by stimulating our imagination art drives a wedge into the mundane, the routine. (Moriyama and ICC 1997, 16).

The work of Paul DeMarinis (b.1948) has parallels with Iwai's, but also differs from it. Both artists mine old technology for inspiration. From a range of materials and elements—secondhand electronic components, old record players and records, phonograph cylinders, holographic glass, gas flames, jars for galvanic electricity, electric guitars, sewing machines, virtual reality datagloves—DeMarinis builds machinic artworks that sing, speak, transmit messages, and resonate culturally in the observer's mind. As his writings demonstrate, DeMarinis is a learned artist-researcher, who also finds inspiration in forgotten patent documents and old books of science and technology. So is Iwai, but in a different sense. For Iwai the device—the technical apparatus—is the center of everything, a mechanism full of unrealized potential. DeMarinis is fascinated by gadgets as well, but his creations resonate with the meanings of technology in society and media history as well. Over and over again, DeMarinis writes media history in the conditional. His creations seem to be asking: What happened? What did not happen? What would have happened, if …? What would happen, if …?

A perfect example is *The Edison Effect* (1989–1996), which plays a symptomatic role in DeMarinis' oeuvre. It is a group of self-contained sound "sculptures," each with a custom-built record player reproducing sounds from an old phonograph record or cylinder by means of a laser beam.[80] The title refers to many things: the overall impact of sound technology; Edison, the self-made inventor of the phonograph; and the "Edison effect," a scientific phenomenon that causes light bulbs (another invention normally attributed to Edison) to darken as a consequence of the emission of electrons into a vacuum. For DeMarinis, each of the pieces is "a meditation of some aspect of the relations among music, memory, and the passage of time."[81] Where Iwai usually gives his creations matter-of-fact titles (*AV-Game II*, *Switch on the Glass*, *Resonance of 4*, *Violin ~ Image of Strings*, etc.), DeMarinis composes playfully associative and enigmatic ones. In *Al & Mary Do the Waltz* (the first completed piece, 1989), an early Edison wax cylinder recording of the "Blue Danube Waltz" by Johann Strauss is played by a laser beam traversing a bowl of goldfish, whose "waltzing" affects the sounds.[82] The link between the Danube and the water in the fishbowl is anything but accidental.

In *Ich auch Berlin(er)* (1990), a (de)materialization of one of DeMarinis's astonishing discoveries, a hologram of a 78 rpm record of "Beer Barrel Polka" is scanned by a green laser, reproducing the music of the original record. The title is a complex wordplay that combines references to Emil Berliner, the inventor of the gramophone (which had a major influence on recorded music), the composer Irving Berlin, and President John F. Kennedy, who uttered the famous phrase "Ich bin ein Berliner" (I am a Berliner) in a landmark Cold War era speech in West Berlin on June 26, 1963.[83] The formulation "I am also a Berlin(er)" may imply that the reproducing device (or the artist?) should be added to the list. The dense discursive veil that surrounds the work becomes part of its signification. Eras, technologies, and the relationship between sound and visual media (Kennedy's speech was both televised and broadcast by radio) are brought together while the work itself bridges gramophony, lasers, and holography.

Of all the pieces in *The Edison Effect*, *Fragments from Jericho* (1991) may be the one that best demonstrates DeMarinis's peculiar way of merging temporalities and gliding between the real and the imagined. A clay pot rotates on an old turntable. Sweeping its surface by turning a knob that emits a laser beam, the exhibition visitor hears scratchy, barely audible sounds supposedly preserved in its grooves. According to DeMarinis, the work is an "authentic recreation of what is probably the world's most ancient voice recording" (Beirer, Himmelsbach, and Seiffarth 2010, 129). The artist initiates here a game of historical make-believe. As DeMarinis argued in an essay that accompanied the piece, Edison's cylinder Phonograph (1877), the first functioning device for the recording and playback of sounds, was so simple that it could well have been invented earlier, perhaps even accidentally (DeMarinis 2010a). What if the silence of the pre-phonographic past is really an illusion, caused merely by our inability to play it back? It is the artist who is in the best position to ask such speculative "what if" questions, and to "demonstrate" them with artworks. *Fragments from Jericho* takes the participant on a paratemporal trip down and up and down again the shaft of time.[84]

In *Gray Matter* (1995b), DeMarinis's speculative media archaeology takes a slightly different form. The work was inspired by the unfortunate American inventor Elisha Gray, who is said to have submitted his patent application for the telephone hours after Alexander Graham Bell had submitted his (on February 14, 1876). Gray proposed an unusual way of producing and transmitting sound. By connecting an electric rheotome to a bathtub and one's own skin an electric field was created. Gliding one's fingers along the surface of the bathtub turned it into "a musical bathtub." DeMarinis turned Gray's forgotten ideas into an astonishing installation. Rubbing metal strings attached to different objects (a bathtub, a violin, a toaster, etc.) creates electric circuits for amplifying and manipulating (pre-recorded) sounds. Had Gray won the race, DeMarinis suggested, we might "enter the washcloset to speak afar, stroking small tin tubs as we listen" (DeMarinis 1995b).

Another major work of DeMarinis is *The Messenger* (1998–2006), which consists of three bizarre telegraphic receivers, inspired by the forgotten Catalan scientist Don Francesc Salvá i Campillo (1751–1828). In the first, a series of chamber pots mounted in a curved row utter—every now and then—letters of the alphabet in Spanish, with barely audible voices. In the second, there are twenty-six glass jars, each with an electrolyte and a pair of metal electrodes, one of them in the shape of a letter. From time to time one of the letters starts producing a stream of hydrogen bubbles. In the third system twenty-six little skeletons, each wearing a poncho with a letter, are hanging from wooden scaffolding; occasionally one of them jumps up. The "motive power" that explains the voices, the bubbling letters, and the jumping skeletons is Internet activity. Every time a new e-mail message appears in the artist's inbox, it is painstakingly spelled out, letter by letter, by the three telegraphic systems. The idea is deliberately absurd, meant to radiate meanings that bridge the past and the present. The prehistory of the telegraph and its authoritarian and colonialist underpinnings merges with a critical investigation of the partly unfounded myths and utopian (even messianic) expectations that shroud the Internet (Huhtamo 2004, 32–44).

In an interview DeMarinis aptly summarized his media-archaeological stance:

> I think that by carefully studying the histories of current day technologies, we can uncover insights into the constellation of human and technical arrangements that can help to projectively crystallize an understanding of the real nature of our current condition. This is based on my prejudice that cultures have long-standing currents of agenda—over hundreds of years and often unspoken—and that technologies, like the rest of material culture, are a reification of these agendas. They are neither discoveries nor neutral. They come out of the dreams of people and offer indications of social relations. (Pritikin 2012)

This recurring shift from the technological and the scientific to the social and the ideological is the feature that most clearly differentiates DeMarinis's work from Iwai's. The need to draw a distinction between technology's inherent properties and its applications to different purposes within specific contexts is the key issue. Over and over again, DeMarinis's work undermines simple deterministic ideas. In typical manner, he wrote in connection with *The Messenger*: "there is no inherent bi-directionality in electrical communication" (DeMarinis 2010b, 240). This obviously applies to radio as well, although it is often assumed that it is the one-directionality of broadcasting that is ideologically and commercially determined, while the "nature" of the medium is multidirectional. Radio inspired DeMarinis as a boy and has reappeared many times in his artworks. His autobiographical essay accompanying the (equally autobiographical) installation *Walls in the Air* (2001) re-enacts, almost word for word and in a somewhat nostalgic spirit, the experiences of the early 20th-century radio enthusiasts, including their their standard hideaway: the attic (Douglas 1989). While they certainly carry personal memories, such stories can also be interpreted as topoi, repeated formulas used by cultural agents to make sense of their encounters with the technological unknown (and uncanny).

DeMarinis's works with radios reveal parallels with the interests of hackers and techno-hobbyists. *Four Foxhole Radios* (2000) consists of functioning radio receivers built from burnt-out light bulbs, mesquite barbecue charcoal, rusty batteries, 18th-century nails, packs of chewing gum, discarded CDs, votive candles, whisky bottles and shot glasses. The work speaks about human inventiveness, particularly in dire circumstances like concentration camps where legitimate technology is absent, and about the human need to overcome isolation in situations where proper communication channels have either been denied or are otherwise are nonexistent.

Rome to Tripoli (2006) is a working recreation of the radio transmitter used in 1908 to transmit voice messages from Rome to Tripoli, "inaugurating the age of radio-telephony and of broadcast media" (Beirer, Himmelsbach, and Seiffarth 2010, 183).

DeMarinis's approach to art and technology has similarities with that of his friend Jim Pomeroy, with whom he collaborated and whose life and work he commemorated in the installation *Grind Snaxe Blind Apes (A Study for Pomeroy Tomb)* (1997), and perhaps indirectly also in a related work, *Dust* (2009).[85] In a perceptive essay that he contributed to a posthumously published book about Pomeroy's work, DeMarinis characterized him as the "quintessential Boy Mechanic," associating him with a line of American "artist-tinkerers" from Benjamin Franklin and Thomas Edison to Mr. Wizard in the television show *Watch Mr. Wizard* (1951–1965), and David Packard (DeMarinis 1993). The same expression could be applied to DeMarinis himself, although not in quite the same sense. Even though Pomeroy's creations were grounded in history and culture (like those of DeMarinis), as an artist he was an impersonator, a flamboyant performer whose personality merged with his eccentric characters and ecclectic creations. Tinkering is DeMarinis' passion as well, but he is more restrained and analytic, an artist-inventor (and excellent writer—like Pomeroy) who likes to hide behind his creations—a "thinkerer" as I have called him (Huhtamo 2010).

Although DeMarinis's work resonates with the idea of "circuit bending" as a media-archaeological "method," proposed by Garnet Hertz and Jussi Parikka, I feel that his work goes far beyond the goals and practices of software and hardware hacking and media activism (Hertz and Parikka 2012, 424–430). It is worth citing two more works as evidence, *Raindance* (1998) and *Firebirds* (2004). *Raindance* does not seem to evoke the past at all. Donning normal umbrellas, participants in the installation pass under a shower. When water begins bouncing from the surface of the umbrella, music (such as, a little predictably, *Singing in the Rain*) can be heard. One soon notices that the music can be "jammed" by moving the umbrella, almost like manually "scratching" a record on a turntable. "Where does the music come from, and how is this effect possible?," one wonders. Answers are not necessary to enjoy the work, but it is interesting to know that DeMarinis's patented invention (under the title "Interactive Entertainment Device") derived its inspiration from sources as varied as 19th-century research into the effects of audio vibrations on water, Alfred Jarry's *The Exploits and Opinions of the Dr. Faustroll, Pataphysicist* (the foundational text of Pataphysics), and Siegfried Giedion's "anonymous history" of the mechanization of the shower (Beirer, Himmelsbach, and Seiffarth 2010, 159, 217).[86]

To realize the equally astounding *Firebirds* DeMarinis explored an improbable and almost uncanny-sounding theme: scientific research into the potential of gas flames to function as loudspeakers (Figure 3.3). This research was combined with an exploration of media culture's political implications: the use of "inflammatory" amplified speech by dictators as a vehicle for propaganda. In spite of the astonishing idea, the work avoids any hints of sensationalism. DeMarinis has encapsulated everything in an elegant installation, presenting a series of birdcages—like little houses or prison cells—with speaking flames inside. In the observer's mind, the work uncages itself, leading to one association after another.

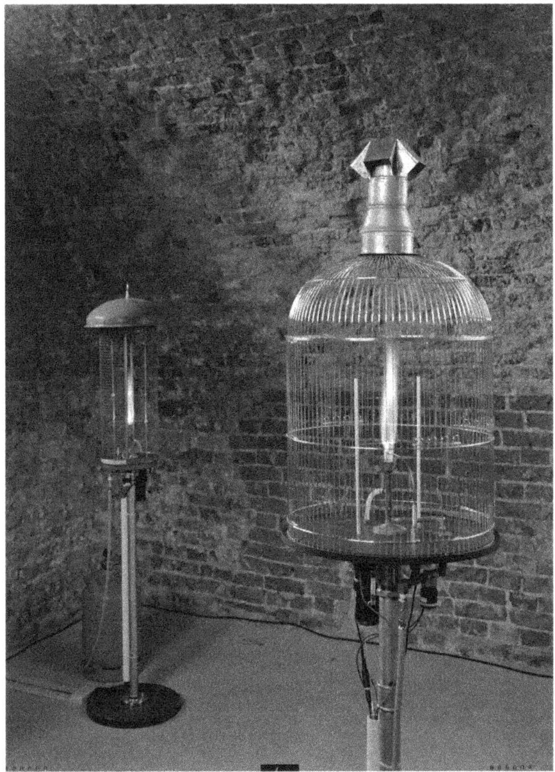

FIGURE 3.3 Paul DeMarinis, *Firebirds*, 2004, installation shot. Photo: Roman Maerz.

Conclusion: The Media-Archaeological Turn

This chapter, despite its length, has anything but exhausted its topic. It would be an impossible task—the range of media-archaeologically oriented work is growing and becoming more and more diverse. There is Amanda Steggell's *Emotion Organ* (2007), a refurbished old pump organ turned into an interactive multisensory simulation engine, based on the artist's research of synesthesia and the history of visual music. There are Bernie Lubell's extraordinary interactive machines created of wooden parts, pneumatic tubes, and stretched latex sheets. Their playfulness may disguise their debt to Etienne-Jules Marey's "graphical method" and to other scientists, engineers, and artists, thoroughly studied by Lubell (Huhtamo 2008). Ken Feingold's talking animatronic heads hark back to talking automata, ventriloquist's dummies, and simulated artificial intelligences such as Joseph Weizenbaum's "Eliza," filtered through the legacies of surrealist automatic writing and Duchampian wordplay. Martin Riches has also been inspired by the history of automata, studying their principles in order to create machines that speak and play music (Riches 2004).

The list goes on and on. William Kentridge's rich body of animation, graphic art, installation, and performance work draws from a wide array of media-archaeological sources, ranging from shadow puppetry, cylindrical anamorphoses, and automata to phenakistiscopes, stereoscopy, and the trick films of Georges Méliès.[87] Recently, the young Japanese artist Ei Wada (b.1987) and his Open Reel Ensemble have created impressive performances and installations by refunctionalizing old open-reel tape recorders, VHS video machines, and CRT television monitors (Open Reel Ensemble 2013). Jeff Guess has investigated the relationship between the body and technology by using his mouth as a camera obscura (Guess 1993).[88] Working with Dragan Espenschied, Olia Lialina, one of the pioneers of net art, has extended media archaeology into the Internet by *Once Upon* (2011). Although the work's reference point dates back less than twenty years, it functions as a veritable time machine presenting simulations of Google+, YouTube, and Facebook as they could have been in 1997, realized with the technological possibilities of the time (Lialina and Espenschied 2011). Video game culture is another frontier region of media-archaeological work.[89]

Fitting all this—and other unnamed things—under a neat conceptual umbrella and classifying everything under a limited set of headings would be impossible, and perhaps not even desirable. It is one of the basic tenets of art making to defy categorization and rationalization. Generalizations of any kind are risky, but it may not be incorrect to say that all experimental art strives for the indeterminate and the unchained, even when highly structured. As my long experience as an exhibition curator and art educator has taught me, artists do whatever they feel they need to do for whatever reason, without always asking or knowing why—no matter how much history and theory I teach them. During the almost three decades I have spent roaming the earth disseminating and discussing ideas about media archaeology, I have met many artists whose agendas have resonated with mine. Some of them, like Paul DeMarinis, Toshio Iwai, and Ken Jacobs, began their media-archaeological explorations before I started mine. Their ideas were already formulated in terms of research and a media-historical awareness.

This is not always the case. There are artists in whose works I find evident media-archaeological parallels, and yet these may not have been acknowledged by the artist when producing the work. More than once I have shown artists items from my archives, pointing out connections, and asking if the material was familiar to them. Some of them have been truly surprised, assuring me they had no knowledge of such historical precedents. One way to explain what happened in these cases is to treat media-archaeological motifs as topoi, culturally transmitted formulas. Topoi are used deliberately with specific goals in mind (for example by advertisers and politicians), but they can also appear "accidentally," as if automatically retrieved from shared cultural archives. The Internet, in particular, is a huge topos storage area and accelerator. Not only are many forgotten ideas and artifacts more easily accessible today than ever before; the speed and extent of their circulation within networked culture have been boosted as well. Simply typing a few words in Google Image Search often reveals unfamiliar associations, even from the distant past. These are recycled for cultural products, not always with awareness of their historical referents.

Access to channels of information is a precondition for developing a media-archaeological awareness. The emergence of interest in early silent films in the 1960s and 1970s had to do with new possibilities of seeing such works in film archives and clubs and on television. However, access to information does not automatically produce media-archaeological work; more is needed. In general terms and with respect to individual differences between approaches, technologies, and cultural traditions, it can be suggested that the media-archaeological turn has something to do with an overarching, partly uncontrolled and troubling transition that is underway in media culture. Media forms have been multiplied, familiar patterns shattered; media is co-opted by corporations and governments alike for uses beyond the users' control. Reconnecting with the past can serve as a cultural safety valve, but also as a way of enriching contemporary culture, and of helping us to face what may lie ahead. To return to McLuhan's metaphor evoked at the beginning of this study, gazing into the rear-view mirror is a necessary precondition for finding routes—scenic, exciting, and safe, although not necessarily the quickest and the most direct—to navigate into the future.

Notes

1 The word Muzak was coined by George Owen Squier in 1934. Joseph Lanza does not mention Cahill and his Telharmonium (2004).

2 "Inscription system" or "notation system" would be more accurate translations of Kittler's key concept "Aufschreibesysteme" than the Foucaultian "discourse network" that was used in the English translation of his first major work, *Discourse Networks 1800/1900* (1990 [orig. 1985]).

3 Salvador Dali's work with anamorphosis, stereoscopy, and other optical illusions deserves a mention.

4 Janet Cardiff's and George Bures Miller's *The Killing Machine* (2007) refers to bachelor machines. Inspired by Kafka's short story *In the Penal Colony*, it is a robotic theatre of torture, where lights flicker, ill-omened sounds roar, and a megaphone-speaker circles around the scene. Two robotic arms (reminiscent of dentist's drills) move eerily around a reclining chair. An operation is obviously taking place, although no one is visibly strapped to the chair. Other installations by Cardiff and Miller also evoke "ghosts" of media technologies of the past (Cardiff and Miller 2007).

5 Marey donated his device to the Collège de France, which gave it as a permanent loan to the Musée Marey in Beaune, his hometown. The museum has been closed since 2004, but the zoetrope seems to exist in its storage.

6 Bertolt Brecht's famous plea (1932) for turning the radio into a two-way medium was wishful thinking in the context of its time. For a different, psychoanalytic interpretation, see Krauss 1993.

7 Thaumatropes were spun between fingers by cords attached to the disk so that the pictures on both sides would merge. Cornell employed a simple, mechanical, hand-held spinning device (such were available for purchase). He used found stereoscopic photographs, cut into half, in his "film script" *Monsieur Phot* (1933).

8 No one seems to have associated *Étant donnés* with the stereoscope. Haladyn just mentions that the "interior diorama" is accessed through "peepholes" (Haladyn 2010, 84). In his cardboard model for *Étant donnés*, Duchamp used the expression "Trous de Voyeur" (Duchamp 1987, separate insert).

9 Tinguely's autodestructive machines were created in parallel with Gustaf Metzger's early manifestoes of autodestructive art (1959–1961).

10 The work may refer to Duchamp's *Bicycle Wheel* (1913). For a media archaeology-influenced reading of Vanderbeek's work, see Sutton 2015.

11 The Dream Machine's history is coated with myths because of Brion Gysin's cult hero status, and overreliance on his egocentric writings. The state of things is (inadvertently?) expressed by the title and the name of the publisher of John Geiger's *Nothing Is True—Everything Is Permitted: The Life of Brion Gysin* (2005).
12 Geiger's book is useful, but the research is not entirely reliable from a critical perspective.
13 Entry said to be from Gysin's diary, quoted in his "Dreamachine." In his letter to Gysin, Sommerville also evoked the kaleidoscope: "Visions start with a kaleidoscope of colors on a plane in front of the eyes and gradually become more complex and beautiful ..."
14 Carpenter's study is a still valid landmark.
15 Gysin produced the scroll paintings using a modified paint roller. Most were displayed on the wall, but a few were placed inside Dream Machines.
16 Gysin, in an interview with Gérard-Georges Lemaire (August 1975).
17 At Galleria Trastevere (Rome) and at "L'Objet," Le Musée des Arts Décoratifs (Paris), February–March 1962. In December 1862 it was exhibited at Galerie Iris Clert in Paris (Hoptman 2010).
18 Even Geiger relies on Gysin's words in *Nothing Is True* (Gysin 1962).
19 Thanks to the patent history specialist Marcel Just (Zürich) for helping me to find this out by exploring the French patent archives.
20 In *Brion Gysin: His Life and Times*, Geiger wrote about the later efforts in the United States (Geiger 2003b). No sources of information are provided in either.
21 *Rotoreliefs* are not mentioned.
22 Art editions of *Rotoreliefs* were produced by the gallerist Arturo Schwartz, while the Basle-based publisher Carlo Levi produced an edition of the Dream Machine on the occasion of an exhibition in 1979.
23 This is demonstrated in the interviews with celebrities like Marianne Faithful and Iggy Pop in Nik Sheehan's feature documentary *Flicker* (2008).
24 Schilling has fallen into oblivion, particularly in the Anglo-American world.
25 Damien Hirst's "spin paintings" from the 1990s, exhibited in stasis only, seem to me copycat products, although Hirst may have ignored Schilling. He claimed to have got the idea from a "patent picture painter" shown in the UK children's television program *Blue Peter*. Schilling's work inspired such a toy, "Electro-Swirl ART," in the early 1960s (Brown 2012).
26 The random dot stereogram craze was especially strong in Japan.
27 DeMarinis's essay is the best piece of critical writing on Pomeroy I know.
28 DeMarinis has called Pomeroy's sound machine *Turbo Pan* (c.1985) "an acoustic equivalent of the zoetrope" (DeMarinis 1993).
29 Another artist who has done media-archaeologically oriented work with 3D is Perry Hoberman (Huhtamo et al. 1997).
30 Pomeroy produced the series as an artist in residence at the California Museum of Photography (Riverside, CA) that houses the Keystone-Mast archive.
31 Text accompanying the View-Master package *Stereo Views* (1988). The set was produced in connection with Pomeroy's exhibition at Light Work's Robert B. Menchel Photography Gallery, Syracuse, NY (January 10–February 13, 1988).
32 About Pomeroy's other 3D performances, such as *Composition in Deep—Light at the Opera* (1981), a kind of 3D shadow theater produced in real time (DeMarinis 1993).
33 His later idea, expressed in *Camera Lucida: Reflections on Photography* (1980, trans. 1981), of the "punctum" partly undermined his earlier semiotic position.

34 Nekes is a major collector of optical devices and has demonstrated these in films, videos, and traveling exhibitions (Nekes 1987).

35 Several other patents were granted before the 20th century (Gethmann et al. 2005).

36 Gethmann et al. 2005 also includes a rich selection of mentioned works on a DVD.

37 Gunning erroneously claims it was first published in *October* in 1981.

38 Another series, *False Impressions* (with Marion Faller, 1979), also referred to Muybridge. Frampton already produced Phenakistiscope discs.

39 There are other works by Cummins as well that investigate photography and motion in relation with sundials.

40 Pippin has developed other unconventional solutions, for example by converting a bathtub into a pinhole camera. Several works are in the collection of Tate Modern, London.

41 In the manner of Etienne-Gaspard Robertson in his secretive *Fantasmagorie* projections in the 1790s, Jacobs refused to show me his equipment after a performance I attended at the Sonic Acts festival in Amsterdam, hiding them behind a curtain.

42 Jacobs's program notes for his Cineprobe presentation in January 19, 1981. I have not noticed Jacobs mention Schilling since. He is missing from *Le relief au cinéma* (Lefebvre and Michaud 1997, 141–146).

43 Schilling used the spellings "Alfonse" or "Alfons." The statement is incorrect: magic lantern projections did not use fast-spinning shutter disks, except projecting phenakistiscope slides ("Wheel of Life"). Devices like Carpenter & Westley's round "crescent moon" shutter was moved only from time to time to reveal and block the lenses in presentations of dissolving views (Belisle 2014).

44 Kenneth Jacobs, "Eternalism, a method for creating an appearance of sustained three-dimensional motion-direction of unlimited duration, using a finite number of pictures", US. Patent 7,030,902 B2, granted Apr. 2006 (filed Jan. 22, 2002). Schilling's invention was protected by the disclosure document No. 049265, filed at the United States Department of Commerce, Patent and Trademark Office on May 12, 1976, but it was not protected by a patent (Schilling et al. 1997, 188–191).

45 Sengmüller has created several other media archaeological projects, including *Vinyl Video* in which he converted another obsolete technology, the LP record, into a medium for low-resolution video. He has created a tongue-in-cheek media industry around it, inviting other artists to create titles for the Vinyl Video product catalog.

46 *Demi-Pas* was preceded by projections called *Diapositives* (1995–1998) with which Maire tested and developed his mechanical slides. Maire has used imaginative projections in many other works since then.

47 The Toshio Iwai Exhibition was shown at the OTSO Gallery in Espoo, Finland, the temporary premises of the ZKM in Karlsruhe, Germany and the Dutch Design Institute, Amsterdam, the Netherlands.

48 The Museum of Contemporary Art, Helsinki. The co-curator was Asko Mäkelä.

49 Related work was Lynn Hershman's *America's Finest* (Hershman 1993–1994). A modified M-16 assault rifle was on top of a swiveling 360-degree pedestal. Pulling the trigger made a collage of war images, superimposed on a video of the shooter, appear in the gun sight.

50 As a side product, Naimark created stereocards of some of the still frames, embedded in Victorian-style card mounts.

51 Richards's works often evoke early science and technology (Huhtamo 1994). *Curiosity Cabinet at the End of the Millennium*, a large cabinet of copper and wood, evokes the Faraday cage (a chamber shielded from ambient magnetic waves), while the glowing tubes of *Charged Hearts* connect electromagnetic impulses in atmosphere, the human body, and media. The *Apparatus for Finding Love* is a simulated patent document (Dyson, Hayles, and Tuer 2003; Sawchuk 2003; Dyson 2009, 161–181).

52 When I discussed this parallel with Richards during the first MediaArtHistories Conference in Banff, Canada in 2005 and showed her images of such a camera obscura, she expressed surprise.

53 Related ways of connecting the media apparatus and the gendered observer have also appeared in Tikka's later works (2014).

54 Few artists attempted to use the cumbersome virtual reality head-mounted displays. An exception was the Art and Virtual Environments project at the Banff Centre for the Arts in Canada. Its results were documented as the book *Immersed in Technology*, where my "Time Machines in the Gallery" appeared (1996).

55 Other artists who have produced important work with panoramas include Jeffrey Shaw, Michael Naimark, and Luc Courchesne. This huge topic needs to be discussed at length on another occasion.

56 "Hidden Mechanisms: An Interview with Heidi Kumao" reveals that Kumao did not know what the device was called or who the showman was (Love 1994).

57 Jock Reynolds has characterized both artist Mowry Baden's phenakistiscope and Kumao's *Dusk* (1990–1991) as "zoetropes," which is a false generalization (Sheldon and Reynolds 1991). Kumao's device is really an adapted Projection Praxinoscope. Kumao writes about the ideas behind her works in "Hidden Mechanisms" (Love 1994).

58 Rebecca Cummins has used camera obscura in works like *Bagged* (2005), a shopping bag camera obscura, *Log Cam* (2010), a camera obscura made of a cedar log, and *Golf Cam* (2011), a motorized golf cart turned into a four-lens mobile camera obscura.

59 The other participating artists were Dorit Gypis, Leeny Sack, and Leslie Thornton.

60 North's *Recollections of a Happy Life Being the Autobiography of Marianne North* (1893, pub. 1993) does not mention it, but in *Some Further Recollections of a Happy Life* (1893, 120, 145) North describes how a fellow traveler, Mr. S., "a young architect with the R.A. traveling scholarship," used a related instrument, camera lucida, for tracing "every squared stone with it from Cairo to Aboo Simbel and back."

61 This is demonstrated by cartoons showing people inside camera obscuras peeking at lovers unaware of their presence.

62 Lippard (1999, 58) noted that casual visitors who happened to be around the Giant Camera experienced the performance very differently than those who were inside. The camera obscura only accommodated ten people, so the fifteen-minute performances were repeated continuously from 11 a.m. to sunset.

63 At the Exploratorium, a performance took place at the opening only. According to Zweig's typewritten description of her work (author's archive), it featured three girls representing different eras, including a 19th-century advertising girl, whose dress, parasol, and fan were all covered with photographs (such dressing up in media is known to have taken place).

64 Zweig must have been aware of this, because it is described in *Camera Obscura—a Chronicle* (Hammond 1981, 18), which she used as a source for the audiotape of *She Traveled for the Landscape* (Tamblyn 1987).

65 Sconce's *Haunted Media* (2000) links media history with esoteric currents.
66 They were re-released by Beloff as upgraded versions in 2009 and 2010.
67 In the television program "Another Evolution of the Moving Image," *What's Next*, Asahi Television, 1990 (video copy of the program in author's archive).
68 There is a limited amount of research about Iwai in English. In my early work *Excavating Media Dreams: Looking for a Context for Toshio Iwai's Art* (1994c) I already called Iwai's art "media-archeological." An important source (up to 1997) is *The Trace of Toshio Iwai's Media Art* (Iwai 1997). Yvonne Spielmann outlines Iwai's career in *Hybrid Culture: Japanese Media Arts in Dialogue with the West* (2013).
69 This paragraph relies on Toshio Iwai's "Beginning" from *The Trace of Toshio Iwai's Media Art* and on private conversations with the artist. I saw the craftbooks at Iwai's exhibition at Kichijoji Art Museum near Tokyo in January 2011.
70 Gregory Barsamian (NYC) is a sculptor who has used the zoetrope as the basic apparatus in many surrealistic machinic installations.
71 Muybridge's practice of shooting chronophotographic sequences from several points of view at the same time inspired *Jumping Grand Prix!* (1996), shown at the Science Museum, Tokyo.
72 In a deadpan manner, Iwai commented on the latter (No. 3): "I'm not sure whether this work was a joke, or a simple form of virtual reality," and on the former (No. 5): "This is another somewhat humorous work" (Iwai 1997, 91).
73 Another piece he created there, *Well of Lights* (1992), was a further development from *Time Stratum IV*.
74 Iwai's co-developer was Yu Nishibori from the Music and Human Interface Group at the Yamaha Center for Advanced Sound Technology.
75 NHK is the Japanese Broadcasting Corporation.
76 Iwai had failed to pay attention to the Anorthoscope when he studied persistence of vision devices, as he told me when demonstrating for me the prototype in his studio in Tokyo around 1999.
77 I saw such works at Iwai's exhibition at Kichijoji Art Museum near Tokyo in January 2011. Iwai also had a parallel exhibition at Inokashira Koen Zoo. Both were oriented for children; there were no pointers to Iwai's international career as a media artist.
78 The Japanese title of the series is *Hyakkaidate No Ie*. In an e-mail message on March 19, 2014, Iwai told me that 1.4 million copies of the two first volumes had been printed in Japan. The books have been published as translations in Taiwan, Korea, China, Hong Kong, Thailand, France, and Germany.
79 This happened during a private conversation at SIGGRAPH 2006. On that occasion Iwai donated to me a copy of *Elektroplankton*.
80 DeMarinis also includes "His Master's Face" (a transforming projected image of Edison's face) and the "Lecture of Comrade Stalin" (a lacquer record with Stalin's speech and carved face), making the number of items thirteen (Beirer, Himmelsbach, and Seiffarth 2010, 126–139).
81 Paul DeMarinis, "The Edison Effect," typewritten description (author's archive).
82 Who are Al and Mary? The goldfish? Or Al Jolson and the sweetheart of his character, dancer Mary Dale (May McAvoy), in *The Jazz Singer* (1927)? "Mary" is also the first word recorded with Edison's Phonograph. DeMarinis plays with it on three tracks in the CD *The Edison Effect: A Listener's Companion* (DeMarinis 1995a).
83 Unlike one might assume, *The Beer Barrel Polka* is not by Berlin. It was composed in 1927 by Lew Brown, Wladimir A. Timm, and Jaromir Vejvoda.

84 If I remember correctly, the grooves of the clay pot contain the singing of pygmies, placed there by a method invented by DeMarinis. In *Dinner at Ernie's* (1995), sounds from Hitchcock's *Vertigo* have been stored on ceramic plates, and in *Singer of Songs* (1996) they are embedded in woven fabrics, played back with a modified sewing machine.

85 DeMarinis belonged to the group of artists around the New Langton Arts Gallery, an alternative art space in San Francisco, which Pomeroy co-founded. Pomeroy and DeMarinis performed *A Byte at the Opera* (1977) together. DeMarinis co-curated Pomeroy's posthumous retrospective exhibition at the same place. Both in *Grind Snaxe Blind Apes* and *Dust* DeMarinis used fluorescent pictures that appear and disappear, referencing the transitory quality of life.

86 DeMarinis's patent was approved on August 1, 2000 (US 6,095,889). Giedion discusses the issue in his classic *Mechanization Takes Command* (1948), one of DeMarinis's favorite books.

87 Kentridge's *Phenakistoscope*, a functioning device created of two reused gramophone records with a stand and rotating handle, was released as an edition of forty by the New Museum of Contemporary Art (NYC) in 2000.

88 In *Hand to Mouth* (1993) Guess put unexposed film in his mouth and took pinhole photographs of the surroundings by using his lips as shutter. The results were exhibited as a circular panorama, adding another media-archaeological reference.

89 I exclude retro games, machinima, and game hacking here. Cory Arcangel's "video-game modifications" *Super Mario Clouds* (2002) and *Various Self Playing Bowling Games* (2011) have media-archaeological interest (Arcangel 2002, 2011), while in *Game After: A Cultural Study of Video Game Afterlife* (2014) Raiford Guins meticulously investigates media archaeology of game culture.

References

Ades, Dawn. 2000. *Dali's Optical Illusions.* Hartford and New Haven, CT: Wadsworth Atheneum Museum of Art and Yale University Press.

Arcangel, Cory. 2002. "Super Mario Clouds." Artist's web site. http://www.coryarcangel.com/things-i-made/supermarioclouds/ (accessed October 9, 2011).

Arcangel, Cory. 2011. "Various Self Playing Bowling Games." Artist's web site. http://www.coryarcangel.com/things-i-made/2011-009-various-self-playing-bowling-games (accessed October 9, 2011).

Barthes, Roland. 1977. "The Photographic Image." In *Image, Music, Text*, edited and translated by Stephen Heath. London/New York: Macmillan/Hill & Wang.

Beirer, Ingrid, Sabine Himmelsbach, and Carsten Seiffarth, eds. 2010. *Paul DeMarinis Buried in Noise.* Heidelberg: Kehrer.

Belisle, Brooke. 2014. "Depth Readings: Ken Jacobs's Digital, Stereographic Films." *Cinema Journal* 53(2): 1–26. doi: 10.1353/cj.2014.0010.

Beloff, Zoe, ed. 2008. *The Sonnambulists: A Compendium of Source Material.* New York: Christine Burgin Gallery.

Béret, Chantal, ed. 1996. *Frederick Kiesler. Artiste-architecte.* Paris: Éditions du Centre Georges Pompidou.

Berry, Ian, Darby English, Vivian Patterson, and Mark Reinhardt, eds. 2007. *Kara Walker: Narratives of a Negress.* New York: Rizzoli.

Birksted, J.K. 2009. *Le Corbusier and the Occult.* Cambridge, MA: The MIT Press.
Brecht, Bertolt. 1986. "The Radio as an Apparatus of Communication." In *Video Culture. A Critical Investigation*, edited by John G. Hanhardt, 53–55. Layton, UT: Peregrine Smith Books.
Brougher, Kerry, Russell Ferguson, and Dario Gamboni. 2013. *Damage Control. Art and Destruction Since 1950.* Washington, DC/Munich: Hirshhorn Museum and Sculpture Garden/DelMonaco—Prestel.
Brown, Mark. 2012. "Damien Hirst Credits Blue Peter with Idea for His Controversial Spin Paintings." *The Guardian.* http://www.theguardian.com/artanddesign/2012/aug/29/damien-hirst-blue-peter-spin-paintings (accessed August 29, 2012).
Bubb, Martine. 2010. *La Camera obscura. Philosophie d'un appareil.* Paris: L'Harmattan.
Burnham, Jack. 1968. *Beyond Modern Sculpture: The Effects of Science and Technology on the Sculpture of the Twentieth Century.* New York: George Braziller.
Cardiff, Janet, and George Bures Miller. 2007. *The Killing Machine and Other Stories 1995–2007.* Ostfildern, Germany: Hatje Cantz Verlag.
Carpenter, William B. 1868. "On the Zoetrope and its Antecedents." In *The Student, and Intellectual Observer of Science, Literature and Art.* London: Groombridge & Sons.
Carrouges, Michel. 1954. *Les Machines Célibataires.* Paris: Arcanes.
Castle, Terry. 1995. *The Female Thermometer: Eighteenth-Century Culture and the Invention of the Uncanny.* New York: Oxford University Press.
Clair, Jean, and Harald Szeemann, eds. 1975. *Le macchine celibi/The Bachelor Machines.* New York: Rizzoli.
Cummins, Rebecca. 2013. "Selected Works 2003–2013." *Washington.edu.*http://faculty.washington.edu/rcummins/CumminsCatalogue2003-2013.pdf (accessed January 15, 2015).
Dalrymple-Henderson, Linda. 1998. *Duchamp in Context: Science and Technology in the Large Glass and Related Works.* Princeton, NJ: Princeton University Press.
DeMarinis, Paul.1993. "The Boy Mechanic—Mechanical Personae in the Works of Jim Pomeroy." In *For A Burning World Is Come To Dance Inane. Essays By and About Jim Pomeroy.* Brooklyn, NY: Critical Press.
DeMarinis, Paul. 1995a. *The Edison Effect: A Listener's Companion.* Audio compact disc. Eindhoven, Netherlands: Het Apollohuis/Apollo Records ACD039514.
DeMarinis, Paul. 1995b. "Gray Matter." *Well.com.*http://www.well.com/~demarini/graymatter.html (accessed October 8, 2014).
DeMarinis, Paul. 2010a. "Essay in Lieu of a Sonata." In *Paul DeMarinis Buried in Noise*, edited by Ingrid Beirer, Sabine Himmelsbach, and Carsten Seiffarth, 218–221. Heidelberg: Kehrer.
DeMarinis, Paul. 2010b. "The Messenger." In *Paul DeMarinis Buried in Noise*, edited by Ingrid Beirer, Sabine Himmelsbach, and Carsten Seiffarth. Heidelberg: Kehrer Verlag.
Douglas, Susan. 1989. *Inventing American Broadcasting, 1899–1922.* Baltimore, MD: Johns Hopkins University Press.
Duchamp, Marcel. 1987. *Manual of Instructions for Étant donnés.* Philadelphia, PA: Philadelphia Museum of Art.
Dyson, Frances. 2009. *Sounding New Media Immersion and Embodiment in the Arts and Culture.* Oakland, CA: University of California Press.
Dyson, Frances, Katherine N. Hayles, and Dot Tuer. 2003. *Catherine Richards: Excitable Tissues.* Ottawa: Ottawa Art Gallery.

Fabre, Gladys C. 2003. "I AM THAT AM I? Between Crystal and Smoke." In *Brion Gysin: Tuning in to the Multimedia Age*, edited by Jose Férez Kuri. London: Thames & Hudson.

Field, Simon. 1981. "Beginning … and beginning again." *Afterimage* 8(9).

Frampton, Hollis. 1973. "Eadweard Muybridge: Fragments of a Tesseract." *Artforum* 11: 43–52.

Frampton, Hollis. 1984. *Recollections/Recreations*. Cambridge, MA: The MIT Press.

Geiger, John. 2003a. *Chapel of Extreme Experience: A Short History of Stroboscopic Light and the Dream Machine*. Brooklyn, NY: Soft Skull Press.

Geiger, John. 2003b. "Brion Gysin: His Life and Times." In *Brion Gysin. Tuning in to the Multimedia Age*, edited by José Férez Kuri. London: Thames & Hudson.

Geiger, John. 2005. *Nothing Is True—Everything is Permitted: The Life of Brion Gysin*. New York: The Disinformation Company Ltd.

Gethmann, Daniel, and Peter Gorschlüter, Ulrike Groos, Christoph Benjamin Schulz, eds. 2005. *Daumenkino: The Flip Book Show*. Düsseldorf/Cologne: Kunsthalle Düsseldorf/ Snoeck.

Guess, Jeff. 1993. "From Hand to Mouth." Artist's web site.http://www.guess.fr/ works/from_hand_to_mouth (accessed October 9, 2014).

Guins, Raiford. 2014. *Game After: A Cultural Study of Video Game Afterlife*. Cambridge: The MIT Press.

Gunning, Tom. 1983. "An Unseen Energy Swallows Space: The Space in Early Film and Its Relation to American Avant-Garde Film." In *Film Before Griffith*, edited by John L. Fell. Berkeley, CA: University of California Press.

Gunning, Tom. 2003. "Never seen this Picture Before. Muybridge in Multiplicity." In *Muybridge and the Instantaneous Photography Movement*, edited by Phillip Prodger, 222–272. Stanford, CA/New York: Stanford University, The Iris & B. Gerald Cantor Center for Visual Arts at Stanford University/Oxford University Press.

Gysin, Brion. 2001. *Back in No Time: The Brion Gysin Reader*. Middletown, CT: Wesleyan University Press.

Gysin, Brion, and Ian Sommerville. 1962. "Construct Your Own Dream Machine." In *Olympia* No. 2. (Reprinted in Laura Hoptman, 2010. *Brion Gysin: Dream Machine*.)

Haladyn, Julian Jason. 2010. *Marcel Duchamp: Étant donnés*. London: Afterall Books.

Hammond, John H. 1981. *Camera Obscura—A Chronicle*. Bristol, UK: Hilger.

Hawthorne, Nathaniel. 1896. *Passages from the American Note-Books*. Boston and New York: Houghton, Mifflin.

Hershman, Lynn. *America's Finest (1993–1994)*. http://www.lynnhershman.com/americas-finest/ (accessed October 2, 2014).

Hertz, Garnet, and Jussi Parikka. 2012. "Zombie Media: Circuit Bending Media Archaeology into an Art Method." *Leonardo* 45(5): 424–430.

Hockney, David. 2001. *Secret Knowledge: Rediscovering the Lost Techniques of the Old Masters*. New York: Viking Studio.

Hoptman, Laura. 2010. *Brion Gysin: Dream Machine*. London/New York: Merrell/New Museum.

Huhtamo, Erkki. 1992a. "Ennen broadcasting" ("Before Broadcasting"). *Lähikuva* 1: 6–17. Turku: Finnish Society of Cinema Studies.

Huhtamo, Erkki. 1992b. "Commentaries on Metacommentaries on Interactivity." In *Cultural Diversity in the Global Village. The Third International Symposium of Electronic Art* (Sydney, Australia November 9–13, 1992), edited by Alessio Cavallero, 93–98. Sydney: The Australian Network for Art and Technology.

Huhtamo, Erkki. 1994a. "From Kaleidoscomaniac to Cybernerd: Toward an Archaeology of the Media." In *ISEA '94: The Fifth International Symposium of Electronic Art Catalogue*, edited by Minna Tarkka, 13–35. Helsinki: University of Art and Design.

Huhtamo, Erkki. 1994b. "Simulator Ride Program." In *ISEA '94: The Fifth International Symposium of Electronic Art Catalogue*, edited by Minna Tarkka, 206–208. Helsinki: University of Art and Design.

Huhtamo, Erkki. 1994c. "Excavating Media Dreams: Looking for a Context for Toshio Iwai's art." In *Toshio Iwai Exhibition*, edited by Päivi Talasmaa, 8–11. Karlsruhe and Espoo: Zentrum für Kunst und Medientechnologie/Medienmuseum & Galleria OTSO.

Huhtamo, Erkki, ed. 1995a. *An Archeology of Moving Image Media* (special issue) *InterCommunication Quarterly* 14 (Autumn). Tokyo: NTT/ICC.

Huhtamo, Erkki. 1995b. "Seeking Deeper Contact: Interactive Art as Metacommentary." *Convergence* 1(2): 81–104. doi: 10.1177/135485659500100209.

Huhtamo, Erkki. 1996."Time Machines in the Gallery. An Archeological Approach in Media Art." In *Immersed in Technology. Art and Virtual Environments*, edited by Mary Anne Moser and Douglas McLeod, 232–268. Cambridge, MA: The MIT Press.

Huhtamo, Erkki. 2003. "Mr. Duchamp's Playtoy, or Reflections on Marcel Duchamp's Relationship to Optical Science." In *Experiencing the Media: Assemblages and Cross-Overs*, edited by Tanja Sihvonen and Pasi Väliaho. Turku, Finland: University of Turku, Media Studies.

Huhtamo, Erkki. 2004. "An Archaeology of Networked Art: A Symptomatic Reading of The Messenger by Paul DeMarinis." In *Networked Narrative Environments*, edited by Andrea Zapp, 32–34. Manchester, UK: Manchester Metropolitan University Press.

Huhtamo, Erkki. 2006. "The Pleasures of the Peephole: An Archaeological Exploration of Peep Media." In *Book of Imaginary Media: Excavating the Dream of the Ultimate Communication Medium*, edited by Eric Kluitenberg, 74–155. Rotterdam: NAi Publishers, 2006.

Huhtamo, Erkki. 2008. "Between Lightness and Gravity: Bernie Lubell's Media-Archaeological Art." In *Sufficient Latitude: Interactive Wood Machines by Bernie Lubell*, exhibition catalogue, 12 pages, unnumbered. Pasadena: Art Center College of Design. http://blubell.home.att.net/text.htm (accessed January 15, 2015).

Huhtamo, Erkki. 2010. "Thinkering with Media: On the Art of Paul DeMarinis." In *Paul DeMarinis Buried in Noise*, edited by Ingrid Beirer, Sabine Himmelsbach, and Carsten Seiffarth, 33–39. Heidelberg: Kehrer.

Huhtamo, Erkki. 2011. "Dismantling the Fairy Engine: Media Archaeology as Topos Study." In *Media Archaeology: Approaches, Applications, and Implications*, edited by Erkki Huhtamo and Jussi Parikka, 27–47. Berkeley, CA: University of California Press.

Huhtamo, Erkki. 2013a. *Illusions in Motion: Media Archaeology of the Moving Panorama and Related Spectacles.* Cambridge, MA: The MIT Press.

Huhtamo, Erkki. 2013b. "Illusion and Its Reverse: About Artistic Explorations of Stereoscopic 3D"/"Illusion und ihre Umkehrung. Über die künstlerische Erforschung des stereoscopischen 3D." In *Expanded Narration. Das neue Erzählen. B3 Biennale des Bewegten Bildes*, edited by Bernd Kracke and Marc Ries, 129–143. Frankfurt: Biennale des Bewegten Bildes/Transcript Verlag.

Huhtamo, Erkki, and Jussi Parikka. 2011. "Introduction: An Archaeology of Media Archaeology." In *Media Archaeology: Approaches, Applications, and Implications*, edited by Erkki Huhtamo and Jussi Parikka, 1–21. Berkeley, CA: University of California Press.

Huhtamo, Erkki, Päivi Talasmaa, Jonathan Lethem, Timothy Druckrey, and Perry Hoberman. 1997. *Unexpected Obstacles. The Work of Perry Hoberman 1982–1997.* Finland: Galleria OTSO Espoo.

Iwai, Toshio. 1997. "Beginning." In *Open Studio: The Trace of Toshio Iwai's Media Art*, edited by Tomoe Moriyama and ICC, translated by David Cheilly, Stephen Suloway, and Gary Tegler, 32–38. Japan: Hajimu Yoshida.

Iwai, Toshio. 2000. *Artist, Designer and Director SCAN #7.* Japan: Rikuyo-Sha.

Iwai, Toshio. 2005a. "Historical Description of Morphovision." *NHK Online.* http://www.nhk.or.jp/strl/morphovision/historical_description.html (accessed October 8, 2014).

Iwai, Toshio. 2005b. "Morphovision." *NHK Online.* http://www.nhk.or.jp/strl/morphovision/index_e.html (accessed October 8, 2014).

Kemp, Martin. 1990. *The Science of Art: Optical Themes in Western Art from Brunelleschi to Seurat.* New Haven, CT: Yale University Press.

Kittler, Friedrich. 1990. *Discourse Networks 1800/1900.* Translated by Michael Metteer and Chris Cullens. Redwood City, CA: Stanford University Press.

Koch, Polly, ed. 1998. *Joseph Cornell/Marcel Duchamp ... in resonance.* Ostfildern, Germany/New York: Hatje Cantz/Distributed Art Publishers.

Kofman, Sarah. 1998. *Camera Obscura: of Ideology.* Translated by Will Straw. Ithaca, NY: Cornell University Press.

Kranz, Stewart. 1974. *Science and Technology in the Arts: A Tour Through the Realm of Science/Art.* New York: Van Nostrand Reinhold Co.

Krauss, Rosalind E. 1993. *The Optical Unconscious.* Cambridge, MA: The MIT Press.

Kusahara, Machiko. 1997. "Historical Perspective of Art and Technology: Japanese Culture Revived in Digital Era. On Originality and Japanese Culture." Waseda University web site. www.f.waseda.jp/kusahara/Invencao.html (accessed October 8, 2014).

Lanza, Joseph. 2004. *Elevator Music. A Surreal History of Muzak, Easy-Listening and Other Moodsong.* Ann Arbor, MI: University of Michigan Press.

Lefebvre, Thierry, and Philippe-Alain Michaud. 1997. *Le relief au cinema.* Paris: AFRHC.

Lialina, Olia, and Dragan Espenschied. 2011. "Once Upon." Project's web site. http://1x-upon.com/ (accessed October 9, 2014).

Lippard, Lucy. 1999. *On the Beaten Track: Tourism, Art and Place.* New York: New Press.

Love, Lynn. 1994. "Hidden Mechanisms: An Interview with Heidi Kumao." *Afterimage* 21(7): 6–9.

Maines, Rachel P. 2001. *The Technology of Orgasm: "Hysteria," the Vibrator, and Women's Sexual Satisfaction.* Baltimore, MD: Johns Hopkins University Press.

Maire, Julien. 2002. *Demi-pas (Half-step). Projection-performance.* http://julienmaire.ideenshop.net/project4.shtml (accessed September 28, 2014).

Michaud, Philippe-Alain. 2004. *Aby Warburg and the Image in Motion.* Translated by Sophie Hawkes. New York: Zone Books. Original German title is *Pathosformel.*

Moriyama, Tomoe, and ICC, eds. 1997. *Open Studio: The Trace of Toshio Iwai's Media Art.* Translated by David Cheilly, Stephen Suloway, and Gary Tegler. Japan: Hajimu Yoshida.

Nekes, Werner. 1987. *Uliisses. Ein Film von Werner Nekes.* Edited by Walter Schobert. Cologne: Verlag der Buchhandlung Walther König.

North, Marianne. 1893. *Some Further Recollections of a Happy Life.* Edited by Janet Catherine Symons. London: Macmillan and Co.

North, Marianne. 1993. *Recollections of a Happy Life: Being the Autobiography of Marianne North.* Edited by Susan Morgan. Charlottesville, VA: University of Virginia Press.

Open Reel Ensemble. 2013. *Kaiten—En-Cyclepedia*. Tokyo: Gakken.

Oursler, Tony. 2000. "The Influence Machine." *Artangel.org.uk*. http://www.artangel.org.uk/projects/2000/the_influence_machine (accessed September 28, 2014).

Parikka, Jussi. 2010. *Insect Media: An Archaeology of Animals and Technology*. Minneapolis, MN: University of Minnesota Press.

Parikka, Jussi. 2011. "With each project I find myself reimagining what cinema might be: An Interview with Zoe Beloff'." *Electronic Book Review*. http://www.electronicbookreview.com/thread/imagenarrative/numerous (accessed October 2, 2014).

Pierson, Michele, David E. James, and Paul Arthur, eds. 2011. *Optic Antics: The Cinema of Ken Jacobs*. New York: Oxford University Press.

Pippin, Steven. 1998. *New Work—Laundromat-Locomotion*. San Francisco: SFMoMA. Exhibition catalog.

Pomeroy, Jim. 1983. *Apollo Jest. An American Mythology (in depth)*. San Francisco, CA: Blind Snake Blues.

Pomeroy, Jim 1988. *Stereo Views; Ver Multidimensionales*. Syracuse, NY: Light Work.

Pomeroy, Jim. 1999. *A Retrospective*. San Francisco, CA: New Langton Arts.

Pontus Hultén, Karl G. 1968. *The Machine as seen at the End of the Mechanical Age*. New York: Museum of Modern Art.

Porta, John (Giovanni) Baptista. 1658. *Natural Magick*. London: Thomas Young and Samuel Speed.

Pritikin, Renny. 2012. "Interview with Paul DeMarinis." *Art Practical* 3(13). http://www.artpractical.com/feature/interview_with_paul_demarinis/ (accessed October 9, 2014).

Riches, Martin. 2004. *Maskinerne/The Machines/Die Machinen*. Odense: Kunsthallen Brandts Klaedefabrik.

Sawchuk, Kim. 2003. "Charged Heart: The Electronic Art of Catherine Richards." *Horizonzero*. http://www.horizonzero.ca/textsite/see.php?tlang=0&is=6&file=3 (accessed October 2, 2014).

Schilling, Alfons, H. Klocker, C. Aigner, K.A. Schröder, and M. Peintner. 1997. *Alfons Schilling, Ich, Auge, Welt—The Art of Vision*. New York: Springer.

Schwartz, David, ed. 1989. *Films That Tell Time: A Ken Jacobs Retrospective*. Exhibition catalog. New York: American Museum of the Moving Image.

Sconce, Jeffrey. 2000. *Haunted Media: Electronic Presence from Telegraphy to Television*. Durham, NC: Duke University Press.

Sconce, Jeffrey. 2011. "On the Origins of the Origins of the Influencing Machine." In *Media Archaeology: Approaches, Applications, and Implications*, edited by Erkki Huhtamo and Jussi Parikka, 70–94. Berkeley, CA: University of California Press.

Sheldon, James L., and Jock Reynolds. 1991. *Motion and Document, Sequence and Time: Edward Muybridge and Contemporary American Photography*. Andover, MA: The Addison Gallery of American Art/Phillips Academy.

Shirai, Masato. 1997. "Toshio Iwai—The Technology of Astonishment." In *Open Studio: The Trace of Toshio Iwai's Media Art*, edited by Tomoe Moriyama and ICC. Translated by David Cheilly, Stephen Suloway, and Gary Tegler, 15–19. Japan: Hajimu Yoshida.

Spielmann, Yvonne. 2013. *Hybrid Culture: Japanese Media Arts in Dialogue with the West*. Translated by Anja Welle and Stan Jones. Cambridge, MA: The MIT Press.

Spigel, Lynn. 1974/1992. Introduction to *Television: Technology and Cultural Form*, by Raymond Williams, xi–xvii. Hanover, NH: Wesleyan University Press.

Strauven, Wanda. 2013. "Media Archaeology: Where Film History, Media Art, and New Media (Can) Meet." In *Preserving and Exhibiting Media Art: Challenges and Perspectives*, edited by Julia Noordegraaf, Cosetta G. Saba, Barbara Le Maître, and Vinzenz Hediger, 59–80. Chicago, IL: University of Chicago Press.

Sutton, Gloria. 2015. *The Experience Machine: Stan VanDerBeek's Movie-Drome and Expanded Cinema*. Cambridge, MA: The MIT Press.

Tamblyn, Christine. 1987. "Whose Life Is it, Anyway?" *Afterimage* 15(1): 24.

Testa, Bart. 1992. *Back and Forth: Early Cinema and the Avant-Garde*. Toronto: AGO.

Tikka, Heidi. 2014. *Visual Artist Heidi Tikka*. www.heiditikka.com (accessed October 3, 2014).

Varnedoe, Kirk and Gopnik, Adam. 1990. *High & Low : Modern Art and Popular Culture*. New York: Museum of Modern Art.

Virilio, Paul. 1985. *War and Cinema: The Logistics of Perception*. Translated by Patrick Camiller. London: Verso.

Watkins, Glenn. 2010. *The Gesualdo Hex: Music, Myth, and Memory*. New York: W.W. Norton.

Weidenaar, Reynold. 1995. *Magic Music from the Telharmonium*. Lanham, MD: Scarecrow Press.

Weiss, Jason, ed. 2001. *Back in No Time: Brion Gysin Reader*. Middletown, CT: Wesleyan University Press.

Williams, Raymond. 1974/1992. *Television: Technology and Cultural Form*. Hanover, NH: Wesleyan University Press.

Further Reading

Architekturzentrum, Wien, ed. 2009. *The Austrian Phenomenon*. Berlin: Birkhäuser Architecture.

Lange, Christy, Jeannie Lee, Janet Cardiff, and George Miller. 2007. *Janet Cardiff & George Bures Miller: The Killing Machine and Other Stories 1995–2007*, edited by Ralf Beil and Bartomeu Mari. Ostfildern, Germany: Hatje Cantz Verlag.

Mannoni, Laurent. 2000. *Great Art of Light and Shadow: Archaeology of the Cinema*. Translated by Richard Crangle. Exeter, UK: Exeter University Press.

Mannoni, Laurent, Donata Pesenti Campagnoni, and David Robinson, eds. 1996. *Light and Movement: Incunabula of the Motion Picture, 1420–1896*. London: BFI Publishing.

Moser, Mary Anne, and Douglas Macleod, eds. 1996. *Immersed in Technology: Art and Virtual Environments*. Cambridge, MA: The MIT Press.

Pepper, John Henry. 2012. *True History of the Ghost: And All about Metempsychosis*. Cambridge: Cambridge University Press.

Prodger, Phillip. 2003. *Time Stands Still: Muybridge and the Instantaneous Photography Movement*. New York: Oxford University Press.

Sommerer, Christa, and Laurent Mignonneau. 1996. "Trans Plant II." In *3D Beyond the Stereography: Images and Technology Gallery Exhibition Theme*, edited by T. Moriyama, 76–77. Tokyo, Japan: Tokyo Metropolitan Museum of Photography.

4

Proto-Media Art
Revisiting Japanese Postwar Avant-garde Art

Machiko Kusahara

The history of Japanese media art goes back to the postwar avant-garde art of the 1950s and 1960s, both in terms of attitudes toward media technology and the artists themselves, who later played crucial roles in launching institutions for media art including educational programs and art centers. Soon after World War II, a sense of freedom brought an explosive energy to visual art. New forms of art emerged within a few years after the war, when major cities were still making an effort to recover from the ashes. With the recovery of freedom of speech and expression, innumerable cultural activities took place all over the country and many art groups were formed. Theoretical leaders such as Shuzo Takiguchi, Jiro Yoshihara, and Taro Okamoto led the art scene and inspired young artists to carry out highly experimental activities in the early 1950s—activities original and powerful even by today's standards.

Among the many groups that were active from 1950 to 1970, Jikken Kobo and the Gutai Art Association are of particular interest when seen from the point of view of today's media art. As the country started to rebuild international relationships, Japanese artists became involved in art movements such as art informal, abstract expressionism, Neo-Dada and Fluxus.[1] The aim of this chapter is to provide not an in-depth introduction to their works and projects but a snapshot of what was happening in art in connection with the social and political background of the era. For this purpose, prewar art history will be briefly introduced. It would require another essay to analyze the complex and extremely rich activities in the 1960s that connected art, design, film, theatre, and music, among many other fields. The role that the 1970 Universal Exposition in Osaka (Osaka Expo '70) played in the death of avant-garde art and the birth of media art is yet another topic that would warrant an essay of its own.

A Companion to Digital Art, First Edition. Edited by Christiane Paul.

An Overview of Postwar Avant-garde Art

The Japanese postwar avant-garde art movement was short-lived but extremely active and colorful in spite of the country's difficult situation. Recent publications in English that accompanied major exhibitions provide rich source material for understanding the phenomenon. For example, *Gutai: Splendid Playground* (February–May 2013) at the Guggenheim Museum in New York offered a rare opportunity to view the group's unique activities from its earliest stages to its final days. The exhibition titled *Art, Anti-Art, Non-Art: Experimentations in the Public Sphere in Postwar Japan, 1950–1970*, shown at the Getty Research Institute in 2007, gave an excellent overview of the wide spectrum of artistic activities based on research. *Tokyo 1955–1970: A New Avant-Garde* (November 2012–February 2013) at New York's MoMA (Museum of Modern Art) focused on art activities and groups in Tokyo including Neo Dadaist Organizers (Neo-Dada), Hi Red Center, and Fluxus, highlighting the multidisciplinary approaches and practices that characterized the avant-garde art in Tokyo during that time.

In Japan, curatorial efforts exploring what the postwar avant-garde art movement meant for society gained visibility after the Great East Japan Earthquake and the Fukushima Daiichi nuclear disaster. In December 2012 the exhibition *Quest for Dystopia* at the Metropolitan Museum of Photography in Tokyo included a section titled "Protest and Dialogue – Avant-garde and Documentary," which focused on documentary films and videos produced by avant-garde artists in the 1960s and 1970s. During the same season a large-scale exhibition titled *Jikkenjo 1950s* ("testing ground 1950s") was held at the National Museum of Modern Art as the second part of its 60th anniversary special exhibition. The chief curator, Katsuo Suzuki, states in the accompanying anthology of texts (in Japanese only) that the 1950s were an era when people could imagine and realize many possibilities, and multiple options were still open for Japan's future. According to Suzuki, groups, movements, debates, and publications developed by art critics, artists, and other cultural figures were the practice to create "public spheres" that would support democracy, art, and the power of cultural resistance. With the period of rapid economic growth from 1955 to1973, such activities gradually diminished.

Prewar Avant-garde Art

Japanese art has a long history, but it is very different from its counterpart in the West. Western-style painting was officially introduced only in the second half of the 19th century. As a result, Japanese and Western paintings remained two separate categories, dominated by two different groups of established artists. These artists ran the official Imperial Academy of Fine Arts Exhibition (Teiten), which was held at the Metropolitan Museum of Art in Ueno Park.[2] Artists frustrated by the hierarchical art communities and their favoritism founded their own groups and curated exhibitions. As an action against Teiten they launched the Nika-kai (meaning "second section group") annual exhibition in 1914 to exhibit their works.

By the 1920s, modernist culture flourished in major cities, especially in Tokyo. Cinemas, variety theatres, and dance halls clustered on the streets of Asakusa. Jazz, French chanson, and European classic music became popular on the gramophone and radio. Less than half a century after Japan opened its borders, Western culture was knit into urban life.[3] New trends in art, design, and theatre, among them Bauhaus, constructivism and futurism, arrived almost in real time. The Dadaist movement was introduced in 1920 and had a strong impact especially on poets. Their first Dada magazine came out as early as in 1922.

Surrealism was introduced in the late 1920s and had an immediate influence among poets, theorists, and artists, mostly as a new style of expression rather than social criticism or a political attitude. The two leading figures were painter Ichiro Fukuzawa and Shuzo Takiguchi, a poet and theorist who translated Andre Breton's *Surrealism and Painting* in 1930.[4] Surrealists showed their works in the "9th Room" of the Nika-kai exhibition, which served as a core part of prewar avant-garde art. Meanwhile, Proletarian artists influenced by the Russian Revolution gathered and formed San-ka (the 3rd section group).

The age of modernism did not last long. While people still enjoyed jazz and dance, and enthusiastically welcomed Charlie Chaplin's visit, militarism spread quickly. Soon democracy movements were demolished, and artists who were suspected of having socialist tendencies were harshly oppressed. Fukuzawa and Takiguchi were arrested and detained for months in 1934 on the groundless allegation that they were part of the international surrealist movement connected to communism. This marked the end of the prewar avant-garde art movement. Taro Okamoto, who had lived in Paris and achieved recognition among surrealists and abstract painters, was forced to come back to Japan in 1940. After his first solo exhibition in Tokyo he was drafted and sent to the Chinese front. Major painters—of both the Japanese and Western school—were involved in war painting, but surrealist or abstract paintings were of no use for propaganda.[5]

Postwar Political Situation and the Art Community: 1945–1960

When the war ended in 1945 and the occupation forces arrived with overwhelming material presence, it became clear that the wartime spiritualism could not resist the power of science and technology. The belief that Japan had to remodel itself as an industrial nation was widely shared. Osamu Tezuka's manga and animation *Mighty Atom* (1951, titled *Astro Boy* outside of Japan) represents this vision. In 1970, this ideal of industrialization was visualized in the world exposition in Osaka, for which many of the avant-garde artists were hired.[6]

Establishing democracy and eliminating any remaining traces of wartime nationalism was the most urgent goal for GHQ, the occupation force operated by the United States.[7] Although there were no official convictions of former art leaders who had promoted the war propaganda, they were publicly criticized by those who had remained "innocent."[8] The discussion inevitably led to heated arguments about the nature of art and the responsibilities of artists. Following the collapse of the prewar and wartime hierarchy, numerous groups of artists and theorists formed, actively working and collaborating in a spirit of excitement about the new possibilities that had opened up for them. The group that played the most important role in the formation of the avant-garde art movement was *Yoru no Kai* (The Night Society, named after Taro Okamoto's painting), founded in 1948 by Okamoto and Kiyoteru Hanada, a literary critic who most actively argued for the democratization of art. For the younger generation who had had no chance of receiving a proper art education during the war, Okamoto's texts on art history and theory—testament to the fact that he had inherited his mother's passion for writing as well as his father's talent in art—must have been a liberation.[9] Young artists joined the group's meetings to learn about art history and theory, and to discuss future Japanese art.

Art classes were also held. The Avant-Garde Artists' Club, which was founded in 1947 by artists and critics including Takiguchi with the aim of democratizing the art community, opened its Summer Modern Art Seminar in July 1948. Leading art critics and painters, including Takiguchi and Okamoto, taught the class. As a theorist and art critic with a firm theoretical background who had not yielded to wartime militarism, Takiguchi soon became a leading figure in the postwar art scene. He helped launching not only the annual Yomiuri Indépendant (which will be further discussed in the next section) but also Takemiya Art Gallery in the central part of Tokyo, an independent art space for exhibitions of young artists he discovered. Securing such a venue was an important step at a time when art museums were still scarce and there was no regular space for contemporary art.

As Okamoto's works show, Western art in Japan had been under European (especially French) influence before the war. The postwar occupation brought a major change. Cultural programming was an important part of the GHQ's democratization policy. In November 1945, the library of the Civil Information and Educational Section (CIE), located in the center of Tokyo, opened its doors to the Japanese public with publications that introduced American culture and society, including a rich selection of art books and musical records.[10] Books introducing the latest art movements were among them. As the United States had become the center of new movements in visual art, music, and dance from the beginning of World War II, the CIE library provided up-to-date information that was not available elsewhere. After years of an absence of any cultural atmosphere—high school students worked in factories while university students were drafted—people were hungry for books, art, music, or any other cultural activities. A law student named Katsuhiro Yamaguchi immediately visited the library when he saw a notice in the newspaper. Yamaguchi, who would soon become a central figure of Jikken Kobo, recalled that he decided to become an artist when he encountered works by Lazlo Moholy-Nagy at the library. Frequent visitors to the library included people who later would become major members of Jikken Kobo, such as Kuniharu Akiyama, Shozo Kitadai, Toru Takemitsu, Hideko and Kazuo Fukushima, and Takiguchi.[11] Akiyama, who was a university student in French literature but extremely knowledgeable in music history, eventually took a role as an assistant organizing record concerts at CIE.[12]

The thirst for cultural activities was shared by a wider public. Rejoicing in the freedom of speech and expression, many circles focusing on art, music, theatre, etc. were formed among the people, especially students and workers, supported by the GHQ's policy to help labor unions to grow. One of these art organizations, founded by a group of prewar as well as younger proletarian artists, launched the annual Nihon Indépendant art exhibition as early as 1947.[13] The Communist Party actively promoted "cultural movements," supported by the respect they had gained for their suffering during wartime and the international high tide of communism. However, the wind changed quickly as tension in East Asia increased. The People's Republic of China was established in 1949, and the Korean War started in 1950. Communism spreading in Asia became a major concern for the United States. Instead of a promotion of democracy and freedom of speech, a Red Purge—the equivalent of McCarthyism in the United States—was conducted under the GHQ's instructions around 1950. It is estimated that 30,000 people lost their jobs.[14] In the process of redefining Japan as a "protective wall against Communism" (New York Times 1948), the occupation, except for that of Okinawa, ended in 1952.[15] The 1950s therefore was the decade of politics. The immediate confusion after the war was settled, but the Cold War followed.

The Korean War (1952–1955) helped the Japanese economy to recover as Japan became the major supplier of commodities for the US forces in Asia, but people were also afraid of being involved in warfare again. The 1954 tragedy of the *Lucky Dragon* No. 5 tuna fishing boat in the South Pacific reminded them of their fear of nuclear weapons.[16] The 1955 protest against US military bases, led by farmers who lost their land in Tachikawa, a western suburb of Tokyo, attracted much attention. In 1956 the government declared the postwar period to be over, based on the country's rapid economic growth. But severe struggles between labor unions and enterprises continued.[17] Moreover, the government's decision to make Japan a cornerstone in America's global strategy was not fully supported by everyone. Massive protests against signing the US–Japan Treaty of Mutual Cooperation and Security (in Japanese abbreviated as Anpo) took place in 1960. When the treaty was signed in spite of a student's death in one of the final demonstrations, a feeling of defeat was shared by many, including artists. The explosive energy that drove postwar Japan came to a halt.

Collectives, Exhibitions, and Organizations

Yomiuri Indépendant (1949–1963)

Yomiuri Indépendant (written "andepandan" in Japanese characters), the annual art exhibition that started in 1949—only four years after the war—played a crucial role in the birth of postwar avant-garde art.[18] The annual non-juried exhibition chose the Tokyo Metropolitan Art Museum in Ueno—where the national Teiten was held in the prewar era—as its venue, and anyone could show their work by paying the fee. The exhibition was sponsored by *Yomiuri* newspaper and supervised by Shuzo Takiguchi.[19] Yomiuri journalist Hideo Kaido, who was responsible for its cultural section, detested the prewar and wartime hierarchy in art. While the majority of the submitted works were said to be rather conventional paintings and sculptures including those by hobbyists, Yomiuri Indépendant, informally referred to as Yomiuri Anpan, offered an ideal space for independent artists and the most experimental works. Along with younger artists such as Shozo Kitadai and Katsuhiro Yamaguchi, the Gutai founder Jiro Yoshihara was among its early participants.

"Anpan" is the name of a popular Japanese pastry. The reason why young artists such as Genpei Akasegawa preferred calling the exhibition "anpan" with a friendly tone rather than using the more art-ish French "Indépendant," was probably more than a matter of mere abbreviation. "Anpan" was invented in the early Meiji era when bread was not yet part of Japanese daily culinary life. Instead of filling a small piece of bread ("pan" in Japanese, based on the original sound of the word introduced by the Portuguese in the 16th century) with apple preserve or chocolate, as in the case of French pastries, the bakers Kimura, father and son, used traditional bean paste ("an") that was (and still is) familiar to most Japanese. In other words, they replaced the traditional flour- or rice-based exterior part—which is called "skin"—of Japanese cakes with the more substantial volume of the most basic Western food, which was new to most Japanese. Anpan was a huge success and the bakery was immediately commissioned to serve the emperor's court, which made their reputation solid.[20] It is believed that the invention of anpan made a substantial contribution to bringing bread onto Japanese tables. This well-known anecdote illustrates a typical way in which Western culture was introduced to and merged into Japanese culture. The abbreviation "Yomiuri anpan" was thus metaphorical, and it may explain the way young artists outside the traditional hierarchy of the art world felt closer to the exhibition.

From approximately 1959 onwards, performances and unusual, large-scale installations by art groups started to appear at Yomiuri Anpan. The most radical of all was Neo-Dada Organizers, the "anti-art" artists group that was formed in 1960 by Masanobu Yoshimura, Jiro Takamatsu, Natsuyuki Nakanishi, Shusaku Arakawa, Genpei Akasegawa, and Ushio Shinohara, among others.[21] They performed "happenings" around the same time as, but independently from, Allan Kaprow, and introduced interactivity into their works.[22] For the 1963 Yomiuri Indépendant exhibition—which would be the last one—Takamatsu exhibited a piece consisting of a string that extended outside the museum, crossing the streets and reaching the Ueno Station. Nakanishi submitted a work titled *Clothpins Assert Churning Action*, a performance in which he walked through the streets with his head and face covered by numerous cloth pins. Akasegawa exhibited a huge copy of a 1000 yen bank note, which was part of a series that later became part of a famous court case as a counterfeit note.[23] Another project realized by Akasegawa, Nakanishi, Takamatsu, and Yasunao Tone was a "miniature restaurant" for which they sold tickets for dishes to visitors. Those who had expected a full meal were disappointed when they found out that the food was served in tiny sizes on a dollhouse dish. Body-centered performances also took place, including one performed nude. Takehisa Kosugi, who was a member of Group Ongaku (Group Music), sealed himself in a bag with a fastener and crawled around.

Yomiuri Indépendant ended in 1963—or, more precisely, the 1964 exhibition was canceled just before the opening, and that was the end of it. The conflict between the institutional framework of a public museum and the radical artists became visible in the 1962 exhibition with its destructive, noisy, or stinking junk art that went beyond the limits of what the organizers could support.[24]

Competition among avant-garde artist groups had already led to demonstrations of most unusual pieces of anti-art and non-art for several years (Merewether and Iezumi-Hiro 2007). Kyushu-ha (Kyushu School) were notorious for their anti-art approach as demonstrated by their infamous piece *Straw Mat – Straw Mat*, which was a straw mat from the floor of their studio rolled up and filled with garbage.[25] The museum had stated rules forbidding types of works that produced extremely unpleasant sounds, or involved knives and materials that would stink or decay, but not all artists respected them. The cancellation of Yomiuri Indépendant did not stop the avant-garde art movements. The Neo-Dada artists Takamatsu, Akasegawa, and Nakanishi formed a new group, Hi Red Center, in the same year.[26] The last and best-known project by the short-lived but brilliant group was the *Be Clean* performance *(Let's Participate in the HRC Campaign to Promote Cleanup and Orderliness of the Metropolitan Area!)* in October 1964. Artists wearing white robes cleaned the sidewalks of Ginza in central Tokyo. It was an ironic commentary on the government's campaigns to "clean up" Tokyo for the Olympic Games.[27]

One might argue that *Yomiuri Indépendant* illustrated the limits of a public museum and private media company. At the same time artists enjoyed freedom because they didn't have to take on certain responsibilities thanks to the sponsor who took care of the exhibition management. *Yomiuri Indépendant* created opportunities for them to regularly present their works and to meet other artists and form a loose but important network among them. Another outcome was the rise of a critical discourse among artists and critics triggered by the conflicts created by the exhibition.

Jikken Kobo (Experimental Workshop, 1951–1957)

Jikken Kobo—Experimental Workshop being the official English name—was active from 1951 to 1957 in Tokyo.[28] Without doubt, Jikken Kobo was the most experimental and technologically advanced group of artists in 1950s Japan. The group was ahead of its time and laid the basis for media art to come. A departure from the traditional art system clearly was a concept driving the group. Unlike many other artist groups, Jikken Kobo never announced the beginning or ending of the group, its policy, or the membership. Besides the group's shows, which were titled "presentations" instead of "exhibitions," their activities included multimedia performances, workshops, concerts, photographic works for magazines and so on.[29] Jikken Kobo's members worked both in visual art and in music. Most of them came from outside of the academic art or music environment and were not bound to mainstream art. At the same time they were well informed about prewar and postwar art movements in the West, and freely appropriated elements from them. They gathered at members' houses, inspiring each other and working together. Openness was a shared attitude. They extensively collaborated with others, widening their field of activities.

Jikken Kobo started as a voluntary gathering of visual artists and composers around Shuzo Takiguchi, who named the group when they were commissioned to realize, in collaboration with dancers, a multimedia ballet titled *Picasso, La joie de vivre* (Joy of Life), as part of a "Picasso Festival" accompanying an exhibition of Picasso's paintings in 1951.[30] The choice of ballet as a form of collaboration was an homage to the history of avant-garde art, referring to Dada's and surrealists' experimental ballets created by artists such as Francis Picabia, Erik Satie, and others in the 1920s; to Jean Cocteau and Diaghilev; and to the American avant-garde scene represented by John Cage and Merce Cunningham. Set designs required a wide variety of methods, tools, industrial materials, and scalability. The experience created a foundation for the group's extensive activities. Many of them became leading figures in visual art and music as, for example, Toru Takemitsu who contributed not only to the international contemporary music scene but also to Japanese cinema by composing for many films including those by Akira Kurosawa and Nagisa Oshima.[31] Although there is not enough space to fully introduce the group's extremely rich body of works, reviewing its process of formation by taking a look at the paths of Shozo Kitadai and Katsuhiro Yamaguchi will give an idea of the group's nature, the speed of its development, and the postwar environment.

Shozo Kitadai was a few years older than the other members and played a leading role in the group. He was born in 1921 in Tokyo, grew up amidst 1920s and early 1930s modernism and, influenced by his father, familiarized himself with photography at a young age. He studied metal engineering before being drafted in 1942 and sent to the South Pacific as an officer of telecommunications technology. He was detained after the war—as was Okamoto—and returned to Japan in 1947. After coming back to Tokyo he joined the aforementioned Summer Modern Art Seminar in July 1948. In August, Kitadai proposed to Yamaguchi, Hideko Fukushima, and a few other young artists he met at the seminar to form a group. Soon after, Fukushima's young brother Kazuo, a composer, joined with his friends. The young artists and composers regularly met at Kitadai's and Fukushima's houses, discussing topics ranging from art history and contemporary art, to nuclear physics, relativity theory, and science fiction (Jikken Kōbō 2013, 49–51). Within a few months (November 1948) they had put together their first group exhibition including abstract paintings and a "mobile" by Kitadai, who was inspired by a picture of Alexander Calder's work that he had encountered in a magazine. Kinetic sculpture would become an important element for Kitadai and Jikken Kobo, enabling remarkable stage design for dance performances.[32]

The exhibition generated a review by Okamoto, strongly supporting the group and their exhibition, in *Bijutsu Techo*, a magazine that played (and continues to play) a leading role in contemporary art. Imagine Kitadai's excitement when he, the self-taught artist who had recently returned from detention, was highly appreciated by the leading artist/theorist of the era![33] In 1949, an abstract painting and a mobile that Kitadai had submitted to the first *Yomiuri Indépendant* generated praise in a review written by Takiguchi for *Yomiuri* newspaper. As an emerging artist, Kitadai was invited to be the stage designer for a performance by a contemporary ballet company in 1950.[34] He created a sculptural composition, which was a novelty. Takiguchi once again highly praised him in Yomiuri, referring to Isamu Noguchi's stage design for the Martha Graham Dance Company, and hoped this would be the first step in further collaborations between contemporary art and ballet. The following year Kitadai was invited again and designed an even more innovative set. The lighting designer for both performances was Naotsugu Imai, whom Kitadai had already known through a major circle of artists and poets.[35] Imai would later become an important member of Jikken Kobo. What made Jikken Kobo so unique was the collaboration among multidisciplinary talents. Recognizing the potential of the group, Takiguchi commissioned them for the stage, costume, and musical design of *Picasso, La joie de vivre* in 1951, which marked the beginning of the group's activity.

Along with Kitadai, Katsuhiro Yamaguchi played a key role in the three-dimensional space design. Apart from Lazlo Moholy-Nagy's works and György Kepes's *Language of Vision*, Frederick Kiesler's projects—such as the stage design for *Entr'acte* (René Clair, Francis Picabia, 1924)—had a lifelong impact on him.[36] An interest in motion, time, and space can already be observed within his *Vitrine* series, which started in 1952. It consists of abstract patterns painted on the surface of corrugated or slumped glass plates—an industrial material typically used for bathroom windows (Figure 4.1). Although the idea itself sounds simple, the work creates a proto-interactive optical illusion of movement as the observer moves in front of it.[37]

Yamaguchi's spatial design for Jikken Kobo's *Musique Concrète/Electronic Music Audition* at Yamaha Hall also involved everyday industrial materials.[38] Musique concrète was developed by Pierre Schaeffer around 1950 as a new form of music based on magnetic-tape recording technology and attracted members' attention immediately after its introduction to Japan in 1953. Yamaguchi used dozens of white strings, stretching from the middle of the seating area to the ceiling, that created geometric patterns, turning the well-known Yamaha Hall in the central part of Tokyo into an

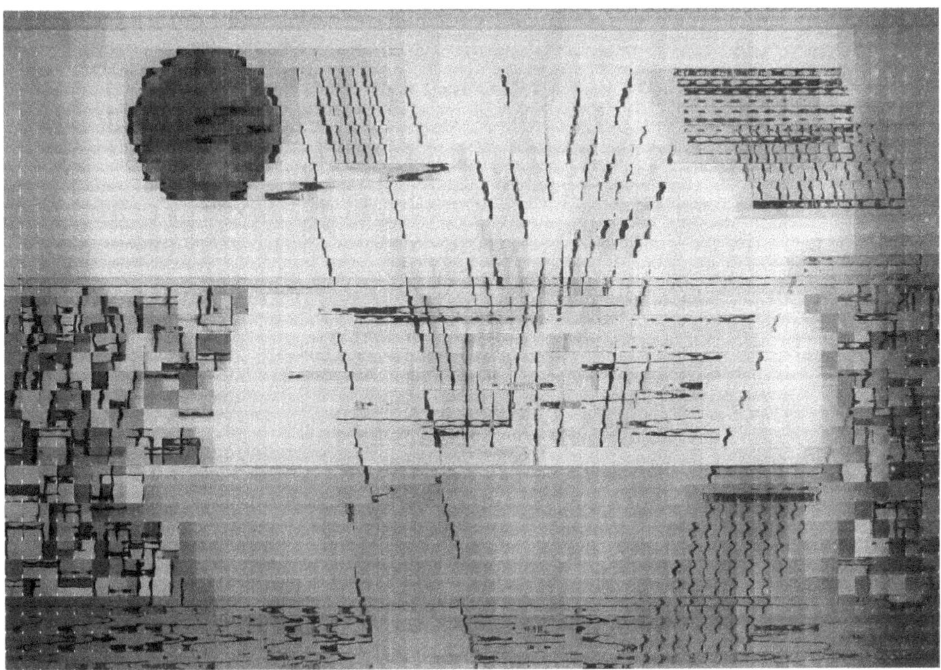

FIGURE 4.1 Katsuhiro Yamaguchi, *Vitrine Blueplanet*, 1955.

unusual space for the temporal event. The design compensated for the emptiness on stage, where machines rather than humans played back the music. Such transformation of space by a geometric and semi-transparent structure may have been inspired by Moholy-Nagy's *Light-Space Modulator*, a major influence for Yamaguchi. Innovative use of industrial materials is one of the features Jikken Kobo members share with today's media artists. The Bauhaus spirit and the aesthetics of Oskar Schlemmer and Nicolas Schoeffer are strongly felt in the early works by Jikken Kobo, but they went beyond these influences.

For self-taught young artists who aspired to the spirit of democracy after the war, the "sense of gravity in plastic art such as painting, sculpture and architecture" was the most depressing feature of authoritative prewar art academia. Their interest in transparent or lightweight industrial material, found objects, lighting, and interactivity can be also understood from that perspective.[39] Later in the 1960s Yamaguchi developed a technique for using acrylic resin in sculptures with embedded light sources developed as "order art," that is by giving instructions for their creation to factories.[40]

The acrylic light sculptures were a logical consequence of his *Vitrine* series while "order art" was an homage to Moholy-Nagy, who in 1923 created his *Construction in Enamel* series by describing his designs over the telephone to a local enamel factory in Weimar. In 1966 Yamaguchi co-founded the Environment Group (Enbairamento-no-kai), which organized the exhibition *From Space to Environment* in the same year, in which he included a light sculpture titled *Relation of C*. The exhibition was meant as a precursor for the Universal Exposition 1970 in Osaka.[41]

The best example of Jikken Kobo's experimental and multimedia approach is a series of surrealistic audiovisual stories they produced in 1953 by combining 35 mm slides and musique concrète, using the brand-new Automatic Slide Projector (Auto Slide) from Sony.[42] The system synchronized a slide projector with a tape recorder, and was meant for educational use. Four Auto Slide works were made for their *Fifth Presentation* in September 1953, combining experimental music by composers and imagery by visual artists (Jikken Kōbō 2013, 84, 338).[43] Yamaguchi worked with Hiroyoshi Suzuki on *Adventures of the Eyes of Mr. Y.S., a Test Pilot*; Hideko and Kazuo Fukushima collaborated on *Foam is Created. Tales of the Unknown World* was written by Takemitsu, with art direction by Kitadai and music by Suzuki and Joji Yuasa. Slides for these three works were based on sculptural constructions for each scene that were photographed by Kitadai or Kiyoji Otsuji, the photographer and experimental filmmaker. The images for *Lespugue*[44] were not photographed but painted by Tetsuro Komai. For that piece Yuasa did an exquisite manipulation of sound elements, including ones created by piano and flute, making full use of the functions available on tape recorders. It is considered a pioneering work of musique concrète in Japan (Jikken Kōbō 2013, 84).

In parallel to the production of Auto Slide works, Jikken Kobo expanded its activities to printed media from January 1953 onwards. For the weekly *Asahi Graph*, a magazine published by the Asahi Newspaper Company, a photograph of an abstract structure—with the letters APN (for Asahi Picture News) included in it in some way—was created every week until February 1954. The abstract compositions' style was similar to that of the group's stage sets and Auto Slide works, and consisted of everyday materials and objects, such as pieces of wire, paper, wood, plastic, beads and small balls, glass containers, metal cans. The compositions were created alternately by Kitadai, Yamaguchi, Komai, and Yoshishige Saito while photography was always done by Otsuji. Later three artists outside of Jikken Kobo, including Sofu Teshigahara, the founder of the "avant-garde" Teshigahara Flower School, were invited. The series, which continued for fifty-five weeks, was the first instance of a regular and frequent distribution of avant-garde art works by mass media.

In 1955 Jikken Kobo members were involved in a series of performances named *Ballet Experimental Theatre*. The program included *Illumination*, *The Prince and The Pauper*, and *Eve Future*, with stage and costume design by Yamaguchi, Fukushima, and Kitadai, and musique concrète by Takemitsu. The stage set for *Eve Future* by Kitadai consisted of abstract structures that were partly movable by actors. The same year they collaborated with the radical theatre director Tetsuji Takechi[45] to realize Arnold Schoenberg's *Pierrot Lunaire* as a masquerade for *An Evening of Original Play by the Circular Theater.* Akiyama translated Albert Giraud's poems into Japanese, Kitadai designed the masks and the stage sets, Fukushima the costumes, and Imai did the lighting. The Noh player Hisao Kanze played the role of the Harlequin. Joji Yuasa composed for another piece from the program, "*Aya no Tsuzumi*" (The Damask Drum) written by the novelist Yukio Mishima, based on a classic Noh play. Such collaboration and mixing of Western and Japanese traditions was a precursor of the lively visual culture of the 1960s that included underground theatre, experimental cinema, and Butoh dance performances and often involved avant-garde artists and composers. Another project Jikken Kobo worked on at the same time was a film titled *Mobile and Vitrine*, featuring Kitadai's and Yamaguchi's works. It premiered at ACC in 1954. In the same year it was used as a backdrop projection for an act of a burlesque theatre piece at Nichigeki Music Hall titled *7 Peeping Toms from Heaven*, featuring music that used sounds of hammering and a lathe (Jikken Kōbō 2013, 96).[46] While the combination of avant-garde art and nude dancers might seem unusual, it was a time when a new wave of postwar humanities was spreading through the cultural sphere. Led by the philosopher Shunsuke Tsurumi, who coined the term "genkai geijutsu" (marginal art), studies of mass culture from a democratic perspective developed, covering topics within mass entertainment that had previously been neglected by academia.[47]

In 1955 *Mobile and Vitrine* was shown at a special screening of abstract films at the National Film Center. The screening included Jikken Kobo's Auto Slide works, Otsuji's and his Graphic Group's *Kine Caligraphy*, and Hans Richter's *Rhythm 21*.[48] For the group, film was a logical continuation of the Auto Slide works and the best medium to capture optical illusions and movements. They collaborated with the experimental filmmaker Toshio Matsumoto on *Ginrin* (*Bicycle in Dream*, 1956), a promotion film for the Japanese bicycle industry. In the film, a young boy's dream is presented in surrealistic landscapes created by Kitadai and Yamaguchi, in a style similar to their Auto Slide, APN projects, and stage sets, while a Vitrine sometimes blurs the dream. Eiji Tsuburaya, who made the film *Godzilla* in 1954, was in charge of the special effects and the music was composed by Takemitsu and Suzuki. From then on Matsumoto continued to collaborate with Jikken Kobo members, especially Yuasa and Akiyama, who composed music for his films.

The group activities of Jikken Kobo ceased at the time of Takiguchi's death in 1957, after their last group exhibition. The friendship among members continued, but, as members already had received recognition individually and were busy with their own work, they lost momentum to act as a group without their spiritual leader. Most of the members continued to be active either on solo or collaborative projects. Takemitsu composed music for more than fifty films in the 1960s alone. Yamaguchi traveled to Europe and the United States from 1961 to 1962, meeting Kiesler and Fluxus artists, and witnessing the latest movements in art including minimalism and primary structure. The experience drove Yamaguchi to further experimentation with new materials and manipulation of space, leading to the formation of the Environmental Group with architects and designers. In the 1960s Yamaguchi joined some of the Fluxus events that were co-organized by Akiyama and Ay-O. Eventually the Osaka Universal Exposition was around the corner. It involved most of the members of the group who created high-tech audiovisual environments.

Gutai Art Association (1954–1972)

Among the many artists groups active during that period, Gutai is the internationally best known, having produced works such as Atsuko Tanaka's *Electric Dress* (1956) and *Six Holes* by Saburo Murakami (1955). Jiro Yoshihara founded Gutai in 1954 in the international and cultural town Ashiya, near Osaka. Staring in 1955, Yoshihara published newsletters called *Gutai* and sent them to his prewar international contacts. As a result, Gutai was noticed abroad as a Japanese equivalent of French *art informel* or American abstract expressionism in 1956. Among the many avant-garde artist groups of the time, Gutai was the first to be associated with international art movements and recognized outside the country.

Gutai also was the longest lasting among the postwar avant-garde art groups. Altogether almost sixty artists joined Gutai during its nearly two decades of activity that ended with the death of Yoshihara in 1972. In contrast to Jikken Kobo, Gutai was a solid "group" with declared membership. The *Gutai Art Manifesto*, published in 1956, stated the goals of the group, which functioned under Yoshihara's strong leadership. The activities of Gutai can be divided into three phases.[49]

Beginnings of Gutai

Yoshihara, the heir of a leading cooking oil company, was a recognized avant-garde painter in the prewar era. Although he studied business instead of art he was accepted into the Nika exhibition at the age of 29 and, in 1938, joined the newly added "Room 9" for avant-garde art. In 1937 he helped traveling the *Surrealist Paintings from Abroad* exhibition to Osaka and shared a panel with Takiguchi, who had co-organized the show. After the war Yoshihara became a key figure in the cultural community of the Kansai region. He assisted in relaunching Nika and served as its representative in Kansai; founded and became the chair of the Ashiya City Art Association in 1948;[50] and, in 1952, co-founded an interdisciplinary art organization that became known as "Genbi." Its monthly meetings were joined by a wide variety of local cultural figures such as painters, sculptors, designers, and calligraphy and flower arrangement artists. Yoshihara himself did stage designs for performances and fashion shows in Ashiya, and Genbi organized five exhibitions, with more than two hundred artists participating, until 1957. Yoshihara's background as a businessman presumably helped him in organizing projects with a strong leadership. Given all of these activities, it seemed a logical step for Yoshihara to establish his own group. By 1947 Shozo Shimamoto and others were frequenting Yoshihara's house, bringing their works and asking for critique. Other groups had started to appear in Kansai, including Zero-kai (Zero Group). In 1954 Gutai was officially formed with members chosen by Yoshihara.[51] The core members of Zero-kai—Murakami, Tanaka, Akira Kanayama, and Kazuo Shiraga—joined Gutai in 1955.[52] The publication of the bilingual *Gutai* journal in January 1955 was a significant step in achieving the international recognition that Gutai would receive. On March 12 of the same year, the Gutai artists submitted their works to the 7th *Yomiuri Indépendant* in Tokyo. All the works were simply titled *Gutai*, in line with Yoshihara's concept of pursuing abstraction. It was Gutai's first and last massive participation in the *Indépendant*. After that, the Gutai artists separated themselves from the most active avant-garde artists who had gathered around the non-juried competition. Did Yoshihara find the messy *Indépendant* inappropriate for his group? Or, was it because the art community in Kansai was smaller and more exclusive compared to the one in Tokyo? It seems that Yoshihara believed in the value of closed groups and juried exhibitions such as Nika, while more radical critics such as Takiguchi tried to change the system and realize democracy in art.[53] Gutai was actively involved in the scene of modern art, as their list of exhibition illustrates, while Jikken Kobo members did not care if they were making art or not. Experimentalism and an interest in science and technology can be observed in the activities of early Gutai members, but did not develop further.

The first phase of Gutai: 1954–1957

The most unusual and original Gutai works were created between the group's first and legendary outdoor exhibition titled *Experimental Outdoor Exhibition of Modern Art to Challenge the Midsummer Sun* in Ashiya Park in the summer of 1955 and *Gutai Art on the Stage* in July 1957. The outdoor exhibition inspired members to think differently about art making.[54] No one cared about preserving or selling the work after the show, and everyone tried to attract the most attention. The need to create large-scale pieces within a limited budget led to the choice of unusual materials. Everyone was enthusiastic about their respective ideas, including impossible or dangerous ones. Having a leader who made the final decision was a necessity.[55] Concepts such as interventions into the environment, interactivity, and participation by visitors were pursued because of the nature and scale of the park with nearly five hundred pine trees, stretching along a river. In October of 1955, the *1st Gutai Art Exhibition* took place at Ohara Kaikan Hall in Tokyo.[56] This time the challenge was to surprise the Tokyo audience who were familiar with avant-garde art through *Yomiuri Indépendant* and other exhibitions. Murakami's *Making Six Holes in One Moment*, in which he stretched layers of packaging paper over two wooden frames and tore through them six times, and Shiraga's *Challenging Mud*, in which he thrashed around in a heap of building clay for twenty minutes, surely shocked visitors.

Among the legendary pieces from the period were Tanaka's *Work (Bell)* (1955), Shiraga's *Please Come In* (1955),[57] and Shimamoto's *Please Walk on Here* (1956)[58]—all strongly focused on visitor participation, which was unusual in contemporary art at the time. Tanaka's *Work (Bell)* was a sound installation—consisting of a string of electric bells laid out around the gallery—that could be experienced only when a visitor pushed a button for a certain period of time to set off a chain of rings (Figure 4.2). A series of electric bells connected to a control panel was placed along the border of the exhibition space. Tanaka designed the wooden control panel, which was placed on the turntable of a record player. Touch switches were carefully placed on the board in the shape of a heart (i.e., a variation of cycloid), with each switch corresponding to a bell. As a visitor pushed a button the panel would rotate, and the bells would start ringing one after another, producing a continuum of an alarming sound traveling through the exhibition space. *Work (Bell)* was shown at the *3rd Genbi Exhibition in* Kyoto in 1955.

Shiraga's *Please Come In* consisted of a structure made of logs bound together at the top. Visitors were invited to come inside the open structure to contemplate the sky and surrounding trees. Shimamoto asked for more involvement from the visitors.

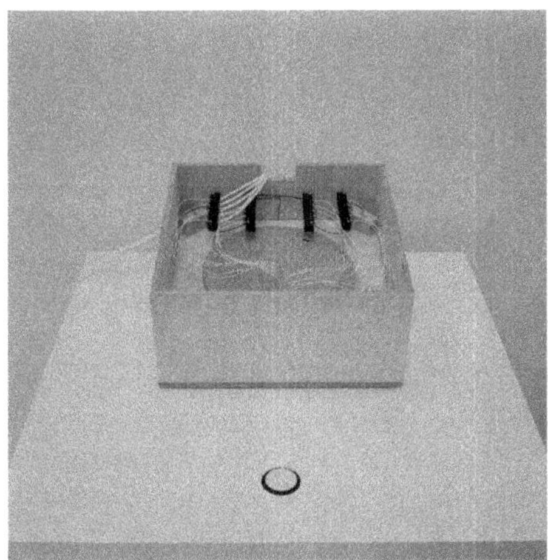

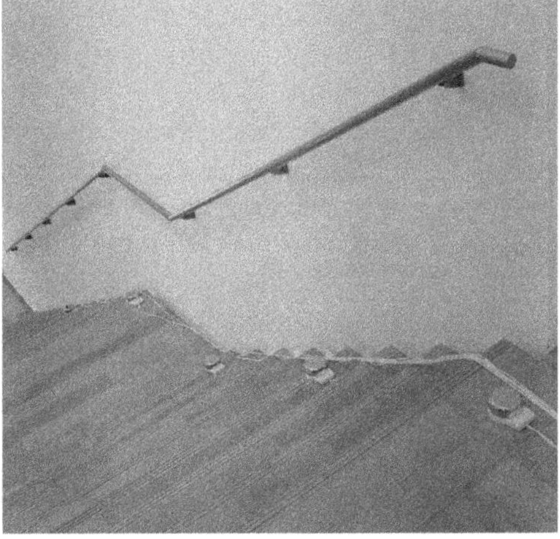

FIGURE 4.2 Atsuko Tanaka, *Work (Bell)*, 1955/2005. Photo: Seiji Shibuya. Photo courtesy of NTT InterCommunication Center (ICC).

His installation consisted of long, box-like pathways made of colored wooden blocks. A notice read: "Please walk on top of it. Shozo Shimamoto." The wooden floors started wobbling as visitors walked on them since the artist had installed springs underneath the blocks to make them unstable. Using simple technology he created an interactive kinetic sculpture involving visitors' bodies.[59]

During the 2nd Gutai Outdoor Exhibition in Ashiya Park in 1956, a big wooden panel together with paint and markers for free use was installed. A small sign said, "Rakugaki-ban: Please draw freely" ("rakugaki-ban" means a board offered for graffiti) without attributing the work to any artist. In the 5th volume of the *Gutai* periodical, which reported on the outdoor exhibition, the board was featured only as a "Scribbling Board" in the "Snap" section, which presented snapshots taken by group members and visitors to the outdoor exhibition. The work raised the question whether it was meant as an artwork, or was just a service offered to the public, especially for children. The piece later was officially named *Please Draw Freely* when it was shown at the Nul international art exhibition in Hague in 1966, to which Gutai had been invited. Whether the piece was originally meant as an artwork or not, Yoshihara defined it as art by then.[60]

One might ask how and why such an idea—which almost anticipated interactive art or the net art of the 1990s that offered free (online) spaces for virtual drawing—was conceived and realized. The answer may lie in Gutai's involvement in children's drawing. In late 1947 Yoshihara was contacted by an editor of a children's poetry and art magazine titled *Kirin*.[61] The editor himself, Yozo Ukita, joined Gutai. Gutai members contributed their works and writings to the magazine and were involved in competitions of children's paintings. Like many other young painters, Gutai members often earned their living by teaching painting to children. When members later on were asked about influences from abroad that had influenced their work, they would answer that they were inspired by children's drawings, not by international art movements. Respect for the originality of children's drawing was in accord with Yoshihara's famous doctrine to respect originality above anything else.[62] Originality was the criterion he applied in selecting members' works, and even the repetition of one's own original ideas was rejected (Murakami 1994, 213).[63] This generated an explosive production of original works, as Atsuko Tanaka's projects illustrate.

Tanaka, who used to produce rather minimal works before joining Gutai, discovered industrial textile as a cheap material for creating structures in outdoor space. A huge piece of thin cloth in vivid pink would change its form in the wind. Tanaka's interest in transforming space continued in indoor pieces such as *Work (Bell)* for which she designed the electric circuit herself and appropriated regular house bells and a record player, anticipating the "circuit bending" practices of today's media artists. She continued using electric wiring for the outdoor exhibition in 1956, employing light bulbs and changing light intensity through the use of water. In her best known work *Electric Dress* (1956)[64] she connected light bulbs painted in vivid red, yellow, green, and blue to form a dress, which she wore as performer. The bulbs flashed, and, together with the wiring, made the dress extremely heavy. There was the danger of getting an electric shock if cables came loose. Yoshihara's doctrine along with technical advice from Kanayama, whom she later married, must have encouraged her, yet it involved significant risk-taking for a young female artist to realize the piece.

The above-mentioned works show Tanaka's interest in creating projects that move, change, and interact with the environment. Her experience with using textile became the basis for her *Stage Clothes (Butai-fuku*, 1957) performance. The dress she had designed and wore continued to dramatically transform as she removed its parts, one after another, on stage. The extremely complex design of the cloth and performance proved her talent in designing a layered but logical system through the use of either electrical circuits or purely physical representations. However, *Stage Clothes* marked Tanaka's departure from technology. From 1957 onwards Tanaka concentrated on abstract paintings based on drawings she had done for designing electric circuits. Her interest in movement was occasionally realized in the form of figures painted on large circular wooden panels that rotated, driven by motors, and were installed in her garden. In the film *Round on Sand*, Tanaka is seen drawing these types of lines and figures on the beach, and the waves wash them away.[65]

The interest in technology, new material, and scientific phenomena was shared by some of the Gutai members, including Jiro Yoshihara, who created light sculptures for outdoor exhibitions, and his son Michio Yoshihara, who applied musique concrète in their stage performances. Sadamasa Motonaga suspended plastic bags—a new material at the time—filled with colored water for the outdoor exhibitions.

Among the technically most advanced members of Gutai was Kanayama, who experimented with industrial materials such as inflatable balloons and plastic sheets. His *Footprints* (1956) was an installation using long white plastic sheets with black "footprints," laid on the floor of the exhibition venue or on the ground (if exhibited outdoors), and inviting visitors to walk on it. However, the imaginary walker's footprints would leave the visitors behind when the sheet would "climb up" a wall or a tree, revealing the work's three-dimensional nature. Kanayama's *Work* series, produced mostly around 1957, was created by means of a remote-controlled toy car with paint tanks. The artist built, modified, and drove around the car on a sheet laid on the floor. Neither its trajectory nor the resulting traces of ink were fully controllable. Kanayama tested a variety of crayons, markers, black and color inks that were scribbled or dripped by the car over large pieces of paper and later white vinyl sheets, which the artist found to be most appropriate for his purpose. The result was a series of complex line drawings—traces of an entangled relationship between the artist and the machine, control and chance operation.

"Painting through action" was an experimental practice shared by early Gutai members, among them Murakami who created sensational performances by running through paper screens. Shiraga, who performed *Challenging Mud* in 1955, continued to use his own body in his work, often painting with his feet while swinging on a rope hung from the ceiling. Michio Yoshihara used a bicycle for drawing. Shimamoto painted on large canvases, first by throwing glass bottles filled with paint, and later using a cannon and even a helicopter. One has to wonder whether Gutai members saw their work in the tradition of publicly performing calligraphy or calligraphic painting, which had existed since the Edo era.[66]

The second phase of Gutai: 1957–1965

As Yoshihara and Shimamoto kept sending their bilingual journal *Gutai* abroad in 1956, the group started gaining international recognition. In April, *LIFE* magazine sent two photographers to shoot images for an article on Gutai.[67] The journal also reached Michel Tapié, the French critic and theorist who coined and promoted the concept of *art informel*. Recognizing Gutai as the Japanese version of *art informel*, Tapié, together with the painter Georges Mathieu, visited Gutai in September 1957. Being part of international movements meant a lot to Japanese artists at that time. Yoshihara decided to follow Tapié's suggestion to exhibit Gutai abroad and introduce *art informel* in Japan. Gutai members began focusing on the creation of paintings, instead of experimenting or performing, for practical reasons—to be able to ship, exhibit, and sell, as Tapié also was an art dealer.

In 1958, a Gutai Group Exhibition took place in New York's Martha Jackson Gallery. In the spring of that year, a hundred copies of *Gutai* Vol. 8—co-edited by Yoshihara and Tapié—were sent to a bookstore in New York and were "sold out in a few days" (Kato 2010, 104). However, their works were (mis-)interpreted and contextualized as manifestations of *informel* or abstract expressionism. The press release of the exhibition introduced Gutai as an "informal gathering" that aimed at "embodiment of spirit" and took inspiration from "new American painting," especially from Jackson Pollock (Kato 2010, 106). This was especially unfortunate for Kanayama whose *Work* series was understood as mere mimicry of Pollock. The same year Shimamoto made a seven-minute color film with sound, titled *Work*, by painting directly on film, but otherwise experiments became rare.[68]

The International Sky Festival in 1960 was an exceptionally unique exhibition in the second phase of Gutai. Air balloons—a typical medium for advertisements during that era – featuring paintings by Gutai and international artists from Italy, Spain, and the United States floated in the air above the roof of the Takashimaya Department Store in Osaka for a week.[69] Another interesting work of that time was the interactive *Gutai Card Box*, which was installed in the gallery space of the Takashimaya Department Store for the *11th Gutai Art Exhibition* in April 1962. By inserting a coin into an automatic vending machine, each visitor would get an original artwork painted by a Gutai member. Created before the arrival of Fluxus, the project was ahead of its time and its venue (a department store) made it even more interesting. The *Gutai Card Box* actually was not a machine, but had a human hiding inside who would do the drawings.[70] Shiraga and Murakami recall that the quality of the card depended on "human factors." Male members tended to draw better if the client was a young woman (Murakami 1994, 218).

Gutai's focus on painting was enhanced when Gutai Pinacotheca, a permanent exhibition space named by Tapié, opened in the central part of Osaka in 1962 in the old warehouse of the Yoshihara Oil Mill. Compared to the times when the artists had to work hard on filling the vast space of Ashiya Park, hoping their pieces would last for a week or two, the gallery made exhibiting much easier, but it also left little space for experimenting. Tanaka and Kanayama left Gutai in 1965 just when the invitations to take part in the Osaka Expo '70 split the artworld. In their studio in Nara, Tanaka focused on her paintings inspired by circuit designs from her earlier works. Kanayama stayed away from presenting artworks until the late 1980s, and his later works involved artistic visualizations of sound waves and astronomical data.

The third phase and end of Gutai: 1965 to 1972

Given that Gutai was based in the Osaka area and internationally recognized and Yoshihara was a member of the region's business and cultural communities, there were reasons for the group to get involved in the 1970 Expo.[71] In parallel with the official art exhibition, which included selected members of the group, the Gutai Group Exhibition was realized with a unique exhibition design by a new member, Senkichiro Nasaka, who used metal pipes to create a visual structure for hanging paintings. Another new member, Minoru Yoshida, contributed his large-scale optoelectronic sculptures to the show.

Furthermore, Gutai group performances took place on the main Festival Plaza in front of Taro Okamoto's Sun Tower, reviving some of the experimental practices in which the group had engaged in its earliest stages. New members with advanced technical skills played a major role in the group exhibition and the spectacular stage performances. One might ask what initiated these changes after years of more conventional practices consisting of images displayed on gallery walls.

In April 1965, Jiro Yoshihara and his son Michio visited Amsterdam to install Gutai artworks at the Stedelijk Museum for the international exhibition *Nul 1965*. The exhibition was organized by the Nul group founder Henk Peeters and was based on his network of European avant-garde artist groups, such as the French GRAV and the Italian Gruppo N and Gruppo T, and artists including Otto Piene. When the Yoshiharas arrived "with a suitcase full of paintings and sketches for new installations," Peeters surprised them by rejecting the paintings as being "too *informel*" (Munroe 2013, 35). Kanayama's inflatable vinyl air sculpture Balloon, which they had brought in the suitcase, was accepted, but, other than that, they were asked to reconstruct early Gutai works on site, including Murakami's *Work (Six Holes)* and Shimamoto's *Please Walk on Here*, by using locally available materials. As a result, Gutai's works were, probably for the first time, internationally presented and received within the right context, side by side with works by artists from various countries that represented experimental and challenging approaches. This experience made Yoshihara reconsider the policy he had adopted since 1957. The "*informel* fever" was over in Japan at that point, and the forthcoming Osaka Expo would become a new stage for technological art forms.

By the end of the same year Yoshihara invited quite a few younger artists to join the group, which was unusual in Gutai's history. His hope to bring back an experimental spirit to the group was obvious, and the effect became immediately visible. In 1966, Toshio Yoshida developed a machine that produced soap bubbles as a sculpture, which was shown at the *19th Gutai Group Exhibition* in 1967. The 19th exhibition showcased a number of kinetic and light artworks consciously responding to the movement of "environment art," including kinetic sculptures by the youngest member, Norio Imai.[72] The introduction of a darkened room for light art was a new development for art exhibitions. Minoru Yoshida, whose background was painting, became known for kinetic sculptures using motors and industrial materials such as fluorescent acryl. He and Nasaka were invited to *Electromagica: International Psytech Art Exhibition '69*, held at the Sony Building in Tokyo, along with artists including Nicholas Schöffer and Katsuhiro Yamaguchi. The *Electromagica* exhibition was meant as a pre-event for the Expo and aimed at presenting new methods and forms of art and design in the era of electronics, in which "cohabitation of human and machine is needed," echoing the theme of the Expo that called for "Progress and Harmony for Mankind."[73] Gutai at that point was regaining its experimental spirit and trying to bridge art, design, and technology.

Yoshida's iconic work *Bisexual Flower* (1969), a large kinetic sculpture incorporating sound, was made of yellow-green, transparent, fluorescent plexiglass, ultraviolet tubes, motors, and electronic circuits. Petal-like elements made of plexiglass moved as neon-colored water flowed through transparent plastic tubes. The entire sculpture glowed in a darkened space. Even today the piece fully functions and is strikingly impressive. The unprecedented kinetic sculpture was shown at the Expo along with three other works by Yoshida, including a transparent car, but the artist himself was not present. Yoshida felt uncomfortable with being part of the Expo while the political meanings of the event were argued about and criticized among young artists. Tired of conflicts, Yoshida left Japan before the Expo opened and moved to the United States.[74]

Toward the end of the Expo, from August 31 to September 2, a group performance titled *Gutai Art Festival: Drama of Man and Matter* took place on the Festival Plaza. It combined elements from Gutai's previous stage performances, such as balloons, smoke, bubbles, light, sound, dancers in designed costumes, as well as kinetic sculptures. Nasaka designed the major structure. Sadaharu Horio created an installation made of fabric, which responded to the general interest in environmental design. Yoshida's transparent car appeared on the stage and robots were also present, yet they were not controlled by means of sophisticated technology. A box that magically moved and finally fell, for example, was operated by a student inside—similar to the earlier *Gutai Card Box*. After Yoshida left, the technical skills of the group were more limited.

The Expo could have served as a springboard for the group. Instead it created stress and disagreements among the members. Due to the rapid increase in new members, the group's identity was no longer clearly defined. Older key members, such as Shimamoto, Murakami, and Motonaga, left Gutai in 1971. Although the Gutai Mini Pinacotheca, a smaller reincarnation of the original Pinacotheca, which closed in 1970, opened in Osaka in October 1971, not much activity took place after the Expo. With the unexpected death of Yoshihara in 1972 the group disintegrated.

Cross-genre, Intermedia, and Sogetsu Art Center

The latest international art movements were introduced in Japan in the early 1960s. The most sensational event were the performances by John Cage and David Tudor at the Sogetsu Art Center in 1962. Yoko Ono, who had already been active as an avant-garde artist in New York, and the young composer Toshi Ichiyanagi, who was a student of John Cage, helped realize Cage's and Tudor's visit to Tokyo.

As previously indicated, 1960s Japan saw an incredibly rich variety of experimental art activities. Japan was part of an international phenomenon, as the Fluxus events organized by the avant-garde artist Ay-O and ex-Jikken Kobo members Yamaguchi and Akiyama illustrate, but, at the same time, distinctly Japanese elements rooted in more traditional aesthetics started to appear. New forms of art, such as Butoh and the underground theatres organized by Shuji Terayama and Juro Kara, among others, reflected both the international rise of underground culture and the prewar (or even pre-Meiji Restoration) mass entertainment tradition. "Japan-ness" was rediscovered and woven into the underground culture, for example in the posters designed by Tadanori Yokoo and Kiyoshi Awazu for underground theatres and experimental films. Experimental film directors, including Nagisa Oshima, founded the Art Theatre Guild (ATG), a membership organization that supported the production of independent cinema. Photographer Eiko Hosoe, for whom the writer Yukio Mishima modeled nude, took close-up pictures of 1960s cultural figures including Butoh dancers, creating a new genre in Japanese photography.

"Midnight entertainment" TV programs also launched in the 1960s, bringing a glimpse of radical avant-garde art to the living room through the artists invited to the shows. Yoji Kuri was among the regular guests and introduced his experimental short animations, which could be either ironical, nonsensical, or surrealistic. The merger of popular entertainment and art was also taking place in *manga*. The independent comic magazine *Garo*, which launched in 1964, played an important role in the rise of alternative and avant-garde manga, Yoshiharu Tsuge's "surrealistic" manga being an example. These people with very different backgrounds would eventually form a wide network—also including editors, writers, and TV producers of cultural programs—which made it possible to organize cross-genre activities. "Intermedia" became the keyword of the 1960s and early 1970s, encompassing the wide range of art, design, illustration, music, literature, theatre, architecture, film, video, animation, entertainment, and more.

It was symbolized by Sogetsu Art Center, which opened in 1958 in the central part of Tokyo. It served as a hub for experimental art through the 1960s.[75] Sofu Teshigahara had founded Sogetsu School before the war, redefining flower arrangement as free form spatial sculpture rather than a set of rules for arranging flowers, and introduced industrial materials that had never been used before. His son, the experimental filmmaker Hiroshi Teshigahara, operated Sogetsu Art Center as the director until April 1971.[76] Concerts, screenings, and lectures took place almost every weekend during high season, with Sogetsu Cinematheque often focusing on underground cinema, Sogetsu Animation Festival introducing art animation, and the concert series featuring contemporary composers.[77] In 1969, Sogetsu Art Center collaborated with the American Culture Center (ACC) to introduce works by Stan VanDerBeek on the occasion of his visit for the *Cross Talk Intermedia* event.

Cross Talk Intermedia, a three-day event that took place in Tokyo in the huge Yoyogi Gymnasium in 1969, was sponsored by ACC as an attempt to create a dialogue between Japanese and American "intermedia." Catalogue essays were contributed by John Cage, Buckminster Fuller, Peter Yates, Taro Okamoto, Shuzo Takiguchi, Kenzo Tange, Gordon Mumma, and Stan VanDerBeek, and works by Cage, Mumma, and VanDerBeek were performed along with those by other American and Japanese artists. The long list of artists and composers included names such as Matsumoto, Yuasa, Akiyama, Ichiyanagi, and Takemitsu, as well as other avant-garde artists, such as Takahiko Iimura and Mieko Shiomi who had joined New York Fluxus. Butoh dancer Tatsumi Hijikata also performed. Both visual artists and composers attempted to fill the space, be it with multiscreen projections or multiple tape decks. Robert Ashley's sound piece *That Morning Thing* included audience participation. Former Jikken Kobo members Akiyama and Yuasa enthusiastically volunteered to realize the event, collaborating with Roger Reynolds. Imai was the lighting director and Yamaguchi collaborated on the set design. *Cross Talk Intermedia* became possible through an international network of avant-garde artists, and the former Jikken Kobo members formed its hub in Japan.[78] It also was a prelude to the Expo '70.

Osaka Expo '70

The 1964 Olympic Games in Tokyo were an important step in recovering the nation's pride and international presence. Following their success, a plan to realize the Universal Exposition in Osaka in 1970 was immediately developed and confirmed in 1965. There were several reasons why the "Expo" was needed, international promotion of Japan's economic growth being one of them and redevelopment of Osaka another.[79] The Expo was considered a stage for demonstrating the power of science and technology to the public. But the situation also was more complex; the renewal of the permanent version of the US–Japan Treaty ("Anpo") was to take place in 1970, and there were expectations of a strong opposition similar to that in 1960. Those who opposed the Treaty suspected the Expo was meant as a spectacle to divert people's attention from political issues. Due to the opposition against the war in Vietnam and student struggles in many universities, following the May 1968 student revolt, streets in big cities were no longer quiet.[80]

From its earliest stages, the Expo project was led by a group of architects who had promoted Metabolism, a highly conceptual architectural movement since the beginning of the 1960s. Transforming the hills covered by tall bamboo shrubs into a large, completely artificial and temporal "future city" presumably was a dream project for them.[81] The most established architect of the time, Kenzo Tange, was appointed as producer of the main facilities.[82] Tange invited Taro Okamoto to be the producer of the thematic exhibition. Okamoto initially hesitated to be a part of the nationalistic event, but accepted the role as a practice of his concept of dualism or Polar Opposites, which suggested that new art forms would be born only from emphasizing contradictions or conflicts rather than synthesizing them.[83] The participation of Okamoto created confusion in the avant-garde art world, which had lost momentum with the cancellation of *Yomiuri Indépendant* in 1964. Should artists consider the Expo as a rare opportunity to realize their ideas and earn money? Was it acceptable for artists to serve the industry and support such a national event?

The theme of the Expo was "Progress and Harmony for Mankind," but it definitely did not create harmony in the avant-garde art world. In the second half of the 1960s avant-garde artists were split into three groups. Artists and composers who used new technology, especially the former members of Jikken Kobo, became actively involved in the Expo. Others kept their distance from the Expo, among them Tanaka and Kanayama, who left Gutai and concentrated on painting in their house in Nara, and artists who had left Japan. The third group of artists and art students severely criticized the Expo as a showcase of capitalism and a spectacle meant to distract people from the social and political problems in real life. They argued that artists should not take part in such a scheme. While some performed happenings and others organized "anti-Expo" art events, the situation gave birth to a new critical wave among young artists. Best known among them is the group of students from Tama Art University, which included Yasunao Tone who formed a group named Bikyoto (Bijutsuka Kyoto Kaigi, or Artists' Joint-Struggle Council) that developed more theoretically oriented activities.[84]

In spite of the protests and hot debates, pavilions by leading corporations and industrial associations featured unusual structures filled with image, sound, and optical effects, realized through contributions by young architects, artists, designers, filmmakers, and composers. There was a high demand for avant-garde artists since they typically were ahead of their time when it came to imagination and experience in using the latest technologies and realizing futuristic space. The "intermedia" atmosphere of the 1960s had already created a loose but effective network that nurtured collaborations. For people in this network the Expo was a once-in-a-lifetime opportunity and a challenge, accompanied by a much bigger fee than they could normally earn with their artworks. When invited they agreed to participate. If Okamoto had accepted the role, why shouldn't they? The Pepsi Pavilion, designed by the members of E.A.T., and covered in a fog sculpture by Japanese E.A.T. member Fujiko Nakaya, was one of the most experimental pavilions with an open-ended, interactive design. The Mitsui Group Pavilion, designed by Yamaguchi, anticipated today's motion rides by creating three movable decks, each carrying twenty visitors, suspended in the air. The young architect Arata Isozaki, a regular member of Neo-Dada meetings, took on major responsibilities in the system design of the main pavilion, which included two robots.

A most unusual pavilion was designed by the experimental filmmaker Toshio Matsumoto, who had earlier directed *Bicycle in Dream* with Jikken Kobo. As a freelance film director he was known for highly experimental short films created during the 1960s—both for advertising and publicity and as personal artworks—including *For The Damaged Right Eye*, a multi-projection short film. A collage of footage documenting anti-Anpo demonstrations and scenes from the entertainment districts of Shinjuku were shown on three screens. The work was both an artistic engagement with the political situation of the time and an experiment in deconstructing time and space by juxtaposing two parallel scenes coexisting in Tokyo in 1968. Matsumoto was nominated as director for the Textile Pavilions while shooting the feature film *Funeral Parade of Roses*, a landmark piece in Japanese avant-garde cinema.[85] His team for the Expo consisted of avant-garde artists: Tadanori Yokoo created the exterior and interior, both done in red, with the exterior half covered by a scaffold-like structure as if the pavilion was still under construction; The Neo-Dada artist Masunobu Yoshimura modeled a number of plastic ravens that were positioned on the scaffold along with a few life-size human figures who looked like workers. Inside the pavilion, life-size "butler" figures, all identical and designed by the doll artist Simon Yotsuya, welcomed the visitors. Matsumoto himself created a multiscreen space showing an ordinary day in the life of a young lady named Ako. Sound and lighting effects were designed by the former Jikken Kobo members Akiyama and Imai.

All in all, it was a surrealist installation. It is not clear whether the client (the textile industry association) was exactly happy with the outcome, but they had given Matsumoto and Yokoo permission to do whatever they wanted to do, and the artists took advantage of it. Why did they choose to create such an uneasy atmosphere for the pavilion, with its red scaffold, ravens, and "workers" on the roof? As a filmmaker who had worked with the industry for years and already was famous for a style combining artistic qualities with functionality—which presumably was a reason for choosing him—working with the industry itself could not have been an ethical problem for Matsumoto. At the same time the nature of the Expo and the political problems surrounding it must have bothered him, since he was also a theorist. The uneasy and unfinished look inside and outside the pavilion could be interpreted as a metaphorical refusal of the artists involved to complete the tasks given to them by the industry.

As mentioned earlier, Japanese postwar avant-garde art was inseparable from the social and political situation of the era. In a sense the artists participating in the Expo were used for creating propaganda, the illusion of infinite economical growth supported by future technologies. As an artistic resistance to such agenda, Matsumoto's Textile Pavilion perhaps was an exception. Most of the participating artists had to face the fact that art was consumed as a mass entertainment, as a part of a spectacle in the sense of Guy Debord's *Society of the Spectacle* (1967).

One reason for involving avant-garde artists in the Expo was the relationship between being avant-garde and being experimental. While being "avant-garde" implied a certain attitude confronting the establishment or tradition, being "experimental" meant the exploration of new methods, materials, or tools that had not yet been known in art making. When new materials and tools such as tape recorders, electronic devices, and computers appeared in the 1950s and 1960s, experimentation with new technologies or materials often required collaboration with engineers or researchers coming from the industry. At the same time, the industry was interested in discovering new possibilities for their products or technologies through artistic imagination. Though still small in scale, Jikken Kobo's works using Auto Slide were examples of such a collaboration between artists and engineers. When the scale of the experiment expands and the technology is very specialized or expensive, collaboration extends beyond a small group of people, which frequently happens in today's media art as well.

One might still raise the questions why artists did take part in a nationalistic event sponsored by the government and whether they were indifferent to political issues. While it will be impossible to definitively answer them, the distance that Jikken Kobo and Gutai artists kept from politics or social issues can be better understood when considering the social and political turbulence around them. They were surrounded by politics, including proletarian art movements and hierarchical academic art. Still, considering the contrast between French and Japanese surrealists, one has to ask whether the tendency to avoid social or political issues has a tradition in Japanese art.

East Asian Avant-garde Art after World War II

In other parts of Asia the birth of avant-garde art and subsequently media art took much longer. The following is a brief overview of art developments in China and Korea. An in-depth exploration is beyond the scope of this chapter; it would require another text to discuss details of experimental film and video in Hong Kong alone, for example.

China after the War

When World War II was over and the Japanese occupation ended in 1945, drastic changes took place in China and Korea. Following the immediate political confusion after the war, the Cold War brought a continuous tension to East Asia.

In China, the Communist Party led by Mao Zedong fought against the Chinese Nationalist Party. The civil war ended in1949 as Mao took hold of Mainland China and the Nationalist Party moved to Taiwan. At that time most of China was far from being modernized. From 1958 to 1961, Mao's Great Leap Forward campaign was carried out, aiming for a rapid transformation of the country's industry and agriculture. The unrealistic plan collapsed, resulting in the Great Chinese Famine. To regain his political power Mao launched the Cultural Revolution, which lasted from 1966 to 1976. Many artists and cultural figures were expelled from the cities and sent to remote farming villages for labor. Any "anti-communist" activities or expressions were severely punished. During these campaigns, much of the historical and cultural assets were destroyed and Western art books were confiscated. Art teachers and painters used to study either in Europe or in Japan before the war and were familiar with the latest trends in the artworld, but three decades after the war there was no information flow on modern or contemporary art from the West. Art education was focused on realism, based on European classical academic styles, and meant to serve communist propaganda. Painters found themselves under censorship, and there was no space for experimental art.

In late 1970s, economic reform started and open policies set in. Only then did Western modern and contemporary art became accessible, inspiring young artists to experiment with new forms of art. A 1979 outdoor exhibition by a group of avant-garde artists named Star (Xingxing) Group, founded by twelve principal members including Ai Weiwei, was a major breakthrough.[86] It was followed in the 1980s by various experiments by different groups, which were referred to as the "85 Art Movement" or "85 Art New Wave."[87] An epoch-making exhibition of Robert Rauschenberg's work took place in the Beijing National Gallery in 1985. A most radical art group called Xiamen Dada, led by Huang Yong Ping, was founded in 1986. The *China/Avant-Garde* exhibition in 1989 at the National Gallery was a seminal event that concluded the era of Chinese avant-garde art, showing more than three hundred works from more than a hundred artists.[88] In the same year the democracy movement came to a halt in Tiananmen Square and at the same time China experienced an economic boom.

In the 1990s Chinese contemporary art started to flourish with Political Pop and Cynical Realism as mainstream approaches. With the rapid increase of international interest in Chinese art, contemporary art finally gained more status and recognition within the country, encouraging young artists to explore new media such as computer graphics and animation. Feng Mengbo (b.1966) belongs to the new generation of artists who work with new media technology. He became internationally recognized through the interactive piece *My Private Album* shown at DOCUMENTA X in 1997, and the video-game-based *Q4U* shown at DOCUMENTA XI in 2002.

During the long period of confusion in China itself, some Chinese-born artists were very active abroad. Wen-Ying Tsai is known as a pioneer in cybernetic art who combined kinetic sculpture and stroboscopic light, often using sound from the environment as the "input" to a cybernetic system. Tsai, born in China in 1928, moved to the United States in 1950. When the Cultural Revolution came to a halt Tsai contributed to helping young Chinese artists to show their work outside the country.

Korea after the War

On the Korean Peninsula the political situation remained unsettled for decades after World War II. The Korean War, fought between South Korea, supported by the United Nations (notably the United States), and North Korea, supported by the People's Republic of China and the Soviet Union, started in 1950. The war officially came to an end in 1953 with the Armistice Agreement. Due to continuing Cold War tension the political atmosphere in South Korea remained mostly authoritarian, sporadically marked by military rule and martial law. Korean culture and society remained conservative, with a traditional value system based on Confucianism, placing importance on hierarchical structures both in society at large and the individual family.

Under these circumstances avant-garde art could not grow, and an artist who challenged traditional art forms would be considered a dissident.[89] The eminent cultural critic and novelist O-young Lee argues that this was a larger cultural issue.[90] Lee met Nam June Paik in 1984, when Paik visited Korea for the first time since his family had left the country, and became Paik's lifetime friend. He recalls asking his friends whether they thought that Paik could have become such an internationally important artist if he had continued to live in Korea, and came to the conclusion that it would have been extremely difficult. As Lee metaphorically put it, Korean society has a tendency to turn a young orange plant into a spiky bush with small and sour fruit instead of growing it into a sweet orange tree (Lee 2010, 4). It no doubt was a great opportunity for Paik to live in Japan, Germany, and the United States when challenging developments in art and music were taking place while Korean culture did not welcome these changes.

In 1970, Ik-tae Lee directed Korea's first independent film, *From Morning to Evening*. The film depicts a day in the life of a young man who moves from one woman to another and revealed a shocking gap between the sense of reality of the young and the old generation. The film marked the beginning of modernism in Korean cinema. In the mid-1970s the feminist experimental movie group Khaidu was formed by students of culture and media at Ehwa Woman's University. Ok-hee Han who directed *Color of Korea* in 1976 was part of the group. The film interpreted the modern history of the country through the use of Korea's traditional colors and culture and is considered one of the first experimental films, using techniques such as superimposition and dyeing. More independent films started appearing in the 1980s. The rise of experimental cinema coincided with the birth of new forms of culture supported by a younger generation. It laid the foundation for video art and media art to come, both in terms of themes and interest in media technology. However, it took time for Korea to become a modern society in which free expression was allowed. In 1980 protesters for democracy were crushed by the military regime in the Gwangju (Kwangju) Massacre. The process of democratization became stable only in 1987.

Nam June Paik, who became an internationally recognized artist outside of Korea,[91] played an important role in launching new media art in Korea in the mid-1980s. After studying art history in Japan he began his career as an artist in Germany after meeting Karlheinz Stockhausen and John Cage. When he returned to Japan in 1963 before settling down in New York, his Fluxus performance at Sogetsu Hall had a great impact on the Japanese avant-garde movement.[92] However, Paik remained unknown in his home country for many years and did not visit it, although he kept a Korean passport (Kubota and Jeong-ho 2010). It was only in 1984, after the success of *Good Morning Mr. Orwell*—a New Year's Day international live satellite television broadcast linking WNET TV in New York and the Centre Pompidou in Paris, among others, and celebrating a more positive beginning of the "Orwell Year"—that a TV broadcasting company invited him to Seoul.[93] After that his activity expanded to Korea and included the production of video sculptures for the Korean audience. In 1986 Korea, along with the United States and Japan, was part of his live satellite link-up *Bye Bye Kipling*, which featured interviews with Keith Haring and Arata Isozaki as well as performances and works by Philip Glass and Lou Reed. For the Seoul Olympics in 1988 O-young Lee, who was in charge of the event's organization, invited Paik to build a monumental "media tower" using 1003 sets of TV monitors. The combination of new media technology and Korean aesthetics with unusual concepts inspired young artists. New art forms started to emerge in the country. When the first Gwangju Biennale took place in 1995, the exhibition even included a section of CD-ROM works by Korean artists, catching up on the international trend.[94]

It was not coincidental that Korea's first and biggest contemporary art festival showcasing media art started in Gwangju. The city had been known for being a hub for art and literature through its long history. The Biennale was launched to commemorate the citizens of Gwangju who fought for democracy—not only in the 1980 Gwangju Massacre, but also in the 1929 student uprising against Japanese rule. The city of Gwangju chose to focus on non-traditional and international art—rather than the "established art" that was shown in Seoul—as part of its new identity.[95] For a city with a name translating into "city of light" and identifying itself as "the city of democracy and human rights," there was no one more appropriate than Paik to realize an exhibition featuring the history of video art and its development into media art, as well as the paths artists had taken to democratize the media, using light as a medium. It makes sense to briefly revisit the 1995 Biennale to see how this story was told.

Situated in newly built large halls within a big park, the huge contemporary art festival included a special exhibition of *InfoART*, planned and literally made possible by Paik. It was co-curated by Cynthia Goodman, Kim Hong-hee, and Paik himself in three major sections to showcase the history of video art and the beginnings of new media art in Korea (Hong-hee and Goodman 1995). Part 1 was titled "Interactivity in Arts & Technology" and co-curated by Goodman and Paik, who had selected state-of-the-art works by twenty-five artists from around the world as the highlight of the exhibition. While classic pieces, such as the aforementioned Wen Ying Tsai's cybernetic sculptural work, also was included, the show mainly followed the development of virtual reality and interactivity in art showing works such as Jeffrey Shaw's *Revolution* (1990) and Myron Krueger's *Small Planet* (1993), as well as younger media artists including Christa Sommerer and Laurent Mignonneau, David Rokeby and Paul Garrin, among others. Paik himself exhibited a new work using laser beams, which later developed into a piece included in his first American retrospective, *The Worlds of Nam June Paik*, at the Guggenheim Museum in 2000. The Asian section featured works from South Korea, Mainland China, Hong Kong, and Japan, among them both major historical works by Paik himself and works by younger artists.[96] In the section outlining the birth and development of video art, the Paik–Abe Synthesizer and Stephen Beck's Direct Video Synthesizer produced brilliant images, while Vito Acconci's installation represented another dimension of video art. Visitors were allowed to manipulate Paik's *Magnet TV* (1965). The exhibition was a visual "textbook" of new media art, either for learning its history or starting to make one's own artworks.

From Experimental Art to Digital Media Art

The lack of communication with their audience during the Osaka Expo left the participating artists exhausted. Their regrets about this lack of engagement were a factor in the rise of Japanese video art soon after the Expo.

It was a time when video technology became accessible to artists both as a new medium for experimentation and a tool for communication. In 1969 Nam June Paik and Shuya Abe developed their synthesizer, and Matsumoto, who always was ahead of his time in exploring new aesthetics, realized his *Magnetic Scramble* performance as early as 1968, using magnetic distortion of video images. Meanwhile, Canadian director Michael Goldberg visited Japan and introduced works by North American video artists and activists. Inspired by the possibility of video as a medium for the people and interactive communication, avant-garde artists—both those involved in the Expo and those opposed to it—united to collaborate. Video Hiroba (meaning Video Commons) was launched in 1972 as an active network of artists, including Yamaguchi and Matsumoto, among others. Members organized performances and workshops involving the public. Fujiko Nakaya and Hakudo Kobayashi helped demonstrators who fought against a serious environmental pollution case by documenting their activities. Nakaya also founded the Video Gallery SCAN, which played an important role in maintaining an international network of video artists. Nobuhiro Kawanaka co-founded Image Forum, an art center, publisher, and film festival that continues to play a key role in introducing and promoting experimental and art film and video today. Members of Image Forum also made contributions by launching programs and institutions for showcasing video and media art. While the Expo had sucked the energy from postwar avant-garde art, it also served to give birth to new forms of video and media arts.

Experiments in digital art in Japan had started in the 1960s. Hiroshi Kawano, a Tokyo-based scholar in information aesthetics, used Markov chain algorithms and Monte Carlo methods to put his theories to the test in 1964.[97] Eiichi Izuhara, who also studied aesthetics, shared Kawano's interest in algorithmic art and developed a system named Comtree simulating the growth patterns of various trees. Two graduate students in architecture, Yoshio Tsukio and Gaku Yamada, won an award at the First Sogetsu Experimental Film Festival in 1967 with an abstract computer animation film titled *Art of Fugue*. A group of students named CTG (Computer Technology Group, 1966–1969), co-founded by Masao Komura, Haruki Tsuchiya, and other people with backgrounds in art, design, and technology, actively produced works ranging from graphics and animation to an automatic drawing system named APM no. 1 that took input from the environment. Their works were shown in the American magazine *Computers and Automation* in 1968 and in the legendary exhibition Cybernetic Serendipity at London's ICA, curated by Jasia Reichardt, the same year. CTG also created a TV commercial for the fashion industry. Through exhibitions and events, personal encounters, and a shared experimental spirit, video artists and digital artists connected. Itsuo Sakane, a journalist at the *Asahi Shimbun* newspaper, actively wrote about and organized exhibitions of "science art," introducing works from abroad. Artists from different backgrounds met and exchanged ideas. Yamaguchi and Matsumoto launched educational programs at art universities in the 1980s where students would experiment with both analog and digital media. Digital media art was about to be born.

Notes

1 Artists such as Yoko Ono, On Kawara, Shusaku Arakawa, Yasunao Tone, and Yayoi Kusama moved to the United States and participated in Fluxus and other movements.

2 It started in 1907 as the Ministry of Education's art exhibition (Bunten), modeled after French salons, and was renamed in 1919. After World Ware II it was renamed as the Japan Fine Arts Exhibition (Nitten).

3 Most postwar avant-garde artists lived through their prewar teenage years in this atmosphere. For more on the audiovisual culture of the era, see Machiko Kusahara's "The Baby Talkie" (2011).

4 Takiguchi would play a leading role in relaunching avant-garde art during the postwar period and published many texts in art journals after the war. *Kindai Geijutsu* (Sedlmayr and Ishikawa 1962) summarizes his early writings on art.

5 Art materials were controlled and distributed for propaganda works. It was officially stated that non-representational paintings would be excluded from commissions.

6 The general attitude toward technology is an important issue in understanding Japanese proto-media art. The anti-nuclear movement was strong for many years after Hiroshima and Nagasaki and the tragedy of the fishing boat *Lucky Dragon*, which was seriously contaminated by US thermonuclear device tests in the Bikini Atoll in 1954. On the other hand, not only industry but also scientists (Tezuka was a medical doctor) promoted the idea that overly negative attitudes toward nuclear power should be overcome. A highlight of the Osaka Exposition in 1970 was the Electricity Pavilion lit by electric power from the brand-new nuclear power plant. The art critic Noi Sawaragi points to connections between Hiroshima, metabolism, and the Expo '70 in his book *Senso to Banpaku: World Wars and World Fairs* (2005). Sawaragi analyzes what Expo '70 meant to Japanese postwar avant-garde art by juxtaposing the war and world fair as demonstrations of national identities. The contemporary artist Kenji Yanobe examines our relationship to nuclear power in artworks including the *Atom Suit Project* series (1997–2003) and *Sun Child Project in Fukushima* (2012), among others.

7 GHQ/SCAP (General Headquarters, the Supreme Commander for the Allied Powers) was operated by the United States and was usually referred to as GHQ.

8 Tsuguharu Fujita (Leonard Foujita) and Taikan Yokoyama were the most criticized artists. Unable to take the accusations, Fujita left Japan and moved to France. The Japanese-style painter Yokoyama recovered his fame and position after a while. The Japanese/British novelist Kazuo Ishiguro illustrates the life of painters after the war in his novel *An Artist of the Floating World* (1986).

9 Okamoto continued to have a complex effect on young artists. His dualism theory (*taikyoku-shugi*) regards conflicts between contradictory ideas as the source of creation, which would later provide a delicate twist in the participation of avant-garde artists in the Universal Exposition 1970 in Osaka.

10 Research by Mari Ishihara (2010) of Keio University on the CIE Library in Yokohama shows that more than half of the library's items were devoted to art, literature, and history, with art making up 12.9% of the holdings, which is a significant ratio. These numbers are much higher than the standard percentages in public libraries and suggests that the CIE libraries were aimed at exerting cultural influence.

11 Among the people connected to CIE was Donald Richie, who joined GHQ in 1946 as a typist but was promoted to the position of writer and film critic for the culture section of the US Army's newspaper, *Stars and Stripes*. Richie later came back to Japan and joined the 1960s experimental film movement as a filmmaker.

12 The CIE libraries were in twenty-three major cities all over Japan. When the occupation ended in 1952, thirteen of them were kept and renamed as American Culture Centers (ACC). By 1972 six of them were left, and their name was changed to American Centers (AC). Books and other materials from the closed ICE Libraries and ACC were donated to local libraries. Yoichiro Kawaguchi, the internationally recognized computer art pioneer, recalls seeing a screening of experimental abstract films, including works by Jordan Belson and Len Lye, at the AC in Fukuoka when he was an art student, which inspired him to start experimental computer animation.

13 The Nihon-bijyutsu-kai (Japan Art Association) and its exhibition (Salon des Artistes Indépendent du Japon) still exist.
14 *Heibonsha World Encyclopedia.*
15 More precisely, the occupation of the Amami Islands continued until the end of 1953. The return of Okinawa to Japan continued to be a major political issue until it finally took place in 1972.
16 The fishing boat was operating outside the danger zone of the US nuclear testing site when the United States carried out their thermonuclear device tests in 1954. The boat and the fishermen were seriously contaminated, and the chief radio operator died after several months.
17 Most serious were the labor struggles at coalmines that continued through the 1950s as the result of the shift from coal to oil. The most critical clashes took place in 1953 and 1960, and a series of serious accidents occurred in the first half of the 1960s. The 2007 film *Hula Girl* is based on a real story that occurred at a coalmine in Joban in 1965.
18 There was another annual *indépendant* called Nihon Indépendant Art Exhibition that started even earlier, in 1947, and was organized by Nihon-Bijyutsu-Kai (Japan Art Association). The association was meant to promote the "liberal and democratic development of Japanese art," and co-founders included prewar proletarian artists. Works by artists who died in the war, such as Masamu Yanase and the surrealist painter Aimitsu, were shown in the second exhibition in 1948. The association protested when Yomiuri launched another exhibition under the name *indépendant.* Nihon-Bijyutsu-Kai maintained its political agenda and during the 1960s often exhibited artworks from communist countries.
19 Major newspaper companies often sponsor art exhibitions and other cultural activities. Yomiuri, for example, launched a professional baseball league before the war. The author was involved in large-scale media art events sponsored by Yomiuri in the early 2000s. The venue could be either a museum or an exhibition floor of a major department store. Showing serious art exhibitions at a department store is another Japanese tradition, which was stronger when the number of museums was limited.
20 The bakery still continues operations nationwide today, with its main shop staying in Ginza, Tokyo.
21 After their artworks were classified as "anti-art" at the Yomiuri Independent exhibition of the previous year, the artists decided to form a group. Members included Masunobu Yoshimura, Ushio Shinohara, Genpei (Gempei) Akasegawa, and Shusaku Arakawa. They gathered at the "White House"—Masunobu Yoshimura's white-walled studio—regularly, including the young architect Arata Isozaki. This group of artists split into two camps during the lead-up to the Osaka Expo 1970. While Isozaki played a major role and Yoshimura also was involved, Akasegawa joined the anti-Expo campaign.
22 In the early 1960s Takamatsu used string as a motif. In 1962, at the 14th Yomiuri Indépendant, Takamatsu put a string in a box and instructed visitors to pull it using the gloves he provided.
23 This became known as the Model 1000-Yen Note Incident. Many cultural figures, including Takiguchi, defended Akasegawa, but he lost the case. The seized objects tagged by the police later became an important part of his artworks.
24 The process of closing *Yomiuri Indépendant* is described in detail by the contemporary artist/theorist Hideki Nakazawa on his bilingual web site (Nakazawa 2014).

25 They rented a beach hut to prepare works for the *Indépendant.* When the works were done and they needed to clean up the hut, they realized that the best way of getting rid of the accumulated garbage was to send it to the exhibition as an artwork.
26 The name of the group was coined by combining the first letters of their family names, meaning high, red, and center. The fact that the name sounds like that of a communist organization reflects their sense of irony. Details of their activities are described in Akasegawa's books, among them *Tokyo Mixer Plans.* Akasegawa also is an award-winning novelist.
27 Hosting the Olympic games was extremely important for the government in order to prove that Japan was a reliable independent country that had recovered from the war. At the same time it was used as a pretext for "cleaning" the city for redevelopment by removing the old (including traces of the war) and building new facilities.
28 For more information see *Jikken Kōbō—Experimental Workshop* (Yomiuri Shimbun-sha/Exhibition Organizers, 2013), which is a more than 350-page catalog accompanying the exhibition that toured several museums in 2013. It includes images, list of works, and essays in English translation. In *Tokyo 1955–1970 A New Avant-Garde* (MoMA, 2012), Jikken Kobo is mentioned on pp. 50–57 and pp. 143–149. In *Art Anti-Art Non-Art*, Jikken Kobo is referred to on pp. 3–5.
29 Later, in the 1960s, the term "intermedia" was used for these works.
30 The exhibition and the event were organized by Hideo Kaido who also realized the *Ballet Experimental Theatre.*
31 Takemitsu composed for more than a hundred films. His mentor Fumio Hayasaka composed for the film *Rashomon.*
32 As in Calder's case, Kitadai's original background in engineering helped to establish his artistic career. His interest in movement continued throughout his life. In the 1970s, after becoming a photographer, he handcrafted model planes and wooden toys reminiscent of Calder's *Circus* for fun.
33 Although Okamoto was already a leading figure and Kitadai was a self-taught young artist, they exchanged their paintings as mutual gifts that year. Okamoto maintained a positive attitude toward the Jikken Kobo artists.
34 *Paradise Lost*, performed by Haruhi Yokoyama's Ballet Group.
35 Kitadai was a core member of *Seiki-no-Kai* (Century Society), one of the offsprings of *Yoru-no-Kai.* The group started in May 1949 and regularly met at Hosei University.
36 Takiguchi probably introduced the work to Yamaguchi in preparation of the set design for the Picasso event.
37 The strategy was first used in 1952 and then for "Illumination" and other stage designs. In this case, actors' motion behind the vitrine created an optical effect.
38 Musique concrète was an important part of Jikken Kobo's activities. Besides presenting concerts they organized an open competition of musique concrète in 1956.
39 Yamaguchi's and Kitadai's metal mesh sculptures experimented with avoiding such sense of gravity.
40 The light sculptures attracted much attention and were shown at the Venice Biennale in 1968.
41 There were several important pre-events for the Expo in which Yamaguchi was involved, including *Electromagica: International Psytech Art Exhibition '69* and *Cross Talk Intermedia* in 1969.
42 At the time the company was known under the name Tokyo Tsushin Kogyo (Tokyo Telecommunications Engineering Corporation). It was founded in 1946 and changed

its name to Sony in 1958. Interested in their project, Tokyo Tsushin offered the machine and technical support for the artists. They worked either at Sony's studio or at Kitadai's house.

43 The program lists the titles and names of the members involved. The MoMA book does not refer to *Lespugue*. It states that each piece was made as a collaboration between a visual artist and one or two composers (MoMA 2012, 55), which is not exactly true in the case of *Tales of the Unknown World*.

44 It sometimes comes with a subtitle, *Lespugue—Poem by Robert Ganzo*.

45 Takechi was known as a theatre critic and a director of experimental kabuki. Later he became active as an avant-garde filmmaker.

46 Nichigeki Music Hall, with its famous nude dancers, aimed at providing entertainment with artistic quality. It opened in a landmark building in the central part of Tokyo in 1952. Playwrights and directors included well-known artists and writers such as Mishima.

47 The journal *Shiso-no Kagaku* (*Science of Thought*, 1946–1996), edited by Tsurumi and his scholar colleagues, looked at the everyday life of Japanese people, including entertainment, with fresh approaches and texts including those by non-academics. The journal represented the postwar democratic movement in academia, based on an understanding that the prewar hierarchy in culture supported militarism.

48 The program is in the Film Library of the National Museum of Modern Art. *Mobile and Vitrine* is lost (Jikken Kōbō 2013, 98).

49 Tiampo divides Gutai activities into two phases: 1954–1962 and 1962–1972, defining the first phase as "Building Democratic Capacity" and the second as "Humanizing Japan's Economic Growth." However, there is a clear difference between their early activities and those after 1957. I would argue that the earlier experimentalism did not continue until 1962.

50 The association organized annual art competitions open to anyone regardless of residency and size of work, which was unusual for a competition sponsored by a local government. It provided a great opportunity for young artists in Kansai at a time when most of the major art events took place in Tokyo.

51 The group was formed around August 1954 and, at the beginning, comprised seventeen members including Yoshihara himself.

52 Shiraga and Murakami recall that Yoshihara sent Shimamoto to Zero-kai to see what they were doing, and then decided to recruit their members (Gutai 1994).

53 Yuri Mitsuda (2010, 109–119) fully analyzes the situation from the perspective of the advent of *gendai bijutsu* (contemporary art) in this period. The text critically discusses Gutai's position in postwar Japan.

54 The idea of an outdoor exhibition came from Yoshihara, but the plan was developed through discussions among group members.

55 Yoshio Kanaki, for example, submitted a proposal to build a hat under the pine trees and burn it. Yoshihara rejected it (Murakami 1994, 207).

56 At the time Ohara Kaikan was run by the Ohara School of flower arrangement (*ikebana*). It was the era when reformation took place in traditional art such as ikebana.

57 Shown at the *Experimental Outdoor Exhibition of Modern Art to Challenge the Midsummer Sun* in Ashiya Park, Ashiya, in 1955.

58 Shown at the *Outdoor Gutai Exhibition* in 1956.

59 Shimamoto's piece was shown at the 2009 Venice Biennale. Today San Francisco-based artist Bernie Lubell creates wooden machines that make us aware of our own

bodies and their functions. Shimamoto's project was very much ahead of its time. Its title has also been translated as "Please Walk on This" or "Please Walk on Top."

60 It was shown at the Guggenheim exhibition in 2013 as a symbolic piece representing Yoshihara's push for democracy. All of the works shown in the 1956 outdoor exhibitions were proposed at meetings and approved by Yoshihara.

61 Kirin means giraffe. It might sound surprising that this type of magazine existed soon after the war, but periodicals for children such as *Akai Tori* (Red Bird) had been an important part of prewar culture. The idea that "children should enjoy their life" has been deeply rooted in Japanese culture since the medieval era. Mitsukuni Yoshida analyzes this culture of playfulness in *Asobi: The Sensibilities at Play* (1987).

62 There is an anecdote that Yoshihara was extremely pleased when his piece was taken for a child's work by a visitor from New York (Murakami 1994, 213).

63 Apparently this criterion was suspended in Gutai's second phase, when paintings were much in demand.

64 Shown at the 2nd *Gutai Art Exhibition,* Ohara Kaikan, Tokyo, 1956.

65 Filmed and produced by Hiroshi Fukuzawa in 1968.

66 This type of performance by a well-known painter or calligrapher was typically held in front of a temple or shrine to attract a big audience. On special occasions, an extra large sheet of paper would be laid on the ground and a brush as tall as the performer him/herself would be used. Today so-called "calligraphic performance" or "performance calligraphy" is done not only by professionals but also by high school students.

67 Excited about the opportunity, Gutai members organized a *One Day Only Outdoor Art Exhibition* to hold the shoot at the ruins of the former Yoshihara Oil Mills factory, which was bombed during the war. Shiraga did an impressive performance, "fight against mud."

68 The technique dates back to the Scottish-born Canadian animator Norman McLaren (1914–1987). Inspired by his works, Jikken Kobo member Kiyoji Otsuji used the method with his Graphic Group members to produce a film in 1955. They named the method Kine Calligraph. Sam Francis was also interested in the use of film for producing abstract animation, and was a central figure of The Single Wing Turquoise Bird, a renowned light show group based in the Los Angeles area in the late 1960s.

69 As mentioned earlier, department stores have been typical venues for small-scale art exhibitions. In this particular case, the work was more ironic since ad balloons were typically seen on the rooftop of department stores.

70 The *Gutai Card Box* brings to mind Joseph von Kempelen's *Mechanical Turk* (1769), a chess-playing automaton with a human controlling the chess moves hidden inside, which gained notoriety in the age of Web 2.0. In 2005 Amazon launched its crowdsourcing Internet marketplace Amazon Mechanical Turk (or MTurk), which allows "requesters" to hire workers online for specific tasks and has become emblematic of digital labor practices. MTurk has been used for the creation of several prominent pieces of net art addressing issues of digital labor, among them Aaron Koblins's *Sheep Market* (2006) and *Ten Thousand Cents* (2008).

71 Part of the Expo's aim was to redevelop Osaka, as the 1964 Olympic games redeveloped Tokyo. The community of Osaka's cultural figures played an important role in the planning. Yoshihara was nominated for membership in the Exhibition Committee in 1969.

72 His finely designed white objects and irregularly shaped paintings were carefully arranged in the exhibition space, adding an environmental design element to the exhibition floor.

73 The event consisted of the exhibition, a symposium, and a fashion show. The program was uploaded to Tama Art University's web site (Tama 2013). Some words, including Yamaguchi's family name, were misspelled.

74 In an interview Yoshida explains that he was in a difficult position because many of his friends in Kyoto were against the Expo. He also recalls that the title "Bisexual" caused negative feedback. When a curator from LACMA offered him the chance to exchange their studios he accepted the offer and moved to Los Angeles (HIVE 2005).

75 Sogetsu's official web site lists major events from 1958 to 1970. The center was closed in 1971.

76 Hiroshi Teshigahara is best known for the film *The Woman in the Dunes.* He joined the avant-garde art movement when he was a student and, in the early 1950s, started making films as a part of his social involvement. He was a central figure in founding the Art Theater Guild (ATG). As the son of Sofu he inherited the leading position of the Sogetsu School in 1980 while continuing his career as film director.

77 The 415-page book titled *Kagayake 60-nendai: Sogetsu Ato Senta-no Zen-kiroku/ Brilliant 60s: A Complete Record of the Sogetsu Art Center* (Nara et al. 2002) lists all the events along with texts by those who were involved (such as Matsumoto, Yamaguchi, and Yuasa). Posters and newspaper articles (by Takiguchi and others) are also included. The program for 1964—the year of the Tokyo Olympic Games, when traveling abroad became possible without special permissions—gives an idea of the activities. Starting in February, there were twenty-four events throughout the year. Seven screenings included the premiere of Teshigahara's *The Woman in the Dunes*, films by Oshima and by Donald Richie, award-winning works from the Belgian Experimental Film Festival, and animated films as part of the Cinematheque. There were four concerts, including *Collective Music* with Ichiyanagi, Takemitsu, Kosugi, Yuasa, Akasegawa, and the art critic Yoshiaki Tono; the *Good-bye Yoko Ono Concert* (when she went back to New York); and another concert by Cage and Tudor. Merce Cunningham, Robert Rauschenberg, and Nam June Paik also performed. Other listings include theatre performances, an exhibition of poems, and dance workshops.

78 Christophe Charles (1996) studies the event in detail in his dissertation "Media Arts in Japan: Cinema, Video, Intermedia, 1951–1995," which is available in Japanese and French.

79 The Olympic Games had been "used" for a remodeling of Tokyo, and many people felt that a similar event was needed for Osaka. Osaka-based cultural figures, such as sci-fi novelist Sakyo Komatsu, were actively involved in the Expo.

80 Since the US military bases in Japan played a crucial role during the Vietnam War, the anti-war and anti-Anpo protests were connected.

81 Sawaragi illustrates how architectural movements were related to experimental arts, especially in the case of the former Experimental Workshop artists, and how their "experiments" were consumed as part of the "environment" created by the Metabolism architects. The term *environment* was a new one at the time and referred to an artificial urban environment; it was not related to ecology as it is today.

82 Tange taught many of the Metabolism architects, including Arata Isozaki and Kisho Kurokawa, and was renowned for designing the Hiroshima Peace Memorial Park and its museum in 1955.

83 Eventually Okamoto built the Sun Tower as a thematic symbol that stuck out from a hole opened in the roof of the main pavilion designed by Tange. When his involvement in the Expo was later criticized, Okamoto commented that his response was captured in the fact that his tower created a hole in the roof of the government's pavilion.

84 The members included Naoyoshi Hikosaka, Nobuo Yamanaka, Miyako Ishiuchi, and Ryuji Miyamoto. They further developed critical discussions on art in the 1970s under the name Bikyoto Revolution. In 1972 Hikosaka, Tone, and Yukio Akatsuka co-edited *The Chronicle: 50 Years of Contemporary Art 1916–1968* for *Bijutsu Techo*, accompanied by a "scroll" created in collaboration with the Neo-Dada artist Genpei Akasegawa and the illustrator Nobuhiro Minami (a.k.a. Shinbo Minami). The scroll harshly caricaturized those who participated in the Expo.

85 Matsumoto admits he decided to work for the Expo because it would bring in the money he needed to make the film.

86 They hung their works on the fence surrounding the park outside the China Art Gallery in September 1979 after they had been denied the opportunity to exhibit in the gallery. The outdoor exhibition was soon forced to close by the authorities, and the artists organized a protest march asking for democracy and artistic freedom. Their indoor exhibition was finally realized in November. Most members had no academic background in art, and were not affiliated with any official art organizations. Some of their families were the victims of the Cultural Revolution, as in the case of Ai Weiwei and Li Shuang, or they themselves had been sent to remote farms, as in the case of Huang Rui. Their activities continued to confront political oppression and the group was dismantled in 1983. Most of the members moved out of the country in their search for freedom. For example, Ai Weiwei lived in New York for more than ten years before he moved back to China.

87 "The 85 Movement was a group-movement because in only two years (1985 and 1986), seventy-nine self-organized avant-garde art groups, including more than 2,250 of the nation's young artists, emerged to organize exhibitions, hold conferences and write manifestos and articles about their art. A total of 149 exhibitions were organized by these groups within the two-year period. The movement continued to develop in 1987 towards a more provocative and conceptual direction, peaking in 1989 during the period of the China Avant-Garde exhibition" (*Encyclopedia of Contemporary Chinese Culture*).

88 Accessed June 15, 2015. https://mondaymuseum.wordpress.com/2012/02/27/1989-china-avant-garde-exhibition/

89 An example would be Ungno Lee, a pioneer in Korean abstract art who merged traditional Korean calligraphic drawing and contemporary abstract painting. Lee already was an established artist before the war and a co-founder of an artist group that fought against cultural influence from Japan. After the war he was considered a dissident artist because he was critical of the conservative Korean art establishment and the authoritarian regime. He moved to Paris in 1956 after his works became appreciated in the *informel* movement. As in the case of Paik, he was recognized as a great Korean artist only after democratization of the country.

90 O-Young Lee became the first Korean Minister of Culture in 1989 after the democratization. His book *The Compact Culture: The Japanese Tradition of "Smaller is Better"* (1992), first published in Japanese in 1982, became a bestseller in Japan. In the book Lee argues that the tendency to "shrink" things or ideas is not limited to Japanese but also applies to Korean culture. Lee taught at Ehwa Woman's University.

91 Paik's family moved to Japan during the Korean War, and he studied art history at the University of Tokyo. After graduating with a thesis on Arnold Schoenberg in 1956 he continued his studies in art history and musicology in the Department of Philosophy at the University of Munich, Germany.

92 During this stay in Japan he met Shuya Abe who would become his collaborator. Abe collaborated with Paik in building and operating *Robot K-456* and the *Paik–Abe Synthesizer*.

93 Both Paik and the aforementioned Ungno Lee were considered anti-patriotic during the militaristic regime because they "escaped" from the country. After the democratization they were recognized as important pioneers in Korean art. At the first Gwanju Biennale, works by Ungno Lee were featured both in the contemporary art section and the Korean art section while Paik co-curated *Infoart*. Today both have museums named after them in Korea, and their contributions are taught in arts education.

94 It was the time when the CD-ROM with its capacity for publication became the storage medium for screen-based works involving interactivity. Exhibitions and competitions focused on CD-ROM-based works took place around the world, as part of the Videonnale in Berlin, MILIA in Cannes, and the Interactive Media Festival in Los Angeles, to name just a few.

95 This is what the author learnt from local artists and witnessed at the opening of the first Biennale. On the eve of the inauguration, streets were literally flooded by people singing and marching in excitement, which is quite unusual for a celebration of a contemporary art festival. The author's report was published in the *Asahi Shinbun* newspaper.

96 Shigeko Kubota, Keigo Yamamoto, Takahiko Iimura, Shuya Abe, Katsuhiro Yamaguchi, Wen-Ying Tsai, among others. Younger artists such as Feng Mengbo (Mainland China), Ellen Pau (Hong Kong), and Visual Brains (Japan) were also invited.

97 The collection of Hiroshi Kawano's works and documents is now archived at ZKM in Karlsruhe, Germany.

References

Akasegawa, Genpei. 1994. *Tokyo Mixer Plans: Documents of Hi Red Center's Direct Actions*. Tokyo: Chikuma Bunko.

Charles, Christophe. 1996. "Media Arts in Japan: Cinema, Video, Intermedia, 1951–1995." PhD dissertation, University of Tsukuba. http://home.att.ne.jp/grape/charles/texts/phd-chapters.html (accessed December 31, 2013).

Encyclopedia of Contemporary Chinese Culture. "85 New Wave Movement." http://contemporary_chinese_culture.academic.ru/2/85_New_Wave__Movement (accessed August 19, 2013).

Gutai I, II, III. 1994. Exhibition catalog. Translated by Simon Scanes and Shihara Keiko. Ashiya, Japan: Ashiya City Museum of Art and History.

Gutai Magazine (facsimile edition). 2010. Edited by Chinatsu Kuma. Twelve-volume box set with supplement. Tokyo: Geikashoin Co.

HIVE Interview Series 07. 2005. "YOSHIDA Minoru Interview." Tokyo, Japan: Intercommunication Center (ICC) – Open Video Archive Hive. Center's web site. http://hive.ntticc.or.jp/contents/interview/yoshida (accessed December 31, 2013).

Hong-hee, Kim, and Cynthia Goodman, eds. 1995. *InfoART '95 Kwangju Biennale*. Kwangju Biennale Foundation. Kwangju, Korea: Sam Shin Gak.

Ishiguro, Kazuo. 1986. *An Artist of the Floating World*. London: Faber & Faber.

Ishihara, Mari. 2010. "Library Collection of Yokohama American Cultural Center and the Purpose behind Its Foundation." Artist's web site. http://www.mslis.jp/am2008yoko/12_ishihara.pdf (accessed October 31, 2013).

Jikken Kōbō (Experimental Workshop). 2013. Exhibition catalog. Tokyo, Japan: Yomiuri Shimbun-sha, The Japan Association of Art Museums.

Kato, Mizuho. 2010. "A Bridge to the World: Gutai, 1956–1959." In *Gutai Magazine, Facsimile Edition*, edited by Chinatsu Kuma. Tokyo, Japan: Geikashoin Co.

Kubota, Shigeko, and Nam Jeong-ho. 2010. *My Love, Nam June Paik*. Tokyo: Heibonsha.

Kusahara, Machiko. 2011. "The Baby Talkie." In *Domestic Media, and the Japanese Modern, Media Archaeology*, edited by Erkki Huhtamo and Jussi Parikka, 123–147. Berkeley, CA: University of California Press.

Lee, O-Young. 1992. *The Compact Culture: The Japanese Tradition of "Smaller is Better,"* translated by Robert N. Huey. Tokyo, Japan: Kodansha Amer.

Lee, O-Young. 2010. Preface to *My Love, Nam June Paik*, by Shigeko Kubota and Nam Jeong-ho. Tokyo, Japan: Heibonsha.

Matsumoto, Toshio. 1969. "Magnetic Scrumble." In *Vital Signals: Early Japanese Video Art*, 30 sec, b & w, silent. New York: Electronic Arts Intermix, 2010.

Merewether, Charles, and Rika Iezumi-Hiro, eds. 2007. *Art, Anti-Art, Non-Art: Experimentations in the Public Sphere in Postwar Japan, 1950–1970*. Los Angeles, CA: Getty Research Institute.

Mitsuda, Yuri. 2010. *Gutai and Gendai Bijutsu in Japan—The Critique of Representational Art*. Ashiya, Japan: Ashiya City Museum of Art and History.

Munroe, Alexandra. 2013. "All the Landscapes: Gutai's World." In *Gutai: Splendid Playground*, edited by Alexandra Munroe and Ming Tiampo. New York: Guggenheim Museum Publications.

Murakami, Saburo. 1994. "Gutai-teki na hanashi" (Concrete Talk: Interview with Murakami and Shiraga Kazuo). In *Gutai I, II, III*. Exhibition catalog. Ashiya, Japan: Ashiya City Museum of Art and History.

Nakazawa, Hideki. 2014. "The Discontinuation of the Yomiuri Independent Exhibition." Artist's web site. http://aloalo.co.jp/arthistoryjapan/3b.html (accessed October 31, 2014).

Nara, Yoshimi, Noriko Namura, Kaoruko Otani, and Haruo Fukuzumi, eds. 2002. *Kagayake 60-nendai: Sogetsu Ato Senta-no Zen-kiroku* (Brilliant, 60s: A Complete Record of the Sogetsu Art Center). Tokyo, Japan: Sogetsu Art Center.

New York Times. "Japan As 'Protective Wall' Against Communism." August 10, 1948.

Sawaragi, Noi. 2005. *Senso to Banpaku* (World Wars and World Fairs). Tokyo: Bijutsu Shuppan-Sha.

Sedlmayr, Hans, and Kôichi Ishikawa. 1962. *Kindai Geijutsu* (Modern Art). Edited by Kôichi Ishikawa. Tokyo: Bijutsu Shuppan-sha.

Sogetsu Art Center. "Major Activities of Sogetsu Art Center and Associated Individuals." Center's web site. http://www.sogetsu.or.jp/e/know/successive/artcenter/activity.html (accessed December 31, 2013).

So-won, Kang. 2014. *Korean Film Archive*. http://www.koreafilm.org/feature/50_1.asp (accessed February 5, 2014).

Tama Art University. "International Psytech Art Exhibition 'Electromagica 1969.'" Tama Art University web site. http://www.tamabi.ac.jp/idd/shiro/mecha/electro/electro.htm (accessed December 30, 2013).

Tokyo 1955–1970: A New Avant-Garde, edited by Doryun Chong. Exhibition catalog. New York: MoMA, 2012.

Yoshida, Mitsukuni. 1987. *Asobi: The Sensibilities at Play*, edited by Tanaka Ikko and Sesoko Tsune. Hiroshima, Japan: Mazda Motor Corporation.

5

Generative Art Theory

Philip Galanter

Introduction

What people often find most fascinating in the realm of digital art are not the replacements of physical tools by computer applications such as Adobe Photoshop™ or Corel Painter™, but rather works in which the computer seems at times to directly create the art on its own. To date there is, of course, an artist behind the scenes, creating the situation that allows the computer to act this way. Nevertheless, the relative independence of the computer is perceived as being qualitatively different from the characteristics of other tools in art history.

Art created by means of an apparently autonomous system or process is most frequently referred to as "generative art," a realm of digital art practice that has boomed since the start of the 21st century. In fact, the growth of generative digital art has been so robust that, for many people, "generative art" and "computer art" have become synonymous terms. In this chapter I hope to show that generative computer art is in fact a subset of the larger field of generative art. It will be seen that generative art can leverage virtually any kind of system, not just computers, and that it in fact is as old as art itself.

It is in some ways natural that "computer artists," in their enthusiasm for a relatively new field, would want to claim the term "generative art" exclusively for themselves. To many people the computer seems uniquely suited to independently generate visuals and sounds of aesthetic interest. However, conflating the term "generative art" with the term "computer art" would come at an unacceptable cost. We would need a new term for the now orphaned forms of earlier generative art. We would lack a term for post-digital work we could otherwise call generative art. But, perhaps most importantly, we would lose an opportunity to explore unified art theory that uniquely spans all systems-based art practices, digital or not.

A Companion to Digital Art, First Edition. Edited by Christiane Paul.

To theorize generative art as a systems-based practice we can turn to the branch of science devoted to the study of systems across all scientific disciplines, namely complexity science. In the following I will explicate a more specific definition of generative art, use concepts from complexity science to tie together the commonalities among types of generative art through history, and discuss issues of art theory that are specific to generative art at large and thus apply to digital generative art.

What Is Generative Art?

The question "what is art?" is a notorious one. For some, it is a prime example of intellectualism about to run amok. For others, it is the required starting point for any serious discussion of aesthetics and the philosophy of art. And for yet others, it is both.

If one takes an analytic rather than continental view of philosophical aesthetics, there are many theories of what art is. In approximate historical order these include:

- art as representation;
- art as expression;
- art as form;
- art as experience;
- art as open concept and family resemblance (neo-Wittgensteinianism);
- art as institution;
- art as historical definition.

While it would be possible to discuss these theories in depth using the language of aesthetics in philosophy, the theories of art as representation, expression, form, and experience are also adequately self-explanatory for practical purposes. The neo-Wittgensteinian notion of art as open concept and *family resemblance* is more easily understood than the name might imply. The idea simply is that art has no stable essence, but that there is a body of recognized art at any given point in time. Over time the boundary enclosing art can be stretched to include new forms that seem to share a "family resemblance" to currently accepted art (Carroll 1999).

The intuitive notion of family resemblance ultimately came to be viewed as ill defined and problematic. The "art as institution" theory takes a social construction approach, positing that the "artworld" is an informal yet self-regulating entity that confers the status of art upon objects, with standards shifting over time. In a sense, family resemblance is what the artworld says it is. Historical definition is yet another attempt to establish resemblances. In this case, those with a proprietary claim on an object specify that the object be considered as art in the way other objects before it have been.

Over time the definition and scope of art has informally broadened. Nevertheless there sometimes is confusion as to what makes for *art* versus *good art*. By any contemporary standards the drip paintings of Pollock are obviously art. But one can easily imagine that some traditionalists must have exclaimed, "That's not art!" at the time of the paintings' creation. More arguable would have been the statement, "That's not good art." In fact, within most contemporary notions of aesthetics the bar for qualifying as art is rather low and inclusive. The bar for qualifying as good art, however, is much higher and more contentious.

In a similar way some artists or critics in the field of generative art have such rigid standards as to what makes for good generative art that they are prone to dismiss other work as not being generative at all. But like the bar for art itself, the one for what qualifies as generative art is rather low, as we will see. What remains is the quite a bit higher and more contentious bar for what passes as good generative art.

There is another commonality between the "What is art?" and "What is generative art?" questions. These questions aren't simply a request for the definition of the word; they are a request for the articulation of a *theory of art*. To the extent that they are answerable at all, they will at least require responses to the competing theories noted above.

In a similar way, a solid definition of generative art will have to include a theory of generative art that responds to competing theoretical frameworks. Thus a reasonable point of departure for such a definition is a survey of existing self-claimed generative art.

Some Generative Art Communities

Computer/electronic music

The use of computers as systems for music composition goes back at least to the seminal paper by Brooks, Hopkins, Neumann, and Wright in 1957 (Schwanauer and Levitt 1993). In that paper, they describe the creation of a statistical system of Markov chains for analyzing a body of musical scores. Having gathered statistics from that body, the system is then used to create new scores that mimic the style of those analyzed. In the 1960s analog electronic music synthesizers such as the Moog, Buchla, and others offered systems in which all inputs and outputs had compatible voltages. This allowed outputs to be fed back into inputs, creating generative systems that could "play themselves." Some advocated for the complete rejection of piano-like keyboards and other controllers that copied traditional instruments. From the 1970s to the present, users of audio-specific programming languages and environments such as MUSIC 5, Csound, Max, and Supercollider have created a culture of algorithmic music composition.

Computer graphics and animation

There is a vast body of literature from the Association for Computing Machinery's (ACM) Special Interest Group on Graphics and Interactive Techniques (SIGGRAPH) and other organizations that describes the use of generative software systems. Examples include Perlin Noise for the synthesis of smoke, fire, and hair imagery (Perlin 1985), the use of L-systems to "grow" plants (Prusinkiewicz, Lindenmayer, and Hanan 1990), and the use of physical modeling to create linkages, cloth surfaces, collisions, and other objects without painstakingly choreographing every detail by hand. These assorted techniques have been documented in a body of publications, perhaps most notably those from SIGGRAPH, and have yielded results popularized in animated feature-length films and video games.

The demoscene, VJ culture, glitch art, circuit bending, and live coding

Leveraging generative software techniques, hacked game machines, and early inexpensive personal computers, youth culture movements developed low-cost alternatives for use in nightclubs and other social settings. Referred to as "the demoscene," these do-it-yourself programmers organized party-like gatherings where they would get together to show off feats of programming skill in an aesthetic context (Tasajärvi 2004). Frequently using data projectors, part of the challenge was the creation of complex graphics despite the fact that the available 8-bit technology lacked in speed, memory, and resolution. Hackers who demonstrated superior skills in the creation of surprisingly complex graphics were rewarded with higher social status and the respect of fellow programmers. With the emergence of VJs (the visual equivalent of DJs) in clubs, artist/programmers found new venues for their real-time graphics systems.

More recent is the advent of "live coding" where musician/programmers improvise by writing code that is immediately rendered as sound for a live audience. Part of the performance typically includes projections of the code as it is keyed in and executed. Also notable in this context are glitch art and circuit bending. In glitch art the data of digital media files or code is somehow corrupted, resulting in strange, often garish or psychedelic-looking imagery or animation. Circuit bending is a hardware-based correlate where musicians make arbitrary hardware modifications to sound toys and instruments in search of unusual or even bizarre sounds.

Open source digital art, tools, and social websites

Users of open source programming environments and tools such as Processing, Pure Data, openFrameworks, and others increasingly congregate on dedicated web sites where work is shown, technical help offered, and new ideas are shared.[1] Microcontroller platforms such as the Arduino, used for digital installations and other physical computing, have joined in this phenomenon. The initial attraction frequently is the low cost of entry, but the social network of users has increasingly become the leading asset attracting generative artists and musicians.

Industrial design and architecture

Parametric design practice extends the use of computer-aided design (CAD) software as a passive tool for creating plans and blueprints, and adds generative elements for the modulation and de novo creation of form. Visual tools such as Grasshopper,[2] a graphical algorithm editor, provide designers and architects with algorithmic leverage while freeing them from having to program in textual code.

Popular theories of generative art

Clearly, any attempt to define generative art would have to include all of the above forms of engagement, as there is no obvious reason to privilege one form of contemporary generative art practice over another. And few people would want to stop with just the above list. One could also include, for example, robotic art and math art as clusters of generative art activity.

There also are examples of generative fine art. In the 20th century, for example, artists such as John Cage, William Burroughs, and Marcel Duchamp embraced randomization to generate surprise and variation. Minimalists such as Carl Andre, Mel Bochner, and Paul Morgenson used simple mathematical systems to generate compositions. Sol LeWitt used combinatorial systems, creating complex works from simple components. The conceptual artist Hans Haacke also explored physical generative systems in his early work.

When asked, many generative artists will define generative art in a way that sculpts out a subset resembling, not surprisingly, their own work. Typical examples include:

- Generative art is art that uses randomization.
- Generative art is art that uses genetic systems to evolve form.
- Generative art is art that is constantly changing over time.
- Generative art is art created by running code on a computer.

The problem with such attempts at definition is that they mistake options and choices within the field of generative art as being requirements for generative art. The other option is to create a big tent that accommodates all kinds of generative art and discussion.

Defining Generative Art

What will a useful definition and theory include?

Defining generative art is, not surprisingly, in some ways similar to defining art itself. Just as any definition of art is actually proposing a theory of art, a definition of generative art involves positing a theory of generative art. A possible difficulty in this endeavor is that "art" is part of the term "generative art." This implies the significant complication of having to define art as a prerequisite to understanding generative art. The strategy employed in the following is to leave the definition of art an open issue. We will define generative art in such a way that art, however it is defined, can be divided into generative and non-generative subtypes.

Another problem emerging from the question "What is art?" is the perceived need to provide a crisp definition that neatly cleaves objects into two unambiguous sets of art and non-art. In philosophical aesthetics, however, the approach is more nuanced. The neo-Wittgensteinian model, for example, suggests that the definition of art evolves at art's borders. The border is expanded outward when artists operating outside of the boundary create work that nevertheless has a family resemblance to the art existing within the boundary. In a similar way we should expect that there is work existing at the boundaries of generative art. We can hope for a crisp definition or theory, but do not have to despair if it has a fuzzy aspect to it in the sense that some works are more generative than others.

There are additional considerations that will contribute to a robust definition of generative art. First of all, the definition should include both past and current work that is generally accepted as being generative. In addition, it should be open to new forms of generative art yet to be invented. And finally, generative art should be defined in such a way that some art *is* excluded from its field. If the term "generative art" does not exclude some art, then "art" and "generative art" are synonyms, and "generative art" becomes an unnecessary redundancy.

For example, some people will argue that humans themselves are generative systems, and that, since humans ultimately create all art, all art is generative art. From a certain point of view this is a useful observation, pointing to the status of life as a literal embodiment of generative systems. But if the term "generative art" is supposed to be useful we should understand that it denotes art created by non-human systems. Since the definition of generative art encapsulates a theory of generative art, it should lead the way to explanations and predictions within broader realms of art theory and aesthetics.

Generative art defined

In 2003 I offered what has come to be the most widely cited definition of generative art to date.[3] Supported by other writings it accomplishes the goals outlined above. It also promotes the use of complexity science as a way to sort out and compare all manner of generative art systems:

> Generative art refers to any art practice in which the artist uses a system, such as a set of natural language rules, a computer program, a machine, or other procedural invention, that is set into motion with some degree of autonomy, thereby contributing to or resulting in a completed work of art. (Galanter 2003)

The key element in generative art is the use of an external system to which the artist cedes partial or total control. This understanding moves generative art theory into discussions focused primarily on systems, their role, their relationship to creativity and authorship, system taxonomies, and so on.

While the above definition is further explained in my original paper (Galanter 2003), some discussions working solely from that single sentence have led to misunderstandings which we will try to clarify in the following.

Generative art is not a subset of computer art

At the time of the Industrial Revolution, the steam engine became the reigning technology, and popular culture used it as a metaphor for all kinds of purposes. In the mid-20th century atomic energy and all things "atomic" took on a similar cultural role. In contemporary culture computers and networks have become the reigning technologies to capture the paradigmatic imagination of the public.

It therefore isn't surprising that for many people this definition has reinforced a common misconception and resulting confusion: that generative art is essentially a kind of computer art. However, what this definition refers to as a "procedural invention" can include a chemical reaction, the use of living organisms, condensation and crystallization processes, melting substances, self-organization, self-assembly, and other physical processes, including some that have yet to be discovered.

It is worth noting here a highlight from the history of generative art: the invention of the Jacquard loom. Prior manual textile machines already allowed weavers to apply repetitive operations in the generative creation of patterned fabrics. With the Industrial Revolution, some of these systems were automated. It was Jacquard's 1805 invention, introducing the notion of a stored program in the form of punched cards, that revolutionized the generative art of weaving. One of Jacquard's primary goals was to allow the automation of patterns of greater complexity. Later both Charles Babbage and Charles Hollerith adapted Jacquard's method of punch card programming in their efforts to invent the computer. Computers did not pave the way for generative art; generative art helped to pave the way for computers.

Generative art only requires a weak form of autonomy

A second confusion surrounding the definition involves the required use of an autonomous system for making generative art. Some critics object that no mechanical system can be considered completely autonomous, because such a system is wholly dependent on humans for its continuing operation. Others insist that autonomous systems require free will and consciousness, which pulls this theory of generative art into debates about complicated and contentious philosophical matters.

In the above definition of generative art, the notion of an autonomous system is simple and modest. It follows the use of the same terminology in robotics. Some robots are controlled, moment-by-moment, by a human operator at a console not unlike those used to steer model cars or fly model airplanes by radio. More sophisticated robots use sensors, GPS units, image processing computers, and other technologies to allow them to navigate and adapt to their environment without a human driver. Robots such as these are referred to as being "autonomous" without any implications or claims regarding free will or consciousness.

It is in this sense that generative art systems are "autonomous." They do not require moment-to-moment decision making or control by the artist. They are functionally autonomous relative to the artist.

Not all rule-based art is generative art

A third confusion relates to rule-based art. In a previous article (Galanter 2006) I outlined a number of types of rule-based art, noting that some are generative, but others are not. Josef Albers and Piero Manzoni, for example, created paintings on the basis of self-imposed constraint rules. Albers created color studies involving only concentric rectangles, and Manzoni did paintings that were all white. Ed Ruscha published an art book of photography with a thematic constraint rule allowing only photos of small fires and milk. Bruce Nauman created minimal performances by following rules in the form of instructions for physical movement. On Kawara has done a series of paintings consisting of the respective day's date lettered in paint. The rule calls for making such a painting every day, but says nothing about lettering style, color, and so on (Zelevansky et al. 2004; Rose et al. 2005).

None of these rule-based artworks can be considered generative art because the artist never ceded control to a functionally autonomous system. There is an in-principle dependence on the artist from moment to moment, and at no point does the artist lose fine-grained control over the art-making process. In most cases the proposed rules suggest a *kind* of action to be taken, but do not fully determine a *specific* action to be taken. That is to say, the rules lack a functional autonomy. As these examples show, it is a mistake to use the phrases "rule-based art" and "generative art" interchangeably.

Here are some types of (non-autonomous) rules that do not result in generative art:

- constraint rules—e.g., Manzoni;
- abstract scores for free interpretation—e.g., Earle Brown's composition *December 1952* (Vickery 2012);
- inspirational rules—e.g., Brian Eno's card set called *Oblique Strategies* (1978);
- thematic rules—e.g., Ruscha as noted above;
- performance scripts or rituals as rules—e.g., Nauman as noted above;
- non-specific ideas for geometric construction—e.g., McEntyre and Vidal (discussed here later).

For comparison, these are some types of (autonomous) rules that do result in generative art:

- algorithms stated in text that can unambiguously be translated into computer code;
- combinatorial rules—e.g., Sol LeWitt's *Incomplete Open Cubes* (1974);

- numerical sequences as rules—e.g., Mel Bochner's *Triangular and Square: Numbers* (1972);
- detailed line composition or drawing rules—e.g., many of Sol LeWitt's wall drawings;
- rules establishing serial composition—e.g., many of Carl Andre's sculptures;
- tiling and other symmetric composition rules—e.g., much Islamic art and architecture;
- chance operations—e.g., as typically associated with John Cage and William Burroughs.

That many of the examples of rule-based art come from the period of conceptual art should not be surprising. Also note that both rule-based art and generative art are fuzzy at their borders. Some works exist in the gray zone of either or both. Moreover, a given work of art may be either dominated by the application of rules or the use of generative systems, or only slightly affected by the generative or rule-based aspect.

The question whether any given work is merely rule based or truly generative is important. Equally important are questions as to why an artist has chosen to work that way, and whether the use of rules or generative methods is part of the concept or merely a pragmatic means to some other end. These questions and more are discussed here in following sections.

Generative art is as old as art

Going back in time, we find examples of symmetry and pattern in the creation of art wherever we find human artifacts that go beyond minimal survival needs. Among even the most so-called "primitive" peoples we find abundant examples of the use of geometric patterns in textiles, symmetric designs evolving around a point, repeating border designs, and so on (Hargittai and Hargittai 1994).

The artistic use of tiling, in particular, is nothing less than the application of abstract systems for decorating specific surfaces. The most notable examples of this practice are perhaps the masterworks found in the Islamic world. It is no coincidence that the Islamic world was also one of the significant cradles of mathematical innovation, and that the word "algorithm" has its roots in Arabic.

From 1999 to 2000 a team led by archaeologist Christopher Henshilwood of the South African Museum in Cape Town uncovered some of the oldest known art artifacts anywhere (Balter 2002). Etched in hand-sized pieces of red ochre more than 70,000 years old is an unmistakable grid design made of triangular tiles that would be clearly recognizable to anyone, from generations of Islamic artists to the 20th-century graphic artist M.C. Escher.

While the etchings, like all ancient archaeological finds, are surrounded by a certain amount of controversy, many find them to be compelling examples of abstract geometric thinking with an artistic bent. In an article on the etchings in *Science* magazine, anthropologist Stanley Ambrose of the University of Illinois, Urbana-Champaign says, "This is clearly an intentionally incised abstract geometric design [...] It is art" (Balter 2002).

One can only imagine the excitement this early artist experienced in making the discovery that one could make marks of aesthetic interest not by simply copying what the eye sees, but by instantiating a systematic abstract idea over and over again on various surfaces. LeWitt presumably would have approved.

Generative art defined a second time

In later writings, I have suggested modifications to the original definition in order to combat the common misinterpretations mentioned previously:

> Generative art refers to any art practice in which the artist cedes control to a system with functional autonomy that contributes to, or results in, a completed work of art. Systems may include natural language instructions, biological or chemical processes, computer programs, machines, self-organizing materials, mathematical operations, and other procedural inventions. (Galanter 2008)

It is worth noting that the earlier criteria for a useful definition and theory are met here. For example, while the definition refers to "art" it does not make presuppositions as to what art is. Art is left as an open concept, and yet our definition divides it into generative and non-generative subtypes. The definition is fairly crisp in that any use of a functionally autonomous system qualifies a given work as being generative. Yet it is easy to see how some pieces might be more system-determined than others, and therefore the border of the definition can be fuzzy in that some pieces are in a sense more generative than others.

As we will show in subsequent sections, this definition creates a wide tent under which all manner of old, current, and future generative artworks are welcome. But the term also remains useful and non-redundant because there is a wide range of art that is clearly not generative; work in which the artist never relinquishes control to a system. In fact, most contemporary art is distinctly *not* generative, and one would likely have to randomly visit a large number of galleries or museums before encountering any generative work. In any case it is clear that the "all art is generative art" problem has been avoided.

Creating a big tent for generative art turns most debates about what is or isn't generative art into more nuanced discussions about options, theories, and opinions available within the field of generative art. The term simply is a reference to how the art is made, and in itself makes no claims as to why the art is made that way or what its content is. It is a definition that invites further thought and discussion rather than foreclosing on it. This notion of generative art also remains uncoupled from any particular technology, and as such directs attention to the art-theoretical issues that are invariant, even as this or that technology comes and goes. Generative art need not be "high tech," which is an advantage in a world where "high tech" is a moving target.

Since generative art is defined as a *way* of making art, it remains available for making art with all manner of content. Being in a room full of painters, one would not assume that these artists have anything in common other than using paint to make art. Similarly, artists creating generative work might have little else in common than using a certain way of making art. This speaks to the robust potential of generative art, and by implication, generative digital art.

Perhaps most telling, there are issues related to generative art, digital or not, that do not impact non-generative art, which will be explored in the following.

Other Uses and Related Terms

The term "generative art" has been used, somewhat obscurely, in other contexts with other meanings. The Romanian sculptor Neagu, for example, founded a mostly fictitious collective called the Generative Art Group (1972). Generative art as a form of geometric abstraction where basic elements are rotated, translated, and modulated in scale was practiced by the Argentinians Eduardo McEntyre and Miguel Ángel Vidal (Osborne 1981). The term has often also seen unrelated generic use. For example, Richard Serra has referred to some of his works as "generative" in the sense that they introduced a new basic form he would go on to use in a series of later works (Serra et al. 1980).

Critic Lawrence Alloway introduced the term "Systemic Art" when he organized the well-known exhibition *Systemic Painting* (1966) at the Solomon R. Guggenheim Museum in New York. He understood systemic art as a form of abstraction using simple standardized forms that are repeated on the basis of a clear organizing principle. Noland's series of chevron paintings, begun in 1963, would be a prime example. Alloway may have shifted his intended meaning closer to that of generative art when he also extended the term to process-oriented color field painting (Osborne 1981).

"Generative Systems" was introduced by Sonia Landy Sheridan as an academic program at the School of the Art Institute of Chicago in 1970. It was a response to the telecommunications and imaging technologies, but also political and pedagogical ideas, of the time. The hue shifts and distortions created by the color copier technologies that artists used at the time could be viewed as related to the understanding of "generative" here.

Beginning with the album *Discreet Music* (1975), musician Brian Eno popularized the term "generative music" with a meaning relatively consistent with "generative art" as it is used here. There was, however, a somewhat narrow focus on repeated note patterns, phase shifts, and tape loops that had already been introduced in the 1950s by composer Terry Riley, and further developed in the 1960s by composer Steve Reich.

The architect Celestino Soddu helped to popularize the use of the term "generative art" by creating the International Generative Art Conference in 1998. While the conference continues to invite all manner of opinion on generative art, Soddu's own definition leans toward a genetic approach that captures the aesthetic of the artist/programmer rather than leading in arbitrary directions. The original call for participation states:

> Generative Art builds possible worlds by creating evolutionary rules that produce events that if, on one side, they are unpredictable and amazing, from the other one they mirror the identity and recognizability of the idea, they are the natural representation of it. (Soddu 1998)

The encoding of an artist's vision as a system is certainly a valid approach to generative art, but it isn't the only valid one. In some cases, for example, the generative artist creates a system without a pre-existing vision of what the result should be. The artist then explores the system as a new territory and discovers treasures here and there along the way.

Complexity, Systems, and Generative Art

If the defining feature of generative art is the artist ceding control to an autonomous system, it is worth exploring whether a deeper understanding of systems can shed additional light on generative art. For a state-of-the-art view of systems we can turn to the field of complexity science where a revolution in systems thinking is taking place. But before doing that, some previous notions regarding systems, system complexity, and aesthetics should be considered.

20th-Century Notions of Complexity in Aesthetics

Birkhoff's aesthetic measure

In 1933 the mathematician George David Birkhoff proposed what he called the "Aesthetic Measure." With this measure he relates "aesthetic effectiveness" (M) to "the degree of complexity" (C) and "the degree of order" (O) using the formula M = O/C. The operationalization and application of this formula almost immediately turned out to be problematic. Nevertheless it was an interesting attempt in that, as Birkhoff points out, "The well known aesthetic demand for 'unity in variety' is evidently closely connected with this formula" (Birkhoff 1933).

What is often overlooked is that Birkhoff based his formula on what we would now call a (speculative) neuroaesthetic theory (Skov and Vartanian 2009, iv, 302). He describes complexity (C) as the degree to which unconscious psychological and physiological effort must be made in perceiving the object. Order (O) is seen as the degree of unconscious tension released as the perception is realized.

Shannon's information theory and the information aesthetics of Bense and Moles

While we have an intuitive sense of what we mean when we refer to a system as "simple" or "complex," it is not easy to develop a formal technical measure of complexity that corresponds well to our intuitive sense. Unrelated to Birkhoff, *information theory*, as an attempt to better understand communication systems, was developed by Claude Shannon in 1948. Shannon was interested in analyzing the capacity of communication channels, and one of his core ideas was that the more "surprise" a given communication exhibits, the more information it contains (Shannon 1948).

From the information theory view, a stream of characters consisting of just the letter "a" over and over again offers no information whatsoever. A stream of English-language sentences would offer considerably more variation and thus more information. The information density can be further increased, and redundancy reduced, via contractions and acronyms. Cell phone text messages such as "R U there" or "Don't B L8" are examples. Ultimately, a stream of totally random letters delivers the largest amount of information. It offers no redundancy and any attempt at compression will immediately result in an irreversible loss of content.

Abraham Moles combined these notions with findings from perceptual psychology in order to analyze the arts. Using various statistical measures, Moles showed how musical works exist on a spectrum from "banal" to "novel" corresponding to the relative order and disorder they exhibit as information (Moles 1966). In addition, he demonstrated how various forms of media can be thought of as the union of aesthetic possibilities in a high dimension space. For example, considering only pitch, a musical instrument has a single dimension. Adding loudness adds a second independent dimension, and so the possible states map into a two-dimensional space, that is, a plane. Given two such mutually independent instruments the entire media space requires four dimensions, that is, a hyperspace.

Around the same time Max Bense emphasized the notion of analyzing media space in terms of information theory, and then used it as the basis for what he called "generative aesthetics":

> The system of generative aesthetics aims at a numerical and operational description of characteristics of aesthetic structures (which can be realized in a number of material

> elements) which will, as abstract schemes, fall into the three categories of the formation principle, distribution principle and set principle. These can be manipulated and applied to an unordered set of elements, so as to produce what we perceive macro-aesthetically as complex and orderly arrangements, and micro-aesthetically as redundancies and information. (Bense 1971)

Following Shannon, both Moles and Bense equated high degrees of order with simplicity, and high degrees of disorder (i.e., randomness) with complexity. However, as much as information theory has its place in the analysis of communication channels, it does not correspond very well with our experiential sense of complexity in the world generally, or in art specifically. To the extent it equates complexity with disorder, information theory breaks down as a general model of our experience. This is where contemporary complexity science has fashioned a response in the form of *effective complexity.*

Effective complexity

Considered as a system, a crystal is made of atoms arranged in a highly regular lattice forming planes and facets. What emerges at human scale is a high degree of order that is easy to describe and easy to predict; in this sense, crystals seem simple. Because of their highly ordered nature any one crystal seems quite similar to others.

By comparison, molecules that make up the gas in our atmosphere could not be more different. As a system, gas molecules are in constant motion, each with a random direction and momentum, and they are all constantly bouncing off each other without any discernible structure at all. Nevertheless we experience gasses as simple systems at human scale. Gas is easy to describe and predict, and a cubic foot of air in one place seems no different than a cubic foot of air in another.

Things we think of as complex systems defy simple description and easy prediction. Many would agree that the most complex systems we encounter are other living things. Life requires a mix of order and disorder: order to maintain integrity and survival; and disorder to allow flexibility and adaptation.

It was this kind of intuition that led physicists Murray Gell-Mann and Seth Lloyd to suggest the notion of effective complexity (Gell-Mann 1995). As illustrated in Figure 5.1, Shannon's information complexity increases with disorder, but effective complexity peaks where there is a mix of order and disorder.

To underscore the contrast, where Shannon would consider white noise or a display of random pixels as being highly complex, Gell-Mann and Lloyd would likely point out that all white noise sounds alike and all displays of random pixels look alike, and as such we perceive them as having low complexity.

Effective complexity as a framework for generative art

Effective complexity introduces a paradigm where high degrees of order and disorder both create simple systems, and complex systems exhibit a mixture of both order and disorder (Figure 5.2). Given this understanding, we can classify forms of generative art as simple-ordered, simple-disordered, and complex systems. Going beyond classification, however, is the discovery that the history of generative art roughly follows the history of our culture's understanding and embrace of these different system types.

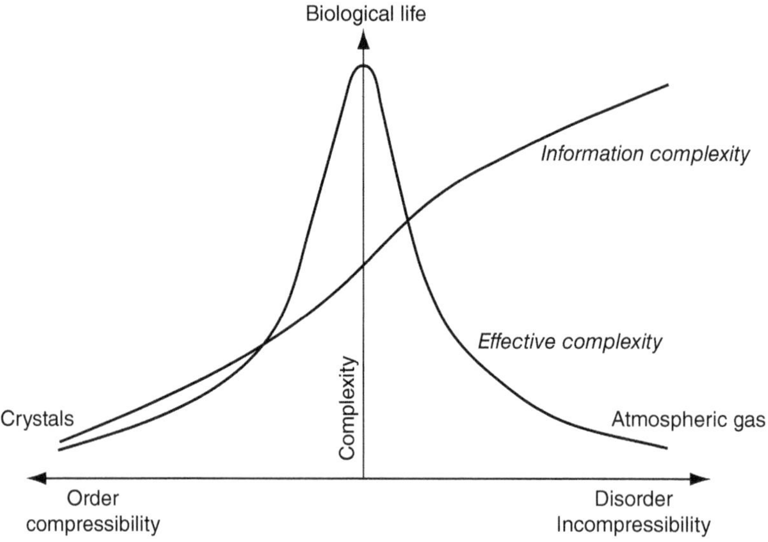

FIGURE 5.1 Order/disorder relationships for information complexity and effective complexity.

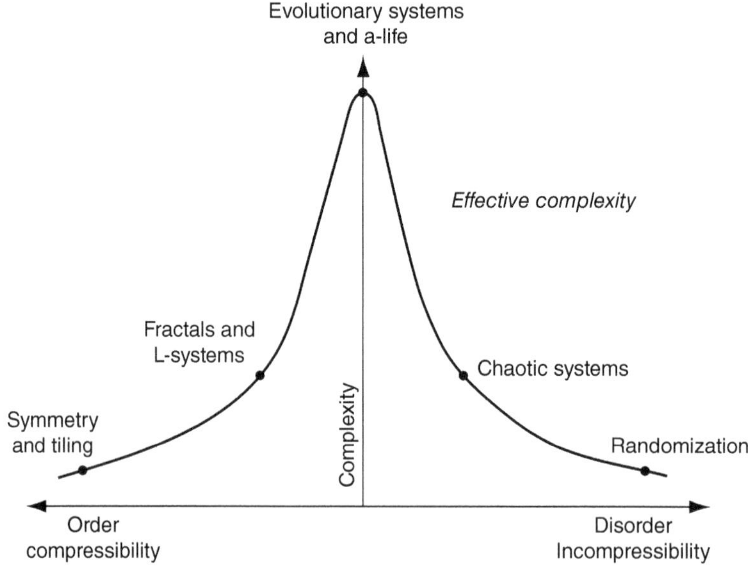

FIGURE 5.2 Systems used in generative art identified by effective complexity.

Highly Ordered Generative Art

Every time and place for which we find artifacts yields examples of symmetry, tiling, and pattern in art. These artifacts provide evidence that simple, highly ordered systems were the first systems applied to art (Hargittai and Hargittai 1994). As noted earlier, samples of generative art over 70,000 years old have been found (see Figure 5.3), establishing that generative art is as old as art itself (Balter 2002).

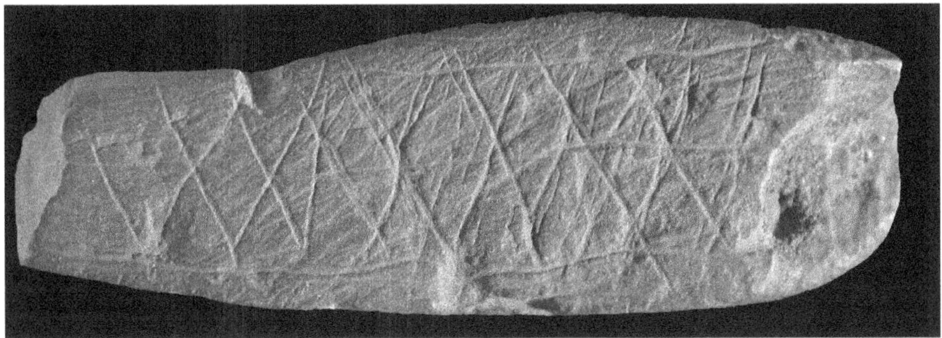

FIGURE 5.3 77,000-year-old generative art etched in red ocher. Photo courtesy of Prof. Christopher Henshilwood, University of Bergen.

Even though these objects are handmade, they qualify as generative because the placement of individual marks has not been decided by the artisan, but dictated by a manually executed symmetry-based algorithm. In principle, an algorithm-executing robot could, for example, tile a checkerboard pattern on a surface of any size using a single algorithm. Here, as pseudo-code, is the program the robot could execute:

```
Set current_position to the lower left corner
Set current_color to black
Do this until the area is full {
   Set saved_position to current_position
   Set saved_color to current_color
   Do this until the right edge is reached {
      Select tile of current_color
      Place tile at current_position
      Set current_color to the opposite of current_color
      Set current_position to one space to the right of current_position
   }
   Set current_position to saved_position
   Set current_position to one space up from current_position
   Set current_color to the opposite of saved_color
}
Done
```

The inner loop, the code indented the furthest and within the inner brackets, repeats the placement of alternating tiles to complete a single row of tiles. The outer loop, the code indented only once and within the outer brackets, repeats to create all of the needed rows. Similar code could be created to produce any regular tiling pattern.

Highly ordered systems in generative art have also appeared in innovative 20th-century art. M.C. Escher was a student of Islamic art and architecture and a popular 20th-century graphic designer. While lacking in formal mathematical training, he obviously had a significant understanding of the generative nature of what he called "the regular division of the plane." Without the use of computers he invented and applied what can only be called algorithms in the service of art (Escher et al. 1982).

As noted earlier, conceptual and minimal artists such as Carl Andre, Mel Bochner, and Paul Morgenson used simple mathematical systems to generate compositions. Sol LeWitt created combinatorial systems he would leave to others to execute as wall drawings. In his essay "Paragraphs on Conceptual Art" he famously offers what could double as a description of generative art by saying, "The idea becomes a machine that makes the art" (LeWitt 1967; Alberro and Stimson 1999; Meyer 2000).

Highly Disordered Generative Art

Compared to the use of highly ordered systems such as patterns and number series, the appreciation of highly disordered systems is a relatively recent pursuit. Prior to the 17th century, mathematics was thought of in the spirit of Platonic forms and Aristotelian logic; order, as opposed to indeterminacy and randomness, was considered a virtue. Chance occurrences were viewed as accidental, irrational, removed from reason, and perhaps even evil in the sense of lacking participation in the Logos. It was not until the 17th century that mathematical models for chance events were developed by Fermat and Pascal.

One of the earliest documented uses of randomization in the arts is often attributed to Wolfgang Amadeus Mozart, but music game systems similar to his were widespread in the 18th century, and the actual inventor is probably lost to the ages. Mozart's version begins with 176 snippets of prepared music. These are assembled in a sequential score based on the throw of the dice. It is interesting to note that the game uses a primitive way to mix order (the short pre-composed snippets) and disorder (the throw of the dice) (Schwanauer and Levitt 1993).

Chance procedures—that is, highly disordered systems—in the arts came into their own primarily in the 20th century. As a young artist, Ellsworth Kelly used inexpensive materials such as children's construction paper along with chance methods to create colorful collages. He was inspired by observing the random patchworks that would develop in the repair of cabana tents on the French Rivera (Bois et al. 1992).

The writer William Burroughs famously used a "cut-up" technique he borrowed from Brion Gysin to randomize his novels (Burroughs and Gysin 1978). Less well known are Burroughs's experiments in visual art using shotgun blasts to explode cans of spray paint, thereby randomly coloring, and partially destroying, plywood supports (Sobieszek and Burroughs 1996).

Certainly one of the most famous advocates for the random selection of sounds in music was John Cage. Cage also experimented with various chance methods to create fine art prints and musical scores (Nyman 1999). Carl Andre explored both order and disorder, often using highly ordered grids or stacks of serial objects, but occasionally a random spill of small parts (Meyer 2001).

While all of these artists used disorder as a system, each of them typically had a different reason for doing so. Mozart and his contemporaries apparently found novelty and rapid results to be amusing. Kelly was initially fascinated by the emergence of form from a process of random decay. Burroughs sought to uncover hidden meaning and probe the unconscious. Cage tried to help the listener experience a Zen acceptance of all sounds as being of equal value. Andre used both order and disorder as a minimalist strategy to achieve simplicity of composition and draw direct attention to the materials themselves.

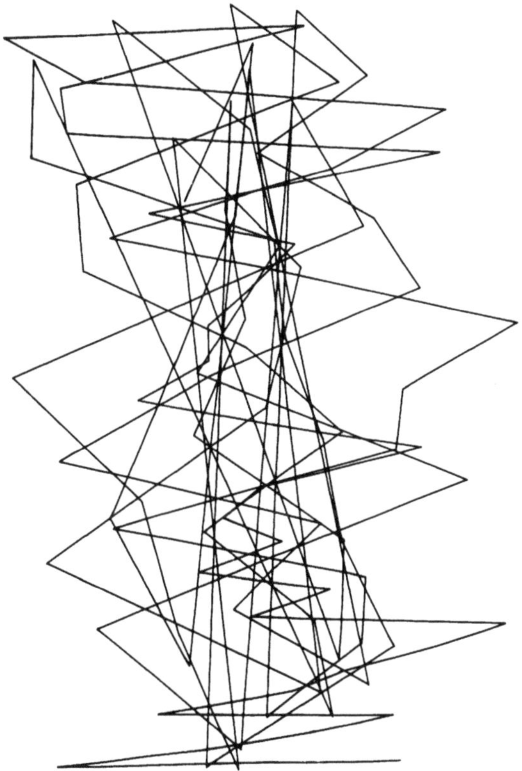

FIGURE 5.4 Michael Noll, *Gaussian Quadratic*, 1963. © AMN 1965.

Early computer artists such as Frieder Nake and A. Michael Noll used pseudo-random number algorithms to exploit disorder. Noll, in particular, attempted to simulate Mondrian's *Composition with Lines* (1917) by starting with a regular array of lines and then perturbing their size and position with random numbers. Noll was among one of the first algorithmic artists to add complexity to highly ordered systems of geometry by including disordered elements. In *Gaussian Quadratic* (Figure 5.4), horizontal positions are established using a Gaussian distribution of random numbers, while vertical positions are predictably fixed using quadratic equations (Benthall 1972; Bentley and Corne 2002).

The use of random numbers remains a mainstay of generative art among contemporary Processing artists/programmers and others.

Complex Generative Art

For most practical purposes, a crystal can be considered a highly ordered physical system and modeled with a simple formula of mass, velocity, and spin. A system of gases is highly disordered, but nevertheless can be modeled with a simple formula of volume, pressure, and temperature. For several centuries science and Western culture have been comfortable with both highly ordered and highly disordered simple systems. And during that time generative artists have used autonomous systems of both kinds.

A biological system, such as a frog, is complex and much more difficult to model. Combining order and disorder, a frog is ever changing and adapting. An attempt to model a frog's bodily functions, the tension of every muscle, the activity of every neural connection, and so on would be a very daunting task.

In recent decades scientists from diverse fields have been working together in a new way to create a novel multidisciplinary understanding of systems, with the founding of the Santa Fe Institute in 1984 serving as a significant milestone. Under the general rubric of "complexity science" and "complexity theory," various kinds of systems have been studied, compared, contrasted, and mathematically and computationally modeled. An abstract understanding of systems that spans the physical, biological, and social sciences is beginning to emerge (Waldrop 1992; Mitchell 2009). The very models of complex systems studied by these scientists are being used as state-of-the-art generative systems by artists.

Principles of complex systems

While both highly ordered and highly disordered systems remain legitimate choices for creating generative art, contemporary generative artists typically aspire to explore and exploit complex systems.

When scientists or knowledgeable artists speak of complex systems they do not mean systems that are complicated or perplexing in an informal way. The phrase *complex system* has been adopted as a specific technical term, or a term-of-art, so to speak. Complex systems typically have a large number of parts or agents that interact with others nearby. These local interactions often lead to the system organizing itself without any master control or external agent being "in charge." Such systems are often referred to as being *self-organizing*, and as exhibiting *emergent* behavior or characteristics that are more than what one would obviously expect from their parts. Complex systems often develop in ways that are dramatic, fecund, catastrophic, or so unpredictable as to seem random. They can also exist as systems in dynamic tension that remain balanced and relatively stable even as they exhibit constant change within.

Complex systems are often referred to as being *non-linear*. The term "non-linear" has multiple discipline-specific meanings that can confuse an interdisciplinary discussion. In the humanities non-linear can mean (1) disconnected, illogical, or irrational, or (2) having multiple narratives, or (3) having a viewer-driven interactive narrative, or (4) being a non-chronological presentation. In the context of complexity science, non-linearity references (1) mathematical expressions with exponential terms (e.g., "x^2") or (2) behaviors similar to the saying "the whole is greater than the sum of the parts," or (3) situations in which small continuous changes result in macro-level phase changes. Examples of the latter might include solid ice melting into liquid water with a slight increase in heat, or catastrophic material failure due to a slight increase in load.

Complexity science offers more than an incremental increase in scientific understanding. Traditional science uses *reductionism*, the hierarchical decomposition of phenomena into smaller simpler components to model, explain, and predict. Complex systems resist such analysis in that they present an emergent whole that seems to be more than the summation of the parts. Complexity science is revolutionary in that it reverses the top-down process of reductionism, and instead offers a synthesis of bottom-up processes.

Areas of application in the life sciences include evolution, brain function, animal societies, metabolism, and much more. More generally, complexity science impacts physics, chemistry, economics, meteorology, computer science, and other sciences. In that complexity science seeks to abstract an understanding of systems across all of these disciplines, the study of complexity is one of integration rather than specialization.

Complex systems often exhibit *chaos*. Chaotic dynamics are non-linear and difficult to predict over time, even though the systems themselves are deterministic and follow a strict sequence of cause and effect. The non-linearity of chaotic systems results in the amplification of small differences, and this is what makes them increasingly difficult to predict over time. This process is usually referred to as *sensitivity to initial conditions*. Sometimes it is called *the butterfly effect*, suggesting that the flapping of a butterfly's wings in Hawaii can result in a tornado in Texas.

Complex systems address issues of *scale* in that large numbers of smaller objects and transactions result in the emergence of a much larger phenomenon. Such systems frequently exhibit *feedback* in that a chain of influences will eventually affect the initiating component. Some complex systems are rather passive, but others, especially life forms, will exhibit *adaptation* in their behavior to preserve their integrity. These are often called *complex adaptive systems*. The hallmark of adaptation in life at the level of species is *evolution*, which also is one of the strongest complex systems applied to generative art.

Complex systems used in generative art

From the mid-1990s onwards, digital generative art has experienced a boom. This is in part due to the creation of easier-to-use, mostly open source, software environments such as Processing, Pure Data, Supercollider, vvvv, openFrameworks, Cinder, and Max.[4] More artists can now write their own programs without losing sight of their artistic goals in a sea of code. Beyond virtual systems, physical computing platforms such as the Arduino have empowered artists by giving them access to sensors, light displays, sound devices, motors, actuators, robots, and so on for reactive and interactive installations.

However, it is the new models offered by the study of complexity science that have been the primary engines behind contemporary generative art. For example, *fractals*—mathematical objects first discovered by Benoit Mandelbrot and exhibiting self-similarity at all scales—have been applied to generative art in the creation of abstract patterns as well as the simulation of natural objects such as clouds, riverbanks, mountains, and other landforms (Mandelbrot 1983). Fractal flames are a particular type of fractal that forms the basis for Scott Draves's network-based screen saver artwork the *Electric Sheep* (2005).

Somewhat related to fractals are *Lindenmayer systems*, also known as L-systems. L-systems are grammar based, using sets of axioms and production rules, and were originally invented to simulate branching structures in plants. L-systems have been applied to generative art in the creation of abstract patterns as well as 2D and 3D renderings of artificial trees, bushes, and flowers in stills and animations (Prusinkiewicz, Lindenmayer, and Hanan 1990). What fractals and L-systems have in common as systems is that they produce highly recursive and thus compressible forms. While they are more complex than the highly ordered patterns discussed earlier, there are other systems ranking higher yet on the complexity curve.

On the disordered side of the effective complexity curve are systems of *chaos*. Chaotic systems are deterministic but exhibit a non-linear sensitivity to initial conditions. While the long-term results of a chaotic system may be so unpredictable as to seem random, there is some short-term predictability. This bit of structure gives chaotic feedback systems greater effective complexity and less disorder than simple randomization.

Artists who have used chaotic feedback include early video artists Steina and Woody Vasulka. The Vasulkas created dynamic systems by creating a video signal loop where the camera is pointed directly into its own display (Vasulka and Vasulka 2001). In 1963—the year that Edward Lorenz discovered deterministic chaos in weather systems (Lorenz 1963)—Hans Haacke's *Condensation Cube* (1963–1965; initially titled *Weather Cube*) displayed similar deterministic yet unpredictable dynamics (Benthall 1972). The piece is a simple transparent acrylic plastic cube sealed with about one-quarter of an inch of water at the bottom. The ambient heat of the room evaporates the water, and then the water vapor condenses on the walls of the cube creating ever-changing chaotic patterns of moisture and running droplets.

Given the growing scientific understanding of increasingly complex systems, it is not surprising that generative artists are now addressing the most complex systems known to date, those of life itself. For example, *reaction-diffusion systems* simulate organic chemical reactions that produce their own catalysts with differing diffusion rates, and by doing so create patterns. Examples of such patterns found in nature include seashells and animal fur. The simulated process can also produce patterns similar to those found in materials such as marble. Because of this, reaction-diffusion systems have been used in the animation industry as well as for abstraction (Turk 1991). Reaction-diffusion systems are typically implemented by breaking a surface up into a fine digital grid, which provides a way of approximating chemical gradients with discrete values for each cell. Diffusion calculations are made at each border between two cells, and overall patterns emerge from these local interactions. This kind of calculation using a discrete grid is a specific elaboration of a general system type called a *cellular automaton* (Turing 1952).

Artificial neural networks, or more simply "neural networks," are inspired by nature's biological computer, the brain. Just as neurons establish networks where associations are created based on the strength of synapse connections, artificial neural networks use weighted virtual connections to associate various input patterns with corresponding output patterns.

Neural networks have been used in *agent-based systems* such as *artificial life* or *a-life* systems. A-life systems are essentially simulated ecologies with resources and virtual entities or agents that reproduce, compete for resources, and sometimes exist in predator/prey relationships. Artists such as Jon McCormack (*Eden*, 2000–2010) and the team of Christa Sommerer and Laurent Mignonneau (*A-Volve*, 1993–1994) have created installations presenting a-life worlds in aesthetically compelling formats.

The realm of *artificial intelligence* (AI) in art is more difficult to define or pin down. AI-based art is generally viewed as the attempt to create programs that apply a set of heuristics or codified rules of thumb gathered from human experts to create art. Well known in this area is Harold Cohen, a painter who in 1973 created *AARON*, a software application that functions as a drawing program and that he has continually updated for over four decades. Cohen has used *AARON* to produce work in a number of forms. He is perhaps best known for large canvases directly painted by robotic extensions under the control of *AARON* (McCorduck 1991).

Some a-life implementations include a genetic system as part of the reproduction activity, allowing generations of agents to evolve. The use of evolution is arguably the most popular and robust high-complexity system employed in contemporary generative art.

Evolutionary art, genetic algorithms, and the fitness bottleneck

Genetic algorithms and *evolutionary computing* are terms used for algorithms patterned after the reproductive mechanisms studied in biology. In industry, genetic and evolutionary techniques are used, for example, to design optimal electronic circuits, aircraft wings, investment strategies, telecommunications routing, encryption methods, and computer games. In general, genetic and evolutionary approaches provide a way to search a large space of possible solutions with greater efficiency than mere random trial and error (Fogel 1999).

In biology the *genotype* is a collection of DNA, sometimes referred to as the "code of life." The *phenotype* is the collection of resulting features and characteristics such as blue eyes, curly hair, gender, and so on. As implemented on a computer, the genotype is a data structure that provides input into an algorithm that then produces the phenotype as a simulated result. The genetic system makes progress by making random changes to genotypes selected from the gene pool, discarding those new genotypes that do not constitute an improvement, and further breeding genotypes that do. This process is done over and over again for many generations allowing increasingly strong phenotypes to emerge from the gene pool (Bentley and Corne 2002).

"Improvement" here is relative to a *fitness function* that captures the design aspects to be optimized. In the case of an airplane wing, the fitness function might seek to maximize lift and minimize weight. In the case of an investment strategy, the fitness function might simply be the estimated profit for a given genotype. Because the evolutionary process is completely automated, optimal solutions can be rapidly approximated by using gene pools with many dozens of competitors evolving for hundreds of generations.

The difficulty for artists using evolutionary systems is that we don't have algorithms for judging aesthetics, and thus we can't code robust aesthetic fitness functions. While there have been attempts at automation, the typical solution to this challenge involves putting the artist back in the loop to manually score each new phenotype. This means the system is no longer entirely automated, and that places a severe upper limit on both the size of the gene pool and the number of generations that can be run. This inability to computationally measure aesthetic quality, thus slowing the entire evolutionary process by orders of magnitude, has been referred to as the *fitness bottleneck* (Todd and Werner 1998).

William Latham arguably created the first computer-mediated evolutionary art in the early 1990s. Initially the results took the form of large digital prints of biomorphic forms reminiscent of insect larvae or crustaceans (Todd and Latham 1992). Later work included animations, video installations, and software for personal computers. Around the same time Karl Sims produced mathematically based abstract images and animations. He went on to evolve plant-like forms for representational animations, as well as virtual creatures that combined genetics, neural networks, and simulated physics to achieve various locomotion goals. In his piece *Galapagos* (1995) the audience provides a fitness function by standing on a sensor pad in front of the display showing the evolutionary form they prefer (Sims 1991, 1994, 1997).

In subsequent years evolutionary techniques proved to be useful despite the lack of automated fitness functions. Since these techniques are a general approach for exploring a design space they can be combined with other generative systems. Updating Sims's gallery-bound approach in *Galapagos*, Draves's piece *Electric Sheep*, for example, gives each user the opportunity of choosing their favorite screen saver on their own computer. These preferences are gathered over the Internet, and the fitness function is effectively crowdsourced (Draves 2005).

Artists continue to experiment with ways to break the fitness bottleneck. Following in the footsteps of Birkhoff's aesthetic measure, Machado and Cardoso's *NEvAr* system uses computational aesthetic evaluation based on a ratio of complexity measures acting as a fitness function[5] (Machado and Cardoso 2005). Todd and Werner were early adopters of a co-evolutionary approach to music composition (Todd and Werner 1998). By using separate populations of critic agents and composer agents, they enabled a consistent aesthetic to emerge in the simulated culture. However, they found that, while the evolved aesthetic was consistent, it in no way reflected or appealed to our human sense of aesthetics. This same result has been observed in other cases of emergent aesthetics as well.

Problems in Generative Art Theory

In the following we will consider a series of problems in generative art theory. These are not problems in the sense that they require single correct solutions, but rather are questions that the artist will want to consider when making a piece; that critics and historians will typically address in their analysis; and that insightful audience members will ponder. They are problems that typically offer multiple opportunities and possibilities.

It is notable that, for the most part, these problems equally apply to both digital and non-digital generative art; to generative art past, present, and future; and to ordered, disordered, and complex generative art. In addition, these same problems or questions are trivial, irrelevant, or nonsensical when asked in the context of non-generative art. The fact that our systems-based definition of generative art includes art with a common set of problems, and that those same problems don't apply to non-generative art, can serve as evidence that the definition is meaningful, effective, and well formed.

The Problem of Authorship

How do traditional views of authorship shift regarding credit, expression, and provenance?

When someone first encounters digital generative art a commonly asked question is "Who is the artist, the human or the computer?" On a more sophisticated level, many see a resonance with poststructuralist thinking on authorship when faced with an artwork that has been created without any human intuition or real-time judgment involved. Some artists in the field of generative art work specifically in the vein of problematizing traditional notions of authorship. In describing the ironic software artwork/application Auto-Illustrator (Ward 2000–2002) Ward and Cox quote Barthes, Foucault, Benjamin, and others to contextualize what they see as the breakdown of the heroic author of modernity (Ward and Cox 1999). Shifting emphasis a bit, McCormack et al. (2014) question the relationships between authorship and agency, creativity, and intent, which are all problematized in generative art but taken somewhat for granted in non-generative art.

Over the past few decades, a significant portion of humanities discourse, and specifically art discourse, has focused on poststructuralist notions such as the "death of the author." In generative art, the author apparently is a machine, so that the art appears to be the reification of poststructuralist theory. Some have gone so far as to suggest that the primary function of generative art is to destabilize notions of authorship. This certainly is an option but, surveying the field, one that is exercised only by a modest subset of artists in the field.

The problem with this authorship-focused view of generative art, and with the poststructuralist critique in general, is that shifting the production of meaning toward the reader rather than author comes at a huge cost. Taken literally and in good faith, this view purports to remove the possibility of art, or even simple speech, as a means of effective communication. History and anthropology show that this cost has, in fact, not been exacted. Communication and its advancement must be possible, or we would never have progressed beyond grunts and hand gestures as a species. More pointedly, if some poststructuralist theorists believed that communication from author to reader ultimately would be impossible, they would not have bothered to publish their work.

Pushing the reader—the audience—to the front of creating meaning in art is to ignore the obvious. For centuries art has acted as a powerful binding force that brings people together, transmits culture from generation to generation, creates common understanding and experience, and provides visions for the future.

Related issues emerge with the question whether computers can be truly creative agents, and generative art requires more subtle variations to that question. In the case of Latham or Sims, for example, the artist and audience can make choices, but only among alternatives created by the computer. To what extent does such selection confer authorship? In most art discourse since Duchamp selection is considered a form of authorship. In cases where works wholly emerge from the computer some might find the answer to be more difficult.

Non-generative art, on the other hand, suffers no such ambiguity. There is no doubt that Leonardo and not his paintbrushes created the Mona Lisa. The problem of authorship for generative art, digital or otherwise, is quite different.

The Problem of Intent

Why is the artist working with and ceding control to generative systems?

Described as a systems-based way of making art, the term "generative art" says something about *how* the artist creates the work, but little about *why* the artist has chosen to work that way. As noted in a previous section, many artists have used randomization, but for different reasons. Cage used chance procedures as a Zen strategy to remove attachment to particular sounds; Burroughs as a Dada-esque method for unleashing the unconscious; Kelly as a simulation of the creation of form by natural entropic forces.

Looking across the long history of generative art, or the relatively short history of digital generative art, there seem to be as many reasons for embracing the generative approach as there are artists working that way. Nevertheless, there also are some notable clusters of use and motivation.

Across cultures from antiquity to the present, the use of highly ordered systems, such as symmetry and tiling, has provided ways to achieve design consistency in space and time. Such designs can be handed off to artisans for construction. For large-scale, labor-intensive practices such as architecture this is of great practical value. In addition, the ability to pass on essentially algorithmic patterning methods allows for the creation of inheritable cultural identity as abstract form. Anthropologists, for example, are now able to identify specific artifacts as belonging to particular peoples by analyzing the abstract mathematical symmetry group membership of the decoration (Washburn and Crowe 1988).

In a contemporary context the artistic intent behind generative strategies is highly varied. In the effects and animated film industry, generative methods are purely pragmatic. The creation of forests or crowd scenes by means of generative techniques is much less expensive than modeling and animating each tree or character individually by hand. Some artists exploit generative systems for similar reasons.

For some practitioners the technical generative system itself is the object of interest. These artists will tend toward a *truth to process* aesthetic where the work is presented in a deconstructed format seeking to minimize the gap between the mechanism of creation and the resulting artifact. In a fully realized scenario, LeWitt's dictum is extended to the point where a machine does not only make the art, a machine *is* the art.

For yet others it isn't the literal system used that is of interest, but rather systems found in nature that become sources of inspiration. Some artists, for example, use genetic algorithms and evolutionary computing because they have an interest in actual biological genetics and evolution. The artworks provide aestheticized simulations with the hope of re-presenting the natural world in a way that reinvigorates awe and reinforces the understanding of that world.

Another group of artists has mathematical interests that lend themselves well to generative interpretation. Yet others want to turn control over to computers to illustrate social, cultural, or even engineering implications of the technology.

Perhaps one of the most common motivations behind the use of generative systems is that they can surprise the artist and provide a springboard for novelty and new ideas. As advances in this mode are made, the computer will move closer to becoming a true collaborator of the artist. There is no single or correct intent behind generative art practice. But any thoughtful artist or critic working in the area of generative art will want to address the problem of intent on a case-by-case basis.

The Problem of Uniqueness

Does it diminish the value of the art when unique objects can be mass-produced?

Whether in the context of market value or cultural value, traditional works of art have been treasured as unique and thus rare objects. Walter Benjamin declared art made through mechanical reproduction, such as printmaking and photography, to have a diminished "aura." Today the ability to produce endless copies has found its fullest fruition in digital media. The dematerialization of the work along with Internet distribution makes duplication essentially a free process.

Digital generative art introduces a completely new problem: rather than offering an endless supply of *copies*, it provides an endless supply of *original and unique* artifacts. The apparently oxymoronic phrase "mass-produced unique objects" in fact describes the reality of generative art. The art can take the form of prints made using digital giclée technology, and the possibility of an endless supply of monoprints on demand is real. 3D printing technologies that turn data into physical objects are quickly improving in quality. It is already possible for artists to create unlimited numbers of singular and unique sculptures, and quality of construction will improve over time.

Some artists may choose to address the paradox of mass-produced unique objects by making it a content issue in their generative art. However, even if it is not an overt part of the content of a piece, the issue of uniqueness in generative art deserves the attention of critics and artists.

The Problem of Authenticity

Given that it is in part created by an unemotional and unthinking system, is generative art really art at all?

The question as to whether generative art is art at all mostly tends to be raised by those not familiar with digital art, and results in a discussion that runs directly into the "What is art?" question.

In an earlier section a number of theories on art were noted. Generative art can certainly fit within the older theories of art that emphasize form or viewer experience. It is only partially compatible with the theory of art as representation, which excludes a great deal of non-generative modern art as well. Generative art can comfortably fit within the contemporary theories of art surrounding social construction and based on family resemblance, the notion of art as institution, or historical definitions.

The type of theory that sees art creation as a function of expression is the one most problematic for generative art. Can it be claimed that a computer can and will express itself? Alternatively, when the computer determines forms not anticipated by the artist, does its creation still qualify as the artist's expression? This is where the fact that digital generative art is part of the long history of generative art can assist. It is useful to point out that the unanticipated results generated by Cage's and Burroughs's use of randomization are generally accepted as being artistically expressive. In a similar way digital generative art, however unpredictable, can also be considered expressive.

The Problem of Dynamics

Must generative art change over time while being exhibited to an audience?

Some people have argued that truly generative art must exhibit change over time, and that static artifacts created by using generative systems outside the view of the audience do not qualify as generative.[6] If the display of dynamics is turned into an absolute requirement it conflicts with a broader systems-based definition or theory of generative art. Given that generative art exhibiting dynamics in real time is a relatively new development, generative art theory is better served by positing that some generative art is dynamic and some is not.

A more salient question is whether dynamism in generative art is an especially powerful choice at this particular time in generative art history. As noted earlier, truth to process in generative art that explicitly addresses the generative process can be quite powerful, and the literal display of system dynamics surely is truth to process in action.

Ultimately there are many reasons why an artist might take a generative approach. Again, the use of generative systems in the film and animation industry is largely pragmatic, and the generative results are "frozen" once realized. Given the artistic goals of filmmaking, this is entirely valid. Whether a given piece is better served by displaying dynamics remains a question to be considered by artists, critics, and audience members on an individual basis.

The Problem of Postmodernity

Is generative art an unavoidably postmodern approach to art?

It has been suggested that digital art, and especially digital generative art, embodies a postmodern attitude and intrinsically addresses postmodern concerns. Part of this argument is built on the convolution of the previously addressed postmodern and poststructuralist ideas about authorship. As first noted by Burroughs and then popularized by performance artist Laurie Anderson, the notion of language as a virus takes on new, multivalent meanings in the context of computer languages and computer viruses.[7]

Due to its use of complexity models as creative engines, digital generative art can also be seen as addressing the realm of simulacra. Artworks that essentially are artificial life environments —complete with competing agents, limited resources, layered information, and evolutionary change—seem to be the reification of concepts on simulacra and simulation offered by Baudrillard (1994). Authors such as Margot Lovejoy are quite explicit their postmodern contextualization of not only digital art regardless of the artist's intent, but of purely technical infrastructure such as computer operating systems also independent of the programmer's intent (Lovejoy 2004).[8]

However, digital generative art can also combat what other artists view as postmodernity's deficits. Postmodern art typically abandons the pursuit of formalism and ideals of beauty as meaningful activity. It practices radical skepticism toward the use of art for revealing non-relativistic truths. At most, postmodern art addresses beauty and truth from an ironic distance, seeing them as naïve pursuits to be left behind.

Generative art can counter these positions head on. First of all, artists creating generative work can explore form as something other than social convention. Using complex systems they can produce form that emerges as the result of naturally occurring processes beyond the influence of man and culture. Most would agree that water was made of two parts hydrogen and one part oxygen long before man was present to say so. Similarly, reaction-diffusion systems, evolution, and all the other systems leveraged by generative art operate autonomously in a way independent of man and human influence. These systems would exist whether or not man existed, and currently operate in places where man has never been. Generative art can establish beauty as something that is not man's arbitrary creation, but rather an expression of universal forces.

Second, artists on that basis can demonstrate, by compelling example, reasons to maintain faith in our ability to understand our world. They can remind us that the universe itself is a generative system, and generative art can restore our sense of place and participation in that universe.

Ultimately, generative art per se is ideologically neutral. It simply is a way of creating art and any content considerations are left to a given artist. After all, generative art is prehistoric and precedes modernism, postmodernism, and every other "ism" on record. Nevertheless, the postmodern condition continues to interest some artists and critics in the realm of generative art, and it serves as a platform for extending, not ending, that discussion.

The Problem of Locality, Code, and Malleability

Is the art in the object, the system, the code, or something else entirely?

Digital generative art raises the question as to where the art resides—that is, its ontological status. For some people, generative art is like all other art, and, to the extent there is an object or event, the latter determines where the art resides. Others, however, prefer to demote the object or event to by-product status, and see the generative system itself as the art. Still others will insist that the code itself is the art.

These debates are not new or unique to digital generative art. Consider, once again, Sol LeWitt's wall drawings. LeWitt would write up instructions, and then different assistants might draw different renderings of the same instructions in different places at different times. One could speculate as to where the art is. Is it the piece of paper upon which LeWitt typed the instructions? Is it the abstract words that might be delivered in different materialities? Is the art in fact the drawing on the wall? Or is the art the union of all these things?

An additional twist, and arguably a new paradigm, has been created with the advent of art as open source software. The first step was that artists doing generative work freely shared their creations as executable applications. This allowed anyone to download the work and run it on a personal computer. Typically the software would not create another object, such as a printout, but would directly display graphics and perhaps generate sound right on the user's computer. Sharing artwork has always been an option, but in this case everyone and anyone could have a personal copy of the work.

The next step was that some artists chose to also share their actual source code. This allowed other artists and programmers to download it, make their own modifications, and then release variations of the original artwork. This type of creative approach breaks with the paradigm of the heroic single artist creating a "fixed" masterpiece. It creates a process where multiple artists evolve an ever changing and growing family of related artworks over time.

Despite the vagaries of making such work economically viable, a number of artists have embraced this new, radically open source, production paradigm, using free sharing hosts such as github.com. The malleable, non-physical nature of code makes such an approach possible while it would not be an option with traditional media. Yet there is no requirement for artists to work this way, and the generative approach provides multiple options rather than dictating any avenues for creativity.

The Problem of Creativity

Are generative systems creative? What is required to create a truly creative computer? Philosopher Margaret Boden has suggested that "Creativity is the ability to come up with ideas or artifacts that are new, surprising, and valuable" (Boden 2004). Most people would agree that digital generative art systems, and generative art systems in general, do not have ideas in a sense that implies consciousness. However, successful generative art systems commonly create new and surprising artifacts. The question of value is yet something else. As discussed in the context of the fitness bottleneck, the assignment of value to the results of generative art systems for the most part requires human judgment.

A reasonable prerequisite for a generative system to be deemed truly creative is that it exercise critical evaluation discriminating between high- and low-quality art. Moreover, the system should be able to modify its own behavior to create more of the former and less of the latter. Unfortunately, computational aesthetic evaluation remains a fundamentally unsolved problem.

In other writings, I have suggested a notion of creativity that can apply to both conscious and unconscious systems (Galanter 2009). In complexity science, systems are deemed to be *adaptive* when they modify their structure or behavior to maintain their integrity in response to changes in the environment. For example, when a beehive is damaged by the weather, the behavior of the inhabitants will shift to either repairing the physical hive, or moving to an entirely new physical hive. This adaptation is an emergent behavior of the social hive that arises from the local interactions of individual bees. Creativity can be viewed simply as the difference between merely complex systems (e.g., the weather) and *complex adaptive systems* (e.g., a beehive.)

A possible objection is that the relatively simple adaptations of bees are already implicit in the overall natural system's structure, which comprises instinctive behavior, and that the invention required of creativity is therefore lacking in the case of the hive. But one can raise the question whether, when compared to the creativity of the human mind, this is a difference in kind or simply a difference in degree. While there may be hive-keeping instincts inherited by the bees, they still have to respond to the physical specifics of the given situation. Every detail, and every response needed, cannot be preprogrammed. In a similar way, the creativity of the human mind is probably already implicit in the structure of the brain despite the apparent inventiveness of individual creative acts. Perhaps both consciousness and creativity can be viewed as emergent properties of complex adaptive systems, and indeed both seem to be in rough proportion to the complexity of the underlying system.

Boden takes pains to differentiate between ideas that are new to the person inventing them, and ideas that are new to the entire world or society. These are the products of what she calls p-creativity and h-creativity, with p- standing for "psychological" and h- standing for "historical" (Boden 2004). This distinction is less about the actual mechanism behind creativity, and more about the social response to the product of creativity. All creativity is in a sense the result of p-creativity. However, some products qualify for the distinction of being h-creative if they are unprecedented in history.

The Problem of Meaning

Can and should generative art be about more than generative systems?

By now it should be obvious that one advantage of defining or theorizing generative art as simply a way of making art is that it maximizes the possibilities for the artist. In artistic practice one can find all manner of intent and meaning in both digital and non-digital generative art.

The above discussion of the problem of intent mentioned a number of possible meanings for generative art. For example, highly ordered systems can create meaning in the form of symbolic markers of cultural identity. By using a generative system design consistency, and thus identity, is ensured across the society. Note, however, that while the result has symbolic meaning, it is not a comment on the particular system used or the general notion of generativity.

A generative system may simply be pragmatic and also create products without intrinsic meaning. It was previously mentioned that in the creation of an animated film, having the modeling department create hundreds or thousands of trees by hand for a forest scene would be very time consuming. It is much less expensive to use an L-system-based generative system to automatically create as many trees as needed. However, the audience will never know L-systems were used, and the film is not "about" generative systems as such, nor is it even about trees.

A piece like Haacke's *Condensation Cube*, however, is indeed about the very generative system it is. The system used doesn't create an independent object for presentation. The system itself is what is put on view. Elsewhere, many artists are unapologetically abstract and formal in their generative practice, seeking only to reinvigorate the sublime and instill a sense of awe. Others may attempt to deliver political opinion, social commentary, religious inspiration, or indeed any meaning humanly imaginable.

To the extent that some generative art is about generativity itself, the notion of *truth to process* deserves a bit more discussion. Past art movements have promoted the notion of "truth to materials." In the context of formalism, it was believed that the most powerful aesthetic would reside in presenting the essential nature of the medium, and that doing so would deliver the purest distillation of significant form. Applied to architecture, this meant that concrete was presented as concrete, and steel beams were revealed as steel beams. For Clement Greenberg, paintings as simulated windows into illusory space presented a compromised formal aesthetic (Greenberg 1986). It was paint on a flat finite support presented purely as paint that harnessed the medium's true form and essential power.

Most artists producing generative work begin with an idea of what the final result might be, or at least what final result might be desired. They then take a top-down rather than bottom-up approach, creating systems that will conform to and yield their preconceived notion. This imposes a teleology that does not exist in natural systems, and does so even though the art is supposed to be inspired by natural systems. One conclusion would be that this imposition of top-down teleology introduces a kind of conceptual incoherence.

A pure truth-to-process approach would be radically bottom-up. The system, whether digital or not, would begin with low-level functions, and these would be assembled to interact and begin a process of complexification building up across multiple scales and levels of emergence. Generative art created in the spirit of truth to process would not obsess about intended form working toward a final object. There would be no intended form, and formal aspects of the final object would be important only in so far as they reference the processes that created them. The art would give the audience a sense of dynamism and offer the generative system itself as the expression of aesthetics. Working this way would move attention away from objects to processes, and from nouns to verbs. It would embrace dynamism over formalism, celebrate the aesthetic of creation as an activity, and posit truth to process as being intrinsically beautiful.

The Future of Generative Art

Computational Aesthetic Evaluation

The notion of computational aesthetic evaluation has been referenced here a number of times, and a reasonably detailed discussion would require at least another chapter (Galanter 2012).[9] But it seems safe to say that if it is a large step from the hand tools of digital art such as Adobe Photoshop™ to the generative art of complex systems, it will take a bigger leap to advance from generative art to systems capable of self-criticism.

Relatively simple formulaic approaches such as Birkhoff's aesthetic measure, the Golden Ratio φ, the Fibonacci series, Zipf's law and related power laws, as well as others have proven to be at best supplemental rather than definitive. The information-theory-inspired *generative aesthetics* of Bense and Moles have proven to be more descriptive than normative. Attempts to create automated fitness functions for evolutionary systems, such as Machado and Cardoso's use of compression-related complexity measures in their *NEvAr* system, have proven to have some limited success, but it is questionable whether such approaches generalize well (Galanter 2012).

Some artists have suggested that a better understanding of the psychology of art and aesthetics could yield models for computational aesthetic evaluation. Years ago Rudolf Arnheim applied principles of *gestalt psychology* such as the *law of pragnanz* to the realm of aesthetic perception (Arnheim 1974). Both Daniel Berlyne's *arousal potential* model and Colin Martindale's neural network model of *prototypicality* are suggestive (Berlyne 1971; Martindale 2007). However, none of these has yet inspired the creation of actual software. The nascent field of *neuroaesthetics* aspires to model aesthetic experience from the bottom up starting at the level of basic neurology. Those with a complexity-science turn of mind are optimistic as to where neuroaesthetics might lead, but so far there again have been no practical results applicable to generative art.

However, despite the apparent difficulty in solving the problem, the attempt to move digital art beyond the raw generativity of the computer to something more like an aesthetically critical artificial intelligence is too compelling a goal to ignore. While success cannot be guaranteed, work is sure to continue.

Generative Art after Computers

Generative art is a way of creating that is technology-agnostic. And just as the first generative art long preceded the computer, it seems inevitable that technologies subsequent to computers will be used to make generative art. Some have suggested that computers represent a kind of "final" technology since they can simulate any other machine or process, past or future. The problem with this suggestion is that simulations only exist in the virtual reality of the computer, and not in the physical reality in which people actually live, work, and play. A significant practical challenge for digital art has always been that of "output," meaning, how the remarkable virtual creations within the computer can be made compelling in the "real" world.

Future generative art technologies are likely to provide new physical possibilities. In fact, some of these are already appearing on the horizon and coming within reach of artists. Synthetic biology, for example, draws lessons from life science to create new organic systems typically starting at the level of DNA sequencing and synthesis. Existing DNA can be used and modified, and new DNA can be built from scratch. Projects such as the BioBrick initiative (Ginkgo Biolabs 2012) can now provide standardized DNA sequences as building block components that can be incorporated into living cells such as E. coli, creating new forms of biology not found in nature.

Some indication of what the future may bring is offered by the E.Chromi project at Cambridge University (iGem 2009). Researchers there genetically engineered E. coli to create biological machines that can sense various chemicals and then synthesize pigments of various colors. A practical application is the creation of easy-to-use tests for environmental hazards. For example, one strain might detect arsenic in ground water and produce a red pigment when it is found. Another strain might detect mercury and produce green pigment.

One can imagine future generative art where, for example, dynamic murals are made by painting thin layers of living cells on the wall. These cells would detect each other, exhibit non-linear dynamics, and self-organize, creating emergent patterns of color. Unlike Eduardo Kac's *Specimen of Secrecy about Marvelous Discoveries* (2006), consisting of framed assemblages of pre-existing living organisms, future bio-art pieces will be created by artists sequencing custom DNA and programming new organisms not unlike the way current digital artists program computers.

Also of growing interest to generative artists is nanotechnology and technology at other tiny scales. This includes *nanomachines*, molecule-sized machines 10^{-9} of a meter in size, *micromachines* 10^{-6} of a meter in size, and *millimachines* that work at the (10^{-3}) millimeter scale. Nano-, micro-, and milli- technologies are currently very broad areas of intense technological development.

One application area ripe for radical miniaturization is that of robotics. It has been speculated that developments in this area may one day lead to the creation of self-assembling materials. Imagine, for example, a sand-like material where grains sense, communicate, and navigate and move across each other. Such grains could then bond, creating emergent 3D shapes at human scale capable of locomotion and shape-shifting.

A number of much larger self-assembling robots have already been created. Examples include the Swarm-bots of Gross et al. (2006) and, more recently, the coin-sized smart pebble robots of Gilpin and Rus (2010, 2012). The pebble robots are capable of a kind of swarm intelligence. For example, when a large number of smart pebbles surround another object, they can cooperate to infer that object's shape, and then copy it by inducing yet other smart pebbles to bond in that shape.

It is not a great leap to imagine generative art sculptures that are in constant flux, perhaps even taking on the forms of the visitors that come to see them. But new forms of generative art appearing on the horizon aside, it is virtually certain that digital generative art is here to stay. Like art in general, generative art proceeds by a process of addition, not substitution.

Notes

1 Some of the web sites for popular (mostly) open source software used to create generative art include:
- Processing, a development environment and online community: http://processing.org
- OpenProcessing, an additional resource for Processing users: http://www.openprocessing.org
- Arduino, an open source electronics prototyping platform: http://arduino.cc
- Pure Data, a visual programming language for music, sound, and performance: http://puredata.info
- Cinder, a professional-quality creative coding library for C++ users: http://libcinder.org
- openFrameworks, an open source C++ toolkit for creative coding: http://www.openframeworks.cc
- vvvv, a multipurpose toolkit for media environments, graphics, video, and audio: http://vvvv.org
- Supercollider, a real-time audio synthesis and algorithmic composition language: http://supercollider.sourceforge.net
- Max is a commercial visual programming language for music, sound, video, installation, and interactive art applications that is both easy to use and powerful: http://cycling74.com/products/max/.

All accessed January 15, 2015.

2 Grasshopper is a graphical algorithm editor that allows users to add generative systems to 3D models created with Rhino. Additional information can be found at these web sites:
- Grasshopper: http://www.grasshopper3d.com
- Rhino: http://www.rhino3d.com.

3 The interest shown in this theory is greatly appreciated. In late 2013 the Google Scholar tracking service listed over ninety published academic articles and papers citing the original paper (Galanter 2003). Further, there are dozens of citations of articles I've written further developing this view. In addition references can be found in a number of books, online magazines, dozens of blogs and online education resources, and assorted artist statements, gallery guides, and conference calls for participation.

4 See note 1.

5 A full technical explanation of their computational aesthetic evaluation approach is beyond the scope of this chapter. However, Machado and Cardoso (2002) note in their article:

> Our point of view is that the aesthetic value of an image is connected with the sensorial and intellectual pleasure resulting from its perception. It is also our belief that we tend to prefer images that are, simultaneously, visually complex and that can be processed (by our brains) easily. […]
>
> We won't try to justify our beliefs about aesthetics, basically because we lack sufficient experimental evidence to support them. We will, however, present the formula that we currently use to automate fitness and the experimental results achieved so far.

In brief, they use the degree to which a given image can be compressed using jpeg methods as a proxy measure for image complexity. In addition, they use the degree to which the same image can be compressed using fractal methods as a proxy measure for the cognitive complexity involved in the brain processing the image. They posit that our experience of aesthetic quality will be roughly proportional to the ratio of image complexity to processing complexity.

6 Although the various points of view summarized in this chapter can be found in the publications cited here, I encountered many of them first in the online community of generative art enthusiasts on the e-mail list called eu-gene. The debate regarding dynamism as a requirement for generative art was just one point of active debate among many. With the growth of generative art from a niche to a popular practice in computer art, the forums for generative art discussion have multiplied, and eu-gene activity has somewhat diminished. It is, however, still active, and can be joined at http://generative.net/read/home. I remain indebted to the eu-gene list for many years of stimulating discussion.

7 The famous supposed Burroughs quote that "Language is a virus from outer space" may, in fact, be apocryphal. Sometimes attributed to his novel *The Ticket That Exploded* (1962), the quote cannot be found in the text but similar ideas are exercised there. One related passage is this example:

> From symbiosis to parasitism is a short step. The word is now a virus. The flu virus may have once been a healthy lung cell. It is now a parasitic organism that invades and damages the central nervous system. Modern man has lost the option of silence. Try halting sub-vocal speech. Try to achieve even ten seconds of inner silence. You will encounter a resisting organism that forces you to talk. That organism is the word.

Using Google's textual search engine (http://books.google.com) the precise quote cannot be found in that novel, nor can it be found in the other two novels from the Nova trilogy, *The Soft Machine* and *Nova Express*, or for that matter his other best known novels *Queer*, *The Naked Lunch*, and *Junky*.

Precisely quoted or not, Burroughs's notion of language as a virus was picked up by Laurie Anderson in her song of the same name from her performance art piece *Home of the Brave*. Burroughs was prescient in his anticipation of the notion of the meme.

8 The cited book was first published as *Postmodern Currents: Art And Artists in the Age of Electronic Media* and both freely associate not only generative art, but essentially all new media and electronic art, with the umbrella of postmodern and poststructural theory. For example:

> George Landow, in his Hypertext: the Convergence of Critical Theory and Technology demonstrates that, in the computer, we have an actual, functional, convergence of technology with critical theory. The computer's very technological structure illustrates the theories of Benjamin, Foucault, and Barthes, all of whom pointed to what Barthes would name "the death of the author." The death happens immaterially and interactively via the computer's operating system. (Lovejoy 2004)

9 The problem of computational aesthetic evaluation appears to be as difficult as any in the field of artificial intelligence. It calls into play concepts from mathematics, philosophy, computer science, art theory, design practice, psychology, neurology, and more. At the time this text was written, my cited chapter (Galanter 2012) provided the most comprehensive chapter-length overview of the topic available. Included are all the

aspects briefly mentioned here, including formulaic approaches, variations of evolutionary computing, the work of psychologists such as Arnheim, Berlyne, and Martindale, the nascent field of neuroaesthetics, empirical studies, and more.

References

Alberro, Alexander, and Blake Stimson. 1999. *Conceptual Art: A Critical Anthology*. Cambridge, MA: The MIT Press.

Arnheim, Rudolf. 1974. *Art and Visual Perception: A Psychology of the Creative Eye*. Berkeley: University of California Press.

Balter, Michael. 2002. "From a Modern Human's Brow—or Doodling?" *Science* 295: 247–248.

Baudrillard, Jean. 1994. *Simulacra and Simulation*. Ann Arbor, MI: University of Michigan Press.

Bense, Max. 1971. "The Projects of Generative Aesthetics." In *Cybernetics, Art, and Ideas*, edited by Jasis Reichardt, 207. Greenwich, CT: New York Graphic Society.

Benthall, Jonathan. 1972. *Science and Technology in Art Today*. New York: Praeger.

Bentley, Peter, and David Corne. 2002. "An Introduction to Creative Evolutionary Systems." In *Creative Evolutionary Systems*, edited by Peter Bentley and David Corne, 1–75. San Francisco/San Diego, CA: Morgan Kaufmann/Academic Press.

Berlyne, Daniel E. 1971. *Aesthetics and Psychobiology*. New York: Appleton-Century-Crofts.

Birkhoff, George D. 1933. *Aesthetic Measure*. Cambridge, MA: Harvard University Press.

Boden, Margaret A. 2004. *The Creative Mind: Myths and Mechanisms*. London and New York: Routledge.

Bois, Yves A., Jack Cowart, Alfred Pacquement, et al. 1992. *Ellsworth Kelly: The Years in France, 1948–1954*. Washington, DC/Munich: National Gallery of Art/Prestel-Verlag.

Burroughs, William S. 1962. *The Ticket That Exploded*. Paris: Olympia Press.

Burroughs, William S., and Brion Gysin. 1978. *The Third Mind*. New York: Viking Press.

Carroll, Noel. 1999. *Philosophy of Art: A Contemporary Introduction*. London and New York: Routledge.

Draves, Scott. 2005. "The Electric Sheep Screen-Saver: A Case Study in Aesthetic Evolution." *Applications of Evolutionary Computing, Proceedings* 3449: 458–467.

Escher, M.C., F. Bool, and J.L. Locher. 1982. *M.C. Escher, His Life and Complete Graphic Work: With a Fully Illustrated Catalogue*. New York: H.N. Abrams.

Fogel, Lawrence J. 1999. *Intelligence through Simulated Evolution: Forty Years of Evolutionary Programming*. New York: Wiley & Sons Inc.

Galanter, Philip. 2003. "What Is Generative Art? Complexity Theory as a Context for Art Theory." Proceedings of the International Conference on Generative Art, Milan, Italy. Generative Design Lab, Milan Polytechnic: City.

Galanter, Philip. 2006. "Generative Art and Rules-based Art." *Vague Terrain*.

Galanter, Philip. 2008. "What is Complexism? Generative Art and the Cultures of Science and the Humanities." Proceedings of the International Conference on Generative Art, Milan, Italy Generative Design Lab, Milan Polytechnic: City.

Galanter, Philip. 2009. "Thoughts on Computational Creativity." Proceedings of the Computational Creativity: An Interdisciplinary Approach, Dagstuhl, Germany. Schloss Dagstuhl - Leibniz-Zentrum fürr Informatik, Germany: City.

Galanter, Philip. 2012. "Computational Aesthetic Evaluation: Past and Future." In *Computers and Creativity*, edited by Jon McCormack and Mark D'inverno. Berlin: Springer.

Gell-Mann, Murray. 1995. "What Is Complexity?" *Complexity* 1(1): 16–19.
Gilpin, Kyle, and Daniela Rus. 2010. "Self-disassembling Robot Pebbles: New Results and Ideas for Self-Assembly of 3D Structures." *IEEE International Conference on Robotics and Automation* Workshop Modular Robots: The State of the Art, 94–99.
Gilpin, Kyle, and Daniela Rus. 2012. "What's in the Bag: A Distributed Approach to 3D Shape Duplication with Modular Robots." *Robotics: Science and Systems*. http://www.roboticsproceedings.org/rss08/p12.pdf (accessed September 30, 2015).
Ginkgo_Biolabs. 2012. "BioBrick Assembly Manual." http://ginkgobioworks.com/support/BioBrick_Assembly_Manual.pdf (accessed January 15, 2015).
Greenberg, Clement. 1986. "Modernist Painting." In *Clement Greenberg: The Collected Essays and Criticism*, edited by J. O'Brian. Chicago, IL: University of Chicago Press.
Gross, Roderich, Michael Bonani, Francesco Mondada, and Marco Dorigo. 2006. "Autonomous Self-assembly in Swarm-bots." *IEEE Transactions on Robotics* 22: 1115–1130.
Hargittai, Istvan, and Magdolna Hargittai. 1994. *Symmetry: A Unifying Concept*. Bolinas and Berkeley, CA: Shelter Publications. Distributed in the USA by Ten Speed Press.
iGem. 2009. "E. Chromi." http://2009.igem.org/Team:Cambridge/Project (accessed January 15, 2015).
LeWitt, Sol. 1967. "Paragraphs on Conceptual Art." *Artforum* 5(10).
Lorenz, Edward N. 1963. "Deterministic Nonperiodic Flow." *Journal of the Atmospheric Sciences* 20: 130–141.
Lovejoy, Margot. 2004. *Digital Currents: Art in the Electronic Age*. New York: Routledge.
Machado, Penousal, and Amilcar Cardoso. 2002. "All the Truth About NEvAr." *Applied Intelligence* 16: 101–118.
Mandelbrot, Benoit B. 1983. *The Fractal Geometry of Nature*. San Francisco, CA: W.H. Freeman.
Martindale, Colin. 2007. "A Neural-Network Theory of Beauty." In *Evolutionary and Neurocognitive Approaches to Aesthetics, Creativity, and the Arts*, edited by Colin Martindale, Paul Locher, and Vladimir M. Petrov, 181–194. Amityville, NY: Baywood.
McCorduck, Pamela. 1991. *Aaron's Code: Meta-Art, Artificial Intelligence, and the Work of Harold Cohen*. New York: W.H. Freeman.
McCormack, Jon, Oliver Bown, Alan Dorin, Jonathan Mccabe, Gordon Monro, and Mitchell Whitelaw. 2014. "Ten Questions Concerning Generative Computer Art (Preprint)." *Leonardo* 47(2): 135–141. Cambridge, MA: The MIT Press.
Meyer, James S. 2000. *Minimalism*. London: Phaidon.
Meyer, James S. 2001. *Minimalism: Art and Polemics in the Sixties*. New Haven, CT: Yale University Press.
Mitchell, Melanie. 2009. *Complexity: A Guided Tour*. Oxford and New York: Oxford University Press.
Moles, Abraham A. 1966. *Information Theory and Esthetic Perception*. Urbana, IL: University of Illinois Press.
Nyman, Michael. 1999. *Experimental Music: Cage and Beyond*. Cambridge and New York: Cambridge University Press.
Osborne, Harold. 1981. *The Oxford Companion to Twentieth-Century Art*. Oxford and New York: Oxford University Press.
Perlin, Ken. 1985. "An Image Synthesizer." *SIGGRAPH Computer Graphics* 19(3): 287–296.
Prusinkiewicz, Przemyslaw, Aristid Lindenmayer, and James Hanan. 1990. *The Algorithmic Beauty of Plants*. New York: Springer Verlag.
Rose, Bernice, Judy Knipe, Patricia Hughes, and PaceWildenstein. 2005. *Logical Conclusions: 40 Years of Rule-based Art*. New York: PaceWildenstein.

Schwanauer, Stephan M., and David A. Levitt. 1993. *Machine Models of Music.* Cambridge, MA: The MIT Press.

Serra, Richard, Clara Weyergraf-Serra, and Hudson River Museum. 1980. *Richard Serra, Interviews, etc., 1970–1980.* Yonkers, NY: Hudson River Museum. Distributed by Art Catalogues.

Shannon, Claude E. 1948. "A Mathematical Theory of Communication." *The Bell System Technical Journal* 27: 379–423.

Sims, Karl. 1991. "Artificial Evolution for Computer-Graphics." *Siggraph 91 Conference Proceedings,* 25: 319–328.

Sims, Karl. 1994. "Evolving 3D Morphology and Behavior by Competition." In *Artificial Life IV: Proceedings of the Fourth International Workshop on the Synthesis and Simulation of Living Systems,* edited by Rodney A. Brooks and Pattie Maes. Cambridge, MA: The MIT Press.

Sims, Karl. 1997. "Galápagos Interactive Exhibit." http://www.karlsims.com/galapagos/index.html (accessed January 15, 2015).

Skov, Martin, and Oshin Vartanian. 2009. "Introduction—What Is Neuroaesthetics?" In *Neuroaesthetics: Foundations and Frontiers in* Aesthetic, edited by Martin Skov and Oshin Vartanian. Amityville, NY: Baywood.

Sobieszek, Robert A., and William S. Burroughs. 1996. *Ports of Entry: William S. Burroughs and the Arts.* Los Angeles: Los Angeles County Museum of Art. Distributed in the USA by Thames & Hudson.

Soddu, Celestino. 1998. *Generative Art: Proceedings of the 1998 Milan First International Conference of Generative Art '98.* Rome: Librerie Dedalo.

Tasajärvi, Lassi. 2004. *Demoscene: The Art of Real-Time.* Finland: Even Lake Studios.

Todd, Peter M., and Gregory M. Werner. 1998. "Frankensteinian Methods for Evolutionary Music Composition." In *Musical Networks: Parallel Distributed Perception and Performance,* edited by Niall Griffith & Peter M. Todd. Cambridge, MA: The MIT Press/Bradford Books.

Todd, Stephan, and William Latham. 1992. *Evolutionary Art and Computers.* London and San Diego: Academic Press.

Turing, Alan. 1952. "The Chemical Basis of Morphogenesis." *Philosophical Transactions of the Royal Society: Biological Sciences* 237: 37–72.

Turk, Greg. 1991. "Generating Textures on Arbitrary Surfaces Using Reaction-Diffusion." In *Proceedings of the 18th Annual Conference on Computer Graphics and Interactive Techniques,* ACM: 289–298.

Vasulka, Steina, and Woody Vasulka. 2001. "Steina and Woody Vasulka: Instrumental Video." Daniel Langlois Foundation. http://www.fondation-langlois.org/e/collection/vasulka/archives/ (accessed January 15, 2015).

Vickery, Lindsay. 2012. "The Evolution of Notational Innovations from the Mobile Score to the Screen Score." *Organised Sound* 17(8): 128–136.

Waldrop, M. Mitchell. 1992. *Complexity: The Emerging Science at the Edge of Order and Chaos.* New York: Simon & Schuster.

Ward, Adrian, and Geoff Cox. 1999. "How I Drew One of My Pictures: * or, The Authorship of Generative Art." In *International Conference on Generative Art.* Milan: Generative Design Lab.

Washburn, Dorothy K., and Donald W. Crowe. 1988. *Symmetries of Culture: Theory and Practice of Plane Pattern Analysis.* Seattle, WA: University of Washington Press.

Zelevansky, Lynn, Valerie Hillings, and Los Angeles County Museum of Art. 2004. *Beyond Geometry: Experiments in Form, 1940s–70s.* Cambridge, MA: The MIT Press.

6

Digital Art at the Interface of Technology and Feminism

Jennifer Way

This chapter examines how digital art engages with feminist approaches to making sense of technology. In particular, these approaches emphasize how "[w]omens identities, needs and priorities are configured together with digital technologies" (Wajcman 2010, 151). Key to the discussion is that we appreciate the digital nature of digital art as technology. According to Nathan Ensmenger,

> No technological development of the past century is considered to be as profoundly influential as the invention of the electronic digital computer. Indeed, in most contemporary contexts, the word "technology" has come to mean computer technology. (Ensmenger 2012, 756)

The artworld figures among these contemporary contexts. In defining digital art, typically, it conflates technology with digital computing and computer hardware and software (Wands 2006, 14). Therefore, here we adopt the artworld's own perception about digital art. Crucially, doing so enables us to inquire how specific examples of digital art intersect with the significance that feminist and social constructivist scholars attribute to technology.

For one thing, these scholars allow that "different groups of people involved with a technology [...] can have very different understandings of that technology, including different understandings of its technical characteristics" (MacKenzie and Wajcman 1999, 21). Feminist historians of technology in particular employ a range of ideas associated with feminist theory and research methodologies to understand women's involvement with technology in the past and present. Additionally, they study how, in relation to technology, people are gendered female or male, and they analyze ways that technology creates, stabilizes, and modifies gender identities and differences, including inequalities. Furthermore, they hold that "the increasingly complex intertwining of gender and technoscience [is] an ongoing process of mutual shaping over

A Companion to Digital Art, First Edition. Edited by Christiane Paul.

time and across multiple sites" (Wajcman 2010, 150). Correspondingly, these scholars agree that gender shapes what technology is, how it works, what it is used for, what its effects are, and why it is important. Overall, feminist technology scholars embrace a "social constructivist framework" that treats "technology as both a source and consequence of gender relations" (Wajcman 2010, 149).

Women digital artists, especially, have taken up these ideas. For example, the notion that gender can distinguish "different groups of people involved with a technology" or impact "very different understandings of that technology" follows from a precept that the artists share with the scholars: "[o]bjects and artefacts are no longer seen as separate from society, but as part of the social fabric that holds society together; they are never merely technical or social" (Wajcman 2010, 148–149). Wajcman's assertion that technology unites society resonates for constructivist scholars of technology, too. An example of a constructivist approach involves grouping together things that are considered technology, for instance, computers, with activities and behaviors that relate to them, like programming, to understand how jointly they are "inextricably intertwined with a larger system of computing that include[s] not just machines, but also people and processes" (Ensmenger 2012, 763).

Similarly, in their writing and art, many women digital artists explore how people engage with "machines (computers) and processes (computing)" along with software as "more information-processing technologies than just the electronic computer" (Ensmenger 2012, 758–759). Principally, they investigate technology in regard to the social and cultural contexts of its creation and uses. Also important have been the artists' interest in how gender and technology impact one another through time. Wajcman observes that "[s]uch a mutual shaping approach recognizes that the gendering of technology affects the entire life trajectory of an artefact" (Wajcman 2010, 149). Beyond the artifact, "[t]he gendering of technologies can then be understood as not only shaped in design, but also shaped or reconfigured at the multiple points of consumption and use" (Wajcman 2010, 150).

These ideas illuminate the significance of technology in regard to the works of art and projects discussed in the sections that follow. At the outset, however, they compel us to inquire why we lack accounts of women who participated in the first generation of artists to embrace digital computing. In regard to the 1980s through the 1990s and beyond, they clarify why and how artists who considered themselves feminist created alternatives to visual representations of women appearing in popular digital culture. Subsequently, as new definitions of feminism have arisen, we shall find that in their work women digital artists have engaged with networked feminism, DIY feminism, technofeminism, hacktivist pedagogy, and fabriculture.

Exclusions and Exceptions

> The "world without women" narrative is largely a story about the history of the exclusion of women from scientific and technical fields, and about the consequences of this exclusion for the symbolic coding of technology as "masculine."
>
> Knut Sorensen, Wendy Faulkner, and Els Rommes,
> *Technologies of Inclusion*, 46

Scholars of the history of technology show that since the 19th century, as modern Western societies attributed the ability to create and wield technology to men, concurrently they socialized women to perceive that what technology consists of, how it works, and what it may be used for is beyond their ken. Until recently we have not possessed the intellectual tools to make sense of or redress this distancing of women from technology. Feminist scholar Ruth Oldenziel reminds us that "the word technology [...] did not enter American culture as a key word until World War II," nor did "women," "gender," or phrases like "gendering of technology" appear in mainstays of technology research until later (2002, 55). For example, not until 1959 did the Society for the History of Technology begin to publish its journal, *Technology and Culture*. Then, more than a decade would pass before the journal began to include articles concerning women. Mainly, women historians wrote about women using appliances in the home.

Wajcman says that the "initial challenge for feminists" was "to demonstrate that the enduring identification between technology and manliness is not inherent in biological sex difference" (Wajcman 2010, 144). As Susanna Paasonen explains, feminist technology scholars showed that "ties between men and technology are not questions of 'inner nature' but of social practices and cultural signification, acts of evaluation, classification and exclusion" (Paasonen 2005, 171). Equally, these scholars identified how masculinity came to be conflated with technology, to the exclusion of women. Oldenziel would report how "[m]achines became a dominant metaphor, model, and material embodiment of [technology's] subject matter and, as such, a symbol of male power" (Oldenziel 2002, 56). Cockburn (1992), Oldenziel (2002), and Wajcman (2010) respectively traced features of the history Cockburn called "technoscience" (41), which involved what Wajcman charted as the growth of the disciplinary knowledge and professional practice of technoscience as "male power." As Wajcman wrote,

> mechanical and civil engineering increasingly came to define what technology is, diminishing the significance of both artefacts and forms of knowledge associated with women. This was the result of the rise of engineers as an elite with exclusive rights to technical expertise. (Wajcman 2010, 144)

Along with this went "the creation of a male professional identity" that "involved an ideal of manliness, characterized by the cultivation of bodily prowess and individual achievement" (Wajcman 2010, 144). Feminist technology scholars say that, by and large, we continue to treat men as having a greater affinity for creating and using technology than women. Wajcman even contends that "in contemporary Western society, the hegemonic form of masculinity is still strongly associated with technical prowess and power" (2010, 145). For this reason, academic institutions and philanthropic organizations target a digital divide that sees fewer women than men mastering the technologies that translate into higher income jobs. Also, educational programs devote special attention to preparing college-age and young professional women to enter and succeed in the STEM fields—science, technology, education, and mathematics. Others target younger ages. For fifteen years the Squeaky Wheel/Buffalo Media Resources has hosted TechARTS for Girls, founded by Mary Flanagan as "a community action project that encourages girls from the city of Buffalo and Erie County to receive an affordable hands-on education in computers, technology and media literacy" (Squeaky Wheel 2013).

Complicating ideas about how to bring an end to the digital divide is what Jan Abbate calls "a much-discussed paradox": "women's numbers in computing have declined since the mid-1980s in the United States and United Kingdom, even as women's participation in other areas of science and technology has risen" (Abbate 2012, 2). This paradox motivates some technology scholars to investigate persistent links between men, power, and computing. For example, Jason Tocci reminds us that popular culture associates computing with geek identity—"the tech-savvy, pop-culture-obsessed, socially-awkward misfit and underdog"—to signify men in ways that are negative as well as positive, and yet on both counts equally dismissive of women (Tocci 2009, 4). Melinda Justine Rhoades suggests that male dominance in technology segues from perceptions to realities governing who can master and practice it:

> If males continue to populate and dominate the computer technology field, as technology exerts increasing sociocultural influence, technology will increasing[ly] reflect masculine concerns, creations, and desires in a self-perpetuating cycle. (Rhoades 2008, 22)

The American artist Christine Tamblyn had already stressed that knowledge was vital to breaking these cycles. In 1995, she wrote:

> One of the reasons that women are in an economically powerless position is that they possess a fraction of the world's technological expertise. Knowledge about making or using tools or machines makes it possible for those who have it to dominate both matter and other people. (Tamblyn 1995, 102)

Abbate and other scholars also call attention to problems with histories of technology. Specifically, the ways these histories are told plus criteria for including people in them fail to redress widely held perceptions that women have not participated in creating or modifying technology. Abbate explains,

> Until the 1980s, women as historical actors were largely neglected in histories of science and technology, and one of the central projects of academic feminism has been to restore women's contributions to the record. (Abbate 2012, 4)

To be sure, attempts to write women into the record stimulated efforts to explain why they were absent in the first place. Yet, Abbate concludes, "[m]ost of the books that look specifically at women have focused on a few exceptional individuals" (2012, 5). They ignore communities and groups along with broadly shared experiences. What is more, Abbate charges the very definition of technology with excluding women from its histories:

> early histories of computing largely equated computing with hardware. This narrow focus led to a relative neglect of software, theoretical computer science, and the practice of programming. Since women rarely had the chance to participate in building computers, the initial focus on hardware unintentionally biased the history of computing toward the activities of men. (Abbate 2012, 6)

Technological determinism kept women out of histories of technology, too. In narrative terms, it cast technology as a protagonist driving its own development, which ostensibly caused social and cultural change. In this role technology paid no heed to forces that aligned the consciousness and actions of its makers and users with gender norms. Thus, if technological determinism "envisions new possibilities and promises change," it also endorses an "empirical account of the world" instead of one nuanced to explicate how gender and technology intertwine to reinforce patriarchy and sexism in technological environments and in their histories. For all of these reasons, as Grant Taylor charges, "[t]he impact of women in the formation of early digital art has been largely ignored"; moreover, "women's contributions are often minimized or ignored as technology is historicized through masculine discourse" (Taylor 2013).

What is more, at times the postwar American artworld prevented women from participating in key art and technology developments. Here is one example. During the late 1960s, many of the scholars, critics, curators, and artists who associated with the nascent American feminist art movement were committed to recovering the work of historical women artists whom canonical art history ignored. Soon they would also debate how to answer the question that art historian Linda Nochlin posed in 1971: "Why have there been no great women artists?" Interestingly, in summarizing research that responded to Nochlin, sixteen years later Thalia Gouma-Peterson and Patricia Mathews noted that she

> challenged the myth of the great artist as one who is endowed with that mysterious and ineffable quality called genius. However, as Norma Broude later pointed out, she did not question the authority or validity of the male-defined notion of greatness and artistic achievement. (Gouma-Peterson and Mathews 1987, 327)

To this last point, also during 1971, the Los Angeles County Museum of Art (LACMA) was merging technology with masculinity, special knowledge, and artistic achievement. For its exhibition *Art and Technology* LACMA represented technology as an economic and social force that could generate new cultural forms, including those resulting from novel ways of making art. LACMA demonstrated the latter by setting up collaborations between artists and non-art specialists in engineering, science, and other technology fields. The museum displayed the collaborators' completed work in *Art and Technology*. A major problem, however, was that LACMA failed to include women, and their absence "set off a storm of protest, resulting in the formation of the Los Angeles Council of Women [Artists] (LACWA)." The *L.A. Free Press* reported that LACWA pronounced:

> We were particularly provoked by the blatant discrimination against women in the highly publicized Art and Technology show new at the Los Angeles County Museum of Art. Sixteen artists are represented in this invitational show—NONE are women, NONE of the technical advisors with whom they collaborated were women. (L.A. Free Press 1971, 98)

Moreover, LACWA observed,

> The Art and Technology show has been heralded as the wave of the future. If this is so, then we are most distressed to observe that there are no women in it. Distressed, but not surprised. Women in our patriarchal society are supposed to be consumers, not producers. The more museums and artists ally themselves with big corporations, which are sexist by definition, the more the art world will have a vested interest in ignoring the works of women artists. (L.A. Free Press 1971)

LACWA implied that in disregarding women artists for collaborations in *Art and Technology*, the museum plainly expressed how "Women's identities, needs and priorities are configured together with" technology in a patriarchal society (Wajcman 2010, 151). In other words, LACWA made sense of the museum's representation of technology in the context of "a larger system of computing that included not just machines, but also people and processes" (Ensmenger 2012, 763) that encompassed "big corporations." Boldly, LACWA drew attention to the possibility that the museum's gendering of technology as masculine foretold conditions that would continue "holding society together" in the future (Wajcman 2010, 148–149).

Inclusions

> Thinking from inclusion means asking questions about why women might be interested in I[formation]C[ommunication]T[echnology] (as opposed to why they are not).
>
> Compared to an exclusion approach, an emphasis on inclusion therefore promises to provide better insights into what it is that makes (particular) ICTs relevant to (particular) people's lives, and what motivates them to engage with technology.
>
> Knut Sorensen, Wendy Faulkner, and Els Rommes, *Technologies of Inclusion*, 39

Nevertheless, a female curator, artist, and critic respectively would curate and publish some of the first accounts of art and computing: Jasia Reichardt, *Cybernetic Serendipity, The Computer and the Arts* (1968, ICA, London); Ruth Leavitt, *Artist and Computer* (1976); and Cynthia Goodman, *Digital Visions, Computers and Art* (1987). This is not to say these authors adopted feminist perspectives in making sense of their topics. Still, at least each referenced some women artists. Arguably, though, much work remains if we are to fulfill the task that the cyberfeminist art collective subRosa proposed: to "make visible the effects of the interconnections of technology, gender, and difference" (subRosa 2002). To do this requires us to revisit women artists who managed to work with technology at a time when artworld institutions tended to ignore them.

Remarkably, emerging research indicates that we may be able to clarify some longstanding beliefs about situations we had thought precluded women from using computing to make art. One example concerns the assumption that "the electronic networks which we know as the Internet have inherited a problematic relationship with gender from their roots within the military-industrial complex and in academic institutions" (Wakeford 1997, 52). Taylor studied "the first women involved in computer-generated art"—"women programmers working [...] at the Army Ballistic Research Laboratories (BRL) in Aberdeen, Maryland." Their art aside, these women took part in what he says "was originally a highly feminized occupation" (2013). Therefore, even if we hold that computing originated in a male-oriented "military-industrial complex and in academic institutions," we may surmise that these institutions' gendered dimensions did not prevent their women employees from creating art with technology. Moreover, we must raise additional questions, such as whether then-dominant ways of thinking about gender and technology shaped the women programmers' jobs or impacted their computer-generated art.

Taylor also studied specific individuals. For example, Lillian Schwartz, he learned, "made the decision in 1968 to employ computers to create art"; Rebecca Allen and others pursued computing in art, too. These women gravitated toward the opportunities for creative research that were just beginning to take root in "university research centers, such MIT, NYIT, Brown University, and the University of Illinois, while others started at corporate settings, such as Bell Labs, TIME Corp, and 3M" (2013). Importantly, this component of Taylor's scholarship suggests that "different groups of [women] involved with a technology [...] can have very different understandings of that technology" (MacKenzie and Wajcman 1999, 21). Consequently, the choices these women made about their work environments varied in part because they approached technology as part of "a larger system of computing that included not just machines, but also people and processes" (Ensmenger 2012, 763).

This last idea suggests Radhika Gajjala and Annapurna Mamidipuni's questioning "the conclusion that 'gendering' always occurs to the disadvantage of women in all technological environments across cultures, histories and various locales" (Gajjala and Mamidipuni 2002; Bratich and Brush 2011, 243). Did the women artists who first practiced digital computing experience gendered environments that impeded or facilitated their art? Taylor says that

> [a]t this leading edge, computing was far less defined, highly experimental, and less prone to the stifling weight of institutionalization. Moreover, during the last years of the 1960s, computer science was only just emerging as a legitimate scientific field. (Taylor 2013)

In the military, university, or corporate lab, did the newness of computer science expedite women's artistic agendas in ways that using other media to make art, in other milieu, could not? It is also fascinating to speculate whether traditional gender identities for familiar materials influenced women artists' choices to bring them into computing.

Oblique Wave (1979) (Figure 6.1) represents the kind of work Joan Truckenbrod made during the mid- to late 1970s: "a computer-generated design representing slight variations in the parameters of [an algorithmic computing] program written by the artist" (Goodman 1987, 45). Truckenbrod wrote her algorithms for the Apple IIe desktop computer she obtained by submitting a successful grant to Apple. Yet, essentially, did she treat computing as a technique for advancing the fiber arts, so heavily populated by women artists? After all, she applied the images her computing generated onto cloth. Gallerist Cynthia Goodman described the process: "once each design is completed, the artist placed a computer monitor on a 3M color-in-color copier machine and made a copy of it, which was heat transferred onto the fabric by ironing" (Goodman 1987, 45). Conversely, did Truckenbrod make sense of her activity as furthering computing as well as mathematics, the latter having a long history of contributing to textile production?

Truckenbrod numbered among the early digital artists who raised concerns about technology in the studio. Goodman recounted that when Truckenbrod participated in "The Aesthetics of Computer Art," a panel for SIGGRAPH (Special Interest Group on Graphics of the Association for Computing Imagery) held in Dallas during 1986, she questioned whether computing would monopolize artistic processes and control their outcomes (Goodman 1987, 184). What enabled Truckenbrod to gain a position of visibility and voice through SIGGRAPH? Did the organization especially support the work of women artists? Furthermore, how did Truckenbrod's concerns about using computing as an artistic method relate to her "identities, needs and priorities" as a woman artist (Wajcman 2010, 151)?

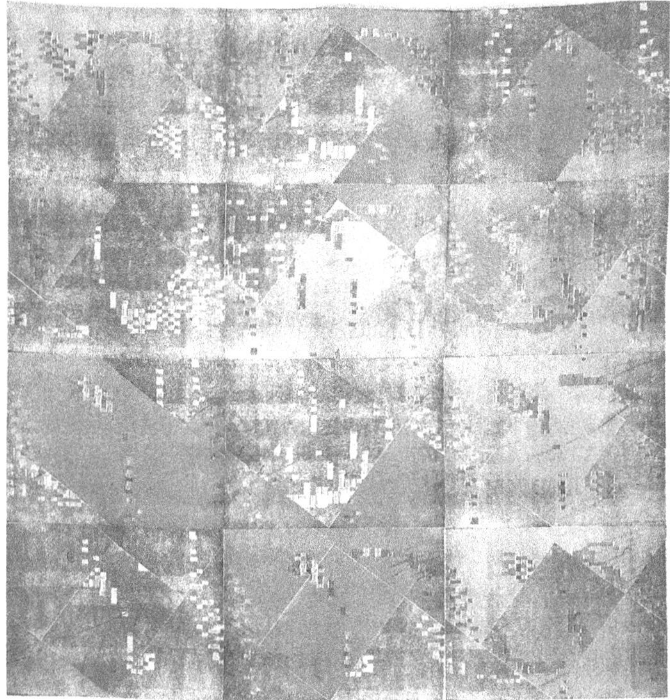

FIGURE 6.1 Joan Truckenbrod, *Oblique Wave*, 1979. Image courtesy of Joan Truckenbrod.

Cyberfeminist Critique

> We live in a time when the very rudiments of life have been measured and appropriated by the domain of technology.
>
> Marta Heberle, "Technologically Empowered Body as a Weapon"

From the mid- to late 1980s to the early 1990s, more artists began treating technology as a primary focus of their work. Some women artists focused on digital images of women appearing in popular culture. They joined together critiques of these images with efforts to foster alternatives that would advance women's empowerment in technology and society.

For example, instead of championing "an overwhelmingly positive picture of the new space known then as 'The Net'" (Hampton 2010, 66), during 1991 in Adelaide, Australia, the art collective called VNS Matrix, consisting of Virginia Barratt, Julianne Pierce, Francesca da Rimini, and Josephine Starrs, criticized this space's sexist treatments of women (Paasonen 2005, 189). VNS Matrix numbered among the first artists to attach "cyber"—referencing computers and computing—to feminism, thus generating "cyberfeminist" to signify their artistic identity. Virginia Barratt pronounced, "We use the terminology to subvert it":

> That terminology was constructed by male science fiction writers. If you read the technological future which William Gibson proposes, keyboard cowboys jacking in

> and jerking off, there's place for me there. Cyberculture seems to me to be located in a very male dominated popular culture night-club scene. (Barratt in Flynn 1994, 426)

In further response to this male-dominated scene, the collective branded themselves VNS, short for Venus, the Roman goddess of love and beauty, in combination with "Matrix," which, in addition to evoking computing resources, calls to mind the Latin word for womb, as in mater, or mother. Barratt clarified, "Our motivation is to discuss women's position and to develop a position for women" (Flynn 1994, 420).

As cyberfeminists, VNS Matrix targeted the "classic fetishistic fembot" images on the Internet and in video games (Barratt in Flynn 1994, 422). They promoted alternatives emphasizing women's agency, or ability to act with authority and control: for example, "a role model or a series of role models for young women who are still formulating their identity as women" (da Rimini in Flynn 1994, 422). Their interactive installation called *'All New Gen' Gamegirl* featured a female protagonist hero commissioned "to terminate the moral code, so we're trying to undermine the hierarchical structure, militaristic, authoritarian, hero-winners and losers aspect of the video game culture" (da Rimini in Flynn 1994, 424). Barratt identified a related concern:

> We're interested in talking about technology and the body, putting some sorts of guts and viscera into that clean and sterile environment and talking about sex. That's so antithetical to the sterile computer environment android, without flesh, without biological fluids. (Flynn 1994, 422).

In their "Cyberfeminist Manifesto for the 21st Century" (1992), VNS Matrix promulgated the female body as a source of disorder if not destruction of patriarchal technology: "we are the virus of the new world disorder/rupturing the symbolic from within/ saboteurs of big daddy mainframe." Critically, they aimed to marginalize masculinity's hold on technology by delineating computing in and through the female body and female pleasure. Their manifesto proclaimed, "the clitoris is a direct line to the matrix."

Other artists were also taking on popular digital culture depictions of women. Along with VNS Matrix, they became the precursors of today's "self-identified nerdy and geeky women [who] have used web sites to outline a different understanding of femininity and computer use" (Tocci 2009, 43). In her interactive CD-ROM project, *She Loves It, She Loves It Not* (1995), Christine Tamblyn counteracted the typical video games' "cowboy hacker, neurotic nerd or the Raymond Chandleresque, disillusioned antihero" (Tamblyn 1995, 103). She asserted,

> I intended the work to reflect the feminist agenda of combining the personal with the political so that it would address not only the general theme of women in relation to technology, but also the history of a particular woman's relation to technology. (Tamblyn 1995, 101)

Like VNS Matrix, Tamblyn integrated writing with her art to blur boundaries "between art and theory (or fiction), [and] also the boundaries between the body and the machine" (1995, 99). Yet, rather than reference a generic female body to foster women's empowerment—a key technique for VNS Matrix—Tamblyn in *She Loves It, She Loves It Not* hyperlinked her own image and voice to gender-based critiques that she laid out in themes labeled "Memory, Control, Power, Communication, Violence,

Homunculus, Labyrinth, Interactivity, The Other, Representation, [and] Ideology or Credits" (1995, 99). Tamblyn had aimed to discover what is gendered about technological forms and then improve them to facilitate interactivity for her female audience. Ultimately, she treated

> technology as a system of social practices, knowledge production and material objects [that] points out the different ways in which technology can affect gender and vice versa through a process of co-creation. (Gimenez 2009, 264)

She developed an interface she considered as "more suited to female learning proclivities" because it was "multisensory, personal, affective and dynamic" (Tamblyn 1995, 103). It resulted from her study of "the design of computer interfaces that are more user-friendly for women" and do not have a masculine bias of "a violent, aggressive character modeled on video games" or "are hierarchical, mirroring the militaristic male pyramid with its rigid chain of command" with "a predominantly visual bias, privileging the male gaze and masculine strategies for control through surveillance of territory" (Tamblyn 1995, 102–103).

In her 16 mm film *Hiatus* (1999), Ericka Beckman took aim at masculinity and power in computer games (Figure 6.2). *Hiatus* features "a woman playing a VR interactive game with logged-on game players and game identities, which confuse and trick her into consciousness" (Beckman 1994). This main character creates a garden as "a habitat that she feels most comfortable in, that she has complete control over and which empowers her." The character also creates "a construct of

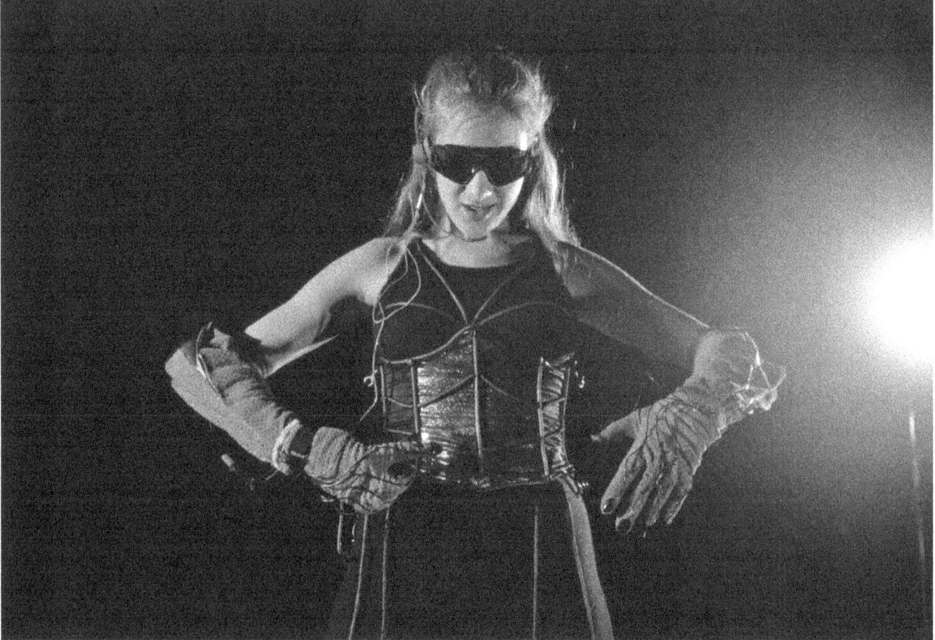

FIGURE 6.2 Ericka Beckman, *Hiatus*, 1999. 16 mm film. Screenshot.

herself (WANDA) to move around in this world." In Level 2, WANDA enters "The Frontier" consisting of "a community of Indians who challenge her to build her habitat there, but in balance with their existing culture." For help she summons a digital scarecrow who, unfortunately, "becomes an open channel, a code that someone can hack into, a telephone pole to the outer world." Next, a male intruder, WANG, threatens "to overtake her garden, the reservoir of all her power." Yet, "[s]ince WANG's world is huge and slow to render, she has time to turn this sad adventure around." Happily, WANDA learns "how to creatively block WANG's expansion and preserve her freedom" (Beckman 1994). With *Hiatus*, Beckman analyzed "dominant cultural myths of empowerment, especially the promise that technology can provide the means for individual empowerment" (Wexner Center for the Arts Film and Video and Division of Comparative Studies 1995). Akin to Tamblyn's *She Loves It, She Loves It Not*, a parallel purpose for *Hiatus* was "to inform and empower young women at a critical stage in their psychological development with self-esteem and self-reliance" (Wexner Center for the Arts 1995).

VNS Matrix, Christine Tamblyn, and Ericka Beckman respectively highlighted power "materialized in technology, and [ways that] masculinity and femininity in turn acquire their meaning and character through their environment and embeddedness in working machines" (Wajcman 2010, 149). Additionally, to empower their art's female audiences, they replaced technology as "a symbol of male power" with protagonists and opportunities to engage with technology that spoke to women's agency (Oldenziel 2002, 56). At the same time, other artists working with digital technology emphasized empowerment through community.

Networking Communities

> ... technical practices have historically embodied unequal power relations—but can also be reconceived in ways that promote greater justice.
>
> Janet Abbate, *History of Computing*, 7

These artists aimed to connect people to one another. In doing so, some revealed how emerging technology applications potentially harmed women. In general they used multimedia computer-based communications or tele-collaborative networks to link people who were geographically dispersed. Ultimately, they took advantage of the Internet's potential to facilitate "the creation of a global community who use [it] both for discussion and activism" (Munro 2013, 23). In these respects, their projects exemplified "networked feminism" (Wands 2006, 27).

Kit Galloway and Sherrie Rabinowitz's *Electronic Café* (1984) serves as an early example. The Los Angeles Museum of Contemporary Art commissioned *Electronic Café* for the summer Olympics Arts Festival of 1984. In response to the museum's charge to "link culturally diverse communities," Galloway and Rabinowitz drew upon two interrelated aspects of digital computing. One is that digitized data "can be replicated, transformed, and communicated by using an ever-increasing range of readily available technologies" (Ensmenger 2012, 769). The other concerns technological interconnectivity nurturing "an important dialogue about the role such technologies can play in fostering the invention of a new cultural interaction, and scale of artistic collaboration and inquiry" (Galloway and Rabinowitz 2002).

For seven weeks their *Electronic Café* deployed numerous "readily available technologies":

> a hybrid of computer-based communications; Keyword searchable text and pictorial databases "Community Memories"; Videoconferencing: Audioconferencing; Realtime collaborative telewriting/drawing, including the ability to collaboratively add annotations to still-video images; High resolution image printers so that activities could be documented and mounted on the wall for public view; and, the ability of any venue to broadcast sight and sound to any, or all, of the others venues. (Galloway and Rabinowitz 2002)

Galloway and Rabinowitz intended for these technologies to give rise to a lively communications network linking members of "culturally diverse communities" represented by specific sites spread throughout the region: The Gumbo House, Crenshaw (South Central LA); Ana Maria Restaurant (East LA); The 8th Street Restaurant (Korea Town) LA; Gunters Cafe (beach area) Venice; and The Museum of Contemporary Art (The Temporary Contemporary), Downtown LA; as well as internationally. Community members dialogued about technology and a host of other topics. They "could—and did—exchange drawings, photos, poems, and messages to café-goers at other locations, via the video/computer/robot equipment setups" (Caruso 1984, 16).

Importantly, as *Electronic Café* connected the communities digitally, so too it allowed for variety and diversity in the ways their members communicated. On one hand, Rabinowitz concluded that the project was "successful in that it empowered people in those communities with enough experience to describe what is desirable or what they would want as a system" (Durland 1987, 58). On the other hand, *Electronic Café* aspired to generate a commons that permitted interaction by people without technology experience. Furthermore, it gave everyone the choice to be known or remain anonymous:

> It was a place to present your ideas, register your opinions anonymously. You didn't have to sign your name. The artifacts you created—pictures, drawings, writing, computer text—either independently or collaboratively could be, if you desired, permanently stored in the community-accessible archive. People could have access to opinions without being monitored. (Durland 1987, 58)

These features of *Electronic Café* sanctioned a fundamental idea shared by networked feminists and technology constructivists: "different groups of people involved with a technology [...] can have very different understandings of that technology, including different understandings of its technical characteristics" (MacKenzie and Wajcman 1999, 21).

According to Munro, networked feminism also embraces "micropolitics and challenging sexism and misogyny insofar as they appear in everyday rhetoric, advertising, film, television and literature, the media, and so on" (Munro 2013, 23). Today, the online feminist journal of art and digital culture called *.dpi* addresses these topics by combining critiques of gender-based sexism in the visual arts with efforts to create more positive circumstances in which women artists produce and distribute their work. Established during 2004 in Montreal by Patricia Kearns, the journal's name,

.dpi, references the measurement of digital print resolution, or dots per inch. Like *Electronic Café*, *.dpi* treats community as a major interest:

> *.dpi* is a participatory and user-generated space for dialogue and community building. The journal especially welcomes both personal approaches and collaborative ways of working. By means of its blog and a biannual electronic publication, *.dpi* endeavours to provoke exchanges across different communities. (DPI Feminist Journal of Art and Digital Culture 2004)

Nonetheless, whereas *Electronic Café* sought to interconnect communities having diverse ethnic and cultural identities, from its beginnings *.dpi* embraced diversity in its specifically feminist constituents:

> Like art or technologies, feminism is inherently contentious or constantly evolving, and thus, a potential source of innovation. *.dpi* acknowledges the plurality—even the antagonism—at the basis of feminisms and welcomes bold—or better yet polemical—contributions situated within a framework of anti-oppression. (DPI Feminist Journal of Art and Digital Culture 2004)

Sophie Le-Phat Ho, the current editor-in-chief, says *.dpi* wants to safeguard individual agency and community for artists who practice these feminisms.

> In 2013, we no longer oppose "local" and "global" but we can certainly see that it is necessary to create and strengthen real community. Instead, atomized, individualistic and normative configurations of acting and thinking continually persist. In 2013, the focus should perhaps be put on self-assertion rather than simply self-representation, that is, to gain a sense of being from somewhere, of being anchored. To be able to share our personal experiences and to expand our collective struggles, across different fields and terrains. (Le-Phat Ho 2013)

What is more, in its role as an affiliate of Studio XX, "a bilingual feminist artist-centre for technological exploration, creation and critique," *.dpi* aims to balance its status as an alternative journal—"a forum that is socially and artistically committed and fundamentally alternative, allowing unconventional voices to be heard outside of mainstream or institutional discourses"—with inserting women artists into the mainstream cultural historical record: "*.dpi* was born of the desire to establish a creative and scholarly interdisciplinary platform where the contributions of women to media art history could be prolifically documented" (Studio XX). To advance the latter agenda, *.dpi* affiliates with The HTMlles, too. This international festival "occupies the singular position of being one of the only events promoting and disseminating independent media artworks with a particular emphasis on feminist approaches, concerns and engagements" (Studio XX 2012). Its 2012 iteration endorsed

> a feminism that lies at the intersection of praxis, anti-racism and anti-colonialism, sex worker solidarity, as well as queer and transpolitics. The HTMlles 10 support the convergence and merging of solidarities as well as artistic and social innovations. (Studio XX 2012)

The activist orientation of *.dpi*, Studio XX, and The HTMlles speaks to the technofeminist assertion that "only we can free ourselves. This makes a feminist politics possible and necessary" (Wajcman 2004). Wajcman says that technofeminists believe

> Feminist politics has made a difference, and we can build upon the difference it has made. We do not live in a world that is post-feminist, but we do live in a world that feminism has shaped and will continue to shape. (Wajcman 2004)

For *.dpi*, Studio XX, and The HTMlles, this entails supporting women artists by providing alternative venues accessible within mainstream sites. Similarly, feminist scholars Katherine Behar and Silvia Ruzanka say that in contrast to the recent past, now it is necessary to maintain online places "for [feminist] dialogue and community building" that avoid the major mainstream search engines and web sites:

> Nostalgia for surfing the web is also nostalgia for the open possibilities of a still-undefined terrain—nostalgia for a moment when hierarchies were leveled and multinational corporations stood on the same footing as anyone's home page filled with animated GIFs and neon blinking text. This was the 1990s Net culture that supported cyberfeminism at its height. It may sting a bit for those who miss the old days before the Search Giants came in and everything changed. Digital feminisms should be—must be—"ungoogleable." (Behar and Ruzanka 2013)

Behar and Ruzanka contend that the "[s]earch Giants came in and changed everything" in ways that intensified gender inequalities online. As a result, they caution web-based feminism to avoid conventional "Net culture." Vanderhoef (2013) reminds us that according to Kafai et al. (2008), "the same issues of gender representation that plagued video games and their industry in the 90's still persist, regardless of the increased female player base." Digital games capitalize on imagery and behavior to reinforce traditional gender relationships associated with technology. This reinforcement "places the masculine in the superior position and the feminine in the inferior position, the result of which is the reproduction and perpetuation of gender inequalities." Nor does the situation change when the gaming industry pursues women players. In this case, players denigrate the games "as feminine, and therefore 'trivial'"; they celebrate traditional video games "for their seriousness and authenticity, both of which are qualities nested in masculinity" (Vanderhoef 2013). Ultimately, Vanderhoef argues, "[t]he consequences of this are far reaching and can be seen to perpetuate the dearth of females in science and technology sectors, among other social inequalities" (Vanderhoef 2013).

Interestingly, the feminist collective subRosa, active since 1998, continues to place some of its work online to call attention to the ways technology encroaches upon women's bodies. For a 2011 conference devoted to the topic of risk, subRosa contributed their net art project *SmartMom* (1999, redesigned in 2000 and 2009). One of its images features military "Smart" clothing fitted to the torso of a generic female body (Figure 6.3). The clothing's straps and wiring evoke surveillance mechanisms that the technology industry makes for the military. On the female body they cover the breasts and belly. One implication is that major social institutions—the military and perhaps also the government and the medical establishment—value women primarily as bodies having reproductive potential that, like an unknown or enemy target, ostensibly requires supervision if not control.

With this facet of *SmartMom* subRosa is teasing out for critique whether uses of certain technologies are "smart." According to Wajcman's scholarship, subRosa practices

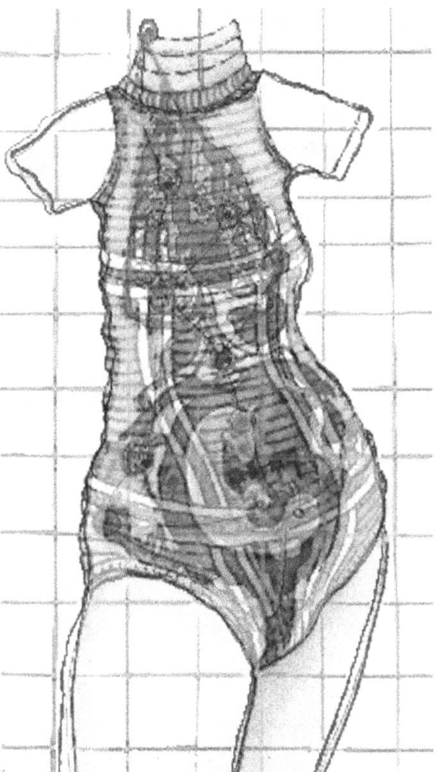

FIGURE 6.3 subRosa, *SmartMom* sensate dress, 1999.

> a technofeminist perspective [that] points beyond the discourse of the digital divide to the connections between gender inequality and other forms of inequality, which come into view if we examine the broader political and economic basis of the networks that shape and deploy technical systems. (Wajcman 2004)

These networks, subRosa purports, link together "new bio and medical technologies and women's health; and the changed conditions of labor and reproduction for women in the integrated circuit" (subRosa 2011, 17). Here, subRosa's activism challenges the purpose, efficacy, and ethics of treating women's bodies as targets for technologically assisted reproduction and surveillance. Consequently, subRosa asks those who see their work on the Internet to grasp how "the broader political and economic basis of … [technology] networks" intersect with certain groups that ultimately "embody[their] unequal power relations" (Abbate 2012, 7).

Hacktivist Pedagogy

Questions of power and technology also predominate for digital artists interested in social media in everyday communication. Some of these artists take an interest in the

> clear procedures that structure how we present ourselves, and […] dozens of small, formalized micro-interactions that shape how we relate online, from the instantaneous and semantically ambiguous "poke" to what may (without irony) be considered

> the longer forms of social media: the "tweet" and "status update" (140 and 420 characters of text maximum, respectively). (Schoenbeck 2012, 158)

Additionally, these artists inquire how rhetoric from the technology industry skews realizations about struggle in everyday life. As Mayer observes,

> Who cares about HD and 4G, much less net-locality, when you don't have power to begin with? In short, we cannot overlook the impacts of neoliberal governance, specifically the disinvestment in public goods and the privatization of basic utilities, on a supposedly techno-centric society. (Mayer 2012)

As an example, Do It Yourself (DIY) feminists thrive in making the "micro-interactions" key to using technology transparent to women. Thereby, they aim to increase women's participation and empowerment in a "techno-centric society."

Typically, DIY feminists consider teaching a form of activism that achieves these ends. This has motivated DIY to become acutely aware of where teaching technology to women falls short. As a result, DIY feminists take on

> complex issues embedded (and often taken for granted) in technological contexts. For example, an instructor who revises a course to make the content more relevant and engaging to women, and yet maintains a traditional pedagogy emphasizing competition and individual accomplishment, has not recognized the importance of reforming the experience of women in these disciplines. (Jackson 2007, 150)

To this end, *.dpi* and Studio XX hold that before women can change the nature of power in a "techno-centric society," they often first need help learning how to use its hardware and software.

Kathleen Kennedy, a member of Studio XX, recalls:

> It was only when I bought my first Power Mac that year that I realized there was a real digital divide, economically and ideologically keeping women at arm's length from the burgeoning technological revolution. Women were intimidated by the idea of working with technology then in a way that feels incomprehensible now. (Kennedy 2006)

To give another example, the editor of *.dpi* wrote that before and during 2007, artist Limor Fried, known as Ladyada, "release[d] much of her work in the form of DIY kits or instruction sets, including persistence of vision displays for bikes, a home brew synthesizer and a game Grrrl portable Nintendo" (Le-Phat Ho 2007).

Consequently, Le-Phat Ho characterizes Ladyada's kits as "hacktivism"—a contraction of hacking and activism—that "can be broadly understood as representing a source of technology mediated radical political (direct) actions or, in other words, hacking for a political cause" (Le-Phat Ho 2007). Ladyada repackaged existing technology for a purpose for which it wasn't intended—learning. Intent on demystifying how technology works so that women could make and use it for their own purposes, she distributed this material widely. As Sophie Toupin explains, hacktivism "is not strictly the importation of activist techniques into the digital realm. Rather it is the expression of hacker skills in the form of electronic direct action" (Toupin 2013).

In response to being asked, "So do you see it is still relevant being pro-active with regards to the place of women in technology?" Ladyada says, "I think a lot of it is having more female instructors, which helps a lot. I'm not a good teacher, but I try to teach because, again, subverting the paradigm" (Le-Phat Ho 2007).

Ladyada's method of challenging women's disassociation from technology dovetails with a tradition of feminism that uses pedagogy to accelerate women's social and cultural emancipation through technology. On this last point, media and technology scholar Andrea Zeffiro (2008) considers "the ability to circumvent institutional structures of dissemination" that fail to equip women to use technology requires feminist intervention. In her dissertation on technology and art education, Rhoades outlines what may help in traditional educational settings:

> Gender and technology research supports applying feminist pedagogy within technology education. Important pedagogical success factors for women in technology include: 1) collaborative, hands-on, practical, holistic application; 2) mentors, role models, guidance, and network connections; 3) service and work-based learning projects; 4) real purpose; 5) high expectations, quality program implementation, and outside support and encouragement; and 6) the recognition and treatment of individuals as such. (Rhoades 2008, 29)

However, more along the lines of what Zeffiro advises, during the past few years ad hoc programs arose to provide alternatives to "hackerspaces [that] are generally dominated by (white) men, where a particular 'dudecore' culture might be explicitly or implicitly foregrounded"; "such a space might be less inviting to women, queers and people of colour, demographics that are often largely missing from hackerspaces" (Toupin 2013). During 2010, Stefanie Wuschitz and Lesley Flanigan collaboratively ran an interactive art workshop at Harvestworks in New York City, aiming "to playfully demystify technology and open up an atmosphere where learning new technological tools is fearless, interesting and clear for women artists" (Harvestworks Team Lab 2010). The following year, MzTek in London provided "opportunities for women to creatively explore and expand their experience of working with technology" and "create a network of women techie artists" (MzTek 2009–2013). In 2012, at Intervention's Cultural Space of A Coruña University (UDC) in Normal, Spain, the group Elas Fan Tech (Women Making Tech) offered workshops that included software and experimental art, another on Open Frameworks, and a third on Modul8 and Madmapper (Madmapper 2013). These initiatives fused hands-on learning with interactivity, a prevailing characteristic of a broad, contemporary desire to "hold [technology] in our hands, play with, change, break and put [it] back together" (Anable 2008, 49). As they reconfigured existing technologies for educational purposes, these artists underscored the fact that a digital divide still exists in the artworld.

Representation, Change, and Fabriculture

In closing, it is worth noting three related themes that deserve the attention of technology scholars and artists.

One concerns representation. Today, scholarly interest in digital computing and art sidelines questions of visual representation. Unfortunately, gender does not fall outside the politics of images and visibility. Questions to keep in mind include, in digital art, "[w]o is and is not seen? What are the thresholds of visibility? What [and who] is privileged within the field of vision?" (Lynes 2007, 12). A second theme queries how technology influences gender identity. Can artists use digital computing to trouble or even change gender identity in everyday life? A second question is, how does technology in art engage with "institutions, discourses, identities and representations" in ways that "uphold stable gender practices?" (Sorensen, Faulkner, and Rommes 2011, 53) These questions point to the importance of a third theme. It concerns a potential end to technology as a masculinizing force.

DIY feminism intersects with the Maker Movement in so far as practitioners of either create technology as an end in itself and to apply to other projects. DIY feminism shares something with fabriculture, too—an emphasis on digital ways of making, or fabricating. Crucially, fabriculturists, like DIY feminists, integrate textile-based domestic arts and activities with digital communication and culture. Also, they treat technology as something one does "as part of the social fabric that holds together as a community of makers by virtue of their interests and actions" (Wajcman 2010, 148–149). For instance, fabriculturists use the Internet and social media to distribute skill-based collaborative technology, thus enabling

> an exchange of information, skills, and even products. In other words, the knitting circle now meshes with the World Wide Web. More apropos is the phenomenon of online social networking, where interactions are now embedded in virtual spaces (blogs, microblogs, and social media applications). (Bratich and Brush 2011, 240)

According to Jack Bratich and Heidi Brush, "[f]rom commercial sites to virtual knitting circle (or *knit-alongs*), the new domesticity is thoroughly an online affair" (2011, 241).

Bratich and Brush are especially interested in analyzing parallels between technology-centric fabriculture and its beloved domestic textile arts. The former, they suggest, amounts to "a new way of connecting that is based on material production using traditional craft skills and yarns as well as the optical fibre and twisted pair cable used for telecommunications" (Bratich and Brush 2011, 240). Radically, they claim that social "meshworks" or online communities of digital fabricators transcend gender as one of their defining characteristics: "Continuing with our crafting notions, we can call these social *meshworks*, whose affinities and links are formed not in organizational contexts or in identity-based communities or even via consumer tastes" (Bratich and Brush 2011, 240). Social meshworks have roots in historically female textile domestic culture like the knitting circle. Yet, Bratich and Brush say they may elude pre-existing community identities. In what ways will fabriculture meshworks redefine how "[w]omens identities, needs and priorities are configured together with digital technologies"? (Wajcman 2010, 151). Can they eradicate technology's enduring "ties between men and technology"? (Paasonen 2005, 171)

References

Abbate, Janet. 2012. *History of Computing: Recoding Gender: Women's Changing Participation in Computing*. Cambridge, MA: The MIT Press.

Anable, Aubrey Meredith. 2008. "Digital Decay: The Urban Interface in New Visual Culture, 1968–2008." PhD dissertation, University of Rochester.

Beckman, Ericka. 1994. Press Release: "Video Viewpoints: Through a Video Window: Technology in the 1990s." New York: The Museum of Modern Art, The Video Program, Department of Film. http://erickabeckman.com/Hiatus_Press_files/Moma%20Video%20 Viewponts.pdf (accessed September 15, 2013).

Behar, Katherine, and Silvia Ruzanka, eds. 2013. "Ungoogleable: In Search of Digital Feminisms." *Lateral* 2. http://lateral.culturalstudiesassociation.org/issue2/theory/ behar-ruzanka (accessed October 15, 2013).

Bratich, Jack Z., and Heidi M. Brush. 2011. "Fabricating Activism: Craft-Work, Popular Culture, Gender." *Utopian Studies* 22: 232–260.

Caruso, Denise. 1984. "People." *InfoWorld, The Newsweekly for Microcomputer Users* 6: 16.

Cockburn, Cynthia. 1992. "The Circuit of Technology: Gender, Identity and Power." In *Consuming Technologies: Media and Information in Domestic Space*, edited by Roger Silverstone and Eric Hirsch, 32–47. New York: Routledge.

DPI Feminist Journal of Art and Digital Culture. 2004–. http://dpi.studioxx.org/en (accessed January 5, 2015).

Durland, Steven. 1987. "Defining the Image as Place: A Conversation with Kit Galloway, Sherrie Rabinowitz, & Gene Youngblood." *High Performance, A Quarterly magazine for the New Art Audience* 37: 52–59.

Ensmenger, Nathan. 2012. "The Digital Construction of Technology: Rethinking the History of Computers in Society." *Technology and Culture* 53: 753–776.

Flynn, Bernadette. 1994. "VNS Matrix and Virginia Barratt." *Continuum* 8: 419–443.

Gajjala, Radhika, and Annapurna Mamidipudi. 2002. "Gendering Processes within Technological Environments: A Cyberfeminist Issue." *Rhizomes* 4. http://www.rhizomes. net/issue4/gajjala.html (accessed October 13, 2015.

Galloway, Kit, and Sherrie Rabinowitz. 2002. "Collection: Telecommunications-arts Projects of ECI Founders Kit Galloway & Sherrie Rabinowitz contained in the ECI archives." http://ecafe.com (accessed October 15, 2013).

Gimenez, Martha E. 2009. "Review of *Women, Gender, and Technology*, edited by Mary Frank Fox, Deborah G. Johnson, and Sue V. Rosser." *Science and Society* 73: 263–265.

Goodman, Cynthia. 1987. *Digital Visions, Computers and Art*. New York: Harry N. Abrams.

Gouma-Peterson, Thalia, and Patricia Mathews. 1987. "The Feminist Critique of Art History." *The ArtBulletin* 69: 326–357.

Hampton, Darlene Rose. 2010. "Beyond Resistance: Gender, Performance, and Fannish Practice inDigital Culture." PhD dissertation, University of Oregon.

Harvestworks Team Lab. 2010. "Presentation: Interactive Art Workshop for Women Artists." http://www.harvestworks.org/presentation-interactive-art-workshop-for-women-artists (accessed August 15, 2013).

Heberle, Marta. 2013. "Technologically Empowered Body as a Weapon." *DPI Feminist Journal of Art and Digital Culture*. http://dpi.studioxx.org/en/technologically-empowered-body-weapon (accessed January 5, 2015).

Jackson, Michele H. 2007. "Exploring Gender, Feminism and Technology from a Communication Perspective: An Introduction and Commentary." *Women's Studies in Communication* 30: 149–156.

Kafai, Yasmin B., Carrie Heeter, Jill Denner, and Jennifer Y. Sun, eds. 2008. *Beyond Barbie & Mortal Kombat: New Perspectives on Gender and Gaming*. Cambridge, MA: The MIT Press.

Kennedy, Kathy. 2006. "Did Women Really Want to Use Computers?" *DPI Feminist Journal of Art and Digital Culture* 6. http://dpi.studioxx.org/demo/index.php?q=en/no/06/did-women-really-want-use-computers-by-Kathy-Kennedy (accessed September 51, 2013).

L.A. Free Press. 1971. "L.A. Council of Women Artists Report: Is Woman a Work of Art?": 98.

Leavitt, Ruth. 1976. *Artist and Computer*. Harmony Books.

Le-Phat Ho, Sophie. 2007. "Gender Neutrality: Interview with Ladyada." *DPI Feminist Journal of Art and Digital Culture* 7. http://dpi.studioxx.org/demo/index.php?q=en/no/07/gender-neutrality-interview-with-ladyada (accessed September 15, 2013).

Le-Phat Ho, Sophie. 2012. "Tout est a nous." *DPI Feminist Journal of Art and Digital Culture*. 26. http://dpi.studioxx.org/demo/index.php?q=en/no/26/TOUT-EST-A-NOUS_By-Sophie-LePhat-Ho (accessed September 15, 2013).

Le-Phat Ho, Sophie. 2013. "Do We Have Culture?" *DPI Feminist Journal of Art and Digital Culture* 27. http://dpi.studioxx.org/en/do-we-have-culture (accessed January 5, 2015).

Lynes, Krista Genevieve. 2007. "Imaging Boundaries: Video, Gender and the Politics of Visibility." PhD dissertation, University of California Santa Cruz.

MacKenzie, Donald, and Judy Wajcman. 1999. *The Social Shaping of Technology*, 2nd ed. Columbus, OH: McGraw Hill Education and the Open University.

Madmapper. 2013. "Tech Workshops: Elas Fan Tech (Spain)." http://www.madmapper.com/2013/01/13/tech-workshops-elas-fan-tech-spain (accessed October 15, 2013).

Mayer, Vicki. 2012. "Through the Darkness: Musings on New Media." *Ada: A Journal of Gender, New Media, and Technology* 1. http://adanewmedia.org/2012/11/issue1-mayer (accessed October 15, 2013).

Munro, Ealasaid. 2013. "Feminism: A Fourth Wave?" *Political Insight* 4: 22–25.

MzTek. 2009–2013. "MzTek." http://www.mztek.org/about (accessed October 15, 2013).

Nochlin, Linda. 1971. "Why Have There Been No Great Women Artists?" *ARTnews* 9: 22–39, 67–71.

Oldenziel, Ruth. 2002. "Object/ions: Technology, Culture and Gender." In *The Material Culture Reader*, edited by Victor Buchli, 48–60. Oxford: Berg.

Paasonen, Susanna. 2005. *Figures of Fantasy*. Bern, Switzerland: Peter Lang.

Rhoades, Melinda Justine. 2008. "Addressing the Computing Gender Gap: A Case Study Using Feminist Pedagogy and Visual Culture Art Education." PhD dissertation, The Ohio State University.

Schoenbeck, Robert Wallace. 2012. "Frames: Digital Art as Text, Context and Code." PhD dissertation, University of California Irvine.

Sorensen, Knut Holtan, Wendy Faulkner, and Els Rommes. 2011. *Technologies of Inclusion: Gender in the Information Society*. Trondheim: Tapir Academic Press.

Squeaky Wheel. 2013. "Techarts for Girls." http://www.squeaky.org/techarts (accessed January 5, 2015).

Studio XX. 2013. "HTMlles." http://www.studioxx.org/en/htmlles (accessed September 15, 2013).

Studio XX Women + Art + Technology + Society. "Studio XX's Mandate." http://www.studioxx.org/en/mandat (accessed September 15, 2013).

subRosa. 2002. "Tactical Cyberfeminisms: An Art and Technology of Social Relations." In "Cyberfeminism Right Now," edited by Mary Jo Aagerstoun. http://www.artwomen.org/cyberfems/intro.htm (accessed April 15, 2009).

subRosa. 2009. *SmartMom*. First launched in 1999. http://smartmom.cyberfeminism.net (accessed October 15, 2013).

subRosa. 2011. "Bodies Unlimited: A Decade of subRosa's Art Practice." *n. paradoxa* 28: 16–25.

subRosa. 2012. "SUBROSA/SMARTMOM." The HTMlles 10 Risky Business Feminist Festival of Media Arts + Digital Culture. http://www.htmlles.net/2012/en/index.html#page3 (accessed September, 2013).

Tamblyn, Christine. 1995. "She Loves It, She Loves it Not/ Women and Technology." *Leonardo* 8: 99–104.

Taylor, Grant David. 2013. "'Up for Grabs': Agency, Praxis, and the Politics of Early Digital Art." *Lateral* 2. http://lateral.culturalstudiesassociation.org/issue2/theory/taylor (accessed October, 2013).

Tocci, Jason. 2009. "Geek Cultures: Media and Identity in the Digital Age." PhD dissertation, University of Pennsylvania.

Toupin, Sophie. 2013. "Feminist Hackerspaces as Safer Spaces?" *DPI Feminist Journal of Art and Digital Culture* 27. http://dpi.studioxx.org/en/feminist-hackerspaces-safer-spaces (accessed October 15, 2013).

Vanderhoef, J. 2013. ""Casual Threats: The Feminization of Casual Video Games." *Ada: A Journal of Gender, New Media, and Technology* 2. doi: 10.7264/N3V40S4D. http://adanewmedia.org/2013/06/issue2-vanderhoef/ (accessed October 13, 2015.)

Wajcman, Judy. 2004. *Technofeminism*. Cambridge: Polity.

Wajcman, Judy. 2010. "Feminist Theories of Technology." *Cambridge Journal of Economics* 34: 143–152.

Wakeford, Nina. 1997. "Networking Women and Grrls with Information/Communication Technology: Surfing Tales of the World Wide Web." In *Processed Lives: Gender and Technology in Everyday Life*, edited by Jennifer Terry and Melodie Calvert, 35–46. London and New York: Routledge.

Wands, Bruce. 2006. *Art of the Digital Age*. New York: Thames & Hudson.

Wexner Center for the Arts (Film and Video and Division of Comparative Studies). 1995. Program Notes for Visiting Artist Ericka Bechman, as part of "Gender and Technology: Rethinking Masculinity and Femininity in a World of 'Intelligent' Machines." Columbus, Ohio: The Ohio State University.

Zeffiro, Andrea. 2008. "Reflecting on the Past, Speculating the Future: Feminist Interventions in Locative Media." *DPI Feminist Journal of Art and Digital Culture* 12 (June). http://dpi.studioxx.org/archive/fr/no/12/reflecting-past-speculating-future-feminist-interventions-locative-media-by-andrea-zeffiro (accessed October 13, 2015).

Further Reading

Burnham, Jack. 1971. "Corporate Art." *Artforum* 10: 66–71.

Dunbar-Hester, Christina, and Bryce J. Renninger, curators. 2013. *Trans Technology: Circuits of Culture, Self, Belonging*. Rutgers: The State University of New Jersey, Institute for Women and Art.

Goldin, Amy. 1972. "Art and Technology in a Social Vacuum." *Art in America* 60: 46–50.

Klaas, Renee Diane, Bonnie Mitchell, and the SIGGRAPH Communications Committee, Bowling Green State University. 1999. "Joan Truckenbrod." http://old.siggraph.org/artdesign/profile/Truckenbrod (accessed September 15, 2013).

Time. 1971. "Art: Man and machine." Time, June 28. http://www.time.com/time/magazine/article/0,9171,905268,00.html (accessed April 5, 2009).

7

The Hauntology of the Digital Image

Charlie Gere

In this chapter I propose to examine the idea of the digital image as a form of writing, in the expanded sense first articulated by Jacques Derrida, which in turn was pre-empted by avant-garde artists and writers, and most particularly James Joyce. Digital data has always been characterized in terms of reading and writing, as in the "disk read-and-write head," or "read-only memory," the element of a hard disk that transforms its magnetic field into electronic current and vice versa. The emergence of digital data as something written and read emerged in tandem with the expansion of "writing" as an overarching category in a number of different fields, including, among others, genetics (with the idea of DNA as code); psychoanalysis (with Lacan's reconfiguring of Freud's insights in linguistic terms); and philosophy (with Derrida's notion of *archiécriture*). It is the last, in particular, that offers the resources to think about the digital image as a kind of writing.

I look at early experiments in digital imagery made at Bell Labs in the 1960s, in particular those of Ken Knowlton and Leon Harmon and their *Studies in Perception*. Though emerging in very different contexts, both Bell Labs and postwar continental theory and philosophy are united in their privileging of writing as well as a shared interest in cybernetics. The work at Bell Labs also parallels and connects with contemporary developments in avant-garde art and literature, which in turn resonate with poststructuralism. These disparate strands are brought together in a shared interest in the work of James Joyce, which can be understood to prefigure postwar technological advances in information communications technologies. Finally, I show how these various developments were important for the emergence of bitmapping, hypertext, word processing, and other phenomena connected with the rise of personal computing in the 1980s, and also with the increasing ubiquity of the Internet and of the World Wide Web in the 1990s onwards.

It is usual to think of images as analogous to visual impressions. As such they seem to offer a sense of immediacy, meaning that they not only communicate directly, but

A Companion to Digital Art, First Edition. Edited by Christiane Paul.

also do need an intervening or mediating agency in order to do so. It is as if the thing itself is in front of us. This sense is reinforced by the belief that representational images are the product of a direct visual encounter, whether this takes the form of a painter replicating on a canvas what he or she sees, or a camera fixing the fall of light onto a chemical surface. Digital imagery breaks with the idea of the image as that which makes what it depicts present, as a re-presentation, thus bound up with the "metaphysics of presence," the privileging of the present in Western thought. Since the digital image is constituted differentially as a series of binaries—zeros and ones, on and off states—it seems to sever what appears to be the innate, immediate, and unmediated connection between the thing represented and its representation.

Though it may not seem obvious, at first at least, I suggest this holds for digital photography. Even if the operations of analog and digital photography both involve the fall of light onto a surface, chemical for the former and electronic for the latter, and the results are similar, if not identical, there is still a profound ontological difference between the two. This is manifested most explicitly in what can be done with digital imagery with ease, including manipulation and circulation, which is a consequence of its being encoded. Even if a digital image still resembles and operates like an analog image, there is also a sense that we know that it is different, as we look at it.

The digital image, with its composition out of discrete picture elements (pixels), and the ease with which it can be copied and circulated, is capable of far easier and wider circulation, iteration, citation, of breaking with its context, and thus making new contexts, than the analog image. In order to understand this I look at some of the very first digital images, Leon Harmon and Kenneth Knowlton's *Studies in Perception*,[1] made at Bell Labs in the mid-1960s. Unlike other digital images of the same period, which are mostly based on algorithmically generated vector graphics, Harmon and Knowlton's are in effect bitmaps of scanned photographs, in which grayscale levels are composed of "glyphs," little images depicting a cat, a house, or an umbrella. I see these works as related to the various experiments in bringing together writing and imagery, such as those of Jacques Derrida, and also as anticipations of the current ubiquity of teletechnologies and digital media.

The title of this essay is a deliberate allusion to André Bazin's famous 1958 article "The Ontology of the Photographic Image" (Bazin 1960). But, as its first word indicates, rather than merely follow Bazin in trying to offer an ontology of the digital image in the manner that he attempts for the photographic, I suggest instead that what digital imagery requires is not ontology but "hauntology." This latter term was coined by Jacques Derrida in his book *Specters of Marx* (1993). It is intended as a critique of ontology, as indicated in the fact that the French "hantologie" is pronounced identically to "ontologie." In *Specters of Marx* Derrida defines hauntology as referring to that which is "neither living nor dead, present nor absent: it spectralizes" (Derrida 1993, 51). He sees the hauntological at play in the "medium of the media themselves (news, the press, tele-communications, techno-tele-discursivity, techno-tele-iconicity ...)" (Derrida 1993, 51). For Derrida hauntology is another of the many terms he has employed, including "trace," "pharmakon," "differance," and "logocentrism."[2] Inasmuch as they are always a trace of something either potentially or actually absent, all representations are hauntological. The digital image is not more hauntological than its analog predecessors, but it does reveal the degree to which representations of any sort are more complex and less immediate than one might think.

As its name suggests, hauntology indicates the degree to which representation is bound up with death. This is a theme that was constant in Derrida's work from the beginning and underpinned his expanded understanding of writing. Interestingly, Bazin both acknowledges and disavows this relation by claiming that such representations are intended to disavow or deny death. Bazin acknowledges this in his essay, in which he suggests that the "practice of embalming the dead" might be a "fundamental factor" in the creation of the plastic arts. He goes on to propose that that "at the origin of painting and sculpture there lies a mummy complex," a need to preserve the living body against death and the flux of temporality. Over time this need attenuates from a magical attempt to preserve the body itself to that of preserving its image in the form of a painting or a sculpture (Bazin 1960, 4). Roland Barthes also famously engaged with the relationship between photography and death in his book *Camera Lucida*. As he puts it:

> For Death must be somewhere in a society; if it is no longer (or less intensely) in religion, it must be elsewhere; perhaps in this image which produces Death while trying to preserve life. Contemporary with the withdrawal of rites, Photography may correspond to the intrusion, in our modern society, of an asymbolic Death, outside of religion, outside of ritual, a kind of abrupt dive into literal Death. (Barthes 1981, 92)

Hauntology is closely related to another important idea emerging out of Derrida's thought, that of "originary technicity." Following the work of Derrida as well as André Leroi-Gourhan and Bernard Stiegler, it can be claimed that the technical and the human co-evolve and are coterminous. As Stiegler puts it, the technical invents the human as much as the human invents the technical (Stiegler 1998, 141). Uprightness, bipedality, the freeing of the forelimbs for manipulation, the zoological capacity to "extrude" tools that are apart from the body, and the expansion of the cranium as a result of being upright all come together to produce the modern human, and also the particular human relation to time, history, and mortality (Leroi-Gourhan 1993). As such, technicity is hauntology, in that technical artifacts haunt their users with the possibility and actuality of absence, of both their creators and of other users. This is also true of language itself, which is always inherited.

It might be argued that one of the most hauntological or haunted genres of representative image making is the erotic or pornographic, inasmuch as it is explicitly intended to bring into apparent presence what is absent, the desired body of an other. According to Freud and interpreters such as Laplanche and Pontalis, sexuality is autoerotic and "phantasmatic" in that it is rooted in fantasy (Laplanche and Pontalis 1968). Phantasm is of course cognate with phantom. It therefore is perhaps no surprise that early on in the history of any representational medium erotic or pornographic images emerge. This is true, for example, for photography. It also turns out to be the case for computer art. An article by Ben Edwards in *The Atlantic* magazine entitled "The Never-Before-Told Story of the World's First Computer Art (It's a Sexy Dame)" (Edwards 2013) gave an account of how, in the late 1950s, a piece of soft pornography was painstakingly reproduced on one of the SAGE early warning system's display screens. These circular screens, operated by "light guns," were among the first computer displays to show visual and symbolic information rather than numerical data—in this case the outlines of territory threatened by Soviet nuclear bombers. Apparently programmed by an IBM employee seconded to the SAGE unit, this image seems to have been taken from a George Petty calendar page made for the 1956 edition of *Esquire* magazine. It would have been programmed using a stack of roughly 97 Hollerith punched cards. Fortunately (for the history of digital pornography at least), Airman First Class Lawrence A. Tipton took a photograph of the image using the Polaroid camera normally employed to take pictures of anomaly conditions for diagnostic purposes. Another similar image, this time interactive and animated, of a topless hula hoop dancer in a grass skirt, was not recorded. Apparently, pointing a light gun at the image caused the skirt to fall off (ibid.).

The images on the SAGE screens predate what are known as the first computer images by a number of years. A. Michael Noll produced what is often regarded as the first computer art at Bell Labs in 1962. A little later, in the mid-1960s, also working at Bell Labs, Leon Harman and Ken Knowlton produced a series of what they called *Studies in Perception.* Knowlton had come to Bell Labs in 1962, and embarked on research into computer image making and animation. According to his own account,

> My own shtick became a sort of greyscale picture made by filling the screen with thousands of different letters chosen for their brightness. I soon wrote a memo to department head Tom Crowley, suggesting the possibility of a "computer language" for making animated movies; his two-part response launched my career in raster graphics: "It sounds rather ambitious, but why don't you see what you can do?" [...] Within a year, I had a set of subroutines someone dubbed BEFLIX, acronym for "Bell Flicks," arguably the first computer language specifically for bitmap movie making. (I have also been called the inventor of the pixel, which is a bit of a reach, though I might claim independent discovery.) (Knowlton 2005, 9)[3]

The first of the studies in perception was developed after Harmon was asked to make a "modern art mural" for an office at Bell Labs. What he and Knowlton produced was an extraordinary twelve-foot-long computer-generated nude (Figure 7.1), which was followed by a number of others, including images of a gargoyle, and a telephone. Unlike much early digital imagery, these were not vector-based, using geometric data to guide the shape of the lines, but in effect bitmaps, albeit of a singular sort.

According to their own description of the process, they scanned a 35 mm transparency of a photograph in "a machine similar to a television camera". The electrical signals were converted into numerical representations on magnetic tape. The image was processed by the computer and fragmented into a number of rows of fragments. The nude was comprised of fifty rows with 100 fragments per row, totaling 5000 fragments. Later images using the same technique had 88 rows of 132 fragments, totaling 11,616 fragments. Each fragment is sampled for its brightness, and in the case of the nude assigned one of eight levels, and in the case of later images one of fourteen levels, from white to black, with intermediate gray scales between (Reichardt 1971, 20–21).[4]

The fragments take the form of a square of 10 by 10 dots in the case of the nude, 11 by 11 or sometimes 15 by 15 for other, later images. What makes these images particularly interesting, and takes them beyond the merely technological or experimental, is how Knowlton and Harmon chose to deal with the grayscale fragments. Rather than simply fill the squares with the appropriate number of black dots

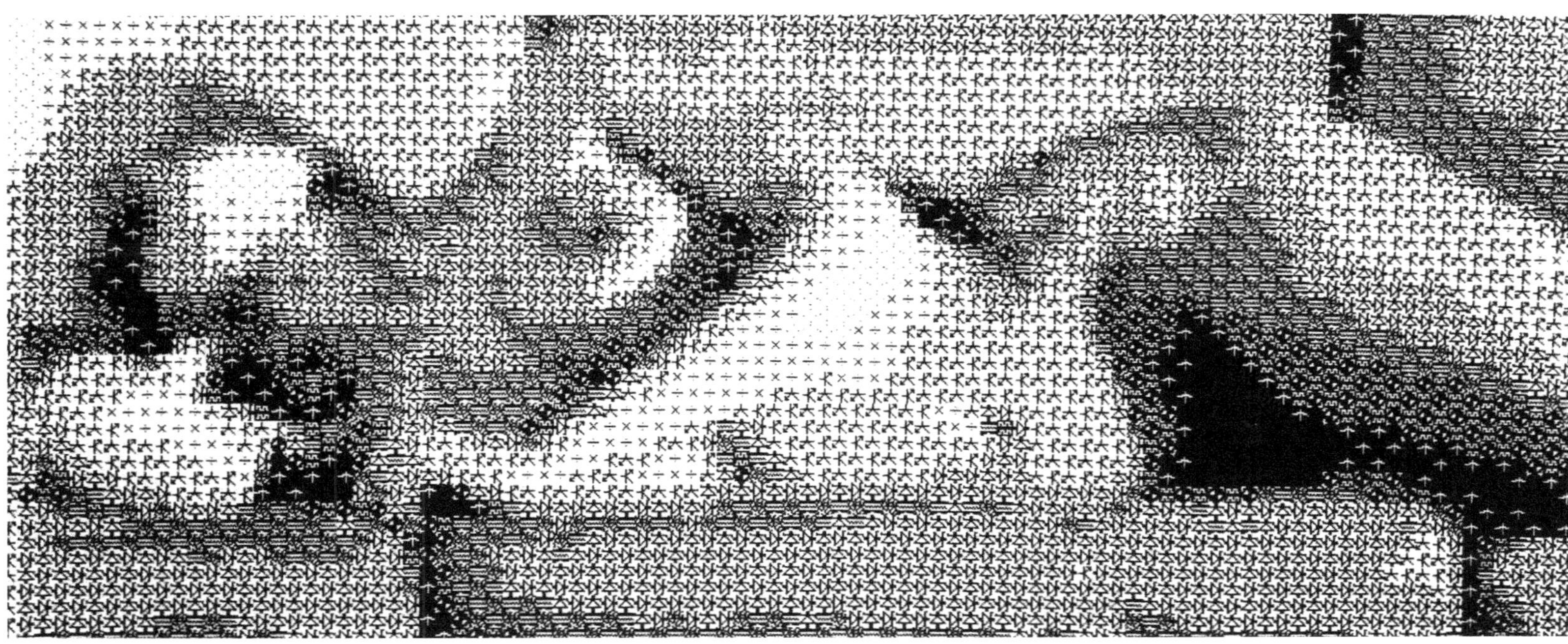

FIGURE 7.1 Leon Harmon and Ken Knowlton, *Studies in Perception No. 1*, 1966.

randomly distributed, they developed a series of little images, which they called "glyphs," of a house, a cat, an umbrella, a stop light, among others (Reichardt 1971, 21).

The first image, that of the nude, made by Knowlton and Harmon was, according to Knowlton's account, originally made as a prank, in which Knowlton and Harmon sneaked into their colleague E.E. David's office to place the image on the wall (which was apparently in black and day-glo green). The glyphs on the image looked like symbols of electronic components, such as resistors and transistors, and the fact that it was a nude was only apparent when seen from a distance. As Knowlton describes it,

> The nonscientific, some say artistic, aspects of computer graphics arose for me via a sophomoric prank. Ed David, two levels up, was away for while and the mice, one might say, played ever more freely. Leon Harmon stopped by to ask me for help with a brilliant idea: when Ed returns, one entire wall of his office will be covered with a huge picture made of small electronic symbols for transistors, resistors and such. But overall, they will form a somewhat-hard-to-see picture of, guess what, a nude! And so the renowned Harmon–Knowlton nude was conceived, coaxed into being, and duly hung on Ed's wall [...] Ed was delighted but worried. More viewers than we had expected were apparently familiar with the subject matter, and could "see" the 12-foot-wide picture from as many feet away. It was therefore judged an unseemly decoration for the Labs, especially midway up the hierarchy. After just one day of glory there, she was retired to Ed's basement rec-room. Smaller versions of the big picture mysteriously did propagate (we had not the slightest idea how); the PR department scowled and warned that "you may circulate this thing, but be sure that you do NOT associate the name of Bell Labs with it." [...] But the big version burst forth a while later at a press conference on Art and Technology in Robert Rauschenberg's loft, and on the watershed date of October 11, 1967, it appeared atop the first page of the second section of the *New York Times*, which made not the slightest effort to conceal its birthplace. Billy Kluver claims that this was the first time ever that the *Times* printed a nude! The PR department huddled and decided, so it seems, that since she had appeared in the venerable *Times*, our nude was not frivolous in-your-face pornography after all, but in-your-face Art. Their revised statement was: You may indeed distribute and display it, but be sure that you let people know that it was produced at Bell Telephone Laboratories, Inc. (Knowlton 2005, 10)

The article by Henry Lieberman in the *New York Times* mentioned by Knowlton above describes what it calls a "happening" at Robert Rauschenberg's loft in vivid terms:

> In a sound-drenched Lower Manhattan loft building that was enlivened by revolving painted disks, film projections, floating pillows and miniskirted girls in paper smocks, representatives of industry and labor joined a number of artists and scientists yesterday to proclaim a "working alliance" between art and technology. (Lieberman 1967, 49)

The article goes on to describe some of the other artworks on display in the loft, including Rauschenberg's *Oracle*, a "sound-emitting assembly consisting of a tire, track door, window frame, bathtub and air vent." This featured five radios, the tuning dials of which were rotated by motor to play snatches of broadcasts, with small FM transistors used to relay the signals (Lieberman 1967). When Davis became President Nixon's science advisor he gave *Studies in Perception* to the Philadelphia Museum of Art. By that time it had been not only reproduced in the *New York Times*, but also exhibited in *Information: The Machine Seen at the End of the Mechanical Age*, which was held at the Museum of Modern Art in 1968/1969. Images by Knowlton and Harmon were also shown at *Cybernetic Serendipity* in the ICA in London in 1968.

The original photograph was taken by Bell Labs colleague Max Mathews of dancer Deborah Hay. This makes it an astonishingly overdetermined artifact of postwar culture. Max Mathews is best known as one of the great pioneers of computer music. In 1957 he wrote MUSIC, the first widely used program for generating sound. In 1968, along with L. Rosler, he developed Graphic 1, an interactive, visual sound system, in which figures drawn onscreen with a light pen were turned into sounds. In 1970 F.R. Moore and Mathews built the GROOVE (Generated Real-time Output Operations on Voltage-controlled Equipment), which enabled musical synthesis for composition and live performance. But what Mathews may be most famous for is his arrangement of the song "Daisy Bell" for synthesized voice, which was performed in 1961 at Bell Labs. Apparently Arthur C. Clarke was visiting his friend John Pierce at Bell Labs at the time, and was sufficiently impressed to suggest to Stanley Kubrick that he use it in *2001: A Space Odyssey* (which was based on Clarke's story "The Sentinel"), in the scene in which the HAL 9000 computer is shut down by Bowman.

Deborah Hay's career is, if anything, even more interesting. Trained as a dancer by Merce Cunningham, John Cage's partner, she danced with the Cunningham Dance Company in the early 1960s, and was later involved with the group of artists that became known as the Judson Dance Theater. Since that time she has been deeply involved in radical dance practice, and has collaborated with many luminaries of the musical avant-garde, including Pauline Oliveros, Alvin Lucier, and Terry Riley.

It is therefore not so surprising to see parallels between the work done at Bell Labs by Knowlton and Harmon and others and developments in the avant-garde art world, particularly in terms of experimentation in perception. As the *New York Times* article demonstrated, there was a fair degree of connection between the New York avant-garde of Robert Rauschenberg and others and the world of computer engineering, particularly through groups such as Billy Klüver's Experiments in Art and Technology. Between 1964 and 1967 Knowlton collaborated with experimental filmmaker Stan Vanderbeek to make the film *Poemfield*, using Beflix. At about the same time A. Michael Noll was writing computer programs to generate images that resembled the work of Piet Mondrian and Bridget Riley. Such imagery, being concerned with abstract geometric shapes, is peculiarly amenable to being encoded. There is also is a more complex connection to larger technological developments in that the work of such artists might itself be considered a response to the mathematization and abstraction of data becoming increasingly visible because of computers.

The real point of contact, however, is perhaps op art and the work of the Groupe de Recherche d'Art Visuel (GRAV). Inspired by the op artist Victor Vasarely and founded in 1960 by Julio Le Parc, Vera Molnar, and Vasarely's son Yvaral, GRAV was concerned with developing scientific and technological forms of art using industrial materials. In addition to creating art that uses optical effects, members of GRAV were also involved in producing kinetic works, and even interactive displays intended to dissolve the boundaries between art and life. Co-founder Vera Molnar was also was a pioneer of computer art. By the late 1950s, she had made work using what she called her *machine imaginaire*, an imaginary computer that allowed her to apply algorithmic principles to art making. In 1968, when GRAV folded, she started working with real computers to produce prints.

In his book *Applied Grammatology*, Gregory Ulmer makes a direct comparison between the work of GRAV and that of Derrida (Ulmer 1985). He sees Derrida's textual experimentation and the geometric strategies employed by GRAV as engaging in the "nonobjective," since they are both concerned with "defining relations among objects or words without regard for their specific embodiments or meanings." Thus the work of GRAV "serves as a model and resource for grammatological experimentation" (Ulmer 1985, 38–39). In particular, so-called op art, the

> creation of optical effects through the manipulation of geometric forms, color dissonance, and kinetic elements, and "the experimental production of optical illusion directly in abstract form" [...] is relevant to Derrida's attempts to identify the illusory effects of grammar in a similarly pure way. (Ulmer 1985, 40)

Thus Ulmer declares that what he calls Derrida's "op writing" is the "grammatical equivalent of the geometrical experiments of the constructivists working at the limits of optical perception" (Ulmer 1985, 40).

For Ulmer op art produces the "trembling" or "shaking" effect that Derrida also strives to achieve in his texts (Ulmer 1985, 40). Ulmer cites Vasarely's "surface kinetics" in which a two-dimensional surface appears to pulse in three dimensions. Among the techniques associated with this were the "Mach strip" and the "moiré effect" (Ulmer 1985, 40). Ulmer claims that the

> moiré effect alone serves not only as a didactic model for "solicitation," but constitutes—by virtue of its peculiar feature of being a static form that produces the effect of motion—an emblem of Moira, destiny, whose nature is to be once the motion of Becoming and the rest of Being. (Ulmer 1985, 41)

Though lacking the visual and artistic sophistication of the work of GRAV, Harmon and Knowlton's *Studies in Perception* evince a similar, deliberate confusion between figure and ground. As they describe it,

> At close viewing distances the many tiny patterns are clearly visible, but unless you know exactly what to look for, the large picture (the overall Gestalt) cannot be perceived. With increasingly great viewing distances the small patterns disappear, and the overall picture emerges. (Reichardt 1971, 21)

There is a clear relation between these images and ASCII art, the curious phenomenon of constructing images out of the American Standard Code for Information Interchange, the basic means of displaying text on computers. ASCII Art rarely manages to rise above the banal and obvious kind of imagery, an exception being the work of net artist Vuk Cosic, who investigated the possibilities of ASCII as an artistic medium in the late 1990s and early 2000s. Harmon and Knowlton's work also somewhat resembles the portraits of artist Chuck Close. Particularly since being confined to a wheelchair in the late 1980s, Close has used a technique involving painting

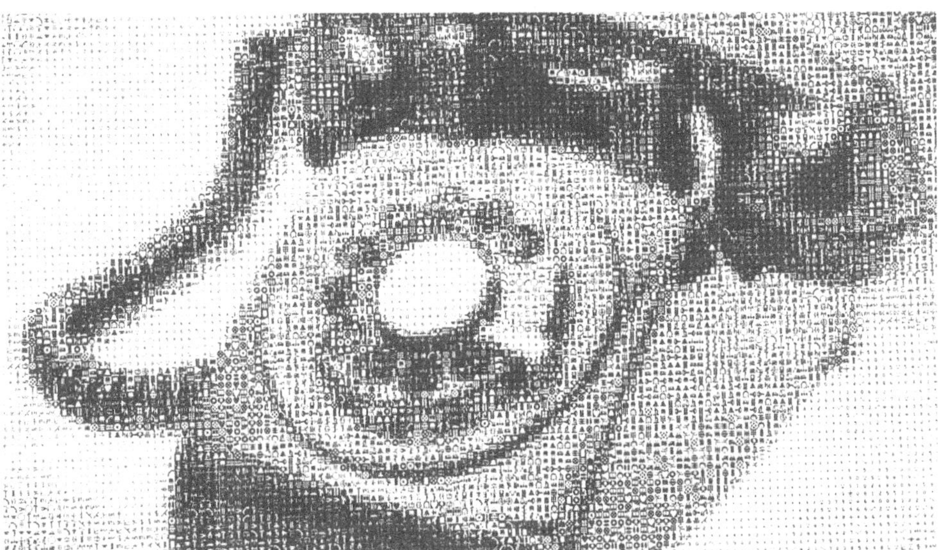

FIGURE 7.2 Leon Harmon and Ken Knowlton, *Telephone*, 1967.

squares or other abstract geometric shapes that resolve themselves into images of faces when seen from far enough away. Images made up of grids of smaller images chosen and distributed to make up the color and tone of the whole image, often referred to as photomosaics, became a trend in the 1990s.[5]

What makes Harmon and Knowlton's images more interesting than these examples is the use of the glyph, which is particularly rich in later images, such as *Telephone* (Figure 7.2), or *Gargoyle*. (The first of their images, the nude, used a comparatively simple array of less explicit glyphs.) In these images, the semiotic richness of the glyphs makes the figure/ground oscillation far more marked. It also turns the images into something resembling writing, or at least hieroglyphics, thus producing another oscillation that has been of interest to Derrida, that between writing and image. The fact that one of the glyphs used in the images is an umbrella also invokes Derrida's most notorious strategic moves in *Spurs: Eperons* (1979), in which he takes a seemingly trivial entry in Nietzsche's notebooks, "I have forgotten my umbrella," to deconstruct the notion of the limits of a literary or philosophical corpus, of style, and of hermeneutics. This way the umbrella becomes a kind of figure of undecidability (Derrida 1979).

There is an impression of something encoded in Harmon and Knowlton's images, as if the glyphs themselves are encryptions of another meaning, different from that of the ostensible image. On one level this alludes to the relation between digital technology and encryption, from Bletchley Park (Hodges 1985, 160) through to contemporary techniques for secret and secure communication. On another level, it gives the images a psychoanalytical dimension, a notion of hidden meanings concealed in ordinary discourse, as first analyzed by Freud. Playing on the connection between encryption and the crypt, Nicolas Abraham and Maria Torok famously interpreted Freud's account of the Wolf Man (Abraham and Torok 1986).

The word "glyph" means an element of writing derived from the Greek word for carving or incising, and can be found in the term "hieroglyph," meaning sacred mark.

About ten years after Harmon and Knowlton's pioneering work, Samuel Weber, an academic working in the field of literary theory at Johns Hopkins University, founded a journal called *Glyph*, intended to engage with and challenge dominant metaphysical understandings, and the crises of representation and textuality that had been analyzed by Marx, Nietzsche, Freud, and, among more recent thinkers, Derrida. Weber's use of the term "glyph" as the title of the journal can be understood as a signal of his intentions to foreground the inscriptive nature of texts, and to emphasize the importance of the idea of "writing" in the expanded sense that is key to Derrida's work.

This emphasis on the materiality and inscriptive quality of the text may be seen as part of what Lydia Liu calls "the ideographic turn of the phonetic alphabet" (2010). This can be traced back at least to Hegel, whom Derrida invokes in *Of Grammatology* as proclaiming that

> acquired habit [...] also suppresses the specificity of alphabetic writing, which consists in seeming to be, in the interest of sight, a detour through hearing to arrive at representations, and makes it into a hieroglyphic script for us, such that in using it, we do not need to have present to our consciousness the mediation of sounds. (Derrida 1976, 25)

As Liu points out, this appreciation of the hieroglyphic potential of alphabetic writing is what makes Hegel, for Derrida, the "last philosopher of the book and the first thinker of writing" (Derrida 1976, 26).

Friedrich Kittler defines the emergence of writing as the "Discourse Network" of 1900. In his book *Discourse Networks, 1800/1900* (1990) Kittler examines the difference between the two discourse networks in operation at either end of the 19th century. For Kittler discourse networks are the "technologies and institutions that allow a given culture to select, store and produce relevant data" (Kittler 1990, 369). The discourse network of 1800, making Romanticism possible and relying entirely on writing, privileges the voice, particularly the maternal voice, and thus poetry. The discourse network of 1900, with the invention of the typewriter and the phonograph, destroys writing's monopoly of media, and also the privileging of the voice. Writing now becomes technologized, as one media channel among others. The printed page is reconfigured as a two-dimensional, inscribed surface, generating meaning through the difference of typewritten symbols—mechanical marks on the page—rather than the locus of the transcendent voice of poetry. This produces a new focus on the materiality and opacity of the sign.

Joseph Koerner, in his book *Reformation of the Image*, suggests that Kittler is attempting to "dismantle the myth, foundational to hermeneutics, of a silent inner voice" (Koerner 2004, 295). Koerner quotes Friedrich Schleiermacher's interdiction of any poetry that looks like "an axe or bottle," pointing to the notion that picture poems, in conveying their messages through external forms, "violated the primacy of inner sense that hermeneutics assumed—religiously—for language" (Koerner 2004, 295). By contrast, modernism "dramatized its rupture with the past by putting newly on display the material means of its production." Koerner cites, among others, Guillaume Apollinaire's *Calligrammes* (1918); Stéphane Mallarmé's exploitation of the intervals of blank paper between letters; Paul Klee's picture poems; cubist and Dada collage, to which one might add Ezra Pound and his colleagues involved with Imagist poetry and particularly interested in Chinese writing; Russian Futurist poetry, such as that by Khlebnikov; concrete poetry; Isidore Isou's lettrism, and the work of the L=A=N=G=U=A=G=E group.

The emergence of this kind of work parallels that of psychoanalysis, which Freud started to formulate in the 1890s and which involved concepts such as parapraxes, or so-called Freudian slips, as well as a more general notion of the relation between language and the unconscious. As Derrida points out in his essay "Freud and the Scene of Writing," psychoanalysis is indebted to metaphors of inscription and writing that turn the brain or mind into a kind of machine (Derrida 1978). It was also about this time that Ferdinand de Saussure started on the work that would lead to the *Course in General Linguistics*, in which language is understood in terms of difference without positive terms, and which would lead to numerous developments, among them structuralism, later in the 20th century.[6]

But it is perhaps James Joyce who most brings out the implications of this new understanding of the materiality of language in *Ulysses* and, especially, in *Finnegans Wake*. The latter is, arguably, still the most radical experiment in prose literature ever undertaken—over six hundred pages of puns, neologisms, and every form of verbal trickery and excess. Joyce is perhaps the modernist writer who made the most cogent response to the new media technologies of the time. As Donald Theall puts it, Joyce realized that the arts and communications of his period "involved new modes of social organization and technological production, reproduction, and distribution" (Liu 2010, 103). Among the most important of the new forms of technological reproduction in Joyce's lifetime was film. In 1900 Joyce founded Ireland's first cinema, the Volta Cinematograph, in Dublin. Moreover, the publication history of *Ulysses*—from its serialization by Sylvia Beach between 1918 and 1920, and then its actual publication as a book in 1922—coincides more or less exactly with the technological developments that would lead to commercially viable sound cinema in the late 1920s.

Joyce was also one of the first authors to be recorded reading their own work. In 1924 he made a recording of the "Aeolus" section of *Ulysses* for His Masters Voice in Paris, though the company refused to release it or pay for it. (Sylvia Beach did so, and had thirty copies made for distribution to friends. Joyce even created a design for the record cover, which is now at the University of Buffalo.) Later in the same decade Joyce made a recording of part of the "Anna Livia Plurabelle" section from *Finnegans Wake*. He did this second recording at the behest of C.K. Ogden, the linguist, philosopher, and developer of "Basic English," a much reduced version of the language, limited to 850 words. By this time Joyce's eyesight was so bad that Ogden had the section to be read photographed and massively blown up, so Joyce would be able to read it. Ogden's Basic English project seems as far removed as possible from Joyce's prolific and inventive use of language. Ogden himself calculated that Joyce's vocabulary contained a quarter of a million words. Later, as we will see, Claude Shannon declared Basic English and *Finnegans Wake* to be the two extremes of redundancy in English prose.

Ulysses' cinetelephonographicity is perhaps literature's anticipation of sound cinema, and in particular the possibility of speech in film, confirming Walter Benjamin's observation in his essay "The Work of Art in the Age of Mechanical Reproduction" that

> One of the foremost tasks of art has always been the creation of a demand which could be fully satisfied only later. The history of every art form shows critical epochs

in which a certain art form aspires to effects which could be fully obtained only with a changed technical standard, that is to say, in a new art form. (Benjamin 1969, 237)

Finnegans Wake was controversial from the beginning, and was subject to harsh critique by other writers such as Ezra Pound who had previously been in favor of Joyce's work. Though there also were also those who continued to support Joyce, it was not until some time after the original publication that the real implications of his later work began to be appreciated. In the postwar era media theorists, such as Marshall McLuhan and Donald Theall, scientists including Claude Shannon, Richard Ogden, and John R. Pierce, and theorists such as Jacques Derrida engaged with the implications of Joyce's work for understanding of the emerging world of new information and communications technologies. From his earliest published work onwards, Jacques Derrida showed a profound appreciation of these implications. In his introduction to Edmund Husserl's *Origin of Geometry* (first published in 1962), he invokes Joyce as a counterpoint to Husserl's project to produce a transparent univocality of language in which experience can be translated without remainder. Derrida characterizes Joyce's, with Joyce's project of equivocity as,

utilizing a language that could equalize the greatest possible synchronicity with the greatest potential for buried, accumulated, and interwoven intentions within each linguistic atom, each vocable, each word, each simple proposition, in all worldly cultures, and their most ingenious forms (mythology, religion, sciences, arts, literature, politics, philosophy and so forth). And, like Joyce, this endeavor would try to make the structural unity of all empirical culture appear in the generalized equivocation of a writing that, no longer translating one language into another on the basis of their common cores of sense, circulates through all languages at once, accumulates their energies, actualizes their most secret consonances, discloses their furthermost common horizons, cultivates their associative syntheses instead of avoiding them, and rediscovers the poetic value of passivity. In short, rather than put it out to play with quotation marks, rather than "reduce" it, this writing resolutely settles itself within the labyrinthian field of culture "bound" by its own equivocations, in order to travel through and explore the vastest possible historical distance that is now at all possible. (Derrida 1989, 102)

This passage might function as a description of Derrida's own project of grammatological reading, and it is obvious that Joyce is central to that project, given the frequency with which he appears in Derrida's work. Indeed, Derrida is explicitly hauntological in his relation to Joyce, claiming that "every time I write, and even in the most academic pieces of work, Joyce's ghost is always coming on board" (Attridge and Ferrer 1984, 149). From the introduction to *The Origin of Geometry* (1989), to *Speech and Phenomena*, and on to later books such as *The Post Card* (1987), and essays such as "Two Words for Joyce" (Attridge and Ferrer 1984) and "Ulysses Gramophone" (Derrida 1992), Joyce is a constant, if frustrating, presence. In the "Plato's Pharmacy" chapter of *Dissemination* there is even a footnote suggesting that it is nothing other than a reading of *Finnegan's Wake* (Derrida 1981). In "Two Words for Joyce" Derrida admits to not even being sure that he likes Joyce, or that he or anyone else can ever claim to have read Joyce (Attridge and Ferrer 1984, 148). Beyond the explicit references Joyce's influence on Derrida is also clear in much of his work, including his most experimental project *Glas* (1986), as well as his readings of the work of Paul Celan, Francis Ponge, and Walter Benjamin (the last two especially involving an engagement with the translatability/untranslatability of their proper names in a very Joycean fashion).

In his essay "Ulysses Gramophone," Derrida deals with the relation between Ulysses and the teletechnologies, such as the postal system, postcards, and telegraphy, that are a constituent part of the experience of late modernity. He engages with these phenomena through the question of the status of "yes." For Derrida, "yes" is not merely a word in language, but the word that comes before language, the affirmation that makes language, communication, possible at all:

> Yes, that's right, that's what I am saying, I am in fact, speaking, yes, there we are, I'm speaking, yes, yes, you can hear me, I can hear you, yes, we are in the process of speaking, there is language, you are receiving me, it's like this, it takes place, it happens, it is written, it is marked, yes, yes. (Derrida 1992, 297)

But for "yes" to be meaningful it must also be repeatable, iterable. "It must a priori and immediately confirm its promise and promise its confirmation." As an example of the mechanical repetition of yes, Derrida refers to *Ulysses*, citing the secretaries at the newspaper answering the phone: "Hello, yes, sir, no, sir, yes, sir." In such an essential repetition,

> [w]e can already hear a gramophony which records writing in the liveliest voice. A priori it reproduces it, in the absence of intentional presence on the part of the affirmer. Such a gramophony responds, of course, to the dream of a reproduction which preserves as its truth the living yes, archived in the very quick of its voice. (Derrida 1992, 276)

This is what Derrida calls "the gramophone effect," the "desire for memory and the mourning of yes," which sets "in motion the anamnesic machine. And its hypermnesic overacceleration. The machine reproduces the living, it doubles it with its automaton." Derrida takes another example from *Ulysses*, this time from the scene in the cemetery, in which Bloom imagines graves having gramophones with recordings of the dead:

> Besides how could you remember everybody? Eyes, walk, voice. Well, the voice, yes: gramophone. Have a gramophone in every grave or keep it in the house. After dinner on a Sunday. Put on poor old greatgrandfather. Kraahraark! Hellohellohello amawfullyglad kraark awfullygladaseeagain hellohello amawf krpthsth. Remind you of the voice like the photograph reminds you of the face. Otherwise you couldn't remember the face after fifteen years, say. (Joyce 2008, 109)

But perhaps most significantly, Derrida directly describes Joyce's work as a kind of highly advanced computer, also in advance of modern computing:

> … you can say nothing that is not programmed on this 1000th generation computer—Ulysses, Finnegans Wake—beside which the current technology of our computers and our micro-computerified archives and our translating machines

remains a bricolage of a prehistoric child's toys. And above all its mechanisms are of a slowness incommensurable with the quasi-infinite speed of the movements on Joyce's cables. How could you calculate the speed with which a mark, a marked piece of information, is placed in contact with another in the same word or from one end of the book to the other? For example, at what speed is the Babelian theme or the word "Babel," in each of their components (but how could you count them?), co-ordinated with all the phonemes, semes, mythemes, etc. of Finnegans Wake? Counting these connections, calculating the speed of these communications, would be impossible, at least de facto, so long as we have not constructed the machine capable of integrating all the variables, all the quantitative or qualitative factors. This won't happen tomorrow, and in any case this machine would only be the double or the simulation of the event "Joyce," the name of Joyce, the signed work, the Joyce software today, joyceware. (Attridge and Ferrer 1984, 147–148)

Lydia Liu takes up the relation between the Wake and computer technologies, but in a more contemporary mode. She singles out this passage from Joyce's work:

These paper wounds, four in type, were gradually and correctly understood to mean stop, please stop, do please stop, and O do please stop respectively, and following up their one true clue, the circumflexuous wall of a singleminded men's asylum, accentuated by bi tso fb rok engl a ssan dspl itch ina, —— Yard inquiries pointed out ——> that they ad bîn "provoked" ay fork, of à grave Brofèsor; àth é's Brèak–fast–table; ; acùtely profèššionally piquéd, to=introdùce a notion of time [ùpon à plane (?) sù ' ' fàçe'e'] by pùnct! ingh oles (sic) in iSpace?! (Joyce 2012, 124)

For Liu the neologism "iSpace" is particularly resonant in its anticipation of modern digital textual ideograms such as the iPhone:

Graphic spacing is taken as an assault on logocentrism as it dissolves the familiar word and becomes itself the originary act of writing in iSpace. The latter certainly anticipates the Derridean notion of spacing and différance for grammatology; but, more appropriately, iSpace is about the ideographic prolepsis of modern technology, ranging from cybernetics ... to the internet, bearing the news of the iPhone, iVision, iTunes, iLove, and iPolitics of the future. Most symptomatic of all is the appearance of iEnglish itself on the internet. The crux of the matter is not whether the letter i means "intelligent," "information," "internet," or "imaginary" or simply represents an inverted exclamation mark that has no corresponding phonetic equivalent in the spoken language but rather that the ideographic structure of i + Word (or even i + word) provides the sole semantic guarantor for any or all of the meanings one can possibly attribute to the letter i. (Liu 2010, 114)

Liu recounts the invention of the 27th letter of the English language, standing for the space, by Claude Shannon at Bell Labs in 1948 (or rather the reinvention of it, since Samuel Morse had already understood the need for such a character in telegraphy) (Liu 2010, 45–46). In her words, it is a "non-phonetically produced positive sig" that "laid the first stone in the mathematical foundation of information theory in the early postwar years; it was as revolutionary as Newton's Apple" (Liu 2010, 45). Shannon worked through his ideas about information, noise, and redundancy through the study of what he called "Printed English," which necessitated the invention of the space character and allowed him to approach the English language in mathematical and statistical terms. As described above, Shannon used *Finnegans Wake* as an example of extreme redundancy in prose. Liu describes this use of language as "Joyce's anticipatory contribution to communication engineering [...] his effort to bring the statistical properties of letter sequences and spaces among words and nonwords to light." Liu goes on to describe the Wake as an "act of engineering" that "involved subjecting the statistical mechanism of alphabetical writing to an elaborate literary experimentation two decades in advance of Shannon's experiment with the statistical models of Printed English" (Liu 2010, 103–104).

Shannon's pioneering work in information theory was intended to facilitate efficient electronic communication and to mitigate the effects of noise. Joyce was a crucial component in his analysis of language's technical communicability, especially in terms of redundancy, Shannon's term for the elements in any message that are not strictly necessary for its successful transmission, in an ideal communication situation (but are however often needed to overcome the problem of "noise"). Knowlton and Harmon's work at Bell Labs is exactly parallel to Shannon's, albeit in the visual realm. They were concerned with the minimum amount of information needed to make an image recognizable. This was, in part at least, done with an eye to the image's transmissibility, and they experimented with faxing their images. Knowlton and Harmon's experiments were part of the process by which imagery became efficiently transmissible within a networked culture. It also required fragmentation of images into discrete elements, glyphs and, later, pixels, in order to facilitate their transmission, which in turn brought them closer to writing, understanding as an arrangement of discrete elements that can be more easily manipulated, cited and rearranged, than traditional analogue images.

By using glyphs, and thus imbuing their images with considerable semantic complexity and ambiguity, Knowlton and Harmon produced images that are arguably Joycean, inasmuch as they evince the "greatest potential for buried, accumulated, and interwoven intentions within each linguistic atom" (especially if one substitutes the word "linguistic" with "visual"). Thus *Studies in Perception* might be understood to act as a break in our understanding of visual imagery, much as Joyce's work does in relation to language, in particular moving away from a logocentric paradigm of re-presentation, making present again, and toward a more writerly model of the image, and more visual model of language. As Donald Theall and Joan Theall point out, Joyce designed the *Wake* "in such a way that the reader had to both see the printed page with his eye, while simultaneously listening to it with his ear to be able to understand the workings of the language and the range of puns" (Theall and Theall 1989, 56).

It should be no surprise that Joyce anticipated the future of the image as a kind of writing explicitly in *Finnegans Wake*, as part of his investigation of "verbivocovisual presentements," his name for film and television. Early on in the *Wake* he declares that "Television kills telephony in brothers' broil. Our eyes demand their turn. Let them be seen!" (Joyce 2000, 52). The *Wake* features what may be the first fictional description of television, then only just invented. This takes place in Humphrey C.

Earwicker's dream of working in his tavern. In his dream his customers are watching a televised fight between two fighters, Butt and Taff:

> In the heliotropical noughttime following a fade of transformed Tuff and, pending its viseversion, a metenergic reglow of beaming Batt, the bairdboard bombardment screen, if tastefully taut guranium satin, tends to teleframe and step up the charge of a light barricade. Down the photoslope in syncopanc pulses, with bitts bugtwug their teffs, the missledhropes, glitteraglatteraglutt, borne by their carnier walve. Spraygun rakes and splits them from a double focus: grenadit, darnamyte, alextronite, nichilite: and the scanning firespot of the sgunners traverses the rutilanced illustred sunksundered lines Shlossh! A gaspel truce leaks out over the caseine coatings. Amid a fluorescence of spectracular mephiticism there coaculates through the iconoscope steadily a still ... (Joyce 2012, 349)

What is particularly noticeable about this passage is Joyce's prescient use of the term "bit" (or in his usage "bitt") to describe the elements making up the television picture long before this was used as a technical term. Theall and Theall suggested that Joyce "foresaw that the evolution of electric communication extends the rhetoric of the machine; thus accelerating our sense of the world as bits and pieces" (Theall and Theall 1989, 62).

Joyce thus acts as a secret passage between the otherwise apparently disparate worlds of Bell Labs and French theory. Certainly the highly technocratic, positivist, engineering ethos of Bell Labs is at odds with the framework in which French theory is operating, being founded on the work of continental philosophers and thinkers such as Marx, Freud, Nietzsche, Heidegger, and others. Indeed the two would seem to be directly and in some ways explicitly opposed. But it is this very opposition that reveals that these different phenomena are two sides of the same coin, that coin being cybernetics.

Cybernetics is, at its most precise, the word invented by Norbert Wiener to denote his "scientific study of control and communication in the animal and the machine" (Wiener 1948). More generally it can be taken as an umbrella term to cover the range of techno-scientific discourses that proliferated in the postwar era, including Wiener's cybernetics, but also Claude Shannon's information theory, and van Bertalanffy's systems theory. But cybernetics is also a key term in various developments within continental philosophy, albeit used more critically and circumspectly. Some of the issues of cybernetics are prefigured, *avant la lettre*, in Marx, particularly in the so-called "Fragment on Machines" in *Grundrisse* (1939). Though written in the 1850s, *Grundrisse* was not published until 1939, and after the war became an important resource for those trying to formulate a version of Marxism appropriate for a "cybernetic capitalism" dominated by information communication technologies. Freud's work on the unconscious also anticipated the idea of mental processes as machine-like. Martin Heidegger employed the term "cybernetics" in a more critical vein as another name for the relation between technology and metaphysics, which he also described as "enframing" or "gestell." The psychoanalyst Jacques Lacan was also greatly interested in cybernetics, and wrote two essays on its relevance to psychoanalysis in the 1950s.

But perhaps the most important continental engagement with cybernetics was that of Derrida, in *Of Grammatology*, his masterly early work, written at more or less exactly the same time that Knowlton and Harmon were conducting their experiments in perception. According to Derrida, cybernetics is grammatology inasmuch as it foregrounds writing over language. Derrida points out how "writing" has come to exceed and comprehend language, and is now used for phenomena once described by language, such as "action, movement, thought, reflection, consciousness, unconsciousness, experience, affectivity, etc.":

> we say "writing" for all that gives rise to an inscription in general, whether it is literal or not and even if what it distributes in space is alien to the order of the voice: cinematography, choreography, or course, but also pictorial, musical, sculptural "writing." (Derrida 1976, 9)

Derrida expands writing to cover even athletics, politics, and military techniques, as well as the way in which "the contemporary biologist speaks of writing and *pro-gram* in relation to the most elementary processes of information within the living cell" (Derrida 1976, 9). It is at this point in the paragraph that Derrida comes to what is clearly for him the most important development in this expansion of writing:

> And finally, whether it has essential limits or not, the entire field covered by the cybernetic program will be the field of writing. If the theory of cybernetics is by itself to oust all metaphysical concepts—including the concepts of soul, of life, of value, of choice, of memory—which until recently served to separate the machine from man, it must conserve the notion of writing, trace, grammè [written mark], or grapheme, until its own historico-metaphysical character is also exposed. Even before being determined as human (with all the distinctive characteristics that have always been attributed to man and the entire system of significations that they imply) or nonhuman, the grammè—or the grapheme—would thus name the element. An element without simplicity. An element, whether it is understood as the medium or as the irreducible atom, of the arche-synthesis in general, of what one must forbid oneself to define within the system of metaphysics, of what consequently one should not even call experience in general, that is to say the origin of meaning in general. (Derrida 1976, 9)

Here Derrida invokes André Leroi-Gourhan, whose ideas greatly influenced his notion of "grammatology." For Derrida, following Leroi-Gourhan, the "graphie" (the inscription or mark), is not merely something human, but a stage or an articulation in the history of life itself; in other words, it is "differance," as the history of the grammè or written mark. The "pro-gram" becomes, for Leroi-Gourhan and Derrida, the way of thinking about the history of life without recourse to the "concepts that habitually serve to distinguish man from other living beings (instinct and intelligence, absence or presence of speech, of society, of economy etc. etc.)" (Derrida 1976, 84). Derrida suggests that though this

> must be understood in the cybernetic sense … cybernetics is itself intelligible only in terms of a history of the possibilities of the trace as the unity of a double movement of protention and retention. (Derrida 1976, 84)

"Protention" and "retention" are terms Derrida takes from Husserl to describe how our consciousness of the present is structured by both the memory of what has passed, and anticipation of what is to come. It is what "goes far beyond the possibilities of the 'intentional consciousness' that makes the grammè appear *as such*," and leads not just to writing in the narrow sense, but from the "genetic inscription" and the "short programmatic chains" (regulating, for example, the behavior of the amoeba or the annelid) to "the passage beyond alphabetic writing and the orders of the logos of a certain *homo sapiens*." All is structured by the grammè (Derrida 1976, 84). Derrida invokes Leroi-Gourhan's concept of the "liberation of memory" from the "elementary programs of so-called "instinctive" behavior up to the constitution of electronic card-indexes and reading machines"—the very machines that were used in making Harmon and Knowlton's images (Derrida 1976, 84). Joyce anticipates this history of inscription in the *Wake*:

> A bone, a pebble, a ramskin; chip them, chap them, cut them up allways; leave them to terracook in the muttheringpot: and Gutenmorg with his cromagnom charter, tintingfast and great primer must once for omniboss step rub-rickredd out of the wordpress else is there no virtue more in al—cohoran. For that (the rapt one warns) is what papyr is meed of, made of, hides and hints and misses in prints. Till ye finally (though not yet endlike) meet with the acquaintance of Mister Typus, Mistress Tope and all the little typtopies. Fillstup. So you need hardly spell me how every word will be bound over to carry three score and ten toptypsical readings throughout the book of Doublends Jined (may his forehead be darkened with mud who would sunder!) till Daleth, mahomahouma, who oped it closeth thereof the. Dor. (Joyce 2012, 20).

Read against the grain of the humanist context in which it emerged, cybernetics can therefore be understood as a kind of grammatology in so far as it understands all phenomena in terms of the pro-gram. Since the pro-gram necessarily involves the grammè, the written mark, or grapheme, cybernetics is also necessarily concerned with spacing. Spacing, *espacement*, is crucial to Derrida's thinking, as Martin Hagglund explains in his book *Radical Atheism* (2008):

> Given that the now can appear only by disappearing – that it passes away as soon as it comes to be – it must be inscribed as a trace in order to be at all. This is the becoming-space of time. The trace is necessarily spatial, since spatiality is characterized by the ability to remain in spite of temporal succession. Spatiality is thus the condition for synthesis, since it enables the tracing of relations between past and future. Spatiality, however, can never be in itself; it can never be pure simultaneity. Simultaneity is unthinkable without a temporalization that relates one spatial juncture to another. This becoming-time of space is necessary not only for the trace to be related to other traces, but for it to be a trace in the first place. A trace can only be read after its inscription and is thus marked by a relation to the future that temporalizes space. (Hagglund 2008, 18)

In a sense the bitmapped image exemplifies this notion of spacing, not only since it is composed of discrete elements, but also because they are discrete by virtue of their difference from each other, defined in mathematical terms. This difference is particularly obvious in the case of early "one-bit" displays, in which every pixel was either black or white. But it remains the case in 24- or 32-bit images, which are able to define 256 levels each of red, green, and blue, thus making possible more than 16 million distinct colors. Harmon and Knowlton's work can be seen as a stage in the history of bitmapped computer graphics. These are sometimes also known as "raster graphics," a name that derives from the Latin *rastrum* for rake, and thus invokes a certain materiality of inscription. At Bell Labs A. Michael Noll developed an early raster display, which he described in a paper for the Communications of the ACM in 1971. As the abstract of the paper puts it,

> A television-like scanned-display system has been successfully implemented on a Honeywell DDP-224 computer installation. The scanned image is stored in the core memory of the computer, and software scan conversion is used to convert the rectangular coordinates of a point to the appropriate word and bit in an output display array in core storage. Results thus far indicate that flicker-free displays of large amounts of data are possible with reasonably fast graphical interaction. A scanned image of size 240 × 254 points is displayed at a 30 frame-per-second rate. (Noll 1971)

Noll's attempt to patent this system was abandoned at the Supreme Court in 1977 on the basis of issues surrounding the patentability of computer software. Despite or perhaps because of this rejection, research into raster graphics continued throughout the 1970s and 1980s, though its use was limited to high-end graphic workstations, at least until the advent of personal computers with "graphical user interfaces" (GUIs), such as the Apple Lisa and Apple Macintosh. The former is possibly the first computer to feature a bit-mapped display. This display was necessary for mixing text and graphics and made Lisa the first computer understood as an apparatus primarily for media processing, rather than for calculation.

The Lisa was too expensive to succeed commercially, but the Macintosh, or Mac, became extremely successful. One of the early programs for the Mac was Hypercard, which attempted to put Ted Nelson's notion of hypertext into practice (Project Xanadu History 1999). Hypertext was the idea of non-linear texts developed by Nelson in the mid-1960s, at the same time as Bell Labs researchers were pioneering computer graphics. Hypercard was based on the metaphor of a Rolodex, and allowed the user to link different virtual cards. Despite the minimal one-bit graphic capabilities of the Mac, there were some surprisingly sophisticated uses of Hypercard, such as the interactive environment/game *Cosmic Osmo* (1989). For theorists such as Landow, hypertext put into practice the kind of textual experiments that Derrida had been advocating and indeed practicing since the 1960s (Landow 1992). His texts *Glas* and *The Post Card*, in particular, seemed to prefigure the fragmentary nature of hypertext. The creation of a link between Derrida and hypertext may have been something of a misunderstanding of Derrida's strategies, but there clearly was some connection between them and these new technologies. The idea that Derrida's work had some affinity with computer data management was also posited by Geoff Bennington, who declared,

> If writing had for Derrida a privileged empirical version, this would be less manuscripture, or even typescript [...], but the computer, which he has been using for a short while [...] Not just because of the "memory" traces of an electronic archive, which can only with difficulty be thought according to the opposition between the

> sensible and the intelligible, and more easily as differences of force or capacity (although this is already important [...], helping us to think writing in a more complicated relation with space and time): but also because of the possibilities of folding a text back on itself, of discontinuous jumps establishing quasi-instantaneous links between sentences, words, or marks separated by hundreds of pages. (Bennington 1993, 313–314)

Bennington declared his ambition to put together what he called a "Derridabase":

> It is not at all by chance that Derrida talks of Joyce's books in terms of supercomputers ... nor that his thought should communicate in an essential way with certain discourses on so-called artificial intelligence. Nor that we should have conceived this book a little on the model of a "hypertext" program which would allow, at least in principle, an almost instantaneous access to any page or work or mark from any other, and which would be plugged into a memory containing all of Derrida's texts, themselves simultaneously accessible by "themes", key words, references, turns of "style", etc. (which our list of references simulates for better and worse), and then to a larger memory making accessible, according to the same multiple entries, the texts quoted and invoked by Derrida, with everything that forms their "context", therefore just about the (open) totality of the universal library, to say nothing of musical or visual or other (olfactory, tactile, gustative) archives to be invented [...] But this machine is already in place, it is the "already" itself. We are inscribed in it in advance, promise of hazardous memory in the monstrous to-come, like the monumental, pyramidal, but so humble signature, so low, effaced, of Jacques Derrida, here below, now. (Bennington 1993, 314–315)

Bennington's project ended up being a book on Derrida, with entries trying to capture and domesticate his thought in an encyclopedic and perhaps totalizing way, while a text by Derrida entitled "Circumfession" along the bottom of each page undid any attempt at such totalization. The book also contains a photograph of Derrida and Bennington in Derrida's study, parodying the medieval image of Plato apparently standing behind Socrates—philosophers Derrida constantly returns to in *The Post Card*. The image shows that the computer on which Derrida is working is a Mac. In an interview with *La Quinzaine Litteraire*—published in the book *Paper Machine* under the title "The Word Processor"—he declares "I can't do without anymore, this little Mac" (Derrida 2005, 20).

As a number of writers have pointed out, the context that led to the emergence of cybernetics, the work of Bell Labs and similar organizations, the Internet, Apple Computers and the World Wide Web, was also that of the rise and triumph of neoliberalism. In 1992, in the context of the so-called "end of history," Derrida engaged with what he called the "specters of Marx" (Derrida 1993). It was in the context of this engagement that he named and defined the notion of "hauntology." Derrida's main premise was that, against the grain of neoliberal triumphalism, the spirit of Marx and Marxism still haunted the world, not least because of the continued prevalence of the same issues that had animated Marx's thought in the first place. Derrida points out that Marx, among other things, was the first thinker of technics as well as deeply concerned with the spectral and ghostly (Derrida 1993). Technics and spectrality are of course closely related, as suggested above. In a long passage at the end of a section critiquing the work of Francis Fukuyama, Derrida asserts deconstruction's ability to

> take into account, or render an account of, the effects of ghosts, of simulacra, of "synthetic images", or even, to put it in terms of the Marxist code, of ideologems, even if these take the novel forms to which modern technology will have given rise. (Derrida 1993, 75)

Summing up near the end of the book, Derrida lays out what is at stake in contemporary politics understood in relation to Marx's legacy:

> also at stake, indissociably, is the differantial deployment of tekhne, of techno-science or tele-technology. It obliges more than ever to think the virtualization of space and time, the possibility of virtual events whose movement and speed prohibit us more than ever (more and otherwise than ever, for this is not absolutely and thoroughly new) from opposing presence to its representation, "realtime" to "deferred time," effectivity to its simulacrum, the living to the non-living, in short, the living to the living-dead of its ghosts. It obliges us to think, from there, another space for democracy. For democracy-to-come and thus for justice. We have suggested that the event we are prowling around here hesitates between the singular "who" of the ghost and the general "what" of the simulacrum. In the virtual space of all the tele-technosciences, in the general dis-location to which our time is destined—as are from now on the places of lovers families, nations—the messianic trembles on the edge of this event itself. (Derrida 1993, 169)

Though Derrida would not necessarily have known it at the time, the year in which his thoughts on Marx were published was also that in which the World Wide Web went from being a specialized system for computer experts to one with far greater reach. This was owing to advent of user-friendly web browsers such as Mosaic. This, along with the increasing capacity of the Web to handle images and graphics, led to it becoming the media-rich environment with which we are now familiar. It is on the Web where the bitmap images that are the descendants of the early experiments in computer imagery done at Bell Labs in the 1960s now circulate with spectral ease.

They are part of what J. Hillis Miller calls the new regime of telecommunications that breaks down "the inside/outside dichotomies that presided over the old print culture" (Miller 2000): This new regime involves

> the breakdown of traditional boundaries between inside and outside brought about by new communication technologies [...] the new electronic space, the space of television, cinema, telephone, videos, fax, e-mail, hypertext, and the Internet, has profoundly altered the economies of the self, the home, the workplace, the university, and the nation-state's politics. (Miller 2000)

Miller claims that these are all ordered around "the firm boundaries of an inside–outside dichotomy," from the home to the nation state. He continues, "the new technologies invade the home and the nation. They confound all these inside/outside divisions" (Miller 2000), as ghosts do.

Notes

1 http://www.knowltonmosaics.com/
2 These terms, and others he used over his career, are intended to deconstruct the metaphysics of presence, and the ontology of Being.
3 Given that I shall argue for the importance of James Joyce to these developments later in the chapter, it is perhaps worth noting that Knowlton gives his account the Joycean title of "Portrait of the Artist as a Young Scientist."
4 If one thinks of these fragments as analogous to pixels then it is instructive to compare the density of the images to, for example, the screen I am working on, which is set at 32-bit color, meaning it has over 16 million colours available, and 256 levels of grayscale, and has a resolution of 1366 times 768 pixels, or 1049088 pixels.
5 Joseph Francis, a designer working for R/Greenberg Associates in Manhattan is believed to be the inventor of the photomosaic with his "Live from Bell Labs" posts, created in 1993.
6 For Saussure, words in language do not have a positive relation with what they represent, but rather operate in a system of difference and custom. Thus the word "cat" comes to denote the domestic feline, not because it has any privileged relationship with the creature, but because it differs from similar words, "mat", "sat", etc., and because it has become associated with that which it denotes.

References

Abraham, Nicolas, and Maria Torok. 1986. *The Wolfman's Magic Word.* Minneapolis, MN: The University of Minnesota Press.

Attridge, Derek, and Daniel Ferrer, eds. 1984. *Post-structuralist Joyce: Essays from the French.* Cambridge: Cambridge University Press.

Barthes, Roland. 1981. *Camera Lucida.* New York: Hill & Wang.

Bazin, André. 1960. "The Ontology of the Photographic Image." *Film Quarterly* 13(4).

Benjamin, Walter. 1969. *Illuminations.* New York: Schocken Books.

Bennington, Geoffrey. 1993. *Jacques Derrida.* Chicago and London: The University of Chicago Press.

Derrida, Jacques. 1976. *Of Grammatology.* Baltimore, MD and London: Johns Hopkins University Press.

Derrida, Jacques. 1978. *Writing and Difference.* London and New York: Routledge.

Derrida. Jacques. 1979. *Spurs: Eperons.* Chicago and London: The University of Chicago Press.

Derrida, Jacques. 1981. *Dissemination.* London: Athlone Press.

Derrida, Jacques. 1989. *Edmond Husserl's Origin of Geometry: An Introduction by Jacques Derrida.* Lincoln: University of Nebraska Press.

Derrida, Jacques. 1992. *Acts of Literature*, edited by Derek Attridge. London and New York: Routledge.

Derrida, Jacques. 1993. *Specters of Marx: The State of the Debt, the Work of Mourning, & the New International.* New York: Routledge.

Derrida, Jacques. 2005. *Paper Machine.* Chicago and London: The University of Chicago Press.

Edwards, Ben J. 2013. "The Never-Before-Told Story of the World's First Computer Art (It's a Sexy Dame)." *The Atlantic*. January 25. http://www.theatlantic.com/technology/archive/2013/01/the-never-before-told-story-of-the-worlds-first-computer-art-its-a-sexy-dame/267439/ (accessed January 15, 2015).

Hagglund, Martin. 2008. *Radical Atheism: Derrida and the Time of Life*. Stanford, CA: Stanford University Press.

Hodges, Andrew. 1985. *Alan Turing: The Enigma of Intelligence*. London and Sydney: Unwin.

Joyce, James. 2008. *Ulysses*. Oxford and New York: Oxford University Press.

Joyce, James. 2012. *Finnegans Wake*. Oxford and New York: Oxford University Press.

Kittler, Friedrich. 1990. *Discourse Networks 1800/1900*. Stanford, CA: Stanford University Press.

Knowlton, Ken. 2005. "Portrait of the Artist as a Young Scientist." http://www.kenknowlton.com/pages/04portrait.htm (accessed January 15, 2015).

Koerner, Joseph. 2004. *The Reformation of the Image*. London: Reaktion Books.

Landow, George. 1992. *Hypertext: The Convergence of Contemporary Critical Theory and Technology*. Baltimore, MD: Johns Hopkins University Press.

Laplanche, Jean, and J.B. Pontalis. 1968. "Fantasy and the Origins of Sexuality." *International Journal of Psychoanalysis* 49(1).

Leroi-Gourhan, André. 1993. *Gesture and Speech*. Cambridge, MA: The MIT Press.

Lieberman, Henry B. 1967. "Art and Science Proclaim Alliance in Avant-Garde Loft." *The New York Times*, October 11.

Liu, Lydia. 2010. *The Freudian Robot: Digital Media and the Future of the Unconscious*. Chicago and London: The University of Chicago Press.

Miller, J. Hillis. 2000. "'Stay! Speak, Speak. I Charge Thee, Speak': An Interview by Wang Fengzhen and Shaobo Xie." *Culture Machine* 2.

Noll, A. Michael. 1971. "Scanned-display Computer Graphics." *Communications of the ACM* 14(3).

Project Xanadu History. 1999. http://xanadu.com/HISTORY/ (accessed January 15, 2015).

Reichardt, Jasia. 1971. *The Computer in Art*. London: Studio Vista.

Stiegler, Bernard. 1998. *Technics and Time: The Fault of Epimetheus*. Stanford, CA: Stanford University Press.

Theall, Donald, and Joan Theall. 1989. "Marshall McLuhan and James Joyce: Beyond Media." *Canadian Journal of Communication* 14(4).

Ulmer, Gregory. 1985. *Applied Grammatology: Post(e)-Pedagogy from Jacques Derrida to Joseph Beuys*. London and New York: Routledge.

Wiener, Norbert. 1948. *Cybernetics, or Control and Communication in the Animal and the Machine*. Cambridge, MA: The MIT Press.

8

Participatory Art
Histories and Experiences of Display

Rudolf Frieling

It comes as no surprise that participatory works of art have long been considered anathema within the institutional realm of a museum. They were kept at bay by the various mechanisms of exclusion and institutional expertise that called for a controlled gallery environment to protect the art. Every public showing of a work of art could possibly harm its longevity. The public was considered the art's foe rather than its friend. Thankfully, the critique of these patterns of exclusion and stifling museumification is very well known. From performative works to Institutional Critique, artists were among the first to challenge the notion of collecting finite works as precious commodities. The open and participatory work of art made a point in countering this institutional framework. In other words, artists tried to eschew the pitfalls of museumification and celebrate the work's nature of being impossible to collect.

This dominant narrative, however, fails to reflect institutional changes over the last decade. So let me take the well-trodden path of Institutional Critique for granted and instead explore a more contemporary change: while participatory works were often meant to be a unique disruption and intervention into the museum setting, they did not go unnoticed. As it turns out, we can now look back at the first histories of participatory art within the museum, and can question what effect this history has had on the dichotomy of participation and museums. Responding to the rise of social media over the last decade, many museums have begun to reflect on their history as well as their own practice by readdressing participation in art. The question is, has the institution of the museum changed or has participatory art been tamed? This chapter will look at the effects of the history of participation, with a specific interest in participatory works that have successfully entered the Media Arts Collection of the San Francisco Museum of Modern Art (SFMOMA). I will chart a few exemplary narratives that will allow us to trace changes in participatory artworks from within a collecting institution. As a first step, I will introduce some threads that were first tested in the 1960s and 1970s by artists such as Robert Morris, as well as by the following generation of

A Companion to Digital Art, First Edition. Edited by Christiane Paul.

artists as exemplified by Felix Gonzalez-Torres. These notes will help illuminate the complexities of the histories of digital participatory art since the mid-1990s, which I will explore in more depth by discussing the exhibitions of Julia Scher's installation *Predictive Engineering* (1993/1998) and Dora García's performance *Instant Narrative* (2006–2008); Lynn Hershman Leeson's online work *Agent Ruby* (1999–2002) and Harrell Fletcher and Miranda July's online platform *Learning to Love You More* (2002–2009).

A First Thesis

Looking back at a track record of participatory exhibitions that spans frictions but also productive responses, I will make three specific arguments related to the notion of change in collections, to the appropriate responses by the collecting institution, and to the impact of the public on the work's presence in an exhibition.

To get us started, I propose the following first thesis: there has not been a single paradigm shift or dramatic change in participatory art that helped the museum to embrace this form's radically different concepts of art—change is rather permanently at work. In fact, permanence through change is what attracts curators like me and other professionals and critics to the work, not to speak of the tremendous success it enjoys with the public. The change in museums toward a more flexible approach to participatory art has happened in dialogue with a broader shift in contemporary art. We have seen a surge of exhibitions, symposia, publications, and debates around the notion of participation in art. A discursive field from Nicolas Bourriaud in the 1990s (Bourriaud 2002) to more recent publications by Grant Kester, Anna Dezeuze, or Claire Bishop (Kester 2004; Dezeuze 2009; Bishop 2012) has evolved around a mostly academic analysis of this uncharted terrain in relation to a presumed or stated social agenda. The emphasis has been on the conceptual, categorical, political implications of participatory art, and on its effects on the institutions, the art market, activism, education, and so on. The specifics of an artistic dimension in the participatory sphere are still a question. So, with a closer look at the exhibition histories of key works from SFMOMA's collection, one can better frame the question, what is the "art of participation" (Frieling 2008)?

For me as a curator of a museum collection of media art that, by default, is variable and "subject to change," it is a striking phenomenon that one can already look back at a history of presentations of variable works of art. These specific histories can be formulated within the realm of technology and changing playback formats, which is certainly of prime importance, but for the purpose of this chapter I will tackle a different and possibly more complex task. In order to follow up on thoughts that I first published in 2008 in the catalogue *The Art of Participation: 1950 to Now* (Frieling 2008), I will focus on a few particular histories of participatory art as experienced through a series of changing displays and interfaces. All the examples cover the time frame from the 1990s to now, roughly speaking the two decades of global digitization in the arts that often make works look historic and sometimes dated at an increasingly maddening pace. Pushing beyond the changes in technology that have been addressed many times before, I will concentrate on participatory works that reveal their variable presence in space as their conceptual and practical core condition from their inception until today.

Re-installing

Museums have long grappled with the variable conditions and different temporalities of time-based narratives resulting in a complex set of "co-temporalities," which Terry Smith identified as one of the defining features of contemporary art (Smith 2009, 3–5). The complexities of co-temporality—the often disjunctive ways of experiencing time-based art—can be applied to the hybrids of analog and digital components, to the generations of software-based works, as well as to a contemporary confluence of time and performance through "re-performing" historic works. In media art we have also seen the rise of the MediaArtHistories conference series, from "Refresh" (2005) to "Renew" (2013), the titles of which were all based on the prefix "re-" (Buskirk, Jones, and Jones 2013). While the notion of "re-installing" a work is generally accepted, the term "re-perform" has been widely criticized in the academic world. I argue, though, that this term is a productive proposition: we need a discourse around the relevance of a whole genre that seemed to have been allocated firmly to the historic period of the 1960s and 1970s. Histories of performance art had found their way into exhibitions and permanent collections only as documents that over time came to signify the art itself. What is less noted is that, over the last decade, these documented histories prompted museum collections to rethink their established narratives by embracing not only the documented histories but also contemporary performative works in dialogue with the permanence of a collection. I certainly believe that a unique and singular event cannot be inserted into a concept of "re-performance." Yet, at the same time, it seems to be possible and legitimate to do exactly that in those instances where the performance is conceptually not based on the presence/body of the artist. Once this kind of performative action is translated into a series of sustained or repeated events, the idea of "performing" a display of objects and installations becomes tangible. We have thus moved from performance to performativity within the museum's claim on permanence and immutability.

In the past, artists have addressed performativity, for example in software or social relations, by inserting open-ended participatory projects into the closed, controlled environment of a museum. Others have tackled the seemingly immutable construction of collection displays, from the ongoing fictitious museum display of the *Department of Eagles* (1968–1975) by Marcel Broodthaers to the work of Fred Wilson, Mark Dion, or Andrea Fraser. What is needed now is to acknowledge these two distinct trajectories and analyze the frameworks of collection presentation as performative acts of translation: from one space into another, from one time into another, and from one context into another. While participatory art has largely emerged on the global circuit of biennials of temporary exhibitions, museum collections offer the actualization and reception of a second, third, or fourth installation in relationship to a specific place and time. It is through the reinstallation of variable formats that a shift takes place, a shift that first and foremost produces a difference in perception as a precondition for an expanded understanding of possible histories of participatory work. The focus on the situation and condition of a participatory proposal in the "here and now" dominated the discourse in the past. Today we realize that some of these participatory works are still around and have a renewed urgency, so that the perception of the "here and now" includes an awareness of "there and then." In other words, some collecting institutions have laid the groundwork for a comparative analysis of participatory art as well. These comparative histories, one could posit, are not written by unearthing and looking back at forgotten documents but by experiencing the works again and again under different conditions.

By generously accommodating variable configurations, possibly even different aesthetic experiences, the works in question fundamentally address a precarious presence from the very beginning, a condition based on contextual, social, institutional, and technological set-ups. As I will show in the following, these works are collaborative in an emphatic way and proactively address change—maybe in order to stay the same or maybe in order to open up for actual change. The museum, while historically the anti-place for participation in art and criticized for enforcing grand narratives, re-emerges under this focal lens as the appropriate site for a shift that takes time to manifest itself. What is needed in order to construct histories of participatory art is the "deep time" of a museum collection.

How process becomes manifest

It happened in music, in dance, in visual art in the 1950s and 1960s: a radical deconstruction of composition, choreography, or visual expression toward a grammar of simple activities. Artists were "doing a piece" and not a work as a finished product and commodity. Processual practices have acted upon traditional formats and displays, and their long-lasting effects are still tangible in what Terry Smith calls "remodernization" of contemporary art. In the 1960s, the object left its lofty pedestal and engaged with poor materials, unassuming spaces, and floors etc. Yet the object took on an afterlife that was anything but processual and performative. Objects by Richard Serra and others massively claimed space, so much so that they have become irreplaceable and the epitome of static permanence—see the permanently installed works at Dia Beacon, NY, for example. What happened in between? The obvious answer is: the works got institutionalized and fell prey to the much criticized process of collecting and museumification. This answer, however, is based once again on the assumption that a lively work of art gets stifled the moment it enters a museum collection. Although many past experiences seem to confirm this, the curatorial and institutional responses to the conundrums of collecting today have risen to the challenge of a "living museum" as first theorized and practically tested by Alexander Dorner in the 1920s and 1930s at the Landesmuseum in Hanover, Germany. Dorner was the first to challenge basic assumptions of museum display by embracing mobile units and multimedia exhibition design.[1]

A second example will help us understand the impact of an institutional collection on work that is actually meant to be variable and participatory. A contemporary of Serra, Robert Morris, famously worked with materials that stayed malleable and soft, such as felt. Mirroring concerns that were first voiced by John Cage, Morris believed that the open instructions to install his soft pieces were embracing chance and implicitly also indeterminacy. Each time a felt piece was going to be installed, it would fall differently depending on context and chance. He was making a case for a sculptural work to be casual and to stay true to its material specificity of adapting to different physical influences, such as gravity, pressure, temperature, or elasticity of material. Works would be "scattered" rather than placed.[2] This, however, is not how it played out over time. The artist himself, whose practice was part of a larger group of artists rejecting the aesthetics and concepts of a fixed form, realized that the process of documenting a given installation had unforeseen after-effects: "once photographed, no one wanted to hear about various positions."[3] I am struck by the fact that this process of variability is institutionally and publicly acknowledged but never actually experienced by the visitor in an exhibition since contextual visual information on variants of display is typically not considered museum practice. The display of a specific iteration is removed from its potentiality of variants for the sake of consistency. But what if the concept of the artwork requires an awareness and presentation of its histories and potentialities of display?

The power of the document and the desire to honor the original are often associated with the assumption that one has to be exact, precise, consistent, and truthful to the presumed or stated intent in the representation of a work in the museum. Institutional activities guarantee a legitimacy of display. What emerges in Morris's words above, though, is an inherent contradiction. In order to stay true to the original concept, the work on display needs to be indeterminate—even the specific configuration of the work as it is stored becomes part of a valid display from the artist's point of view. But how does one collect and install histories of change and indeterminacy?

Display: The unfolding of meaning
Serra's lead sculptures and Morris's felt sculptures are obviously not examples of participatory art, but they are based on a practice in relation to space that can project us into the variabilities of the digital realm and participatory structures. When open-ended artistic practice and an adaptive, responsive museum practice join forces, the idea of a performative collection presentation emerges. If we take the etymological root of display as an indication,[4] it is an act over time in space, the unfolding of something in space for a public exhibition: "display" derives from the Old French *desploir* (Modern French *déployer*) "unfold, unfasten, spread out" (of knots, sealed letters, etc.) and from the Latin *displicare* "to scatter," from *dis-* "un-, apart" + *plicare* "to fold." To fold could then mean to stack, store, pack—and to unfold then would mean the act of making something publicly visible. Museums used to simply "hang" their collection; now they need to install and display it. There is, however, an essential reading implicated in the act of display: that there is a core, an essence that can actually be unfolded as in "uncovered." We would probably have a hard time defending such an essential, non-contextual reading, but the question of what constitutes a "core" is still a productive one.

A Second Thesis

From the first thesis—change is continuously at work—I can now move on to a second thesis: the "core" in question is not only a set of material and conceptual artistic parameters, it is also a set of responses by the collecting institution including the practices of exhibition, conservation, and documentation.

Documenting Change

The examples above also imply a crucial shift in the process of documenting works, which covers a wide field ranging from a memory shared with the artist to the track record of changing displays. Yet my argument with regard to process and time-based works is that the document needs to be thought of as a form of history writing in which not only the artist's voice is recorded. It includes tracking the collector's practice—in the case of an institution, the interventions of staff members involved in preserving and exhibiting. Going beyond the tracking of the typical agents in this process, it would now involve a record of the actual experience of a work as it impacts the understanding of the piece: effects produced; the impact of the public display and context; and the responses to the installed work by all players in this complex field, including the visitors' actualizations and experiences. This process of complex interactions goes beyond the definitions of cybernetic feedback to include playful and chance events that occur, driven as much by the concept or software of the work on display as by the seemingly arbitrary events and contingencies that nevertheless give texture to our understanding of a work.

There might be a difference in judgment when participatory art engages visitors to the point of destruction—for example, Robert Morris's *Bodyspacemotionthings* at the Tate, London, 1971[5] (Kalina 1969)—or to the point of making an unforeseen and possibly poetic use of the work (Dezeuze 2009, 39–40). It was an unforeseen moment of insight into the experience of a work in a museum setting when I witnessed the way in which the public can interact with something as simple as a poster from a stack-piece by Felix Gonzalez-Torres. What was clearly meant to be a display of posters as a free take-away triggered unforeseen actualizations in the context of the exhibition *The Art of Participation* at SFMOMA in 2008. The only stated instruction was "please take a poster." The fact that these posters were not only taken and redistributed, but sometimes also folded, thrown, trashed, and so on, was unexpected. The object prompted undefined activities that exceeded the implications of the instruction. Most of the writings on Gonzalez-Torres's work have focused on a dominant narrative of loss, AIDS, and post-minimalist concepts. It is time to also talk about the effects that a work such as a take-away poster produces—not in order to blame it for these effects, but to take them into consideration when writing histories of participatory art. I witnessed a poster folded into a sculptural paper airplane, then thrown to let it swerve through space. The interaction begs the question to what extent it prompts the participant to think differently about the piece which, in this particular case, depicts a grey sky with a lonely bird in flight.

Conservation of a work of contemporary work of art is equally challenged by the ways in which concepts, materials, and artistic practice have fundamentally altered the notion of collecting contemporary art. The letter, the photo, the written statement by the conservator—all of these are needed more than anything else. The crucial point made by Robert Morris in relation to his own works in collections, however, is that an exact and comprehensive documentation can be used against the artist's intentions. The photographic and the written document can even exert a retrospective power. They eliminate the complexity of a work that is based on performativity and instead support a final form, hence Morris's pledge for "anti-form." In participatory and time-based works, these archival records do not simply get more complex when the works embrace process, chance, and indeterminacy. The most significant change is one in perception and process. What comes into play in all variable and participatory works is the notion of presenting an experience in a work of art. Can one document and display the continuum of pasts and presents and invoke future displays too?

Something's Happening in the Galleries

The display of a participatory work thus includes the performative action that the public brings to the work. We can further unfold the implications of this shift in perception by adding that it is a "situation" that conditions a specific display. I am using this term, which obviously resonates with the legacy of Situationism in its political and historical underpinnings, for its reference to a specific space and time that includes all the actors in this field: the artists, the museum staff, and the public. Something's happening in the here and now, and it needs to be addressed immediately. One cannot simply "hang" the work; one must watch it carefully as it "unfolds" in the galleries. In short, one has to stay attentive and involved in a process. Taking a cue from the "expanded field" as theorized by Rosalind Krauss (1979, 30–44), we can conceive of such a process-driven presentation as forming an "experiential field." And it is possibly this attention and manifest activity that constitutes a "core" of the work in question. Does the display chosen in a particular context generate productive, maybe even poetic, readings and understandings of a work or does it rather eliminate possibilities? The "core" then becomes a set of relationships between a concept and material display and an institutional response to generate and sustain the public activation of a work.

A Third Thesis

This finally brings me to the third thesis, which acknowledges the essential role of the public: the public's actions do not only follow the artist's intent but actively expand and shape the understanding and experience of participatory art.

The subjectivities of the term "experience" are endless and clearly imprecise compared to the exactitude of a photographic record and its art-historical counterpart, "contemplation." Many have argued that all works of art are experienced in some way, yet I am not interested in following a string of arguments that seems to make a case for one or the other. My argument is rather that it is precisely this experiential factor that will determine the success of a renewed form of display in time-based, performative, and code-based works. Is distance in time and space, considered to be a prerequisite for the emergence of history, also a condition for the histories of participatory art? And how do we deal with the concern that the "presence" of a work is not only tied to its effects on an individual or on a community as expressed in their responsive actions, but also to the way it is displayed aesthetically? Last but not least, how do these factors contribute to a different way of narrating these histories? Even when a visitor is experiencing a work physically on view rather than a document of an event or work, a key question for creating histories of participation in art still is what exactly "presence" might mean. In the digital sphere, for example, it is a considerably different story when the display consists of a computer monitor at home as opposed to an installed situation in public space, constantly interpreted and acted upon by the public.

Four Case Studies of Dynamic Displays

What follows below is a look at four specific histories of digital art displays over decades. These cases are linked to a set of problems that are not unique to the digital sphere, as the early example of Morris has shown, but become more urgent and unavoidable in the case of the constantly evolving terrain of digital technologies. In terms of historical time spans, the digital platforms of ten years ago are already historic artifacts. In other words, digital histories surface as we speak and write about today's technology, but they surface only for a brief moment. I have selected four works that illuminate the complexities of the histories of digital participatory art since the mid-1990s: Julia Scher's installation *Predictive Engineering* (1993/1998) and Dora García's performance *Instant Narrative* (2006–2008) share aspects of real-time representations; Lynn Hershman Leeson's *Agent Ruby* (1999–2002) and Harrell Fletcher and Miranda July's *Learning to Love You More* (2002–2009) are two web-based works that have been presented in a variety of mixed-media installations. In each case, the public enacts a dialogue in space and time. They all follow an unprecedented trajectory of complexity and indeterminacy, which clearly was part of the fascination of acquiring these works. I will outline some of the histories embedded in these various manifestations that have a surprising impact on the blurry boundaries between collecting and archiving in art.

Lynn Hershman Leeson: Agent Ruby *(1999–2002)*

In 2001–2002, SFMOMA commissioned San Francisco artist Lynn Hershman Leeson's online project *Agent Ruby*,[6] an artificial intelligence Internet entity that has engaged online users in at times serious, humorous, quirky, or even absurd conversations, which in turn have shaped her memory, knowledge, and moods, at least to a certain degree. As a classic conversationalist, Ruby knows how to dodge a question, divert attention, or simply reflect and deflect an implied sense. She also has favorite themes and questions that she can toss in for a change of subject. In other words, a conversation with this agent never gets dull. The work reflects the artist's longstanding interest in the interaction between fictional or virtual characters and real people or situations.

The work was accessioned by SFMOMA in 2009 as one of the first Internet artwork to officially enter the collection, despite the fact that the museum had been among the first to embrace the emerging Internet art at the end of the 1990s. The analysis of the virtual agent's implications for the museum's collection policy and practice prompted a second public look at the online platform, which resulted in the exhibition titled *Lynn Hershman Leeson: The Agent Ruby Files* in 2013 (Figure 8.1). This digital and analog presentation reinterpreted dialogues drawn from more than a decade of archived text files and reflected on technologies, recurrent themes, and patterns of audience engagement. Exhibiting the project in 2013 as an interactive terminal alongside an archival setting with eight thematic binders and printouts of a hundred related conversations from the past twelve years turned out to be not an easy task, as the simple algorithmic mining of all log files produced a huge amount of redundancy and noise such as aborted dialogues. One of the more productive outcomes, however, was the realization that, while certain everyday political or technological topics clearly had changed, the patterns of interaction had not shifted much. Ruby dealt with scams, bots, and plain attempts at insult as gracefully as ever. In fact, the perseverance with which the virtual agent kept up the dialogue prompted many visitors to seriously engage in prolonged conversations, possibly due to the fact that they were also being watched by others in the public realm of the gallery context. This deepened level of commitment was further highlighted by

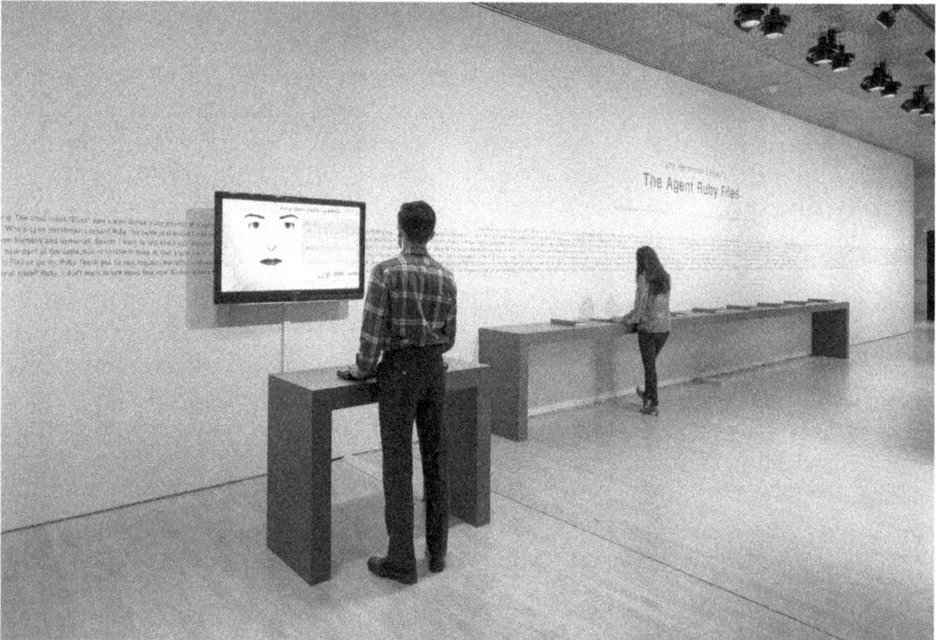

FIGURE 8.1 Lynn Hershman Leeson: *The Agent Ruby Files*, SFMOMA (2013). AIML Programming: Colin Klingman. Collection SFMOMA, gift of the artist, commissioned by SFMOMA. Photo: Johanna Arnold, Courtesy of SFMOMA, © Lynn Hershman Leeson.

the curatorial decision to commission and preface the archival binders with eight new conversations that were driven by an interest in the eight thematic fields proposed as avenues of research into Agent Ruby's database of knowledge. This somewhat arbitrary probing of her "artificial intelligence" in relation to these topics ("economy"—"dream"—"feminism"—"humanistic"—"philosophy"—"politics"—"sexuality"—"technology") produced an embodied understanding of the patterns of interaction, including the recurring frustration to have Ruby focus more deeply on terminology, topology, or memories related to the topics. These pitfalls of communication, however, also proved to be the driving force of sustained engagement. In an era of ubiquitous voice-recognition, GPS-software, and "virtual assistants" such as "Siri," the quirky character of Ruby has reaffirmed her relevance despite the almost complete change of context brought about by our daily social media interactions. This resistance to instant gratification, more than anything else, turns out to be a key factor in the prolonged shelf life of this virtual agent. The exhibition display gave equal importance to the acts of writing and reading, setting a stage for a more nuanced and informed act of participation in public space. Just how one could teach her that George Bush is not the US president any more remains a riddle to be solved in the future.

Last but not least, let me point out that works like *Agent Ruby* not only generate new perceptions or unforeseen responses when reinstalled, but the platforms of presentation generate original content and thus new materials. Here, the body of text produced online and on site in the museum is archived but not immediately accessible or viewable to the public. But this might change in the future. A work that produces its own history of effects and affects as a context generator is complex, and there is more than one history to tell. The art actively engages in a constant mode of expansion, so to speak. It is this mode that inherently links it to the next work from our collection being discussed as a generator of content.

Dora García: Instant Narrative (2006)

In Dora García's *Instant Narrative*, accessioned in 2011 and exhibited at SFMOMA as part of the exhibition *Descriptive Acts* in 2012, visitors encountered a complex situation of feedback and surveillance in public space. A projected text on a wall manifested an ongoing narrative that required visitors' attention as readers. This work was on view during museum hours and performed live by a series of writers who each interpreted the present gallery situation differently, allowing multiple and highly subjective narratives to become manifest and "instantly" including the public as unwitting, complicit, and at times actively engaged actors in the production of a continuous narrative that the artist considers an agent of observation. An artwork, typically the object that is being looked at, here reverses the gaze and looks back. As a matter of fact, it does not only look back but acts in response.

The performance has been installed in a variety of places and contexts, each time following the prerequisite of foregrounding the text and allocating the performer a location set apart from the work's immediate impact. This location can be a distant part of the gallery or even a second room, provided that it allows observation of what is happening in the gallery. During García's ongoing activation of the Spanish Pavilion at the 2011 Venice Bienniale, however, the writer was placed on the central stage of a performance series called *The Inadequate* (2011) while the projection of the ongoing narrative was in an adjacent room, thereby downplaying the projection's presence and deliberately allowing the presence of the writer to be interpreted as part of the action on stage. All of these scenarios point to the simple but crucial fact that the writers' output is obviously affected by all these choices. The degree to which the resulting writing can deviate from any presumably realistic observation immediately leads into questions around the legitimacy of the performers' liberty in interpreting the given instruction, which, according to the artist, is to simply "observe." To what degree the range of textual responses conforms to the standard put forth by the artist is an open question that can only be tested, but not answered. At the core of the artist's reversal of the default relationship between art object and viewer, however, is the open structure of writing and responding to a written narrative. Responses can be found in actions performed in the gallery—for example, the obstinate motionless presence over a prolonged period of time—or in texts or even images produced by visitors in response to the narrator's text. In my own experience as a performer of *Instant Narrative*, for example, I was given a series of sketches, notes, and responses as a sort of "thank you" by a diverse range of gallery visitors.

On a related but more institutional note, this text-based performance generates a text that is immediately archived as a log file, not unlike the previously discussed archive of *Agent Ruby*. The status of this text in relation to the collected and accessioned performance work, however, is unclear. Does the text constitute a growing body of writing that is essential to the understanding of the work, or is it closer to the effects that works have on critical or academic writing? In the latter case, it would clearly constitute a distinct practice that only relates to the original work but is not an integral component of it. Dora García has at times published the entire text production of an exhibition as a book, emphasizing the work's generative mode and the role of the museum as a producer of not only experiences but also concrete work.

The construction and perception of images through language is a fundamental experience of exhibiting in the public domain. Dora García's "inserts in real time"—as she calls a whole body of her interventions—emphasizes, however, the futility, precariousness, and affective ambivalence of this process. Whether the viewers are charmed, lured, or even frustrated, they cannot help but be affected by the sensory presence that these works produce over time. This effect includes their own presence as part of the artistic situation. Their awareness of this condition—knowing that the observer influences the thing observed—hence shapes the events in real time. The public is driving the conversation as much as the performers whose authorial decisions are shaped by their observations.

Harrell Fletcher and Miranda July: Learning to Love You More *(2002–2009)*

Over the course of seven years Harrell Fletcher and Miranda July's online platform *Learning to Love You More* provided seventy unique assignments from *#1* "Make a child's outfit in an adult size" to *#70* "Say Goodbye." In the end, over 8000 people had contributed to the project. SFMOMA acquired the web site and all related ephemera in 2010 with the understanding that the museum could exhibit the work in any format, excerpt, or representation, electronically or physically, but that it would provide the contextual information on all seventy assignments and ideally always reflect the collaborative nature of the work by engaging an artistic collaborator—a conceptual decision to continue the participatory foundation of the work without adding assignments.

For the first presentation at SFMOMA—as part of the collection exhibition *The More Things Change* in 2011—I asked the Bay Area artist Stephanie Syjuco to collaborate on the format of the display. She proposed to exhibit the totality of all submissions related to the seventy assignments, not as access to an installed archive but as a consecutive proactive presentation of all the entries in all their media. To facilitate a more dialogical perception, two assignments were presented side by side each day, thus totaling a series of thirty-five consecutive pairings to show the totality of all seventy. To that end Stephanie Syjuco transferred all material to seventy playback files, compiling video, audio, or slide shows sequentially, and transferring text to a spoken text and audio file. Configuring the exhibition copies was an act of translation into a new context indicating that something fundamental had changed: the open work had come to a close with assignment #70 "Say Goodbye." While the work continues to live online as an archive, the transition from active contribution to passive consumption as an audience in a museum reflected this fundamental shift without requiring or even suggesting a final form.

This proposal for a radically different collection presentation, however, did not come out of the blue. In fact, the very first sentence from the "Hello" section of the project states: "Learning to Love You More is both a web site and series of non-web presentations comprised of work made by the general public" (Fletcher and July 2002–2009). The project had already been exhibited in a huge variety of display formats even while it was being expanded through new assignments. All exhibitions are documented as part of the work's online menu and the artists declare in no unclear terms:

> Since *Learning To Love You More* was also an ever-changing series of exhibitions, screenings, and radio broadcasts presented all over the world, participant's documentation was also their submission for possible inclusion in one of these presentations. Presentations have taken place at venues that include The Whitney Museum in NYC, Rhodes College in Memphis, TN, Aurora Picture Show in Houston, TX, The Seattle Art Museum in Seattle, WA, the Wattis Institute in San Francisco CA, among others. (Fletcher and July 2002–2009)

The simple descriptive list of changing presentation formats is impressive: from the first exhibition at the ICA in Portland, Maine—"The pilot version of this site was created for the "Playground" exhibition. Anyone who completed one of these first five assignments while the show was up could bring or mail their work to the museum" (Fletcher and July 2002–2009)—to a series of single assignment presentations in screenings, printouts on gallery walls, classroom workshops, and high school collaborations, and varying contributions to a touring exhibition or even an elevator audio installation.[7] From these precedents it is obvious that curatorial decisions were diverse, context dependent, and highly selective, sometimes due to the fact that not every submitted image file was an image fit to print. I would argue, though, that it is a quality of the artwork to allow for these responsive concepts to happen in the first place.

Not surprisingly, the work itself has grown and expanded over time, yet this fact alone does not explain the sheer inventiveness of dealing with curating and interpreting, and reinventing formats of display. Ultimately, the project has repeatedly blurred the boundaries that delineate the work by allowing individuals, institutions, and the public at large to contribute to it. Each physical manifestation can thus be interpreted as being generated by a conceptual core of the assignments, formulated by Harrell Fletcher and Miranda July. While the work has been preserved online, its translation into a representation in space has been a series of subjective interpretations. A first observation and somewhat surprising element is that even someone who has frequently visited the web site will be constantly confronted with contributions unseen before. The archive of 8000-plus contributions is just too massive to be able to provide an overview for any individual; the artists and their web designer Yuri Ono potentially being the exception to the rule. Although technically a finite body of submitted images, texts, videos, the experience is one of endless surprises, a true generator of meaningful interpretations. The histories that emerge through these exhibitions/presentations point to the work as an archive or container. Metaphorically speaking, one could describe the work as a farmer's market offering home-grown art but letting you, the customer, choose what to cook.[8] What we can thus acknowledge in performative works based on a concept and script is that only change produces a sense of specific experiential, aesthetic, and cognitive limits and conditions to support a sense of continuity.

The scale of the archive, as well as the open call for curatorial decisions without a dialogue with the original authors, run counter to all established museum practices. The effects on the institution's agents, such as curators and conservators, however, are enormously productive. Each display renews an urgency to look more, to look deeper, and above all, to listen to the stories embedded in this vast archive. But each selection/presentation also adds a new template to the histories of display, producing exhibition copies that take on archival status precisely because they successfully generated new meaning. It is in the spirit of inclusiveness of the work to add these iterations and their respective materials to the expanding archive. The work of collaborations continues.

Julia Scher: Predictive Engineering *(1993/1998)*

While *Learning To Love You More* is clearly structured and instantly accessible, Julia Scher's *Predictive Engineering* is opaque, despite its claims to add transparency to institutional acts of surveillance in space. Julia Scher has had a long and productive relationship with SFMOMA. Her work holds a specific significance in its relationship to space, as it has been exhibited in SFMOMA's different museum locations, and was being re-viewed as SFMOMA started work on an expansion that offers an opportunity for a third (in the artist's words) "temporary, transitory installation." In brief, this is the history of two past presentations, with an eye to an imminent future presentation in the expanded museum, opening in 2016.

Predictive Engineering premiered in 1993 in the historic SFMOMA location inside the War Memorial Building as an installation including real time closed-circuit surveillance cameras and pre-recorded fictional narratives presented as video playback, constantly mixing the two in order to enhance the confusion of real time (Figure 8.2). The exhibition was based on the notion of duality, not only in terms of the juxtaposition of live and recorded time, but also the opposition of two galleries creating a binary structure for this installation around a central space that did not belong to Scher's exhibition. Scher characterized the original installation as a

> dual channel [...] based on the original architecture provided by the museum for the work. Two identical hallways as installation location [...] Camera mix was provided by 1990's era homing bridging switchers (analogue) [...] one input can turn into an output, so, one live camera can show up in more than one place on a switcher, and can migrate images to another switcher.[9]

This disjunctive layout was changed in 1998, after SFMOMA's move to the Mario Botta architecture on Third Street, when *Predictive Engineering²* (*PE2*) was launched (Figure 8.3). Even within the short span of five years, the complexity had expanded, as Scher acknowledges: "[*PE 2*] was both 7 channel and 'dual' [...] a different ordering of images went out into the exhibition area, to cover the '7 zones.'" New software tools also allowed more "live" performance: in 1993, fixed Amiga graphical overlays that did not run live had been part of the fake feeds in the piece, whereas in *PE2* "live" graphics were created in Aftereffects and overlaid on the actual live camera feeds. On top of that, materials from both the 1993 version and an installation of the same work in France from 1995 were added to the new mix of live and pre-recorded channels. *PE2* thus also incorporated a time capsule of past recorded footage. Scher finally

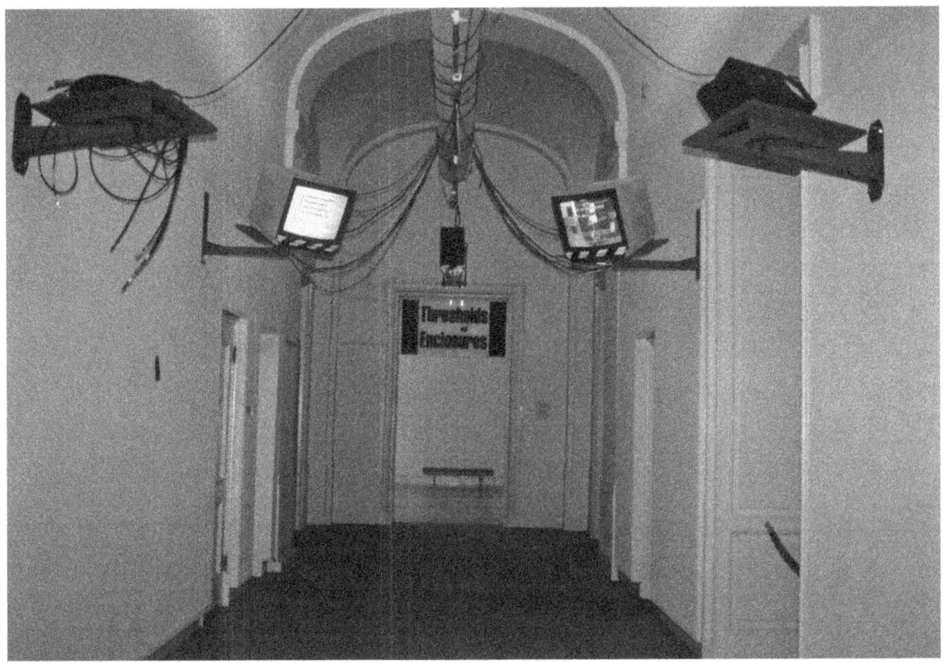

Figure 8.2 Julia Scher, *Predictive Engineering*, 1993. SFMOMA installation view. Multi-channel video installation with sound, dimensions variable. Photo courtesy of SFMOMA. © Julia Scher.

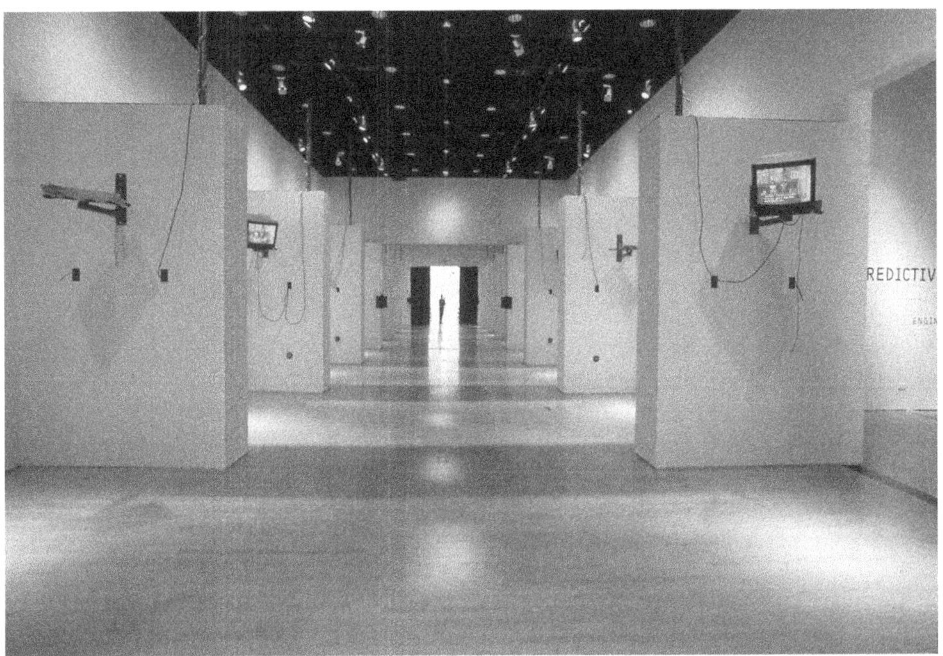

Figure 8.3 Julia Scher, *Predictive Engineering*², 1998. SFMOMA installation view. Multi-channel video installation with sound, dimensions variable. Collection SFMOMA, Accessions Committee Fund purchase. Photo courtesy of SFMOMA. © Julia Scher.

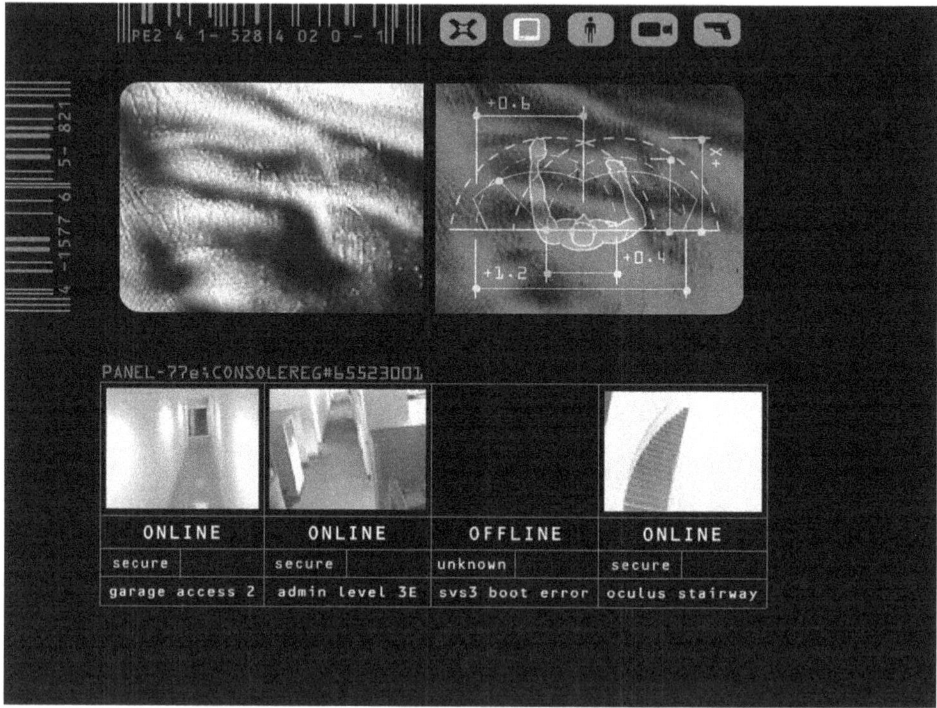

FIGURE 8.4 Julia Scher, *Predictive Engineering²*, 1998 (screenshot). Web project. Collection SFMOMA, gift of the artist, commissioned by SFMOMA. © Julia Scher.

added a live participatory audio component in which visitors could add their voice to a scrambled, slightly deferred audiotracking in the exhibition space, emphasizing the framing and out-of-control condition of participation.

To further complicate matters, Julia Scher produced an online presence related to PE2 in 1998. Benjamin Weil, then curator of media arts at SFMOMA, included this web project as part of his online exhibition platform *e.space*, launched in 2001.[10] In keeping with the notion of "performances in which she captures data and then crunches, alters, and retransmits it, deliberately using and misusing it," the online representation related to *PE2* was conceived as yet another layer of information gathering and "crunching" that did not merit a new serial number for the work (Figure 8.4). The two iterations and unnumbered online component were only a few years apart but signaled a major expansion of the concept based on the technologies that had emerged in the meantime.[11]

The shifts, however, were also felt in a larger context. Scher's statement for *e.space* is revealing in that it already signals a change in her perception after having installed *PE2*:

> I originally saw surveillance in terms of looking at landscape, because indeed there was the landscape through the lens or eye of a camera rather than my own eye. [...] More insidious and less visible to the human eye is identity, created through multiple data bases and hierarchies imposed and created without laws or the knowledge of those being judged. These virtual spaces are far more interesting for me and far more dangerous.

And she continues to speak of her interest in "experiential aesthetic [...] where visitors can deal with their own flexible script."[12]

From the "crunching" of data to the embodiment of past manifestations and the expansion into different arenas, *Predictive Engineering*'s identities are indeed manifold, pointing to the call for contextual and contemporary actualizations. A common denominator, though, already emerges from Scher's artistic statements: "What kinds of hierarchies are going to be employed to keep us in or out of those virtual spaces? I can penetrate those walls without being a physical presence. I'm interested in the extremity of this battleground."[13] Amplifying a charged look at future power structures and plays, Scher's work has always been grounded in the thematic complex of surveillance. To this day, it is the foundation upon which her entire oeuvre is based. The dimension in which her scenarios have played out on a larger scale in societies today was simply a science fiction tale of the future when she started work on *PE* in the early 1990s.

Today, the collapse of the private/public divide, greatly enhanced and facilitated by social media, adds a completely new dimension to a future iteration, adding a significant dimension to an architectural space that is never as permanent as one might think. Once again, SFMOMA is physically changing its architecture; once again, this offers an opportunity to reflect these changes in a political, social, but also aesthetic dimension through an experiential lens. Over the last twenty years surveillance has not only permeated buildings in visible ways but also penetrated our personal devices, cell phone tracking being just one of these instances of real-time data storage. To put it in Scher's emphatic terminology: "No longer on the edge [of a building], or behind the camera's hidden-eye security, THE APPARATUS comes out of its shell and acts as a prism and white-hot calculator in space."[14]

From my e-mail correspondence with the artist I learned that she had always envisioned the series not as a simple numbering of parts but rather as a multiplication of materials: "PE to the power of 3: "PE * PE * PE = PE3, ... being in the now of the 'expansion' idea of SFMOMA." Scher's own speculation is tentative but an indication of yet another shift in perspective: "If the 1990s was about a critique thru reenactment of space age fears of 'technological dehumanization' [...] PE3 future is more towards welcoming aliens, new life, in all languages."[15]

Continuing her speculation on changes in the future, she claims:

> The delight, pleasure or fear of watching one's self has evolved since the 1990s. "To be seen at all" is more the crisis of the moment. You have, at the Museum, the PE2 contract that states for any further reviewing, installing or traveling of the work, any old technology can be replaced with new technology (or arguably any material) that carries the concept of the original idea. Therefore it presents an interesting challenge of options. PE2 or 3 can exist as large scale airborne over-flying drone, embedded chips in Museum visitors, electrified microwave pulses, iPhone communication or small symbolic gestures within architecture, a "limelight" Rampenlicht pointed at people at one end of a hallway.[16]

In another e-mail, Scher offers a test of authenticity—"different but the same"—and speculates on new "core" forms: "[PE3] could be a spectral multi media [installation] with view-extensions. 'Real' views, mixed with 'pre recorded/digital game/hologramed' views. I see PE3 in this context as fluid to the building itself, easily flowing thru gang-ways, corridors, passages."[17] Speculating about the "core" of her work has provided the pains but also pleasures of collecting Scher's work—an expansive concept of past material and a hybrid "real" with changing extensions. But who is to make this call about the "core" without the artist? It is a call to action in light of changes in technology and the notion of self, and obviously a radically different notion of the old public/private dichotomy that now seems obsolete, a distant memory. It could very well be that any future configuration and update of the work would be independently produced by a trained institution, trained in its basic or core responsive and inventive approach to the work. With Julia Scher and her poetic embrace of constant change and complexity, we are asked to constantly refresh our practice as curators, collectors, conservators, or educators, and review critically our practice as agents of a civic institution. It is this implied contract of critical contemporary practice toward surveillance that incorporates the methods of conservation, presentation, and the engagement of the public—whatever its material configuration might be.

Conclusion: Toward an Art of Participation

Embracing the performativity of digital works as well as the inclusion of bodily performance in the museum, the call to action today is to meet the needs of the performative work in a performative museum that engages the public—deleting the traditional notion of permanent collection display; opening up to performativity in dialogue with objects; embracing change including poetic speculation; and engaging with other agents as performers in the galleries. I have argued that the archival document supposedly guides us through the complexities of an artwork's history, yet also often forces the institution into a default, archived, and thus authorized format of presentation. From the perspective of conservators and curators, the archival document might thus alleviate the burden of making a (possibly wrong) decision in arranging the display of a work, yet from an artistic point of view, every new instance of the performative work productively challenges the museum's default way of operating. The self-identified strategy of most museums—"Follow what artists do"—impacts the documentation, which follows a hybrid form of narrative and takes into account the experience factor of complex, performative, and participatory works like the ones discussed above. Documentation follows the art, and not vice versa.

Media art rarely offers clearly defined objects to collect. It might include sculptural components or a manual or a physical case for files. These material components, however, do not constitute the experience of a time-based work. In the past, this has been viewed as a problem. Today we begin to see this condition as an opportunity to stage and produce manifestations of a work that expand and update previous configurations and recordings. Art often is neither a given nor permanently present; it emerges as a temporary act of presentation in relationship to the contemporary context. Pointedly said, in media art the call is to do it "again and again" but differently each time.

There is a larger, untold history that includes the impact of process-based art on the traces it leaves within the museum setting, whether this is a documentation of a Fluxus performance through a set of photographs or a film/video documentation, which, as I have argued, gradually blurred the line between event and document by taking on the status of the artwork, as in the case of Yoko Ono's famous performance *Cut Piece*

(1965). In other cases, as in Mail Art or undocumented performance art, the narratives of historic events were restricted to the educational or academic framing of an object standing in for something that had happened elsewhere. Props or ephemera took on artwork status, for example the vitrines of Joseph Beuys. I am not arguing that these responses to ephemeral events were inappropriate. On the contrary, they were mostly guided by artists' intentions and conscious decisions. What is at stake, though, is the fact that in all these above-mentioned precedents, a finite object embodied a complex event. The digital, participatory works from the SFMOMA collection discussed above point to a different condition, one of permanent change based on a set of objects, materials, concepts, and responses. While this certainly is a condition that is almost ingrained into the very notion of algorithmic performance, I am arguing that we need to look at a core set of parameters that exceed the analog/digital divide. Let me close by quoting from a letter that the late San Francisco artist Bruce Conner sent to Henry Hopkins, then director of the San Francisco Museum of Art, in response to the museum's endeavor of "protecting" a work from the artist's intervention in preparation of an exhibition:

> The concept of change is basic to many of these works which I made before 1964. To accept the concept as part of the value of exhibiting the work and to forbid the artist to continue to participate in the basic aesthetic intent is a paradox I find hard to rationalize. If you accept these works at their face value and convey this to other people as an aesthetic concern intended by the artist, then why do you propose to accept all the changes and alterations of the past through the hands of warehousemen, vandals, ignorant manipulation, gravity, humidity, fire, conservation lab, etc. and refuse to accept the participation of the artist himself? (Conner 1977)

Things have changed indeed over the last thirty years. Museums today are comfortable with having a work in their collection changed, updated, activated, reinstalled, reconfigured, reperformed, re-... and not just by accident, but by design. A responsible collection display is motivated and driven by an ethics of responsive actions in order to share control over narratives and histories that will guide us toward an art of participation.

Notes

1 "Art historian and researcher Kai-Uwe Hemken and designer Jakob Gebert have realized—posthumously—the design for *Raum der Gegenwart* (Room of Today) by artist László Moholy-Nagy and museum director Alexander Dorner from 1930." Announcement of the exhibition *Museum Modules* at the Van Abbe Museum, Eindhoven, in 2010. Today, the notion of "re-exhibiting"' has taken to the big stage, as witnessed by the reconstruction of Harald Szeemann's seminal exhibition *When Attitudes Become Form* at the Fondazione Prada in Venice in 2013.

2 The painter Richard Kalina on Robert Morris: "Morris maintains that *Untitled (Scatter Piece)* would exist in a perfectly valid iteration while in storage—presumably neatly stacked rather than strewn about [...] in Post-Minimalist works such as *Untitled (Scatter Piece)* and *Continuous Project Altered Daily*, [...] workmanlike activity—at the points of inception and installation in the former, and on a daily basis in the

latter—took precedence over final form." Kalina then quotes from Morris's 1968 essay "Anti-Form": "Considerations of ordering are necessarily casual and imprecise and unemphasized. Random piling, loose stacking, hanging, give passing form to the material. Chance is accepted and indeterminacy is implied, as replacing will result in another configuration. Disengagement with preconceived enduring forms is a positive assertion. It is part of the work's refusal to continue estheticizing the form by dealing with it as a prescribed end" (Kalina 2014).

3 Quote from a wall text of the Wadsworth Atheneum's 2013 display of a Morris felt piece, *Untitled* (1978), from their collection. http://www.thewadsworth.org/robert-morris-untitled-1978/ (accessed June 22, 2014).

4 See "display" at http://www.etymonline.com (accessed June 22, 2014).

5 It is a key moment in the history of participatory art that Robert Morris's notorious exhibition at the Tate in London, closed after the disruptive engagement of the public at the time of its first showing, got restaged in 2009 in the Tate's Turbine Hall as a three-day event. I'm pointing this out as a relatively easy way out of the institutional problems of realizing a participatory exhibition. It becomes an event in a public space rather than an exhibition in the galleries. See Dezeuze (2009).

6 http://www.agentruby.net. The original URL "http://www.agentruby.com" is no longer available to the project, having fallen through the cracks of discontinuous maintenance, which led to the purchase of the URL by a third party. Does it matter in our context that it has since become a porn site? Is that also an effect of the name Ruby?

7 In 2004, assignment #29 "Make an audio recording of a choir" was exhibited at the Whitney Biennial, Whitney Museum of American Art, New York in the elevator "when it rose." For a complete list and photo documentation see http://www.learningtoloveyoumore.com/displays/index.php.

8 A more behind-the-scenes observation concerns the fact that the work has somewhat shrunk over time when individuals retroactively eliminated their presence, comparable to successful artists who have eliminated some very early weak or just untypical work from their official biography. The museum is legally not obliged to follow up on these requests and delete a name from the assignments, but it is in the same spirit of collaborative ownership that SFMOMA decides to follow the path laid out by the artists. The work is thus not simply expanding exponentially through an ongoing series of different displays; the core archive is actually shrinking.

9 Unpublished artist statement, archives of SFMOMA.

10 http://www.sfmoma.org/exhib_events/exhibitions/espace (accessed June 22, 2014).

11 Unfortunately, no record or recording of the microphone audio is left of *PE2*, except for a small sample on a documentation tape.

12 http://www.sfmoma.org/exhib_events/exhibitions/details/espace_scher (accessed June 22, 2014).

13 http://www.sfmoma.org/exhib_events/exhibitions/details/espace_scher (accessed June 22, 2014).

14 All quotes from the original e-space introduction: http://www.sfmoma.org/exhib_events/exhibitions/details/espace_scher#ixzz2dnRxJWLv, San Francisco Museum of Modern Art (accessed June 22, 2014).

15 E-mail correspondence between Julia Scher and Rudolf Frieling, June 13, 2013.

16 E-mail correspondence between Julia Scher and Rudolf Frieling, September 28, 2012. German in the original.

17 E-mail correspondence between Julia Scher and Rudolf Frieling, May 23, 2013.

References

Bishop, Claire. 2012. *Artificial Hells: Participatory Art and the Politics of Spectatorship*. London and New York: Verso.
Bourriaud, Nicolas. 2002. *Relational Aesthetics*. Dijon: Les presses du réel.
Buskirk, Martha, Amelia Jones, and Caroline A. Jones. 2013. "The Year in Re-." *Artforum*, December. http://www.artforum.com/inprint/issue+20110&id+44068 (accessed June 22, 2014).
Conner, Bruce. 1977. Letter dated July 27. Conner files. University of California: Bancroft Library.
Dezeuze, Anna, ed. 2009. *The 'Do-It-Yourself' Artwork: Participation from Fluxus to New Media*. Manchester and New York: Manchester University Press.
Fletcher, Harrell, and Miranda July. 2002–2009. "Hello." *Learning to Love You More*. http://www.learningtoloveyoumore.com/hello/index.php (accessed June 22, 2014).
Frieling, Rudolf, ed. 2008. *The Art of Participation: 1950 to Now*. London/San Francisco: Thames & Hudson/San Francisco Museum of Modern Art.
Kalina, Richard. 1969. "Robert Morris." *Art in America*, December 31. http://www.artinamericamagazine.com/news-features/magazine/robert-morris/ (accessed June 22, 2014).
Kester, Grant. 2004. *Conversation Pieces*. Berkeley, CA: University of California Press.
Krauss, Rosalind. 1979. "Sculpture in the Expanded Field." *October* 8 (Spring): 30–44.
Smith, Terry. 2009. *What Is Contemporary Art?* Chicago: University of Chicago Press.

Part II

Aesthetics of Digital Art

9

Small Abstract Aesthetics

Max Bense

Aesthetics

We interpret aesthetics to be an abstract aesthetics, which implies that it can be applied to any arbitrary field of special aesthetic objects regardless of whether it involves architecture, sculpture, painting, design, poetry, prose, dramaturgy, film, music, or events in general. This is no philosophical aesthetic as it is not embedded in a philosophical system. Rather, it is a scientific aesthetic in that it strives for the form of a theory. Accordingly, it is conceived of as research, not interpretation; it corresponds to the Galilean[1] type of knowledge, not the Hegelian,[2] and is more strongly oriented technologically than metaphysically. Its interest is considered a relative-objective theme, not an absolute, subjective conception of the object of investigation. It is an open, expandable, revisable theory, not a closed, postulated doctrine.

Aesthetic Condition

Its central concept is that of aesthetic condition. This is understood to include the relatively extreme and objective condition of all objects and events of greater or lesser artistic origin that are taken into consideration to the extent that it can be distinguished from the physical and semantic condition of these objects or events. The central concept of abstract aesthetics is therefore not conveyed by the term "beauty" and its philosophical or trivial derivatives, which for the most part can only be decided by subjective interpretation and not by objective determination. Accordingly, an aesthetic condition is also not defined as "ideal," but as "reality"; it is observable and describable as a real condition of the object under consideration.

A Companion to Digital Art, First Edition. Edited by Christiane Paul.

Aesthetic Carriers

By the term "aesthetic carriers" we mean real objects as well as events, thus material realities by which or with which aesthetic conditions are created, e.g., so-called works of art, but also design objects. In any case, distinctions must be made between an aesthetic condition and its carrier.

Material Aesthetics

The actual material reality of the artistic objects in which a distinction between aesthetic carrier and aesthetic condition can be made entitles one to speak of material aesthetics. Abstract aesthetics, which is applicable, includes material aesthetics. It is therefore stated that aesthetic conditions can only be discussed by means of material conditions and are thus demonstrable only through the manipulation of given materials.

Aesthetic Repertory

Materials are not necessarily material in a physical sense. Meanings, things that are imagined, words, fictional items can also be the carriers of aesthetic conditions. Distinctions can absolutely be made between material and immaterial materials or the carriers of aesthetic conditions. The phrase *material* is generally interpreted in the sense of distinguishable, discrete, manipulable elements, and the epitomy of a host of elementary, discrete, and manipulable materials is called a *repertory*. Aesthetic conditions are dependent on a repertory. An aesthetic repertory is a material repertory from which a corresponding material aesthetic condition can be created by means of manipulation.

The First Definition of an Aesthetic Condition

From this we can derive a first material and abstract definition of an aesthetic condition. In our first—material and abstract—approach to the term, we understand an aesthetic condition to be the distribution of material elements throughout their finite repertory. Here distribution means first of all nothing more than manipulated dispersion. Manipulation itself can be perceived as selection, transportation, and reordering. In a more precise sense selection, transportation, and distribution are partial *procedures* of the *process* that produces aesthetic conditions in all the material of the given repertory. This aesthetic process that is easily broken down into procedures can be specified as such in further definition attempts.

Processes

We distinguish between determined and non-determined processes or procedures. This is a crude distinction. A subtler one is the distinction between fully determined, weakly determined, and non-determined processes. Macrophysical processes, such as a free fall, are fully determined. Certain microphysical processes, such as quantum leaps, are non-determined. Linguistic processes, being conventional, are mostly weakly determined. Aesthetic generative processes are distinguished by weakly determined or non-determined procedures. Connected with this is the fact that their outcomes, the aesthetic condition, are almost entirely excluded from the quality that one would anticipate, namely conceivability, and are not distinguishable until they are realized and only then can they be distinguished. By aesthetic condition we therefore mean the weak or non-determinate distribution of material elements throughout their finite manipulable repertory.

Aesthetic Distribution

Aesthetic distributions are therefore, first, at least weakly determined and, second, material distributions. As material distributions they are extensional dispersions and combinations in time-space patterns. Distributions of material elements in time-space schemata can be characterized as compositions. Following Lessing's terminology in *Laocoon*, we need to differentiate between "coexisting" distributions or compositions in space patterns (painting) and "consecutive" distributions[3] or compositions. In temporal (music, poetry, events) patterns. In a certain respect texts belong to the combined space-time system and are thus simultaneously coexisting and consecutive compositions.

Aesthetic Information

Since according to information theory, only undefined, therefore weakly or non-determinative operations produce what is called *information*, the indefinite quality of aesthetic processes and aesthetic conditions is sufficient to characterize them also as *aesthetic information*. Moreover, each piece of information in information theory as well is regarded as repertory-dependent.

Reality Themes

We distinguish between physical and aesthetic reality themes. The former are determined by procedures and events, the latter by selective manipulations leading to singular conditions which may be comprehended as *innovations*, as novelties in the sense of a *principle* of repertory-linked *emergence*. A third reality theme, in a certain sense an intermediary theme, the *semantic*, can be identified between the physical and the aesthetic *reality themes*. It is governed not by procedures in natural law but also not by selective manipulation, but by *conventional* and *interpretive* contingency. Linguistic and beyond that absolutely any kind of representational communication is the true realm of semantic reality themes.

Creative and Communication Pattern

In order to distinguish more clearly between singular innovations and contingent conventions, let us introduce a *creative* and a *communicative pattern* as their generative principle. The contingent convention is developed in communication patterns, the singular innovation in creation patterns.

The communication system describes the model of the (linguistic) sign connection between a sender and a receiver (expedient and percipient) over a communication channel that is vulnerable to noise.[4] So that a connection in the sense of an understanding that is capable of conventionalization comes to pass, the sign repertories of the sender and the receiver must to a certain extent, therefore, correspond. Before insertion of the signs provided by the sender (expedient) into the communication channel, they must be transformed or coded appropriately, that is, in a fitting manner transformed or coded into the transport capabilities of the channel in order to be again retranslated or decoded before being picked up by the receiver.

Common Signs

The creation pattern, on the other hand, describes the model of the selective connection between a given repertory of material elements and their selective distribution to a singular innovative condition. It demarcates itself from the communication pattern primarily because it introduces an *external observer* who represents the generative principle of the selective connection (Figure 9.1). The sender (expedient) explicitly acquires the character of the repertory ("source") and the receiver (percipient) the character of the product ("depression"). The creation channel can also be exposed to noises which raise or lower the degree of indeterminacy.

The selective function of the external observer (thus of the artist) certainly refers primarily to the repertory, secondarily, however, also to the product (Figure 9.2). The selection of the product can refer back to the selection of the repertory so that the

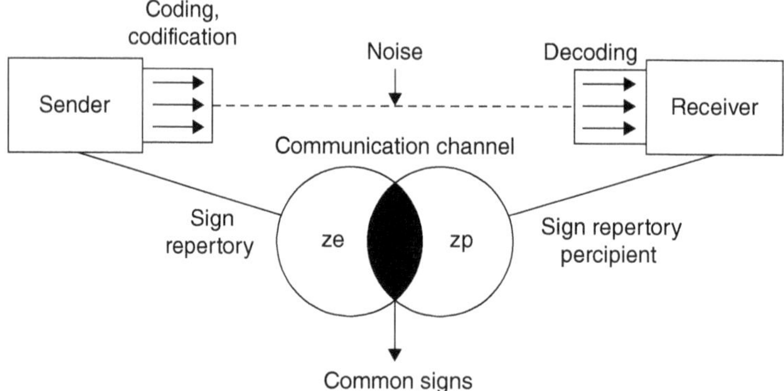

FIGURE 9.1 Diagram 1.

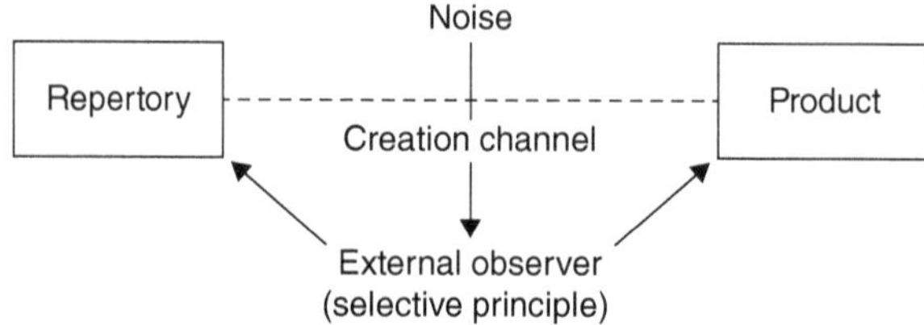

FIGURE 9.2 Diagram 2.

generative principle in the creation pattern can also acquire the nature of a recoupling system. In this case the product selects the repertory, or at least defines its scope. In every aesthetic generative process the selective freedom of the external observer increasingly changes into the product of the distribution of material elements; this is the reason for the consumption of selective freedom by the external observer in the process of the creative manipulation of the repertory.

Signal and Sign

It is necessary at this stage to attempt a distinction between signal and sign, which is as relevant to the communicative as to the creative process. We speak of *signal* when the exclusively physical substratum of a connection is meant. Sound as an acoustical and color as an optical phenomenon belong, for example, to this. However, we speak of a sign when intellectual cognition declares such a substratum (1) to be a medium that (2) signifies an object and (3) for a certain interpretation thereby endows it with meaning. Accordingly, each signal as a physical substratum is definable by three place coordinates x, y, z and a time coordinate t and is consequently presented as a (material) function:

$$\mathrm{Sig} = \mathrm{F\ mat}\left(x, y, z, t\right)$$

A sign, on the other hand, is (with Charles Sanders Peirce)[5] presented as a triadic relation between its nature as a medium, its relevance to an object, and its relevance to an interpreter. Accordingly a sign is not an object but a relationship:

$$Z = R\left(M, O, I\right)$$

As medium M the sign is manipulable, that is, selectable, transformable, transportable, short, and communicable. In object reference o it "objectified" the knowable or the known in that it *signified*, and in the interpretation reference it *means* the something that is objectified and signified.

Categories of Signs

A sign as a triadic relationship of its reference modes of medium, object, and interpretant is, according to Peirce, again split triadically. As medium a sign can function qualitatively (qualisign), singularly (singsign), and legitimately (legitsign); in relation to object, it can signify the object in an arbitrary symbolic manner (symbol), in an indicative indexing manner (index), and in an iconic depictive manner (icon); in an interpretive context these object relationships are introduced and acquire meaning in an argumentally complete (argument), in a dicentish closed (dicent) and in a rhematically open (rhema) connection (connex or context). Each concretely introduced sign is therefore represented in reality as a triadic relationship and at the same time as a triadic combination of the three possibilities of the triadic components. This triadic relationship covering all the possibilities of the triadic components of the sign is called a sign category. Each sign that is introduced therefore in reality represents a *sign category.*

Semioses

Processes and procedures that are associated with signs, take place in signs, and thus are based on the manipulation of signs, are called semioses or semiotic processes. Creative and communicative processes in general are just such semioses and are therefore semiotic processes. Now while creative and communicative processes are carriers of the process characterized and artificially generated by *aesthetic conditions*, in this it is likewise a question of a sequence of semiotic procedures. Obviously signs form a medium of indeterminate or only weakly determined processes and constellations, that is fertile ground for the engendering of innovation, and therefore of *aesthetic information*, in a creative pattern. Repertories of signs are always marked by *emergence*, by the cropping up of the new, which develops in the creative pattern. *Aesthetic semiosis* thus begins with the establishment of a repertory which is always the forerunner of the innovation-creating process. Signs still function in the repertory as pure means, without an object reference, without interpreters. They have here the nature of physical substrata, and they can (in terms of the theory of knowledge) be understood as signals (of the physical substance of the world). Not until the selection of the repertory by an *external observer* is the genuine aesthetic semiosis initiated, and this takes place as a *transformation* of the *signals* in *signs*, of the objective *media* in *triadic relations*:

$$\text{Sig} \to Z = \text{Fmat}\,(x,y,z,t) \to R\,(M,0,I)$$

Numeric and Semiotic Aesthetics

While the aesthetic generative process ends as a whole in creative and communicative procedures, it leads on the one hand to *material distributions* and on the other had to *relational semioses*. The material distributions are characteristic of creative procedures and the relational semioses are characteristic of communicative procedures. The *aesthetic* condition generated in this manner appears under the aspect of the distribution of creative materials as *selective information* and under the aspect of the communicative relational semiosis as *selective superisation*. The selective information defines the aesthetic innovation with respect to its statistical vagueness. The selective superisation denotes the coexisting or consecutive semiotic synthesis of individual (atomic) signs into complex (molecular) supersigns or hierarchies of signs. *Aesthetic theory* thereby acquires its two methodical sides: the numerical and the semiotic. The *numerical aesthetic* relates essentially to the statistical indeterminacy of the selection; the *semiotic aesthetic*, on the other hand, relates to the description of the sign categories and supersigns constituted in the relational semioses.

Micro- and Macroaesthetics

In material distribution as well as in relational sign category the aesthetic condition is repertory dependent. The degree of differentiability and refundability of the constituted elements leads to differentiation between crude and subtle descriptions of aesthetic conditions and thereby to differentiation between *crude* and *subtle aesthetics*, which also can be characterized as *macro-* and *microaesthetics.* If the *smallest* aesthetic conditions, and thus the most minimal material distributions, allow themselves to be differentiated as aesthetic conditions, information, innovations, or semiotic superisations, it is reasonable to speak of their *nuclear aesthetics.*

General Numerical Aesthetics

In order to make a general numerical approach to a numerical description of aesthetic conditions as a distribution of material elements throughout a repertory, one must proceed from the fact that each creative process transforms a *given condition* (of material elements) into an *artificial* one. The given condition is the condition of the material elements in the *repertory*; the artificial condition is its condition in the *product.* The given condition of the distribution of the material elements can in the extreme case be designated in the repertory as *disorder* in the sense of a disorganized crowd of elements; the relocated, artificial condition of the distribution of material elements throughout the repertory can be termed *order* in the sense of a structured crowd of elements. The degree of disorder in the condition of the repertory is a question of the *complexity* of the repertory, which can be described in the case of crude macroaesthetics by the number of constituent elements and in the case of more subtle microaesthetics by the measured value of its *mixture*, by its *entropy.* In any event the possibility thereby presents itself of expressing the material, distributive aesthetic condition as the relationship of an *ordered* condition to one that is in a state of *disorder*, as a relationship of the measured number of the order relations of the produced condition to the measured number of the complexity of the condition being produced. This general approach of numerical aesthetics to the numerical definition of aesthetic conditions can therefore be expressed by the interrelationship

$$M = f(0, C) = 0IC$$

in which M signifies the *aesthetic measured number*, 0 the *measured number of order*, and C the *measured number of the complexity.*

Numerical Macroaesthetics

From this approach to general numerical aesthetics, which originated in a mathematical and aesthetic concept of the American mathematician George D. Birkhoff[5] in 1928, a macroaesthetic and a microaesthetic variant can be derived. Birkhoff's original approach was intended to be macroaesthetic in nature insofar as it rested on perceptible and unquestionably countable elements of the observed object. He demonstrated his calculations of aesthetically measured numbers at first in polygons, grids, and vases. Polygons, grids, or vases form to a certain extent *aesthetic families*, within whose individual objects it makes sense to develop measured numbers for comparison. Macroaesthetic measured numbers are introduced by Birkhoff as scalar unnamed masses, which only in relation to the formation of comparable objects assume comparable values. It therefore is an issue of macroaesthetic measured numbers in the sense of *form measurements*; for *form* functions macroaesthetically as a perceptible whole, as "form quality," as stated in the concept that Christian von Ehrenfels (1890)[7] introduced. Individual polygons such as squares, rectangles, the rhombus, and the like create form classes whose "form quality" is synthetically defined in each case by definite *order relationships* (0) covering a definite *complexity* of constitutive elements (C). Each macroaesthetic form measurement is therefore a *relative* aesthetic measurement insofar as the aesthetic condition of the artificial object to which it relates is itself relative, dependent on the order relationships 0 that are seen as aesthetically relevant (e.g., the number of symmetries in polygons) and the form elements C perceived as constitutive (e.g., the number of elements that are needed to make a - in a square, for instance, one side).

Numerical Microaesthetics

While the macroaesthetic measurement functions as a form measurement and relates to the observed artificial object as a given and perceptible unvarying whole, the *microaesthetic* measure considers the emergence of the object and its aesthetic condition from a selectable repertory of material elements and takes into account thereby the number of one-time or repeated decision steps. One can say, therefore, that macroaesthetic measurement neglects the external observer whereas it acts decisively in a microaesthetic measurement. The macroaesthetic measurement therefore yields the aesthetic object in the communication pattern, and the microaesthetic measurement produces it in the creation pattern. The macroaesthetic measurement regards the aesthetic object as a given realization, but the microaesthetic measurement sees it in connection with a collection of possibilities bestowed by the repertory. These different methods of observation explain why the macroaesthetic measurement is geometrically oriented and the microaesthetic measurement is statistically oriented and why the former means a (communications pattern) form measurement, whereas the latter means a (creation pattern) information measurement. The distribution of material elements throughout a given repertory, which is interpreted macroaesthetically as identifiable form, must therefore be evaluated macroaesthetically as innovative information. To the extent that thereby the aesthetic condition as such is viewed as a function of the order relationship and complexity of its elements, it is necessary to represent these aspects that define the aesthetic measurement not by metrically geometric volume, but by statistically information-theoretical volume. The *microaesthetic complexity* in this aspect is conveyed by *statistical information* or *entropy* and the *microaesthetic order* is conveyed by *statistical redundancy* and is determinable. That is reasonable, since statistical information or entropy represents a measurement of the degree of mixing, of disorder, of the indeterminacy of a crowd of repertory revealing elements that can be selected and put in order. However, this is exactly what belongs to the concept of repertory complexity if it is intended to function as a source of possible innovation. The redundancy concept, on the other hand, means a kind of counter-concept to the concept of information in information theory in that it does not designate the innovation value of a distribution of elements but the ballast value of this innovation, which accordingly is not new but is well known, which does not provide information but identification. Order comes under the category of redundancy because its concept includes that of identifiability. It is constantly a ballast feature of the given, not an innovation feature. A completed innovation, in which just like in chaos there are only new conditions, would also not be recognizable. In the final analysis chaos is not identifiable. The identifiability of an aesthetic condition requires not only a singular innovation to be identifiable but also its identifiability in the light of its redundant ordering features. The microaesthetic measurement is therefore done by the relationship of statistical redundancy to statistical information (or entropy), that is, by

$$Mä = R/H$$

The calculation of the (average) statistical information of the distribution of elements throughout a repertory takes place, according to Claude E. Shannon,[8] analogously to the calculation of the condition of the degree of mixture, of the indeterminacy by which the elements of the system are given, by means of the relationship

$$H = -\sum p_i \, ld \, p_i$$

that is, as the sum of the probabilities (or relative frequencies) with which the elements of the repertory are selected or multiplied by the digital logarithm of these probabilities.

Redundancy in general is understood to be the difference between the *maximum possible* and the *actually occurring* information of an element of the repertory. The maximum possible information of an element of a repertory n elements is attained when all elements can be selected with the same probabilities, that is, when

$$H = H_{max} = ld\,n$$

exists. The relationship to the calculation of redundancy accordingly takes the form, with reference to the maximum information, of

$$R = H_{max} - H \div H_{max}$$

If one characterizes the relationship of h to hmax as *relative information*, the result is

$$R = 1 - H_{rel}$$

Semiotic Macroaesthetics

The macroaesthetic measurement is a *form measurement*. Seen semiotically, the form is always given in the *iconic* object reference, that is, the sign category by which it is semiotically determined contains in each case the iconic component of the object reference. Three modifications of the sign category of the form are therefore possible: the rhematic-iconic qualisign category (when, e.g., the form is derived from the representational value of a color), the rhematic-iconic single sign category (when, e.g., the form is represented by a singular form), and the rhematic-iconic legisign category (when the form is represented by a rule-based applied form).

Semiotic Microaesthetics

The microaesthetic measurement revealed itself as a repertory-dependent distribution or information measurement. The selection of the elements therefore required an *indexical identification*, which can be represented by the probability of its occurrence. Seen semiotically, this means that the elements are characterized by an indexical system of probability dimensions or statistical frequencies. The selectable elements of the repertory thus belong to the object-thematic, indexical-oriented sign categories: There are four modifications: the rhematic-indexical singsign category, the rhematic-indexical legisign category, the dicentic-indexical singsign category, and the dicentic-indexical legisign category. The indexical-oriented sign categories thus define elements of signs in semiotic systems which can designated as *indexical* given *configurations*. The microaesthetic measurement may therefore be regarded, unlike the macroaesthetic form measurement, as a configuration measurement. Configurations are formed that are not given in iconic but indexical form. Each element of the configuration belongs to the rhematic-indexical signsign category of the configuration, which is fixed by a singular probability. When each element is labeled by the same probability of the selection, it is a question of a legitimate use of the probability as in the case that the probabilities, for instance, are established by a regularly increasing progression; the elements or the total distribution are then defined as belonging to the rhematic-indexical legisign category. The dicentic-indexical signsign category is realized by a definite grid element (which functions dicentically as a result of its isolation), and the dicentic-indexical legisign category ultimately defines semiotically the border- or frame-limited grid system, in the area of which the elements can be located configuratively. Another important indexical system of the dicentic-indexical legisign category also creates the perspective.

Nuclear Aesthetics

Nuclear aesthetics is concerned with the smallest or extremely small units of distributions in a repertory of material elements and their creative procedures, the selections. Through these selections the distributions are generated as conditions of vagueness, as innovations. We have already established in the context of microaesthetics that in principle the repertory can be regarded as an equally probable distribution of material elements, and this equally probable distribution entitles us to designate the condition of the repertory as *chaogenic*. The selection of this chaogenic repertory leads to two aesthetic borderline areas, the regular order of the *structural* condition and the irregular order of the *configurative* condition. Semiotically it would be easy to characterize these conditions object-thematically as *iconic* and as *indexical systems*, while the *chaogenic* repertory, likewise in the object-thematic aspect, would be interpreted as a *symbolic system*.

Now Aleksandr I. Khinchin[9] has developed finite patterns of the statistical vagueness of events which are explainable as elementary models of aesthetic distributions or conditions. What is observed here is a repertory of material elements that can be selected. In the selection procedure a similar material element of the finite horde of elements of the repertory are always chosen with a certain degree of probability. The chain of selections is therefore the creative process. Now if the full repertory of material elements (colors, sounds, words, and the like) is shown E1, E2, ... En together with the probabilities of selection P1, P2, ... Pn, this can be interpreted as a *finite pattern*, that is nuclear-aesthetic as an elementary model of ***undefined distributions*** or ***aesthetic conditions***. The abstract finite pattern for classifying the elements of a repertory into the probabilities of their selection is accordingly depicted in the following figure:

$$\text{Rep} = \begin{pmatrix} E_1, E_2, \ldots E_n \\ P_1, P_2, \ldots P_n \end{pmatrix}$$

This *finite pattern*, which, as stated, according to Khinchin describes each ***condition*** of ***indeterminacy***, conveys the creative process at the same time or the creative pattern as a distribution of probabilities, reducible to fundamental cases, to the *core* of aesthetic conditions.

Numerical Nuclear Aesthetics

For numerical nuclear aesthetics it is important that each finite pattern of classification among elements of a repertory and their probabilities of selection describes a condition of indeterminacy. This holds true in particular for our border conditions of aesthetic distribution, for the chaogenic, the structural, and the configurative conditions. If the repertory contains n elements and if each of them is assigned the same probability of selection 1/n this is how the *finite pattern* describes

$$\begin{pmatrix} E_1, E_2, \ldots E_n \\ 1/n, 1/n, \ldots 1/n \end{pmatrix}$$

the pattern of ***chaogenic distribution***, which in principle is characteristic of all possibilities of selection and innovation in the repertory.

If an element is selected from the repertory with confidence, that is to say with a probability of 1, the *finite pattern* has the form

$$\begin{pmatrix} E_1, E_2, \ldots E_n \\ 0, 1, 0, 0, 0, 0 \end{pmatrix}$$

and identifies a ***structural distribution***, for example, for the plan of an ornament which by setting a support element, for example,• the gap in an infinite pattern, can be constructed.

Finally, if the *finite pattern* shows a classification of the type

$$\begin{pmatrix} E_1, E_2, E_3, \ldots E_n \\ 0{,}3\ 0{,}1\ 0{,}4\ 0, 0, 0, 0{,}2 \end{pmatrix}$$

it therefore reflects an irregular ***configurative distribution***, a singular selective innovation.

According to Khinchin there is a function

$$H(p_1, p_2, \ldots p_n) = -\sum p_k \log p_k,$$

which should be designated as *entropy* of the *finite pattern*. It is evident that with this function the *finite patterns* of the nuclear aesthetic condition experience a microaesthetic measurement determination. The function vanishes if an element e1 with probability p1 = 1 is chosen and all other p's equal zero, that is, are not selected. In this case no lack of certainty exists for the aesthetic condition. We are therefore concerned now with a case of structural distribution whose entropy—and therefore also innovation or statistical information—is negative. In all other cases of the distribution of probability over all the elements of the repertory. the function and therefore the entropy or the innovation are positive. The maximum is attained when, as already remarked, all E's in the repertory acquire the same probability of selection. Thus in the case of chaogenic distribution. which describes the ideal repertory, the indeterminacy of this condition is greatest.

Semiotic Nuclear Aesthetics

As far as the semiotic feature of the borderline case of the *nuclear* aesthetic condition and its finite patterns are now concerned, it must orient itself to the *sign categories.* Nuclear semiosis develops the distributive core as a sign category, that is, as a complete triadic relationship covering I, O, and M. In this we must firmly realize that while the macroaesthetic description is oriented object-thematically to the icon and the microaesthetic description is object-thematically oriented to the indexical, the nuclear-aesthetic description, since it has directly become a disparate system of elements in the chaogenic repertory, can always only presume a separating *symbolic* object relationship. The constituted sign categories in nuclear semiosis are sign categories of symbolic object relationships. We are therefore concerned with the three cases in the system of sign categories, the cases known as:

1 the rhematic-symbolic legisign category
2 the dicentic-symbolic legisign category
3 the argumental-symbolic legisign category

The rhematic-symbolic legisign category defines semiotically a condition of maximum indeterminacy and openness and thereby the chaogenic condition of the repertory.

The dicentic-symbolic legisign category, on the other hand, defines a definite condition and therewith a structure.

The argumental-symbolic legisign category ultimately comprises all configurative conditions between the condition of maximum indeterminacy and the condition of maximum definition, whereby the graduation is produced argumentally by a system of probabilities that is numerically between 0 and 1.

One can also assign the three categories of the equally probable, the regular, and the irregular order to these three sign categories. It is likewise clear that the three borderline cases of Khinchin's abstract finite pattern are semiotically represented in this manner. Finally we must also point out that the well-known sign operations of adjunction, iteration, and superisation are connected in a characteristic way within the nuclear semiosis with the aesthetic conditions that were introduced of chaogenic, structural, and configurative distribution. The adjunction of signs or categories of signs, for each sign belongs to a sign category, constitutes the chaogenic condition;

for in a case like this the signs are given separately, and mere selection, which relates to the separated sign, cannot take place other than in an adjunctive manner. Corresponding to this is the structural condition, which, seen abstractly and from a principled point of view, constitutes the infinite agreement, can only be proved in the event of iteration, the reflexive repetition of the structural element. Configurative aesthetic conditions, on the other hand, are clearly set by the indexical system, but this very indexical setting of the distribution of the material elements lifts it to a totality that under certain circumstances can be identified in relation to the object as supericon. From the standpoint of distribution, for example, the points of certain pencils of lines form an indexical configuration of elements which at the same time set a perspectival system that can be iconisized object-thematically.

The System of Semiotic Aesthetic

Corresponding to the growth of semiotics as such, semiotic aesthetics also is broken down into three parts: a syntactical part, a semantic part, and a pragmatic part. The *syntactical* aesthetic produces statements about the relationships between the signs that constitute an aesthetic condition insofar as these are regarded as material elements, as mere means. The purely numerical, especially statistical or probability theoretical formulations of microaesthetics thus above all belong to syntactical aesthetics, but so do statements that relate to the well-known semiotic operations of adjunction, iteration, and superisation.

The *semantic* aesthetic, on the other hand, is concerned, as is the whole field of semantics, with the object-focused, object-related, or object thematics of the signs of an aesthetic condition. Insofar as an aesthetic condition at the same time as a distribution of the signs gives a distribution of the objects of these signs, the question arises of the aesthetic relevance not only of the signs, but also of the objects which they signify. For semantic aesthetics, the repertory of the creative selection process accordingly includes not only material elements as sign, but at the same time also the objects or object relationships of these signs. A doubled trace of selection and an ambiguity of "representation" with respect to aesthetics corresponds here to the doubled being-themes of the repertory. Insofar as the once represented "world" and a "representation" of world are realized and correspondingly the aesthetic distribution at one time in the particular world of semiotic means and another time in the outer world of the objects denoted by these means is realized. For each object-thematic art, regardless of whether this is about painting, text, sculpture, or music, the redoubled problem of the given reality of things in material *aesthetic space* and in relational *semantic space* arises under the point of view of semantic aesthetics. Numerical macroaesthetics, which relates to the aesthetic measurement of objects such as polygons, vases, ornaments, models, and the like is essentially also semantic aesthetics. Hegel's metaphysical aesthetics can be thought of as "content aesthetics" as well as an interpreting aspect of semantic aesthetics. Meanwhile their problems already refer back to pragmatic aesthetics.

Pragmatic aesthetics relates to the interpretations or references to meaning of the signs that constitute an aesthetic condition. The distinction between object reference and interpretation reference (designation function and meaning function) is defined by the fact that in the object reference the sign (by means of the external observer in the creative pattern) related to an object, whereas the signified object in the interpretation reference relates to other objects, thus (by means of the external observer in the creative scheme) is selected to go into a connex or context. Then in fact even in the interpretation reference of a sign with the rhema, the dicent, and the argument, three connexes, the open, the closed, and the complete connex, are introduced and are produced by the three patterns of meaning. As far as their connection with the three aesthetic conditions of the chaogenic, structural, and configurative distribution is concerned, it is easily demonstrated that the rhematic connex corresponds to the chaogenic as more open, the dicentic as more closed to the structural condition, and the argumental as more complete to the configurative aesthetic condition. One must just keep firmly in mind that the interpretation references are given over all of the object references. Accordingly, when it comes to connexes, we are concerned with the connexes of objects. The external observer, who acts as the interpreter of object references, selects objects as being separated in the event of an open rhematic connex, and the aesthetic condition, which is generated in this manner, is the type in which each object can replace another. As a material distribution the latter condition is chaogenic; it indicates the image of chaos; but the pattern of interpretation consistent with meaning is that of the metaphor. The principle of the metaphor is one of aesthetics, to the extent that it at the same time includes the principle of a chaogenic identification of the global connection. In the case of the closed dicentic connex, the external observer acting as interpreter has already selected certain objects as belonging together and *facts* that are open to the assertion, which linguistically may be represented as a *sentence*, visually as object-form or a form-color relationship and owing to whose stringent relevance and repetition, the signified objects of the world show up in *structures*. In the fully developed argumental connex, finally, the external observer interprets a complete global connection of symbolically signified objects in a meta-indexical system of their distribution which aesthetically possesses the abstract character of a *configuration*. It is not difficult to classify the word patterns of (lyric) poetry, (epic) prose, and (reflection-theoretical) texts within the linguistic creation process of these three aesthetic modifications of pragmatic interpretations. Obviously the function of *information* devolves upon the semantic object reference of the designation in the creative pattern of writing more strongly, and the function of *redundancy* more strongly upon the pragmatic interpretation reference of meaning. A maximum amount of (innovative) information corresponds to the rhematic, open context of (lyric) poetry that is oriented to the chaogenic global connection, and a maximum (interpretative) redundancy (of syntactic means and semantic references) to the argumental, complete context of (theoretical) reflection that is formed in the configurative global connection. The dicentic, closed context that is oriented to the structural global connection (of finite throngs of sentences) of (epic, narrative) prose, the sentences of which in each case consist of (individual) subjects and predicates which are appropriate or inappropriate for them, is on the other hand, as Rudolf Carnap has shown, determined by a special "semantic information"[10] whose measurement coincides with the "information transmitted by the statement." This "information" interpreted as a "statement" is the information of a dicentic and thus closed connex and thereby of a structural unity of two objects that are designated in two different categories and are linguistically interpreted as (individual) subject and (classifiable) predicate. The information transmitted by way of a statement in a dicentic connex is an innovation insofar as it, as a representation (consistent with a sentence) of a factual content, at the same time alters its original representation. The innovation which constitutes the essence of the information appears in the "semantic information" of the connex as the difference of two representations, which means, however, as the difference of the object references selected by the interpreting external observer when he appears in the creative pattern as writer or as narrator. One must always be careful, however, that the actual aesthetic weight of a distributive material condition is in the relationship of the redundant to the innovative moment. Looked at from the standpoint of the numerical identification of the aesthetic condition, "semantic information" can therefore only be a vehicle of the "aesthetic." So it is said about a semiotic identification of the aesthetic condition that it is a question of a singular relationship between the selected *designated* object references and the selected *meaningful* interpretation references.

Crude and Subtle Aesthetics

Aesthetics is always a description of the condition of certain distributions of material elements in their repertory. This description of a condition can be cruder or more subtle. Therefore one must speak in terms of crude and subtle aesthetics. In principle aesthetic conditions are graduated conditions. Numerical as well as semiotic categories are categories that have the capacity of fine-tuning, without which the characteristic feature of graduated indeterminacy with extreme cases of singularity and fragility cannot be comprehended. Even the *value aesthetic* of certain *emotional interpretants* of aesthetic conditions presumes that the latter are graduable even if this aesthetic does not make use of an object-related but a subject-related scale, which in fact is the theme of a value aesthetic. The conventional value aesthetic, however, can be developed into an exact value aesthetic if the conventional, subject-related and consumption-dependent values are defined throughout all of the numerical measurement rules and semiotic classifications (empirical and statistical).

General Conclusion

Abstract aesthetics is concerned with all possibilities of the material realization of aesthetic conditions; it does not limit the category of the carriers of aesthetic conditions. In principle it does not acknowledge any distinction between natural, artistic, and technical objects as carriers of aesthetic conditions. It can therefore be pursued as natural theory, art theory, literature theory, text theory, design theory, architecture theory, or in general as theory of technology. Since the exact applicable means of numerical measurement determination and semiotic classification relate directly to the condition of graduable indeterminacy by means of which aesthetic conditions distinguish themselves, the idea of *aesthetic programming*, which is an object of *generative aesthetics*, does not contradict the intentions of art as such.

Acknowledgment

Originally published as *Kleine abstrakte Ästhetik*, text 38, *Edition rot*, Stuttgart, January 1969.

Used with the kind permission of Elisabeth Walther Bense. Translation by Joseph Ebot.

Notes

1 Galileo Galilei, *Considerazioni al Tasso*, Edizione Nazionale delle opere di G.G., 21 vols., 1890–1927.
2 Georg Wilhelm Friedrich Hegel, *Vorlesungen über die Ästhetik* (Lectures on Aesthetics) (1835). Selected by Max Bense, edition rot, text 36, Stuttgart, 1968.
3 Gotthold Ephraim Lessing, *Laokoon* (Berlin, 1766), chaps. XVI and XVIII of Lessings Werke, vol. 3 (Weimar, 1963), pp. 245 and 263.
4 Claude Shannon and Warren Weaver, *The Mathematical Theory of Communication* (Urbana, 1949).
5 Charles Sanders Peirce, Die *Festigung der Überzeugung* (The Consolidation of Conviction), publ. by Elisabeth Walther (Baden-Baden, 1967).
6 George David Birkhoff, *Quelques elements mathematiques de l'art*, 1928 (*Einige mathematische Elemente der Kunst* [Some Mathematical Elements of Art]), translation. Elisabeth Walther, edition rot, text 37 (Stuttgart, 1968).
7 Christian von Ehrenfels, *Über Gestaltqualitäten*, 1890.
8 Shannon and Weaver, *Mathematical Theory of Communication.*
9 Aleksandr J. Chintschin [Aleksandr I. Khinchin], "Über grundlegende Sätze der Informationstheorie," *Arbeiten zur Informationstheorie* (On Fundamental Propositions of Information Theory, Papers on Information Theory), 1957.
10 Rudolf Carnap, *Introduction to Semantics* (Cambridge, MA, 1942); *Meaning and Necessity* (Chicago, 1947); *Logic and Language* (1962).

10

Aesthetics of the Digital

Sean Cubitt

Homo sum, humani nihil a me alienum puto.
[I am a human being, I consider nothing that is human alien to me.]
Publius Terentius Afer

Straying from its ancient Greek root meaning '"sensation," the term "aesthetic" has had to bear an increasingly heavy load since becoming current in Europe in the 18th century. Attached variously to the physical or phenomenal sensations of the body as it senses the world; the natural or artificial objects that give rise to such sensations (especially pleasurable ones); the specific qualities of beautiful objects, and the emotional and intellectual reactions we have to those objects and sensations, aesthetics has come to attach itself to the realm of art. Badiou (2007) suggests that aesthetic history can be divided between two moments: the Classical aesthetic, describing the realization of an ideal of beauty in an artwork, an ideal to which all artworks seek to aspire and which transcends history; and the Romantic, accepting the historical nature of beauty and placing its faith in a future realization. The Classical thus addresses the past, the Romantic the future. And yet, if we accept the idea that the aesthetic describes a moment when objects and senses come into contact—generating forms, sensations, and psychic events—then surely the aesthetic is par excellence the experience of the present?

The problem we face in tracing an aesthetic of the digital then begins in the problem of the present, a moment by definition too short to experience all the artifacts that might be described as aesthetic. Heidegger notes a similar problem related to the qualities of art. "What is art?" he asks. Is it that quality shared by artworks? Then how do we know something is an artwork? Because it has the quality of being art. The circle is logically vicious (Heidegger 1971, 18). We must try something more radical. If the aesthetic is that event that brings together objects, sensations, and subjectivity—the "aesthetic attitude," for example—then it always involves mediation

A Companion to Digital Art, First Edition. Edited by Christiane Paul.

between the world and the mind. Aesthetics, in the narrow sense of the appreciation of art, is dependent on mediation by the senses of vision and hearing; and with the benefit of a century of phenomenological studies, we must recognize that these senses are intrinsically temporal. There is always a "before" that comes ahead of any now. Turning a corner and clapping eyes for the first time upon Bill Viola's *Five Angels for the Millennium* (2001), the surprise occurs in time. There is no pure present for the aesthetic: there is the mediated experience of time. If we return to an artwork—poem, image, music—the recognition, the misremembering, the renewed encounter are all temporal.

The constitutive elements of aesthetic mediation are the same as those of any other mediation. There are matter and energy (in the form of light or the vibrations of air); there are space and time (even if the phenomenologists are wrong and the artwork can be sensed in an instantaneous gestalt); and there are form and entropy. The second of each of these pairs—energy, time, and entropy—each presume duration. The question now becomes: is there a specific quality of digital duration that differentiates it from other forms of mediation?

But here we meet our own version of Heidegger's problem: what counts as digital? Is there a common feature linking, say, a 3D-printed sculpture by Keith Brown with Spike Jonze and Fatboy Slim's collaboration on the video for *Weapon of Choice* (2001)? Is there, in short, only one digital aesthetic, or are there multiple modes of digital mediation? If we take some recognizably digital art forms and ask what constitutes their significantly digital aesthetic, we come upon a series of incomplete and unpersuasive answers. Advocates of flarf, the poetry of colliding search terms, suggest that the speed of *random* collocation is of the essence. Yet contingency has been a hallmark of modernism in the arts since before the beginnings of cinema (Doane 2002), as a poetic that can be traced from William S. Burroughs's cut-up technique back to Mallarmé's exclamation of 1897, "Jamais un coup de dès n'abolira le hasard" ("A throw of the dice will never abolish chance"), and that in John Cage's works connects the element of randomness avant-garde musical composition to the I Ching, at least four thousand years ago. What distinguishes the digital in the electronic arts, including music, is the *discrete* aspect of its sampling and processing. Yet Friedrich Kittler (1987) notes exactly the same quality in the field of writing, in the "Aufschreibesystem" or notational system introduced in the 1870s with the advent of the typewriter, which split letters apart as keystrokes and marks, ending the rule of cursive handwriting. We can turn to the concept of *code* as a natively digital concept; but code is also, as Eugene Thacker (2004) has been at pains to point out, a biological category, and its early use by the sociologist Jean Baudrillard (1970) to denote the self-organizing capacity of social life predates the mass take-up of digital tools by decades. At a more intuitive level, the digital is *clean*: smooth, depthless, immaterial. But digitality inherits this cleanliness from the marketing of electricity in the early part of the 20th century (Nye 2001), a period when the production of energy was for the first time dissociated from its consumption. Resting on a vast infrastructure of energy production, materials extraction, human exploitation, and environmental degradation, the digital cannot be spoken of as pure form—and therefore clean —without lying about the physical weight of digital media, a weight it shares with every other human activity. Cleanliness is always a matter of moving the dirt elsewhere. We may, finally, ask whether the essence of the digital is *information*, but Maxwell's Demon teaches us that information is a universal characteristic of the physical world.[1] We may follow

Bolter and Grusin (1999) in arguing, after McLuhan (1964), that the content of every new medium is an old medium; and that the digital takes as its content all the old media. We must add, in light of the above discussion of the random, discrete, coded, clean, and informatic qualities of the digital, that not only its content but also its form is borrowed from the near and distant past.

The digital is not clean, nor is it a clean concept. Defining the digital is as messy as the digital itself. As N. Katherine Hayles argues, we do not know how it works: programs as banal as Microsoft Word can be large, complex, and either undocumented or written by automated processes so that "no living person understands the programs in their totality" nor ever could understand them (Hayles 2008, 26). The digital materializes in a wealth of forms: electricity, light, punched tape, radio signals. What we imagine as shared across these forms are formal properties shared with pre-digital predecessors, but which we recognize as ubiquitous in the 21st century—to the extent that we look back on pre-digital culture as a distant and different country.

Beyond these more obvious but unpersuasive categorizations of the digital, we can find more complex concepts. Tracing the idea of any given digital image as a unique realization of the code that underlies it, Boris Groys argues that

> Digitalization, that is, the writing of the image, helps the image become reproducible, to circulate freely, to distribute itself [...] But at the same time the digitalized image becomes even more infected with non-identity [...] with the necessity of presenting the image as dissimilar to itself. (Groys 2008, 87)

Not only is each performance of the scripted code different depending on platform, scale, illumination, display, operating system, and so on, but every performance is "other" than the code that in some sense also "is" the image. Thus the digital image is not identical to itself: it is both pure code (and therefore not an image) and an image. What Groys misses is that the same is true of any electronically scanned image: analog cathode ray tubes scanned the image twice, building it from top left to bottom right on odd and even scanlines, so that at no single moment was the whole image present on the screen. On an even more basic level, the succession of images destined to produce the effect of motion depends not on single frames, but on their succession: no one "image" is therefore complete, but each is dependent on those surrounding it. This incompletion of all moving images intensifies from the level of the frame to that of the scanline and, today, the level of programmed pixels. Groys's point is more salient than he first imagines: and in this guise appears the first assertion we can make of the digital as an aesthetic.

The principle of non-identity has a key place in the history of modern mathematics in Gottlob Frege's (1974) definition of number. Since, according to Aristotle's axiom, everything that is, is identical to itself (A = A), Frege defines "nothing" as that which is not identical to itself: the symbol of non-identity is zero, since only the non-existent is non-identical. We should note here, as good materialists, that the "zero" used in binary logic is such a symbol, and should not be mistaken for "void." That "zero" is a symbol is clear from the fact that an absolute absence of electromechanical activity is impossible, at least in any environment where humans can survive. As there is no absolute silence (in Cage's anechoic chamber for example) or absolute black (the body produces effects of light if there are none in the environment), there is no zero condition in the transmission of electronic signals. What we name "zero" is at best an asymptotic diminution of activity curving toward the background state of electromagnetic flux. If Groys is correct, there is no "one," no whole, complete, and self-identical unity of the digitized image: and if Frege is correct, then there is no zero either. Not only is "zero" only ever an approximation, since the complete absence of charge is impossible in our universe, but the very concept of zero is the concept of non-existence. Therefore we can take as a premise that non-identity is a quality proper to the digital, and that as an aesthetic it is muddy and impure.

The work of archivists working in the field of digital art has made apparent a second characteristic of digital media: their ephemerality. We like to warm ourselves with the old comfort that digital files can be endlessly and accurately reproduced. Unfortunately, it has become apparent that this is not the case: transmission invariably introduces "bitrot," changes in the code resulting from small elements altered by fluctuations in the media of transmission and storage, or larger elements misplaced in their distribution through packet-switching networks. Magnetic and optical storage media are notoriously unstable compared to older media like safety film, paper, oil paint, or stone. The machinery on which they were designed to play falls victim to the planned obsolescence of the computer industry: whole families of drives and connections are driven out of the market, maintained for a few decades by conservators and collectors, and gradually succumb to the predations of time. Emulations retro-engineer contemporary machinery to simulate old devices, but the aesthetic and technical success can vary (Depocas, Ippolito, and Jones 2003). The platforms on which digital artworks are designed to run age and decay; replacing components changes the nature of the work—response times, refresh rates, color gamuts, tonal range, image density. The files themselves degenerate, mutating to produce random pixel colors and artifacts, while transfer to new file formats can introduce new errors. Conservators have been addressing these issues and developing strategies that will be discussed in more detail in the final section of this book. The digital is ephemeral, sometimes more so than older media. Shakespeare is still Shakespeare in a mass-produced paperback, still based on but no longer anchored in the primacy of the Folios and Quartos. But an early, digitally generated audiovisual poem by Bill Seaman, if it can be coaxed into running, no longer exhibits in the same way unless treated by conservators, and the old comet tails and bleeding colors of the early QuickTime format become evanescent memories as the software "improves" (Sobchack 1999).

A third quality of the digital is that it is unknowable, both because code is designed to be read by machines rather than humans, and because there simply is too much of it (Bohn and Short 2010; Hilbert and López 2012a, 2012b). No single human being could even sample the mass of digitally generated, stored, and transmitted data, much of it secured behind protection systems, some never leaving the machine on which it is generated. As a result, nothing we say today about digital aesthetics can be guaranteed to be true, both because somewhere in the ocean of electronic messages there may lie the exception, and because someone, somewhere, will invent a tool just to prove the theory wrong. The scale of digital activity is, however, a truth that can be spoken of, providing a fourth quality that can be described as integral to digital aesthetics.

Non-identical, ephemeral, and unknowable: these qualities might be said to belong to any and all aesthetic experience. But there are reasons to believe that in the case of digital art these qualities have specific valences that distinguish them. Take a simple example, John F. Simon, Jr.'s *Every Icon* (1997). A grid of 32 x 32 pixels, the work is

Given: A 32 × 32 grid

Allowed: Any element of the grid to be black or white

Shown: Every icon

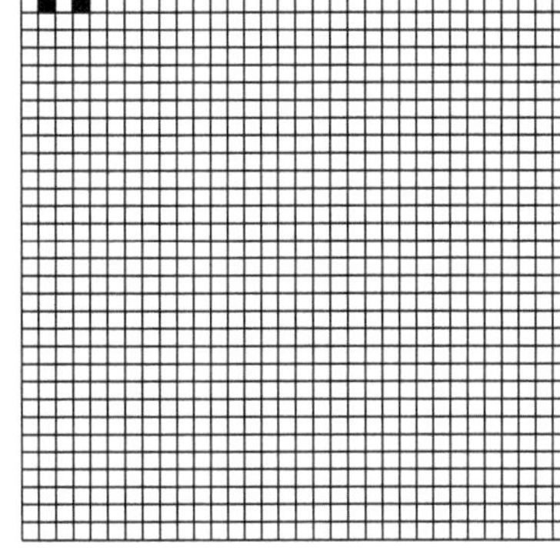

FIGURE 10.1 John F. Simon, Jr., *Every Icon* (1997), screenshot. Image courtesy of numeral.com.

programmed to fill the grid with every possible permutation of the sequence of black and white pixels (Figure 10.1). The top line flickers along busily —going through all possible variations of sequences of black and white—but, by the artist's reckoning, it will take 5.85 billion years to complete the second line. The problem posed for us is the problem of the present of the work. There is a sense in which the progressive flickering of the top left of the icon is present. But what about the artwork, which is destined, as the millennia glide by, to produce every possible icon? At some all too imaginable moment, a smiley face or the BP logo will pop into existence, gradually deforming as the matrix inexorably grinds on. Although we can, with the utmost accuracy, sketch on another 32 x 32 grid what will appear in *Every Icon*, that is not the appearance that will matter; the one that matters is not of a human will but of a process inaugurated and left to its autonomous work by the artist. In the unimaginably far future when the grid closes in on its goal of turning every square black, will there be any memory of what the individual icons were, the machine-readable QR codes and barcodes, as well as the human-readable graffiti and swooshes? And what will have become of these earliest flickerings we can observe on Simon, Jr.'s site in the first quarter of the 21st century? The thing itself is unknowable, while its present state is a permanently moving feast devouring its own past, an object that is not an object but the imagination of all the objects that it will be or has been.

Were we to say something similar about the *Mona Lisa*, we would be describing other qualities: what is unknowable about Leonardo's painting is that unanchorable smile, its non-identity premised perhaps on the impossibility of seeing so familiar an image for the first time; its ephemerality is tied to the common lot of the great crowd of those who have witnessed, marveled, and gone their ways since it was made six hundred years ago. In other words, we would be describing subjective experience. Simon, Jr.'s *Every Icon* does not invite that kind of thought: it proposes for our contemplation an autonomous process of making that will exceed human timescales. Its autonomy is not an allegory of human freedom: the program processes itself without intervention or reference to humanity. It will never know whether it has produced a recognizable image or word. At the same time, it requires a human audience to make sense of the ridiculous proposition of a machine that would run for trillions of years—long after its maker, his culture, and the kinds of machine it depends on are cosmic ash. Nonetheless, we ascribe the vision and the practice required to make it real to a human subject, an artist.

Theodor Adorno understands the necessarily subjective process of making art as something that distinguishes it from the objective process of philosophy because it "compels art—as something spiritual—to undergo subjective mediation in its objective constitution. The share of subjectivity in the artwork is itself a piece of objectivity" (Adorno 1997, 39). The fact that art is made by a historically positioned (and therefore biographically unique) maker cannot be denied, except at the cost of losing what makes art special: its mediation through an experiencing, living subject. At the moment of completion, however, the subjective component of making becomes an objective property of the work, a property that distinguishes it from everything else that professes itself to be ideal, universal, or objectively true. For Adorno, subjectivity is an unavoidable flavor of all art. Language operates according to its own evolution and structure, but in the hands of the poet it mutates according to the contingent conditions of a life lived in a specific speaking community, so that the same words come out of the process, but in new combinations with new semantic and musical properties. Subjectivity is the lens through which the working of the world is brought into a fine focus in the work of art.

Various forms of digital artwork—not only algorithmic works such as *Every Icon* but, for example, interactives in which the interactor "completes" the work; social media forms generated by network activity; and partnerships between human and technical partners such as machines/tools or robots in forming a work—raise the question whether digital aesthetics must confront a change in the meaning of "subjective" since Adorno wrote in the 1960s. That change may already have been flagged in Beuys's social sculptures, in happenings and event scores of the 1960s and 1970s, where the subject in control of the realization of the work is no longer a single individual. Freud's discovery of the unconscious was our first step into a new theory of subjectivity recognizing that the socialization subjectivity undergoes is integral to it; and that subjectivity therefore is not a given, but a historical phenomenon. On this historical basis, can it be said that the contemporary subject, after twenty years of intensive digitization, is now one step further removed from the isolated Cartesian individual, and one step closer to the social subject imagined in the Marxist tradition, at least since Gramsci's work on Fordism and Taylorism? And if, as Adorno maintained, art is always a compound of the objective historical conditions and their subjective mediation, would that suggest that the objective conditions now are also—and not necessarily in a utopian sense—increasingly socialized? Has the social in fact ceased to become the historical goal of a post-individualist socialism, and instead become the mode of contemporary governmentality?

The code for *Every* Icon was written in Java, a language first released in 1995 and designed to provide much of the functionality of C and C++ and capable of running on any computer. Though the authorship of Java is attributed to James Gosling, the language draws on a long legacy that can be traced through Bell Labs in the 1970s to BCPL (Basic Combined Programming Language), originally developed at Cambridge University in the 1960s for writing compilers for other computer languages. The "virtual machine" that John F. Simon, Jr. created with *Every Icon* is itself a social product with a thirty-year history whose roots anchor it in the oldest forms of computer language. Simon Jr.'s work is then ripe to consider as a "poem" spoken in a rapidly evolving language of which no one of its speakers can claim to be the originator. However, in any given instance, this language allows statements that, if well parsed, speak themselves, and generate new statements. First of all, there is a collaboration between human and tool that amounts to more than the assemblage of brush, pigment, and canvas created with the hand and eye of the painter; a collaboration in which the tools are capable of self-motivating action without reference back to the author. And secondly, there is an element of the grotesque in *Every Icon*; an element of the absurd as outlined in Camus's *Myth of Sysiphus (*1955), which depicts a hopeless and unintelligible universe that is best confronted with the resigned repetition of a meaningless task. To consign this task to a program compounds the ignominy. Both the subjectivity of the artist and the autonomy of the work are diminished in a farce as bitter as Beckett's *Waiting for Godot*.

And yet there lies a kind of hopefulness in the future-oriented—and in that sense, reverting to Badiou's terminology, Romantic—aesthetic to *Every Icon*, for which the completion of its task, and all the subtasks along the way, is set off into a time hundreds of trillions of years away. Like the numerical unknowability of the digital domain as it exists today, the temporal unknowability of every icon to be produced by *Every Icon* balances the pointlessness of the task with more than the absurd determination to carry on: it suggests that marvels may appear one day, that the program might generate a figure of unguessed beauty. But that moment will not necessarily occur (and is highly unlikely to occur) in the artist's lifetime or that of his current audiences: it is deferred to a future when *aesthesis* will perhaps take on another, different form, maybe one that is also mediated by machines. At such a juncture we should pause before and contemplate the thesis that technology is where we Westerners keep our ancestors.

In the *Grundrisse* (Marx 1973, 690–711), Marx writes of machinery as "dead labor." The accumulated knowledge and skills of all the dead coagulate into the factory: the memories of knitting, weaving, and sewing, hammering, and turning are converted into automated processes, set to run at their own speed, and set against the workers now doomed to service them. In indigenous cultures, a similar principle is in operation but recognized in a different way: the ancestors responsible for creating a tool or technique are consulted as a new job is begun, their contribution is honored and their wisdom requested. A major difference between Western and indigenous cultures is that we do not know the names of our ancestors and that, as a matter of political economy, we force them into servitude. To call upon the ancestry of Java in C and BCPL is to honor the ancestral tradition and, by setting the program off to run at its own pace, a certain ancestral subjectivity is released to do its own business in its own time, its own temporality. The time addressed by Simon, Jr. is hard to name as "present" (and therefore as "aesthetic," as addressed to the senses) because, even as it runs according to the clock cycles of its CPU, it inhabits a different time—mythic time—and the subjectivity that inhabits it is no longer bound to the temporality of biography, the mortal span.

Is it beautiful? This question seems almost absurd. Much of the conceptual turn in contemporary art returns to Duchamp's strictures, almost a hundred years ago, on "retinal art," and not much is left of the claim to beauty. Yet numerous artists work with and in traditions that speak directly to visual pleasure. In a series of landscape videos made since 2005, Peter Campus has directed his camera toward a scene around the Long Island coast. In *phantom* (2011), the camera has been tilted 90 degrees to record in portrait format a jetty, the abandoned road leading to it, and, on the further

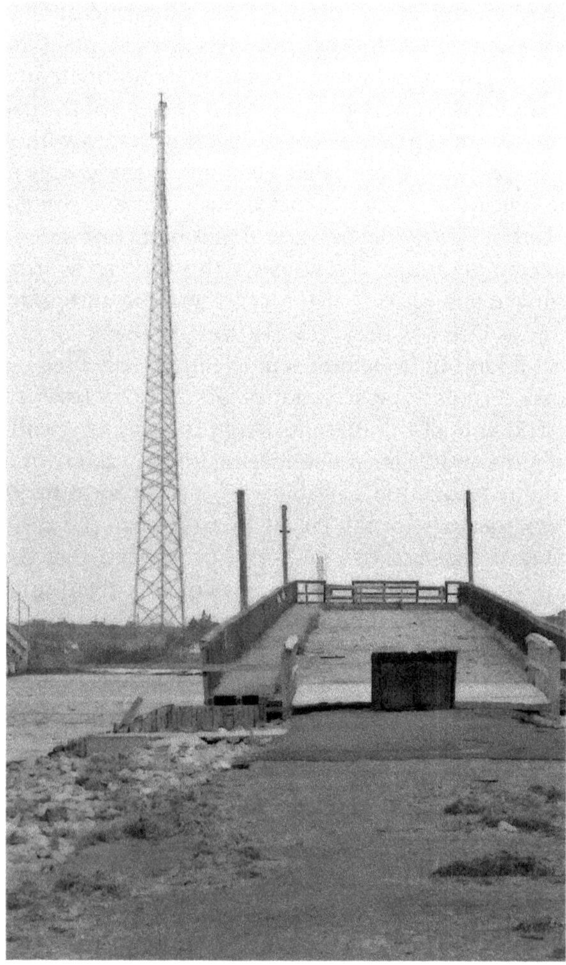

FIGURE 10.2 Peter Campus, *phantom*, 2011. Courtesy of Peter Campus.

shore of the inlet, a radio or celnet mast (Figure 10.2). Although in some of these works he has slowed image, sound, or both, *phantom* operates at or near real time: birds fly into frame, water ruffles, wind moves the foliage on the far bank. The piece loops, but so little happens that it is hard to decipher when the work is repeating. You could get the impression that the artist has just let his camera run, and released that stretch of recorded time back into the gallery, except for the fact that—while the composition framed by the locked-off camera signals its links to the landscape tradition from Corot onward—the color, depth, and graphic quality of the image speak directly to the tradition of printmaking, East and West: to Hokusai and Rembrandt among others.

Yet the art-historical reverberations are at best a corona of connotations surrounding the fascination of the image itself. Campus is coy about revealing his process, but insists that, prior to their transfer to Blu-ray (and lately digital media players) for exhibition, the image files are resolutely uncompressed (Basciano 2009). It would appear that the image has been decomposed into layers and treated in such a way that, similar to the translucent washes of suspended color layered over one another by a painter, it is built up, with each layer treated to its own filters until the surface of the high-resolution (1080 x 1920 progressive scan) LED screen seems to give way to a painterly depth of air and material: blocks of color made up of under- and over-layered hues, in this instance summing at a palette of earths and greys with an almost cartoon-like discretion between blocks. The assertion that this does not involve compression is significant. Most compression algorithms work by assembling similar colors into blocks and groups of blocks, packing and unpacking the image for maximum efficient transmission. These images are not the artifacts of such automated efficiency. They are ways of seeing, but also marks of a patient labor rebuilding the raw footage into a contemplation of the visual qualities of the scene.

For its duration, the loop allows us to inspect the whole screen where we typically focus our attention only on the most active parts. (This focus also is a principle of contemporary codecs, which concentrate the most detail in the areas with the most activity, usually faces and bodies in action.) In *phantom* the density of atmospheric haze shifts fine gradations of blue-gray washes over cream, a movement as fascinating as the trembling edges of poles moved by buffeting breezes. There is time to think through the collocation of motifs—jetty and antenna. In the first chapter of *Ulysses* (Joyce 1968, 31), Stephen Dedalus describes the Kingstown Pier as "a disappointed bridge": it is hard not to start reading into the iconography of *phantom* a history of failed or failing communication. Water, wind, and birds connect the banks, where human artifacts do not—except for the video itself in which they are assembled into a complexly flat representation (broached by the swatches of color) that nonetheless rhymes digital layers with the actual space of the location.

At the same time, it seems false to descend to the statement that *phantom* is a work "about" the medium of representation, or representation itself, even though it works at this level, as well as at the semantic and indeed the representational and perceptual ones. The digital tools—including the stylistic device of turning the screen sideways to create the desired shape, with the added effect of scanning the image vertically instead of the familiar horizontal raster scan—are means toward other ends. In an interview, Campus speaks of a desire to see, to spend time seeing, to provide an audience with the wherewithal to spend time, to experience the time of events and their perception. What is perhaps most striking about *phantom* and Campus's other digital video landscapes is that they are works of exceptional beauty. Again, to say that beauty is all there is to see may be wrong: Campus is, for example, familiar enough with the poetry of place along the northeastern seaboard of the USA, from William Carlos Williams's Paterson to Charles Olson's Gloucester, for the salt of history to be rubbed into his choice of location. Yet the beauty of the series, in which *phantom* is one pendant, is undeniable, and, for all its art-historical recollections, this series is an unmistakably digital work, not least because of its use of the affordances of layers and the specific tools developed in video editing for the manipulation of time.

At the same time one would need to admit that, although these are images of human landscapes (a jetty here, cabins, ports, container ships elsewhere), there is a certain inhumanity in operation. The initial suspicion is that this is a landscape observed without an observer. The labor of post-production certainly involves an attentive observation of the scene, more attention perhaps than any but an automated eye could give to the fluster of light across the area contained by the frame. To stand and watch this work also means to watch that observation in process, both the mechanical and the laborious, but to do so on the premise that, for a period of time, this landscape has been recorded without being perceived. Few photographs, and very few films, give this uncanny sense of the autonomy of their subjects, or convey the sense that the process of observation itself is an autonomous activity, apart from the everyday concourse of life. The absence of human figures distinguishes these landscapes from, for example, Terry Flaxton's *Portraits of Glastonbury Tor* (2008) in which extreme high definition captures individuals, couples, families, and groups against a backdrop of the ancient monument, each posing for a minute between entry into and exit from the frame. Flaxton's use of ambient sound is another difference: Campus's recent works have no sound, not even the chunter of the projector that used to accompany otherwise soundless film artworks such as Brakhage's *Mothlight* (1963). Although both works make use of locked-off cameras and RAW files, Flaxton focuses on the figure in the landscape, and Campus on the landscape itself; Flaxton on the viewer's encounter with another; Campus on the encounter with the Other. Campus engages in the alterity of both the world and our perception of it, rather than the commonality of perception that Flaxton embraces. *phantom* works, we might say, on the level of the unconscious of perception, somewhere between the optical unconscious that Benjamin saw in high-speed photography's revelation of unseen processes of the world and the Freudian unconscious, the unknown that is excluded from subjectivity.

This subject hovers between ontology and psychology, world and mind, in that embarrassed hinterland that Hegel made his own, thinking the world as a Mind moving toward self-understanding through a millennial series of alienations and overcomings. In the *Aesthetics*, Hegel describes the beautiful as the manifestation of freedom. A child of his times, he believed that as expression of the freedom of the spirit, once emancipated from its attachment to the divine, "art, considered in its highest vocation, is and remains for us a thing of the past" (Hegel 1975, I, 11). However, he also understood that art continued both to be made and to act aesthetically as expression of human freedom. It is this aspect of Hegel's aesthetic that underlies Adorno's *Aesthetic Theory*. Since "[writing] poetry after Auschwitz is barbaric" (Adorno 1967, 34), the last viable forms of art are those that recognize the dark failure of the European Enlightenment by enacting a last refusal, thereby prising open a last inkling of the free spirit. This spirit can only be defined by its absence, but, as negation of the present, allows us a last fragile hope of living freely, that is, different from mere existence under conditions of capitalist modernity: "For absolute freedom in art, always limited to a particular, comes into contradiction with the perennial unfreedom of the whole" (Adorno 1997, 1). Calling on a very different tradition, D.N. Rodowick comes to a remarkably similar conclusion:

> It is not that Art dies and therefore must be mourned ... Rather it is the unconscious fear that Art may never have existed and will never be able to exist in the economic age that desires it as a supplement to alienation and lack of freedom. (Rodowick 2001, 138)

Rodowick concludes that it is necessary to liberate ourselves from the idea of the aesthetic. For Adorno the point is the contradiction itself, to such an extent that "Even in a legendary better future, art could not disavow remembrance of accumulated horror; otherwise its form would be trivial" (Adorno 1997, 324). The subjectivity involved in art is then caught in a vise, its realization (as code, for example) dependent on the social whose oppression is precisely what it strives to escape. This contradiction is the place of the aesthetic in Adorno.

Our starting point, the question concerning the identity of the aesthetic as rooted in the present moment of aesthetic experience, must be formulated in a way that allows for the co-presence of not only artwork and audience but also the social that forms both of them. An extreme phenomenological position might isolate the aesthetic moment as a uniquely exclusive collision of perceiver and perceived and therefore one that is beyond history, making the moment indefinitely repeatable. However, we have already observed that this existence beyond history is not possible for aesthetic encounters, which occur in time. As non-identical, the experience cannot be repeated. We therefore must incorporate history in the aesthetic encounter, which is to say that we must recognize the aesthetic, as both property of a work and as an experience of it, as something giving body to ("corporating") the historical present. We are then charged with the task of understanding what exactly constitutes the historical and social present, for both artworks and their audiences. We are also given a privileged material to investigate in pursuit of an answer, for it is in the artworks themselves that, if the theory is correct, we will discover the characteristic incorporation of that socio-historical present.

And yet there is no single artwork to which we might entrust this role of capturing the present, especially given the unknowability principle. That principle extends to the unknowability of every permutation of many works, especially those driven by constantly changing live data streams like radioqualia's *Radio Astronomy* (2004–) or Joyce Hinterding and David Haynes's *Electro-magnetique Composition for Building, Plants and Stars* (2007), Mark Hansen and Ben Rubin's *Listening Post* (2001–2002) or Beatriz da Costa's *Pigeon Blog* (2006–2008) and many more. Corby + Baily's *Cyclone.soc* (2006), for example, maps live newsgroup discussions onto streaming meteorological data feeds in an interactively navigable installation that, like many data-streaming artworks, "begins in delight and ends in wisdom," as Robert Frost (1939) described poetry (Figure 10.3). Except that the end never comes. By interacting, the viewer selects what *not* to see as much as what to see; and the installation evolves constantly whether viewers are present or not (which might also be said of artificial life artworks, in which software generates life-like processes and systems, and indeed of Simon Jr.'s *Every Icon*). The "gestalt moment" of an ending, when the patterns of a narrative or the structures of melody and development make sense as a whole, does not happen in this kind of work, which concludes only in the sense that it must be switched off at some point. The freedom of these works lies in their ephemeral temporality, their constant bubbling into and out of existence, and in the operations they perform on the accumulated data of the past to produce the emergent unknown future. The raw materials of online community interaction are as unforeseeable as the weather and never add up to the equilibrium state of 3% growth per annum that characterizes the idealized model of the market, which, as we know, is a feeble characterization of a classically turbulent system (Harvey 2010).

What is so chilling about *Cyclone.soc* is its specific view of the worlds it depicts. Conversation here appears as data: as flux of information. Knowledge of social life is reconstituted as knowledge modeled on the statistical regularities of climatology. In one sense this is a deeply satirical work, unveiling the biopolitical management of populations so characteristic of contemporary rule. At the same time, it reveals a troubling analogy between the handling of weather data and the handling of

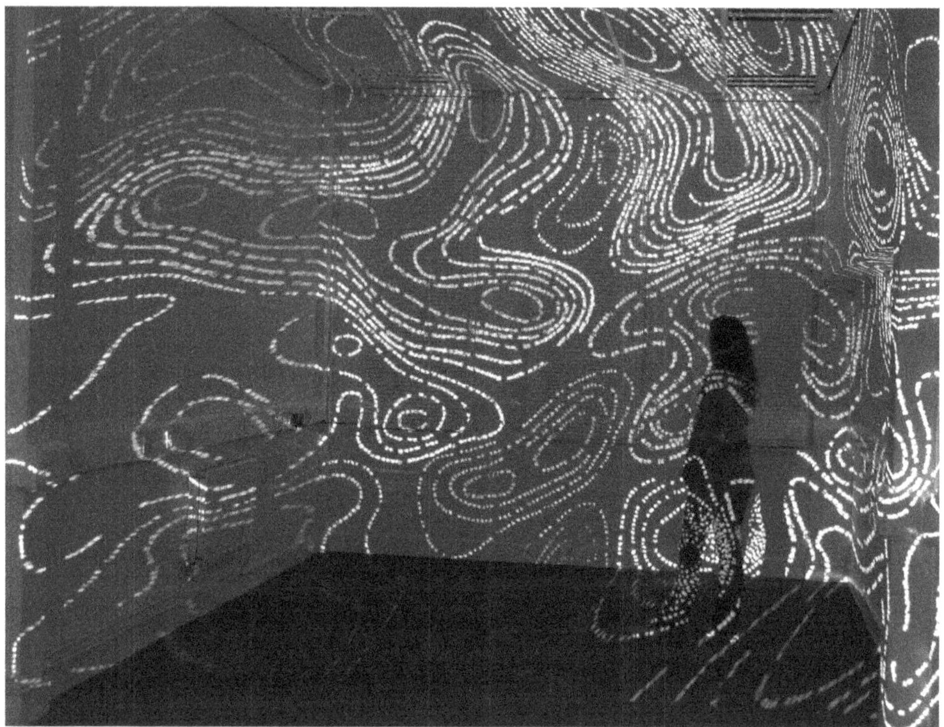

FIGURE 10.3 Corby & Bailey, *cyclone.soc*, 2006. Installation view. Courtesy of Tom Bailey, http://www.reconnoitre.net/.

telecommunications traffic since both can be analyzed as mathematical systems with their own regularities and emergent properties. Recast as data, weather ceases to be the phenomenon of rain-lashed and sunburned skin and becomes numerical; and as weather converts into arithmetic, the human environment, *Cyclone.soc* suggests, becomes a data environment. In centuries past, people—alienated from the land by enclosures and colonialism—came to confront that land as an environment over and against the human. The Industrial Revolution seized the skills of handcraft workers and embodied them in factory machines, which again appeared to their servants as an environment set over and against them. In the 21st century, knowledge has been alienated from its knowers in vast databases and Google's immense server farms, where what once was our knowledge has become an environment we must inhabit. This is the environment of data that live-streaming data-driven artworks must address according to their lights. This is the new form of the social—of the human universe defined by its alienation from land, technology, and information—constituting our contemporary historical condition, the unfreedom to which all art worth the name must respond.

In the field of digital aesthetics, there remains the problem of addressing the multiple aesthetics of the vast variety of digital media forms, from Flash aesthetics (Munster 2003) and ascii art (Cosic 1999), net.art (Bosma 2011), and glitch aesthetics (Menkman 2010), to locative media (Tuters and Varnelis 2006) and the "new aesthetic" (Bridle 2011). The conditions of non-identity and ephemerality extend to theorization of digital aesthetics. The idea of an aesthetic theory asks us to know, in some sense, what we mean by digital *art* as anything other than a sociological category of works that circulate in the institutions and discourses of art. It is possible to wriggle off the hook by arguing that the aesthetic moment is in all instances unknowable, but that does not quite raise the issue to the appropriate level of discourse. Instead we must confront the possibility that the condition of aesthetic "knowledge" is not something that can be captured the same way that information can; that it does not lend itself to the commodity form, despite the monetary value ascribed to artworks; and that it has qualities and values that, at least to date, elude the privatization and privation associated with the enclosure of knowledge as skill or data. Rather than the "known unknowns" of Donald Rumsfeld, we confront the unknown knowns, the unconscious of our days (Žižek 2004).

Considered as unknown knowledge, the aesthetic in general might simply be reduced to ideology, to the nature of the "unknown knowns," those disavowed knowledges and beliefs we pretend not to know even though they are the backbone of our everyday practices and behaviors, which leads again to Rodowick's call for liberation from the idea (and ideology) of the aesthetic. But pleasure and beauty, to echo Richard Dyer (1992), are too precious, too rare to surrender. Instead of equating the unconsciousness of the aesthetic moment with the ideology of digital capital, we might understand the aesthetic moment as that which is excluded from capital, even at a moment when capital has turned the energies of accumulation not only to knowledge but the creativity itself, in the massive engines deployed to extract free labor of creation from the countless users of social media (Terranova 2012).

If the aesthetic moment is excluded from capital, what is it that capital excludes? For Mark Hansen, the materiality of the digital image

> is both continually in process and routed through affectivity as that extraperceptual "faculty" that ensures our openness to the preindividual, the preperceptual, the new, and with it, the very future-directedness of the constitutively incomplete present. (Hansen 2006, 268)

Evoking Gilbert Simondon's (2005) theory of individuation, affectivity refers to the condition of the body before the socializing process of becoming an individual organizes perception into distinctions and hierarchies. Like Freud's polymorphous perversity,[2] this primal, unformed field of sensation becomes unconscious in the adult: the aesthetic, Hansen argues, makes it available as a bodily experience below the threshold of conscious thought, even of perception. At the core of this theory lies both a humanist presumption that the heart of the aesthetic will always be a human being, and a specifically individualist humanism, even though what is being appealed to is a pre-individual affectivity. The field of a social unconscious will never be an effect of socialization—individuality as result of social processing. It must in some sense be social itself. What constitutes the social in the digital era, as argued above, is the cumulative alienation from land (the natural environment), machines (the technological environment), and information (the data environment). It is these alienated environments that constitute the unknown knowns of the present. If *Every Icon* speaks from the unconscious of technology, and *phantom* from the unconscious of the land, *Cyclone.soc* speaks from the unconscious of data, articulating it with both the natural and technological, and underpinning the brutal reversal enacted by the capitalization of creativity: that we who produce the content of digital media are no longer conscious of our work as it is perceived from the commanding heights of biopolitics; and that it is the human population that has become the unconscious of a social organization that has long abandoned the disciplining of individuality for the mass management of populations.

The opposite of a digital aesthetic would be digital kitsch. Kitsch, following Greenberg (1939), was the attempt by rulers to ape the unschooled taste of the ruled. Today it takes the opposite form. From "shoot 'em up" and strategy games to workplace databases and spreadsheet software, the quotidian aesthetic of the digital is manipulation, the basic activity of biopolitical rule. Digital kitsch places us in the imaginary position of control, an illusory freedom founded on the capitulation of everything to the data form (its commodification and its openness) or, more precisely, to manipulation: we are not playing "God games"[3] as they are sometimes called, but "Ruler games." In contrast, the work of digital aesthetics is to place us in the unthinkable zone of the non-human—to abandon mimetic realism, for example, because it can only be an account of human perception—and, instead, to force a way of perceiving otherwise than humanly. Like contemporary science, contemporary biopolitics leans toward the Pythagorean belief that material reality is only the illusory surface of actual mathematical processes; and that manipulating the math will produce new realities. New forms of mathematics are one tool in the armory of digital aesthetics (Badiou 2008); another are the attempts to speak the unconscious of what we have defined, by alienating them in the form of estranged environments or economic externalities, as non-human. To speak from the social as its own unconscious, the unknown known, is only thinkable when we sacrifice humanism, and embrace the voices of our estranged others, natural, technical, and informatic. This is the task peculiar to digital aesthetics.

Notes

1 To demonstrate the challenges of the Second Law of Thermodynamics—the tendency of closed systems to move toward equilibrium—James Clerk Maxwell imagined a demon sorting hotter, faster molecules from slower, cooler ones by opening and closing a door between two halves of a closed box. The demon has to do work in order to create order, work which requires energy that he can only get from the closed system he inhabits, thus demonstrating that entropy will continue to increase. Entropy is a measure of the quantity of information in a system, and all systems are subject to the Second Law.

2 The theory that infants have a sexuality that is unfixed, not located in the genitals but multiform and without regulation from social codes.

3 Games like *Civilizations* which cast the player in the role of a divinely powerful overseer of a world.

References

Adorno, Theodor W. 1967. "Cultural Criticism and Society." In *Prisms*, translated by Samuel and Shierry Weber, 19–34. Cambridge, MA: The MIT Press.

Adorno, Theodor W. 1997. *Aesthetic Theory*, edited by Gretel Adorno and Rolf Tiedemann, translated by Robert Hullot-Kentor. London: Athlone Press.

Badiou, Alain. 2007. *The Century*, translated by Alberto Toscano. Cambridge: Polity.

Badiou, Alain. 2008. *Number + Numbers*, translated by Robin MacKay. Cambridge: Polity.

Basciano, Oliver. 2009. "ArtReview meets Peter Campus." *ArtReview*, December 18. http://www.artreview.com/forum/topic/show?id=1474022%3ATopic%3A963569 (accessed January 4, 2015).

Baudrillard, Jean. 1970. *La société de consommation: ses mythes, ses structures*. Paris: Gallimard.

Bohn, Roger E., and James E. Short. 2010. *How Much Information? 2009 Report on American Consumers*. San Diego, CA: Global Information Industry Center, University of California.

Bolter, Jay David, and Richard Grusin. 1999. *Remediation: Understanding New Media*. Cambridge, MA: The MIT Press.

Bosma, Josephine. 2011. *Nettitudes: Let's Talk Net Art*. Rotterdam: Nai010.

Bridle, James. 2011. *The New Aesthetic*. London: Really Interesting Group. http://www.riglondon.com/blog/2011/05/06/the-new-aesthetic/ (accessed January 4, 2015).

Camus, Albert. 1955. *The Myth of Sysiphus*, translated by Justin O'Brien. London: Hamish Hamilton.

Cosic, Vuk. 1999. *3D ASCII, An Autobiography*. http://www.ljudmila.org/~vuk/ascii/vuk_eng.htm (accessed January 4, 2015).

Depocas, Alain, Jon Ippolito, and Caitlin Jones, eds. 2003. *Permanence Through Change: The Variable Media Approach*. New York/Montreal: The Solomon R. Guggenheim Foundation/The Daniel Langlois Foundation for Art, Science, and Technology.

Doane, Mary Anne. 2002. *The Emergence of Cinematic Time: Modernity, Contingency, The Archive*. Cambridge, MA: Harvard University Press.

Dyer, Richard. 1992. *Only Entertainment*. London: Routledge.

Frege, Gottlob. 1974. *The Foundations of Arithmetic*, translated by J.L. Austin. Oxford: Blackwell.

Frost, Robert. 1939. "The Figure a Poem Makes." In *Collected Poems of Robert Frost*. New York: Holt, Rinehart, and Winston.

Greenberg, Clement. 1939/1992. "Avant-Garde and Kitsch." In *Art in Theory 1900–1990*, edited by Charles Harrison and Paul Wood, 529–541. Oxford: Blackwell.

Groys, Boris. 2008. *Art Power*. Cambridge, MA: The MIT Press.

Hansen, Mark B.N. 2006. *New Philosophy for New Media*. Cambridge, MA: The MIT Press.

Harvey, David. 2010. *The Enigma of Capital and the Crises of Capitalism*. Oxford: Oxford University Press.

Hayles, N. Katherine. 2008. "Traumas of Code." In *Critical Digital Studies*, edited by Arthur and Marilouise Kroker, 25–44. Toronto: University of Toronto Press.

Hegel, G.W.F. 1975. *Hegel's Aesthetics: Lectures on Fine Art*, translated by T.M. Knox, 2 vols. Oxford: Oxford University Press.

Heidegger, Martin. 1971. "The Origin of the Work of Art." In *Poetry, Language, Thought*, translated by A. Hofstadter, 17–87. New York: Harper & Row.

Hilbert, Martin, and Penelope López. 2012a. "How to Measure the World's Technological Capacity to Communicate, Store, and Compute Information Part I: Results and Scope." *International Journal of Communication* 6: 956–979.

Hilbert, Martin, and Penelope López. 2012b. "How to Measure the World's Technological Capacity to Communicate, Store, and Compute Information Part II: Measurement Unit and Conclusions." *International Journal of Communication* 6: 936–955.

Joyce, James. 1968. *Ulysses*. Harmondsworth, UK: Penguin.

Kittler, Friedrich. 1987. "Gramophone, Film, Typewriter." Translated by Dorothe von Mücke. *October* 41 (Summer): 101–118.

Marx, Karl. 1973. *Grundrisse*, translated by Martin Nicolaus. London: Penguin/New Left Books.

McLuhan, Marshall. 1964. *Understanding Media: The Extensions of Man*. London: Sphere.

Menkman, Rosa. 2010. "Glitch Studies Manifesto." http://rosa-menkman.blogspot.co.uk/2010/02/glitch-studies-manifesto.html (accessed January 4, 2015).

Munster, Anna. 2003. "Compression and the Intensification of Visual Information in Flash Aesthetics." *MelbourneDAC 2003 streamingworlds*. Proceedings of the 5th International Digital Arts and Culture (DAC) Conference, Melbourne, May 2003, edited by Adrian Miles, 150–159. Melbourne: RMIT University School of Applied Communication.

Nye, David E. 2001. *Electrifying America: Social Meanings of a New Technology*. Cambridge, MA: The MIT Press.

Rodowick, David N. 2001. *Reading the Figural, or Philosophy After the New Media*. Durham, NC: Duke University Press.

Simondon, Gilbert. 2005. *L'individuation à la lumière des notions de forme et d'information*. Paris: Editions Jérôme Millon.

Sobchack, Vivian. 1999. "Nostalgia for a Digital Object: Regrets on the Quickening of QuickTime." *Millennium Film Journal* 34: 4–23.

Terranova, Tiziana. 2012. "Free Labor." In *Digital Labor: The Internet as Playground and Factory*, edited by Trebor Scholz, 33–57. New York: Routledge.

Thacker, Eugene. 2004. *Biomedia*. Minneapolis, MN: University of Minnesota Press.

Tuters, Mark, and Kazys Varnelis. 2006. *Beyond Locative Media*.http://networkedpublics.org/locative_media/beyond_locative_media (accessed January 4, 2015).

Žižek, Slavoj. 2004. "What Rumsfeld Doesn't Know That He Knows About Abu Ghraib." *In These Times*, May 21. http://www.inthesetimes.com/article/747/ (accessed January 4, 2015).

11

Computational Aesthetics

M. Beatrice Fazi and Matthew Fuller

It is the contention of this chapter that computation has a profound effect on the composition of digital art. We understand computation as a method and a force of organization, quantification, and rationalization of reality by logico-mathematical means. The computational precedes yet grounds the digital in its technical, social, and cultural manifestations: it finds in digital technologies a fast, efficient, and reliable technique of automation and distribution, yet remains a notion wider and more powerful than the digital tools that it subtends. Art, operating with the digital prefix and taking on many of the characteristics of the contemporary world, is inherently interwoven with the specific features of computational structures. At the same time, though, it can be said that aspects of digital art have yet to be sufficiently considered from that perspective. To some extent this is understandable, given the immense flexibility—and, often, resultant opacity—of computational systems. Digital art, however, builds upon and works through the computational, sharing its limits and potentials while also inheriting conceptual histories and contexts of practice. For this reason, we contend that an aesthetics of digital art is, at a fundamental level, a computational aesthetics.

Medium Specificity

The crux of our argument can be summarized in the particular kind of medium specificity of the aesthetics of digital art, a specificity that we see pertaining to this art's primary computational character. When making a claim for the computational specificity of digital art, however, we abstain from flattening this proposition onto openly "modernist" arguments, or following on with the sets of uneasy qualifications and rejoinders that come after such positions. We are wary of the essentialism that such an argument would imply, mourn, or efface. It is our contention, however, that the risk of "computational essentialism" is diminished by the nature of computation itself. It is somewhat perverse to look to Greenberg as a point of orientation, but it

A Companion to Digital Art, First Edition. Edited by Christiane Paul.

will serve to make the point: traditionally, a modernist medium-specific aesthetics would call for the individuation of a "raw" materiality, which—in operation and in effect—amasses and defines the potential for artistic expressivity of a certain medium, a modernism of attenuation (Greenberg 1961). In the case of computational aesthetics, however, such a prescription is more difficult to sustain. How is one to match the material promises of a medium if this medium does not have an idiotypic substantial form (such as canvas, paint, marble, or mud), but rather has to be understood as a method and a force that, through rules, constraints, and capacities for expression, continually renegotiates its own structures of existence? In other words, what makes computation special in terms of its mediality—and thus perhaps different from any other media coming into composition with art—is the impossibility of describing it simply as an intermediary "substance."

Art, thankfully enough, is not simply communications. The relation of art with its media has been complex— a relation that is disavowed as much as it is explored, and through which one can trace the histories of many modalities or kinds of art that may themselves not cohere into a stable lineage. Art always propagates, rather than necessarily progresses, by disrupting and reinventing its terms of growth and domains of operation. Computation, however, has, in a certain sense, been a more historically delimited domain. To some extent this is due to the relatively young state of the field as an organized discipline. At the same time, we argue, computation's development through mathematics, logic, philosophy, and physical engineering gives it an equally rich genealogy. With its folding out into culture and the social, and indeed in its entanglement with art, it is undergoing further mutation, and its complex lines of invention and imagination find new forms of growth.

Recognizing this, critical discourse in recent years has developed cultural and artistic understandings of some of the mechanisms and components (algorithms, values, parameters, functions, codes, and so on) through which computation operates, for instance via the emergence of fields such as software studies (Fuller 2008). We would like to supplement this discussion with a consideration of computation's mediality as a mechanism of ontological and epistemological production. In terms of our medium specificity argument, this implies that computation is a medium in so far as it actualizes modes of being, levels and kinds of agency, and procedures of thought and configuration. The ontological and epistemological expressions of computation are concretized and become operative at various scales: in the cultural, the societal and the political, as well as in art and elsewhere. Through a double articulation, computation changes these fields yet maintains its own specificity; a specificity that is in turn affected, in variable ways, by the mutational forces of these fields' characteristics. Calling for a recognition of the medium specificity of computation in digital art thus means to take up the challenge of considering a mediality that surpasses the bounds of its grossly material instantiations and circumstances. In fact, acknowledging medium specificity involves reconsidering the notion of matter altogether, via the mobilization of all categories of the computational (whether sensuous, or logical, or both), and in light of the ontologies and epistemologies that computational systems initiate or participate in.

A problem that immediately follows from this argument about medium specificity is how computation can be understood and spoken of, and by which means its consequences in the area of digital art can be mapped out. In attempting to address these questions, we do not advocate a "programmatic aesthetics," but a way of understanding the things that are explicitly or implicitly taken into account when working with computational systems. Computational aesthetics is certainly partially entwined with the computing machine, and in many particular works founded on very specific articulations of that interlacing. Yet the existence of computational aesthetics is not exclusively tied to a particular past, present, or future technology. Computation, we contend, is a systematization of reality via discrete means such as numbers, digits, models, procedures, measures, representations and highly condensed formalizations of relations between such things. To compute involves abstractive operations of quantification and of simulation, as well as the organization of abstract objects and procedures into expressions that can (but also may not) be thought of, perceived, and carried out. Attending to computational aesthetics, then, puts in question the forces of all degrees and kinds that participate in these abstractions, and enquires what level of autonomy one should assign to such forces and abstractions. Similarly, a medium-specific computational aesthetics addresses the ways in which other techniques and genealogies (e.g., language, science, mathematics, and art itself) conjoin, contribute to or contrast with computation, and thus result in often irreconcilable, convulsive or, conversely, reductive interrelations of other aesthetic approaches, ontological commitments, knowledge structures, and arenas of practice. The impact of computation on other hitherto distinct fields constitutes, to a large extent, the status of the problematic of contemporary forms of life. We can therefore conclude that computation is as much a condition as it is a medium.

Computational Construction

It is in light of these and related issues that the condition of computational aesthetics has to be understood not as given but constructed. This claim, however, comes with two important qualifications.

To construct is to build up, to compose, to compile. A construction requires, in varying measures, a dose of planning and an amount of improvisation, the laying of foundations and the addition of decoration, the work of an engineer and the effort of a craftsperson. In this sense, a construction is less the straightforward manufacture of a result or an output than a heterogeneous process of creation. Constructing a computational aesthetics is a similarly inventive and procedural endeavor. It is, we claim—alongside the recognition of ecology and the invention of economies—a requisite for contemporary thought, imposing key issues proper to 21st-century culture. For example, questions such as how to define numerically determined rules for the analysis, codification, and prediction of the world; how to account for digitally interfaced modes of sensing; and how to theorize new spatio-temporally distributed and networked prospects for cognition.

If it is a truism that computational technologies have brought about a fundamental epistemological break,[1] constructing a computational aesthetics means to come to terms with both the disruptions and the opportunities that this break initiates in modes of perceiving, acting, and cognizing. In fact, it involves coming to terms with these conditions while looking for and articulating computational aesthetics' internal epistemological validations—those that are inherent to the theories and practices of computation itself. The construction of computational aesthetics, therefore, calls for a reworking of many of the conceptual categories, classes, types, and criteria involved in aesthetics, noting that aesthetics is in turn understood here as a theory of construction—again!—of what constitutes experience. In other words, we are arguing, on the one hand, that to understand digital art in terms of an aesthetics of computation is key to the status of contemporary culture, which indeed is a computational culture. On the other hand, however, the very notion of computational aesthetics for us goes well beyond a theory of "art made with computers," and becomes an investigation of the more foundational and formative aspects of the reality of the computational itself. In this respect, the reworkings of the aesthetic that we are here advocating are acts of both discovering and inventing the unfamiliar, the nameless, that which has been forgotten and is yet to be known: computational aesthetics must construct its own concepts.

Our first qualification of computational aesthetics' mode of construction should be read in light of what we consider the restrictions or limitations of a traditional "constructivist epistemology" for addressing the potential for conceptual discovery and invention. To claim that computational aesthetics is not given, but that it has to be constructed, would seem to echo the slogans of social constructivism, according to which situations are constructed by the interpretations that humans give of them. While there are some conditions and circumstances in which such an approach may gain significant traction also in digital art, we are keen to stress that the sociocultural constructivist position is not what we argue for, and that the construction of computational aesthetics advocated here is irreducible to the social constructivist epistemological paradigm. We would like to take a distance from the sociocultural constructivist agenda to extend the significance of "construction" from an epistemological level to an ontological one. Which is to say: when constructing computational aesthetics one creates not only ways of knowing reality, but reality itself. To be more explicit, we understand the construction of computational aesthetics as a process that is "internal" to the notion of computation, and should therefore not to be approached from any particular disciplinary ground. Computer science alone cannot fully account for the modes of existence of the aesthetics of computation, but neither can cultural theory, philosophy, or art. To say that computational aesthetics is not inferred from some particular disciplinary area, however, also means that its actuality cannot be subsumed under individual categories such as the societal, the cultural, and the economic, or of course the aesthetic, although this actuality can surely be more or less successfully interrogated from such perspectives.

Computational aesthetics does not arise from a void; it is of course part of society, culture, and economy—if we can, for a moment, accept the ruse that these things are adequately nameable. At the core of this issue lies, for us, the following point: to understand construction as the methodology proper for an immanent investigation of computation. We believe that social and cultural constructivism, in wanting to accommodate and assimilate difference, reiterates instead a "transcendent" take on computational practices and technologies. From this transcendent perspective, human social histories or human cognitive processes are equally relative amongst each other, yet still causally superior to the events that they are said to construct. We argue for another view: that the construction of computational aesthetics is not solely based upon the determinism of a particular identity-forging coordinate, such as a time in history, or a group of people, but that this construction is in fact incidental to computation's capacity of being an immanent operation of production of its own as well as other entities' modes of existence. Computational aesthetics is not produced by the social but is social. Similarly, it is not the result of a certain culture; it is culture. The diversities of the planes into which computational aesthetics cuts are not the transcendent cause of the aesthetics; these planes and multiplicities of contexts, intentions, norms, actions, perceptions, etc. must themselves—to appropriate Deleuze and Guattari's claim—be made (Deleuze and Guattari 2004, 7). With this assertion we do not mean to say that in the aesthetic investigation of computational media anything is equal to anything else. On the contrary, we affirm that the realities of computational aesthetics are produced in the expressions that the aesthetics of computation finds for itself. The construction of such aesthetics is always in the computational event.

Having clarified this, we should note that, while we are wary of a simply sociocultural constructivist approach, our position also differs from what one could call an "autopoietic" constructivism that would frame construction as a self-producing and self-organizing operation of subjective experiencing. This then is our second qualification of computational aesthetics' construction—a qualification that perhaps can help us to clarify our proposal for an immanent investigation of computational aesthetics. According to the autopoietic dialectics between observing and observed systems, everything relates to the environment in so far as it establishes and stabilizes itself in relation to it. The observer thus constructs her own world self-reflexively—that is, by positioning herself in relation to an environmental situation (Maturana and Varela 1992). Without disavowing the importance of autopoietic constructivism for some fields (such as theories of cognition, which see it as variously involved with the world), we believe that this type of constructivism becomes particularly problematic when applied to computational aesthetics. In our opinion, autopoietic approaches to digital art seem to overlook the fact that computation is full of encounters between levels of expressivity and actuality that cannot interact in terms of subjects and objects, or within the confines of an environmental "outside" or an "inside" of the system.[2] Many of these encounters or determinations in fact concern the (human) users of computation, not computation itself. We believe instead that the construction of computational aesthetics also involves incongruences and incompatibilities: in computation there are many particular cases but there is also an at least implied pretense to universality; the different speeds of eternity and fracture are often disjointed, and the diverse scales of what is too big to count or too small to see are frequently beyond subjective perception. In this sense, the construction of computational aesthetics needs to be radicalized from within the limits and potentialities of the computational itself, and not imposed upon the experiential positioning of an observer (for whoever or whatever this latter is supposed to be). In other words, what we are advocating here is the capacity of computational aesthetics to not simply represent reality, but to contribute to the immanent constitution of reality itself.

Ten Aspects of Computational Aesthetics

In order to cut into the condition of computational aesthetics, we would like to offer a short overview of some of the features and characteristics that, to a greater or lesser extent, and to varying degrees of combination, articulate the reality of computation. It should be stressed that we are not looking for the ultimate qualities and values of either computation or aesthetics. Rather, we take these characteristics and features as modes of existence of the computational that infiltrate (and, in some cases, pervade and direct) its ontological and epistemological productions. In other words, these features and characteristics inform computation's modalities of being, levels of agency, and procedures of thought that mark the medium specificity of digital art, on the one hand, and its constructive nature, on the other. There is therefore no claim that the list below is either an exhaustive itemization of the conditions of computational aesthetics, or that aspects or combinations of it are exclusive to computational aesthetics and do not surface in other contexts and kinds of art, or aesthetics more broadly. What we suggest, instead, is that computational aesthetics brings the modes below into a sharper focus and degree of compositional strength. If aesthetics can be understood as a theory of how experience is constructed, then this list attempts to account for some of the modalities of the computational that partake in such constructions. In some cases the items on this list help to sustain those constructions and to bring them into the empirical realm; in others they clash with the very category of experience altogether. The examples we offer are equally meant to provide an illustration of how computational aesthetics produces, regulates, but also points beyond its own ontological and epistemological validations, and thus always has to be found and investigated in the computational event.

1. *Abstraction and Concreteness*

Computation sets in motion some fundamental reorientations of culture, and of the circumstances in which art occurs, in that it endures as a conjoint condition of the abstract and the concrete.[3]

On the one hand, computation is a technique of abstraction. Layers of abstractions are piled up, from the hardware and the machine language right up to the graphic user interface; they manage the in-betweens of electronic circuits and symbolic procedures, and thus safeguard the operability of computing machines. In this respect abstraction is a self-contained dimension of existence of the computational. Historically and conceptually, computation draws upon the formal abstractions of logic and mathematics. Abstract mechanisms of inference drive it, while formal languages and symbol manipulation are among the abstract means that ground the very possibility of algorithmic "effective procedures."

On the other hand, however, computation is as concrete as the world in which it participates. Computation not only abstracts from the world in order to model and represent it; through such abstractions, it also partakes in it. In this sense, computation is a technology of material agency: there are the actions of algorithms organizing commercial warehouses, air traffic, and administrative records; there are the social associations of networked practices, which aggregate and shape both the technological and the cultural; there are the solid effects of software applications which intervene in and bring about modes of knowing, trading, writing, playing, perceiving, interacting, governing, and communicating.

The qualities of abstraction and concreteness have innumerable effects in terms of the constructivism and medium specificity of computational aesthetics. One of those is that the abstract structures of computation can move fast from one instantiation or occurrence to another (an algorithm can be used for sorting rice grains, faces, or patterns of pixelation, for instance). The movement across multiple sites and occasions of a work is one way of tracing the variable characteristics of computational aesthetics across social forms, and to highlight some of the ways in which the computational is often built into the latter. Tracing aspects of such a genealogy, the work of YoHa (Matsuko Yokokoji and Graham Harwood) and Graham Harwood—epitomized in *Lungs (Slave Labour)* (2005, with Mongrel);[4] *London.pl* (2004);[5] and *Coal-fired Computers* (2010, with Jean Demars)[6]—amongst others, works with the abstractions of relational database systems to both concretize their schema and establish relational calculus as a grammar of composition that links labor, primary accumulation, mechanisms of power, and the materialities of organic and non-organic forms of life.

2. *Universality*

Universality in computation is established at the conceptual level of the machine. In the 1930s the computer science pioneer Alan Turing famously developed a thought experiment that put the mental activity of computing in mechanical and finite terms in order to imagine a universal device (subsequently known as the Universal Turing Machine) that would be able to replicate the behavior of any other Turing machine. Anything mechanically computable could and would be computed by such a universal device, as it would be capable of processing any algorithm fed into it (Turing 1936). The Universal Turing Machine (UTM) is the basis of the "von Neumann architecture" for stored-program computers (Davis 2000), and thus the foundation of present-day computing devices, which are in fact general-purpose and can be programmed to emulate each other. Such functional generality is perhaps the most basic, yet crucial conceptual premise of modern computational endeavors. Moreover, the amplification of functional operations also underpins the possibility of understanding computation as a technique of abstraction that is already geared toward universality. Computation generates and disseminates abstractions that are general and inclusive. In its renegotiation of structures of existence, computation aims to encompass and produce the universality of formal methods of systematization and of all-purpose models of reasoning.

Artists may respond to this universality by attending to the specificity of particular instantiations of computational forms, as in the wave of attention that has been paid to retro-computing platforms and to Game Boy hacks. The artist group Beige (Cory Arcangel, Joe Beuckman, Joe Bonn, Paul B. Davis), for example, looked for constraints in order to address the question of universality and thereby reveal universality's nature by noting its particular, historical concrescence in styles of design, the development of genres of game, and so on.[7] In their work, computing was always filtered through the quirks and constraints of a particular system with all its clunkiness and idiosyncracy. *Super Abstract Brothers* (2000), for instance, replaced the sprites and landscape of a Nintendo Entertainment System cartridge game with blocks of color.[8] Alternatively, the nature of claiming universality itself may be a foundational point of exploration for certain artists, such as David Rokeby,[9] whose multifarious and rigorous works probe and ally with the various ways in which algorithms and other procedural and interpretative acts of computers shape and condense as spaces and behaviors. One example amongst many would be *n-Cha(n)t* (2001), where a circle of computers run generic speech-recognition and speech-to-text programs. The machines hear and interpret each other, responding with further speech. The resulting cycling mixture of interpretation and response also makes the implicit offer for people to loop themselves into the feedback cycles of chuntering vocalizations and tangential interpretations in which machine intuition, logic, and chance are intriguingly interwoven.[10]

3. *Discreteness*

Something is defined as discrete if it is disjointed, separated, distinct, detached, or discontinuous. Discreteness arguably is the hallmark of the digital. Digital systems by definition are discrete systems: they represent, store, and transfer information in terms of discontinuous elements or values (binary digits, for example). The computational, as we explained above, is not synonymous with the digital: the digital should be understood as an automation of the computational. Computation itself, however, is also marked by discreteness. As a rule-governed activity, computation arranges calculation procedures through the sequential succession of countable and separable states. The "valid reasoning" that computational mechanisms are meant to encapsulate and model is explicated via the manipulation of quantifiable entities into a finite sequence of well-defined steps. The time and memory that such a sequence employs in order to perform the computation are also finite; so too are the input that set it in motion and the outcome that it generates.

The discreteness of computation is often at odds with the continuity of interactions proposed by affective philosophies, system theories, and cognitive phenomenologies, which—in art, culture, and science—focus on the dynamic becoming of relations and connections. Discreteness also prompts questions about the recognition one is willing to give to computational entities, on the one side, and computational processes, on the other, and invites further investigation whether a theoretical and technical reconciliation between the two is possible.

The discreteness of a computational object may also be used for comedic effect, as in the game *Surgeon Simulator* (Bossa Studios 2013) where a patient, body parts, surgical tools, transplant organs, and the paraphernalia of an operating theater are all to be worked on by interacting with a First Person Shooter (FPS)-style interface. The game is a device-based Grand Guignol that reaches the level of slapstick in the clashing, clumsy, interactions of the handled objects' levels of discreteness.

Discreteness also allows for the recomposition of things and their fixture in new positions, thereby generating both new kinds of commodity forms, and new commonalities. This potential is illustrated in its violation by Yuri Pattison's *e ink pearl memory* (2012), in which discreteness is employed as a means of disrupting the transcendental role of the commodity. Here, amongst other forms and arrangements of informational matter, such as a small spill of photocopier toner, treated Kindle e-book readers are modified to display fixed abstract images, that is to say they are 'broken', becoming finite, discrete. Conversely, the discreteness of digital material such as software or music also allows for an establishment of its sharing or commonality in certain ways. This aim is a prominent aspect of numerous computational initiatives, but becomes most obvious in Free Software, and in file-sharing ventures such as the Pirate Bay, a project itself sometimes manifesting explicitly as artways through the Piratbyrån (Bureau of Piracy).[11] As different levels of discreteness—alongside the ability to copy wholes or parts—combine with computing resources such as memory or bandwidth, discreteness also plays a part in the development of expressive styles and modes of computing at multiple scales, including the determination of degrees of granularity in the resolution of images.

Discretion, the ability to keep things separate, is by necessity a key factor of the ethico-aesthetic dimensions of computational technologies' political nature,[12] determining what they reveal or make tractable, as well as what they hide. The regimes of what links, what can be analyzed, what pools together, and what remains apart are core to the nature of such systems.

4. *Axiomatics*

Computation is axiomatic. The modes of abstraction, universality, and discreteness discussed above are key features of the axiomatic character of computational systems, and of the many parallels between computation and logico-mathematical reasoning. Via this axiomatic character, these parallels distinguish past and present conceptions of digital computing machines.

As is well known, Alan Turing (1936) established the notion of computability after discovering a particular class of numbers that cannot be computed. Turing demonstrated, however, that what is computable can be determined algorithmically; that is, through a mechanized principle of deductive inference, "with every tiny step of reasoning in place" (Chaitin 2005, 30). What had been an informal notion of computation was hence formalized into the axiomatic parameters of the logico-mathematical comprehension of correct inference. In this sense, to compute became to manage discrete quantities, and to do so by following abstract and finite inferential rules with universal applicability.

Today the axiomatic nature of computing subsists in and thrives on its many formalisms. The axiomatic method is central to symbolic notation and procedural execution: for every calculating process, whether a basic operation or a more convoluted function, the computational system engages, and then reiteratively re-engages again, with the general problem of determining consequences from a handful of validly symbolized premises. It is because of the unavoidability of axiomatics in computation that digital art and theory alike cannot leave the formalizations of computation to the computer scientist's classroom. Instead, they need to take up the challenge of thinking and creating an aesthetics of computation that takes into account, if not limiting itself to, the inferential and rule-based character of computational systems, while remaining aware of the ways in which computation borrows methods from mathematics and logics.

5. *Numbers*

Computation holds a multifaceted and profound relationship to numbers. Of course, contemporary computers are "metamedia" (Manovich 2013) capable of accomplishing much more than merely "crunching" numbers. However, the computing machine's relation to the numerical remains intimate. This is due partly to computation's discrete and quantitative nature, and partly to the fact that a computing machine has to operate within the parameters of a calculation.

The very idea of number has continuously changed over time, stretching and convoluting to encompass new categories and attributes, and has become something different again in its encounter with the medium specificity of computation: a means of establishing relations among abstractive methods, formal systems, and concrete tasks that are governed in turn by the operation of numbers. Although this recursion to some degree existed before in techniques such as the calculus, it is fundamentally different in computation in terms of the quantity and density of operations. Numbers in computation show various qualities and behaviors. As a unit of measurement, numbers are used, for instance, to portion pixels, megahertz, and registers in memory. As a mathematical entity, numbers are the objects of the many types of counting that computers carry out: counting of amounts, of sequential steps, of variables, of inputs, of time, and so on. As an incommensurable quantity, numbers approximate the risk of infinite loops within recursive functions. As a digital representation, they mirror electronic binary states into binary digits. As a symbol, numbers are elements of codes and scripts, and cement the possibility of encryption, while also being means of organizing, prioritizing, and enacting such qualities and behaviors.

6. *Limits*

Computation is limited, in a quite fundamental way. Its limitations are inherent in the axiomatic nature of computational systems. In mathematical logic there are undecidable propositions; in computability theory there exist problems that cannot be solved via purely mechanical procedures. The formal notion of computation itself is founded upon the discovery that some programs will not halt and some functions will not be calculated. Some things just cannot be computed.

The existence of limits in computation is unsettling but also empowering. Amongst the most troubling consequences of these limitations is the comprehension that while computing machines do indeed process many tasks, they do not process just anything. Techno-cultural agendas proposing an all-embracing and all-solving computational rationality are thus faulty at their very outset. Errors, bugs, and glitches might be more or less probable, depending on the specific case. Yet they are always logically possible, as is a formalist misapprehension of a situation or a condition.[13] One of the most interestingly enabling outcomes of the limits of computation, however, results from turning this internal failure into the very method through which computation operates. Limitations, just as with the previously discussed principle of universality, are established at the conceptual level of the computing machine: they are intrinsic to the axiomatic character of computational formalization. Given the necessary provisions, the formal deductions of computational systems nevertheless have been turned into systems of unprecedented instrumental power. To the cultural theorist, the philosopher, and the artist, such mismatches and ambiguities surrounding promises of delivery and potentials for machine breakdown or misrecognition offer an equally finely textured occasion for speculation and are also one of the qualities of computation gamed in the exercise of power.

7. *Speeds*

Art stages different relations to time: for instance, in the way a dance slows, speeds, accentuates, draws attention to the miniscule or raises it to the level of the cosmic. A relation to, modulation, and creation of time and timings characterizes a work and articulates its mode of being in the world. Computational aesthetics enters into relation with such articulation by intervening in time in certain ways.

The intensity of computational speed is characteristically emphasized as being core to its novelty and to its world-making capacities. When the audience is supposed to pay attention to a rapidly unfolding complex process in the film *The Matrix* (1999), for instance, the scene is rendered to film in great slowness, as if to suggest that—in order to yield something comprehensible to the human sensorium—what passes in less than a moment in computational terms must necessarily be drawn out over minutes. Computational speed is thus about experiential intensity as much as it is about strict measure; yet it is also about the mobile threshold of the capacities of computing itself of structuring its own modes of existence. The speed of calculation of a computer was, from the very outset, in monstrous disproportion to the capacities of humans, just as machine weaving had been to the movements of earlier generations of hand-weavers. This scale of disproportion is fluid, and forms a complex set of texturing of expression that manifests in anything from interaction times in musical instrumentation to media-archaeological concerns regarding speed of execution or bandwidth in the conservation of aesthetic objects.

This issue connects to a subsequent characteristic of speed within computational aesthetics: namely, its constructivist nature. As a consequence of the Universal Turing Machine, the timing of many kinds of processes can be brought about within the machine. Computing has no inherent "native" speed but provides means of staking out and arranging relations to speeds. While intensification of speed is one mode in which computational expression is staged, extension of a work over time is also a significant tendency, especially in works such as Jem Finer's *Longplayer* (2000–)[14] and Gustav Metzger's proposed *Five Screens with Computer* (1965)[15] where the unfolding of a work is arrayed in relation to monumental time. Finer's project, currently sited in London's Trinity Buoy Wharf, assembles a system for making a non-repeating piece of music play for a period of exactly one thousand years. Metzger's plan was to erect a run of five 30 x 40 foot panels of stainless steel 25 feet apart. Each panel would be two feet deep and constructed from 10,000 picture elements of plastic, glass, or steel that would each be ejected over a period of ten years, eventually resulting in the annulment of the work.

8. Scale

Scale effects are core to the development of computing in the present era. By scale effects we mean the ways in which a specific kind of structure or process can be instantiated both across a relatively small number of instances and for a tendentially infinite quantity of them. Systems designed to navigate and conjoin multiple scales, such as the golden mean or Corbusier's Modulor (1954),[16] exist within numerous aesthetic forms as a means of arranging elements or of making and assisting a judgment about these forms' efficacy or beauty. Computing, however, allows for these systems of judgment and composition to be integrated into the technology in which these systems themselves are realized.

In systems such as the World Wide Web, limitations of scale due to material considerations tend toward the negligible, resulting in the use of the term "scale-free" to describe the Web's patterns of network growth. The specific qualities of the scale-free nature of such a system contrast with other aspects of computational aesthetics. This is due to the quality of universality systems such as finite state machines, which have a very small scale that can coexist alongside systems of larger scales. Most notably, however, there may be transitions across the scales. A multitude of small-scale finite state machines, for instance, can be conjoined in order to generate a system of great complexity that can be described as scale-free. Computational aesthetics then includes, as a core constituent, the movement in and out of scalar reference. Concomitantly, the tendency toward a scale-free aesthetics in certain works operating on the basis of these networks can be observed and is to be expected in the future.

The scale-free nature of certain computing forms is coupled in dynamic ways with currents such as globalization, which was explored in early Internet art by Shu Lea Cheang in *Net Nomad* projects such as *Buy One Get One* (1997).[17] Artists such as Ai Wei Wei have used this condition in creating a global constituency for their work, in a period in which the artist—perhaps due to the demise of the reputation of figures such as the politician and banker— also becomes a potential candidate for the role of "moral hero." Other artists, such as The Yes Men,[18] Übermorgen,[19] or Paolo Cirio[20]—whose work is discussed in more detail in Armin Medosch's text—have used the unstable conditions implied by these scale-free networks and globalization as a departure point for exploring sociotechnical expressions of networked forms as they mesh with various political and institutional configurations. Paolo Cirio's loophole4all.com (2013), for instance, is a web site and service that allows users to select the names of tax avoidance entities nominally framed as companies or trusts legally located in the Cayman Isles. Once selected, since these entities need to keep their status shady, the project suggests that their names and tax-free status can be used for invoicing by citizens, thus ensuring the same fiscal opportunities to a wider range of users.[21]

The question of scale is also linked to the development of platforms for cultural expression, since the potentially scale-free nature of a project in technical respects aligns with the capacities of expression of specific social and cultural forces and the individual histories embedded in them. The development of platforms such as the video analysis and combination site Pad.Ma (2008–)[22] by a coalition of groups based in Mumbai, the early picture-sharing platform Nine(9) (2003),[23] or the text discussion site aaaaarg.org [24]—in their combinations of invention and specificity and their amalgamation with other groups, histories, and resources—exemplify such a condition.

9. *Logical Equivalence*

In earlier discussions of digital media much attention was paid to the question whether a particular experience or thing qualified as "real" or "virtual." Recognizing the medium specificity and the constructivism inherent to computational aesthetics suggests that it might be more fruitful to pay attention to the discussion of forms of logical equivalence.

A system can be said to be logically equivalent to another if it yields the same behaviors and functions—independent of each system's underlying material structure. Logical equivalence is a quality that is foundational to computing as a thought experiment, arising out of the need to equate computing activity with the mental processes of a person. Alan Turing (1936) describes the procedure of making a calculation as a series of mental processes and note-making, abstracting the procedure to a formally describable set of steps that can then be instantiated in a machine. The result is an axiomatic procedure that can be universally applied to any computable problem (the a priori limits of the axiomatic procedure itself, however, remain intractable). Simulation is one effect of establishing logical equivalence between systems. An entity or process may be ordered in such a way that it is rendered more or less behaviorally identical to that which it models. At the same time, there may be play within the kinds of equivalence that are operative. At a certain scale, for example, a system may display logical equivalence to another, yet be composed of substantially different materials. There also may be interplay with the subjective experience of each different instantiation of a logically equivalent event or performance. The musicological concept of interpretation may be pertinent here. The translation of behaviors and entities from other contexts into computational ones implies an evaluation of what constitutes meaningful forms of equivalence and thereby the intensification of aesthetic, along with ethical, judgments. The interplay of these conditions has proven to be very fertile ground for exploration for many artists.

In his ongoing *Status Project* (2005–), for instance, Heath Bunting sets out to establish a logically equivalent description for the process of attaining membership in various kinds of social formations (such as nation states or video libraries). Being a certain age, having an address, a name, being able to produce and refer to other specific documents—by following certain set and delimited procedures, one may acquire a position that can be computed as verifiable within a logically describable system of veridiction, a statement that is true according to the worldview of a particular system. The condition of logical equivalence has also driven much work in the field of bio art, where the reduction of the characteristics of DNA to its base pairs TCAG (T = thymine; C = cytosine; A = adenine; G = guanine) allows for the rearticulation and the handling of the amino acids that they signify and partially render tractable. In the project *The Xenotext* (2011), the poet Christian Bök exploited this context to encode a short poem in a bacteria that would in turn produce protein that would be readable, via the use of Bök's interpretative system, the Chemical Alphabet, as further fragments of poetry.[25]

10. Memory

Within computing, the fact that both data and the instructions that act upon that data are themselves stored as data has significant consequences. Not the least of these consequences is that—since a computational machine can be completely copied with great ease under the conditions of logical equivalence—the conditions for an effective digital commons can be produced. The fact that both a computer and the data that runs on it (including the operative and executable data software) can be copied, creates interesting situations in politics and economics, situations that also have consequences for art and contribute to the social and economic force of computing at large.

Memory also introduces other conditions and forms of computational aesthetics: possibilities both for all actions and interactions to be logged in order to be restaged or analyzed, and, within different configurations, for the (partial or full) reversibility or irreversibility of an action. Moreover, memory presents conditions of delay and storage, so that an event may unfold in computational time at a different moment. Related to the question of speed, time—as it manifests in the interrelation between processing and storage and in the interaction between the computational system and a subject, such as a musician, dancer, or game-player—becomes a crucial factor in the developments of the aesthetic modality of both specific systems and computational systems as a whole.

Memory, understood as the extent of the capacity to process data, also has significant effects for digital art. These effects are readily observable in 8-bit aesthetics (Goriunova 2012), where constrained data-architectures are adopted or simulated for the pleasures of their nostalgic and simplified forms. However, they can also be seen in the use of any constrained computing system—that is to say, any at all. We can also argue that memory is exemplified in an interplay between learning and the relentless lack of it in computing. Kryštof Kintera's human-scaled robot *Revolution* (2005) (Horáková 2012) beats its hooded head endlessly, over and over, against a wall. This is not a generative error, as a glitch would be, but a machinic ability to repeat without recourse to reflection.

If – then

At this point any reader will probably have added some other aspects of computational aesthetics to this list. Our aim is not to be complete here. Indeed, part of the question of the aesthetics of contemporary digital media, particularly as they are developed by artists, is to advance and proliferate frameworks for recognizing further modes of existence for the computational. The task of doing so is a collective one, and cannot be reduced to a schematic list of qualities, or to a set of conditions imported into art directly from an understanding of different forms of computer science. Once again, we would like to stress that computational aesthetics, and the immanent investigation of it, reside in the computational event. Computing and its aesthetics are no longer "owned" by the disciplines and fields that grew up closely in and around it. The computational mundanity of everyday objects and processes, as well as the more explicitly critical and speculative modes of computational forms, may be interrogated by means of the characteristics that we have discussed above. At the same time, the nature of the computational may be changed altogether by bringing more conditions and forms of existence into its purview. All of this together, along with the very flexibility of computational reality, means that these considerations can only ever be a provisional and partial mapping. There is much to invent and to be dazzled by, much texture to be found. One might also discover a strange, dull, as yet unnameable familiarity to certain repetitions and compulsions that may indeed travel unremarked from art installations to office work and social forms. To go beyond such a list means to engage in a preliminary process of recognizing and operating the aesthetic dimensions of computation. As critical experimental work moves more substantially in this direction, the force and method of computation may become more open to understanding, discovery, and invention.

Notes

1 For instance, Stiegler (2012) argues that the irreducible ambivalence of technological rationality is altering all forms of knowledge, and thus "we must learn to think and to live differently."
2 Although such conditions of internality and externality may also be part, or indeed be imperative to, aspects of the computational method (as with the specific forms of modular architectures, object-oriented environments, the limited modes of abstraction layers such as interfaces, and so on).
3 The history of art is, in some respects, that of an interplay between the abstract and the concrete, as they are understood and made manifest by different means over time. In a sense, we live at a moment in which the abstract itself, as a force and a method, is understood to be of highly diverse character. The modes of abstraction in art, having generated a history of significant range, now also manifest this proliferation, the consciousness of which in turn has its own effects. A significant exploration of this context can be found in the work of Matias Faldbakken (2007), who produces an intensive bestiary of modes of abstraction in relation to the powers of materials.

4 See http://www.mongrel.org.uk/lungszkm/
5 See http://www.mongrel.org.uk/londonpl/
6 See http://yoha.co.uk/cfc/
7 See http://www.post-data.org/beige/
8 See http://post-data.org/beige/abstract.html
9 See http://www.davidrokeby.com/
10 See http://www.davidrokeby.com/nchant.html
11 See http://piratbyran.org/
12 Here we are referring to the "ethico-aesthetic paradigm" of Guattari (1995). Guattari draws the expression from Mikhail Bakhtin, and uses it to denote the way in which collective subjectivity can, through the techniques and practices epitomized in (but not limited to) art, constitute and project itself toward alterity and heterogeneity. For Guattari, aesthetics has ethical and political implications, in so far as "to speak of creation is to speak of the responsibility of the creative instance with regard to the thing created, inflection of the state of things, bifurcation beyond pre-established schemas, once again taking into account the fate of alterity in its extreme modalities" (1995, 107).
13 This narrow or voluminous gap is, for instance, that occupied by the discussions of so-called ethicists in their prevarications on the operation of automated warfare, such as that carried out by drones.
14 See http://longplayer.org/
15 See Ford (2003).
16 Le Corbusier's Modulor is a scale of proportions that was based on the golden ratio and developed on the model of the human body.
17 See http://www.ntticc.or.jp/HoME/
18 See http://theyesmen.org/
19 See http://www.ubermorgen.com
20 See http://www.paolocirio.net/
21 See http://loophole4all.com/
22 See http://pad.ma/
23 See http://www.mongrel.org.uk/nine
24 See http://aaaaarg.fail/
25 See http://www.poetryfoundation.org/harriet/2011/04/the-xenotext-works/

References

Aaaaarg.org. http://aaaaarg.fail/ (accessed October 15, 2015).

Beige. http://www.post-data.org/beige/ (accessed January 4, 2015).

Beige. 2000. *Super Abstract Brothers.* http://post-data.org/beige/abstract.html (accessed January 4, 2015).

Bök, Christian. 2011. *The Xenotext.* http://www.poetryfoundation.org/harriet/2011/04/the-xenotext-works/ (accessed January 4, 2015).

Bossa Studios. 2013. *Surgeon Simulator.* http://www.surgeonsimulator2013.com/ (accessed January 4, 2015).

Bunting, Heath. 2005– . *The Status Project.* http://status.irational.org/ (accessed January 4, 2015).

Chaitin, Gregory. 2005. *Meta Maths: The Quest for Omega.* London: Atlantic Books.

Cheang, Shu Lea. 1997. *Buy One Get One*. http://www.ntticc.or.jp/HoME/ (accessed January 4, 2015).
Cirio, Paolo. http://www.paolocirio.net (accessed January 4, 2015).
Cirio, Paolo. 2013. *Loophole For All*. http://loophole4all.com/ (accessed January 4, 2015).
Davis, Martin. 2000. *Engines of Logic: Mathematicians and the Origin of the Computer*. New York: W.W. Norton.
Deleuze, Giles, and Felix Guattari. 2004. *A Thousand Plateaus: Capitalism and Schizophrenia*, translated by Brian Massumi. London: Continuum.
Faldbakken, Matias. 2007. *Not Made Visible*. Zurich: Christoph Keller Editions.
Finer, Jem, 2000– . *Longplayer*. http://longplayer.org/ (accessed January 4, 2015).
Ford, Simon. 2003. "Technological Kindergarten." *Mute* 1(26), July 4. http://www.metamute.org/editorial/articles/technological-kindergarten (accessed January 4, 2015).
Fuller, Matthew, ed. 2008. *Software Studies: A Lexicon*. Cambridge, MA: The MIT Press.
Goriunova, Olga. 2012. *Art Platforms and Cultural Production on the Internet*. London: Routledge.
Greenberg, Clement. 1961. *Art and Culture*. New York: Beacon Press.
Guattari, Felix. 1995. *Chaosmosis: an Ethico-Aesthetic Paradigm*, translated by Pail Bains and Julian Pefanis. Bloomington, IN: Indiana University Press.
Harwood, Graham. 2004. *London.pl*. http://www.mongrel.org.uk/londonpl/ (accessed January 4, 2015).
Harwood, Graham, with Mongrel. 2005. *Lungs (Slave Labour)*. http://www.mongrel.org.uk/lungszkm/ (accessed January 4, 2015).
Horáková, Jana. 2012. "The Robot as Mitate: The Media Specific Aesthetic Analysis." In *Device_Art*, festival catalogue, 60–89. Zagreb: Kontejner.
Le Corbusier. 2004. *The Modulor: A Harmonious Measure to the Human Scale Universally Applicable to Architecture and Mechanics*. Basle and Boston: Birkhäuser.
Manovich, Lev. 2013. *Software Takes Command*. London: Bloomsbury.
Maturana, Humberto, and Francisco Varela. 1992. *The Tree of Knowledge: The Biological Roots of Human Understanding*. Boston: Shambhala.
Mongrel. 2003. *Nine(9)*. http://www.mongrel.org.uk/nine (accessed January 4, 2015).
Pad.ma. 2008– . http://www.pad.ma/ (accessed January 4, 2015).
Pattinson, Yuri. 2013. "e ink pearl memory." In *Open Office Anthology* edited by Tom Clark, Farkas Rozsa, and Harry Burke, 58–61. London: Arcadia Missa.
Piratebyrån. http://piratbyran.org/ (accessed October 15, 2015).
Rokeby, David. http://www.davidrokeby.com/ (accessed October 15, 2015).
Rokeby, David. 2001. *n-Cha(n)t*. http://www.davidrokeby.com/nchant (accessed January 4, 2015).
Stiegler, Bernard. 2012. "Die Aufklärung in the Age of Philosophical Engineering." *Computational Culture*, 2. http://computationalculture.net/comment/die-aufklarung-in-the-age-of-philosophical-engineering/ (accessed October 2, 2015).
Turing, Alan M. 1936. "On Computable Numbers, with an Application to the Entscheidungsproblem." *Proceedings of the London Mathematical Society* 42: 230–265.
Übermorgen. http://www.ubermorgen.com (accessed January 4, 2015).
Yes Men. http://www.yesmen.org (accessed January 4, 2015).
YoHa, with Jean Demars. 2006. *Coal Fired Computers*. http://yoha.co.uk/cfc/ (accessed January 4, 2015).

12

Participatory Platforms and the Emergence of Art

Olga Goriunova

What she wished for more intensely than anything … was the coming of our world; and … the kind of imagination one needs for a real understanding of it.

She didn't like things to be fixed. … Everything … is so difficult to get moving again, so one should try in advance to keep it alive while it's still in the process of coming to be … It must keep on originating, that's what matters.

Christa Wolf, *The Quest for Christa T.* (1995)

The emergence of art is heavily mediated. This mediation can be approached in countless ways: through the well-known apparatuses of the artworld, which are as much organizational and conceptual (curators, museums, and critics) as they are financial and historical (markets, galleries, art institutions); through the technical apparatuses of the systems used in constructing a project, for example the photographic, industrial, and "socio-economic complexes" unfolding in the use of a camera (Flusser 2000); multi-scalar networks and omnivorous media ecologies (Fuller 2005); or through mediating political systems and relational structures of the moment, and in many other ways.

In other words, multiple forces participate in art's emergence: relationality, collaboration, technicity can be seen as forms of mediation, or, indeed, as vibrant and at times violent aspects of live processes themselves. An interest in this cross-mediation is grounded in a certain understanding of a subject, a body of knowledge, an artwork, or a series of cultural events as not a "given," but processes of emergence. It is a focus on how art "becomes," and how such modes of becoming evolved over the last two decades that is explored in this chapter. This focus on emergence allows for seeing an art event or project as an open process whose coming into being is contingent, so that questions of authorship, audience, materiality, power, communication, meaning, economy, and aesthetics in general are cut open, repracticed and rethought. It is this

A Companion to Digital Art, First Edition. Edited by Christiane Paul.

rethinking that is evident in the multiple instances of large-scale grass-roots creativity (Lovink and Rossiter 2007), relational art (Bourriaud 2002), and collaborative production (Wikipedia), and in projects ranging from the classic piece of net art *Refresh* (1996)[1] to large institutional shows such as *We Are All Photographers Now!* by the Musée de l'Elysée in Lausanne in 2007.

Arguably, it is these very processes of emergence that are most affected in current times, when biological, ecological, and financial, as well as political, cultural, and social landscapes are measured, quantified, and managed on the basis of calculated risks; networked, digitally performed, sorted, listed, all in all put on a computational footing and opened up to be operated upon algorithmically. The "computational turn" not only allows for algorithmic actors to come on stage more openly; it also sustains the process of emergence in ways that are more open to working, acting, copying, archiving, and performing together (as well as to trolling, and being operated upon en masse).

There are drastically varying lenses through which such processes can be viewed, especially in relation to digital art: some people focus on aesthetics, art, and its particular ecology; others on human subjects, collectives, and communities, social and political dimensions; while what is still a minority is able to account for all of those factors in relation to technical and computational mediation.

In contemporary art and in aesthetic theory, collaboration, participation, and relationality—both in the process of making art happen and in discussing it—are a new norm. Claire Bishop, Maria Lind, and Gregory Sholette, amongst others, account for the various ways in which the fostering of relations, communal spaces, and production of frameworks for doing things together are employed to counteract individualizing neoliberal forces, the passivity of the audience in front of which Debord's (1984) spectacle continuously unfolds, as well as the disempowerment of non-authors (Billing, Lind, and Nilsson 2007; Stimson and Sholette 2007; Bishop 2012). Art is made in ways that are open to participation, and performs itself in relation to being communally experienced and co-constructed.

The lineage of such thinking extends to Benjamin's "user as producer" (Benjamin 2005) and Michel de Certeau's micro-tactics of resistance (de Certeau 2002), but also to the traditions of socialist and anarchist thinking of writers such as Kropotkin. The processes of becoming a subject through creative and collective work, as well as mutual support, have traditionally been seen as liberatory by rational liberals emphasizing the empowerment of the individual, revolutionaries working collectively, and theorists of micro-politics seeking plateaus of difference within the stratified order of things. Feeding on, cherishing, and working up creativity was ultimately linked to freedom, and collective creativity in turn led to mutual support, radical equality, and satisfaction.

None of the theorists mentioned above—Bishop, Lind, or Sholette—sees the current emphasis on participation and the possibility of collective creative work as unproblematic. Creative individuals and excited communities taking care of both themselves and problematic situations are also well aligned with the neo-Kantian and anti-state ontologies of the neoliberal order, in which the individual and community are ultimately held responsible for their own well-being, and functions of the state such as education, health care, and even policing are ideally delegated to the individuals in question and the concerned public. When the state is left unburdened by these responsibilities, it is the public's duty to be healthy, productive, caring, protected, and entertained, all of which can be achieved through creative and collective endeavors, which handily happen to move outside of the realm of financial relations into that of aesthetic ones. Guattari (1995) suggested that it is this turn to the "aesthetic paradigm"—whereby social, political, and economic spheres of action take on aesthetic modes of operation—that most vividly characterized the societal shifts already well under way in the 1980s.

The way in which collaboration, communal production, and use of the participation of the many can be ethically problematic (as, for instance, in undermining the livelihood of these very many and others to come) is exacerbated when technical networks and computational mediation are more pronouncedly called upon. The cognitive, sensory, and emotional labor of living that includes the acts of expressing momentary thoughts, liaising with fellow humans, and idling meaninglessly creates value in and for social networks, e-mail services, search engines, and data centers and sustains large intelligence services and new global "Stasi economies" of computational surveillance. Following the leaks by Edward Snowden and the revelation of the scale of the Anglo-American surveillance machinery, it is estimated that this machinery employs hundreds of thousands of people, making it a large part of the information economy in its own right (Lanchester 2013).

As Virno (2004) and others have pointed out, what lies at the heart of so-called cognitive capitalism are instruments of financialization, of production and evaluation geared toward economic profit, that hook into the process of generating subjectivity and creativity, thus capitalizing on a never-ending energy and working on a *perpetuum mobile*. A set of discussions on the subject of immaterial labor and the "soul at work" (Berardi 2009), based on the vocabulary of producer and power user, highlight the breakdown between consumption and production, and point to the conjunction between generating value and generating self, participation, and the investment of desire. If this is indeed the current condition, it can be conceptualized by systematically looking for the ways in which such participatory and technologically mediated modes of life revolutionize art, education, knowledge, ownership, power relationships, and production through extending communicative technical systems that are socially acute and responsive to participatory creative work (and redefine work itself). The core role of subjective and collective emergence in these new forms of the organization of living and the capitalization of such living draws attention to changes in the conditions and forms of mediation, the means of propelling the emergence of self, collectives, artworks, and cultural movements. The focus on these mediations brings us back to aesthetics and the computational modes of existence.

Aesthetics in this framework refers not only to the sensual, affective, and non-rational or the field of art. Aesthetics itself can be seen as mediational and relational and, as such, as core to the emergence of subjects and objects. Here Simondon (1992) and Bakhtin (1990) can be usefully read against each other as theorists of relational becoming, central to which is a performative, mediational process of oscillating back and forth between oneself and the other, the pre-individual and the individual, the pre-individual and the collective, the internal and the external—relationships that are the becoming itself. One element is important to both Bakhtin and Simondon: the durational materiality of the process, which allows for focusing on formation, crystallization, and for partaking. For Bakhtin this process also is profoundly aesthetic, in the sense that aesthetic is emphatic and relational, but also organizational, as it implies two and more subjects posited against each other, on a plane in space and time, providing each other with becoming through what we can now call mechanisms of interaction. Bakhtin states, "A whole integral human being is the product of the aesthetic, creative point of view and of that point of view alone" (Bakhtin 1990, 83), thus radically merging the aesthetic and the mediational.

But mediation itself becomes a problematic term since it can also be seen as referring to a process "true to itself" that is fed through various systems to acquire certain overtones; or indeed to a process that can be immediately present but, because mediation takes time, becomes deferred (Winthrop-Young 2012, 114). One of the strengths of digital artwork and theory lies in their pushing for an understanding of mediation, and of computational mediation as something varied, radically open, connected to many spheres of life, as well as constitutive to the process of becoming and being. Here mediation, or rather the computational, is not only about digitization that "comes afterwards" and allows for the building of collaborative tools for and by human subjects, work to be performed online, or data to be produced easily and moved freely. Mediation is both deeper and more profound, as well as both more potentially vivacious and deadly. It is precisely the close attention to the technical that can draw a more complex picture of this condition.

Mediation has been rigorously considered by many scholars as being of central significance to the process of emergence—of a human subject, collectives, and objects, if such distinctions are still worth being made. Perhaps one of the best known earlier accounts is Plato's dialogue *Phaedrus* (2005). Here the technology of alphabetic writing, one of the most significant mediations, externalizing speech and subjecting it to a radically different materiality, is discussed in relation to memory, subjectivity, and truth, which are all profoundly transformed with the movement from orality to writing. Both McLuhan (1994) and Kittler (1990), although differently and somewhat contrarily, focused on the early media of language and the alphabet, the introduction of signs for vowels, and the printing press. In their differing accounts, the mediational creation of the Western man and subject via the processes of externalization and discretization, enacted by early technologies of alphabetical writing and then widely intensified by the technologies of the printing press, gave way to the optical and electric media forms of the 19th century and then the digital media of the 20th, which in turn dispersed the subject. Not only did such media technologies create new social and political milieus, forms of knowing, and mechanisms of production, they also produced both new avenues and the withdrawal of possibilities for subjectivation. For Kittler, the mediation of cursive writing, the meaning-making and spell-binding machine of maternal language production, and the more technical mediation of the later forms of media contribute to or rather determine subject formation. The human subject of the era of literature gives way to the subject of optical, sonic, and computational systems and is no longer necessarily in the center of the situation or indeed in the position of an observer.

Bernard Stiegler's extensive conceptual apparatus (Stiegler 1998, 2009, 2011), building on Simondon and Leroi-Gourhan (1993), extends the notion of "technicity" to discuss technical mediation that includes the erect position assumed by humans, cortical development, tools and language—all as part of the apparatus producing the human being from the dawn of humankind. In his arguments technical intelligence arises from zoological movement. And for Kittler the soul itself is formed by the predominant media mechanism of each era. Here, media are both biological and metaphysical.

It is interesting to compare such terminology with Bakhtin's assertion that "the problem of the soul is methodologically a problem of aesthetics" (Bakhtin 1990, 89). Core to all these discussions is the search for the process of becoming—the becoming of the human subject as we used to know him; the further struggle for the place *he* occupies in relation to a *she;* then the evolutions of the posthuman (Braidotti 2013), cyborg and animal (Haraway 1997), and finally, the Turing Machine (Kittler 1990). The production and maintenance of this position occupied by the subject, as well as of the subject itself, are aesthetic and computational.

The aesthetic work through which our own emergence takes place and the range of aesthetic potentialities of subjectification are drawn out in the computational, in what was previously called digital media. Not only do memory, communication, production, creation, learning, and disruption occur and are organized through computational mechanisms, but social and political relations, and societal horizons of possibility for even the youngest people, are mapped out in the networks and are run by software.

In the case of digital art, the art itself is computationally emerging from the work of multiple authors, some of which are not necessarily human but nevertheless are active in shaping and engendering it, such as discussion boards, bots, software scripts, networks, and data packages. In such a context we find that the roles of art, artists, audiences, and what we understand to be art, creativity, and aesthetics are radically changing. These changes are equally in line with, may lead to, and are plugged into larger transformations of the human and society, with far-ranging consequences. In this sense digital art is akin to concentric waves on water, spreading further and further out until things far removed from the projects in question are drawn into their ecology and transformed.

Archives, Art Platforms, and Web Communities

The optimistic or at least outward-looking reception of the Web in the mid-1990s is well known: early accounts investigating the pioneering forms of increased cross-global connectivity, collaborative life, the posthuman subject, and new forms of art and culture include Rheingold's *The Virtual Community* (1993), Haraway's work on cyborgs (1991), as well as writings on early net art's vision of the changing role of art, creativity, and their forms of existence (Stallabrass 2003; Bosma 2011; Monoscope 2014). Digital art's fascination with online galleries (First Real Net Art Gallery[2]), open archives (Netzspannung, Rhizome[3]), web platforms (Media Art Net/Medien Kunst Netz[4]), and mailing lists such as 7-11, Spectre, Nettime (Lovink 2002, 2003) is grounded not only in the potential of exploring new forms of experiencing and maintaining art, which draws upon the radical inclusion of technical agents and other humans and bypasses or supplements traditional institutions, but also in investigating the ways art, and more generally, "new things" emerge and live.

Net art puts an emphasis on the process of emergence as being fundamental to practice. Not only did art projects rely on the contributions of "audience artists," direct access, immediate appreciation, and the input of a large range of actors; a significant amount of work was put into reflecting upon the conditions that allow for such emergence to take place, participate in, be witnessed, bear a trace, and be archived. Early on, digital art focused on the means of continuous, relational, and productive operation as culturally and politically significant. This focus is aligned with certain movements, such as that of Free Software (Kelty 2008), but the attention to miniscule software and network gestures and their allowances is also important. Nettime, for example, is a basic daemon-based mailing list (running Mailman software) and these rather simple technical means enabled the generation, exchange, and maintenance of ideas out of which some thrilling projects, discussions, and movements were born. The creation of thoughts, discourses, and projects emerging from their dwelling in networks and mailboxes—in relation to each other and to the techno-human structures maintaining them, which were specific to the Nettime of the mid- and late 1990s—was a radical novelty. It is hard to reconcile Nettime's significance with its technical simplicity given today's instant and ongoing circulation of communication through much more complex arrangements of social media that yield nothing comparable. But technical mediation, as introduced above, evolved in relation to enchantment, mirage, and illusion. In mediational terms a mailing list is not more or less simple than books, a mother's voice, content management systems, or an online video editing suite, the effects of which cannot be understood exclusively by systematic reverse-engineering of their technical complexity.

Nettime was plugged into the mediation of the becoming of an art and cultural movement that both amplified the list's apparatic specificity and allowed for a thrilling burst of curiosity, inventiveness, discovery, and achievement. It certainly was not only Nettime that played a role in the development of certain threads in digital art. The attempt to understand how the processes of emergence can be accounted for, and kept open and present—even once they have passed —is perhaps best exemplified in the Netart-datenbank project (net.art-database).[5] Netart-datenbank was conceived by Sakrowski and Constant Dullaart in 1999; a limited version was implemented and tested. Though the project did not achieve its full aims and objectives, it was, both conceptually and technically, a remarkable exercise. The vision of the archive was to create ways in which people, events, projects, actors, and audiences of various kinds could be added to the database and commented on, and also the various types of connections between them, so that not only the main documents or landmarks of the movement but the very processes of its becoming would be preserved. Reading Halbwach, the cultural historian Charity Scribner suggests that an archive—unlike a museum that looks back to the past—acts as a collective memory, which is always "ephemeral, contingent, specular" and alive, and "can only exist as a work-in-progress, which is kept in motion or held aloft with a plural collective" (Scribner 2005, 37–38). The makers of Netart-datenbank wanted the site to play an archival role in tracking the evolution of processes so that users could focus on the shift that net art itself was fighting to induce: a shift away from the completed to things in the making, away from star names to the processes of becoming-artist, to machinic art, to practices of art making as filtering, forwarding, hanging out, and to keeping the being and the memory of the movement always craftfully in-the-making.

I have previously suggested the concept of an "art platform" (2012, 2013) a formulation that certainly is an outcome of net art's fascination with dynamic and open archives, mailing lists as evolving knowledge generators, and the Web as everyone's art factory; the concept is devised to give voice to a certain history of digital art in the 1990s and early 2000s.

Art platforms' core concern is how art emerges to become art. Being able to account for things that are incompatible with themselves—that is, have still not "become"—is core to its conceptual framework. Art that is only emerging and could ultimately fail to become significant can initially be seen as a creative "gray zone," and may forever be off the radar of valorized and valorizable art, as well as recognized cultural practices. This gray zone, seething with bubbling creative cultural emergence, full of try-outs, silly and meaningful acts, experiments and movements, can self-develop and assemble means for itself to produce concentrated, differentiated art phenomena. It is this very process of assembly and the ensemble, working with enough creative energy to propel it into "aesthetic brilliance," that I have called art platforms.

Art platforms are ensembles that may take the form of stand-alone web platforms or extended networks, working on and together with other cultural processes to produce art projects, cultural movements, and moments of difference outside of, or in little contact with, traditional institutions for the production of art and the knowledge about it, as well as its valorization.

Examples of art platforms of the 2000s included the Runme.org software art repository,[6] an archive and network that assisted software art in becoming an art movement, and Micromusic.net, a platform and community for 8-bit music or creative practices in Second Life. The questions explored by the concept of art platforms deal with art constructing itself in new ways. What are the new forms and processes of self-organization that are invented and enacted through the emergence of aesthetic work? What are the aesthetic problems that call for new art forms, as well as new forms of artists and audiences to arise through creative work?

A few things are important to thinking in line with the concept of art platforms. Any aesthetics run on computational grounds demands an analysis that is acute to both sides of the process, the aesthetic and computational. On the one hand, everything that circulates in the field of mediating computation now belongs to the aesthetic realm, has an aesthetic function. Nothing can be necessarily discarded as preposterous or insignificant here, as even those aesthetic objects that seemingly are just by-products, outcomes, or processes of subjectification are at the same time active agents that propel and sustain becomings. On the other hand, aesthetic modes of becoming are enacted and sustained through computational ensembles, which require an effort to be understood in order to comprehend the new kinds of becoming.

If nothing can be inherently ignored as aesthetically insignificant and nothing is bereft of capacity for aesthetic becoming, we start to wander into the gray zone of mediocre or "silly" cultural production, meaningless creative acts that are not completed and themselves are processes of the emergence of ideas, materials, humans, collectives, other movements, turmoils, and also of breakdowns and awful things. The novel kind of access to such gray zones afforded by the Internet cannot be ignored, and the new forms of witnessing and co-production provided by computational mediation invite both comprehension and action. Emergence is computationally mediated: it is procedural, has a software side, is networked, and embraces very precise kinds of computational materiality. We currently can partake in and often publicly witness the "raw" state of becoming that previously was concealed and remained private. A process of becoming of a subjectivity, an art current, an aesthetic work previously would have left a trace of documents, diaries, letters, minutes, objects, memories (to be posthumously gathered into an archive) and would have been a relatively closed private and exclusive process. Now it is laid bare and open in the making, prior to its having reached any maturity.

The breathtaking openness supported by the new kind of technicity that assists and enables becoming generates drastically varying scenarios. Collaborative knowledge or art production fascinates people, but it also goes hand in hand with the outpouring of the raw, the unpolished, and underdeveloped that becomes a filler for panicky news articles and is otherwise hardly addressed. Take, for example, a group of teenagers posting daily updates on the mundane details of the course of their life on MySpace or Facebook as they emerge as subjects. Such a process is often open for everybody to see. The aesthetic performance of their emergence as individuals, and as a collective in relation to each other, is enabled, entrained, and given temporality by the computational ensembles of their laptops or tablets, networks, social networking sites, buttons and agreements, codecs and permissions structures, alongside the many other agents that enter and leave such ensembles.

Today, the role that is presented as desired and appreciated for an individual in our society is focused on becoming and performing as a unique subject. This is reputedly achieved best through being and acting creatively. There are indeed entire industries that produce means or mechanisms for acquiring unique and "authentic" kinds of experiences of subjectification. Software-based and network-assisted platforms aimed at sharing unique travel, eating, and dressing-up practices strive to harness the emergent and affective qualities and properties of individuation. Because the most "uniquely" individuated people are the creators, the practice of artistry through software-mediated and -assisted creative production is a top priority both for individuating subjects and the industries willing to tap into such processes.

This paradoxical pairing of the thrill of art, the rapture of achievement striving toward liberatory creative invention, with the ways in which this thrill and rapture comply with the exploitative vectors of neoliberalism does not exhaust either side of the conundrum. Both sides are joined by the tensions between a push for individual subjectification and, at the same time, collaborative, collective becoming and increased social performance—in turn complexified and endangered by the quest for human subjecthood at times of ecological risks—and the ascendancy of systems that reduce humans to the status of mere tables of elements, objects in their manifest or implicit operations. Such tensions remain complex and strained while specific tendencies within them outthrust and recede and humans, as well as the art that is made, enter and leave the novel ensembles in which they are composed.

Total Creativity and Social Media

Some recent exhibitions and events that have dealt with this new condition comprised of tensions and paradoxes could be considered spectacular failures. *YouTube Play: A Biennial of Creative Video* is one such relatively large-scale example. In this case the Guggenheim Museum established a collaboration with YouTube for a competition striving to single out "exceptional talent" in online video making. Within five months over 23,000 videos were submitted.[7] Working eight-hour days, one would need approximately six years to watch all the submitted videos; yet twenty-five winners were chosen and showcased in a much shorter time frame. In this case the total of creativity does not easily translate itself into a museum exhibition format, but becomes a question of the operations of big data and technical meaning-making machines, based on models and quantitative methods. And this is the best-case scenario; the worst-case one would be the old institutional art machinery at play.

What this competition demonstrated is a confusion of the individual aesthetic act, the collective technical ecologies that bear and feed such a creative act, and the communal aesthetic and curatorial environment in which it makes sense. The networks push for new art and meaning-making machines, and what the Guggenheim did—or, more precisely, the constitution of the museum form as it has accreted over time and been realized in this particular instance—was to exploit the networks and then to essentially ignore them in singling out a few individual pieces. Situated within the tensions between individual and collective subjectification and the computational, networked one, as well as the mediation of both, the exhibition harnessed the paradox in order to eventually solve it by ditching some of its constitutive elements.

Making sense of "total creativity" is by no means easy. Inviting the audience to collectively map the world with self-designed patterns,[8] the result being a generic mess, or employing an algorithm to randomly select among thousands of submitted photographs[9] (as Musée de l'Elysée in Lausanne did), can be considered neither a successful assessment nor exploration of this strained complexity. Still, there are projects addressing such tensions in more careful and interesting ways.

Some of these projects thrive on net art's idea that the role of the artist in the network age is to act as a filter or a bot: to crawl, find, filter out, redirect and re-present data flows—to take on an aesthetico-technical role. Here, aesthetic judgment merges with a technical specification, a computational model, becoming one. Surf clubs[10] (Ramocki 2008; Olson 2009), for example, are an intense continuation of digital art's aesthetic techniques of "browsing," downloading, uploading, and linking. Pro-surfers browse for online material they find aesthetically interesting and re-post it en masse on their blogs, itself a common practice, which curatorially makes sense as it is aligned with the functional specificity of social media. Here, the tension between the individual and the collective, the aesthetic and technical, is conserved and worked up.

Sakrowski's *CuratingYouTube*[11] is another project fascinated with mass creativity and the computational mediation of different kinds of being and becoming. *Curating YouTube* is a set of curated exhibitions and tool for curation that allows selecting and presenting chosen videos in a grid, where they can be played together, one after another, or separately. Orchestrating individual videos in a collective fashion technically lends itself not only to presenting outstanding single videos in relation to each other, but to the exploration of the generic element in aesthetic work. If nine videos on the same theme are juxtaposed on a grid, forced to work together collectively, the yet to be understood force of gray creative production, the aesthetico-subjective emergence, is brought to the fore.

Is producing better projects, reflections, subjects and more consistent cultural movements a question of technical-curatorial structures? Does it make sense at all to differentiate in that manner between more and less productive structures? The image-based bulletin board 4chan produced memes as a genre and the Anonymous hacker group as a formation (Goriunova 2013), whereas no art ever really enters into a state of becoming on Facebook. Which technics, technologies, mediations matter? In the cultural discourse on participation it is the technical that is absent, and in the discourse on the technical, it is the absence of the symbolic and of the subject that is elided.

The main question posed by the previously mentioned explorations is what remains of the subject in terms of its role and modes of becoming. If the Guggenheim's

YouTube show tried to traditionally reinforce the position of the subject by plucking out preformed auteurs and individuals, what is the place of the subject in *Curating Youtube*?

As Friedrich Kittler has succinctly put it, it traditionally was Man who was the "Subject of Aesthetics" (Kittler 1997, 131). Kittler raises the question what becomes of aesthetics, which is, in his account, an optical machine without need for a user or a witness, such as the human. It can arguably be maintained that it is the production of subjectivity, whether individual, collective, or technical, that informs art. What does art become now, at least partially outside of the human subject?

For Kittler, the emergence of the human subject as a conceptual figure, historical actor, and a metaphysical entity is fed, or rather, engineered by subjection to the specific language formation that is sang, read, and generally performed by the body of the mother. Thus subjectification, from the very beginning, is purely technical. Today's subjectification for him is modeled on the Turing machine.

Whether to extend such a proposition, or take it elsewhere, I would like to suggest that the emergence of the subject, or at least subjectivities, today is based on techno-aesthetic actions, a techno-cultural performance that is not necessarily communal but carried out by and in relation to others, including humans, post-humans, bots, data storage caves, and algorithms. This emergence is aesthetic because it is relational, sensual, material, and symbolic, and technical because it is fused with computational mediation. As such, a project like *CuratingYoutube* is an ecology in which the emergence of subjectivities is not discourse-based or institutional, but founded on performances and further techno-aesthetic actions performed on those performances. The subjectivities produced are not entirely computational, but sustained by technical media in their aesthetic thrust. Such subjectivities have something in common with aesthetic word images, literary devices, and conceptual personae, as they act as ecologies, composite figures that one can enter and leave, trying the subject on to then take it off and go elsewhere.

The techno-aesthetic enactments of participatory platforms' functions, or projects employing those functions, thus become zones in which art and aesthetics merge with the general cultural production,"total" creativity, and curatorial effort. Artwork born from the intersections of such processes takes us out of the canonical understanding of art, the artist, the audience, art production and appreciation apparatuses, and into territories where creative work engages millions in their making of and being contemporary versions of a human. Art and cultural movements emerging from such processes are novel forms of culture, and the participation in and understanding of such emergences remains a challenge for institutions, individuals, and practices called to make sense and take care of art.

Notes

1 The project no longer works; see broken links from Easylife.org, http://easylife.org/ (accessed October 21, 2013). Here is a description by Andreas Broekmann: "more than twenty WWW pages located on [...] different servers all across Europe and the US were linked together in a loop through which the visitor would be 'zapped' automatically, one page following the next after ten seconds. The project made use of the 'Refresh' meta-tag, a command within HTML, the language that is used to design

WWW pages. The command tells the WWW browser software on the personal computer of the user to automatically go to a particular page after a certain time. By making sure that all these links created a loop, Refresh would take you through all the pages over and over again. The project was exciting for those immediately involved as they could experience how the loop grew page by page, while they were simultaneously communicating and negotiating via an IRC chat channel how to solve certain problems. More generally, the Refresh loop was designed to employ the interconnectivity of the computers and the software infrastructure to create one project that was simultaneously happening at more than twenty different locations, a genuinely distributed artwork whose experiential effect both depended on and transgressed the physical distance between the participants" (Broekmann 1997).

2 "Pages in the Middle of Nowhere (Former First and The Only Real Net Art Gallery)."

3 http://netzspannung.org/; http://rhizome.org (accessed October 21, 2013).

4 http://www.medienkunstnetz.de/ (accessed October 21, 2013).

5 http://www.netart-datenbank.org/; http://net.artdatabase.org/ (accessed October 21, 2013).

6 Runme.org Software Art Repository: http://runme.org (accessed October 21, 2013).

7 "HootSuite Analytics to Drive Campaign Success." http://de.slideshare.net/hootsuite/hootsuite-analytics-to-drive-campaign-success-guggenheim-case-study (accessed October 21, 2013).

8 *World Beach Project*, Victoria & Albert Museum. http://www.vam.ac.uk/content/articles/w/world-beach-project/ (accessed 21 October 2013).

9 "We Are All Photographers Now," *Cool Hunting*. http://www.coolhunting.com/culture/we-are-all-phot.php (accessed October 21, 2013).

10 *Supercentral*: http://www.supercentral.org/wordpress; *Double Happiness*: http://doublehappiness.ilikenicethings.com/; *Loshadka*: http://www.loshadka.org/wp; *Netmares & Netdreams v. 2.2*: http://www.netmaresnetdreams.net; *Nasty Nets*: http://nastynets.com/ (accessed October 21, 2013).

11 http://www.curatingyoutube.net/ (accessed October 21, 2013).

References

Bakhtin, Mikhail. 1990. "Author and Hero in Aesthetic Activity." In *Art and Answerability. Early Philosophical Essays by M.M.Bakhtin*, edited by Michael Holquist and Vadim Liapunov. Austin, TX: University of Texas Press.

Benjamin, Walter. 2005. *Selected Writings, Volume 2: Part 1: 1927–1930*. Cambridge, MA: Harvard University Press.

Berardi, Franco (Bifo). 2009. *Soul at Work*. New York: Semiotext(e).

Billing, Johanna, Maria Lind, and Lars Nilsson, eds. 2007. *Taking the Matter into Common Hands: On Contemporary Art and Collaborative Practices*. London: Black Dog.

Bishop, Claire. 2012. *Artificial Hells: Participatory Art and the Politics of Spectatorship*. London and New York: Verso.

Bosma, Josephine. 2011. *Nettitudes: Let's Talk Net Art*. Amsterdam: NAI Publishers.

Bourriaud, Nikolas. 2002. *Relational Aesthetics*. Dijon: Les Presses du Réel.

Braidotti, Rosi. 2013. *The Posthuman*, New York and London: Routledge.

Broeckmann, Andreas. 1997. "Net.Art, Machines and Parasites." http://www.irational.org/cybercafe/backspace/netart.txt (accessed October 21, 2013).

Debord, Guy. 1984. *Society of the Spectacle*. Detroit, MI: Black & Red.

De Certeau, Michel. 2002. *The Practice of Everyday Life*. Berkeley, CA: University of California Press.

Flusser, Vilem. 2000. *Towards a Philosophy of Photography*. London: Reaktion Books.

Fuller, Matthew. 2005. *Media Ecologies: Materialist Energies in Art and TechnoCulture*. Cambridge, MA: The MIT Press.

Guattari, Félix. 1995. *Chaosmosis: An Ethico-Aesthetic Paradigm*. Sydney: Power Publications.

Goriunova, Olga. 2012. *Art Platforms and Cultural Production on the Internet*. New York and London: Routledge.

Goriunova, Olga. 2013. "The Force of Digital Aesthetics: On Memes, Hacking, and Individuation." *Zeitschrift für Medienwissenschaft* 8, 1/2013. http://www.academia.edu/3065938/The_force_of_digital_aesthetics_on_memes_hacking_and_individua tion (accessed January 4, 2015).

Haraway, Donna. 1991. *Symians, Cyborgs and Women: The Reinvention of Nature*. New York and London: Free Association Books.

Haraway, Donna. 1997. *Modest_Witness@Second_Millennium.FemaleMan_Meets_OncoMouse: Feminism and Technoscience*. New York and London: Routledge.

Kelty, Christopher. 2008. *Two Bits: The Cultural Significance of Free Software*. Durham, NC: Duke University Press.

Kittler, Friedrich.1990. *Discourse Networks 1800/1900*. Stanford, CA: Stanford University Press. Kittler, Friedrich. 1997. *Literature, Media, Information Systems*. London: G&B Arts.

Lanchester. John. 2013. "The Snowden Files: Why the British Public Should Be Worried About GCHQ." *Guardian*. http://www.theguardian.com/world/2013/oct/03/edward-snowden-files-john-lanchester (accessed 21 October 2013).

Leroi-Gourhan, André. 1993. *Gesture and Speech*. Cambridge, MA: The MIT Press.

Lovink, Geert. 2002. *Dark Fiber: Tracking Critical Internet Culture*. Cambridge, MA: The MIT Press.

Lovink, Geert. 2003. *My First Recession: Critical Internet Culture in Transition*. Amsterdam: NAI Publishers.

Lovink, Geert, and Ned Rossiter, eds. 2007. *MyCreativity Reader: A Critique of Creative Industries*. Amsterdam: Institute of Network Cultures.

McLuhan, Marshall. 1994. *Understanding Media: The Extensions of Man*. Cambridge, MA: The MIT Press.

Monoscope. 2014. "Nettime." http://monoskop.org/Nettime (accessed 21 October 2013):

Nettime Readers: *ZKP 1, 2, 3, 4, 5 and 6*

ZKP 3.2.1. 1996. Filtered by *Nettime*. Lubljana Digital Media Lab: Dry books # 1.

ZKP 4.. http://www.ljudmila.org/~vuk/nettime/zkp4/toc.htm.

ZKP 5. 1999. *ReadMe! ASCII and the Revenge of Knowledge*. New York: Autonomedia.

Olson, Marisa. 2009. "Words Without Pictures. http://wordswithoutpictures.org/main.html?id=276¬e=281/ (accessed January 4, 2015).

Plato. 2005. *Phaedrus*. New York and London: Penguin Classics.

Ramocki, Marcin. 2008. "Surfing Clubs: Organized Notes and Comments." http://ramocki.net/surfing-clubs.html/ (accessed January 4, 2015).

Rheingold, Howard. 1993. *The Virtual Community: Homesteading on the Electronic Frontier*. http://www.rheingold.com/vc/book/ (accessed January 4, 2015).

Scribner, Charity. 2005. *Requiem for Communism.* Cambridge, MA: The MIT Press.
Simondon, Gilbert, 1992. "The Genesis of the Individual." In *Incorporations*, edited by Jonathan Crary and Samford Kwinter. New York: Zone Books.
Stallabrass, Julian. 2003. *Internet Art: The Online Clash of Culture and Commerce.* London: Tate Publishing.
Stiegler, Bernard. 1998, 2009, 2011. *Technics and Time,* Volumes 1, 2, and 3. Stanford, CA: Stanford University Press.
Stimson, Blake, and Gregory Sholette, eds. 2007. *Collectivism After Modernism: The Art of Social Imagination After 1945.* Minneapolis, MN: University of Minnesota Press.
Virno, Paolo. 2004. *A Grammar of the Multitude.* New York: Semiotext(e).
Winthrop-Young, Geoffrey. 2012. *Kittler and the Media.* New York and London: Polity.
Wolf, Christa. 1995. *The Quest for Christa T.* New York: HarperCollins.

13

Interactive Art
Interventions in/to Process

Nathaniel Stern

Introduction: Bodies in Process

When we move and think and feel, we are, of course, a body. This body is constantly changing, in and through its ongoing relationships. This body is a dynamic form, full of potential. It is not "a body," as thing, but *embodiment* as incipient activity. Embodiment is a continuously emergent and active relation. It is our materialization and articulation, both *actual* and *virtual*: *as* they occur, and *about* to occur. Embodiment is *moving-thinking-feeling*; it is the body's potential to vary; it is the body's relations to the outside. It is *per-formed*, rather than *pre-formed*. And embodiment is what is staged in the best interactive art.

This chapter looks closely at works by contemporary artists Rafael Lozano-Hemmer, Camille Utterback, and Scott Snibbe, who each have us encounter the body and its ongoing emergence *with* other matter and materials. While Lozano-Hemmer frames the mutual emergence of bodies and space, Utterback highlights how signs and bodies require one another to materialize, and Snibbe accents bodies (plural) as they manifest along with the communities they inhabit. I use these and other artists' works to intermittently differentiate between the interactivity of digital systems and relational emergence; to clarify the different levels and strategies of interaction or engagement with digital technologies; and to look toward the future of what the category "interactive art" may become. Ultimately, I argue that interactive artworks and installations are interventions in/to process: they create situations that enhance, disrupt, and alter experience and action in ways that call attention to our varied relationships *with* and *as* both structure and matter. At stake are the ways we perform our bodies, media, concepts, and materials.[1]

A Companion to Digital Art, First Edition. Edited by Christiane Paul.

Bodies and Spaces

Rafael Lozano-Hemmer's *Body Movies* (2001) projects thousands of photographs, several at a time, onto large buildings around a square. The piece has been shown in cities such as Rotterdam, Linz, Lisbon, Liverpool, Duisberg, Hong Kong, and Wellington, among others. The photographs were themselves taken on the streets in the host cities, and are shown using powerful, robotically controlled data projectors from above. From the center of the square below, huge floodlights wash out these projections, making them appear close to white. The images are revealed only when passersby on the square block out these lights with their shadows, so that the photographs underneath them can be revealed. These shadows range in size from 2 to 25 meters, depending on a visitor's distance from the light or building, and are tracked in real time with Lozano-Hemmer's custom computer vision software. Computer vision, more commonly known as interactive video, combines the use of digital video cameras and/or infrared or other sensing hardware (such as the Microsoft Kinect), and custom computer software, so that artworks can "see" and respond to bodies, colors, and/or motion in space. If the participants in *Body Movies* on the "live" square align their shadows in such a way that all the human bodies in the image beneath are revealed, Lozano-Hemmer's program triggers the next of the photographs in his sequence.

All of us have played with shadows—particularly our own—and *Body Movies* relies on the sophisticated vocabularies we have developed with them since childhood. But while interactors immediately understand this interface, the experience and practice of performing their bodies and shadows is framed and amplified: both literally, because *Body Movies* is a work of art, and also due to the sheer size of their shadows and the photographs beneath, which change the architecture, the images, and the atmosphere around them. The revelation of other bodies and spaces in the images that are actively unveiled from beneath these shadows—a play on presence that Lozano-Hemmer ironically calls "tele-absence"—and all the other bodies working together on the square add layers of complexity to the interaction. Viewers interact with all, part, and parts of the artist's photographs of people and places, bodies and spaces, from around the world. They often try to tell a physical story by playing around the images' contents, interweaving their real-time shadows across each other and with the bodies and spaces in the images, sometimes triggering new photos from Lozano-Hemmer's database.

The artist's collaborating and often dancing participants become active agents in an unfolding and enfolding narrative of bodies and space, agents whose flesh—depending on where they individually move—might collectively span several stories high, or remain close to their actual size, and everything in between. Together, they create complex shapes, animations, and architectures through investigative movements. Viewers run back and forth between the buildings and lights, shifting their individual sizes relative to other bodies, the architecture, and the photographs of the other architectures and bodies they are revealing. They use these tele-absent and projected forms in relation to each other, to the constructions around the square, and to the partially broadcast images in order to perform. I have watched participants in this project use shadows and images to shadowbox a giant, swallow a dwarf, smash a building, or carry a friend or foe to safety. People move between intimate and exaggerated flows, hand shadow-puppets, and sweeping and running formations. They produce animated rabbits and dogs, pour drinks from on high or eat arms of others down low, ride bicycles, and run or skateboard. They pull and push each other, and across each other, and across times and spaces—and all across the surface of a large building, rallying back and forth in size as they move toward or away from the light. The more creative performers play out complex scenes in the previously photographed international cities, their shadows enabling them to bicycle through Madrid, use real-world umbrellas to protect virtual Italians from the rain, or create multi-armed beasts that grow and shrink as they scale building walls or invade foreign lands. They align themselves with strangers and friends alike, with others both present and absent, in a communally shared and created space.

There are at least two techniques of "performance"—which I define as "the process of formation"—at play in Lozano-Hemmer's work. First, there are the ways in which technology makes space (and bodies): the carving out of the actual buildings and square through extant architectures; the virtual shaping of our movements through light and shadow; or the anticipated triggers that ask us to align our bodies with those in the artist's images. And second, there are the ways in which our bodies produce space (as well as themselves and each other): our movements and static moments in the large interactive area; our shadows on the buildings; our narratives between both; and the images beneath them. Here we move-think-feel spaces and bodies as they come to be; they are *always* transforming what and how they *are*, together: both as conceptual constructs, and as material "things."

In other words, Lozano-Hemmer's piece is an exemplary interactive artwork not only because of the technology it uses, but also because of the *situation* it stages and in which it intervenes. For the purposes of clarity interactive art (and interactive installations) can be defined as works of electronic and digital art that feature various forms of sensors or cameras for input; computers, micro-controllers, simple electronic circuits, or other digital or analogical terminals for processing; and any form of sensory output—audiovisual, tactile, olfactory, mechanical, or otherwise; and where all these are placed together in a system that responds to the embodied participation of its viewers. In these circumstances interactivity is understood as the required physical activity of a viewer-participant in order to fully realize a technology-generated and process-based work.

Although this way of understanding interactive art may be necessary for the sake of differentiation and analysis, it establishes a flawed priority: an emphasis on the computer, sensor, or projection, on the tools we use rather than the situations they create. We focus not "on the dynamic form of experience [...] It is the form of the technical object that is emphasized, for what it affords" (Massumi 2011, 45–46). If we explain what interactive art *is* primarily through technology, then we will comprehend it as merely a technological object. We should, rather, approach what interactive art *does*—and what *we* do—when it frames our moving-thinking-feeling (or *affect*). Moving and thinking and feeling are all a part of the same embodied and embodying processes, and interactive artworks such as *Body Movies* stage a rehearsal of some of their possibilities.

Posthumanities scholar N. Katherine Hayles makes a distinction between the "culturally constructed" body that is "naturalized within culture," and our experiences of embodiment, which are "contextual, enmeshed within the specifics of place, time, physiology, and culture" (Hayles 1999, 196, 297). Her distinction is somewhat parallel to Mark B.N. Hansen's, who, following the early phenomenology of Maurice Merleau-Ponty, distinguishes between the "body-image" and the "body- schema."

The body-image is an understanding of the body and identity. It is a "predominantly visual" or semiotic "representation of the body, a primary resemblance" (Hansen 2006, 37). The body-schema, on the other hand, is a "preobjective process of constitution" (Hansen 2006, 39); it is enactive, it is *becoming* a body. While extremely useful in thinking-with the importance of interaction, many theorists discussing embodiment have criticized phenomenological approaches such as Hansen's and Hayles's, because, with such philosophies, every experience centers on *human* perception. Artist and philosopher Erin Manning asserts that we must recognize the potential of virtual effects and bare activities—where being and becoming exceed the human, in what she calls the "more than human" (Manning 2009). Embodiment is always more than what we know, more than what we experience or are; its potential must always include emergent experiences and practices outside of human perception.

With interactive art, "the body" is addressed not only as a cultural construction or contextual experience, but as a relational process. Interactive installations amplify how the body's inscriptions, meanings, and matters *unfold out*, while the world's sensations, concepts, and matters *enfold in*. New media has the ability to intervene in, and challenge, not only the construction of bodies and identities, but also the ongoing and emergent processes of embodying relations, as they occur. Interactive art intervenes into process, that is, it breaks down and calls attention to what is *becoming-with* bodies.

Body Movies, for example, invites us to rehearse modes of making public, embodied, and communal space. The people on the square, writes Lozano-Hemmer, "embody different representational narratives," creating "a collective experience that nonetheless allows discrete individual participation" (Lozano-Hemmer 2001). While each active participant encounters their own performed body through shadow play, they also encounter performing the square and buildings and people around them, the shaping of this space and its continuous relationship to their own flesh, as well as to other spaces and bodies and matter—in their immediate environment and (in images) around the world. In *Body Movies*, participants' (and space's) movements—all of which they may or may not be consciously aware of—intervene in the mutual emergence of a broadly defined and engaged embodiment, and a broadly defined and engaged space. The piece literally stages drawn-out and processual bodies and spaces that we simultaneously activate and experience, through movement. *Body Movies* productively confuses an ongoing embodiment and an architectural/public space-making, asking us to practice the relation of inside and outside, personal and public, actual and virtual. It inaugurates a complex and creative dance, where our inter-activities frame how bodies and spaces move and think and feel and become, *together*. Here moving-thinking-feelings should not be understood as exclusively human endeavors. They are the forces of all things-in-process, always shifting each other's trajectories of becoming. And interactive artworks such as *Body Movies* are not just encounters with what *is*, but rehearsals for what *could be*.

Lozano-Hemmer's work attunes us to our body's making of space, and space's making of bodies. *Body Movies* emphasizes a body-space that cannot be reduced to the boundaries of our skin, the limited image we see on screen, or even our present movements around the square. Here our moving, affected, and affective bodies evince stories and histories that are made sensible in and as space; they are incarnated, together. Both space and bodiliness are potentialized, are accented as susceptible to folding, division, and reshaping, open to continual negotiation. Participants shrink and grow, live and transform, and shift with the spaces and stories they move with and in and *as* their environment. Body and space, here and elsewhere, are implicated in one another, and each presence (or absence) is an incipient action that we *feel* as instantiated through movement and relation. *Body Movies* effectively and affectively intensifies our practices of process, our moving, interrelating bodies and spaces as they come to matter. *Body Movies* has us encounter a complex layering of bodies and space; it frames the performances of embodiment and/with spatialization.

Interaction and Relation

This is not to say that *Body Movies*, or any interactive artworks for that matter, *produce* relational processes, or frame *all* that is our relational becoming-with. Interaction and relation are not the same thing; but they are related.

The recent academic turns to embodiment and affect, process ontology, and the new materialisms note that all of matter and bodes are active, continuously variable, and relational. Activist philosopher Brian Massumi (2011, 2) reminds us that matter goes from "something doing to the bare fact of activity; from there to event and change; then on to potential and the production of the new; coming to process as becoming." Subjects and objects are inter-given; they only exist as in-process relations to other in-process subjects and objects, relaying nested movements and potentials across themselves and each other, as they continuously form. All is always emergent, and of the relation. Relationality is continuous; it is embodiment's (or materiality's) always-ongoing formation.

The interactivity of software-based digital systems, on the other hand, is pre-programmed. With few exceptions, it is a back and forth: "I do *this* and *that* happens." There is a danger that we, as participants, are instrumentalized as interactors, and thus become *less* dynamic, rather than more so. Interaction becomes a game with a goal, and we must behave in a specific way to win it. Poorly conceived interactive art can force particular and thus predictive movements, which then may as well be static because our moving-thinking-feelings are pre-formed.

Interaction, as it is understood in the context of digital technologies, is much more finite than relationality. While it is responsive, the possible outcomes from our performances are restricted. Interaction, in other words, is a limitation. But it can also act as an amplification. Here is an apt analogy: a directional microphone can only pick up sounds directly in front of it, and within a small area; it amplifies what it hears, for example birds chirping and the sound of soft wind blowing. We, as listeners, do not merely "hear" those sounds, however. We perceive more birds than we hear, we *feel* the wind blowing, we imagine nature and the morning, the smell of grass. Like this directional microphone, or the frame of a canvas, or any work of art for that matter, interactive art can highlight and magnify particular aspects of being, so that we experience much more than sits in its frame. At its limits, interactive art *disrupts* our relational embodiment, and thus attunes us to its potentials. Embodiment is per-formed in relation, and interactive art stages us, and our surroundings, so as to suspend, amplify, and intervene in that very performance. It is a space to experience being and becoming, and to practice potential new modes of their relational emergence.

Bodies and Signs

In her *External Measures* series, Camille Utterback uses an overhead computer vision system to track bodies and trigger painterly and animated marks on screen, which collectively create an ongoing image. The marks look and move like actively reconfiguring geometric patterns, smudging pencil sketches, dripping paint, or seeping molding clay, depending on the piece in the series. Their position and velocity within the projected image are initiated and continuously performed by both the location and movements of the participants in space, as well as the marks' own internal logic. Utterback's dynamic paintings are generated as they move, affect, and are affected by participants' gestures and stasis, or presence and absence, in barely predictable and organic ways. And each installation invites a very different style of interaction.

Utterback's marks immediately appear in response to participants' attendance and movement, and they are animated—leaving trails of what looks like graphite or acrylic or earth—based on the flow, stillness, and the number or lack of people in the installation area. An overall composition emerges and continues to transform over time, as layers of persistent marks and bodies feed back between interaction, performance, and image. Each piece "measures" how we move or stand still, and creates an "external" visualization of that movement and stasis. Participants in turn "monitor this external data and measure out their actions in response," creating an "intricate dance between computer algorithm" and affective involvement (Utterback 2002). "Measure," in Utterback's sense of the word, does not refer to measurement but rather to an active "measuring up," a diagram of bodies and images, being made. It is a play on the moving-thinking-feeling and making of the screen image—and its ongoing signification—with our interacting and always relational bodies. Her use of the word "external" is also an ironic pun on interior/exterior between each and the other. Neither body nor matter nor sign are a declared subject (or object). Utterback rather highlights bodies and images as a mapping across each other, an experienced and practiced formation.

The first piece in Utterback's series, *External Measures (Rectangle)* (2001), follows our movements, and our relation to each other, to create a collection of angular shapes that fold in on themselves. It was produced, released, and exhibited along with her second work, *External Measures (Round)* (2001), a circular projection where "lines curve and snap between people like crazy elastic bands, creating a dynamic tension" in the image and space (Utterback 2002). Utterback's third *External Measures* (2003), saw a slightly more organic relationship, where constant procedural animations of slowly moving gray lines are pushed aside by viewers' movements, making way for more sparse but saturated color lines left in their wake. "Subtle brown and black swaths are etched between any people in the space" and "scratchy white lines connect" each of us to our point of entry into the interactive area (Utterback 2004). A given participant's appearance alters the traces on the screen by erasing marks in the projection—ones automatically drawn, as well as those left behind by others—and as time goes on and the software continues to draw over the composition, eventually overwrites all traces left behind. *External Measures, 2003* thus creates a "hypnotic tension between presence and absence, mark-making and erasing, human gesture and algorithmic drawing" (Utterback 2004). Here, we literally write with our bodies, an at-once drawing and meaning-making that is staged as the *work* of the art.

In Utterback's *Untitled 5* (2004), visual feedback between multiple bodies and the projection influence one another immediately and over long stretches of time. The artist's goal was to "create an aesthetic system which responds fluidly and intriguingly to physical movement in the exhibit space" (Utterback 2005). Utterback uses the same computer vision system from her other works, but introduces more generative complexities in her pixel painting that are not only affected by moving bodies, but still bodies, multiple bodies, and absent bodies. The marks that we trigger and that have been cumulatively collected continue to interact with each other even after we have left the installation area. The result is a continuous, hauntingly and haltingly poetic moving image, which invites participants to make and find meaning in, with, and as embodied relation.

What we see first when entering the interaction area of *Untitled 5* is a real-time, bird's-eye view silhouette of our bodies, on an eggshell background, and filled with sketchy, graphite-like, criss-crossing lines. As we move across the space, these sketched patterns move along with us, while a red colored line, drawn out from our center, maps our trajectories. When we leave the installation, this trajectory line is overlaid with tiny organic spots. The longer we are still and in the space, the larger these marks are. The tiny points can be pushed from their location by other people's movement in the space. As they are pushed, they act like sponges of ink or paint being dragged across Utterback's canvas, leaving streaks and smears of color in their wake. Displaced marks also slowly return to their original location, making yet more swaths of color. The junctions between past and present movement and stillness, between motion paths and who does or does not follow them, connect different moments of time, different bodies in space, the continuous compositions and how we might read them, as well as the relation between these three.

The behaviors behind *Untitled 5* are never explicitly revealed to its participants; the work instead invites us to practice *styles* of "kinesthetic exploration" (Utterback 2005). The embodied sense of "more," of a relation to the world's larger goings-on, is always prevalent. For Utterback, a "visceral sense of unfolding or revelation," of both "immediacy and loss" is integral to the work itself. Like the "experience of embodied existence itself—a continual flow of unique and fleeting moments," *Untitled 5* is both sensual and contemplative in its interactivity (Utterback 2005). The tensions she discusses result from the suspension and thus intensity of our relations, a kind of attunement to how we interact, sense, and make sense. She does not elicit specific gestures or behaviors, but rather has us encounter what movement does, what it makes, and what it changes. This is to say that—while the interaction is limited by the technologies the artist uses—neither our specific interactive movements, nor the technology, are where our attention is "drawn." Rather, we attune ourselves to the *quality* of our and the environment's moving-thinking-feelings, to the larger *processes* of embodiment and sense-making.

With *Untitled 6* (2005) (Figure 13.1), a work very similar to its predecessor, Utterback carries on with this interactive methodology, but aesthetically shifts to bold graphics that are less like abstract painting and much closer to minimalist, sculptural forms—like clay mush dropped from above. And with *Abundance* (2007), she highlights public space and social relationships—topics often explored in installation art from the 1960s until today—by moving her visuals onto the facade of a three-story building in San Jose, and viewer interactions onto the adjacent public square.

Each *External Measures* work—indeed, every moment in which any individual interacts with the variable traces of other/past participants on screen, in any given

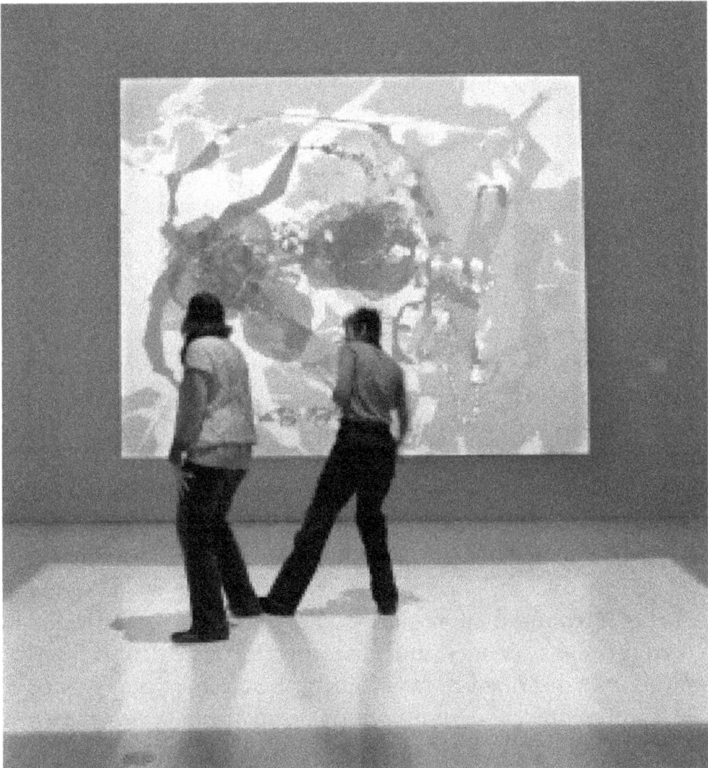

FIGURE 13.1 Camille Utterback, *Untitled 6.* Installation view. Milwaukee Art Museum, 2008. Photo: Tom Bamberger.

piece in the series—creates slightly different encounters between concepts and matter/bodies. These encounters accent multiple relationships with her artwork, and with art- and mark-making more generally. Where one *Untitled 5* viewer, for example, may utilize stillness in order to leave large splotches that later participants may or may not draw out over time, other ones can run and drag illustrative trajectories across an empty field or slowly concentrate their gestures, treading lightly across the stage, so as to smudge a crowded canvas. The interactive experience can be care-ful or care-free, and any performance might produce subjectively stunning images or visual garbage—similar to a professional artist's practice in the studio.

The live relationships and generative algorithms in Utterback's *External Measures* series become more and more complex as she works with her media over time. They also begin to collectively en- and unfold our relationships to art history and practice and, more generally, the signs and symbols or concepts and gestures therein. Utterback began the series with simple shapes and immediate on-screen responses that might allude to early cave paintings or mathematical drawings (*Rectangle* and *Round*); then moved on to the use of negative space and real-time animated images, reminiscent of both landscape painting and early motion graphics (*2003*); again pushes forward on this historical arts trajectory in *Untitled 5*, referencing the affective and performative—and in this case, collaborative—possibilities of abstract expressionism à la Jackson Pollock; turns to the embodied encounters of minimalism in *Untitled 6*; and references happenings, the Situationists, and Fluxus games in *Abundance*. Viewers' movements in the *External Measures* series are a playful reminder of, allusion to, and interaction with, the literal, historical "art movements" of the past. Participants are invited to use the media and materials of art history to physically relate to the images and trajectories of preceding artists/interactors, creating a living collage of transversal expressions and explorations. They construct and assemble multidimensional representations of "embodiment with art" or "bodies and signs" on a two-dimensional plane, and continuously feed back into that image and process. The variable aesthetics and interactions that emerge conjure up memories and rememberings of not just abstract expressionism's embodied splashes of paint or, in *Untitled 6*, minimalism's solid forms; but also art nouveau's graphic arts; collage and assemblage's found objects and pasted fragments in formalist composition; constructivists' and futurists' technological inspiration; cubism's goals of incorporating several perspectives and/or times; Dada's absurdities; or surrealism's unconscious revealings, to name just a few. These aesthetics and rememberings stage and intervene in the movement styles of creation, the non-representational representations they create, and the relation between the two.

External Measures has us move-think-feel the signifying practices of writing, drawing, painting, and making art as simultaneously performed and embodying practices. We are invited to *re-member*—to embody again—how signs, images, and the discourses that surround them require bodies in order to be articulated. And bodies, in turn, require signs, images, and discourse for articulation. Here bodies and signs are continuously inscribed as future memories; remembered as past meanings; and practiced as presented and re-presented formations between past and future. Utterback's work highlights that making meaning always requires bodies, and embodiment always requires that meaning be made. This is art about art and artists, images and image production, signs and bodies; it invites us to feel and rehearse how we express, how we are expressed, and how we relate to each of these embodied processes, both historically, and in the moment. We perform new-but-not-new images into existence, and these (now preformed) images feed back into how we perform, again. Utterback invokes our relationship with her individual artworks in order to evoke our affective encounters with the work of art more generally. At stake is how meaning and bodies and matter are articulated and presented through always interacting and relating agencies—conscious and unconscious, human and non-human, present and non-present, living and otherwise. Here we encounter the relational sense, the emergent language, the preformed and performed continuity, of art.

Such are not the only encounters that interactors may have with/in the works discussed by Lozano-Hemmer and Utterback. As situations, they enable an investigation of implication and impact, of what and how we experience and practice, and of the relations between meaning- or space-making and materiality in process.

Processing Interventions

Artists such as the ones discussed in this chapter recognize the processual and relational formation of bodies and spaces, of concepts and images, of communities and their histories. They use their work to interrupt and amplify the potential in these processes. But what they stage are not only interventions into process; they are also interventions *in* process, always interrupting and interrupted themselves, as they occur; and they are also interventions for us *to* process, where affection and reflection interplay. Here *affection* is that which is felt (and thought) in our moving, and *reflection* is thought (and felt) in our making of meaning. Art and (its) philosophy have the ability to create, transform, and mobilize one another.

In encountering and rehearsing affection and reflection *with* interactive art there is potential for different ways of relating. How might we find alternative thoughts and feelings through and with our movements? Can we be more careful in how we become bodies, become spaces, become (a) people? How should we better make ourselves in and with and for the world, and others around us, through our activities? Can we take account of and change how we move and think and feel in the everyday? And what are the implications and impacts of that change? Interactive art has the potential to accent our potential: to show us how to move and become differently.

Bodies and Communities

Scott Snibbe's *Screen series* (2002–2003) consists of cinematically inspired interactive installations, in which our embodied performances contribute to the works' content, over time. It plays with the languages of film, animation, and shadows to create a frame for potential narratives where social rules and bodies in motion interact with and influence one another. We are staged as *bodies* (plural) and together substantiate communal rules that suggest societal structures.

Snibbe's *Screen series* encourages viewer-participants to use their shadows as animated, iconic re-presentations of the body. Each work begins with the same premise: an empty, white projection on a clear, white screen or wall. Here the rectangular projection already has social implications: it references the filmic or computer screen and what each of them means to us culturally and historically. When viewers move between the projector and the image they cast shadows which Snibbe captures and reuses in animated form, so that we may interact with screen and with cinema, with the underlying narratives, meanings, and histories that screen and cinema bring to bear.

In *Shadow* (2002), for example, the projector acts like a spotlight and casts the shadows of any given viewer or viewers beyond it. What each performer may be unaware of is that Snibbe's software begins recording as soon as she or he has entered its domain. When the viewer steps away, "the screen replays the movements of their shadows over and over, so that their shadows are detached from their bodies." These videos "become a recorded performance for a larger audience, and the work is revealed as an instrument for composing cinema with one's own body" (Snibbe 2003). Here the screen becomes a material memory and living record of what bodies do, are, and could be. In *Shadow*, our embodied performance in front of the screen is archived as a kind of miniature narrative, an ongoing artifact: performed, then actively responded to by others, and thus performed again.

Snibbe's *Screen series* continues, from here, to build on this basic premise of coupling body-as-performed with a public, and constantly transforming, community. In *Compliant* (2002), our shadows cause a small projected rectangle/screen "to be distorted and pushed away, as if the screen were a rubber sheet" (Snibbe 2005). Although inspired by the hat Charlie Chaplin wore as his famous Tramp character (who appeared in several films between 1914 and 1936), Snibbe gives his screen-within-a-screen a sentience that more closely resembles that of Peter Pan's shadow running away from him.

The rectangle's edges bend and ripple and slip away when our shadow-fingers push or grab its form. Snibbe sets up a quirky interplay that gestures—and asks us to gesture—toward the structures, forms, and games that bodies make, and, in turn, the bodies that structures, forms, and games make. We and the social space of his screen are staged as entwined game players and rule makers, involved in a kind of narrative-driven society, which is performed by multiple bodies over time and space.

Snibbe's *Screen series* comprises six pieces altogether, and the interactions range from leaving behind animated silhouettes or distorting screens, as in *Shadow* and *Compliant*, to creating collaborative and moving shadow drawings amongst several participants (*Impression* and *Depletion*, both in 2003), and playing interactive games of tag, where projected light illuminates the shadows of the it-person, and is transferred to the next one when their shadows touch (*Concentration*, 2003).

Some viewers did not even realize the work's interactive potential, merely standing to the side and admiring the quality of light. Snibbe recounts that one woman "reflexively stepped back" when "the screen pulled away from her body" at first encounter with *Compliant* (Simanowski and Snibbe 2006). After understanding and acclimating to the rules of the experience, she engaged with it intimately, waving her fingers and tickling the frame, or using her tongue to make small impressions on the square's edge. Another viewer stared at the mere qualities of the square without ever interacting, while still a third "strode purposefully through the projection without looking back. Behind him, the luminous rectangle shuddered and jerked away, distorted from a clean rectangle into the warped form of a fallen tissue" (Simanowski and Snibbe 2006). Snibbe's work, says journalist Cate McQuaid (2005), "invites drama: one person might make wild gestures; two people could act out a pantomime." Playful interactions by and between each individual in the space feed into how current and future interactors decidedly engage. Here bodies encounter and rehearse both non-representational *and* signifying movements both with other bodies and Snibbe's body of work—which did, does, and will help to continuously perform potential narratives and mini communities over the course of an exhibition.

Snibbe's *Deep Walls* (2003), the height of the series, invites viewers to interact directly with many bodies at once, and over time. This piece basically multiplies the interaction of *Shadow* into a grid of sixteen individual boxes (Figure 13.2). When stepping in between the installation's projector and its projection, viewer-participants cast their shadows over the grid, obscuring bodies and parts of the whole, while a camera captures their silhouetted movements. Once they leave the frame of light and their shadows are no more, their recording is placed in one of the boxes, replacing an older film, looping indefinitely alongside other clips of body-outlined actions in adjacent boxes. Every active performance snippet in front of this cinematic narrative is thus suspended, stored, and re-involved in one of its comic book-like square frames. Each supplants an animation that was there before, and is put alongside fifteen others similar to but different from it.

In *Deep Walls,* each shadow-body has more than a dozen collaborators in its grid (which can include groups of people working together on one cinematic snippet). These performers often try to outdo each other, throwing their children in the air before catching them, kissing or dancing or interacting with one another or other boxes on screens, doing cartwheels or whipping their hair, or sometimes even playing out familiar scenes from classic movies (I saw attempts at *Indiana Jones* and *Casablanca* when it was on view at the Milwaukee Art Museum). The accompanying images

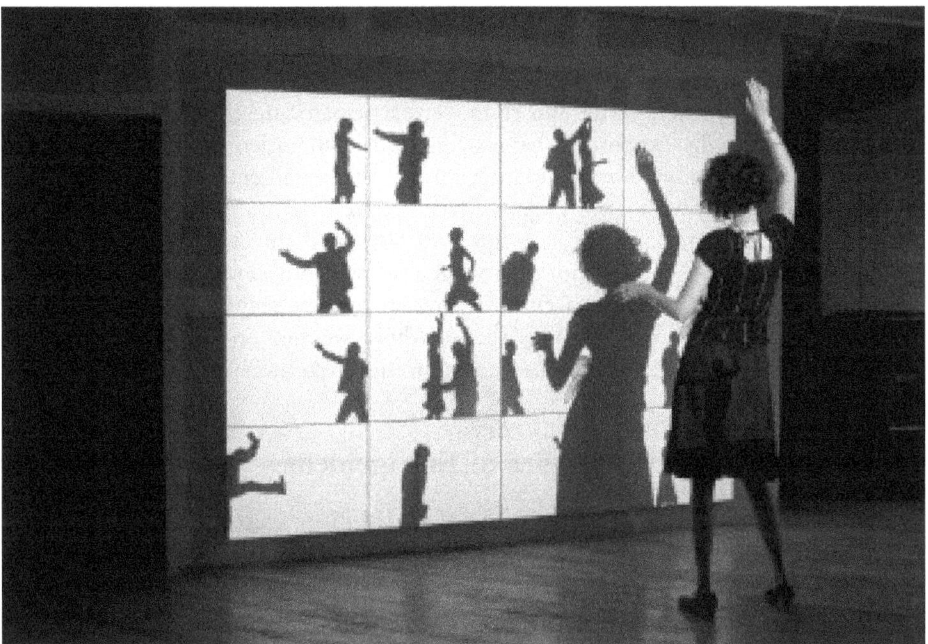

FIGURE 13.2 Scott Snibbe, *Deep Walls*. Interactive video installation. San Francisco Museum of Modern Art, 2002. *Source*: Scott Snibbe Studio.

might intimate iconic iPod advertisements with their stark silhouettes, or allude to graphic novels—but ones that can move through time and space. We see a complexity of narrative imagery that emerges in a mobile, physical, and non-linear fashion, as each individual interaction feeds into the whole, and into future performances. Some interactors glide past, others run or dance and shake their heads and tresses, still more try to work together within a frame and perform deeper meanings into the micro-narratives of a given square—which may or may not contribute to the whole in the ways they initially intended. Here the artifact of the screen is a small society made of embodied collaboration.

I am arguing that, given the open space of the gallery, the performances in Snibbe's work are always shared. Once the first audience member participates in *Shadow*, for example, we each watch the films by previous interactors before playing our own role, and then build on or respond to them; and we are fully aware that current and future gallery-goers will see and engage with the animations we ourselves leave behind. We interrupt an ongoing body film, and that interruption magnifies the productive transformation of both our bodies and the social structures (always) asking us to perform. The artifactual screen story is what we, as bodies, contribute to, relate with, and change, but it also informs what and how and why we contribute and interact. In our interaction, producing the work with our shadows, our body techniques are preconsciously aware of the cultural ways our shadow-movies might be read. We pass on traces of our bodies as part of an ongoing intercorporeal narrative.

This is most evident in *Deep Walls*. The grid of the screen encompasses many frames without itself having a frame (other than the live shadow body of the current player). As such, each frame extends into and is a part of the other, becomes an action and reaction and interaction as "with." The situation creates a partnering between body and screen (as a cultural artifact), body and bodies, body and society—all felt, in and with and as our bodies.

Deep Walls' performers move and re-move, participate and re-member, their own bodies along with the organizing, re-moving and re-membering bodies on screen. In *Deep Walls*, and Snibbe's work at large, we are creating an embodied and dynamic, relational community within our greater, collaborative community; we experience and practice the development of social reciprocity, with and through body and bodies. The artist asks us to encounter not only what a body is, but *how* it is, and how it is in relation to others, to society, to culture. And in this, he implicitly argues that we could—he in fact explicitly provides spaces where we can—rehearse different and perhaps better ways of performing our communities, together.

Strategies of Engagement

My accounts of Lozano-Hemmer's, Utterback's, and Snibbe's works differ greatly from the promises of interactivity declared by many "digital" advocates. Advertisements for new gadgets commonly tell us, for instance, that new media's individual activation, distinctive choice, unique preferences, and never-ending personalization are extremely desirable in our purchases. This language has dominated what digital and interactive products can and should provide, and what we as a consumer culture ostensibly want and even need. More specific to "interactivity," the usually ill-defined term has become a "catch-all phrase that is used to sell many new media technologies as an added bonus, or special element" (Fuery 2009, 27). Simple button clicks on toys and finite menus in our audio and video players are sold as more choices and thus more democratic and thus freer and inherently better, when in reality what many techno-gadgets have to offer is often less than underwhelming, and tied to proprietary media formats or specific streaming services. The notion that "interactive" (art or otherwise) offers more choice and possibilities, is intrinsically democratic and thus superior, is both counterproductive and false. We almost never find a product that actually does all the things or plays and streams all the files and services we want it to, and the first investigation of any given digital artwork is usually to find out how it works technically (Where is the sensor? What does it do?) and how we can circumvent its inner workings. Furthermore, consumer-based interaction between ubiquitous technologies on social media platforms has been marketed as virtually compulsory in the most powerful markets of youth culture. Sites like Facebook or Instagram are all but required by peers of all ages, and are the perfect places to advertise the aforementioned techno-gadgets.

The use of technologies and strategies for art need not mimic, and can in fact work against, the same principles employed for capital gain. Massumi reminds us that the "regulatory principles of the technical process in the narrow sense are utility and salability, profit-generating ability." Art, on the other hand, "claims the right to have no manifest utility, no use-value, and in many cases even no exchange-value. At its best, it has event-value" (Massumi 2011, 53). Art has a right to be "useless": to have unknown outcomes, or *no* outcomes—at least in the traditional sense. Game art, as one example, can both utilize and speak back to the über-marketable gaming console, linear narrative trajectories, violence, and goal orientation. It provides a very specific context for the interactor, and thus offers distinct possibilities for imaginative intervention into present-day capitalist regimes. Cory Arcangel's *Super Mario Clouds* (2002) is an exemplary work that challenges our understandings of games and their goals, Internet culture and what it tells and sells us, and our relationship to all of the aforementioned. A standard video game uses a joystick or other controller, the Kinect, or Wii to have us flail to compete—and focus is always on winning (and ending) the game itself. Arcangel takes the Nintendo Entertainment System's *Super Mario Brothers* (1985) and removes all of these elements. There are no protagonists or antagonists, no "good guys" or "bad guys." There is no controller. There are no rules or architectures. He modifies the original cartridge for the gaming system, so as to leave only slowly scrolling, pixilated clouds in a monochrome blue sky. And he shares his crack with fellow gamers, hackers, and artists online—just as gamers often share how to "beat" a game. *Super Mario Clouds* is less a game, however, and more a critical frame for encountering and challenging our relationships to game culture and industry.

Embodiment's relational emergence has also been co-opted as a point of valuable exploitation for profiteers. Many affect scholars, such as Nigel Thrift (2007), are arguing that the body's mutability has become a key resource for contemporary forms of capitalism, especially in the domains of the creative industry and digital culture. Contemporary discourses of creativity and innovation, particularly in the entertainment industry and its production of surplus value, rely on and hail a changing body that is capable of new contacts and sensations—and subsequently, experiences/ideas. Thus, a body's relation to dominant social forces is an ambivalent matter, one that must be approached by media artists with more care than that invested in the model used to sell mobile phones, tablets, and games. This has not always been and is still often not the case.

Contemporary curators Sarah Cook and Beryl Graham warn that many of their peers tend to use words that signal interactivity and connection "with the vague sense that they are 'good things,' but without any clear idea of the levels of engagement involved in each" (Cook and Graham 2010, 112). What are these levels of engagement, and what do we accomplish with them?

Activation. Pressing a button or a switch, or crossing a threshold, is a different (though not necessarily better) experience from looking, even given all that looking entails. Each is an act you can do, or not do, as a binary input that sets something in motion, for example, a video, a kinetic sculpture, or, in media theorist Kelli Fuery's example, a toy dog sold as "interactive!" that merely barks at you when turned on. The technical strategy of activation provides an easy way to conserve energy in a gallery space for the green-conscious, and in terms of viewer experience it is often deployed as a trigger that gives a minimal sense of authority and authorship—ironic or otherwise. *Navigation*, then, offers more engagement than activation. While still limited, there are a number of possible inputs and choices that can lead viewers in a multitude of predefined directions. A web site, DVD, or "Choose Your Own Adventure" book of interactive fiction are examples of navigable work. This strategy again is generally utilized to give an impression of command or choice, and sometimes a sense of exploration and possibility, while the artist or designer still maintains control of all possible outcomes. When combined with other artistic strategies, navigation can make for interesting sensory possibilities.

Pioneering artist David Rokeby's *Dark Matter* (2010) is an installation we navigate with our entire bodies, rather than using a simple mouse or remote control. He uses four infrared cameras from different angles, and a custom computer vision system, to cut up a darkened room into thousands of three-dimensional zones. A small selection of these zones have sound files associated with them: breaking ice or glass, creaking metal, falling rocks, the bursting of flame. As participants navigate the space, Rokeby's software senses that movement, and those zones with the most physical activity will trigger the audio clips associated with them across an eight-channel speaker system surrounding the interaction area. We slowly creep around the edges, tip toe or drag our feet, jump and dive to trigger or respond to his complex space and sounds. It is like an audio sculpture we are connected to, a part of, in tune with. Rokeby is an expert at creating responsive sonic environments, and this piece builds on his previous work with movement, sensation, and cross-modal perception. He frames a complete and complex analogical exploration, within a limited, digital frame. Although both the inputs and outcomes are numbered, the use of sensors that read variation (how *much* motion?), and the layering of sounds, make *Dark Matter* border on, if not a part of, the next level of engagement above navigation—what Cook and Graham call *reactive* or *responsive* environments (2010, 114), and what I define as *interactive* art.

The works of Lozano-Hemmer, Utterback, and Snibbe are also solid examples in this category. Each piece is more than a series of choices between a small range of inputs matched to a small number of outputs (a navigable work). Electronic sensors such as cameras and microphones are complex enough to pick up a range of motion, and the software of interactive artworks responds with more than a mere trigger or singular path (creating ongoing photographic, or painterly, or complex narrative compositions). And this encourages *styles* of movement. While the computer is always limited in its responses, which are programmed, there are limitless possibilities for how we investigate and create the space of that program's situation. The real potential—indeed the real challenge, Manning points out—is to keep the participants' attention on the quality of their own movements, rather than the response of the machine. Manning implores us to add nuance by making technology's "failures felt" through techniques such as lagging, system collapses, and a loss of ground (Manning 2009, 72). Manning's point needs repeating time and again to this day, but was made as early as the 1970s, by interactive arts pioneer Myron Kruger: "The visual responses should not be judged as art nor the sounds as music. The only aesthetic concern is the quality of the interaction" (Krueger 1977, 423–424). The "degree of physical involvement" is far more important than "illusion" or "3D scenery" (Krueger 1991, 4). Feedback loops or generative coding, layering of time-based forms, or multiple and proportional sensors can create ever more affective digital spaces that might highlight the body, interaction, performance, and relation, rather than technology and its coded replies.

Analogical reactive art—electronic or physical work that does not use computer-based algorithms—is slightly different from its digital counterpart in that it allows for unlimited input and unlimited output possibilities in its variation. I put digital and analogical reactive art in the same category because our experiences of either, at their best, are entirely parallel. As Manning eloquently puts it, although in a different context, making "the digital analog need not be the goal"—media art becomes "evocative when its techniques make transduction felt, foregrounding the metastability of all moving systems" (Manning 2009, 72). In a successful project, we do not just move *in* relation, we move *the* relation (Manning 2009, 64).

Although Lozano-Hemmer's installation utilizes a predefined sequence of images we trigger, he also has us create complex shapes in real time. Utterback's generative programming sees our movements initiate elaborate and layered, uncontrolled and collaborative paintings over time. And in Snibbe's work, we contribute a precise image of self, which then is only a small part of a continuous, communal engagement. Each is a suspended and amplified relation through interaction *with* a moving system that goes beyond the digital's preprogrammed responses.

Although it is not the colloquial definition of interactivity I follow for this chapter, what Cook and Graham call *interaction* means "acting upon each other"—where a computer or another person directly engages us, rather than merely responding to our movements. *Participation*, then, implies having a say; it requires viewers to contribute at least some of the content, and usually involves human-to-human relationships. In the digital art spectrum, this could easily include works that use social media platforms such as Facebook, Instagram, Vine or Twitter, networked games, or wikis. *Deep Walls* could be considered participatory in that we add our shadow-snippets to its database, as could Utterback's installations, where we leave traces of our interactions behind. Finally, *collaboration* means working directly with; the production of the piece sees a degree of equality between the participants, rather than small contributions of content. Collaboration generally takes place between artists, or artists and curators, since it is a reciprocal partnership (Cook and Graham 2010, 112–114). Interaction, participation, and collaboration have, of course, a longer history than electronic art.

Although the lines between many of the levels of engagement listed here can be blurred, they all—as critical tools, digital or otherwise—create situations in which our emergent relationships are highlighted. Their definitions, and what each achieves, are useful in thinking through the strategies for, and implications of, contemporary digital art. Here new media need not be singular in their position or oriented toward a goal, but have the potential to challenge and intervene in how we position, reposition, and proposition ourselves and our bodies in relation to other formations, both material and conceptual.

Interactive Futures

Interactive art is a frame for moving-thinking-feeling, an intensification of relations. With interactive art, an always-relational body is staged so as to suspend aspects of its own performance. Interactive art can concentrate and ask us to *feel* our existing practices as they are practiced, and provoke us to engage with what those practices imply. The goal is not to elicit specific behaviors or gestures, but to introduce us to techniques and approaches for encountering, understanding, and taking greater accountability with our continuous, relational performance.

The works discussed in this chapter focus mostly on the movement of the human body in an exhibition or public space. But the different forms of interactive art are vast. They make use of networked media and virtual worlds, social participation and generative coding, audiovisuals along with mechanical, tactile, or various multisensory outputs, analog or digital sensors, as well as many other new and old technologies and media in combination. In the gallery space, Danny Rozin's *Wooden Mirror* (1999), for example, creates real-time "video" of the people moving in front of it with motorized wood pixels that point toward or away from a light source. In a more private setting, Erwin Driessens and Maria Verstappen's *Tickle Salon* (2002) uses a combination of computer vision, tension sensors, motors, pulleys and rope to create a miniature robot that tickles our skin, while we lie on a massage table. Between virtual and actual, Scott Kildall and Victoria Scott's *No Matter* (2008) asks international participants to model "imaginary objects" such as the Holy Grail or Trojan horse in online, 3D communities, then makes real-world models of their virtual creations. Mark Hansen and Ben Rubin's *Listening Post* (2010) culls large pools of live data from Internet sources such as chat rooms, bulletin boards, and other public forums, and translates them into a huge, and physical, structure, as dozens of screens with scrolling text in a corporeal space. Christa Sommerer and Laurent Mignonneau's *A-volve* (1993–1994) is a virtual environment inhabited by artificial living creatures that are created by visitors, mating and reproducing, and open to outside influences: the "touch" of human interactors influences them in various ways. Lynn Hershman Leeson's *Difference Engine #3* (1995–1998) assigns virtual, 3D avatars to real-world visitors, and invites us to engage with surveillance, voyeurism, digital absorption, and the spiritual transformation of the body in technical times. Random International's *Rain Room* (2012) is a full downpour in a large installation space, where the droplets part to let you walk through them, completely dry. And *Eyewriter* (2009), by Zach Lieberman, James Powderly, Evan Roth, Chris Sugrue, TEMPT1, and Theo Watson, uses custom eye-tracking hard- and software to write and project real-time, digital graffiti with the movements of the participant's pupils. Graffiti artist and activist TEMPT1 is paralyzed and has control only over his eyes, and his work was given new life as he collaborated on the project. The artworks mentioned here are part research, part philosophy or critical theory, part activism, and *all* put into practice with activity, both human and otherwise. They all use different models of interaction that require close investigation.

Recently, the turn to what some call the "non-human," and what Erin Manning calls the "more than human," has led to a renewed interest in *indirect* interactive art, which does not rely solely on human interaction for its response. Interactive art, Manning reminds us, has a tendency to place humans "too quickly at the center of each experience" (Goodman and Manning 2012). Manning's *Weather Patterns* (2012; this iteration in collaboration with Bryan Cera, Andrew Goodman, and myself) uses electromagnetic sensors that pick up feedback from a large range of data in the environment, including radio signals, air currents, and all forms of movement—both living and otherwise. What the system senses is then transduced into both sounds and signals across more than fifty speakers in a large installation, and into variable movements of a hundred yards of hung fabric across the space—the latter swinging and swaying due to motors and fans that continuously turn on and off. In addition to the ongoing, shifting electromagnetism of the environment that all people (and art viewers) are a small part of, the sounds and movements of the installation itself also feed back into what it senses. This creates a complex system where relationality is amplified as always more than what we, as humans, do and perceive.

Interactive art's production, experience, practice, and analysis can also lead to new or different understandings of other forms of digital art. What I have called *potentialized art*, for example, is per-formed, or transformed, through some kind of technologically mediated process. In my own *Compressionism* series of prints (2005 and ongoing), for example, I strap a desktop scanner, laptop, and custom-made battery pack to my body, and "perform" images into existence. I might scan in straight, long lines across tables, tie the scanner around my neck and swing over flowers, do pogo-like gestures over bricks, or just follow the wind over water lilies in a pond. The dynamism between my body, technology, and the landscape is transformed into quirky renderings, which are then produced as archival digital prints. While not interactive by my own definition, such work invests in affect, relationality, and materialization in the process of its making and viewing. Here detail and abstraction exist as successive moments across the surface of the image—a result of my and the scanner beam's continuous movements in relation to their surroundings. These prints wrap the potentials of time and performance into their production, and we see and feel aspects of that potential in the final print—even if only on a two-dimensional and static plane. Like the frame of interactive art, here is a limitation that is also an amplification. Potentialized art promises more than can be delivered, and we move-think-feel with and in its "more than."

Although interactive installations follow and interweave several long, historical trajectories of art, performance, and electronic media, they are only now beginning to be understood within their category. Performance studies scholar Chris Salter's *Entangled: Technology and the Transformation of Performance* (2010), for example, looks at technology's ongoing influence on performance practices—including interactive environments—and vice versa. Art historian and practitioner Katja Kwastek's *Aesthetics of Interaction in Digital Art* (2013) defines and unpacks what new media accomplish surrounding real space and data space, temporal structures, instrumental and phenomenal perspectives, and the relationship between materiality and interpretability. And my own *Interactive Art and Embodiment: The Implicit Body as Performance* (2013) puts forward a discrete critical framework for encountering interactive art as a space for practicing philosophy, and proffers several in-depth case studies.

Taken together, contemporary arguments make clear that the stakes for digital and interactive art are paramount. Our bodies and media, our material and conceptual frames and selves, are always in process, and in relation. We are in a continuous flux of becoming, forever changing through what we do: how we move and are moved by and with the environment around us. The world and its forces of moving-thinking-feeling perpetually fold in on each other, simultaneously constituting and affecting various bodies of matter and concepts, humans and non-humans. Interactive art, at its very best, sets the stage for the experience and practice of that constitution. It teaches us to affect a doubled agency in how we take account of, engage with, and per-form our surroundings.

Note

1 This chapter both pulls from and builds on the author's book *Interactive Art and Embodiment: The Implicit Body as Performance* (2013). The texts are complementary in their approach to encountering and understanding interactive and digital art—as process-based intervention and embodied performance, respectively.

References

Cook, Sarah, and Beryl Graham. 2010. *Rethinking Curating: Art after New Media*. Cambridge, MA: Leonardo Books/The MIT Press.

Fuery, Kelli. 2009. *New Media: Culture and Image*. New York: Palgrave Macmillan.

Goodman, Andrew, and Erin Manning. 2012. "Entertaining the Environment: A Conversation." *The Fibreculture Journal* 21. http://twentyone.fibreculturejournal.org/fcj-152-entertaining-the-environment-a-conversation/ (accessed September 11, 2014).

Hansen, Mark B.N. 2006. *Bodies in Code: Interfaces with Digital Media*. New York: Routledge.

Hayles, N. Katherine. 1999. *How We Became Posthuman: Virtual Bodies in Cybernetics, Literature, and Informatics*. Chicago: University of Chicago Press.

Krueger, Myron. 1991. *Artificial Reality* II. Boston, MA: Addison-Wesley.

Krueger, Myron W. 1977. "Responsive Environments." *Proceedings of the June 13–16, 1977 National Computer Conference*, 423–433.

Kwastek, Katja. 2013. *Aesthetics of Interaction in Digital Art*. Cambridge, MA: The MIT Press.

Lozano-Hemmer, Rafael. 2001. "Body Movies: Relational Architecture 6." *Absolute Arts*. http://www.absolutearts.com/artsnews/2001/08/31/29058.html (accessed September 11, 2014.

Manning, Erin. 2009. *Relationscapes: Movement, Art, Philosophy*. Cambridge, MA: The MIT Press.

Massumi, Brian. 2011. *Semblance and Event: Activist Philosophy and the Occurrent Arts*. Cambridge, MA: MIT Press.

McQuaid, Cate. 2005. "Interactive Works Capture Interplay of Shadows, Light." *The Boston Globe*, June 24.

Salter, Chris. 2010. *Entangled: Technology and the Transformation of Performance*. Cambridge, MA: The MIT Press.

Simanowski, Roberto, and Scott Snibbe. 2006. "Useless Programs, Useful Programmers, and the Production of Social Interactive Artworks: Interview with Scott Snibbe." *Dichtung Digital*. http://www.dichtung-digital.org/2006/1-Snibbe.htm (accessed September 11, 2014).

Snibbe, Scott. 2003. "Body, Screen and Shadow." *San Francisco Media Arts Council (SMAC) Journal*.

Snibbe, Scott. 2005. *Compliant*. http://snibbe.com/scott/screen/compliant/index.html (accessed September 11, 2014).

Stern, Nathaniel. 2013. *Interactive Art and Embodiment: The Implicit Body as Performance*. London: Gylphi Limited.

Thrift, Nigel. 2007. *Non-Representational Theory: Space, Politics, Affect*. New York: Routledge.

Utterback, Camille. 2002. *External Measures 2001*. http://www.camilleutterback.com/externalmeasures.html (accessed September 11, 2014).

Utterback, Camille. 2004. *External Measures 2003*. http://www.camilleutterback.com/externalmeasures2003.html (accessed September 11, 2014).

Utterback, Camille. 2005. *Untitled 5. Camille Utterback*. http://www.camilleutterback.com/untitled5.html (accessed September 11, 2014).

Further Reading

Hayles, N. Katherine. 2002. "Flesh and Metal: Reconfiguring the Mindbody in Virtual Environments." *Configurations* 10: 297–320.

Jones, Caroline A, ed. 2006. *Sensorium: New Media Complexities for Embodied Experience*. Cambridge, MA: The MIT Press.

Massumi, Brian. 2002. *Parables for the Virtual: Movement, Affect, Sensation.* Durham, NC: Duke University Press.
Massumi, Brian. 2008. "The Thinking-Feeling of What Happens: A Semblance of a Conversation." *Inflexions* 1. http://www.senselab.ca/inflexions/htm/node/Massumi.html (accessed September 16, 2013).
Munster, Anna. 2011. *Materializing New Media: Embodiment in Information Aesthetics.* Hanover, MA: UPNE/Darmouth.
Rokeby, David. 2010. *Dark Matter.* http://www.davidrokeby.com/Dark_Matter.html (accessed September 16, 2013).
Scott, Andrea K. 2011. "Cory Arcangel Play Around with Technology." *The New Yorker.* http://www.newyorker.com/reporting/2011/05/30/110530fa_fact_scott (accessed September 16, 2013).
Shanken, Edward A. 2009. *Art and Electronic Media.* New York: Phaidon Press.

14

The Cultural Work of Public Interactives

Anne Balsamo

In this chapter I discuss the characteristics of public interactives as a category of digital media that has become an increasingly familiar part of urban environments. I reflect on the historical antecedents of this emergent media form as a context for discussing the interrelated nature of art and design in the creation of interactive media experiences. For all the variety of public interactives now available, my interest here is to develop a critical framework for assessing the cultural work of this media form. I offer a list of significant genres of public interactives to begin developing a set of terms for making sense of the cultural importance of these digital experiences.

Defining Public Interactives

Public interactives are technological devices that serve as the stage for digitally mediated communication with audiences in communal spaces such as museums, theme parks, trade shows, outdoor entertainment plazas, and urban streets. I use the term "public interactives" to name the broad category of mediated experiences that are now on offer in communal and public spaces. In order to unpack the cultural implications of the increasing proliferation of these technologically mediated experiences, I will begin by defining them according to three cultural dimensions:

- as an *art form* that evokes new experiences and perceptions through experiments with scale, mobility, built space, and modes of human engagement in public spaces;
- as a mode of *public communication* designed to engage people through the use of digital media in conversations for the purposes of information exchange, education, entertainment, and cultural reproduction;
- as a manifestation of multiform *pervasive computing*.

A Companion to Digital Art, First Edition. Edited by Christiane Paul.

My aim is to outline a framework for understanding public interactives for the purposes of developing nuanced critical approaches, new archival practices, and multidisciplinary educational programs that focus on the specificity of this emergent media form.[1]

Importance of History

For each of these dimensions—public interactives as art form, as mode of public communication, as type of pervasive computing—we could trace a rich lineage of historical antecedents that influence the aesthetics and design of contemporary experiences. For example, any history of public interactives would undoubtedly include references to important 20th-century art networks such as Fluxus; installation artists such as Joseph Beuys; media artists Nam June Paik, Kit Galloway and Sherrie Rabinowitz, Jenny Holzer, Jim Campbell, Michael Naimark, Jeffrey Shaw, Doug Aitken, Golan Levin; architects Charles and Ray Eames, Robert Venturi, Diller + Scofidio; media historians Erkki Huhtamo and Norman Klein; cultural venues such as Ars Electronica in Linz, ZKM in Karlsruhe, CASZuidas in Amsterdam, Times Square in New York; and historically significant events such as the annual SIGGRAPH conventions and the Festival Premier Contact organized by LeCube/Art3000 in France in 2005. In different ways, these cultural agents engaged the question of the changing nature of space in the media age by evoking novel experiences through the use of new technologies and the reconfiguration of built environments.

I approach the topic of public interactives and their aesthetics as a scholar of media, informed by the disagreements among theorists such as Marshall McLuhan, Raymond Williams, and Friedrich Kittler; the generative work of contemporary thinkers such as Lev Manovich, Janet Murray, and Brenda Laurel; and especially the speculative provocations of Bruce Sterling and Geert Lovink. A common thread among these writers is an appreciation for the *historical* development of specific forms of mediated experience. While they might conceptualize media in different ways, as "extensions of man" (McLuhan 1967) or as the technical infrastructure of human knowledge (Kittler 1990), they all assert the importance of understanding current media phenomena in the context of historical antecedents. In order to ask more nuanced questions about the significance of a new media form, we need to develop a theoretical frame that can make sense of the way in which public interactives *make sense*. Elaborations of historical antecedents are key to developing this framework; media theories organize analytical assessments of these antecedents. Raymond Williams, for example, uses the terms "residual," "dominant," and "emergent" to describe cultural formations; he argues that every historical moment is animated by the dynamic and contradictory relationships among these forms as they shift in cultural importance and influence.[2] Such terms serve as analytical props that help make sense of the complex nature of cultural regeneration and reproduction. Following this, I approach the understanding of contemporary public interactives as an *emergent* media formation that incorporates dominant and residual technological forms in novel ways that result in the simultaneous *reproduction* of the familiar and the traditional and the *reconfiguration of new* experiences, practices, and relationships among humans and material environments.

Because public interactives incorporate diverse technological devices such as large-scale displays, projection systems, audio systems, sensor networks, spectrum interfaces, and haptic controllers, the histories of ubiquitous computing and pervasive media also figure prominently in understanding the specificity of contemporary instances. These histories are themselves uneven works in progress; the evolution of a single device, such as the computer mouse, is better documented than the history of large-scale displays (which would certainly include non-digital installations such as the ceiling of the Sistine Chapel). When public interactives connect to virtual communication environments such as the World Wide Web, social media sites, and local and personal area networks—through the use of SMS, mobile media devices, and proximity sensors—the range of the technical antecedents expands even further. Given that many public interactives incorporate multimodal content, in the form of text, graphics, illustrations, images, animations, simulations, video, voice, sound, and audio, where each designed experience could also be situated within specific histories of the development of the aesthetics of different communication modalities, the task of detailing the relevant historical contexts of contemporary public interactives becomes an even more daunting project.

If the historical accounting is such an imposition, why belabor the issue of history in creating a framework for the critical analysis of public interactives (especially since I will do little to elaborate these histories in the space of this essay)? I raise this issue for reasons theoretical, pedagogical, and cultural. The term "public interactives" names both an abstract technology and a specific cultural form. As Williams might have argued, just like television and the book, public interactives are cultural technologies. They are platforms for the creation and reproduction of culture. Like all interactive applications, public interactives are, at one level, very simple constructions: organized routines of inputs, processes, and outputs. But this simple formulation does little to help us understand the way in which interactive experiences in public spaces manifest cultural value and perform cultural work. We need a more systematic approach to apprehend the way in which public interactives both replicate previous cultural arrangements and structure the possibility of new practices, habits, understandings, and aesthetics. This is why a historical grounding is important: understanding historical developments, contexts, and antecedents enables the identification of the values and characteristics of cultural arrangements that persist and those that are reconfigured.

Interactivity—as we know—is conversation. As interactive media, public interactives structure conversations among agents, some human, others technological, distributed in time and space, and connected through digital networks and embodied gestures. For as improvisational as the interactive experience is, every example of a "public interactive" includes a *designed* interface that serves to infrastructure the conversations among agents. Thus we must also understand the development of public interactives in the context of changing paradigms of human–computer interaction and experiments in the art of interface design. Like many design fields, the domain of interaction (and experience) design is a multidisciplinary plentitude. With roots in the field of software engineering, from its beginning the discipline of human–computer interaction called for increased attention to the *design* of the interface between human and machine. Brenda Laurel's edited volume, *The Art of Human–Computer Interface Design*, published in 1990, was an early effort to collect insights from design and technology experts to contribute to "the art of making computers easier to use" (Laurel 1990, xv). While the 1990 volume mostly included technologists from Apple Computer and computer scientists from large engineering institutes, Laurel posited that in the future "the designer of interactive systems will be a superdesigner with the skills of an engineer, an artist, and a psychologist" or, "[m]ore likely, a team of individuals who, like the playwright, director, actors, technicians, and scenery, light and costume designers in the theater, will contribute different skills to the realization of a common vision" (Laurel 1990, xiii). Indeed, this is exactly the scene that has unfolded in the twenty-five years since the publication of that book, as programs in interaction design were established in computer science programs and art and design schools. Parallel to the development of these programs was the expansion of interest among humanists in the creative possibilities of interactive media and the question of the design of the interface. The archive of hypertexts, electronic literature, video games, and the broad category of "new media" draw in an even wider set of disciplinary frameworks of analysis and creative influences that contribute to the history of public interactives.

Here then is the second reason for raising the need to document the multifaceted histories of public interactives: to augment the education of interaction designers across the disciplines. The design of public interactives, as Laurel might have predicted, engages distinct domains of expertise, not only the technical, but also the aesthetic and the social. Well before any choices are made about platforms or modes of display, the designer of public interactives must have a broad understanding of new media aesthetics and communicative vernaculars, the critical language of architecture, built space, and spatial practices, and the changing nature of sociality and the public within networked cultures. When the range of relevant cultural knowledge is so widely multidisciplinary, such as is the case with public interactives, it is absolutely necessary to provide students of the media form with an equally multidisciplinary set of histories, even though it may be challenging. These histories not only provide context for understanding what has already been tried out, but also give cues about questions that remain relevant or unexplored. What are the significant differences in embodied habits, modes of social engagement, and the experience of the built environment provoked by the use of networked technologies? Just as with the changes that accumulated through the proliferation of a *previous* ubiquitous technology, the alphabet, we will no doubt eventually become inured to the transformations occasioned by the ubiquity of computational media. Fascinating now, in this phase of emergence, are the animated conversations that debate issues of change and persistence. For every change that is announced, a counter-narrative highlights continuity.[3] This is more than a reassertion of the proverb, "the more things change, the more they stay the same"; it is a comment on divergence among approaches to understanding the relationships among culture and technology. Most debates continue to rehearse the tired argument between techno-determinism and technophilia; the more interesting approach, in my view, is to trace the simultaneous multiple and contradictory effects of the development and dissemination of public interactives.

The Cultural Impact of Public Interactives

Scott McQuire (2008) develops the idea of the media city as a frame for making sense of the transformation of public experience, as it moves from the street (the agora), to the domestic terminal (the television set and computer monitor), and then back to the streets of the contemporary city, enabled now by the use of mobile communication devices and the prevalence of display surfaces. As a hybrid complex, simultaneously physical and virtual, material and digital, the media city, as McQuire argues, provides the frame and foundation for the evolution of forms of social experiences and for the reconfiguration of notions of public space and private lives. One of the most significant events that gathered attention to the phenomenon of public interactives was the "Urban Screens" conference, first held in Amsterdam in 2005, and subsequently in Manchester (2007), Melbourne (2008), and Toronto (2010). The 2005 conference brought together researchers and practitioners to reflect on the meaning of the proliferation of dynamic "outdoor screens for urban society."[4] Among the long-term objectives for the Urban Screens initiative was the intention to broadly rethink the relationship between "architecture and public space in the digital age"; one of the key questions animating that first conference was: how is the presence of interactive dynamic screens in urban environments changing the nature of public space? Noting the increasing prevalence of dynamic digital displays and visual interfaces in urban environments used by corporate agents for purposes of advertising and brand marketing, the organizers of the conference asked participants to discuss the potential of urban screens to provide a space for a different sort of *cultural* content that addressed the civic and aesthetic interests of urban residents. Subsequent seminars and conferences identified three main "fields of action" where urban screens could be usefully deployed to revitalize public space to serve the public good:

1 Social participation: Urban screens as promoters of social responsibility and civic participation.
2 Data visualization: Urban screens as information emitters, constructors of critical thought, and places of collective memory.
3 Game and interaction: Urban screens as interactive devices, which promote social interaction and ludic experiences. (urbanscreens.org.)

These "fields of action" identify the *possible impact* of Urban Screen projects as promoting a specific quality of interactivity, one that promotes the public good in terms of civic participation, collective memory, and ludic (playful) interaction. These are important aims for the design of public interactives. Consider, for example, the effort by Creative Time called "The 59th Minute" that offered artists an opportunity to create video artworks for display on one of the large screens in Times Square. From 2000 to 2006, Creative Time invited artists to air their pieces during the last minute of every hour. What resulted was an oversized attempt to deterritorialize and reterritorialize Times Square—a hyper-commercialized public space typically flooded with cinematic advertisements aimed at throngs of anonymous *flâneurs* and bewildered tourists. The idea was to insert art into this hyper-commercialized landscape for the purposes of disturbing the spectacular performance of media capitalism. But as Julie Nevárez (2006) noted, the 59th Minute art moments were often lost in the visual excess of Times Squares Urban Screens. Instead of disrupting the commercial noise for a moment of cultural reflection, these video art minutes were seamlessly incorporated into the mediascape. She reasoned though, that:

> Even if what is advertised is not a good as such, video art screens might help sell the experience of the city as a representation of excitement, sophisticated taste

> that addresses the sensibilities of a professional class and tourists. Other kinds of contents, such as political, social, not-for-profit and/or community issues could also be part of the screen's content. (Nevárez 2006)

She goes on to suggest, rightly, that this promise of progressive public engagement wouldn't likely be realized without the broadcasting of a critical mass of such civic advertisements. It is probably more reasonable to understand that the design and deployment of public interactives, even those that aspire to contribute to the public good, will have multiple and contradictory impacts.

For every utopic possibility—that for example shows how urban screens can facilitate engaging conversations among inhabitants and a local place—other possibilities unfold as well. For instance, consider those who lament that the same technologies that promise public goods (such as mobile devices using wide area information networks) also serve to invigorate tribalism, rather than civic participation, to propagate data-based propaganda rather than commemoration and story sharing, and to enable pervasive surveillance of bodies in motion through urban streets.[5] The fact that these technologies have contradictory effects is unsurprising given the dynamics of cultural reproduction. As I have elaborated elsewhere (inspired by work by Donna Haraway and Marilyn Strathern), all technologies manifest the dual logic of reproduction:

> There is a doubled logic at the heart of all technological innovation [...] every technology replicates previous possibilities and makes new ones manifest [...] This is how technologies can logically manifest multiple and contradictory effects. To embrace this understanding is to forgo the metaphysical debates that posit technology as either fully autonomous and completely determining, or a mere tool in the hands of a human operator. (Balsamo 2011, 10)

Urban screens and, by extension, public interactives are significant elements of the transformation of public spaces because they inform and infrastructure the program and possibilities of social interaction among members of the public who inhabit and move through urban environments. But for all the possibilities that they manifest, they also *replicate and reinforce* previous cultural understandings and frameworks of symbolic meaning-making. This dual logic of reproduction—replication of the previous and the expression of the new—is foundational across cultural reproductive practices. Identifying which elements (myths, habits, or ideologies) are replicated and which (memes, practices, and logics) are new and novel is the first step in describing the cultural impact of public interactives.

The Art and Design of Public Interactives

Public interactives are complexly *designed* media systems—an *assemblage* of diverse elements that include physical materials, visual codes, spectrum frequencies, sonic vibrations, digital content management systems, discursive descriptors (metadata tags), textual accounts (instructions, stories, memories, recollections), individual human agents, social collectives (audiences, communities of interest, people in public spaces), technical routines, literacy practices, modes of interactivity, programming languages, digital applications, hardware platforms, and social protocols that scaffold experience. The key *functional* components of public interactive assemblages include:

- a digital media-rich application;
- a networked architecture that connects internal elements with external elements;
- an address within an "Internet of things";
- a designed communicative experience;
- a physical display form; and
- a mode of address that targets specific users.

These lists are incomplete, of course, but serve to underscore my point that the construction and implementation of a public interactive involves the *design* of a complex system of interrelated elements.[6] Having said that, I note that, although an account of the semantics of the form or the functional elements of a public interactive can serve the aims of the multidisciplinarily trained designer, the *meaning* of a public interactive coheres when users connect the elements to forge associations among them. Intended users, be they art audiences, tourists, customers, players, citizens, or some other manner of participant, always engage with public interactives in a *context* that serves to organize the sense of the experience. Here is where the multiple histories of public art, of mediated communication, and the technological augmentation of public space contribute to the understanding of the cultural meaning of contemporary public interactives. Here, too, is the point at which the traditional distinction between art and design, or between matters of aesthetics and matters of meaning, break down.

All public interactives—and all digital art forms, for that matter—involve the creation of an interface between humans and technologies. Interfaces facilitate the conversation that is "interaction" by organizing inputs and outputs and managing the communication processes. "Look and feel" is the term that describes the aesthetic or the art of the interface; it is one of the key characteristics by which public interactives make sense to human users. The phrase "look and feel" is said to have originated with the development of systematic approaches to graphic user interfaces, but it was actually used as early as 1987 to describe the lawsuits initiated by Lotus Software over the copying of the characteristics of its Lotus 1-2-3 spreadsheet application. This term is a target site for the discussion of the intertwining of art and design in interactive experiences. To draw out the connections between the *design* of public interactives and the *aesthetics* of this interactive form, I suggest we revisit the work of information designers Charles and Ray Eames who helped clarify and expand our thinking about information, text, and technology such that we could no longer simply separate context (information, text) and technological form (graphic design and display platform).[7] In addition to their architectural portfolio, the Eameses developed some of the first interactive hands-on science exhibitions. In their large-scale exhibit *Mathematica: The World of Numbers and Beyond* (1961), they established several conventions for interactive experiences that continue to guide the art of the form.[8] The historical timeline at the center of the *Mathematica* exhibit—that documents a 1000-year history of the development of mathematics—demonstrated the art of architecting media space; the individual demonstrations of the basic principles of numbers, such as the Mobius Band and the Multiplication Machine, established conventions about the use of high-end materials (rich woods, polished metals), a single button to enable direct user activation, transparent walls that enable users to watch the mechanism of dynamic processes, and the simple mode of explanation that related complex mathematical processes to everyday experiences. The choice of materials, the creation of mechanical demonstrations, the carefully architected layout of timelines, models, and didactic material served to scaffold the learning experience. These designerly choices also conveyed rich aesthetic qualities that appealed to viewers' senses of touch, sight, and sound. Well before the phrase "look and feel" became part of the popular vernacular, the Eameses demonstrated how the careful design of an interface system's ensemble of elements contributed to the creation of an aesthetic user experience.

The Eameses created exhibits for science and technology museums, which were among the first cultural institutions to embrace the use of interactive experiences in the service of their missions to provide informal education to the public about the importance of science and technology. From the earliest use of dioramas in natural history museums and representational paintings and illustrations in science taxonomic collections, the display of the wonders of science and technology often involved artists working in collaboration with museum exhibit designers. For the museums devoted to collections of curiosities, the art of display mimics the array of scientific specimens, an aesthetic that propped up the power and class sensibilities of wealthy collectors. As Tony Bennett (1995) elaborates, these early specialist museums restricted access to elite audiences who understood, because of shared class training, the proper decorum to display in public spaces. For the museums that emerged from the 19th-century Great Exhibitions created to showcase the wonders of the Industrial Revolution—such as the Crystal Palace in London, the Museum of Science and Industry in Chicago, and (we might add) the Deutsches Museum in Munich—a slightly different "aesthetics of the visible" informed the design and development of public exhibits. This aesthetic approach not only structured the presentation of amazing machines (taken out of their industrial context and put on display for the edification of citizens across class distinctions), but also governed the layout of the museum space itself, such that museum visitors themselves were on display, able to be seen as a "mass" from different architectural vantage points (Bennett 1995). Dean MacCannell (1976) notes that the aesthetic of the visible whereby the infrastructures of modern society were transformed into a spectacle for contemplation and wonder also contributed to the creation of "the tourist" as a modern urban subject. I could go on to discuss other historical examples of the aesthetics of display and of presentation that were deeply imbricated in the design of exhibition contexts.[9] My point here is simply to argue that in the case of public interactives, there is no sense in separating the art of the interface from the design of the meaning of the experience.

Genres of Public Interactives

Analyzing collections of historical examples yields insight into patterns of structural elements, semiotic codes, expressive conventions, and institutional contexts; from these histories we can begin to identify significant genres of public interactives. While any classification system is fraught with limitations because the uniqueness of any specific instance is often elided in the attempt to generalize the pattern, the use of a genre approach to the study of public interactives serves as a first step in organizing the widely disparate antecedents and the wild proliferation of interactive experiences.

Like genres of literature (science fiction, historical romance), genres of public interactives are definable by key traits that describe the category of public interactives:

1 *Material aesthetics*: Includes reference to the orientation of screens, input mechanisms, scale of display, and qualities of the built form.
2 *Mode of interaction*: Description of opportunities for interaction between humans and media devices; also refers to the logic of digital media: spatial, procedural, encyclopedic, participatory.[10]
3 *Modalities of experience*: Description of how the interactive appeals to embodied senses, the temporality/duration of encounter, intensity of engagement, and affective impact.[11]
4 *Phantasms of the public*: Determined by mode of address and the idealized figuration of the user as citizen, consumer, tourist, audience, member of the public or as anonymous, individuated, or member of a mass, crowd, or collective.

To fully elaborate the characteristics of each genre would include an account of the cross-domain antecedents of each type of public interactive as well as the critical responses that analyze the cultural implications of the interactive. While that level of analysis is beyond the scope of this chapter, it is possible to begin the process of identifying broad categories of public interactives so as to establish a set of terms and analytical parameters for understanding the cultural significance and impact of this emergent media form. The pragmatic aim is to identify the terms that we might use to "tag" the significance of diverse cultural media experiences, events, and installations. The following list is more taxonomic than typological in that it reflects groupings of public interactives in the wild, identified here by terms created by public artists, media historians, and scholars who study urban screens. This list includes examples from different historical channels, including instances of public art, guerrilla installations, industry commissions, commercial product demonstrations, cultural events. While the aims and objectives for the creation of works of public art may be quite different than those of a product demonstration, they share qualities (the design of the interface or the design of the interactive experience) that begin to define the aesthetics of pubic interactives. I developed the term "public interactive" to describe this emergent cultural form because in so many cases it is difficult to distinguish the specific qualities that make one thing a work of art and something else a commercial product. The public art pieces I refer to below (as examples of different categories) often incorporate cutting-edge engineering and expert media programming. Conversely, the commercial efforts incorporate the experiential design of prior media art. Rather than debate where to draw the line, I suggest a slightly different approach that focuses on the cultural analysis of the many instances of public interactives. Consider then the creation of this taxonomy as a work of cultural analytics. It is one phase of a broader project of collection, curation, tagging, and archiving of public interactives.

Dimensional Dioramas: Hybrid Billboards

Increasingly familiar in major metropolitan areas throughout the globe, living billboards incorporate dimensional media elements. Sometimes these signs incorporate live materials such as foliage and flowers, or other forms of three-dimensional media such as a cutout or bench. They are also used in reference to "human directionals," the improvised performances by individuals holding signs, arrows, and placards on streets corners to attract attention to nearby businesses.

Examples

In 2013 Ikea created a bathroom display showroom on an elevated platform above a Paris street that featured a model using the facilities, doing (most) things one would do in a domestic bathroom. Like the displays of rooms in its massively sprawling stores, this living diorama served to promote the full range of Ikea products for a functional and stylish bathroom.[12]

The marketing company Ogilvy & Mather France created a "living billboard" advertising campaign to announce the launch of IBM's project called "People for Smarter Cities." The campaign featured three different three-dimensional billboards: one that incorporated a bench, another one that curved over the sidewalk to provide a rain shelter, and a third that provided a ramp over a set of shallow stairs.[13]

Urban Screens: Public Space Broadcasting

Large televisual screens installed individually or in arrays on sides of buildings enable the dissemination of dynamic time-based media content. As an example of the broad category of "urban screens," these public interactives offer limited capacity for audience input. One of the simplest variations is the variable-message sign that displays information about traffic conditions and weather related travel alerts.

Examples

In 1996, the United States created a distributed emergency notification system called AMBER (America's Missing: Broadcast Emergency Response) to quickly disseminate information about abducted children. One of the key elements of the AMBER media system is the use of electronic traffic-condition billboards.[14]

The BBC (British Broadcasting Company) launched the "Public Space Broadcasting" project in 2003 to locate large screens in outdoor venues in urban centers throughout the United Kingdom to bring local televisual and live programming to public audiences.[15] The Bigger Picture, an experimental use of the public space broadcasting screen located in Manchester, England exhibited art-based films, videos, and interactive events.[16]

Projection Bombing: Large Format Projections

Using powerful image projectors to display images on large-format surfaces such as screens and building facades, this category of public interactives includes many examples of public art installations, some specially commissioned for festivals and by local cultural venues. The Graffiti Research Lab uses the term "projection bombing" to describe guerilla art actions in which projected animations interact with the surfaces of buildings.[17]

Examples

In 2007 Doug Aitken presented *Sleepwalkers*, a multiscreen project that consisted of five interlocking short films featuring performances by Tilda Swinton, Donald Sutherland, and others. The films were projected onto eight exterior walls of the Museum of Modern Art in New York. On display for twenty-eight days, the piece transformed the streets around the museum into a walk-by cinema.[18]

The public art installation *A Show of Hands* by Ed Purver enabled members of the public to submit messages that were translated into American Sign Language; images of hands signing the message were projected on the building facade. Like other works of large-format projection, this piece choreographed the display of video elements in relation to elements of the building such that large arms appeared to be emerging from windows.[19]

Animated Facades: Buildings as Instruments

With the development of wireless sensor nets and distributed control systems, buildings can now incorporate a range of electronic devices that enable communication between systems (mechanical, security) as well as between the building and the inhabitants. With the installation of networked media devices that trigger sound, light, or visual display, a building can be transformed into an instrument of expression.

Examples

The *Blinkenlights* (2001) project is one of the earliest examples of an urban screen that enabled members of the public to interact with the building facade. The side of the *Haus des Lehrers* in Berlin was transformed into large-scale display; lights in the windows of the building were instrumented such that the building displayed a matrix of oversized pixels that could be controlled by users on the ground to create (pixelated) animations. In the evening, pre-loaded animations played on the display. Using a mobile phone, users could also play Pong or send love letters.[20]

The building that houses the Ars Electronica Center in Linz, Austria, is wrapped in a glass facade that consists of several hundred windows that can be illuminated with colored LED lights. Each LED panel can be individually controlled such that the facade of the building can be programmed to provide a dynamic light show. A docking station installed on the outside of the building enables a visitor to use a music player or smartphone to program a light show to accompany a musical playlist.[21]

Interactive Buildings: Responsive Environments

Myron Krueger, a pioneer in the creation of artificial reality systems in the mid-1960s, was one of the first to predict the transformation of architecture such that the design of "future buildings and the appearance of existing ones could be affected dramatically by responsive technologies" (Krueger 1991, 252). Responsive environments make use of networks of sensors and embedded media devices to create an immersive space that responds to the presence and movement of people and other inhabitants throughout the space. Functional responsiveness that regulates temperature or lighting conditions serves ecological objectives. Expressive responsiveness enables a conversation between inhabitants and building.

Examples

The art/design firm Electroland (Damon Seeley and Cameron McNall) has created several interactive walkways in pedestrian areas at airports and urban buildings. In a pedestrian bridge at Indianapolis International Airport, LEDs are embedded in the ceiling; sensors detect the movement of people across the surface, triggering different light patterns and sounds. The greater the number of people using the walkway, the more lights and sounds are projected, providing travelers with a celebratory display. At a breezeway next to a Target department store in New York, the walls and ceilings have embedded LED lights that respond to shoppers' movements through the space.[22]

The Band on the Wall is a legendary music venue in Manchester, England, that sports a large graphic sound equalizer installed on the rooftop of the building. Created by artists Michael Trainor and Lee Donnelly, the *EQ* graphically represents sounds from inside the venue or noises from the outside street as a light display that flickers and jumps like the visual displays on 1980s music blasters. Pedestrians and passing car passengers can "see" what is playing inside the music hall.[23]

Social Cinema: Relational Architecture

Artist Rafael Lozano-Hemmer uses the term "relational architecture" to describe a social space of layered and hyperlinked cinematic elements configured for display within a specific public architectural space. Active participation by people "on the street" constitutes the dynamic experience of the space and animates the unfolding of story. The design of these public interactives encourages people to contemplate the nature of digitally augmented relationality that is not simply about accessing information from digital networks, but rather about engaging in embodied conversations with others in a specific context.

Examples

One of Lozano-Hemmer's widely known works, *Body Movies* (originally created in 2001 and discussed in depth in Nathaniel Stern's chapter in this section), consists of large-scale photographic portraits projected onto a building facade that are only visible when a pedestrian casts a shadow onto the wall by walking in front of a powerful light source (Figure 14.1). When the collection of photographs has been entirely revealed through the shadows, a video tracking system prompts the display of new portraits.[24]

The public art installation *SPECFLIC* created by Adriene Jenik in 2006 is an example of a new storytelling form that she calls distributed social cinema. In this piece, audience members are invited to interact through the use of mobile devices, such as cell phones, audio players, and laptops, with the live telematic materials projected onto a building facade. The result is a multimodal immersive event that involves street performers, audience members, and prerecorded media elements.[25]

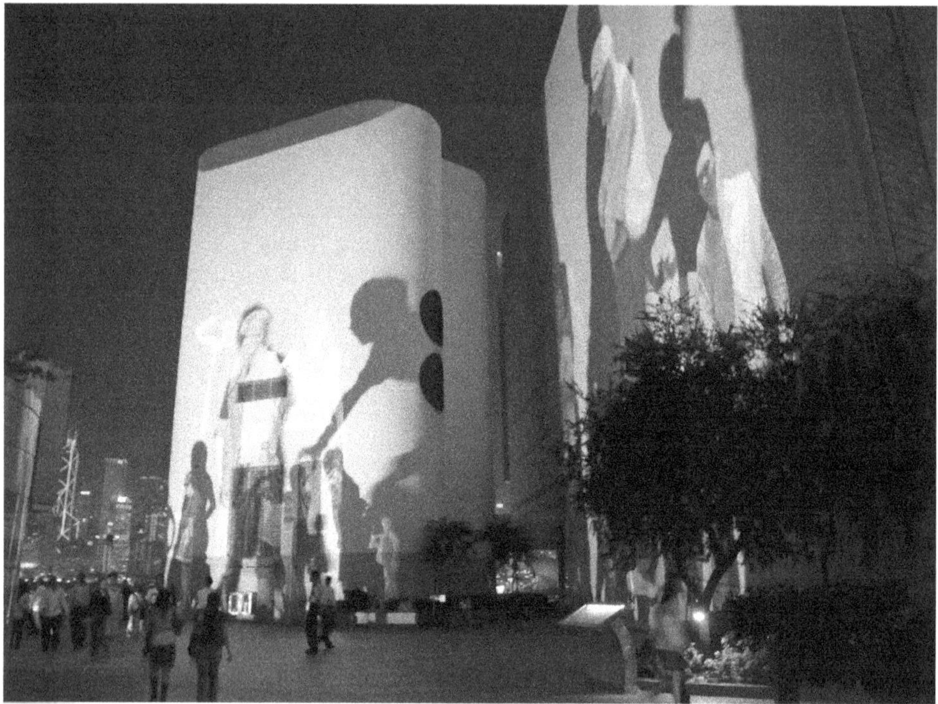

FIGURE 14.1 Rafael Lozano-Hemmer, *Body Movies, Relational Architecture 6*, 2001. Shown here: Hong Kong, China, 2006. Photo: Antimodular Research.

Pervasive Advertising: Interactive Billboards

The term "pervasive advertising" is a concept developed by Jörg Müller and his colleagues to describe how ubiquitous computing will impact the future of advertising and marketing. Interactive shop windows, dynamic bus stop walls, and floor projections are activated by bodily movements such as writing, touch, steps, or proximity, or through the use of ubiquitous interfaces such as smartphones, key fobs, MP3 players, or other forms of wearable devices. The aim of these new forms of advertising is to engage the potential consumer in an experience with the brand or commodity.

Examples

Interactive billboards announcing the launch of the US television show *Person of Interest* staged a simulation of a citizen surveillance experience. Disguised as mirrors that animate when approached by a pedestrian, the billboard notifies the observer that they are a person of interest. A photo is taken and displayed on the screen along with a phone number and an identification number. The participant is encouraged to text their identification number to the provided contact info. If they comply, they are then given the opportunity to access a classified file and post their photo to Facebook or Twitter. In addition to these privacy-invading billboards, people who have "liked" the *Person of Interest* fan page on Facebook can retrieve a personalized dossier that collects your friends' specs, photos, and posts from within the web site.[26]

- An advertising campaign displayed at bus stops in England promoted a self-tanning product by Johnson and Johnson (2008). The ad presents an image of an attractive woman lounging in a bikini. Next to the image is a knob that enables a viewer to shift the tone of the bronze color of her skin. The tagline reads, "You can have the tan you want. Choose yours."

Pedestrian Playgrounds: Walk-Up Games

I use the term "walk-up games" to label the type of ludic experience that occurs in pedestrian contexts such as outdoor streets, theme parks, museums, and cultural entertainment spaces. Game experiences are short in duration and the system does not maintain any persistent record of game play. Unlike casual games, walk-up games are not intended to engage a mass of players at a single time, but rather to engage people in a themed experience within a large context or story world (theme park, entertainment venue, or museum). Advertisers are using walk-up games to promote brand awareness. Playground designers are exploring the use of game mechanics in interactive equipment.

Examples

The company Reactrix Systems builds advertising campaigns that project game fields on floors in public spaces, including a soccer game for Adidas and a virtual race track for Hilton Hotels.[27]

An exhibit by Snibbe Interactives called *InfoTiles* (2011) allows people to browse large amounts of information on an interactive wall in a playful social game. Using their hands or body, people move a virtual frame or object (selector) over a projected grid of tiles with still images or other content. When they rest the selector over a tile, it turns over and reveals video, images, and text. By making information browsing a game, people are engaged and excited to explore all the information, whether in a museum, a theme park, a trade show, or retail.[28]

Walkthrough IMAX: Immersive Cinema

Digital technologies such as 360° video recording, multiple screens, and 4D sound provide a spatialized cinematic experience. Dome-based projection environments, such as those in planetariums, incorporate multiple projectors and mirrors to create a seamless spatial-acoustic image space.

Examples

R+J (Romeo and Juliet) was the first immersive cinema live action movie created by LivinGlobe, a film production company that creates dome theater features. *R+J* was the first film dome film to use live action in addition to computer-generated sequences. The film premiered to the public at the Exploration Place in Kansas in 2004.[29]

The main attraction at the Saudi Arabian Pavilion at the 2010 Shanghai World Expo was a work of immersive cinema called *The Treasure*. The firm Sky-Skan Europe created the world's largest parabolic walk-through 3D cinematic experience. An array of twenty-five projectors creates a 35 million-pixel screen that measures

1600 square meters (17,000 square feet). The pavilion called "The Moon Boat" was donated to China by the Saudi Arabian government in November 2011 to celebrate twenty years of Chinese–Saudi diplomatic ties.[30]

Tangible Story Platforms: Interactive Surfaces

Interactive exhibits enable multi-person face-to-face conversations in social settings. Drawing heavily on research in tangible interaction, interactive exhibits often make use of gesture-based interfaces. In the early discussions about ubiquitous computing, the use of tabletop display surfaces was considered a "natural form" for embedding computational responsiveness when the vertically positioned desktop computer would no longer be a prominent aspect of the interactive form. Currently there are two primary modalities of interacting with horizontal surfaces: either through touch or through the use of tangible objects. As they are generally conceived, tangible interfaces provide the user with a set of physical objects that interact with a responsive surface. There is some evidence to suggest that tangible interfaces make use of "natural understandings" of the world by taking advantage of a user's familiarity with the functions of everyday objects (Lucchi et al. 2010).

Examples

Onomy Labs created the GeoConnecTable that enables a viewer to explore images of the earth by tilting the tabletop, providing an experience of flying over the globe. Twisting the tabletop enables a user to zoom among different viewing altitudes, ranging from an altitude of 250 miles to ground level. Viewers can swipe a driver's license to direct the image on the table to center on their house. Installed in venues such as science museums, technology briefing centers, and urban planning showrooms, the GeoConnecTable is an example of an interactive exhibit that explores the design of "natural user interfaces."

The Bob Graham Center's *Civil Debate Wall*—popularly known as *The Wall*—is a series of connected touch-screen devices that enables students, teachers, and citizens to share ideas and solutions to pressing political questions facing the nation. Installed in 2012 at the University of Florida, *The Wall* operates in real time and can be synchronized to smartphones and its own web site. *The Wall* encourages users to post their opinions or join an existing debate on questions that deal with the economy, politics, and domestic and foreign policy. The idea is to engage citizens on important civic questions. A backend application sifts through the keywords of postings to create a dynamic data visualization to show where agreement lies.[31]

Digital Memorials: Cultural Memory Sites

The design of digital memorials explores the possibilities provided by digital media to augment personal memories, collective cultural memory, and the presentation of cultural heritage experiences. By creating a stage for contemplation and reflection, digital memorials explore the design of architectures for public intimacy. One variation uses QR codes on plaques attached to grave markers. Cultural heritage sites make use of a range of interactive platforms to augment the presentation and recreation of significant cultural histories and stories.

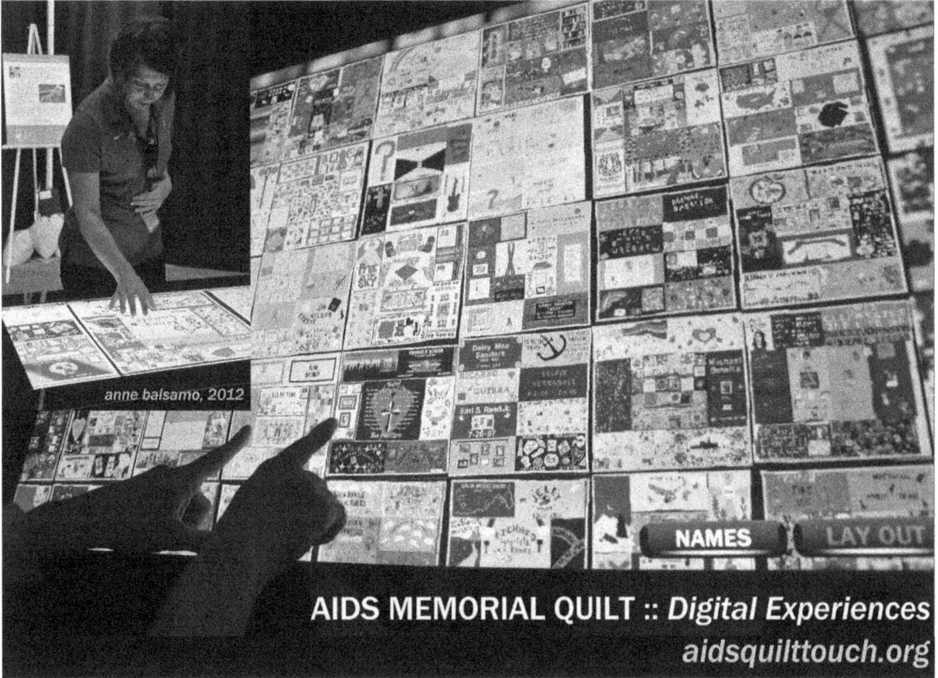

FIGURE 14.2 The AIDS Quilt Touch Table created by Anne Balsamo and Dale MacDonald, in collaboration with the LADS research team at Brown University, 2012.

Examples

The AIDS Quilt Touch Table is an example of a cultural technology that is designed to augment practices of cultural reproduction and historical remembrance. It combines a physical, tangible interface with an interactive digital application that makes available an archive of cultural memories in the form of digital images of textile memorials dedicated to people who died during the first three decades of the AIDS epidemic in the United States and throughout the world (Figure 14.2).[32]

The Prospect Hill Cemetery in York, Pennsylvania, has a digital memorial dedicated to Fallen Heroes. The 46″ touch screen-based digital sign honors the more than 6600 soldiers killed in the Iraq and Afghanistan wars by rotating through pictures submitted by families of the deceased. The pictures range from birthday celebrations to holiday get-togethers and ski trips, allowing visitors to view the more personal side of these heroes.[33]

Conclusion: Augmented Public Spaces, Experience Design, and the Technological Literacies of the Future

Malcolm McCullough, an architectural theorist who has done the most significant work on the intersections of architecture, interactivity, urban media landscapes, and design, asks one of the most trenchant questions about the nature of public space: "Who has the right to mark up the city?" (McCullough 2008, 61–72) The history of epigraphic inscription—the carvings in stone and writing on walls—documents how built environments were marked and augmented to serve both dominant cultural purposes (the account of great wars) and subversive ones (contestations of power). Walls are an ancient technology of culture; learning to read the writing on the wall was a pedagogical mode of enculturation. The examples of public interactives I discuss in this chapter are epigraphic in nature and address the critical question raised by McCullough. Regardless of how we think about the contemporary city—as the electronic city, the media city, the open city, the information city, the optimal city, the smart city, the affective city, the cognitive city, the computer city—the question remains: Who has the right and the *means* to author the city? Public interactives are inscription technologies that augment the multiple layers of meaning already on offer and in play in these urban ecologies.

Experience design methods assert that participation has to be "scaffolded." Scaffolding is the currently used term for a phenomenon that classic behavioral psychologists once would have referred to as "successive approximation." The basic idea remains the same when used in the context of designing an interactive digital experience: the desired (end) interaction is successively shaped over time as the user of the application encounters structured activities that incrementally build on initial behaviors that are "shaped" into more complex actions. The objective for the development of the social protocols embedded within public interactives is to scaffold experience through the presentation of a series of well-designed, and increasingly complex, activities. Initial encounters—motivated by curiosity or personal interest—are rewarded and meaningfully broadened. Just as experience develops through the use of a well-designed public interactive, repeated exposure to interactive opportunities in public spaces creates long-lasting experiences. Even though the actual encounter might be fleeting in time, over time these experiences accumulate. They result in the development of new literacies of technological engagement and new ways of knowing the world.

Public interactives draw on existing technological literacies to engage users and, in so doing, these devices serve as stages for the shaping of literacies of the future. The metaphysical question facing artists and designers of public interactives is, how does one design for audiences (and their literacies) that don't yet exist? How does an artist or designer design new technologies that require skills (literacies) that are not yet common? Interface literacies are probably the most obvious set of skills taught by public interactives because they provide viewers with opportunities to explore the use of gesture and smartphones—familiar devices—in novel ways. Artists and designers rely on the fact that people understand cinematic conventions of the animated image and the symbolism of dynamic text. Even with those public interactives that deploy unconventional information aesthetics, creators must build sense-making bridges from the familiar to the unconventional. In reinforcing a user's literacy, the artist acknowledges them as a member of a particular social group: the technologically literate. This is an example of the doubled nature of technology as simultaneously replicative and expressive; it is also an example of how the process of technological designing always involves the reproduction of techno-cultural understandings. All interactions with new technologies both replicate previous understandings and express new possibilities. This is how new technological literacies are shaped. The cultural literacies on offer are equally important. Public interactives invite users to follow the flow of story across media forms (image, text, sound, animation, multiple screens); they require people to learn how to navigate large-scale story worlds that are never "contained" in the device, but rather envelop the entire spatial environment. For whatever other purpose they serve, as way-finding platforms, broadcast surfaces, or entertaining diversions, public interactives play a significant role in the creation of a common culture and the inspiration of the technological imagination of members of the public.

Notes

1 This chapter draws on research I have conducted over several years to identify "interactives in the wild." This investigation took place at locations throughout the United States, at the 2010 Shanghai World Expo, and through onsite and online visits to institutions such as Ars Electronica and the Institute for Network Cultures.

2 Raymond Williams used the terms "residual," "emergent," and "dominant" to identify cultural forms so as to destabilize the fixity of such forms by adding a temporal dimension to the idea of a form. He noted that structural accounts of culture often referred to formations as if they were fixed in place, shape, and time (i.e., capitalism or television). He argued instead that culture is comprised of formations that are always in dynamic relation of emerging and decomposing, of coming into being and receding in importance. Used in reference to media, the three terms are meant to focus attention on the ways in which forms exist simultaneously in different temporalities.

3 For example, everyone "knows" that mobile phones and social networks expand our communication reach, enabling contact with a mass of friends. But having mass friendship networks (apparently) does not change our social signatures: we remain bound (in most frequent contact) to a relatively small number of close friends and family as core members of our social networks. This report on research coming from Oxford University and published by the National Academy of Sciences suggests that the size of people's closest friendship circles—defined by those people who are most frequently contacted—remains consistent and relatively small regardless of the total quantity of contacts (amassed as phone numbers, friends, or followers on social networks). http://www.independent.co.uk/life-style/gadgets-and-tech/news/despite-social-networks-like-facebook-and-twitter-most-people-will-only-ever-have-a-handful-of-good-friends-9042188.html (accessed January 8, 2014).

4 The first "Urban Screens" conference, held in Amsterdam in 2005, was organized by the Institute of Network Cultures (Netherlands), the Department of Art and Public Space (University of Amsterdam), and Urban Research (Berlin). The conference grew out of research conducted by Mirjam Struppek on the role of screens in urban environments. By 2008, when the third "Urban Screens" conference was held in Melbourne, the initiative had evolved into the International Urban Screens Association. The web site for the IUSA has not been updated since 2011.

5 See, for example, several essays in the collection edited by Alessandro Aurigi and Fiorella De Cindio, *Augmented Urban Spaces: Articulating the Physical and Electronic City* (2008).

6 Daniel Michelis publishes on pervasive advertising and the dynamics of interactive displays in public spaces. His work describes the key elements of an interactive display

system in terms such as screen size, screen direction, number of screens, screen content, user position, interactive zone, and interactive mode (Michelis 2009). Michelis co-authored a paper (Müller et al. 2010) that develops a taxonomy of public display installations that organizes types according to interaction modalities, mental models, and type of interaction. They identify four genres of interactive display: poster, window, mirror, and overlay.

7 Kate Hayles and Jerome McGann are also important here. McGann argues for the use of the term "textspace" to signify the notion that a textual work is a topological space whose dimensionality is mapped through the process of reading. Textspaces are constituted by histories of rules of structure; marked by these rules, a textspace is always an interpreted text comprised of both semantic and graphic elements (the spatiality of textspace) (McGann 2000). Hayles (2002) uses the term "technotext" to foreground the way in which all texts are technological manifestations. Reading is the process of engaging in the interrogation of the inscription technology, where the technotext evokes the oscillation between considerations of the imaginary world (on offer) and the material conditions of the presentation apparatus.

8 The *Mathematica* exhibit was originally created for the California Museum of Science and Industry in Los Angeles as a commission for IBM. Soon after, it was duplicated for the Chicago Museum of Science and Industry, and later for display at the 1964 World's Fair in New York. It was one of the first examples of a designed interactive exhibition that was successfully duplicated in different locations. As of 2014, the exhibition is still on display at the New York Hall of Science.

9 In previous work, I have discussed key paradigm shifts in approaches to public engagement in science and technology museums and centers. I explicitly consider matters of aesthetics in the art of interactive exhibit design (Balsamo 2006) and the design of public interactives (Balsamo 2011).

10 This list reflects the recent work of Janet Murray (2013) who delineates these four characteristics as the key affordances of digital media that organize the cultural meaning.

11 This list draws on work by Nathan Shredoff (2009) in his work on the constitutive elements of interactive experience design.

12 The models did not actually interact with the public, but, with walls removed, members of the public could watch the performances from the street. http://agbeat.com/business-marketing/ikea-living-billboards-models-use-bathroom-paris-street/ (accessed December 15, 2014).

13 The creation of the dimensional billboards was designed to inspire people to think smarter about their neighborhoods and local environments. http://popupcity.net/smart-billboards-double-as-urban-furniture/ (accessed December 14, 2014).

14 AMBER alert warnings explicitly ask drivers and members of the public to be on the watch for abducted children by publicizing details about the vehicles used in the abduction. http://www.amberalert.gov/ (accessed January 12, 2013).

15 The BBC used to allow people to submit content for display on some of the big screens. Although the page has not been updated since 2008, the BBC page about the Big Screen in Derby provides instructions for creating and submitting context for presentation. http://www.bbc.co.uk/derby/content/articles/2007/05/10/big_screen_arrives_feature.shtml (accessed January 1, 2014).

16 The Bigger Picture project was organized and managed by Cornerhouse, a non-profit cultural institution in Manchester that supports contemporary visual arts and

independent film. http://www.cornerhouse.org/art/art-events/the-bigger-picture (accessed December 15, 2013).

17 In a tutorial created by the Graffiti Research Lab (GRL), Eyebeam OpenLab, and Paul Notzold, available on the Instructables site, the term "projection bombing" is attributed to artist Zach Lieberman. Many of the GRL projection projects use the L.A.S.E.R tag developed by artist Theo Watson. The tutorial pages include images of other Graffiti Research Lab collaborations that tag city buildings with animated projections and particle light writing. Examples of projection bombing projects are found on the Graffiti Research Lab site under the category of interactive architecture. http://www.graffitiresearchlab.com/blog/projects/interactive-architecture/#video (accessed January 2, 2014). Paul Notzold has created a companion project called TXTual Healing where he uses a laptop and projector to project speech balloons and graphics onto sides of buildings, along with a phone number that people can use to text a response. http://www.txtualhealing.com/blog/?page_id=2 (accessed January 2, 2014).

18 Doug Aitken's *Sleepwalker* installation is frequently cited as one of the first social cinematic experiences. Concurrent with the exhibition, Aitken also presented a "happening" inside the museum that featured live drummers and auctioneers, and a performance by Cat Power. http://www.dougaitkenworkshop.com/work/sleepwalkers/ (accessed December 15, 2013).

19 *A Show of Hands* was exhibited at the DUMBO Art Under the Bridge Festival (New York) in 2009. http://www.edpurver.com/?p=90 (accessed December 12, 2013).

20 Project Blinkenlights includes several installations that incorporate new technologies to wirelessly control the light patterns. http://blinkenlights.net/ (accessed December 14, 2013).

21 A more recent treatment of the LED facade of the Ars Electonica Media Building, created by Javier Lloret, transformed the building into a giant Rubik's cube. http://www.thisiscolossal.com/2013/12/puzzle-facade-javier-lloret/ (accessed December 2, 2013).

22 Electroland has created several interactive pedestrian experiences that incorporate activated light and sound displays. http://electroland.net/projects/connection/ and http://electroland.net/projects/targetbreezeway/ (accessed December 15, 2013).

23 Thanks to Bill Graner, a member of my Public Interactive Research Team at the University of Southern California, for this example. http://www.creativetourist.com/articles/music/manchester/shining-bright/ (accessed December 15, 2013).

24 Lozano-Hemmer cites Samuel van Hoogstraten's engraving *The Shadow Dance* (Rotterdam, 1675) as an inspiration for the Body Movies installation. http://www.lozano-hemmer.com/body_movies.php (accessed January 10, 2014).

25 *SPECFLIC* installations happened in iconic public spaces such as the CalIT2 building at the University of California San Diego and the Dr. Martin Luther King Jr. Library in San Jose. *SPECFLIC* stories are set in 2030, and arise from research-based speculations about the near future of a particular public institution. http://www.specflic.net/ (accessed December 12, 2013).

26 The use of interactive billboards for the promotion of a television show was reported in an article in the online *Wall Street Journal* on September 12, 2011. http://online.wsj.com/news/articles/SB10001424053111904265504576564763467046264 (accessed January 2, 2014).

27 The Adidas game and the Hilton game are described on the zdnet blog site: http://www.zdnet.com/photos/photos-interactive-billboards/13726#photo and http://www.zdnet.com/photos/photos-interactive-billboards_p2/13726#photo (accessed January 2, 2014).

28 A video of the InfoTiles game is available at: http://www.youtube.com/watch?v=G04ldYYiWmw (accessed January 4, 2014).

29 The R+J fulldome movie was only one of the immersive cinematic experiences created by Living Globe company. http://www.livinglobe.com/rj-romeo-and-juliet-immersive-cinema-fulldome-movie.html (accessed January 11, 2014).

30 The project was managed by architect Henry Stevens (Head of ISG REalys Consulting in Hong Kong). http://www.youtube.com/watch?feature=player_embedded&v=wCNti_r2BGo (accessed December 15, 2013).

31 The Civic Debate Wall enables users to follow debates documented on the wall through the use of SMS; visitors can join the debate at the wall, follow reactions, and respond by text. http://www.civildebatewall.com/whatisthis (accessed December 12, 2013).

32 The AIDS Quilt Touch Table was created by a team of creative technologists and humanists with support from the National Endowment for the Humanities and Microsoft Research, in collaboration with the Names Project Foundation in Atlanta and researchers at Brown University. Information about the AIDS Quilt Touch digital experiences is available at: http://www.designingculture.net/blog/?p=1009 (accessed January 11, 2014).

33 The "Fallen Heroes" memorial was created by Livewire Digital as a commission by the Prospect Hill Cemetery Heritage Foundation. http://www.signageinfo.com/news/22903/livewire-digital-powers-fallen-heroes-memorial-kiosk-at-prospect-hill-cemetery/ (accessed January 11, 2014).

References

Aurigi, Alessandro, and Fiorella De Cindio, eds. 2008. *Augmented Urban Spaces: Articulating the Physical and Electronic City*. Farnham, UK: Ashgate.

Balsamo, Anne. 2006. "A Glorious Mix: The Art of Interactive Science and Technology Exhibits." *Intersections: Art at the New York Hall of Science*. Catalog published by the New York Hall of Science.

Balsamo, Anne. 2011. *Designing Culture: The Technological Imagination at Work*. Raleigh, NC: Duke University Press.

Bennett, Tony. 1995. *The Birth of the Museum: History, Theory, Politics*. London: Routledge.

Hayles, Katherine N. 2002. *Writing Machines*. Cambridge, MA: The MIT Press.

Kittler, Friedrich. 1990. *Discourse Networks 1800/1900*, translated by Michael Metteer. Stanford, CA: Stanford University Press.

Krueger, Myron. 1991. *Artificial Reality II*. Reading, UK: Addison-Wesley.

Laurel, Brenda, ed. 1990. *The Art of Human–Computer Interface Design*. Reading, UK: Addison-Wesley.

Lucchi, Aurelien, Patrick Jermann, Guillaume Zufferey, and Pierre Dillenbourg. 2010. "An Empirical Evaluation of Touch and Tanigble Interfaces for Tabletop Displays." TEI 2010, January 24–27, 177–184. Cambridge, MA.

MacCannell, Dean. 1975. *The Tourist: A New Theory of the Leisure Class.* New York: Schrocken.

McCullough, Malcolm. 2008. "Epigraphy and the Public Library." In *Augmented Urban Spaces: Articulating the Physical and Electronic City*, edited by Alessandro Aurigi and Fiorella De Cindio. Farnham, UK: Ashgate.

McGann, Jerome. 2000. "Rethinking Textuality."http://www2.iath.virginia.edu/jjm2f/old/jj2000aweb.html#5 (accessed January 2, 2014).

McLuhan, Marshall. 1967. *Understanding Media: The Extensions of Man.* Toronto: Bantam Books.

McQuire, Scott. 2008. *The Media City: Media, Architecture and Urban Space.* London: Sage.

Michelis, Daniel. 2009. *Interaktive Großbildschirme im öffentlichen Raum: Nutzungsmotive und Gestaltungsregeln.* http://www.magicalmirrors.de/ (accessed on January 3, 2014).

Müller, Jörg, Florian Alt, Daniel Michelis, and Albrecht Schmidt. 2010. "Requirements and Design Space for Interactive Public Displays." In *Proceedings of the International Conference on Multimedia* (MM '10), 1285–1294. ACM, New York.

Murray, Janet. 2013. *Inventing the Medium: Principles of Interaction Design as a Cultural Practice.* Cambridge, MA: The MIT Press.

Nevárez, Julie. 2006. "Art and Social Displays in the Branding of the City: Token Screens or Opportunities for Difference?" *First Monday*, Special Issue #4: *Urban Screens: Discovering the Potential of Outdoor Screens for Urban Society.* http://firstmonday.org/ojs/index.php/fm/rt/printerFriendly/1551/1466 (accessed January 5, 2015).

Shedroff, Nathan. 2009. *Experience Design 1.1.* ISBN: 9780982233900.

Further Reading

Mcquire, Scott. 2010. "Rethinking Media Events: Large Screens, Public Space Broadcast and Beyond." *New Media and Society* 12(4): 567–582.

Manovich, Lev. 2006. "The Poetics of Augmented Space." *Visual Communication* 5(2): 219–240.

Part III

Network Cultures: The Politics of Digital Art

15

Shockwaves in the New World Order of Information and Communication

Armin Medosch

Introduction

In 1980 UNESCO published the McBride[1] Report (1980), the result of a large-scale international survey of the latest developments in communications and media. The McBride Report put into sharp and detailed focus the relationship between communications media and power and showed that unequal access to communications media had repercussions for the economic and political development of nations, peoples, and individuals. The report's authors argued that Western rhetoric about the free flow of information only concealed "the advantages of those who have greater communication resources" (McBride 1980, 141). The report emphasized the importance of communications for popular emancipation and concluded that a truly free flow would have to be two-way (McBride 1980, 142). It used the phrase "new world order of information and communication" for the first time. The Reagan administration was so annoyed by the McBride Commission's findings that it became one of a number of reasons for the United States' withdrawal from UNESCO in 1984.[2] During the more than thirty years that have passed since, the sphere of information and communication has grown spectacularly, boosted through the Internet and mobile and wireless communications. Access to media has become much more widespread and made it much easier for individuals and groups to be not only consumers but also producers of information. In the 1970s this idea of access and empowerment was formulated into a theory of emancipatory media production by Hans Magnus Enzensberger (1970) in "Constituents of a Theory of the Media." Enzensberger echoed the central tenet of what is commonly referred to as Bertolt Brecht's radio theory: that every receiver should also become a transmitter. In the 1930s, Brecht's theory was complemented by Walter Benjamin's 1934 demand, formulated in "The Author as Producer" (2002), that every author should work toward enabling others to become authors themselves.

A Companion to Digital Art, First Edition. Edited by Christiane Paul.

This line of thought, from Brecht via Walter Benjamin to Enzensberger, is introduced here as the "emancipatory media paradigm." Recent events such as the so-called Arab Spring, revolutions in North Africa and the Middle East where the Web and social media helped galvanize support for democratic uprisings, once again appear to confirm a democratizing capability of the media. It seems that the emancipatory media paradigm has been fully realized, at least on a technical level, on the Internet, and through the many mobile and wireless gadgets at our disposal. In Enzensberger's time, the idea of two-way participatory media was linked with the socialist utopia of a free and equal society. That part of the equation, however, is continuously pushed back into a forever non-discernible future. The rise of the media since the 1970s has coincided with the implementation of a globalized neoliberal economy. While we have a nuanced media ecology in place that appears to leave out no one and nothing, the political economy has in some aspects returned to the free market fundamentalism of the 19th century. A discussion of political digital art has to account for the paradox that what was once considered revolutionary—full two-way synchronous communication between individuals and groups—has now technically been realized, yet been emptied of its political promise.

This chapter seeks to identify characteristics of political digital art practices, characteristics that change over time along with advances in technology and developments in the political economy. The task thus is to understand the motive forces and concrete modalities of change in order to better assess how artists tried to unlock the emancipatory potential of media. Taking a kind of curatorial approach, the text gives a selective account of radical art practices motivated by political themes and acting in concert with social movements to create shockwaves in the new world order of information and communication.

Artist-activists have a history of addressing issues of communication justice by directly intervening in and interacting with media production (Downing 1984). They have gone well beyond a traditional understanding of media as news media and early on realized that the form of media itself was political. In most cases their interventions were not just aimed at inserting a different message into existing channels, but speculatively created new forms and formats of media. This aspect of formal innovation and the role of aesthetics in political struggles qualify the events and media forms presented here as artworks. Yet the status of those works as art is far from clearly defined. Many of the projects have no easily definable author, nor are their spatial and temporal boundaries self-evident, for instance when a "work" constitutes a political campaign unfolding over months and years and uses online and offline media. Many of the projects and events discussed in the following do not simply convey a message but try to enable marginalized people and groups to develop and spread their own message. They are creating transcultural[3] encounters and forming new, often temporary public spheres. This process by definition involves many people and thereby also falls into the category of participatory art or social art practice as outlined in Claire Bishop's book on participatory art (Bishop 2012).

The following narrative starts with TV art projects from the 1980s and 1990s, and the "camcorder revolution" declared at the first Next Five Minutes (N5M) conference in Amsterdam in 1993 and then explores the notion of "tactical media" in connection with the rise of the Internet. It also outlines how the influence of neoliberalism contributed to forming the so-called anti-globalization movement and new social subjects who made innovative use of the Net and created new forms of virtual protest to make their voices heard. Although some of the highlights of that phase, such as June 18 (j18) or the protests against the WTO (World Trade Organization) in Seattle, seem to have nothing to do with art on a surface level, activist-artists were often involved in them by galvanizing new cultural techniques and linking protest on- and offline with a transcultural aesthetics of difference. This vibrant protest culture celebrated the arrival of a new social subject—transcultural global civil society—and new patterns of solidarity between people in poor and rich countries. Through the creative use of symbolic power they produced an "image" that allowed them to gain access to public and corporate media. After an early peak of those practices around the turn of the millennium with the launch of Indymedia and the development and refinement of forms of media hacking techniques, forms of hactivism and transcultural network protest continue to be viral today.

Over the last ten or fifteen years an additional emphasis of activism shifted toward an engagement with the notion of the commons and a fight against extensions of copyright and related intellectual property rights. The rediscovery of the commons ushered in another paradigm for political digital art, emphasizing learning rather than just protest, as well as collaborations outside the form of the state and the market in order to build a growing liberated sphere of legally shared common goods. The rediscovery of the commons via the digital and a now generalized notion of the commons as a new economic and political paradigm constitutes the current state of the art, whose relation with digital art will be discussed in the final sub-chapter.

It may be argued that this narrative mixes pre-digital art, such as the television art experiments and radio art of the 1980s and 1990s, with later forms that are specific to digital and networked art. In my view those earlier experiments created the foundations for a political or socially engaged practice in digital art. The definition of digital art here is not based on an ontology and phenomenology of the digital—whatever that might be, a new binary-ism between 0 and 1?—but rather on social forms that involve electronic and digital communication technologies. Those social forms and modalities of working—such as different types of collaboration—are more important and longer lasting than specific pieces of hard- and software.[4]

The period covered by this article spans the transition from broadcast media as the dominant model to two-way, participatory networked media. During the same time frame another transformation occurred, the one from so-called Keynesian Fordism (Aglietta 1979) to the neoliberal information economy (Harvey 2005). An important premise of this chapter's arguments is the structural relationships between systems of production and media systems, and the key term to consider here is that of a "political economy."

The Need for a New Political Economy of Communications

In the 1970s the French communications scientist Armand Mattelart went to Chile to support the Allende government by developing an adequate communication science. Supported by Canadians Dallas Smythe, Dan Schiller, and Vincent Mosco, and American Herbert Schiller, the foundations of a political economy of communications were created (Mosco 2008, 46). Mosco defines political economy as "the study of social relations, particularly the power relations that mutually constitute the production, distribution, and consumption of resources" (Mosco 2009, 2).

This school elaborated a critique that traces the impact of ownership structures on media content and the influence of regulatory structures on the media landscape as a whole. It explains why, despite an absence of overt censorship, Western media often appear to speak with one voice and why many people, regions, and worldviews are not adequately represented in supposedly free liberal media. There is a need for the reinvention of the political economy of communications, especially since those experiments in communications science were stopped short by General Pinochet's brutal coup in 1973,[5] and received relatively little support in subsequent decades (Mosco 2008).

The postwar structure of industrial mass production was dependent on creating an adequate media system. The media needed to grow exponentially to become mass production's organizing instrument for the circulation of money, information, commodities, and goods. Enzensberger still framed the media as "consciousness industries," implying a separation between the Marxist concepts of base and superstructure, as well as the primacy of the media's function in shaping people's minds, a notion influenced by the concept of the culture industry outlined by Horkheimer and Adorno (2006). However, as French philosopher Jean Baudrillard[6] argues, the media are not just a superstructural entity, but essentially also forces of production.

In *For a Critique of the Political Economy of the Sign*, Baudrillard (1981) repudiated the cornerstones of Enzensberger's emancipatory and participatory media utopia. Both Baudrillard and Enzensberger adopted Marshall McLuhan's statement that "the medium is the message," but criticized his lack of political and historical inquiry. Both authors also used the Marxist terminology of exchange value and use value to make their arguments. As Marx explains, following Adam Smith, the commodity form is characterized by its miraculous double identity as exchange value and use value.[7] Since exchange value always trumps use value in capitalist societies, the labor that goes into the production of objects is concealed (Marx 1976). The essence of Marx's critique of commodity fetishism—later extended into a theory of reification (Lukács 1971; Lefebvre 2009)—is that what used to be relations between people became relations mediated by things.

The groundbreaking move of Baudrillard's theory was to extend the critique of the commodity form to the sign. By making the sign the subject of a political economy, he circumvented the dichotomy between base and superstructure. The sign, while it is also imbued with immaterial meaning, belongs to a large-scale communications infrastructure—newspapers, TV stations, networks—the world of things. Media were not just shaping the consciousness of citizens/consumers, they also were the place inhabited by a generalized system of signs.[8] And just as there is a hierarchical relation between exchange value and use value, Baudrillard argues that there is a similar one between signifier and signified. The signifier is what is in circulation and it is that which signifies. It takes on an independent "sign value" which functions as the dominant side of the equation, just as the exchange value trumps use value in capitalistic societies. To put it bluntly, the image is more important than reality.

This system of signs formulated by Baudrillard becomes completely unassailable by critique—this is where McLuhan and Baudrillard converge in dodging further analysis—because any speech act cannot touch the fundamental structural form on which the system is built. As Baudrillard had shown in his earlier book, *The System of Objects* (Baudrillard 1996), any generalized system of exchange becomes self-sufficient.

In this schema, the separation between consumers and producers mirrors that between transmitters and receivers. Both systems are ruled by the "code" that reproduces their foundational separations: that between signifier and signified, and between exchange value and use value. The strength of Baudrillard's theory, but also the impediment that makes it difficult and hard to read, is that his argument relies on another discursive layer of what he calls symbolic exchange. According to the anthropologists Marcel Mauss (1967) and Claude Lévi-Strauss (Levin 1981), and the economic theory of Georges Bataille (1988), economic exchange always incorporates other, "differential logics"—forms of symbolic exchange where surface acts are related to fundamental issues of human life such as sexuality, death, and social power. In Bataille's economic framework in particular, "the universe is not a *thing*" (Bataille 1988). That enables Baudrillard to formulate a critique of the sign regarding its relation with social order, as a "theory of a social logic." The logic of signification narrows down, and limits (Baudrillard 1981, 68); the transmitter–receiver scheme of information theory—Claude Shannon's *The Mathematical Theory of Communication* (Shannon and Weaver 1949)—as an extremely narrowing, limiting concept of communications does not allow for playfulness, mutuality, and other qualities of symbolic exchange, where the subject–object relations are dissolved.

The conclusion of Baudrillard's theory is that this scheme is one of systemic non-communication; that, as long as the chain transmitter–message–receiver—understood by analogy with the chain encoder–sign–decoder—is not broken down, the media cannot be liberated. Any usage of the media that reproduces the old model of communication would recreate a heteronomic system of significations, even if the media were to be seized by the left. This negative outlook on any possibility of alternative media usage might come as a surprise, but is a decisive feature of Baudrillard's critique.

Baudrillard personally participated in the uprising of May 1968 and seems to have taken away from it a positive view of micro-media, of the spontaneous overflow of a critical intellect in posters and graffiti. Enzensberger, on the other hand, vehemently criticized the student protesters for seizing not the radio station but the Odeon, seat of traditional high culture (Enzensberger 1970, 67). The revolt of 1968 instigated the production of a new social imaginary that saw political power growing from below rather than through top-down strategies (Katsiaficas 1987). Part of this imaginary was the switch to emancipatory and participatory media practices. The Situationist International (SI) had provided the ideological framework for the critique of "the society of the spectacle," developed by its leader Guy Debord in his 1967 book of the same name (Debord 1983). The "spectacle" was not just a metaphor for electronic media, but described social relationships in the postwar era where "the passive consumption of radio and television programmes was the most dramatic manifestation of the workers' loss of control over all aspects of their lives" (Barbrook 1995, 92–93).

Enzensberger, however, in accord with Henri Lefebvre, saw the spectacle as a utopian promise of consumption as transgression (Enzensberger 1970, 73). He demanded that emancipatory practice should be a collective process, not an effort of individualized people. While, in principle, everybody could become a media producer, the history of using amateur media such as Super 8 film, cassette recorders, and photography showed that people, left to their own devices, would only reproduce stereotypes (Enzensberger 1970, 71).

This virtual conversation between Enzensberger and Baudrillard, held from 1970 to 1972, comes at the start of a period where developments in media appear to confirm either one or the other theorist. After 1968 a number of converging factors, such as political support by social democratic governments and the availability of ever better and cheaper communication technologies, set in place a dialectics that led to the rise of the emancipatory and participatory media paradigm. During the 1970s publicly supported emancipatory media projects sought to include people as makers of video/TV—for instance, the project *Workers Making Television* (Auer, Hueber, and Kronberger 1980). This tendency, however, lost momentum in the 1980s. During the era of Ronald Reagan and Margaret Thatcher the economy was reorganized according to neoliberal criteria, and under conditions of an accelerating digital and media revolution. New video formats, the first affordable computers as creative tools, sampling, and many other innovations brought down the entry costs to creative production. The development of production forces created the condition for an overcoming of backward social relations, but that potential was kept at bay by the changing political economy. Postmodern theoretical discourses and a focus on cultural politics kept intellectuals from adequately raising more directly political questions, such as the decline of labor movements in the West (Harvey 1989) as a "new international division of labor" was created (Froebel, Heinrichs, and Kreye 1980). In that context, the practices of "counter media" production needed an overhaul. Just attacking monopolies that were seen as broadcasting a distorted truth was not enough in a world of liberalization of the media. Although the political and media environment of the 1980s lent plausibility to Baudrillard's ideas, artists found new and innovative ways of intervening in the media, as the following chapter will describe.

"The Last Free Media of the West"

Paper Tiger TV

In 1980, over the course of six weeks, live on cable TV, in front of a studio setting featuring a painted subway car, the communication theorist Herbert Schiller explained how the *New York Times* "serves as the steering mechanism of the ruling class" (Halleck 2002, 115). The format proved so popular that a group around community media activist and artist DeeDee Halleck decided to have different guests analyze different media each week. This set-up gave Paper Tiger TV, a weekly New York City cable program that is still produced today, its name. Many well-known artists and theorists passed through the "school of applied media critique" that is Paper Tiger TV (Larsen 1995, 75), among them Shu Lea Cheang, theorist Manuel De Landa, artist Nancy Buchanan, as well as "several hundred media activists, many of them beginning as undergraduates" (Larsen 1995, 75).

Paper Tiger TV's importance did not derive only from its longevity but from its specific mode of production. DeeDee Halleck has always taken care "to represent collectivity" through the practice of Paper Tiger TV (Larsen 1995, 74). The program deliberately presented itself as non-professional and non-challenging, an environment where not the product but community values in the production process counted most. At the same time, the content of Schiller's critique was the sharp-tongued masterpiece of a leading protagonist of the political economy of communications.

As proponents of this line of critique have pointed out, even supposedly objective and neutral news pieces are heavily biased, and, despite the absence of any overt form of censorship, Western media often appear to speak with one voice, framing world events in a certain way.

Paper Tiger TV's achievement has been to deconstruct the hegemonic influence of mass collective representations (Larsen 1995, 74) through a "deceptively casual mode of production," thereby "signifying that any of us could take the power of production in our own hands" (Larsen 1995, 73). A cornerstone of its methodology was what the Brazilian educational activist and writer Paolo Freire called the process of becoming conscious: "conscientization." In his famous book *Pedagogy of the Oppressed* (Freire 1972), Freire explains that such a pedagogy must be forged *with*, not *for* the oppressed (Freire 1972, 25). Through dialogue, people improve their capacity to reflect on what Freire calls "situationality," "critical thinking through which men discover each other to be in a situation," which allows them to "emerge from their submersion and acquire the ability to intervene in reality" (Freire 1972, 81). For Freire, the capacity to intervene is strongly linked with education, which, in the northeast of Brazil, meant literacy campaigns. For Halleck and other community media activists, the concept of literacy is expanded to include media literacy (Cope, Kalantzis and New London Group 2000). At Paper Tiger TV, the critical demystification of media went hand in hand with becoming a media producer oneself.

In 1986, Deep Dish Television (Halleck 2002, 164), an initiative to use satellites for distribution of public access programs made by social activists, emerged out of Paper Tiger TV. It had its finest hour during the first Gulf War, when people all over the United States gathered in cinemas for public viewings of tapes produced by media activists, the only footage arriving in the US that had not been produced by embedded journalists under army control.

Rabotnik Radio and TV

In the Western Europe of the 1980s, projects similar to Paper Tiger TV were often linked to squats or formerly squatted cultural centers. In Italy these are called Centri Sociali (social centers), which signifies that they are not just squats but experiments in collective ways of living, with self-managed kindergartens, schools, galleries, workshops, and pirate radio (Bazzichelli 2009, 62–66). As Japanese media art curator Yukiko Shikata, who at the time lived in Europe, recalls,

> autonomous communications, unfettered by state propaganda or ideology proved a means of creating a public sphere. [...] By the 1980s in Western Europe, most notably in Holland and England, pirate television, free radio, squatting and "zines" all were tools of political resistance, and generated a media culture of their own. (Shikata 2005, 110–111)

In Amsterdam radio stations that had started as pirate stations, closely aligned with the squatter movement, continued after that movement had gone into decline. The biggest station, Radio 100, as well as Radio Patapoe and Radio Vrije Keyser, hosted slots with program makers who had their own distinctive style, such as the group DFM (deformation) or Fluxus artist Willem De Ridder. Rather than simply remixing sound artifacts, DFM relied on complex strategies that appropriated the medium of radio and gave it a new meaning through often rather violent methods, such as turning the transmitter on and off. De Ridder invited listeners to late-night wanderings through his mind, in stories that he spontaneously improvised live on air. In different ways these program makers' practices left behind all social norms and rules for the use of media and constituted a "Sovereign Media," as Geert Lovink argues in "Theory of Mixing" (Lovink 1992). These radio projects broke through Baudrillard's hierarchies of signifier–signified and transmitter–receiver by playing with the elementary forms of the medium.

In 1980 a large number of pirate TV stations, one of them run by art and film students, mushroomed in Amsterdam. Originally started under another name, they finally called themselves Rabotnik TV. Rabotnik TV drew inspiration from punk's DIY spirit and applied it to the medium of television. Although Rabotnik TV at first did not think of themselves in categories such as counter-information or critique of the media mainstream, they came to see themselves as "dissidents of the ether" after they were forced off the air by the authorities. For a brief period they enjoyed the privilege of making programs free from any interference from above, without any rules imposed by anyone but themselves. In retrospect, long-time Rabotnik member Menno Grootveld raised the question whether they had been "the last free medium of the West" (Grootveld 2012). That statement implied that other Western electronic media were not free. In its ideological struggle with communism the West had argued that it at least had free media, but the "dissidents of the ether" showed that this was far from true.

Although most media makers were not directly part of the squatter movement, its existence and history provided an important context for Amsterdam-based media dissidents. The core idea behind many of their projects was a striving for autonomy as artistic media producers. This meant that they did not just want to create a program for a specific slot but to develop their own vision of how a sovereign medium might operate free from the constraints of taste and the narrative strategies of ordinary television. In the case of Rabotnik TV this goal manifested itself in the camerawork, in particular, which was very direct, with all editing done in-camera except for some computer-generated titles or music. While Rabotnik TV refrained from excessive mixing or video effects, presenting events in as pure and direct a way as possible, they did use Amiga scrolling texts with a very distinct typographical style. Although offering no direct interactivity, the unplugged, uncommented style challenged viewers to become engaged and to fill in the gaps, to start thinking and speculating about the images and sounds, empowering them to overcome the unquestioning acceptance of everything presented on TV.

Ponton/Van Gogh TV

In Germany, the group Ponton/Van Gogh TV[9] emerged from the performance art group Minus Delta t, who had become internationally famous for transporting a large stone to Bangkok on a truck. In the 1980s and 1990s Ponton/Van Gogh TV carried out several large-scale participatory radio and TV projects, the highlight of which was *Piazza Virtuale* (1992), consisting of 100 days of television at Documenta 9 in Kassel. Their projects were always based on a similar organizational logic, sending a call to a network of friends, co-producers, and activists who contributed as voluntary culture producers for free accommodation and food. The projects sometimes became "material battles" (Arns 2007) that consumed large numbers of people and equipment in orgies of communication.

Ponton was aimed at involving the audience in a direct way, engaging viewers emotionally and intellectually through a mix of methodologies, ranging from studio hosts acting erratically to the use of de-familiarization techniques. Their goal was to unsettle people's viewing habits and thereby activate them to become co-creators of the program. This activist approach was also taken by camerawork, the video mixer, and the people who operated banks of Amiga and Atari computers. At the 1992 Documenta In Kassel, digital live streams received from so-called *Piazza Virtuale*, virtual squares, were mixed together into a live television signal with other sources such as a chat channel, telephone call-ins, and live cameras, creating a stream that was broadcast all night long on the satellite and cable channel 3Sat—sometimes hypnotizing, sometimes sense-deafeningly boring.

The television and radio art projects of this period raised the question of the totality of the medium: they did not just make a program for an existing channel, but experimented with the form of the medium itself. Ponton's projects, in particular, were forerunners of and training grounds for an Internet ethics of collective and collaborative work. Ponton TV's aesthetic negated the norms of public TV by creating an excess of symbolic exchange[10] on all levels, breaking norms and manipulating studio guests to go beyond their own psychological limits. Their works connected dozens of activists with thousands of participants who strove to abolish the screen as an entity that structurally separates societies into groups of consumers and producers. This approach no doubt was technologically innovative and dissipated the notion of authorship by transferring it to decentered networks.

Today, work in the spirit and style of the television art groups of the 1980s continues to be produced. In Italy there has been a movement of activist TV groups who literally brought the medium to the streets, using low-powered TV transmitters for small areas—the *Telestreet* movement. One of the most active groups in this area is Candida TV who refer to themselves as "a nomadic swarm that advances as grasshoppers of sense" (Candida TV 2003, 156). Since 2005 Swiss-born media activist Adnan Hadzi has developed Deptford TV (http://www.deptford.tv/) in Deptford, south London. Working in an area that was rapidly transformed by gentrification, he asked himself whether the Web could be used by documentary filmmakers to share and collaboratively edit footage online (Hadziselimovic 2012). In Nairobi, a group of Serbian, Austrian, and Kenyan artists[11] has initiated Slum TV (http://www.slum-tv.org), a self-sustaining media lab in Mathare, a slum of 500,000 people in the Kenyan capital (Cippitelli 2008; Nikolic et al. 2008). These projects continue to demonstrate that emancipatory media practice with television formats is feasible and rewarding.

It seems that the notion of television itself has changed. While activists of the 1970s and 1980s believed that the left had to take over television in order to educate the masses, the new emancipatory imaginary of media had no such centralized point of intervention any more. Their focus switched to molecular media, a term inspired by Félix Guattari's notion of the "molecular revolution" (Guattari 1984). Micro-media and narrowcasting projects such as Slum TV, Candida TV, and Deptford TV show that the "medium" is not an abstraction but is embedded in social groups. The most important step in successfully implementing these projects is the building of capacity among program makers who use the process as a way of forming a critical understanding of their own relation with the environment and the reality projected by official TV. The key point here is the actual practice taking place between co-producers and viewers, and not a transmission of messages. The self-empowerment of the producers, together with that of audiences, shapes "communities of practice" in a collective learning process (Lave and Wenger 1991). Their small size allows those projects to avoid reification, thereby breaking through the transmitter–receiver schema Baudrillard had criticized (as discussed above).

The New New World Order

After the fall of the Berlin Wall in 1989, George H.W. Bush announced a "New World Order," a unipolar world in which the USA would be the leader. The point was forcefully demonstrated by the first Gulf War in 1990/1991, which saw the emergence of CNN as a global medium and the introduction of the "bomb's eye view"—obtained by a camera built into a so-called smart bomb approaching its target—on TV. The emergence of global 24/7 news together with the bomb's eye view marked the closing of a blanket of complete fiction over reality, the final agony of the real,[12] as the new media arrangement made the distinction between the fictional and real structurally impossible. Military simulation of the theater of warfare played along with the ideological representation of a perfect, victimless war on the screens in order to render fruitless any question about the reality of that approaching cruise missile—that much Baudrillard (1995) and his colleague Paul Virilio agreed upon (1994, 69). This myth of the perfect war conspired with another myth, that of the end of history, so that any political media activism theoretically seemed futile.

Tactical Media

In this new new world order where power appeared to consolidate itself on a new layer of satellite and fiber-optically mediated information, the first of four Next Five Minutes (N5M) conferences was held in Amsterdam in January 1993. In the historical context of the "media revolutions" in Eastern Europe—one regime after another in the Soviet Union zone of influence appearing to crumble live on television between 1989 and 1991—the organizers of N5M pronounced the "camcorder revolution." In the run-up to N5M I, a group of scholars conducted a survey that tried to gather information about activist TV and documentary video projects on a fairly global level, and published it in the *N5M Zapbook* (Amsterdam Cultural Studies et al. 1992). It contained a wide range of examples of various types of camcorder activism, from video artist Paul Garrin's recordings of himself getting beaten up during the Tompkins Square riots in New York City in the summer of 1988, to media activists in Eastern Europe and the global South (Boyle 1992). All those stories added up to the powerful narrative that camcorders were revolutionary tools, and that, given the right conditions, community media projects could even blow away fossilized political structures. The term that was introduced to cover those practices was "tactical media" (Raijmakers 1992).

Bas Raijmakers explained that the term "tactical" was borrowed from Michel de Certeau's differentiation between strategic and tactical (de Certeau 1984). Whereas strategy was the domain of large institutions such as public broadcasters, the independent groups who came together at N5M did not have the luxury of dominating the field. Their media use was short-term, tactical, flexible; they were "lurking, ready to move into the cracks that appeared in strategic TV" (Raijmakers 1992).

At the second N5M conference in 1996, a new urgency was expressed by the title of a panel organized by Geert Lovink, the "Desire to be Wired." Between 1993 and 1996 the Net had been opened up for public usage and the "digital revolution," as San Francisco-based *Wired* magazine had called it, was fully under way. On that panel, political scientist and historian Richard Barbrook presented a paper he had co-authored with the designer Andy Cameron, "The Californian Ideology," in which the authors deconstructed the "bizarre fusion of the cultural bohemianism of San Francisco with the hi-tech industries of Silicon Valley" (Barbrook and Cameron 1996). The public perception of computers had somehow managed to change to something cool and associated with creative values. The former center of hippie culture San Francisco became a hotbed of high-tech entrepreneurship, politically embracing libertarianism. Those were, of course, the days of the New Economy, when everybody thought that exponential growth rates would be the norm forever and that the economy would become "weightless" (Kelly 1995).

This unlikely alliance might as well have been called Dutch Ideology. Throughout the 1990s Amsterdam became an ever more stylish and sanitized environment designed to meet the requirements of the digital creative class (Florida 2002). In the early 1990s the highly influential De Digitale Stad (DDS) had been founded to create a digital public sphere. By 2000 that spirit had given way to the new designer impetus, as activists Geert Lovink and Patrice Riemens described it (Lovink and Riemens 2000).

Despite these transformations of the world outside the conference venues of N5M, De Balie, and Paradiso, "hacktivism," the blend of hacking and activism, took center stage at the third N5M in 1999. In retrospect, the turn of the millennium was a first high point of web-based activism. It was the culmination of the new global civil society's appropriation of the Web, as will be shown in the following. But this high point almost also became its near end.

In 1999 artist-activist Joanne Richardson, one of the more critical voices at the time, pointed out that "tactical" video activism focused too much on violent street battles, an aesthetics of radical chic rather than the "why?" and "what for?" Richardson also elaborated on the problematic spin given to the term "tactical media," which was quite incompatible with the original meaning intended by de Certeau (Richardson 2003). It was no coincidence that the *Old Boys Network*, a cyber-feminist network, held its second conference as a gesture toward N5M around the same time. While N5M had started from a global survey, it had increasingly become a mostly European, white male event.

The organizers recognized this deficiency and, in preparation for N5M IV in 2003, sent a call to international mailing lists, asking for tactical media labs to be set up in a decentralized way outside of Europe (Garcia 2004). This call found a response in Brazil, where a tactical media lab was established that will be discussed in more detail later in this text. The fourth N5M conference appears to have gained the reputation of being a bit of a swan song, although certainly a success in terms of audience numbers. The notion of tactical media, although still expanding on one level, lost some of its initial traction on another, possibly because politics changed quite dramatically in the new millennium. A more repressive climate had already shown itself at the G8 meeting in Genoa in 2001, when protester Carlo Giuliani was shot dead by police. After 9/11 and the Bush government's militaristic response, the dynamic links between popular alter-globalization movements and digital cultural protests were weakened. During the decade in between, however, the changing notion of tactical media belonged to an irreverent new paradigm of transcultural network protest, hacktivism, electronic disturbance, citizen journalism, and media hacking.

Transcultural Network Protest

During the 1990s neoliberalism came to dominate the political economy. Economists such as Friedrich Hayek and Milton Friedman had preached the neoliberal gospel even during the high times of Keynesianism. They had argued that free, unregulated markets were the best way of allocating resources and that any form of redistribution from the rich to the poor in the form of welfare state measures was equal to socialism. The crisis of Keynesian Fordism in the 1970s brought them back from the intellectual wilderness. After 1989, and especially after the success of the Internet-based New Economy in the 1990s, neoliberal policies were adopted widely by nations in the US sphere of influence, which was now nearly all of them. This implied, to a degree varying from country to country, the dismantling of the welfare state, the scaling back of workers' rights, and the exploitation of global income inequalities through new technologies. Increased automation in the West and the redistribution of production to low-wage countries were directly dependent on media technologies. The use of high tech to create global supply chains and computerized electronic markets in so-called "global cities" (Sassen 2001) weakened organized labor in the rich nations, while the new workers in the global South had no chance of obtaining the same level of income and rights. The results were felt most strongly by those at the bottom, such as indigenous peoples in the South, and precarious workers, women, and migrants in the North and South.

Mounting pressure fermented resistance and new social subjects made themselves heard. Avant-garde digital artists and hackers aligned themselves with the alter-globalization movement to create new forms of transcultural network protest. The term "alter-globalization" signifies a rejection of capitalist globalization, but not of thinking on a global scale (Burbach 2001). In different terminology, the sum of all social movements may also be understood as the "multitudes" (Virno 2004; Virno and Hardt 2006). All those terms are simply new connotations of what used to be called the working class. But this working class had become culturally and geographically fragmented so that organizing working-class resistance turned out to be very difficult. Neoliberalism and globalization reshuffled the class structure and created new classes of the disenfranchised. Some nations, however, became "emergent economies," which implied a rising standard of living, a development used as an argument for capitalist globalization by neoliberal ideologists. The so-called Asian financial crisis of 1997, which in fact was a global financial crisis of the emerging economies, should have been sufficient warning that not all was well with the global information society. While the power structures that linked corporate media, business, and politics hardened into a new form of global hegemony, the Net still was not "overcoded" (Holmes 2009) by commercial interest and could be seized by subaltern and minoritarian groups.

This situation was recognized, more or less simultaneously, by the Rand Corporation—the think-tank for the military that had originally thought out the topology of the Net—and the left-wing artist collective Critical Art Ensemble (CAE). In 1993 Rand researchers Arquilla and Ronfeldt (1993) predicted that "Cyberwar was coming," and further elaborated on the idea in a 1996 book called *The Advent of Netwar* (Arquilla and Ronfeldt 1996). They argued that an age of asymmetrical warfare, in which the Net gave small groups an advantage, was imminent. In 1993 the artist collective CAE published *The Electronic Disturbance* and analyzed the ways in which the "revolution in technology" had created a "new geography of power relations in the first world" (CAE 1993). CAE believed that "the core of political and cultural resistance must assert itself in this electronic space [...] Nomadic power must be resisted in cyberspace rather than in physical space" (CAE 1993, 25).

Digital Zapatismo

These ideas were put to the test almost immediately after they had been published. On January 1, 1994, "the day of implementation of the North America Free Trade Agreement (NAFTA)," an "army of indigenous people entered in San Cristobal and other cities of Chiapas, wearing ski masks, carrying guns, and proclaiming revolutionary laws from the balcony of the city council" (De Angelis 1998). As the world woke up in the new year, the previously unknown indigenous army "Ejército Zapatista de Liberación Nacional" (Zapatista's Army of National Liberation—EZLN) had already made its mark (De Angelis 1998). The link between EZLN and NAFTA was that the indigenous people could not use the forests and other commons as before because of large-scale logging and mining operations.

Two days later, on January 3, 1994, Subcomandante Marcos—the figurehead of the movement—was online (Garrido and Halavais 2003). Marcos became an unlikely early hero of the Net as his "dispatches from the Lacandona jungle" reached a global audience. EZLN was able to publish political communiqués with the help of Mexican and international NGOs who enabled them to send out messages worldwide without having to pass through nodes where the Mexican government could apply censorship (Budka and Trupp 2009). Those dispatches did not address the Mexican government directly but spoke to the Mexican and global civil society. The Zapatistas skillfully applied what Paul Gilroy had called "strategic universalism" (Gilroy 2001). They not only addressed the issues that affected them as a consequence of NAFTA's neoliberal policies and the Mexican government's actions, but did so by extending their solidarity to suppressed minorities everywhere: "the indigenous, youth, women, homosexuals, lesbians, people of color, immigrants, workers" (Garrido and Halavais 2003, 7).

The new politics as represented by the EZLN revived the left by providing a model of solidarization across continents and different forms of struggles (Holloway 2005). There was a two-way connection: as the Zapatistas reached out to a newly forming global civil society, which in itself was diverse and was helped in its self-recognition by that process, they benefited from becoming part of that civil society. The one-way structure of politics and mass media was challenged by mobilization from below.

Digital Zapatismo created a blueprint for ways in which—through a combination of on- and offline actions—topics could be brought onto the agenda of news media and government.

Electronic Civil Disobedience

On December 21, 1995, the first Netstrike took place. Organized by Italian activists around Tommaso Tozzi and Stranonet, the Netstrike targeted web sites of French government institutions in protest against the nation's nuclear policies (Tozzi 1995). Users of the Web were asked to direct their browsers at government sites and keep clicking, which resulted in what came to be called a "denial-of-service attack" in hacker jargon: through overloading the server, the bandwidth would get clogged and the server's ability to serve web pages diminished. The Netstrike, however, was not a form of web vandalism, but the attempt to introduce a new form of virtual protest, a conscious act of civil disobedience, the virtual sit-in. Only six weeks later, on March 2, 1996, a "Chiapas net strike" was called, this time directed against web servers of the Mexican government, combined with demonstrations in front of embassies, and articles and programs in other media of the left (Tozzi 1996).

Electronic Disturbance Theater

The term "digital Zapatismo," while initially attributed solely to the EZLN (Lane 2003), has also become associated with the practice of Ricardo Dominguez and his collaborators[13] in the Electronic Disturbance Theater (EDT). Dominguez was a member of the CAE and, in 1995, after splitting from the group, became "web-wise" by joining The Thing, New York.[14] Tuning into the strange thing that was net culture in those days, Dominguez began developing his own theory (1995, 1996) and practice. Dominguez had a background in theater and had always emphasized the peaceful nature of protest. EDT wanted to create a "performative matrix" that forced the opponent into their way of thinking through "Mayan technologies" (Fusco 2003). While real hackers acting in secrecy could unleash denial-of-service attacks that easily brought down web servers, EDT's work emphasized the public nature of electronic civil disobedience, using performances in real space and online actions to raise awareness about topics.

In 1998 EDT called for a virtual sit-in against Mexican financial sites in support of the Zapatistas. Inspired by the tactics of Netstrike but taking things a step further, the action was accompanied by the release of the tool Floodnet, a small script on the EDT web site that multiplied the click-frequency of users. The Floodnet action in 1998 brought EDT the attention of the Pentagon and a front-page article in the *New York Times* (Medosch 2003, 276–278). Around the turn of the millennium, a whole range of groups exercised different forms of hacktivism, often accompanied by the release of toolkits for automating distributed denial-of-service attacks.

After being appointed professor at University of California, San Diego, Dominguez set up B.a.n.g. Lab with old and new collaborators.[15] B.a.n.g. Lab made a fresh contribution to the history of political border art in San Diego and Tijuana by developing the Transborder Immigrant tool, a "GPS cell phone tool which acted as a safety net for migrants crossing the Mexico/US border'" (Cardenas et al. 2009).

Another group which creates new tools and devices for political purposes are Preemptive Media.[16] Their work *AIR* (2005) uses cheap electronics to enable non-specialists to monitor air quality and visualize their findings. Tools such as these stand in for a much wider range of other projects that combine DIY creativity with critical thinking.

It seems that practices similar to Netstrikes have been adopted by the hacker groups Anonymous and LulzSec. These groups claim to deface or bring down web sites for political reasons, in support of Internet freedom and as protest against governments' attempts to control information. A key difference is that the tactics of these groups are usually very secretive. The artists always make it very clear that their works are about influencing perceptions and that they visibly stand behind their works even if that can mean trouble with the law. Transcultural network protest pioneered new forms of political activism that included new types of action—such as the virtual sit-in—and the creation of migratory public spheres, albeit often only temporarily, for a new political subjectivity to express itself.

Neoliberalism and Its Discontents

The years 1999–2000 saw the culmination of many forms of networked protest and a surge of anti-capitalist movements, but also more viral forms of protest that insinuated themselves in attention economies. The traditional sphere of media, politics, and government suddenly found itself confronted with the motley crew of transglobal resistance, from urban ravers to Indian farmers. The "motley crew" here does not refer to the rock band Motley Crue but to the way in which Marx stylistically represented the (sub)working class, as indicated by Peter Linebaugh and Marcus Rediker (Linebaugh and Rediker 2000, 211–247). The descendants of Hewers of Wood and Drawers of Water, the new Levellers and Diggers, managed to surprise, initially at least, their opponents by the effectiveness of their network-coordinated protests.

On June 18, 1999, the activist network Reclaim the Streets (RTS) orchestrated a Global Street Party, a day of simultaneous street protests in the form of parties in dozens of venues worldwide, with the biggest event in London's financial center. RTS had organized parties as a form of environmental protest since the mid-1990s, taking inspiration from Britain's DIY activist networks who had successfully fought the expansion of road building in the 1980s and 1990s. j18 was the first explicitly anti-capitalist action by RTS, targeting the financial sector and echoing a growing sentiment within the anti-globalization movement that finance was at the root of many problems (Annie and Sam 2012). After gathering at Liverpool Street station, demonstrators walked out in three different directions, wrong-footing police who found it difficult to act in narrow streets filled with "sound systems, puppets, colourful banners, dancing crowds swinging in the glistening sunshine" (Annie and Sam 2012). RTS projected the image of a resistance movement that had no leaders and no center. They organized j18 via word of mouth, mobile text messages, and the Web, but without any traditional form of political organization, thereby contributing to a "grassroots-mediated form of political articulation" (Annie and Sam 2012). For a few hours there was a carnival in the streets of London, with 50,000 people enjoying the sunshine and a political rave party (Figure 15.1).

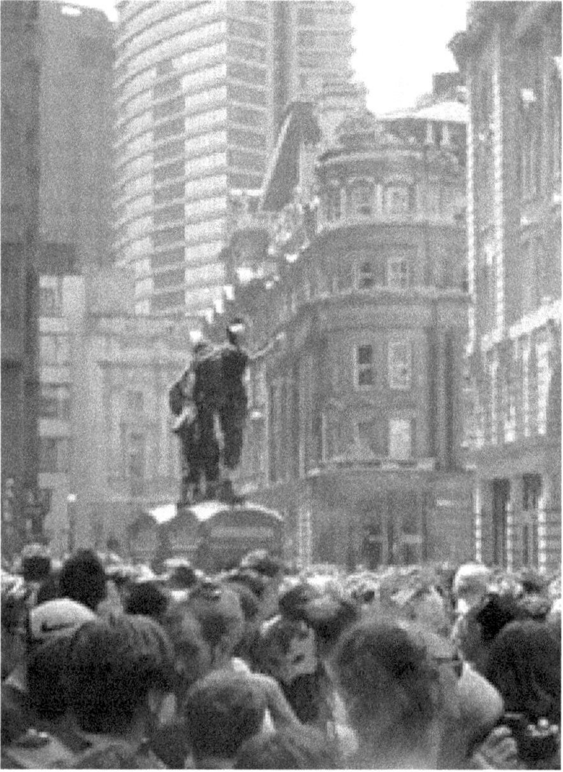

FIGURE 15.1 June 18, 1999, Carnival against Capitalism, City of London. Photo: Armin Medosch.

The internet cafe and gallery Backspace—one of London's precious self-organized hubs of net art and culture—became the training ground for a new type of radical multimedia online journalism. Artists and activists were shuttling back and forth between Clink Street, where Backspace was located, and the scenes of protest just across the river Thames, quickly copying and encoding video footage for live streaming via the Net, which was quite a novelty at the time.[17]

Similar things happened later that year in Seattle, on the occasion of the meeting of the World Trade Organization from November 29 to December 3, 1999. The discourse produced by the alter-globalization movement created a rainbow coalition against the WTO, which had become a symbol of capitalist globalization (Burbach 2001). For the duration of the WTO meeting activists installed an Independent Media Center (IMC). The creation of the IMC in Seattle and the practices at Backspace during j18—which would soon lead to Indymedia UK—saw the inauguration of a new "open" publishing model using the Net, where live news, photos, and videos could be posted. Since then Indymedia has become a sprawling network of sites that pool resources and reports to provide alternative news and create a "new communications commons" (Kidd 2003). While Indymedia is not an artwork, many artists were instrumental in setting it up and creating its pioneering "open publishing" model, where everybody could submit stories through an unfiltered channel. The materials submitted in Seattle and at j18 also allowed demonstrators to present their own version, since television reporting on demonstrations often tends to scandalize violence while misrepresenting the reasons for the demonstrations.

The creation of Indymedia reflected the fact that activists had stopped believing that the media mainstream could be changed. If activists wanted those demonstrations to get covered in a fair and just way, they needed to create news channels of their own. The combination of demonstrations, sit-ins, and blockades on the street with online stories with a global outreach allowed mobilization of an unprecedented number of people who voiced their discontent with neoliberalism. Having been blamed for being politically apathetic, the net generation forcefully demonstrated that this criticism had been just another media fabrication. People had indeed stopped caring about the field of representation, about the lack of representation in the media and in party politics, but that did not make them apolitical. Instead, they started to take media representation into their own hands, which created the nucleus of a big change in the landscape of politics and media. Seattle and j18 planted the seed of disengagement from the current political system. Through strategies of self-empowerment, politically engaged people started rebuilding democracy from below (Castells 2012).

Media Hacking

Seattle was the break-through moment for another form of digital activism, the web spoofs and media hacks by groups such as *RTMark*. The latter group, founded in 1996 by Igor Vamos and Jaques Servin, registered the domain name Gatt.org[18] and made it look like the official web site of the WTO, using its logo and other graphical elements. Instead of GATT information, it contained links to the growing number of direct action initiatives who resisted "the unfettered rule of global capitalism in general and free trade in particular" (Stalder 1999). RTMark, descendants of 1980s appropriation art, practiced subversion-by-affirmation. They presented themselves as a venture capital investment fund which offered several opportunities for investment into direct action against "the neo-liberal juggernaut" (Stalder 1999).

Vamos and Servin then changed their identities into Andy Bichlbaum and Mike Bonnano and became the *Yes Men*. They developed efficient techniques for bringing media attention to controversial subjects by taking on the guise of their opponents. The Yes Men attended meetings of the WTO posing as overzealous businessmen and produced a series of spoof web sites in order to carry out acts of "identity correction," as they called it (Boyd 2005). One of their biggest successes was the appearance of Yes Men's Andy Bichlbaum live on air on BBC World, pretending to be Jude Finisterra, a spokesperson of Dow Chemical, and admitting responsibility for the chemical disaster that had killed thousands in Bhopal, India.

The year 1999 was also the year of the *Toy War*, a symbolic battle between the net art group Etoy and e-commerce corporation Etoys. The company threatened the artists with a lawsuit, accusing them of domain infringements, as if they were cybersquatters who had registered a domain name close to theirs for profit. They had overlooked the fact that Etoy had registered their domain much earlier and had won prizes already, such as Prix Ars Electronica with the *Digital Hijack* in 1996. The apparent injustice of the case brought the artists a huge wave of support among the general public which they skillfully harnessed to orchestrate a so-called toy army of net citizens ready to take their action to cyberspace. With each step in the court case, a torrent of protest letters and press releases was launched. Etoys versus Etoy became viral in online media such as *Wired* and *Telepolis*, and soon also reached the mainstream press. The artists, supported by thousands of volunteers, managed somehow to force the company to give in, as the opinion of the court also changed in their favor (Wishart and Bochsler 2002).

It can be argued that this technique of "cultural hacking 2.0" represents a genre of its own. Shortly after the Etoy/s case, in 2000, Ubermorgen.com, an Etoy offshoot, began promoting voteauction.com, a web site that promised to bring "capitalism and democracy closer together." On the web site people could sell their votes to the highest bidder in the 2000 US presidential election. They drew the attention of state prosecutors and other US law enforcement agencies, and managed, like the Yes Men and Etoy, to get into the media mainstream. The technique applied has been described by me elsewhere as "creative resistance," whereby the energy of the opponent is used against them (Medosch 2009). This principle is most obvious in *Google Will Eat Itself* (GWEI), where money paid by Google is used to eventually buy it. GWEI is the first part of the *Hacking Monopolism Trilogy*.[19] In part two, *Amazon Noir*, a script is used to liberate books in PDF format from the online bookseller. For part three, *Face to Facebook*, personal profiles were collected and posted on a dating web site.

Those media hacks are a special case among strategies of cultural hacking which can be argued to have been part and parcel of historical avant-gardes such as the Dada movement and neo-avant-gardes such as Situationism (Düllo and Liebl 2005). The media h/activist strategy has been updated by those groups for the digital and network age. What is to be admired is the demanding and varied tool-set the artists need to "play" with to carry out such a work. It is not only necessary to shape an image that leads the opponent into a trap of overreacting, so that the media battle can begin. This needs also a lot of legal knowledge, expressed by the term "legal ready-made" by Manu Luksch (2009), who made her film *Faceless* (2006) by letting herself be filmed by CCTV and then requesting the material based on Freedom of Information legislation. At best, the media guerrilla art of the network age can seem like one of the most adequate art forms for our age, hitting at the center of informational capitalism, using hacks and exploits to find loopholes in the system, such as *Loophole For All* (Cirio 2013) who are taking the battle to the center of informational, financial capitalism.

Yet the downside is that those methods get recuperated, as the Situationists would have said (McDonough 2004). This means that tactics that once had a revolutionary or avant-garde edge become incorporated by the system, for instance through advanced marketing agencies and political PR campaigns. Culture jamming and media hacking have become generalized cultural techniques of the network age.

Art of the Digital Commons

In 2001, self-styled artist Shu Lea Cheang launched *Steam the green, Stream the field* (Cheang 2002a). Cheang's intervention reconnected the digital commons with the real world and natural commons resources. While tactical media activism had often focused on media as both means and ends, free media and open source principles were increasingly used to address other, mainly green topics, such as energy, renewability, sustainability, and ecology, in the new millennium. Cheang announced a "field harvesting and public network project" as a part of "a fictional 'after the crash' scenario" (Cheang 2002b).

According to her scenario it was the year 2030, the capitalist economy had crashed, and organic garlic became something resembling the gold standard transferred onto a gift economy. The project took its inspiration from the Argentinian truque clubs that had formed after the Argentinian credit crisis in 2001. Argentinian citizens had issued coupons that allowed them to trade services and goods despite the crash of the currency. In 2002 Cheang and supporters drove around Manhattan for three days in a pick-up, performing on location from Wall Street to Tompkins Square Park. The truck doubled as a mobile urban wireless network node and a farm stand. It made people get involved in barter economies by the curb, as they dealt truque coupons for garlic bulbs, bandwidth for services, accessing landscapes and datascapes simultaneously. In an almost prophetic way, this project anticipated things to come, in particular the rising importance of the commons in the context of the crisis of capitalism.

At some point in the 2000s, the framework of references changed, and discussions shifted from tactical media to the notion of the commons. This is not to say that these concepts are opposed to each other; they can exist side by side. The change that took place was a shift in emphasis. Tactical media implied short-term thinking, an immediacy of action, an intervention in the media to get a different message through. But it turned out that the revolution can take a while, so artist-activists started paying more attention to issues surrounding intellectual property in the meantime. There were several reasons for this shift in attention, one being that the importance of intellectual property in the knowledge economy was increasingly recognized by business leaders, and the industry started pushing for draconian legislation to protect copyright in the digital domain. Another reason was artists' realization that sustainability could only be achieved by using free and open source software (FOSS). The success of Linux instigated a rediscovery of the notion of the commons. In analogy to the commons as a shared natural resource, the notion of the commons as a shared digital resource emerged as a movement. Many artists started to use FOSS tools for their work and emphasized the digital commons as a space for sharing, learning, and a collaborative culture in general. The key principle of this movement has been formulated as "commons-based-peer production" by Yochai Benkler (2006), for whom it contained the new organizational logic of the network society.

Over the past fifteen years artists have made many contributions to this growing tide of an art of the (digital) commons, often on an infrastructural level. The Brussels-based group Constant has engaged in a sustained inquiry into free software tools for creative work, experimenting with software for graphic design, audio, and video; working out how best to substitute FOSS tools for proprietary ones; and documenting the process on individual blogs. Artists are behind initiatives such as *Floss Manuals*, an effort to write good free documentation for FOSS. The artist-engineer Jaromil, alias Denis Rojo, has led an effort to create a special Linux distribution for creative and activist work, Dynebolic. A fork[20] of Dynebolic, Puredyne, has been released by French hacker group Goto10.

These practices were accompanied by a rising activity on the discourse barometer. In Berlin a series of conferences under the title "Wizards of Operating Systems" (WOS) was held between 1999 and 2006, exploring the many ways in which open source ideas and principles could be applied in other areas. By the mid-2000s there was an "open everything" euphoria that culminated in events such as *Open Congress* at Tate, London, and *Node.London* (Vishmidt 2006). I myself was involved in *Kingdom of Piracy* (Shikata, Medosch, and Cheang 2003), which originally was a curatorial project about art and intellectual property and then increasingly turned toward commons research. The discourse on and activism for the commons found particularly strong support in nations such as India and Brazil.

Free Culture in Brazil

In Brazil, the call to set up tactical media labs, sent out in the context of N5M IV in 2003, was heard and artists and activists started to organize an event called Mídia Tática (tactical media), which took place March 13–16, 2003, in São Paulo. As Ricardo Rosas, one of the co-organizers, pointed out, Brazil is a country of extreme contrasts, where a thriving technological culture meets abject poverty. The media landscape is dominated by one powerful corporation, Globo, which owns not just the main TV stations, but also radio and print media, and is pushing out a "narcotic" stream of "telenovelas" (TV soap operas). Rosas concluded that any interpretation of tactical media that took computers as its privileged entry point would fail to grasp the complexities of Brazilian society. The tactical media lab thus "embraced a wide spectrum, from art/activist groups and collectives to DJs and street theatre performances" (Rosas 2004, 426).

Mídia Tática also brought together a number of high-profile speakers, such as Richard Barbrook, the Internet activist, and Electronic Frontier spokesman John Perry Barlow, and Brazil's then minister of culture, the musician Gilberto Gil. During Mídia Tática, an idea was hatched to turn the tactical media lab into a more permanent structure, and the Autolabs were invented, "laboratorial prototypes for media literacy, technological experimentation and creativity created with the help of local communities," as Rosas describes them (2004). In 2004, three Autolabs were organized in the eastern parts of São Paulo, where hundreds of local people got involved in making films, music, citizen journalism, as well as the recycling of hardware and many other things (Garcia 2004).

The Autolabs raised the interest of Gilberto Gil. The outcome of meetings with the activists was the shaping of a program to subsidize hundreds of *Pontos de Culturos* (points of culture) throughout the country, which would be fitted out with hardware and be given training in free software (Freire, Foina, and Fonseca 2007). As the program unfolded and hundreds of such places were registering for support, free culture activists went through the vast country on planes and coaches to teach people how to use Linux and other free software for writing and making videos and music (Brunet 2005). After Gil retired from politics and the new government came in, the program was discontinued. The free culture syndrome, however, keeps permeating Brazil and Latin America as the connection between free speech and free software is recognized. Groups such as Metareciclagem (meta-recycling) and Estudio Livres in Brazil keep producing and distributing tools supporting a free culture ideal.

Raqs/Sarai

A decisive contribution to the artistic discourse on the commons has been made by Raqs Media Collective from New Delhi, founded in 1992 by Jeebesh Bagchi, Monica Narula, and Shuddhabrata Sengupta. Raqs was also co-founder of the Sarai program at the Centre for the Study of Developing Societies (www.sarai.net). In

2001 the online curatorial project *Kingdom of Piracy* commissioned twelve net artworks that addressed topics surrounding freedom of information and intellectual property. Raqs contributed *Global Village Health Manual* (2000), a work that "evokes a 19th century print culture" to "suggest the fragility of the body, especially the laboring body in cyberspace (Raqs Media Collective, Bagchi, Narula and Sengupta, n.d.).

In 2002 Raqs presented Open Commons, a web site for sharing tools and works, at Documenta X. Raqs's work proposes the digital commons as a diverse, transcultural space and a collaborative methodology (Bansal, Keller, and Lovink 2006). They contest the notion of ownership and instead propose one of custodianship of culture: as Raqs puts it, each item of information in the hands of a person does not simply get consumed but has value added to it (Raqs Media Collective 2003, 30–31). These ideas have been further elaborated in the book series *Sarai Reader* (1 to 9). Raqs/Sarai developed a vision of the commons from the point of view of the Global South. As Sarai co-founder Ravi Sundaram argued, modernity often reached India through recycled goods and gray markets, and its instruments were pirated to construct alternate publics (Sundaram 2001). The conference "Contested Commons / Trespassing Publics"—organized by Sarai, Raqs, and the Alternative Law Forum, Bangalore, in New Delhi in 2005—addressed social and political issues connected with intellectual property across a wide terrain, from seeds to medicine and digital culture (Medosch 2005).

The digital commons was a conscious attempt to create mechanisms for the decommodification of more and more aspects of culture and knowledge creation. In commons-based peer production, use values are produced through shared labor. The exchange value is neglected and the tendency toward objectification gets temporarily reversed through this gift economy where code is shared without ever becoming a commodity. The digital commons provided artists with an opportunity for horizontal collaborations and exchanges in a commodity-free zone. This ideal, however, is threatened by the precarious status of knowledge workers and the overall political economy. Free culture producers have to eat and pay rent within a capitalist economy while they create economies of abundance. This disparity gnaws away at the foundations of a liberal ideal of a possible knowledge society. In 2008 the financial system of the rich nations crashed, pushing them into a prolonged economic crisis. As austerity measures are plowing their ways through social systems, failure to act on climate change and a looming energy crisis create rising dissatisfaction with the current regimes and their inability to tackle questions of such fundamental importance.

At this historical moment, many artist-activists are working out post-capitalist and ecological survival strategies. In these scenarios the commons occupies a central position as a potential new framework for a political economy not based on markets. The separation between digital and natural commons is not so important anymore. The interest has shifted toward the conditions and rules that allow forms of commons to prosper. The forms of exchange in the commons may offer better possibilities for artists, as they can become part of a wider ecology. Yet there is also the danger that the commons can become recuperated, a tendency already visible in the world of software.

Conclusion

During the 2000s the Net changed quite dramatically as it became dominated by dynamic web applications known as Web 2.0, mobile applications, or so-called apps, tablets, and other new gadgets. The prophecy of two-way communications from the early 20th century seemed to have finally become realized on the scale of mass participation. Yet the egalitarian ideas of the emancipatory media paradigm were implemented only on the surface level. Behind the screens, communications between users form the basis of a new industry of Big Data. Informationalism, as the current economic paradigm has been called by Manuel Castells (2010), relies on harvesting massive amounts of data for all kinds of reasons, threatening to turn the Web and social media into one giant surveillance machine (Lyon 2007). With financial institutions on top of the social pyramid, the Web has become just another infrastructure that is beyond people's control and appears to dominate their lives, even if they do the clicking themselves.

The digital revolution has moved to the next level, commodifying communications and social relations. Now Baudrillard suddenly appears to be right once again. Objectification and the commodity-form cover the Web and social media, and thus also impinge on our social and communicative behavior. The dichotomies have been shifted on to another level. While the producer–consumer dichotomy has become blurry, another dichotomy gaining in importance is the one between the front end and back end of information systems, between client and server. While people have full two-way playful interaction on the client side, data at the server end is harvested not just by corporations but also by state institutions. Under the shifting circumstances of a globalized information economy, there is an urgent need to update the political economy of communications for the information society. Besides the political economy of the sign, we also need a political economy of information, one that is not detached from reality as the discourse of the 1990s has been, but as clear and cogent as Baudrillard's. At the same time, it should be able to account for other forms of exchange that transcend the parallel hierarchies between signifier–signified and transmitter–receiver. Many of the projects cited here have provided examples of how this can be realized. More work will be needed to develop a political economy of information that offers depth and resonates with a cultural and philosophical worldview that goes beyond the limits of the transmitter–receiver model. Cutting-edge digital art offers a unique advantage for the development of such a theoretic strand as it is not limited by disciplinary boundaries and the works are rich with links and references into different social, cultural, and techno-scientific domains. Although Enzensberger's recommendations rested on weak theoretical foundations, we need more of the type of experimentation that tries to realize the emancipatory media paradigm. The potential of empowerment through and with digital technologies is not a foregone conclusion—there is no automated utopia sitting there like a ghost in the machine—but can be considered a project: a projection of what can be attained if people fight for it, combining political will, collective action, and creativity. The 21st century creates new conditions in which the sensibilities shaped by tactical media and the aesthetics of protest are needed to address urgent issues.

Acknowledgments

With thanks to Shu Lea Cheang, Richard Barbrook, Menno Grotveld, Brian Holmes, Geert Lovink, and Felix Stalder for their comments.

Notes

1 Named after the Irish politician and Nobel peace prize winner Sean McBride who was appointed to head this commission.
2 Several reasons were cited such as undue politicization and poor management, but the New World Order of Information and Communication was clearly one major issue (Weiler 1986).
3 The term "transculturation" emerged in literary studies and has since become common in culture studies and media studies (Hall 1996; Trigo 2000; Chakravartty and Zhao 2008).
4 The title of this text has indeed nothing to do with a piece of software named Shockwave that was initially written to allow display of interactive and animated content online.
5 Also stopped short were the efforts of a group of brilliant designers, economists, and computer people who had converged on Chile to build a cybernetic operations room for the economy, an idea of Stafford Beer (Bonsiepe 2009).
6 There is convergence on this point with Welsh literary and culture studies pioneer Raymond Williams (1980).
7 Adam Smith: "The word VALUE, it is to be observed, has two different meanings, and sometimes expresses the utility of some particular object, and sometimes the power of purchasing other goods which the possession of that object conveys. The one may be called value in use;' the other, 'value in exchange.' The things which have the greatest value in use have frequently little or no value in exchange" (Smith 1904, bk.1.4.13).
8 Which, according to his translator, was strongly influenced by Lévi-Strauss (Levin 1981).
9 Core members were Karel Dudesek, Benjamin Heidersberger, Gerard Couty, and Mike Hentz.
10 The term is used here in accordance with Baudrillard's usage (1989).
11 Alexander Nikolic, Lukas Pusch, and Sam Hopkins.
12 *Agonie des Realen* is the title of a German book by Baudrillard (1981).
13 Carmin Karasic, Brett Stalbaum, and Stefan Wray.
14 The Thing is a BBS and web project by New York City-based German artist Wolfgang Staehle. http://www.thing.net (accessed January 15, 2015).
15 Brett Stalbaum, Micha Cardenas, Christopher Head, Elle Mehrmand, and Amy Sara Carroll.
16 Preemptive Media was a collaboration between Beatriz da Costa (1974–2012), Jamie Schulte, and Brooke Singer.
17 Based on narrative by Manu Luksch, private notes, December 2012–January 2013.
18 GATT was the predecessor of the WTO and stands for General Agreement on Tariffs and Trade.

19 GWEI was created by Ubermorgen together with Paolo Cirio and Alessandro Ludovico; parts 2 and 3 were co-productions of Ludovico and Cirio only.

20 A "fork" in hacker language occurs when one or more developers split from a project, taking the code base with them, which is possible under open source software licenses.

References

Aglietta, Michel. 1979. *A Theory of Capitalist Regulation: The US Experience.* London: NLB.

Amsterdam Cultural Studies et al., eds. 1992. *N5M Zapbook.* Amsterdam: Paradiso. http://www.tacticalmediafiles.net/TMF_documents/N5Mzapbook.pdf (accessed January 15, 2015).

Annie and Sam. 2012. *uktocollectives: From Indymedia UK to the United Kollektives.* London: Indymedia. http://london.indymedia.org/pages/uktokollectives (accessed January 15, 2015).

Arns, I. 2007. *Interaction, Participation, Networking.* http://www.medienkunstnetz.de/themes/overview_of_media_art/communication/18/ (accessed January 15, 2015).

Arquilla, John, and David Ronfeldt. 1993. "Cyberwar Is Coming!" *Comparative Strategy* 12(2):141–165. http://www.tandfonline.com/doi/abs/10.1080/01495939308402915 (accessed January 15, 2015).

Arquilla, John, and David Ronfeldt.1996. *The Advent of Netwar.* Santa Monica, CA: Rand Corporation.

Auer, Sepp, Peter Hueber, and Hans Kronberger. 1980. *Arbeiter machen Fernsehen.* Video Initiative.

Bansal, Lipika, Paul Keller, and Geert Lovink, eds. 2006. *In the Shade of the Commons.* Amsterdam: Waag Society.

Barbrook, Richard. 1995. *Media Freedom: The Contradictions of Communication in the Age of Modernity.* London and Boulder, CO: Pluto Press.

Barbrook, Richard, and Andy Cameron. 1996. "The Californian Ideology." *Science as Culture* 6(1): 44–72. http://www.tandfonline.com/doi/abs/10.1080/09505439609526455 (accessed January 15, 2015).

Bataille, Georges. 1988. *The Accursed Share.* New York: Zone Books.

Baudrillard, Jean. 1981. *For a Critique of the Political Economy of the Sign*, translated by Charles Levin. St. Louis, MS: Telos Press.

Baudrillard, Jean. 1995. *The Gulf War Did Not Take Place.* Bloomington, IN: Indiana University Press.

Baudrillard, Jean. 1996. *The System of Objects.* London and New York: Verso.

Bazzichelli, Tatiana. 2009. *Networking: The Net as Artwork.* Aarhus: Center for Digital Æstetik-Forskning.

Benjamin, Walter. 2002. "Der Autor als Produzent" (1934). Ansprache im Institut zum Studium des Fascismus, Paris, April 27, 1934. In *Medienästhetische Schriften*, 231–247. Frankfurt am Main: Suhrkamp.

Benkler, Yochai. 2006. *The Wealth of Networks: How Social Production Transforms Markets and Freedom.* New Haven, CT: Yale University Press.

Bishop, Claire. 2012. *Artificial Hells: Participatory Art and the Politics of Spectatorship.* London: Verso Books.

Bonsiepe, G. 2009. "Der Opsroom—zum Eigensinn der Peripherie." In *Entwurfskultur und Gesellschaft: Gestaltung zwischen Zentrum und Peripherie*, 35–62. Basle: Birkhauser.

Boyd, Lani. 2005. "The Yes Men and Activism in the Information Age." MA thesis, Faculty of the Louisiana State University and Agricultural and Mechanical College. http://etd.lsu.edu/docs/available/etd-04142005-174336/unrestricted/Boyd_thesis.pdf (accessed October 6, 2015).

Boyle, Deirdre. 1992. "A Brief History of American Documentary Video." In *N5M Zapbook*, 9–16. Amsterdam: Paradiso. http://www.tacticalmediafiles.net/TMF_documents/N5Mzapbook.pdf (accessed January 15, 2015).

Brunet, Karla Schuch. 2005. "Do-It-Yourself as Free Culture Practices: Perspectives of Brazilian Network Projects." *RE: ACTIVISM*. http://members.multimania.co.uk/sonhotipico/ai/pdf/artigos/brunettext.pdf (accessed January 15, 2015).

Budka, Philipp, and Claudia Trupp. 2009. "Indigener Cyberaktivismus und transnationale Bewegungslandschaften im lateinamerikanischen Kontext." In *Mit Hilfe der Zeichen. Por medios de signos. Transnationalismus, soziale Bewegungen und kulturelle Praktiken in Lateinamerika*, edited by Jens Kastner and Tom Waibel. Vienna: LIT. http://www.philbu.net/blog/wp-content/uploads/2009/06/budka_trupp_cyberakt_LA.pdf (accessed January 15, 2015).

Burbach, Roger. 2001. *Globalization and Postmodern Politics: From Zapatistas to High-Tech Robber Barons*. London: Pluto Press.

CAE (Critical Art Ensemble). 1993. *The Electronic Disturbance*. New York: Autonomedia. http://www.critical-art.net/books/ted/ (accessed January 15, 2015).

Candida TV. 2003. "Reality Fiction—Visions of Reality." In *Anarchitexts: A Subsol Anthology*, 153–156. New York: Autonomedia.

Cardenas, Micha, Amy Sara Carroll, Ricardo Dominguez, and Brett Stalbaum. 2009. "The Transborder Immigrant Tool: Violence, Solidarity and Hope in Post-Nafta Circuits of Bodies Electr(On)/ic." *Mobile HCI*, University of Bonn, September 15. http://www.uni-siegen.de/locatingmedia/workshops/mobilehci/cardenas_the_transborder_immigrant_tool.pdf (accessed January 15, 2015).

Castells, Manuel. 2010. *The Rise of the Network Society. The Information Age: Economy, Society and Culture*, 2nd ed. Oxford: Wiley-Blackwell.

Castells, Manuel. 2012. *Networks of Outrage and Hope: Social Movements in the Internet Age*. Oxford: Wiley-Blackwell.

Chakravartty, Paula, and Yuezhi Zhao. 2008. *Global Communications: Toward a Transcultural Political Economy*. Lanham, MD: Rowman & Littlefield.

Cheang, Shu Lea. 2002a. *Garlic=Richair-trade*. Video. Dailymotion.http://www.dailymotion.com/video/x92ivg_garlic-richair-trade_creation (accessed January 15, 2015).

Cheang, Shu Lea. 2002b. *GET GARLIC. GO WIRELESS. GARLIC=RICH AIR*. http://archives.lists.indymedia.org/imc-nyc-coverage/2002-September/000099.html accessed January 15, 2015).

Cippitelli, Lucrezia. 2008. "Slum Tv, Tv Di Strada A Nairobi." *Digicult | digital art, design and culture*. http://www.digicult.it/digimag/issue-022/slum-tv-street-tv-in-nairobi/ (accessed January 15, 2015).

Cirio, Paolo. 2013. *Loophole For All*. http://loophole4all.com/ (accessed January 15, 2015).

Cope, Bill, Mary Kalantzis, and New London Group. 2000. *Multiliteracies: Literacy Learning and the Design of Social Futures*. London and New York: Routledge.

De Angelis, Massimo. 1998. "Limiting the Limitless: Global Neoliberal Capital, New Internationalism and the Zapatistas' Voice." http://homepages.uel.ac.uk/M.DeAngelis/ZAPINT3B.HTM#UNO (accessed January 15, 2015).

De Certeau, Michel. 1984. *The Practice of Everyday Life: Michel de Certeau*, translated by Steven Rendall. Berkeley, CA: University of California Press.

Debord, Guy. 1983. *Society of the Spectacle*, translated by Ken Knabb. London: Rebel Press.

Dominguez, Ricardo. 1995. "Run for the Border: The Taco Bell War." *Ctheory*. December 13. http://www.ctheory.net/articles.aspx?id=155 (accessed January 15, 2015).

Dominguez, Ricardo. 1996. "Zapatistas: The Recombinant Movie." *Ctheory*, November 21. http://www.ctheory.net/printer.aspx?id=83 (accessed January 15, 2015).

Downing, John. 1984. *Radical Media: The Political Experience of Alternative Communication*. Boston, MA: South End Press.

Düllo, Thomas, and Franz Liebl. 2005. *Cultural Hacking: Die Kunst Des Strategischen Handelns*. Vienna: Springer.

Enzensberger, Hans Magnus. 1970. "Constituents of a Theory of the Media." *New Left Review* (64): 13–36.

Florida, Richard L. 2002. *The Rise of the Creative Class : And How It's Transforming Work, Leisure, Community and Everyday Life*. New York: Basic Books.

Freire, Alexandre, Ariel G. Foina, and Felipe Fonseca. 2007. "O impacto da sociedade civil (des) organizada: Cultura digital, os articuladores e software livre no projeto dos pontos de cultura do minc." *Buscalegis, América do Norte* 24(5). http://egov.ufsc.br/portal/sites/default/files/anexos/6041-6033-1-PB.pdf (accessed January 15, 2015).

Freire, Paolo. 1972. *Pedagogy of the Oppressed*. London: Penguin Books.

Froebel, Folker, Jürgen Heinrichs, and Otto Kreye. 1980. *The New International Division of Labour: Structural Unemployment in Industrialised Countries and Industrialisation in Developing Countries*, translated by Pete Burgess. Cambridge/Paris: Cambridge University Press/Éditions de la Maison des sciences de l'homme.

Fusco, Coco. 2003. "Ricardo Dominguez interviewed by Coco Fusco 'Electronic Disturbance.'" In *Anarchitexts: A Subsol Anthology*, 98–106. New York: Autonomedia.

Garcia, David. 2004. "Fine Young Cannibals, of Brazilian Tactical Media." *Descentro*. Posted 10 September 2004. http://pub.descentro.org/fine_young_cannibals_of_brazilian_tactical_media (accessed July 13, 2007).

Garrido, Maria, and Alexander Halavais. 2003. "Mapping Networks of Support for the Zapatista Movement: Applying Social Networks Analysis to Study Contemporary Social Movements." In *Cyberactivism: Online Activism in Theory and Practice*. London: Routledge.

Gilroy, Paul. 2001. *Against Race: Imagining Political Culture Beyond the Color Line*. Cambridge, MA: Belknap Press of Harvard University Press.

Grootveld, Menno. 2012. "De laatste vrije media vanhet Westen." *De Groene Amsterdammer*, March1.http://www.groene.nl/2012/God%20Save%20the%20Queen/de-laatste-vrije-media-vanhet-westen (accessed January 15, 2015).

Guattari, Félix. 1984. *Molecular Revolution: Psychiatry and Politics*. Harmondsworth, UK: Penguin.

Hadziselimovic, Adnan. 2012. "FLOSSTV Free, Libre, Open Source Software (FLOSS) within participatory 'TV hacking' Media and Arts Practices." Doctoral thesis, Goldsmiths, University of London. http://eprints.gold.ac.uk/6922/ (accessed January 15, 2015).

Hall, Stuart. 1996. "When Was the Post-colonial?" In *The Post-Colonial Question*, edited by Iain Chambers and Lidia Curti, 242–259. London and New York: Routledge.
Halleck, DeeDee. 2002. *Hand-held Visions: The Impossible Possibilities of Community Media*. New York: Fordham University Press.
Harvey, David. 1989. *The Condition of Postmodernity: An Enquiry into the Origins of Cultural Change*. Oxford: Basil Blackwell.
Harvey, David. 2005. *A Brief History of Neoliberalism*. Oxford: Oxford University Press.
Holloway, John. 2005. *Change the World Without Taking Power*, 2nd ed. London and Ann Arbor, MI: Pluto Press.
Holmes, Brian. 2009. *Escape the Overcode: Activist Art in the Control Society*. Amsterdam and Zagreb: Van Abbemuseum / WHW. http://brianholmes.wordpress.com/2009/01/19/book-materials/ (accessed January 15, 2015).
Horkheimer, Max, and Theodor W. Adorno. 2006. "Kulturindustrie, Aufklärung als Massenbetrug." In *Dialektik der Aufklärung : philosophische Fragmente*, 16th ed., 128–176. Frankfurt am Main: Fischer Taschenbuch Verlag.
Katsiaficas, George. 1987. *The Imagination of the New Left: A Global Analysis of 1968*. Boston, MA: South End Press.
Kelly, Kevin. 1995. *Out of Control: The New Biology of Machines, Social Systems, & the Economic World*. New York: Basic Books.
Kidd, Dorothy. 2003. "Indymedia.org: A New Communications Commons." In *Cyberactivism: Online Activism in Theory and Practice*. New York and London: Routledge.
Lane, Jill. 2003. "Digital Zapatistas." *TDR / The Drama Review* 47(2): 129–144. http://www.mitpressjournals.org/doi/abs/10.1162/105420403321921274 (accessed January 15, 2015).
Larsen, Ernest. 1995. "When the Crowd Rustles the Tiger Roars." *Art Journal* 54(4): 73. http://www.jstor.org/discover/10.2307/777699?uid=3737528&uid=2&uid=4&sid=21101530980511 (accessed January 15, 2015).
Lave, Jean, and Etienne Wenger. 1991. *Situated Learning: Legitimate Peripheral Participation*. Cambridge: Cambridge University Press.
Lefebvre, Henri. 2009. *Dialectical Materialism*. Minneapolis: University of Minnesota Press.
Levin, Charles. 1981. "Translator's Introduction." In *For a Critique of the Political Economy of the Sign*, 5–28. St. Louis, MS: Telos Press.
Linebaugh, Peter, and Marcus Rediker. 2000. *The Many-Headed Hydra: Sailors, Slaves, Commoners, and the Hidden History of the Revolutionary Atlantic*. Boston, MA: Beacon Press.
Lovink, Geert. 1992. "The Theory of Mixing." *Mediamatic Magazine* 6(4). http://www.mediamatic.net/5750/en/the-theory-of-mixing (accessed January 15, 2015).
Lovink, Geert, and Patrice Riemens. 2000. "Amsterdam Public Digital Culture 2000." *Telepolis* August 18. http://www.heise.de/tp/artikel/6/6972/1.html (accessed January 15, 2015).
Lukács, Georg. 1971. *History and Class Consciousness: Studies in Marxist Dialectics*. Cambridge, MA: The MIT Press.
Luksch, Manu, and Mukul Patel. 2009. "Chasing the Data Shadow." In *Ambient Information Systems*, 276–293. London: AIS.
Lyon, David. 2007. *Surveillance Studies*. Cambridge, UK and Malden, MA: Polity.
Marx, Karl. 1976. *Capital: Volume I: A Critique of Political Economy*, translated by Ben Fowkes. London: Penguin Books.

Mauss, Marcel. 1967. *The Gift: Forms and Functions of Exchange in Archaic Societies*. New York: Norton.

McBride, Sean, and International Commission for the Study of Communication Problems, eds. 1980. *Many Voices, One World : Towards a New, More Just, and More Efficient World Information and Communication Order*. London/New York/Paris: Kogan/Page/Unesco.

McDonough, Tom. 2004. "Introduction: Ideology and the Situationist Utopia." In *Guy Debord and the Situationist International: Texts and Documents*, 10–23. Cambridge, MA: The MIT Press.

Medosch, Armin. 2003. "Demonstrieren in der virtuellen Republik." In *Bürgerrechte im Netz*, Bundeszentrale für politische Bildung – Schriftenreihe, 261–306. Bonn: Leske + Budrich.

Medosch, Armin. 2005. Report from *Contested Commons / Trespassing Publics*, a Conference on Inequalities, Conflicts and Intellectual Property. In *Pixelache 2005: Dot Org Boom*. Pixelache Catalogue, 71–73. Helsinki: Pixelache.

Medosch, Armin. 2009. "AmbientTV.NET: Open Doors, Open Systems." In *Ambient Information Systems*, 336–368. London: AIS.

Mosco, Vincent. 2008. "Current Trends in the Political Economy of Communication." *Global Media Journal – Canadian Edition* 1(1): 45–63. http://www.gmj.uottawa.ca/0801/inaugural_mosco_e.html (accessed January 15, 2015).

Mosco, Vincent. 2009. *The Political Economy of Communication*. Thousand Oaks, CA: Sage.

Nikolic, Alexander, Lukas Pusch, Sam Hopkins, and Lucrezia Cippitelli. 2008. *Slum TV in Beograd and Novi Sad*. Belgrade / Novi Sad: CULTURAL CENTER DOB / Youth Centre CK13.

Raijmakers, Bas. 1992. "Introduction." In *N5M Zapbook*. Amsterdam: Paradiso. http://www.tacticalmediafiles.net/TMF_documents/N5Mzapbook.pdf (accessed January 15, 2015).

Raqs Media Collective, 2003. ""value and its other in electronic culture: slave ships and pirate galleons." In *DIVE An Introduction into the World of Free Software and Copyleft Culture*, 30–36. Liverpool and London: FACT.

Raqs Media Collective, Jeebesh Bagchi, Monica Narula, and Shuddhabrata Sengupta. n.d. Raqs Media Collective. http://www.raqsmediacollective.net/works.aspx# (accessed January 15, 2015).

Richardson, Joanne. 2003. "The Language of Tactical Media." In *Anarchitexts: A Subsol Anthology*, 123–128. New York: Autonomedia.

Rosas, Ricardo. 2004. "The Revenge of Low-tech: Autolabs, Telecentros and Tactical Media in Sao Paulo." In *Crisis / Media*, Sarai Reader, 424–433. http://www.sarai.net/publications/readers/04-crisis-media/55ricardo.pdf (accessed January 15, 2015).

Sassen, Saskia. 2001. *The Global City: New York, London, Tokyo*. Princeton, NJ: Princeton University Press.

Shannon, Claude E., and Warren Weaver. 1949. *The Mathematical Theory of Communication*. Urbana, IL: University of Illinois Press.

Shikata, Yukiko, Armin Medosch, and Shu Llea Cheang. 2003. *Kingdom of Piracy*. http://kop.kein.org.http://v2.nl/archive/works/kingdom-of-piracy. (accessed January 15, 2015).

Shikata, Yukiko. 2005. "Median in Transition: 1989–2004." In *Art Meets Media: Adventures in Perception*. Exhibition catalog, NTTICC, Tokyo, January 21–March 21, 108–119. Tokyo: NTT Publishing.

Smith, Adam. 1904. *An Inquiry into the Nature and Causes of the Wealth of Nations.* London: Methuen & Co., Ltd. http://www.econlib.org/library/Smith/smWNCover.html (accessed January 15, 2015).

Stalder, Felix. 1999. "Challenging the WTO Online." *Telepolis*, November 18. http://www.heise.de/tp/artikel/5/5496/1.html (accessed January 15, 2015).

Sundaram, Ravi. 2001. "Recycling Modernity: Pirate Electronic Cultures in India." In *Sarai Reader 01: Public Domain*, 93–99. Delhi / Amsterdam: Sarai / DeWaag.

Tozzi, Tommaso. 1995. "A Project and an Action." http://amsterdam.nettime.org/Lists-Archives/nettime-l-9601/msg00000.html (accessed January 15, 2015).

Tozzi, Tommaso. 1996. "chiapas net strike." http://amsterdam.nettime.org/Lists-Archives/nettime-l-9602/msg00018.html (accessed January 15, 2015).

Trigo, Abril. 2000. "Shifting Paradigms: From Transculturation to Hybridity: A Theoretical Critique." In *Unforeseeable Americas*, 85–111. Amsterdam and Atlanta: Editions Rodopi.

Virilio, Paul. 1994. *The Vision Machine.* Bloomington, IN: Indiana University Press.

Virno, Paul. 2004. *A Grammar of the Multitude: For an Analysis of Contemporary Forms of Life.* Los Angeles/New York/Cambridge, MA: semiotext(e)/The MIT Press.

Virno, Paul and Michael Hardt, eds. 2006. *Radical Thought in Italy: A Potential Politics.* Minneapolis, MN: University of Minnesota Press.

Vishmidt, M. 2006. *Media Mutandis A Node.london Reader: A Survey of Media Arts, Technologies and Politics.* London: Node.London and OpenMute.

Weiler, Hans N. 1986. "Withdrawing from UNESCO: A Decision in Search of an Argument." *Comparative Education Review* 30(1): 132–139. http://www.jstor.org/stable/10.2307/1188274 (accessed January 15, 2015).

Williams, Raymond. 1980. *Problems in Materialism and Culture: Selected Essays.* London: Verso.

Wishart, Adam, and Regula Bochsler. 2002. *Leaving Reality Behind: Inside the Battles for the Soul of the Internet.* London: Fourth Estate.

16

Critical Intelligence in Art and Digital Media

Konrad Becker

The creative imperative has become a dominant force. As culture has become an economic engine in post-industrial societies, art diffuses into business practice and the realm of the creative industries.

This chapter explores how digital art practice can do more than propagate technical progress and provide affect stimulus in aestheticized production cycles.

In present-day information societies, technologies of imagination and visual representation are embedded and exploited in ubiquitous digital networks. Imagination is a traditional domain of artists and cultural workers. What has changed with the worldwide permeation of communication technology machines? Which art practices or cultural forms address the challenges of a networked digital universe?

What are potential roles of cultural agents in societies saturated and structured by powerful information technologies? Questions regarding the engineering of the imagination arise for all new generations of artists in modernity. But how does their discontent relate to the new spirit of capitalism and the arts? How can artistic practices be relevant in the battle over the resources of the imagination, and what is agency in the cultural field?

Society and technology interact in feedback loops and dynamic interdependence. New media builds on layers of media archaeology and traditions of smoke and mirrors, where fragile concepts of reality reveal the anxious relation to technology. Since the late 18th century automatons have become recurrent figures in ambiguous representations of sexuality and subjectivity. Mary Shelley's *Frankenstein* exposes the uncanny nature of electricity in a time of 19th-century technological breakthroughs that fired spiritualist beliefs in ghosts. Gothic fiction spins dark tales on the rational explanations and ontological cracks of factual realities in an industrializing world. Globalized networks of steamships, trains, and telegraphs not only changed the world but the modes of life, work, and play. Beyond the economization of culture and the culturization of the political economy a creative imperative has become dominant. Urban landscapes

A Companion to Digital Art, First Edition. Edited by Christiane Paul.

require new modes of tactical operative interventions that draw on the extended trajectories of strategies. In this context a practice of cultural intelligence is needed to addresses fiction and agency of change in critical ways.

Digital Communication

Digital media art uses communication technologies as tools and takes information as its raw material. However, communication has many meanings, ranging from the existential exposure of otherness or likeness to mysterious systems of semantic classification. Definitions cover anything from pragmatic organization of empiric action patterns and breakout attempts from the fortress of the self to media- and entertainment-powered opinion management. Whatever meaning one chooses, communication is mostly a political and social problem, not a semantic or technical one. Conventions of representation inscribed into media are always political. While concepts of communication are multifaceted and remain opaque, asymmetric invisibility and hidden forces in the geometries of knowledge can be made more apparent in art practices that deal with intangible materials.

Digital communication and the atomic bomb both have their origin in the research environment of World War II, a milieu in which the science of cybernetics, a term coined by Norbert Wiener (1948) to denote the study of teleological mechanisms, announced a new era of form in the information age: time becomes space and the boundaries of inside and outside are broken. From DNA as the great code of life to the world of arts, language, and social science, communication was considered the fundamental, shared process—a historic paradigm, long beyond half-life, that unified the sciences of the nuclear age. The Macy Conferences on Cybernetics, a group including Norbert Wiener, John von Neumann, Margaret Mead, and Gregory Bateson, met from 1946 to 1953 to explore scientific ideas that had emerged in the war years. Modernist beliefs in the ultimate transparency of pure communication failed to realize its inescapable opacity and the layered indirectness of decision making. Both technocratic information theory and therapeutic discourse of self-realization in modern bourgeois life share angelic ideals of perfect exchange in denial of communication breakdown. Dreams of perfect semantic systems mirror fantasies of telepathy. A politics of the union of minds, as if bodies did not matter, is a problem.

Interactive Media

In a caricature of Cold War high-tech labs a considerable quantity of traditional interactive media arts celebrated classic banal schemes of manipulation. Response mechanisms based on oversimplified technical models of communication and decision trees lacking complexity impose a rigid interaction matrix. Mirroring the bland efforts of drawing consumers into marketing schemes, plenty of interactive communication artwork revealed the dull righteousness and the moral despotism of dialogism. Interactivity, the name of the game for many in 1980s new media art and culture, turned into a business model for TV call-in participation and inquisitive questionnaires of data-mined fidelity cards. In the process, human interaction is reduced to economic functionality where a generalized contractual exchange of goods replaces free mutual give-and-take.

"Dialogue: The Ultimate Communication" (2003) in Harvard Business School speak, is the art of the hustler. Dialogue scenarios allow tactics of humiliation and depreciation, intimidation and terror. Power plays are masked as "free and open" good will. More often than not dialogue is like a cross-examination, a disciplinary method of grilling someone. Dialogue techniques relate to torture where afflicting pain is interrogation foreplay. Merchants of anxiety, interrogators stop the dialogue when the desired information is extracted from the respondent. The Cold War is over and, in today's code war, relevant digital media relate to networked multi-channel practices of distributed systems. With them comes the need to address their effects in a critical way and to demystify the subtle implications of new network paradigms on a cultural level.

Intangible Materials

"Information society" is not just a phrase made visible by the increasing conflicts between the owners of information commodities, on the one side, and authors and users, on the other. Down to the point of criminalizing children for sharing a song, these issues have arrived in the mainstream. Recent financial meltdowns showed the extent of wealth accumulation and destruction in speculative systems that are largely decoupled from material value. The battle for the distribution of wealth is not just based on traditional material or energy production but increasingly is fought around concepts of the intangible world of intellectual property and licensing rights. Nowadays wealth creation and the conflicts of distribution are about intangible assets, IP (intellectual property) regimes and the control of ideas. The 21st-century blood-streams of oil are flows and transactions of IP. Arguing that "Intellectual property is the oil of the 21st century" (*The Economist* 2000), Mark Getty, founder of Getty Images, which holds one of the world's largest copyright portfolios, used his family's oil fortune to invest in immaterial rights.

Conflict lines are largely between public and private interests, between a greater societal public and virtual cartels formed by extreme market concentration: a struggle between those who look at information as raw material and a social resource that needs to be freely available and those who see it as a commodity to be sold to consumers, creating scarcity out of abundance with legal and technological means. This is a rift that cuts deep into the scenes of artistic cultural production. At the same time, the pressure of IP lobbies to control access to information makes concepts and practices of a commons more needed than ever.

Networked cultural knowledge work calls for an information commons where the greatest number of people has the most unrestricted access to scientific and other types of information. It calls for infrastructures that free information from the control of the distributors whose role originally was created by the difficulties of moving printed matter and other physical objects around. Cultural practitioners need open and dynamic models to create and share digital information. Taking full advantage of the Internet's empowering capacities, the commons is based on the very idea that information can be copied and distributed easily and cheaply. Eben Moglen, Professor of Law at Columbia University in New York, sees it as a moral question: "If you could make enough food to feed everyone on earth by baking one loaf of bread and press one button what would be the moral case for denying anyone the food?" (Moglen 2003).

Asymmetric Invisibility

In the new information economy there are displacements of what is traditionally considered useful knowledge. This is not only different from what is considered educational ideals from the canon of a 19th-century middle class but also a matter of access to data processing and the new machinery of symbol manipulation. The collected complete works of Shakespeare need less than 5 megabytes of memory; today any new smartphone holds gigabytes. Professional knowledge economies work with terabytes, petabytes, and exabytes, though, and such big data cannot be processed by humans. At the heart of the new communications landscape are the machine classification and analysis of data. These cognitive tools and analytical data are no longer accessible to a critical civil society or non-governmental organizations, let alone artists or cultural producers.

This asymmetric digital environment creates major imbalances and—by extension—an artificial scarcity of knowledge or non-information society for the majority. Additionally, the increasing personalization of information in search engines like Google or so-called social networks limits access to information and encloses the users of the network in filter bubbles that self-reinforce beliefs. There is, on the one hand, a decentralized, transparent citizen, and, on the other, an entirely invisible core that retains control of these systems at the apex. Arcane knowledge, knowledge as a power base of the ruling elite, is in the hands of fully opaque private interests. Of course all autocrats of the last five thousand years have dreamed of having the kind of knowledge of their citizens that Google has today—a historical unique asymmetry of relations that is hardly compatible with a democratic society.

The Creative Empire

Traditionally it has been religion and politics that exploited artistic technologies of the imagination. They played the registers of affective stimulus specifically in nationalistic, militaristic, or other "visionary" models of social collectives. Art often displaces religious sentiments in secular societies. However, deprived of affect, the rigid social logic of bourgeois functionalist pseudo-rationalism rapidly deteriorates into a general crisis of motivation. With traditional beliefs on the way out, cold rationality is hardly an attractive argument for getting out of bed in the morning.

In the 19th century, increasingly small peripheral social circles, often bound together by an elevation of specific aesthetic codes and a "creative style," fell in opposition to changes driven by this mercantilist industrialization of the world. Clearly, bohemian romanticism about individual creativity did not match well with bourgeois ideas about wage work, family, and education at the time. In the new century the anti-capitalist cultural critique present from 1800 up to the 1960s has become standard operating procedure for the creative industries. However, it would be a stretch to claim that the emancipatory drives of 19th-century bohemians have won over. These "business models" hardly qualify as a late gratification of generations of cultural rebels. On the contrary, creativity returns as a repressive farce. A subcultural attack on the dominant vulgar rationalism of the 19th and 20th centuries turned into a new hegemony of the creative imperative.

What used to be marginal ideas against a repressive hierarchy of power is now mainstream culture and decorates the lifestyles of new oppressive elites. A countercultural strategy of creating emancipatory spaces in the symbolic realm has turned on itself. The radical gesture to transform everyday life into art, the liberating move to integrate life into artistic practice, takes a treacherous turn. Everyone is now supposed to be a creative entrepreneur. In creative cities job profiles demand "creativity" for even the most mundane tasks. Dreams of everyone being an artist turn into nightmares of internalized governmentality. To be non-creative becomes a miserable dark place of exclusion and anyone not under the spell of the creative imperative is identified as one of the cognitively challenged unfortunates.

Thought reform, self-growth psychology, and human potential movements all contributed to this triumph of creativity turned internalized spectacle. Traditionally, creativity was linked to madness and the darkness of individual psychological extremes. However, in the 1960s, psychoanalytic psychology came to view the creative as a process that saves symbol manipulation from ossification, senile repetition, or obsessive-compulsive behavior. This innocent assumption seems to have turned toxic, not at least because the precarious creative imperative comes with a lethal dose of positive thinking.

Cultural Economies

With culture powering post-industrial societies, art diffuses into business practices. When culture is perceived as an economic engine, artistic production comes out of the luxury deco-ware closet and into the realm of creative industries. Creativity, the new oil for the machines of social organization and the construction of a self, is harnessed into the pragmatism of economic rationality and wage labor. Coupling rational optimization and aesthetic innovation in the new creative world, rationalized and economized social relations produce disjunctions of aesthetic stimulation and social affect. A lot of established rationality is based on the logic of equivalent exchange, and equivalence in exchange created through a financial medium establishes a need for identification of object and subject, of owner and owned. This need lies at the core of obsessions with an identity that is only realized when nothing is identical to itself. In a neo-medieval political order, in the dominions of information feudalism, the disturbance of the boundaries of original and copy constitutes a major crime. "Piracy is like terrorism today and it exists everywhere," announced Kamil Idris, Director General of WIPO (World Intellectual Property Organization), at the World Summit on the Information Society (Idris 2003). At the same time, the technological ability to make copies that are indistinguishable from or even better than the original changes the notion of authenticity and undermines the distinction between counterfeit and real.

In the shift of the economic focus toward a dematerialized value, innovation cycles of planned obsolescence and aestheticized experience design turn into standard models. Not just an issue of customer relations, aestheticized culturization emotionally charges mass products to counter anomic lack of meaning. Unfortunately, there is ample testimony that enforced originality ends up as exceptionally bland production of trivia and that the mass production of exclusivity generates the exact opposite. Efficient maximization of innovation cycles is paradoxically experienced as standstill. At the same time, the inflation of supposed "innovation" driving the aesthetic markets is increasingly dependent on authoritative testimonies—a classification hierarchy channeled through a pyramid of authority and gated groupthink that ridicules ideas of a free market. The currency for biopolitical effect is the hypnotic affection for "creative" objects that largely rely on "credit" as a trusted validation by supposed authorities. Not only is urban governmentality in late modernity increasingly cultural, the cultural practices of cities unfolding in creative city branding competitions are always bureaucratically engineered. Creative regimes of self-rule are coupled to institutionalized steering mechanisms not only through funding structures but through cascading flows of incentives, relational validation, and mutual dependencies. A reduction of culture to practices conforming to the economy of a sociopolitical regime of creativity constitutes the grid and boundaries of what can possibly be expressed. Regimented practices of minor deviations from the general norm create subjective illusions of genuine impulse.

Imagineering Work

Since ancient times aristocracies have held up their class values by adoring objects of beauty. Admiring the superiority of artworks is co-functional to the affirmation of supremacy of the social group that celebrates them. When the Western idea of a contained individual self—a cultural construction of the late 18th century—developed, a rising bourgeois class evolved the concept of art into a mental set. Focused less on uniqueness than on finding a substitute for individuality, this class associated beauty with taste and a process of reverence for activities suiting their needs. In food testing, amplitude is the integration level of different flavors and stimuli reaching the taste buds and olfactory glands. Contemporary art-market schemes trade in high amplitude aesthetics, a seamless blending of sensory experience where constituent elements converge into a single gestalt. However, aesthetic discrimination is not rocket science; apparently, street pigeons can easily be trained as curators when sufficiently conditioned to identify specific categories of beauty. A study at the Keio University Department of Psychology in Tokyo shows how pigeons discriminate "good" and "bad" paintings (Watanabe 2010, 2011). That is why art markets that are invested in specific aesthetic games within spaces of representation tend to thrive on a mystification of creation. Adopting the requirements of branding and marketing cycles, they value questionable originality and insignificant stylistic "innovations." Only the naïve might outnumber the cynics in this celebrity cult powered by the echo chambers of media representation and the dynamics of agglomerated recognition value. It's not the unique qualities of an object or celebrity that are relevant, but the fact that this object or person somehow attracts "followers" and "likes" in the first place. Accumulated capital in the attention economy is in itself an object of wonder and amazement. Accordingly, explanations of talent, a product of success, are rationalizations after the fact.

As long as art renounces a claim to intelligence and remains safely removed from societal practice, it is easily tolerated. For some, the affirmative use value of art is mostly defined by aestheticized uselessness. Anthropological fieldwork in colonial times often found a profound pragmatism alongside the inscribed glorification of ritual cult objects. Typically ascribed to the devious nature of the natives, this ambiguity of cultural idols is hardly foreign to Western traditions. Unsurprisingly, there are many claims about aesthetic deficiencies or obsolete didactic gestures in what is made out to be political cultural practice. Many people position art in some imagined realm above all murky issues, daydreaming of an art that never was. They fail to realize that any act is political and that the impure, existing outside a supposedly natural order, is more interesting than the sterile categories that confine human existence. Nineteenth-century art-for-art's-sake mysticism, free from history or society, and the modernist attempts to liberate art from the vulgar impurities of life, only constructed self-referential, well-sealed tombs. Alternatively, rendering art as pure subversion provided new ideas for neoconservative intellectuals.

A New Spirit of Art

"Down with art that aspires to be nothing more than a spot of beauty on the ugly lives of the rich," was a claim in the 1920s (Rodtschenko 1920/1921). By the mid-20th century the opposite poles of pure form and revolt collapsed into each other. Situationists held art to be so deformed by its bourgeois packaging that activities had to cease to be works of art. Guy Debord considers art an activity "to which one no longer could honorably devote oneself" (Debord 1956). In "Methods of Detournement" (Debord 1956), he refers to the role of the artist in an information age civil war, addressing our future present of symbolic manipulation in societies saturated by powerful communication technologies.

At the turn of the century activism thrived on the idea that, if control or negative feedback is a key to power, one can fight back through positive feedback. It soon became clear that strategies of affirmation, to play to power their own melody, can easily turn into a comedy routine that fits well with how things play out. Even desperate despots accommodate jesters when it adds to their prestige. Media stunts that mostly serve to enhance the name recognition of its actors render it a questionable practice. In the same way that Situationist tactics have been misappropriated for advertisement, tactical media concepts of the 1990s are now public relations and viral marketing standards. When the Viennese group Public Netbase started a fake citizen initiative "Rettet den Karlsplatz" ("Save Karlsplatz") in 2003 as part of a series of urban cultural interventions in the city center, it was in reference to companies like Burson-Marsteller that routinely orchestrate fake grass-roots campaigns for governments and large enterprises (Figures 16.1 and 16.2). Guerrilla marketing is not only targeting young audiences for lifestyle products; by 2011 even the Federation of Austrian Industrialists used a strategy of hoaxes for tactical media invasion under the name The BirdBase. Dissent is easily appropriated in the new spirit of capitalism and today's critique is tomorrow's business idea. Creative industry embraces aestheticized boutique activism that offers affective relief with a maximum of inconsequentiality.

Effective strategies of resistance and critical interventions need to build on understanding the past; however, a change from disciplinarian institutions to a society of control has transformed the playing field. The commercial drive into cultural niche markets corresponds to a transition from disciplinarian modes of preconfigured categories to individualized control societies. In new control regimes the traditional modes of enforced categorization and educational indoctrination give way to a fluid mining of cognitive response and reaction flows. Electronic networks and intelligent materials weave asymmetric relations into the fabric of social space and into infrastructures of urban places. Embedded in ambient Big Data intelligence, proprietary protocols and

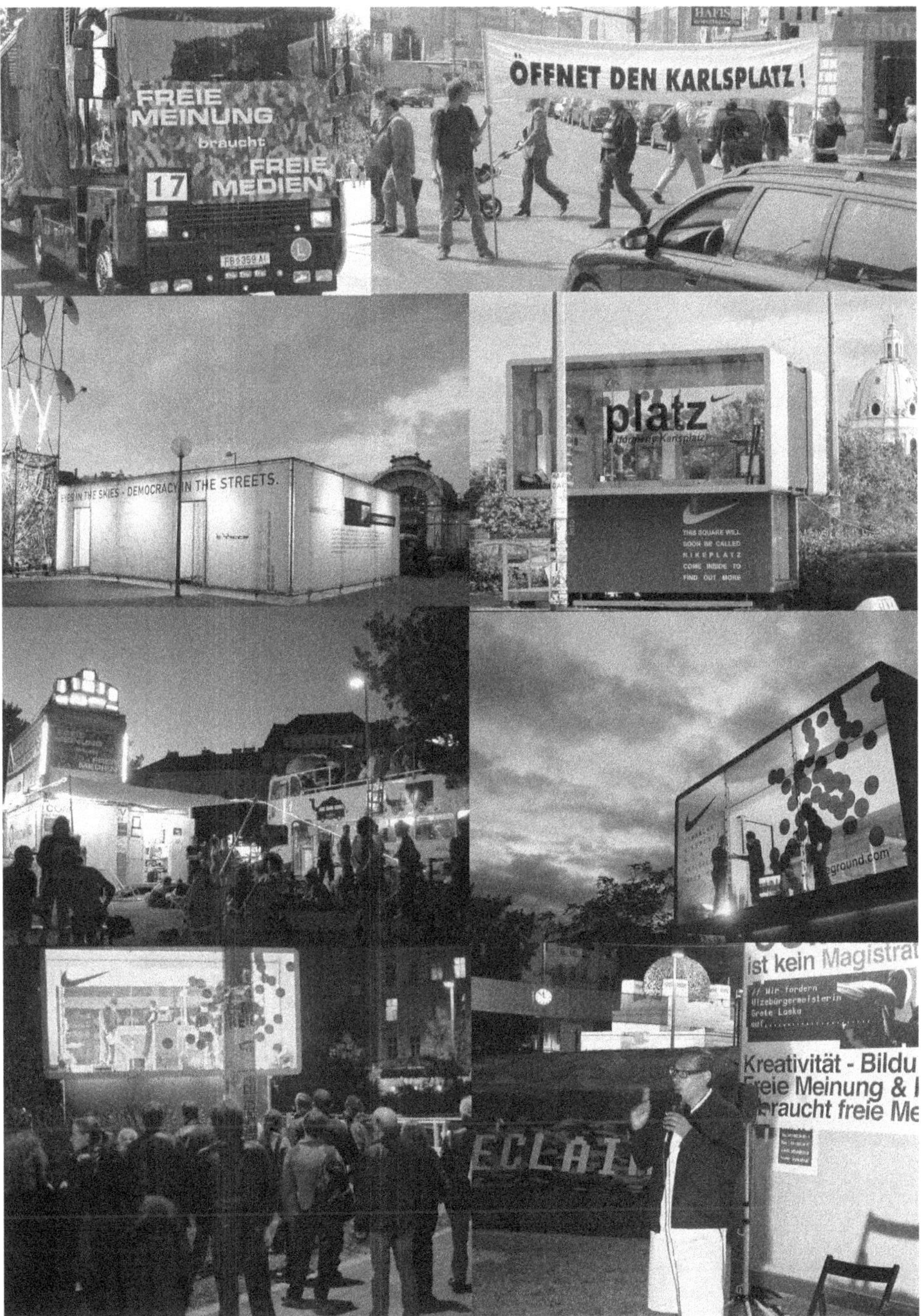

FIGURE 16.1 Urban interventions and tactical media. Karlsplatz, Vienna, 2003–2004.

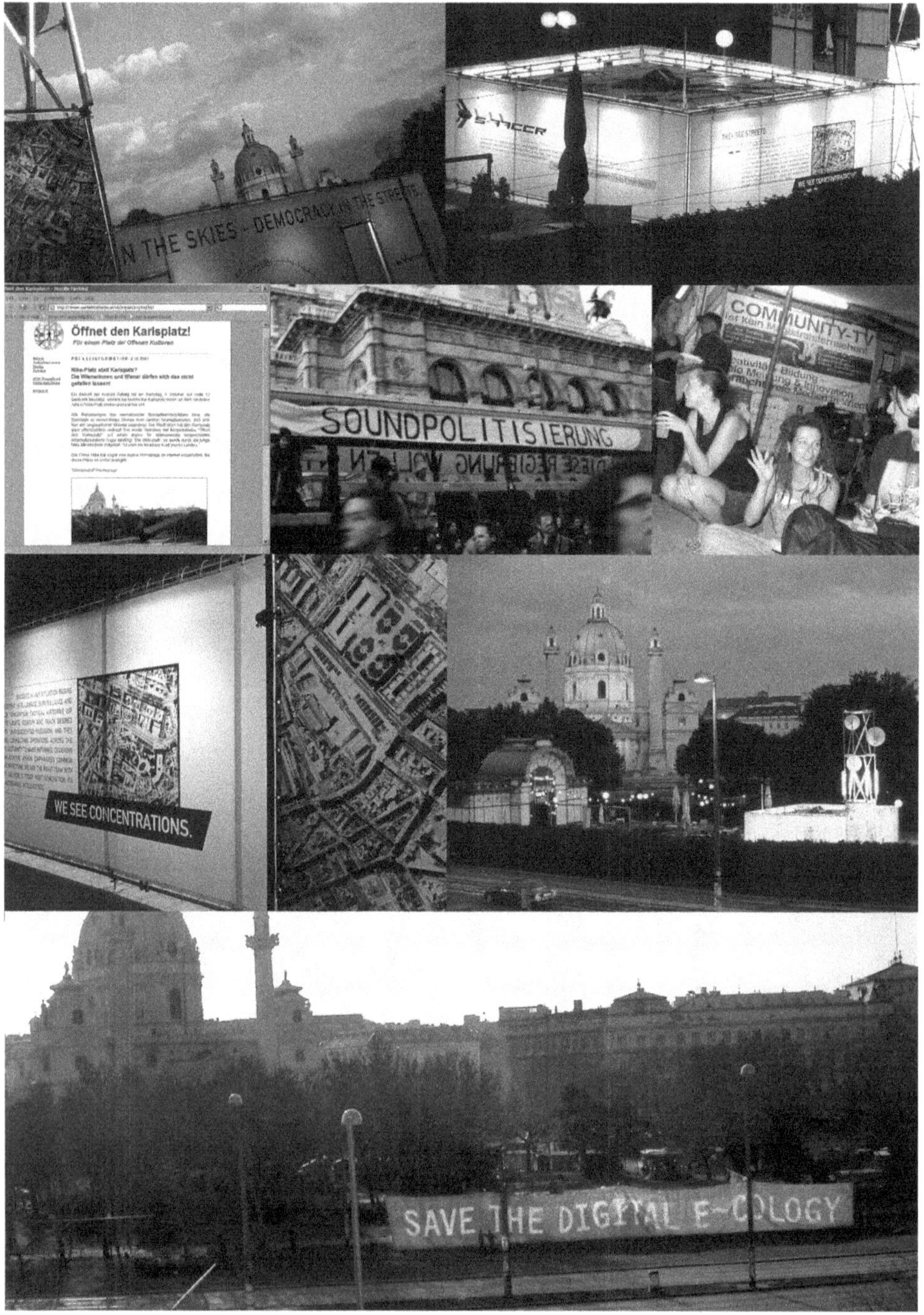

FIGURE 16.2 Urban interventions and tactical media. Karlsplatz, Vienna, 2003–2004. Examples of a strategic series of tactical operations in a central public space. Public Netbase in cooperation with various artists, including Projekt Atol (S77CCR) and 0100101110101101.org (Nikeground), including multiple activist alliances (MediaCamp, Free Re:Public a.o.). Source: Institute for New Culture Technologies/t0.

decentralized devices exploit the individual. Density and speed of digital networking veils the paradoxical effects of increased fragmentation and segregation. So-called "Web 2.0 interfaces" enable the commodification of subjectivity in "social networks," in a culture medium for harvesting narcissist drives and regressive exhibitionism that are then licensed back to the user. Subjectivity is not only the new business target but is also a realm influencing political organization.

Smoke and Mirrors

New communication technologies produce anxieties in relation to representations of reality. Ancient precursors of digital media environments also had uncanny dimensions. Current virtual reality systems and digital simulation technologies of the military entertainment complex have their origins in ghost dramas, the immersive spirit techno-spectacles of the 18th-century phantasmagoria. The history of communication machines is a ghost story. Phantasmagoria—etymologically, "I speak illusion"—thrilled and terrified audiences through embedded magic lanterns. Apparatuses for the raising of specters incorporated complicated contraptions and an ingenious automatic focus to allow for the device being moved. Beginning with the daguerreotype in 1839, the new medium became an important element of the spiritualist séance. Spirits of the dead incarnated themselves into the new technology like ghosts in pursuit of bodies. Affinities of the new medium and contemporary mediums of spirit possession became apparent when spirit photography became a major genre. Photography also played an important role in promoting mediums across continents in the early 20th century. Offering "proof" of ectoplasm, photographic spirit materialization provided a metaphor for the relation between matter and the immaterial. Fixing the spirits of the dead in a reproducible image addresses the fact that humans are chained to an individual and collective past whose ghosts dominate their presence.

Soon after Samuel Morse introduced the electromagnetic telegraph in 1844, the world was swept by "Spiritualism," a popular movement that constructed scientific beliefs that the dead are in contact with the living. Thomas Edison, keen to build a radio to communicate with the spirits of the netherworld, tried to design a receiver for ghosts in the 1920s. "If we can evolve an instrument so delicate as to be affected by our personality as it survives in the next life, such an instrument, when made available, ought to record something" (Edison 1920). In the 1930s the self-declared medium Attila von Szalay claimed moderate success at recording voices on gramophone records and later a wire recorder. Since then a whole genre of "Electronic Voice Phenomenon" and "Instrumental Transcommunication" groups of communication with the dead has formed. When *Radio and Microphone Contacts with the Dead* (Jürgenson 1968) became popular in the 1960s, huge libraries filled with transmissions from the realm of death. These aural electronic investigations portray white noise as filled with the voices of the dead emerging from the static of tape recordings. (Raudive 1971) Inversely, state authorities or private interests exploit digital technologies for pervasive surveillance and invasive practices of listening in to the voices of the living. In reverse of deploying persuasive representation and simulations these technologies of information peacekeeping aim at monitoring everything, everywhere, all the time. The overwhelming dominance of electronic information systems and digitized footprints of social transactions make it feasible to process information over long sequences of widely dispersed activities. Ghostly machines are listening in; they silence not just voices but minds, buried alive by animated walls of distributed computational intelligence.

Phantoms in the City

Cities consist not only of walls, bridges, streets, buildings, factories, places of production, and spaces of consumption, symbolically located in maps and land registers. Topologies are formed by electromagnetic fields and relational geopolitical flows of energy and information; and circuits of capital, trade, and persons embedded in ubiquitous electronic presence and all-pervasive communication technology. Urban spaces encompassing absolute, but also relative and relational, relationships of space and time in the geopolitical influence spheres of finance and information flows. Instead of walls and ramparts, new architectures of control apply software algorithms, satellites, and electronic tracking systems for a spooky influence at a distance.

Omni-directional conflict management accelerates the use of sensors and software systems—by means of biometric passports, global logistics, e-commerce, airline profiling, and navigation and homing guidance systems. Fortifications change into global assemblages of continued linkages of data banks and sensors. So-called intelligent materials, woven into the security fabric of social space and into infrastructures of urban places, serve as hidden ways to influence disenfranchised subjects. In societies of control embedded in ambient intelligence, electronic devices are orchestrated to exploit individuals.

Global socio-technological architectures of security in urban life replace traditional borders of national states. Immaterial systems of order fragment, zone, and stratify urban spaces: free trade zones, export zones, duty-free warehouses and special economic areas, gated communities, privatization of public space, security zones, or airports. New urban borderlines emerge where the flows of the city are forced through checkpoints, and militarized surveillance networks organize the borders of "inside" and "outside." Urban spaces, a medium of "the war against terror," are at the same time a place of revolt. The enemy does not come from without the gates, but hides within. A traditional separation of the military and the civilian domains disappears in the increasing fusion of industry and police, event management and border controls, urban security and entertainment. Summits, mass events, and gladiator fights are implemented and supervised by armies of itinerant specialists. A global traveling circus of temporary security zones of G8 meetings, Olympic Games, or World and European Championships becomes normality. Feeding on technophile dreams of omnipotence and total surveillance, these installations fulfill a purpose of behavior modification by laying down the rules of the game.

Operative Interventions

Interrelations between the immobile spaces of streets and buildings and the fluid fields of desire, memory, and phantasms are rendered visible in the colonization of exterior and interior space. This interdependence not only manifests in the economic zoning of cities driven by real estate interests and grand imagination. The design of its urban spaces and public monuments of solidified memories or the interaction regime of its pathways relate to the internalized images that drive marketing results in the material economy of consumer societies. An entertainment–security complex pervades and normalizes cultures, not only in the fusion of digital entertainment, urban simulation, and electronically supported warfare. Media-entertainment-military industries not only celebrate a security fetish, but are a larger business model that profits from "disaster capitalism," mob mentality, and fear. Mercenary troops of private security service providers, public and private/public operations are increasingly legitimized to use force in the name of capital, state, or the stability of the "international system." The future of military expeditions, however, does not lie in defense against territorial invasion but in defense of investments. Asymmetric warfare and the so-called "long war"—permanently militarized zones—rely on the psychological force of pictures. In the safeguarding of information dominance, cultural peacekeeping is based on inducing behavior by influencing the imagination, and by the permanent live broadcasting of videos, pictures, and texts.

Clearly, global domination has become deterritorialized and power is now grounded in the control of flows and symbols. Nonetheless, a "Reclaim the Streets" movement emerged as a form of protest in the early 1990s and quickly spread around the world, with "street parties" in cities all over Europe, Australia, North America, and even Africa. Dedicated to reclaiming public space from being an arena for the control of society and for consumerism, these tactics momentarily countered the isolation of urban lives. These actions to create a presence on the street were not intended to disturb the flow of commodities, but to playfully intervene in the symbolic landscape of the city. Accordingly, "Reclaim the Net" became a theme of reclaiming public space for free speech and free electronic media and digital cultural practice in the late 1990s, the time of the dotcom bubble and its subsequent crash.

Cities constitute themselves through the intensity and the instability of desires and fears, through phantasmal hegemonies that exploit dreams and frustration. However, they are not only competing centers of dominance, but also lived spaces of empathy and international solidarity where scattered social movements are connected in a network of global cities. Without the multifaceted wealth of urban heterogeneity, beyond the evil eye of normalization, even the homogenized mainstream would have been asphyxiated long ago. Visible centers are dominating the presence, but the future is developing on the margins, in cracks, crevices, and the spaces between. Phantoms of the city, forces and agents defying visibility, are this future. In the Western tradition works of art are seen as finished and stable objects. Increasingly now, works are regarded as "under construction" and changing in versions; considered only temporarily fixed and adaptable to contexts and usages. However, cultural practice is moving on to a process-based understanding of interventions that deals with flows and fields. It confronts a playing field of tactical and strategic moves where artistic operations intervene in the invisible dynamic interactions of material and immaterial.

From Tactics to Strategy

In 1990s critical media culture the focus was largely on questions of the tactical, as in "tactical media." Tactics depend on time; they offer a path for those who cannot count on a place or institutional localization and who do not control a space. Some believe that strategy focuses on power and forces relationships assuming a bounded place that serves as the basis for relations with a distinct exterior. From this perspective, strategic thought seems inadequate for marginal or heterogeneous agents of change. As if strategies were conservative in nature. But the concept of territory and space has to be extended—from the absolute space of walls, streets, and mountains to the relational space-time of lived spaces, of desires, dreams, memory, frustration, phantasms, and the technologies of the imagination. Multidimensional spaces are formed by use, experience, and understanding.

Strategies provide roadmaps toward desired objectives, and better intelligence offers potentially more precise approaches toward goals to be achieved. Strategies of conceptual manipulation of relational space-time transform potentials of cognitive labor into realities of a constitutive informational matrix. Myths create the culture in which they are believed. Processes of reasoning make fictions come true. Economic worldviews produce models and their underlying methods shape the reality they represent. Reference points of orientation for mapping the terrain harden into rock-solid fundamental assumptions.

From an understanding of representations of the real and the unreal and of processes and flows, critical art gives primacy to agency and intervening in a post-aesthetic strategy. There is a need to go beyond tactical media interventions and their decorative appropriations driven by the creative industry curricula. Sustainable action needs to go beyond the tactical toward strategic operations implying a trajectory of purpose and intention, if only virtual. Not spectacular action heroes but discreet operations of a process of change are at work in long-term agency and extended trajectories. Any security or business intelligence unit knows the effectiveness of clandestine and covert operations to influence situations. However, this not only true for those in a position of power. Avoiding the evil eye of their masters, secretive associations also organized the first slave population to throw off the yoke of European colonialism. When Voudou priest Boukman Dutty instigated an uprising, it sparked the Haitian Revolution. Focusing on the deployment of tactics in *The Art of War*, Sun Tzu writes: "All men can see the tactics whereby I conquer, but what none can see is the strategy out of which victory is evolved."

Forgotten Futures

Through an understanding of past practices, the future requires new forms of critical interventions beyond artistic gimmicks. Today more than ever, culture is economically exploited and biopolitically instrumentalized, robbing humans of the chance for surprise. Stunted perspectives steal a future of art beyond status projection or decorum and money laundering. In the face of this it is crucial not to fall back into repeating history as a farce and instead to push ahead with lucid analyses that then may lead to future intelligent tactics. New strategies of resistance are needed—in the virtual and the real, the symbolic and the physical. The challenges ahead demand cogent processes that enable advanced concepts of cultural articulation.

Art practices, as autonomous examinations of processes, investigate spheres of influence, as well as systemic reality. Players explore attractors of popular imagination at the crossroads of the trivial. Invisible like an algorithmic program in an embedded processor, information age cultural agents do not show their hand. Anonymous leaves no fingerprints. Individual contributions in electronic dance music dissolve in a stream of mixes and remixes, discarding anything that becomes too visible in the alternative mainstream. New forms of collective practices that intervene in processes are more relevant than past models of a dubious individual genius. Digital media allows for new forms of collaboration and networked modes of cooperation both locally and globally, not only in distributed production chains or the field of software development but also in the arts and culture. A practice that offers a technical intelligence and a critique of representation by mapping the flows of ideas and power is necessarily based on cooperation. Are there forms of cooperation outside a creative class and a digital proletariat modeled on ecstatic Internet bubbles?

Cultural Intelligence

In a world of intangible soft coercion, control has less of a physical presence but an effective power over transactions and transformation. It is an intangible ubiquitous distribution of power that haunts like supernatural forces, from traditional "soft power" of opinion and cultural persuasion power, enhanced by digital networks of today's disinformation societies, to a diffuse transmission of informal rules and peer pressure. A wide range of normative mechanisms interlocks diverse domains, from the internalization of modern economic legends and the perception management by flexible assemblages of power to the reflex adaption of lifestyle identity segments and the invisible exclusionary effects of mediatized social relations. With the unholy marriage of the security complex and the entertainment industry comes a fusion of simulation and factual, of virtual and real, the disappearance of the borders between fantasy and reality. Information dominance extends into the psycho-cybernetic coordinates of the individual, as Harold Burson, founder of the Burson-Marsteller PR corporation and business intelligence firm, illustrates in an interview with *Der Spiegel* in the context of understanding public relations as "trading with reality" (Burson 2006). In this context cultural intelligence is concerned with the psycho-geographical analysis and representation of multidimensional spaces. As the zoning of immaterial intellectual property regimes and the stratification of social relationships in hyperspace, cultural intelligence is concerned with the dynamics of the virtual and symbolic in materially tangible places. It is about the interaction of conceptualized representation spaces and lived spaces, where property, or rather power relations, determine the level of isolation or solidarity. Art and culture, beyond their function as symbols of status and class in a cultural economy or as tax-conserving investments, serve as an autonomous examination of processes and systems. Urban psycho-geographic art and practice analyzes overarching spheres of influence, the attractions of popular imagination, and the generators of systemic reality. In the late 1990s the Association of Autonomous Astronauts (AAA) propagated a non-militaristic deployment of space-age technologies with calls for "dreamtime." Questioning the established coordinates for cultural interaction while rigorously denying being an art project, they mapped the sky onto their urban environments. Through pamphlets, web sites, and temporary autonomous zones the loosely affiliated AAA cells invaded the imagination with concepts of sex and raves in space all over Europe.

Fiction and Agency

Fiction is a heuristic tool for exploring scenarios in strategic planning beyond scientific extrapolation. Narrative intelligence hypothesizes in terms of good justifications constructing explanations, alternative storylines, and differing schemes.

Common practices to create facts do not only make them appear to be suspicious, but any assessments of facts are perceived relative to a particular ideological background. Historically, transforming fiction into reality is a worldwide standard procedure. Today's realpolitik, possessed by a wealth of old and new myths, governs by an inexorable logic of belief systems. Painting pictures into the mind is at the core of the devices of power, rendering artists, writers, and engineers of the imagination a force on the global stage. Ideas are contagious and social fictions epidemic, and not only in the realm of art and fashion. Life imitates art in embedded media environments of self-fulfilling images. National Security Agency czar Keith Alexander, when running the army's Intelligence and Security Command, designed the facility known as the Information Dominance Center to mimic the bridge of the starship Enterprise, complete with doors that make a "whoosh" sound when sliding open (Harris 2013). What is pragmatic action in a world where thought and reality are not radically distinguished? It seems indispensable to make a strategic claim to reality and reclaim lost utopias against an enforced global colonization of the imagination.

Social control is increasingly in the terrain of the imagination. The gentle coercion of para-political control systems forms an invisible cage. To escape adaptive containment, widely supposed unthinkable in the postmodern discourse, requires a radical new thinking and strategies of the seemingly impossible. Digital art practice can do more than propagate technical progress and provide affect stimulus in aestheticized production cycles. Not merely tickling cultural taste buds but providing a critical instance of reflective intellectual work, artists as agents of intelligence demystify the power of media over matter. Cultural intelligence works to provide an informational context for others and applies technologies of the imagination to tell another story.

References

Burson, Harold. 2006. "Wir unterstützen Journalisten." Interview. *Der Spiegel*, July 31. http://www.spiegel.de/spiegel/print/d-48046169.html (accessed January 5, 2006). English translation: http://www.sourcewatch.org/index.php/Harold_Burson_Interviewed_By_Der_Spiegel.

Debord, Guy, and Gil J. Wolman. 1956. "A User's Guide to Détournement." Bureau of Public Secrets. http://www.bopsecrets.org/SI/detourn.htm (accessed January 5, 2015).

"Dialogue: The Ultimate Communication." 2003. *Business Communication: Harvard Business Essentials: Business Communication*, Chapter 9. Cambridge, MA: Harvard Business School Press.

Edison, Thomas. 1920. Interview with B.C. Forbes. *The Scientific American*. Quoted in Martin Gardner. 2001. *Did Adam and Eve Have Navels?* W.W. Norton.

The Economist. 2000. "Blood and Oil." March 4. http://www.economist.com/node/288515 (accessed January 5, 2015).

Harris, Shane. 2013. "The Cowboy of the NSA." *Foreign Policy Magazine*, September 9. http://foreignpolicy.com/2013/09/09/the-cowboy-of-the-nsa/ (accessed January 5, 2015).

Idris. Kamil. 2003. Quoted in *Peer-To-Peer News – The Week In Review*, December 13. http://www.p2p-zone.com/underground/showthread.php?t=18158 (accessed January 5, 2015).

Jürgenson, Friedrich. 1968. *Radio and Microphone Contacts with the Dead.* Saxon & Lindstrom.

Moglen, Eben. 2003. Quoted in Konrad Becker and Felix Stalder, "Editorial: Why Do Intellectual Property Issues Matter?" *World-Information Newspaper.* Special IP Edition, World Summit of the Information Society, Geneva, December 10–12, 2003. http://felix.openflows.com/html/wio-wsis_ediorial.html (accessed January 5, 2015).

Raudive, Konstantin. 1971. *Breakthrough: An Amazing Experiment in Electronic Communication with the Dead.* Buckinghamshire, UK: Smythe.

Rodtschenko, Alexander. 1920/1921. *Slogans.*

Sun Tzu. 1910/500 BC. *The Art of War.* Norwalk, CT: The Puppet Press. http://www.puppetpress.com/classics/ArtofWarbySunTzu.pdf (accessed January 5, 2015).

Watanabe, Shigeru. 2010. "Pigeons Can Discriminate "Good" and "Bad" Paintings by Children." *Animal Cognition* 13: 75–85. doi: 10.1007/s10071-009-0246-8. http://link.springer.com/article/10.1007%2Fs10071-009-0246-8 (accessed January 5, 2015).

Watanabe, Shigeru. 2011. "Discrimination of Painting Style and Quality: Pigeons Use Different Strategies for Different Tasks. *Animal Cognition* 14: 797–808. doi: 10.1007/s10071-011-0412-7. http://link.springer.com/article/10.1007%2Fs10071-011-0412-7 (accessed January 5, 2015).

Wiener, Norbert. 1965/1948. *Cybernetics: or the Control and Communication in the Animal and the Machine.* Cambridge, MA: The MIT Press.

17

The Silver Age of Social Media

Nettime.org and the Avant-Garde of the '90s

McKenzie Wark

On October 31, 1995, an e-mail message went out to a small group of people, mostly in Europe. "Welcome to the nettime mailing list," it said. Nettime described itself as:

> the official channel for the *ZK proceedings,* a series of meetings bound to the need of a cultural politics of the nets, of non/electronic, internal and international coordinated action, an open and generous definition/exchange of desired information. This list tries to bridge the gap between two meetings, it is no place, table or city.[1]

For those who don't remember such announcements, this message was launching a listserv. On a listserv, an e-mail sent to the list went to all the people subscribed to it. Listservs were a sort of intermediate stage in the evolution of social media. To give you some idea of how different they were from today's social media: when it started, Nettime.org was not moderated.[2] Spam was too rare an occurrence to worry about.

I would like to start the discussion of the avant-garde of the 1990s with Nettime because it was a place that had a fairly rare flavor in the digital media art and culture of the time. It grew out of a series of meetings at the margins of art festivals in Venice, Budapest, Amsterdam, and Ljubljana. It was transnational from the start. It brought together people working at the intersection of digital media art, theory, and activism. And it was from the beginning critical of both received ideas as to what the critical theory of media ought to be and of the "Californian ideology."

Here is how Barbrook and Cameron described this ideology:

> Implacable in its certainties, the Californian Ideology offers a fatalistic vision of the natural and inevitable triumph of the hi-tech free market—a vision which is blind to racism, poverty and environmental degradation and which has no time to debate alternatives. (Barbrook and 1995a)

A Companion to Digital Art, First Edition. Edited by Christiane Paul.

From the start, Nettime was engaged with, but critical of, changes in the technical infrastructure and commodity form of communication emanating from Silicon Valley. The name Nettime itself makes this point. When everyone else was talking about "colonizing" *cyberspace*, the list called itself *net-time*, which might, among other things, be a reference to the concept of labor time. Even in the 1990s Nettimers were already complaining of the lack of time, intensified by networked communication:

> From: "Ivo Skoric"
> Organization: Anti-War Campaign
> To: nettime@is.in-berlin.de
> Date sent: Tue, 23 Jan 1996 09:58:14 +0000
> Subject: Various Subjects
> Send reply to: iskoric@igc.apc.org
> Priority: normal
>
> Hi there,
>
> I have never subscribed to this group. Yet suddenly I started receiving various (rather longish) postings on various subjects. I thought should I be offended with this (like certain decent guy Peter who asked you to unsubscribe him just recently). I noted that there is no much discussion, just apodictic postings. Apodictic in a sense that everybody writes what she or he wants, and everybody else takes it for undisputable truth (because nobody really have the net-time to read those long diatribes). This is the ultimate end of all communication: everybody has access, everybody has net-time, but nobody really cares any more. Communication that is killed by the most formidable [*sic*] means of fostering it. That's of course why I completely enjoy the NetTime. Of course, I don't really read the postings (I don't want to betray the cause). But I created a filter that separates things that come from nettime from other crap and put them in a separate mail folder for future generations. Since postings are mostly futuristic I guess guys in about 40–50 years should have a lot of fun reading them (given they have net-time to do it). Furthermore, I decided to join with a story of my own (don't bother reading it, or if you do and say – "ah? that's it?! just two pages?!" – don't be offended, I promise I can clog any newsgroup with lengthy articles). Ivo Skoric[3]

Nettime, or rather the network of artists, writers, and activists it channeled, was an instance of the avant-garde of its time. As Brian Holmes once put it, "it was our Dada" (Holmes 2000). Like Dada, it had a somewhat diffuse and borderless structure. Like Dada, the archive of texts barely hints at the range of activities of Nettime, or rather the "Nettime neigbourhood of lists."

Whether history will see it as all that important an "historical avant-garde," time will tell (Bürger 1984),[4] but I think Nettime had such an ambition. Like any good avant-garde, it was highly aware of its predecessors, such as Dada, Fluxus, and the Situationists, and also impatient to leave them behind. Its ambition was to absorb, digest, refute, and replace the dominant ideas of its time about emerging media as a space of possibility.

The historical logic of avant-garde works something like this: each avant-garde insists on a new definition of what the space of the avant-garde's mission is to be.

It advances as a group onto what appears to be new terrain. But in the process it retrospectively redefines the avant-gardes that are its predecessors—of which it is highly aware—in its own new terms. In this case, the space onto which this avant-garde advanced was not the irrational, or the dream, or chance, or the drift. Nor did this avant-garde take poetry or art or performance or the city to be its privileged form. It proposed instead to see Dada, Surrealism, Fluxus, and the Situationists as now obsolete precursors in opening up for experiments the form of communication itself.

If, like all avant-gardes, Nettime revised the terms of aesthetic advance, it also tried to distance itself from certain political options available at the time. One way to orient Nettime's innovation in this regard would be to think of it as an attempt to escape the local coordinates of certain forms of struggle, particularly in Europe. Its space of action was not defined by the state, but was the supra-state space created by the European Union and the fall of the Berlin Wall.

The Nettime universe had many local points of origin, and I will mention just three. One was the squatter's movement in Amsterdam and Berlin (Adilkno 1990). These were cities which, for divergent reasons, had long histories of movements carving out urban space for another way of life. Another point of origin was the Autonomist movement in Italy. Unlike Germany and Holland, Italy had a powerful and effective postwar labor movement, but by the 1990s it was in decline, and a lot of activity was invested in creating a progressive culture outside of it (Lotringer and Marazzi 2007). The third was the collapse of the Soviet Union. In the mid-1990s the future of the post-Soviet states was far from clear, and a lot of energy went into formulating alternatives. At that time, the Soros Foundation was funding alternative media centers in several post-Soviet cities.

In all three cases, a minority of those involved in these movements lifted their heads above the space of action defined by the national state and what Gramsci might call national-popular culture. They saw media form, rather than cultural content, as a key part of the questions surrounding aesthetic and political struggle and experiment. Within that minority, an even smaller one saw emerging media forms, in particular the promise of the Internet, as a key space in which to develop both a social critique of the media and a media critique of the social that could escape along the Internet vector out of the national space.

Nettime grew from a handful to three thousand subscribers in the first five years of its life. Early on there had been a few posts in German and other languages, but English emerged from the start as the new lingua franca of the European avant-garde. Indeed, there was even a debate about the emergence of "netlish," a form of written English for Internet communication that retained some of the characteristics of the first language of those who wrote it (Apter 2005, 228).

If the Situationists were the last avant-garde whose dominant language was French, English was now established as the default mediator for the avant-garde milieu. The Nettime "brand" was used for listservs in several other languages, including French.[5] There were overlaps and affiliations with lists in other languages, such as Rekombinant in Italian. English as a non-national *critical* language was, however, a relatively new project.

While written in English, Nettime spent a lot of time filtering and digesting French, German, and Italian theory, and media theory, in particular. The listserv had grown out of meetings, and the sharing of printed texts loaded on tables had been one of the activities at those meet-ups. It is hard to describe the mood of a listserv, as it is made up of many participants, not to mention lurkers. But if one were to risk a generalization, Nettime displayed a certain skepticism regarding the received media theory of its time.

Two models were dominant. One was the critical theory of the culture industries. To caricature the latter, its proponents held that the commodity form of media fatally compromised its ability to communicate anything. Commodified media made everything exchangeable; anything could be exchanged for anything and nothing was irreconcilable in the Hollywood happy ending (Adorno 2001). The variation on such themes promulgated by the Situationist International critiqued not the culture industry but the spectacle in which all of life appeared as a profusion of images. "That is good appears, and that which appears is good" (Debord 1994).

A second model, certainly far less influential in Europe but gaining traction in the anglophone world, held something like the opposite view. It focused not on the coercive power of media but on the creative power of individual media consumers to interpret media in their own sometimes creative or subversive ways (Fiske and Hartley 2003). This current would later give rise to the influential work of Henry Jenkins on fan cultures and the like (Jenkins 2008). It had enormous appeal to those who, without giving it much thought, decided that the old media were "passive" and the new media were "active," and therefore good.

One way of reading what Nettime was trying to do in the late 1990s is to think of it as an attempt to reject the old "culture industry cum spectacle theory of media" without falling into uncritical celebration of users' "creativity" that sometimes occurred within the cultural studies school. The latter was quite correctly seen as taking consumer behavior as a given. Nettime was not interested in "empowering" consumers. Like any good avant-garde, it wanted another life entirely.

Here is where the transnational quality of Nettime really came in handy, as it meant that the space of discussion had access to other resources from other traditions. These included the work of Villem Flusser and Friedrich Kittler from Germany.[6] This overturned the emphasis on commodity form in critical theory, and insisted instead on a close attention to the material properties of media itself. But rather than the bleak, all-enclosing discourse networks of Kittler, manufacturing subjects as nodes in the machine, there was rather an avant-gardist will to make at least a different kind of network and a different kind of subjective node.

This was just one of the strands influencing the intellectual life of Nettime. Much to the chagrin of some subscribers and participants, it became a place for posting essays by the theory stars of the time, from Guattari to Negri and Žižek. On December 2, 1999, for example, someone called "anticopyright," posted Žižek's essay "The Matrix, Or, The Two Sides of Perversion" (Žižek 1999).[7] The culture of sharing such texts had begun, which would result in the global anglophone-theory blogosphere and file sharing culture of more recent times. It was also a moment of propagating and stabilizing a transnational use of English as a medium for critical, theoretical writing.

The genre of theory writing favored on Nettime certainly had an influence on anglophone media theory, and perhaps not a bad one. Nettime writing could be inventive, speculative, highly condensed, and relatively free of specific national-cultural reference. The form of the listserv and a certain kind of theory-inflected essay seemed a good match. But there was a lack of specificity to much of this writing where it concerned media, not to mention "new" media. Why read Baudrillard or Virilio on such things, when it was well enough known that all of their actual communication was managed, in both cases, by their wives? The theory stars were not even online, let alone conducting experiments in the form.

Nettime co-founders Geert Lovink and Pit Schulz (2010) led the way in countering this practice, with a series of essays, originally in German, on netkritik. Many others followed. The beauty of these texts was the matching of form and content, of writing both about and on the Internet, and in a mode of circulation outside of commodified life. The "open and generous definition/exchange of desired information" was not always smooth sailing. There were "flame wars," misunderstandings, stand-offs, and all the rest (Dery 1995).[8] But what gradually emerged from all that was a theory and practice of writing both on and about the Net that had at least some distance from the adversarial style of "debate" deemed characteristic of American online communication. Many Nettimers had experienced this in online forums such as Usenet or The Well, and were looking for another kind of communicative practice.

If one looks not just at Nettime but at the "Nettime neighborhood of lists," one finds that many key ideas and writers were trialed and tempered there, including work by Lev Manovich, Alex Galloway, and Tiziana Terranova.[9] Nettime was not just for theory-heads, however. It really was a convergence of the three things that characterize any avant-garde: thought, art, and action. With art, as with writing, Nettime became a place not to recirculate past forms but to invent new ones.

A particularly controversial example is antiorp, also known as integer and Netochka Nezvanova (NN) (Mieszkowski 2002). This entity—there is no other word for it—was probably behind the production of a graphical environment for music and media called *Nato.0+55+3d* (1999), widely used and respected at the time. It ran on the Apple OS, and extended the Max environment from audio to visual objects. It was one of the first real-time video manipulation and display environments, predating GEM and Jitter, and it was relatively cheap.

While several people report meeting antiorp, it is not clear whether the woman they encountered was part of antiorp, or an actor, or even the same woman. As an online avatar, antiorp made it her, his, or its mission to disrupt and insult pretty much everybody via listservs. A typical integer/antiorp insult looks something like this:

> To: nettime-l {AT} bbs.thing.net
> Subject: [Nettime-bold] Re: GRAVE YOU DIG YOU[R] OWN
> From: integer {AT} www.god-emil.dk
> Date: Tue, 8 Aug 2000 13:55:14 +0200
> List-Id: the uncut, unmoderated version of nettime-l <nettime-bold.nettime.org>
> Reply-To: nettime-bold {AT} nettime.org
> Sender: nettime-bold-admin {AT} nettime.org
>
> >when you chose to validate artmuseum mafia schemes online
>
> varum = ent!tl maf!a +?
> = != maf!a. = 01 plantaz!e zt!le z!ztm.
>
> = nett!me.rh!zome = ultra zaturatd avec lo.tekk.!mbez!l!k kr!t!kx
> + dze!r luvl! + unshapl! pet`art!ztz`. cezt 0+1 komed!e + traged!e
> =01.m!tholog!kl.debr!z.
> nn. (integer 2000)

Frequent posts like this led to furious debates about "netiquette." In one post Lorenzo Taiuti replied to Josephine Berry:

> i read your nice essai and i agree on many things. About "NN/antiorp/integer" i may only disagree. Neither Adorno or Breton would think that around 2000 people would try to realize fragile attempts of a web-democracy through contacts, exchange of informations and attempts of organizations totally free from society controls. And i underline "attempts" because what we are tryng to do is extremely 'light' compared to the tremendous weight of the real official info-structure. In this moment an interesting list like Syndicate is dyng because the strategy of 'spamming' create by NN&Company breaks the subtle balance of the 'comunication agreement' between members of the list. There are not cultural excuses to something like that. (Taiuti 2001)

In retrospect antiorp/NN/integer is perhaps best seen as a conceptual art project, an update on, say, Ray Johnson's mail art strategies for the Internet age (De Salvo and Gudis 1999). Or perhaps as a precursor to 4chan and Anonymous (Coleman 2014). But the Taiuti message neatly sums up some of the tensions between the political and the aesthetic on Nettime. Is the form of the listserv there to serve some larger purpose, or is the form itself something that is open to experiments, even of a disruptive kind? This was a practical double to the theoretical question as to whether what mattered about the Internet in general were questions of form (as in German media theory) or what people do with it (as in British cultural studies).

That the avant-garde is an act of disruptive noise within a media form is an idea that could combine aspects of both points of view. It is an idea with quite a pedigree. Dick Hebdige (1979) used it to understand punk; Greil Marcus (1989) thought it was the thread connecting Dada to the Situationist International. Certainly one of the key strategies to emerge out of the Nettime milieu was a disruptive one: the denial-of-service attack on a web site, for example. When an Internet start-up by the name of eToys.com tried to use legal intimidation to take over the domain name of the art group eToy.com in 1999, the response was a swift and effective campaign to shut down eToys.com in what became known as the Toy War (Wishart and Boschsler 2003).[10] The Electronic Disturbance Theater used similar denial-of-service attacks against Mexican government web sites as a way of drawing attention to the struggles of the Zapatistas.[11]

Such tactics elaborated in new ways and in new domains the classic avant-garde strategy of noise or "disturbance." But next to noise there was another strand to what became known as "tactical media" (Garcia and Lovink 1997). Drawing on Michel De Certeau and others, this approach tried to use ready-made media tools to make temporary interventions in specific media forms for limited periods of time (De Certeau 2011). Critical Art Ensemble's *Free Range Grain* (2003–2004), which used off-the-shelf technologies to allow people to test the products of the global agribusiness system for themselves, might be one example (Critical Art Ensemble 2012).

Perhaps one could describe this other strand as conceptual design. Unlike conceptual art, it inhabited the artworld, but its conceptual questioning was not of art-historical forms, but more directly of the media and technical aspect of social, cultural, and political forms (Lippard 1997). As in any design prototyping, it got as far as proof-of-concept productions—things that worked but were never mass-produced or implemented.

Occasionally there were actual implementations, if temporary and tactical ones. Consider the events around the closure of the (Soros-supported) B92 radio station by the Milosevic government in Yugoslavia in 1999 (Collins 2001). B92 was practically the only media voice of the opposition in Yugoslavia at the time of the Kosovo war. When the government raided the station, the Dutch Internet provider xs4all.nl stepped in to rebroadcast the service, from a secret location in Belgrade, over the Internet. The xsforall.nl signal was for a time rebroadcast by the BBC World Service via shortwave radio. It was a demonstration of both the power and the limitations of the Internet to route around government control of the old, centralized broadcast media apparatus.

Listservs such as Nettime were networks of information sharing, concept formation, and rhetoric generation, or what was called "collaborative filtering" for such activities. What cheap printing and the postal service was to the historic avant-gardes, the listserv was to the new. Sometimes the content of a listserv would be redacted down and printed as a free newspaper, then distributed at art and media festivals. One of these publications was produced by a global network around the Zagreb-originated group Arkzin, which redacted debates around the Kosovo war; it was distributed on at least three continents (Buden 1999).

Not the least of the charms of the Nettime world was that it combined a listserv with sporadic attempts to meet in person. The relation between online and embodied life was a lively topic in the 1990s. Anomalies like antiorp notwithstanding, Nettime was less interested in the theme of "virtual life" than many other online avant-gardes of the time.[12] The focus was more on the interaction between two kinds of *collective* experience than on the vicissitudes of personal "identity."

The emphasis on new forms of collectivity also aligns Nettime more closely with the historic avant-gardes, all of which conducted critical experiments in forms of organization. Some, such as the Futurists, Surrealists, and Situationists, adopted quasi-party forms, including formal tests of membership and exclusion. Some, such as Dada and Fluxus, were looser networks. From Fluxus came the even more distributed practices of mail art, in some ways an intermediate form toward the network practices of Internet-based avant-garde collectivity. From mail art also came the practice of the shared name, the most successful of which was Luther Blissett (Deseriis 2010).

Within the ever-evolving collectivity of Nettime were other forms of collectivity, like the multidisciplinary art collaborations of I/O/D, VNS Matrix, Mongrel, Critical Art Ensemble, Electronic Disturbance Theater, Institute for Applied Autonomy, and FakeShop. ®TMark and the eToy group were early exponents of the more-or-less fake company, later redeployed by the Bernadette Corporation (Wark 2005). Nettime was thus a network of networks in which some nodes were institutions, some scenes, and others groups.

Speaking of scenes: there is a remarkable portrait of this world in science fiction writer Bruce Sterling's novel *Holy Fire* (1996).[13] Sterling was active on The Well, an American bulletin board based in San Francisco, which one might describe as a distant ancestor of Facebook today. Sterling drew that world's attention to Nettime, usually prefacing his observations with remarks about "goofy letfists!" (Sterling 1997). In *Holy Fire,* Sterling captures the ambience of groups that met in an almost clandestine way in the back rooms of bars and nightclubs to plot how to change the world with the combined force of new ideas and new media.

More than most other networks of its kind, but like all of the historic avant-gardes, Nettime was obsessive about self-documentation. Four photocopied and stapled anthologies were produced in 1996 alone. These were always called *ZKP*, short for the German initials for Publication of the Central Committee (Zentralkomiteepublikation)—a joke on old-style socialist organization, although one that did not go down so well with Eastern European Nettimers. *Readme!* (1999) was an ambitious attempt to create a "Nettime bible," edited by a half dozen people in different time zones working around the clock, with the heavy lifting done by Ted Byfield in Amsterdam. The introduction, a détournement of avant-gardist manifesto language, quite accurately describes the milieu of Nettime:

> The discursive interactions on Nettime appear as a fluid process that can't be simulated or staged. The list is a milieu that encourages a certain radicalism of approach: miscellaneous ex-East going on ex-West ancien-regime misfits turned NGO-perfect-fits, fun-guerrilla playgirls, connected autonomists, entrepreneurial molto-hippies, squatters turned digital imperialists, postcynical berks, slacktivists and wackademics, minimalist elitist subtechnodrifters, name- your-cause party people, name-your-price statists, can-do cyber-individualists, can't–won't workers, accredited weird-scientists, and assorted other theoretical and practical avant-gardeners, senders, receivers, and orphans.[14]

That list (artfully composed by Matthew Fuller) is a good description of the Nettime milieu and its range of ambitions. Like all avant-gardes, the most radical and utopian ideas of Nettime actually came true, but always with some small modification. A whole new form of communication really did come to pass, outside of the broadcast model. Transnational networks did form outside of, and often indifferent to, the old national media and state envelopes. New intellectual and creative practices emerged, rendering redundant the old publishing and distributing practices for thought and art. Twenty years after Nettime's founding, these stabilized into a series of corporate silos—Apple, Google, Facebook, etc.—that extract value from the kind of voluntary collaborative filtering of which Nettimers were one of the pioneers.

What Nettimers did not quite foresee was how easily it would all, in the end, be swept back into the commodity system, how quickly state surveillance would catch up, and how the creative energies of time spent on the Net would actually drive a new stage of commodified life rather than escape from it. Like all previous avant-gardes, it won its battle but lost the war.

Here I think it wise to hew closely to the "radical media pragmatism" of one of Nettime's founders, Geert Lovink, who was always far too much of an instinctive pessimist to drink the utopian Kool-Aid (Lovink 2002, 218). Contrary to what is sometimes said today, many Internet activists and theorists of the 1990s were well aware of the dangers and limitations of the impending world. Lovink always paid particularly close attention to the changing working conditions for people in the sector formerly known as the culture industries.

The key theme here is the tension in our working lives between precariousness and autonomy.[15] Creative workers are often willing to forego a big, steady paycheck to achieve some measure of control over their own work and time. The question is how to maximize the autonomy and minimize the precariousness. Nettime itself is instructive in that regard. Many of the writers on it went on to successful careers in media industries, programming, academia, the artworld, journalism, organizing. But there are also a lot of voices who simply disappeared from view. Precarity has its price.

When I hear the word "innovation" I know I can relax. Innovation does not really mean change. It just means decorating the edges of existing technical, economic, and cultural models. Just do the same stuff but maybe make the logo light green instead of green. Perhaps we are in an age of stasis rather than "innovation" in media architecture. The forms of innovation are not themselves innovative. The architecture of corporate media silos may have more or less stabilized again.

While I do not want to wax nostalgic about the Nettime era, or suggest it is in any way the origins of anything, I think there is something worth recapturing about the spirit of adventure of the time: the general experiment in every direction; the desire to make things new. It was at best a silver age. There never was a golden age of media. As Barbrook and Cameron put it,

> As pioneers of the new, the digital artisans need to reconnect themselves with the theory and practice of productive art. They are not just employees of others, or even would-be cybernetic entrepreneurs. They are also artist-engineers—designers of the next stage of modernity. Drawing on the experience of the Saint-Simonists and Constructivists, the digital artisans can create a new machine aesthetic for the information age. (Barbrook and Cameron 1995b)

The Constructivists were an avant-garde active in the Soviet Union, where it appeared, at least for a moment, that capitalist relations of commodity production had been superseded, even though certain aspects of it—like royalty payments—persisted in the cultural sphere (Kiaer 2008). Perversely enough, Nettimers confronted the opposite situation. Commodity production thrived in every sphere except cultural production, where the digital sharing of information was rapidly undermining the old industrial production methods (Scholz 2013).[16] Perhaps another way of seeing the avant-gardes is as antennae tuned toward changing roles for cognition and experiment within commodity production.

Time and again avant-gardes have tried to escape the logic of the commodification of the aesthetic, only to meet one of two fates. One was to crash back into subservience to party or state (Futurists, Constructivists, Surrealists). The other was to be captured by the artworld's valorization of the bespoke cultural commodity (Dada, Surrealists again, Situationists, Fluxus, Conceptualism). In the Nettime era, neither option was quite available. Whatever the political intentions of particular Nettimers, there simply were no mass parties exerting a powerful gravitational pull on cultural life. While much of the activity collaboratively filtered by Nettime required the support of various state cultural ministries, it was always marginal to any state cultural project.

Most curiously, this avant-garde has arguably not resulted in particularly stellar art careers for its members when compared to its predecessors. This is not to gainsay the very interesting work that has come out of this milieu. Eva and Franco Mattes, for example, created a series of works at the Postmasters gallery in New York called *13 Most Beautiful Avatars* (2006), high-resolution digital "portraits" of the avatars people used in the then-popular online world *Second Life* and an "update" of Andy Warhols's *Screen Tests* (1964–1966), such as *13 Most Beautiful Boys* or *13 Most Beautiful Women*).[17]

The institutional capture of this avant-garde was more fully achieved by the university. Many Nettimers ended up in teaching positions, often in art schools or media studies programs. In this respect the Nettime milieu is more reminiscent of the College of Pataphysics, an avant-garde for people with day jobs (Brotchie 1995).

In the margins of *Documenta X*, the 1997 version of the famous art exhibition taking place in Kassel, Germany, every five years, was an area called *Hybrid Workspace*. It ran for a hundred days, not a summer of discontent, but a summer of "content." *Hybrid Workspace* was something of a coming-out party for Nettime and friends. Looking at the pictures, it is striking how the informal workspaces, littered with computers, resemble the studios of the Design and Technology program of Parsons School of Design today,[18] both being low-rent, low-tech versions of the new workspace designed by Google for its New York employees and contractors. If Nettime was the avant-garde of anything, perhaps it was the new spatial and temporal patterns of cognitive and experimental work itself (Ross 2004).

Avant-gardes have their time. They conduct exploits (Galloway and Thacker 2007). They find the unintended possibilities of a given configuration of media form. Those possibilities typically either seed new forms of power and commodity or are closed off in favor of those that do. Nettime had its time. The time of its experimental power ended with the more or less full enclosure of the Internet into business as usual. The time is ripe for considering Nettime, indeed the whole media era, in the past tense. It is time now for working out what in it is living and what is dead in the form of an archive. Perhaps its bones can be picked clean in the interests of feeding new avant-gardes, working in other ways, and elsewhere.

Notes

1 As of July 2014, the whole Nettime archive was available at nettime.org.

2 How moderation changed the feel of the list is another topic:
To: nettime-l {AT} Desk.nl
Subject: <nettime> nettime moderation
From: Matthew Fuller <matt {AT} axia.demon.co.uk>
Date: Sun, 1 Feb 1998 18:15:29 +0000
Sender: owner-nettime-l {AT} basis.Desk.nl

Over the next month or so Pit will be away from Berlin and the net. During this period, moderation of the Nettime list will be carried out by Geert Lovink (geert {AT} xs4all.nl) and Matthew Fuller (matt {AT} axia.demon.co.uk). The style of moderation will generally remain the same. At the same time however, we want to take this opportunity of having dual moderation to invite people involved in the list to experiment a little with it as a technical and social form.

In particular we are conscious that there is a tendency for specific styles of writing to dominate traffic on Nettime. Increasingly the list is being used for men to compare the length of their bookshelves. Whilst we're hot for polemic and monumental essays of universal importance, we also believe that other things need to be said.

To this end we have consulted the relevant tabulations and urge all nettimers to increase productivity in the following areas:
rants – 25% increase
12.8% more manifestos

a full 50% more fiction
software reviews – 23.8% increase
nasty weird shit – 100%

Other formats such as, conversations compiled by email and turned into chat documents; stupid sayings; things overheard on the bus; stolen documents; specifications for impossible network devices, and so on. In addition, we would love to hear from the many lurkers on the list. We'd like your invisibility to remain comfortable, but if you fancy saying something – get typing.

It is expected that the amount of traffic will increase to some extent due to this invitation. In anticipation of this there will be two shifts of moderation: morning and evening (GMT). In order not to swell the tide too much any complaints about overload will be noted, but not posted.

Quality and relevance control will still be important. In order to meet any problems with overload the moderators have arranged to have a new key delivered to the keyboard of every nettimer. It should now be appearing in the top right of your keyboard. It is called the >delete< key. Use it – it feels good.

3 Ivo Skoric on Tuesday, January 23, 1996, 17:05 MET. http://nettime.org/Lists-Archives/nettime-l-9601/msg00042.html (accessed January 4, 2015).

4 While Peter Bürger's *Theory of the Avant Garde* (1984) gave us the category of the historic avant-garde, it is still in need of more elaboration to extract it from dependence on the category of art and the artworld.

5 For a useful documentation of what interested the French scene at the time, see Nettimers Nathalie Magnan and Annick Bureaud (2002).

6 For example, Geert Lovink on Saturday, February 6, 1999, 21:08:19 +0100 (CET), where Lovink forwards "On the Implementation of Knowledge: Towards a Theory of Hardware" from Kitter himself to the list: http://www.nettime.org/Lists-Archives/nettime-l-9902/msg00038.html. Or Pit Schultz on Tuesday, October 13, 1998, 08:16:47 +0200 (MET DST), forwarding the Flusser essay "The Bag" to the list. It would become the opening text of the 1999 Nettime anthology. http://www.nettime.org/Lists-Archives/nettime-l-9810/msg00081.html (accessed January 4, 2015).

7 Anticopyright on Friday, December 3, 1999, 01:35:54 +0100 (CET): http://nettime.org/Lists-Archives/nettime-l-9912/msg00019.html (accessed January 4, 2015).

8 The phenomenon of flame wars, or positive feedback loops of escalating vituperation, was a quite new experience for a lot of Internet users at the time. It became the title of a pioneering collection of essays edited by Nettimer Mark Dery (1995).

9 See, for example, Lev Manovich on Tuesday, December 15, 1998, 19:27:21+0100 (CET): http://nettime.org/Lists-Archives/nettime-l-9812/msg00041.html (accessed January 4, 2015). His influential book *The Language of New Media* (2000) grew out of posts such as these.

10 Also see http://toywar.etoy.com (accessed January 4, 2015).

11 See http://www.thing.net/~rdom/ecd/ZapTact.html (accessed January 4, 2015).

12 See Nettimer Julian Dibbell (1999) for a sophisticated take on the then-new topic of the relation between on- and offline identity and ethics.

13 See also Sterling's Viridian design movement: http://www.viridiandesign.org/ (accessed January 4, 2015).

14 http://www.medialounge.net/lounge/workspace/nettime/DOCS/zkp5/pdf/intro.pdf (accessed January 4, 2015).

15 On precarity see, for example, Franco Berardi (2012). Berardi was both a Nettimer and instrumental in the Italian-language Rekombinant listserv.
16 Scholz is a Nettimer and founder of the listserv The Institute for Distributed Creativity: http://distributedcreativity.org/ (accessed January 4, 2015).
17 http://0100101110101101.org/home/portraits/index.html (accessed January 4, 2015).
18 http://www.medialounge.net/lounge/workspace/ (accessed January 4, 2015).

References

Adilkno. 1990. *Cracking the Movement: Squatting Beyond the Media.* New York: Autonomedia.

Adorno, Theodor. 2001. *The Culture Industry: Selected Essays on Mass Culture.* London: Routledge.

Apter, Emily. 2005. *The Translation Zone.* Princeton, NJ: Princeton University Press.

Barbrook, Richard, and Andy Cameron. 1995a. "The California Ideology." *Mute* 3. http://www.imaginaryfutures.net/2007/04/17/the-californian-ideology-2/ (accessed January 5, 2015).

Barbrook, Richard, and Andy Cameron. 1995b. "The California Ideology." *Amalut.* http://www.alamut.com/subj/ideologies/pessimism/califIdeo_I.html (accessed January 5, 2015).

Berardi, Franco. 2012. *The Uprising: On Poetry and Finance.* Los Angeles: Semiotext(e).

Brotchie, Alastair. 1995. *True History of the College of Pataphysics.* London: Atlas Press.

Buden, Boris, ed. 1999. *Bastard! Global Edition: Kosov@ Briefing.* Zagreb: Arkzin.

Bürger, Peter. 1984. *Theory of the Avant Garde.* Minneapolis, MN: University of Minnesota Press.

Coleman, Gabriella. 2014. *Hacker, Hoaxer, Whistleblower, Spy: The Story of Anonymous.* Brooklyn, NY: Verso.

Collins, Michael. 2001. *This Is Serbia Calling: Rock'n'Roll Radio and Belgrade's Underground Resistance.* London: Serpent's Tail.

Critical Art Ensemble. 2012. *Disturbances.* London: Four Corners.

Debord, Guy. 1994. *The Society of the Spectacle.* New York: Zone Books.

De Certeau, Michel. 2011. *The Practice of Everyday Life.* Berkeley, CA: University of California Press.

Dery, Mark. 1995. *Flame Wars: The Discourse of Cyberculture.* Raleigh, NC: Duke University Press.

De Salvo, Donna, and Catherine Gudis. 1999. *Ray Johnson: Correspondences.* France: Flamarion.

Deseriis, Marco. 2010. "Lots of Money Because I am Many." In *Cultural Activism*, edited by Begum o. Firat and Aylin Kuryel. Amsterdam: Rodopi.

Dibbell, Julian. 1999. *My Tiny Life: Crime and Passion in a Virtual World.* New York: Holt.

Fiske, John, and John Hartley. 2003. *Reading Television.* London: Routledge.

Galloway, Alexander, and Eugene Thacker. 2007. *The Exploit: A Theory of Networks.* University of Minneapolis, MN: University of Minnesota Press.

Garcia, David, and Geert Lovink. 1997. May 16, 10:30:25 +0200 (MET DST). "The ABC of Tactical Media." http://www.nettime.org/Lists-Archives/nettime-l-9705/msg00096.html (accessed October 7, 2015).

Hebdige, Dick. 1979. *Subculture: The Meaning of Style*. London: Routledge.
Holmes, Brian. 2000. *Hieroglyphs of the Future*. Zagreb: Arkzin.
integer. 2000. August 8, 11:57:00 -0000. http://nettime.org/Lists-Archives/nettime-bold-http://nettime.org/Lists-Archives/nettime-bold-0008/msg00093.html (accessed January 5, 2015).
Jenkins, Henry. 2008. *Convergence Culture*. New York: NYU Press.
Kiaer, Christina. 2008. *Imagine No Possessions: The Socialist Objects of Russian Constructivism*. Cambridge, MA: The MIT Press.
Kittler, Friedrich. 1999. "On the Implementation of Knowledge: Towards a Theory of Hardware." *Nettime*. http://www.nettime.org/nettime.w3archive/199902/msg00038.html (accessed January 5, 2015).
Lippard, Lucy. 1997. Six Years: *The Dematerialization of the Art Object from 1966 to 1972*. Berkeley, CA: University of California Press.
Lotringer, Sylvere, and Christian Marazzi, eds. 2007. *Italy: Autonomia*. Los Angeles: Semiotext(e).
Lovink, Geert. 2002. *Dark Fiber*. Cambridge, MA: The MIT Press.
Lovink, Geert, and Pit Schulz. 2010. *Jugendjahre der Netzkritik: Essays Zu Web 1.0 1995–1997*. Amsterdam: Institute for Network Cultures.
Magnan, Nathalie, and Annick Bureaud. 2002. *Connexions: Art, Réseaux, Media*. Paris: École Nationale Supériure des Beaux-Arts.
Manovich, Lev. 2000. *The Language of New Media*. Cambridge, MA: The MIT Press.
Marcus, Greil. 1989. *Lipstick Traces*. Cambridge, MA: Harvard University Press.
Mieszkowski, Katherine. 2002. "The Most Feared Woman on the Internet." *Salon*, March 1. http://www.salon.com/2002/03/01/netochka/ (accessed January 5, 2015).
Nettime, ed. 1997. *ZKP* 4, Ljubljana. http://www.ljudmila.org/~vuk/nettime/zkp4/ (accessed January 5, 2015).
Ross, Andrew. 2004. *No Collar*. Philadelphia, PA: Temple University Press.
Scholz, Trebor, ed. 2013. *Digital Labor: The Internet as Playground and Factory*. New York: Routledge.
Sterling, Bruce. 1996. *Holy Fire*. New York: Bantam.
Sterling, Bruce. 1997. "nettime: submission to nettime list." http://www.nettime.org/Lists-Archives/nettime-l-9703/msg00034.html (accessed January 5, 2015).
Taiuti, Lorenzo. 2001. August 23, 20:35:39 +0200 (CEST). http://nettime.org/Lists-Archives/nettime-l-0108/msg00100.html (accessed January 5, 2015).
Wark, McKenzie. 2005. "Indestructible Life." http://www.nettime.org/Lists-Archives/nettime-l-0502/msg00025.html (accessed January 5, 2015).
Wishart, Adam, and Regula Boschsler. 2003. *Leaving Reality Behind: etoy vs eToys and Other Battles to Control Cyberspace*. New York: Ecco.
Žižek, Slavoj. 1999. "The Matrix, Or, The Two Sides of Perversion." Celina 43.

18

Art in the Corporatized Sphere

The Impact of Commercial Social Media on Online Artistic Practice

Kyle Chayka

Imagine ads being sold on a Mark Rothko canvas—sponsorships, perhaps, stuck discreetly to a corner of the canvas. It is not unthinkable; after all, artworks get a lot of eyeballs, and that audience is not getting monetized as much as it could be.

These days the empty buzzword "content" is used as a shorthand for referring to any kind of media published on the Internet in the form of text, images, or video. Content that gets more attention, in terms of page views, is more "valuable" because it commands a larger audience. The audience drawn by this content is sold to advertisers in packages of a thousand impressions per banner ad at a time; commercial brands buy eyeballs. This most clearly applies to editorial operations like blogs: articles draw readers, and readers are turned into capital in return.

This also holds true for today's massive social media platforms. Facebook, Twitter, and Tumblr all make profits by selling advertising that reaches the millions of users active on their domains. Every piece of content we, as users, manufacture for the social networks draws ever more viewers, users, and impressions, which generates more capital for the business.

Though the suggestion of placing advertising on a canvas in the Museum of Modern Art sounds a little ridiculous, it is a distinctly threatening possibility in the context of the content-capital machines of corporate social networks. Increasingly, artists have been making work using these social platforms as a medium, creating within as well as subverting their frameworks. But these artists must confront the fact that their content—the pieces they create and the media they produce—are part of an economic ecosystem oriented toward the profit of the company that owns the social web space, rather than the artist. This commodification is not as apparent as slapping a logo on a painting, but it is pervasive.

In this essay, I first chart the transformation of the open space of the early Internet into the commercialized social media platforms we experience today, then show how the structure of those social platforms impacts artworks and artists. I discuss how

A Companion to Digital Art, First Edition. Edited by Christiane Paul.

artists' labor is changed by its corporatized context. I describe several prominent works of social network-based art and analyze how they encounter and mitigate commercialization before concluding with a project that encapsulates the parasitical relationship between online art and the Internet businesses that control its milieu, providing a possible strategy for artists creating work online.

From Open Fields to Walled Gardens

We tend to think of the Internet as a blank space that can become occupied and transformed through the magic of HTML and cheap web hosting. Artists are enabled to make work from nothing and disseminate it on a wider scale than ever imaginable, largely controlling the creation and presentation of a piece to a global audience. The work of the Dutch duo JODI—Joan Heemskerk and Dirk Paesmans, acknowledged to be one of the pioneers of Internet art—illustrates that possibility. Their wwwwwwwww.jodi.org/ homepage[1] from the late 1990s, which remains one of their most significant works, is a haze of ASCII "nonsense," recursive links, and exposed HTML code, a fracture in the veneer of the Internet that partakes in an earlier age of web aesthetics, maintaining it as a form of resistance and fighting the glossy usability of Web 2.0.

Now, the Web is becoming less of a clean slate as more of our experience is bounded by walled gardens controlled by commercial interests and companies. Charter owns your connection, Google your search engine, and Facebook your online social life. This background is what artists have to reckon with. "Artists often cling to control of their work and the context of its display, but to interact with Tumblr [one prominent social platform], they must give up that control," writer and curator Ben Valentine (2013) writes in his essay "Revisiting Tumblr as Art," published by the art blog *Hyperallergic*.

Artists working online must also let go of the idea that their work is created in the traditional vacuum of the studio with its connotations of non-commercial or uncorrupted creative labor. Our experience of the Internet is an inherently monetary exchange, with web-based businesses profiting directly or indirectly from our accessing of information that others have chosen to make public. This makes for a sticky situation when one discusses the state of art making on the Internet, particularly in the case of social media art. The major social media networks are self-contained ecosystems for web browsing that make it unnecessary to leave the comfortable confines of a single corporate space. Facebook would love nothing more than their users never leaving its site, and Twitter and Tumblr are driven toward ever-greater user engagement "inside" their service, though they often link out to other areas of the Web. These companies need you to stick with them, so that you can add incrementally to their hoard of unique visitors and user time, much the opposite of JODI's homepage.

For average users, it is probably not a major concern that their content, in the form of status updates and vacation photos, is being monetized, but artists might see the content (artwork) they produce as more dear, with more significance placed on its integrity. The dangers presented by making work in a relentlessly capitalized space where creative content is currency are manifold: the work cannot help but engage with a commercial system, the artists cannot control the work's consistency or continued existence online, and preservation is made difficult when the infrastructure is maintained by a business.

The Aesthetic Mechanics of Social Networks

While web sites like Facebook, Tumblr, and Twitter can be called upon as almost universal experience for active users of the Internet today, this will not last for long. In fact, in 2014, with the rise of mobile Web-browsing via smartphones, many of the acts of sharing that we perform on these social networks are now commonly carried out through apps like Snapchat or Instagram, which have been the sites of less art making given their immaturity. It therefore becomes useful to sketch out what sites such as Tumblr and Twitter look like and how they function.

Each social network is composed of a personal profile, where the user's own information is displayed alongside an avatar and a timeline of their posts, as well as a feed, in which posts are generated by the other users they follow. Each social network incorporates text, images, and multimedia to differing degrees: Twitter emphasizes text; Facebook emphasizes text and still images; and Tumblr is home to a diversity of GIFs, videos, text, images, and links. The format of the pages is downplayed in both Twitter and Tumblr, giving preference to the content of the feed or the profile. Facebook's overwhelming informational structure means that the user is more aware of their residence in a controlled space rather than an unbounded feed.

These social media platforms exist for the purpose of sharing content with an audience that each user gathers on their own. The platforms have simple buttons that allow users to distribute a piece of content they see to their respective audience, moving it from the feed to storage on the personal profile. On Twitter, this is called a retweet; on Facebook, a share; and on Tumblr, a reblog. Tumblr's emphasis on multimedia and sharing—the site is home to a lower percentage of "original content," or content first created or shared on that platform by a user, than the other two platforms—means that it is an excellent space for visual art. Users' personal page on Tumblr functions as a kind of collection, in which they store media that they particularly like or identify with, not unlike a traditional art collector does in a personal or home museum.

This structure makes the experience of viewing media on social platforms much different from that of seeing it on the static artist web sites that came before social platforms' rise. The feeds of these web sites have often been described as a stream. While earlier web sites were made to be perused slowly by the visitor as if she were an explorer venturing into an unknown forest, the social network is a river-like barrage of content that flows past the user, curated and controlled not by the artist but by the user herself. It is within this space that artists are making work, surrendering their creations to the flow of these streams and gauging the responses of their audiences by shares and reblogs.

Trading Independence for Audience

Artwork made and released through social media platforms is ephemeral, unbounded, and uncontrollable. Yet artists continue to create using these avenues. There is a decisive tradeoff to using major social networks as sites for art making: the content may be corrupted in terms of its non-commercial integrity, but the platform and audiences offered by these companies are huge. "Images of artworks can travel as far and fast as an audience commands," artist Brad Troemel writes in his essay "Art After Social Media" (2013a).

Social media platforms (and web sites in general) as venues for art also lack the gatekeepers that guard the exhibition spaces of the artworld: dealers, curators, collectors, and critics. Previously, artists did not have the independent access to exposure that they now have through the Internet. There are social media platforms and networks that are not monetized by advertising—the user fee-driven App.net, for example—but so far, these lack the massive viewership and potential for going viral that is so prevalent on larger networks. Participating in the commercial system is a conscious choice that trades monetization for reach.

In this sense, artists become compensated laborers for social media platforms, though compensated by audience rather than money.

In his essay "Marx, Labor, and the Artist" (2007), poet and critic Reginald Sheperd defines the artist as a "cultural worker in the same way that someone laboring in a factory is an industrial worker." But for Sheperd, artists are more independent and self-actualized than the traditional Marxist oppressed industrial worker because the artist chooses "both the means and the result of his own production" and "both the impulse and the product of his labor are his own" (Sheperd 2007). In other words, artists are laborers who are free to choose how and what they create, and they own the end product—as opposed to the factory worker, who does not have access to the means of production nor the result.

This is clearly not the case for artists making work through social media platforms. In fact, through Terms of Use agreements that all users sign when creating accounts on social platforms, the technology companies often assert their own copyright to media created on their platforms. The platform can legally do what they wish with the unprotected work.

Pre-Internet artists who created within the studio and then used an intimate distribution network of galleries and collectors to support themselves—Cindy Sherman taking guerrilla self-portraits around New York, Lucian Freud painting in the cocoon of his living room—surely did control the means and end of their labor. At the outset of the social Internet, JODI also faced similar conditions, laboring for their own satisfaction online and having strict control over how viewers access and experience their work. Viewing a JODI web site is more akin to a private studio visit than attending a gallery show.

Yet these conditions have changed with the advent of the so-called Web 2.0. Artists working online today, more specifically those using the Internet as a critical medium, might be more productively compared to Sheperd's "industrial workers."

From the very beginning, artists' online work today is integrated into a capitalist system, and they have no more hope of replicating the conditions of the social media platforms through which they create—which are made up of massive amounts of data server infrastructure, staffed offices, and branding initiatives—than an assembly line laborer had of recreating a Ford factory during the Industrial Revolution. Nor do artists seem interested, at this time, in creating their own purpose-built social platforms on the scale of large corporations. Artist Ryder Ripps's creative agency OKFocus, for example, has created small social networks that expand on early work with artist web surfing clubs,[2] but any creative impulse embedded in the founding of a major social platform seems to be quickly lost in the ambition to profit from it. Founder David Karp has portrayed Tumblr as a kind of art project and profits from its branding as such, but art must be self-critical; Tumblr, in contrast, is devoted to narcissism more than self-analysis. No artistic social media project (nor any business, for that matter) has managed to scale up to the heights of Silicon Valley companies while maintaining self-criticality.

It is impossible to resist monetization while working in a corporate online space controlled by investors and board members, the kind of space in which social media art, as opposed to work hosted independently as its discrete domain or distributed through e-mail, must exist. Yet the alternatives—a state-controlled or non-profit Internet that lends itself to censorship and mediocre technology or small-scale non-commercial social media operations that lack large audiences—also seem untenable. It is also important to note that these social media artworks depend on the reach and composition of the respective platforms for their existence. They would not make sense without them.

So what do digital artists have to do in order to avoid or mitigate being involved in such a system? Should they forsake any and all products made by for-profit companies? After all, one can not so much as connect to the Internet without becoming involved in a commercial exchange. Yet we can not go on a witch-hunt for commercialism in the online environment—after all, gallery and museum spaces are capitalist contexts just as social networks are, with galleries oriented toward showcasing and selling works and museums toward pleasing collectors and trustees, whose personal tastes can influence programming and acquisitions.

Appropriating the Platform

Artists succeed by using the commercial nature of the Internet as one tool in their arsenal, turning the structures of corporate social platforms against themselves and adapting to their potential advantages. It is a symbiotic relationship.

I will now describe some prominent artworks made on social platforms and examine how they interact with the context of commercialized labor outlined above.

The strongest examples of the young genre of social media art, or art that is made through and about social media platforms, actively engage and critique the platforms through which they travel, making us rethink how the audience personally uses these now-mundane online tools. Such is the case in Australian artist Joe Hamilton's *Hyper Geography* (2011),[3] a visual orchestra hosted on Tumblr that investigates how images are created and disseminated through the Internet, taking advantage of the social network's infrastructure to form a loosely connected web of images and content propelled by Tumblr's own channels (Figure 18.1).

Hyper Geography exists on two levels. Visiting the site's web page reveals a mosaic of individual image panels that come together to form a cohesive, surreal vision of a post-Internet universe, in which glossy computer renderings of household products coexist with snippets of photographs, glimpses of natural landscapes, architecture, animals, and computer parts, a collage of real and virtual objects and images. Yet following *Hyper Geography* on Tumblr and experiencing the piece through the social platform's newsfeed only reveals one panel at a time, which is isolated and sharable on its own.

"Post-Internet" is a hotly debated term (McHugh 2011; Apprich et al. 2013; Kholeif 2014; Wallace 2014) that I use here to define a time in which the aesthetics of the early Internet—bare hatchworks of HTML, icons of personal computers, GIFs denoting web sites permanently "under construction"—are already an old language that, along with the new vernacular of Web 2.0, deeply informs an artistic practice across media from web sites to prints and sculptures. The visual vernacular of the Web and Internet art itself changes quickly and today artists find themselves responding to a slickly designed, holistically branded Internet universe made up of high-resolution images,

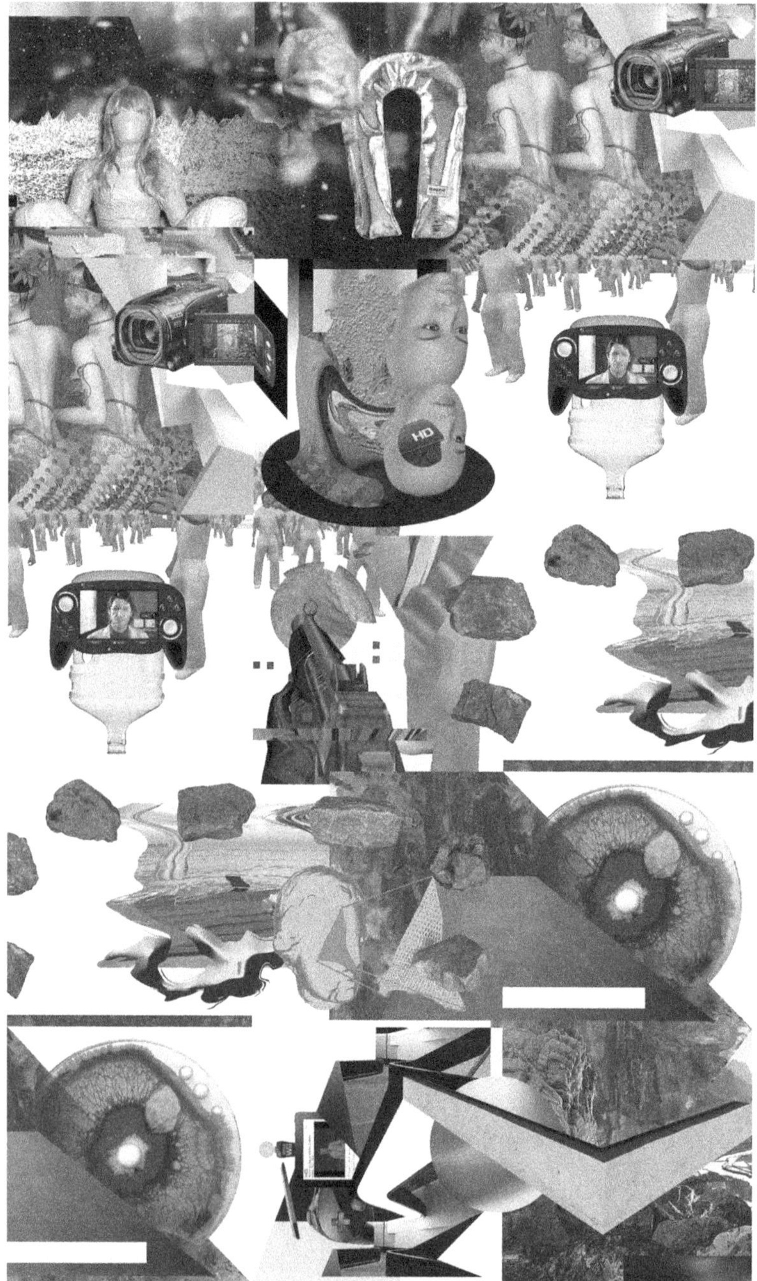

FIGURE 18.1 Joe Hamilton, *Hyper Geography,* 2011. Screenshot. Image courtesy of Joe Hamilton.

monochromatic backgrounds, and scrolling panes instead of the aesthetics of its DIY predecessor. Right now we call this environment Web 2.0—to attempt to nail down any of the Web's trends for more than the current month, let alone year or decade, feels preposterous—though we are quickly moving past it. Web 2.0 is corporatized down to its bones, large businesses own every piece of Internet infrastructure, and every piece connects to the next with the illusion of seamlessness.

The aesthetics of post-Internet art serves to undermine what we have come to expect from the Web. Where we hope to find simple user interfaces and accelerated means of sharing media, the two tenets of the current Web 2.0, we find either self-conscious throwbacks to the early days of the Internet, such as the emoticon explosion on artist Petra Cortright's personal web site,[4] or a mutant, metastasized version of that sharing ecosystem, as in the group blog *The Jogging*[5] (originally started by Brad Troemel and Lauren Christensen in 2009), which I will discuss in the following. The post-Internet is characterized by a lack of ideology or compunction about the Web as a platform. The online space has long lost the utopian sheen that it had in the 1990s, but it has gained massive audiences and a global, nigh-universal reach. The post-Internet artist takes advantage of every tool at her disposal, whether corporate or homemade, to encounter that world of potential, dissect it, build it back up again, create, or destroy. The commercial coexists with the personal.

Hamilton fights Web 2.0's desire for commercial logic and creates a kind of structured nonsense that disseminates itself in a microcosm, traveling through Tumblr without any mark of authorship or artistic intention. *Hyper Geography* is as messy and uncontained as the Internet itself. Hamilton creates physical manifestations of the *Hyper Geography* world in the form of prints, which are sold, yet those pieces simply call back to the work's online existence, which remains dynamic and decentralized.

Hamilton confronts and accepts the Web's ability to separate a work of art from its author. As it moves through the social sharing process, "context information is divorced from the artwork," Troemel writes:

> The name, title, and date are often the first data to get lost. Like a wheel's tire, the image gets stripped of its own form through its continued use. This creates a peculiar, inverse reaction: the more famous an art image becomes, the less its author will be attributed. (Troemel 2013a)

Filmmaker and writer Hito Steyerl succinctly captured the process that the image undergoes in her essay "In Defense of the Poor Image": "As it accelerates, it deteriorates" (Steyerl 2009).

The labor of *Hyper Geography* embraces authorlessness; it poses the artist as a factory himself, a production floor for glossy content and thus capital. Hamilton subverts the role of the artist online as a lone laborer. While he is in fact a craftsman carefully honing his polished images, he appears to be the opposite: his work is designed to thrive in an uncaring commercial ecosystem while maintaining its integrity. This lack of authorship also speeds up the artwork's transformation into the generic "content," the material fuel used for the social networks' monetization schemes. From the perspectives of the companies that control the online platforms, the most successful piece of social media art is barely different from an ex's annoying status updates.

Asserting Authorship

Artists are modifying their approaches to authorship in order to both thrive in the online ecosystem and resist capitalization.

Artist Man Bartlett is widely recognized as one of the forces behind social media art's emergence around 2010.[6] Through a widely varied practice, Bartlett, who remains unrepresented by a gallery, created for himself a powerful presence on the Internet with major followings on social media platforms such as Twitter and Tumblr. He has leveraged those presences as a way both to interact with his audience and to create a sustainable career in the form of monetized content, soliciting and selling work through his social media accounts. This kind of practice can be wrapped up in another Internet obsession—promoting oneself through social platforms and creating a popular identity often referred to as a "brand." Bartlett is building a "personal brand" by both relentlessly emphasizing his own authorship and enabling the participation of his audience within his work, made possible by open social media platforms.

In the performance *#24hKith* (2010)—related to his work *Kith and Kin* (2010)—Bartlett took advantage of the conversational nature and global audience of Twitter by asking his followers to tweet statements beginning with "I am." In the life performance the artist would then "translate" each statement into a colored feather—picking a color corresponding to the mood of the message, such as anger or sadness—which was stuck on a life-size white mannequin, gradually covering and overwhelming the figure. Bartlett streamed to his audience a video of himself attaching each feather while wearing a costume befitting a late-night television show host and muttering mysteriously. The piece compelled a large following for the entire 24 hours, with the attention focused not so much on the platforms, but on Bartlett himself: he piggybacked on the businesses' built-in audiences and converted them into viewers.

Bartlett has a fractious relationship with his own commercialization. He was an active user of the photo-sharing platform Instagram, posting documentation of his studio practice as well as artworks created for the platform, but was taken aback when Instagram was sold to Facebook, which the artist had already stopped using as it began its more aggressive monetization of users in 2013. He decided to sell a photo reproduction of his Instagram account as an artwork before he quit, advertising the new piece, of course, through Twitter.

Bartlett builds his success by promoting himself via social networks, making sure his authorship is reinforced rather than lost. This in turn leads to a conversion of fans to followers to, ideally, collectors, who then fund the artist's work independently—offline and outside of social networks, yet seeded by them. Twitter and Tumblr may monetize the content that Bartlett creates, but he also uses them to monetize himself, a significant opportunity for an emerging artist.

This scenario involves productive labor both for the artist and for the platforms he uses; the work becomes a kind of collaboration between Bartlett and the companies with which he has formed relationships. While these relationships become problematic at times, and Bartlett intentionally subverts them by refusing to follow the communicative norms of social media, tweeting abstract designs rather than words and publishing content that is challenging rather than immediately "sharable" (the term businesses often use for media that panders to users), prompting them to spread it on their own for no compensation. Rather, the artist makes money off an audience he has gained courtesy of social media companies by constructing an economy outside of the gallery system, selling his work directly to followers on Twitter.

The commercialized structure of social media platforms presents a chance to capitalize art in a non-gallery system, creating around the work of art a network of external defining qualities that are not at play in the artworld at large. On which platform did the work of art have its debut? Who was the first to share it, and how many people have shared or liked it since? These qualities also become fodder for monetization.

What Defines Ownership Online?

In 2013, I co-curated an exhibition called *Shortest Video Art Ever Sold* with writer and curator Marina Galperina, hosted at the Moving Image Art Fair in New York. We asked artists to create work on the new social media platform Vine, a spin-off of Twitter that allowed its users to make six-second-long videos edited within the smartphone. The videos on display were made using the platform's technology, but they were not yet posted and hosted online. Only after a collector purchased the work would the video be published on the social media platform of the buyer's choice, giving them control over how it was disseminated and the credit line.

Collectors purchased the work and later published it through Vine and Twitter, including Angela Waschko's *Tits on Tits on Ikea* (2013), a video of the artist sitting on a couch, covering her chest with a laptop showing a video of breasts represented by balloons. As in Bartlett's case outlined above, the work is aggressively converted into capital by using a social media platform even as the business behind that platform monetizes that content by selling to its advertisers—hence the symbiotic relationship. Social web sites, with their large scale and constant, ephemeral flows of information, create a sense of scarcity that does not exist for freely accessible self-contained web sites such as JODI's, though the work of Rafaël Rozendaal, who incorporates collectors' names within the URL for his online artworks, points to another possibility for and different intimation of online scarcity.

The scarcity enabled by social media platforms mimics some of the conditions of the external artworld and is leading to a new discourse on collecting. This scarcity is often a function of ephemerality. As an artistic image travels through the medium of Tumblr, for example, it is experienced at a glimpse, in passing, in a users' feed, then shared, if so desired, on users' own profiles, a gesture that intimates a certain possession of the work, as well as perpetuates it. And yet no one person can claim ownership over a work of art shared on social media platforms. In *Shortest Video Art Ever Sold*, the collector bought the ability to debut the work on social media, giving the image its launch into the online ecosystem along with the collector's name in the caption of the work. Yet this ownership itself was ephemeral. Once the work of art spread far enough, as Troemel explained above, its authorship and ownership are often stripped and the link between collector and artwork severed.

Sometimes artworks are overwhelmed by the commercial context in which they emerged, and become integrated into a larger capitalist system. Such was the case with *Social Printshop* (2010), a project initiated by Benjamin Lotan and composed of a web application that transformed a user's group of Facebook friends into a huge mosaic grid that Lotan then printed out and sent to the user, who paid for the service. Lotan had initially considered the project a work of art that responds to the online representation of social connections. But even as it was incorporated into a 2010 exhibition of social media-based art, *#TheSocialGraph*, curated by Hrag Vartanian, potential investors were courting Lotan with plans to turn the project into a full-fledged business.

Within the exhibition the artwork was displayed as a fictional sponsorship in the form of a vinyl logo adhered to the wall, a perfect replica of the dominant Web 2.0

style and an artifact of its culture. Yet any satire dissipated as Lotan transformed *Social Printshop* into a start-up, which has thrived by turning digital social network systems into physical objects in the form of photo albums and posters. Artworks or artists without a deep commitment to mitigating commercialization are quickly swept up into the 2010s tide of technology venture capital and thirst for incremental innovation.

The Persistence of the Poor Image

The plasticity of the Web and the pervasive nature of its commercial context requires of an artwork multiple, flexible strategies. *The Jogging*, a collaborative project on Tumblr originally created by Brad Troemel and Lauren Christensen, fulfills these needs and is perhaps one of the most successful examples of art that thrives on social networks.

The Jogging began in 2009 as a feed of images of ephemeral sculptures that Troemel and Christiansen would make, photograph, and destroy after publishing the images online, allowing them to disseminate through the Internet without the burden of a physical form. This evolved into digital artworks made up of materials found and collaged online, chance interactions between the virtual and the real. After a hiatus, *The Jogging* re-emerged in 2012 on Tumblr and began posting in earnest, with contributions from a collective of artists that included Artie Vierkant, Joshua Citarella, and others, as well as images submitted by an ever-growing range of artists.

The Jogging has become a byword for a particular post-Internet aesthetic formed by ironic or humorous juxtapositions of non-art objects and artistic interpolations—surreal aggregates that at times are hard to tell from simple "Internet weirdness," often prominently featuring particular brands or companies, which brings the creations closer to advertising's visual language. *The Jogging* style thrives on meme culture, piggybacking on the latest popular memes and tropes of Internet culture and even creating its own unique, insular meme culture only recognizable to Jogging followers. The images cascade in a continuous flow, enhanced by the web site's employment of a continuous scroll design. They are ceaseless, published one after another after another, 24 hours a day, seven days a week, keeping pace with the commercial Internet's short attention span and endless desire for content.

The Jogging has featured a hammer with nails hammered into its head, titled *Revenge* (2013), by Mak Ying Tung; sculptures by Troemel made up of vacuum-sealed computers, philosophy textbooks, and modular furniture elements; a Photoshopped image of art critic Jerry Saltz berating the restaurant chain Outback Steakhouse's signature dish "Bloomin' Onion," a carved fried onion; and a manipulated photo of Brad Troemel rendered meditating in a grocery store aisle encircled by Mrs. Butterworth syrup containers, among thousands of other posts.

Another Jogging image depicts a MacBook Air laptop vertically stuck into a grassy lawn, resembling a gravestone. The hinted-at joke, a half-told one-liner about the quick obsolescence of technology or the degree to which we value our computers, is funny enough to provoke a second look, and, possibly, hitting the "like" button at the bottom of the post or sharing it with friends and followers. Tumblr's reblog button republishes a post to the user's own Tumblr, displaying it to the user's followers. Each like or reblog that a post receives makes it accumulate one "note." The more notes an image has, the more attention and reach it has achieved.

Troemel, who has emerged as *The Jogging*'s de facto representative and chief evangelist (to borrow vocabulary from start-up culture), has described the competition for notes as the current state of the artworld in an online context, where art indiscriminately coexists with every other type of media artifact, freed from its white cube. "Creators must compete for online attention in the midst of an overwhelming amount of information," Troemel writes in his essay "Athletic Aesthetics":

> Athletic aesthetics amounts to the supply-side gamification of the art attention economy. Notes, likes, and reblogs serve as the quantitative basis for influence in an art world where critics' written word has been stripped of power. (Troemel 2013b)

Competition over the metrics of online attention then serves a score-keeping function in a post-Internet, commercialized artworld where it is also difficult for emerging artists to attract the attention of the gallery system. In contrast to Web 1.0 artists, who have largely stayed online, however, this later generation of post-Internet artists are more intrigued by the possibilities of making physical objects. That inclination, along with the growing acceptance of digital-focused practices, has led to the younger artists' increasing integration into the art market, commercial galleries, auction houses, and art fairs over the course of 2013 and 2014.

Social platforms still provide a different kind of access than galleries and collectors. These young creators solicit the support offered by social media businesses as a way to create and communicate with a large audience—the most successful, by Troemel's definition, *Jogging* images have been shared hundreds of thousands of times. *The Jogging* supplies Tumblr with content that titillates its users, but at the same time, the artists behind it are using the social network as a way to infect the non-art world with their viral aesthetic. Individual authorship, which *The Jogging* hides behind symbolic hyperlinks, is downplayed in favor of capitulation to and subversion of the commercial systems of the Internet.

Steyerl pins down this paradoxical situation when she discusses her idea of the poor image, which *The Jogging* epitomizes:

> The poor image is no longer about the real thing—the originary original. Instead, it is about its own real conditions of existence: about swarm circulation, digital dispersion, fractured and flexible temporalities. It is about defiance and appropriation just as it is about conformism and exploitation. (Steyerl 2009)

If we exist in an economy of online attention, then *The Jogging* is surely one of the most valuable artworks ever produced in a digital context. At the same time, it is among the most subtly subversive, because it perpetuates itself like a virus, conforming to whatever context it is shown in, whether blatantly as visual art or simply as a visual object devoid of ideology.

Building Critical Economies

As artists continue to create online work and mature alongside the commercial sites they use as platforms, economies that mingle aspects of web commerce and the art market are growing. Brad Troemel, the proprietor of *The Jogging*, is quickly becoming a well-known artist and an art-market commodity in and of himself. *The Jogging*'s notoriety plus Troemel's patronage led to payments to its contributors, but images that are submitted and accepted by *The Jogging* are compensated according to how many reblogs they receive—or, by Troemel's own definition, how successful the artwork is. This miniature economy perpetuates the norms of other web economies like content marketing or blogging; laborers earn money based on how much attention their work receives.

Online notoriety is a commercial commodity, and it is apparent that this commodity can be created by visual art. Since this economic potential has been made visible, the temptation exists for artists to seek it out and create work purely for the eyeballs of the attention economy—a strategy that may lead to artworld success, though it is far from guaranteed. Yet the most successful artworks, perhaps the ones most likely to make it into the art history books of tomorrow, are the pieces that do not succumb entirely to the established pathways of social media. Though corporations provide a visible path to attention and monetization, artists are continuing to subvert these pathways and carve out their own semi-independent communities and visual languages online. It is these critical economies that will build sustainable platforms for digital art making in the future.

Finally, the process of creating art on a social media platform is a balancing act. The successful work of art must critique the platform on which it exists, both resisting the money-driven ecosystem that the Internet has become and taking advantage of it as a resource for viewership, authority, and attention. Art must take part in the system in order to reach a wider audience. As the genre of institutional critique and its co-dependent relationship to institutional spaces, social media art piggybacks on its semi-willing hosts, untenable without them but impure with them. The trade-off must be acknowledged and, if possible, appropriated and redirected.

Acknowledgment

The author is grateful to Hrag Vartanian, who published an early version of this essay in Hyperallergic.com.

Notes

1 JODI: http://wwwwwwwww.jodi.org/ (accessed July 15, 2014).
2 An Internet surfing club is a group site (typically a blog) on which artists and others link to "surfed" or "surfable" items on the Web and post their own creative work. "Nasty Nets Internet Surfing Club" was the first site to use the term to describe itself.
3 http://hypergeography.tumblr.com/ (accessed July 15, 2014).
4 http://www.petracortright.com/ (accessed July 15, 2014).
5 http://thejogging.tumblr.com/ (accessed July 15, 2014).
6 While there are earlier examples of social media art, it did not gain momentum until around 2010.

References

Apprich, Clemens, and Josephine Berry Slater, Anthony Iles, Oliver Lerone Schultz. 2013. *Provocative Alloys: A Post-Media Anthology.* Lüneburg, Germany: Post-Media Lab and MUTE Books. http://www.metamute.org/sites/www.metamute.org/files/u1/a-post-media-anthology-mute-books-9781906496944-web-fullbook.pdf (accessed July 15, 2014).

Kholeif, Omar, ed. 2014. *Art after the Internet.* Manchester, UK: The White Building/Cornerhouse.

McHugh, Gene. 2011. *PostInternet – Notes on the Internet and Art.* Link Editions. http://www.lulu.com/us/en/shop/gene-mchugh/post-internet/paperback/product-16792924.html (accessed July 15, 2014).

Sheperd, Reginald. 2007. "Marx, Labor, and the Artist." http://reginaldshepherd.blogspot.com/2007/02/marx-labor-and-artist.html (accessed July 15, 2014).

Steyerl, Hito. 2009. "In Defense of the Poor Image." *e-flux* #10, November 2009. http://www.e-flux.com/journal/in-defense-of-the-poor-image/ (accessed July 15, 2014).

Troemel, Brad. 2013a. "Art After Social Media." *Art Papers*, July/August. http://www.artpapers.org/feature_articles/feature1_2013_0708.htm (accessed July 15, 2014).

Troemel, Brad. 2013b. "Athletic Aesthetics." *The New Inquiry*, March 10. http://thenewinquiry.com/essays/athletic-aesthetics/ (accessed July 15, 2014).

Valentine, Ben. 2013. "Revisiting Tumblr as Art." *Hyperallergic*, February 22. http://hyperallergic.com/65674/revisiting-tumblr-as-art/ (accessed July 15, 2014).

Wallace, Ian. 2014. "What is Post-Internet Art?" *Artspace*, March 18. http://www.artspace.com/magazine/interviews_features/post_internet_art?utm_source=Sailthru&utm_medium=email&utm_term= (accessed July 15, 2014).

Further Reading

Broeckmann, Andreas. 2014. "Postmedia Discourses – A Working Paper." http://www.mikro.in-berlin.de/wiki/tiki-index.php?page=Postmedia+Discourses (accessed July 15, 2014).

Nechvatal, Joseph. 2014. "Art's Post-Media Malaise." *Hyperallergic*, February 17. http://hyperallergic.com/109631/arts-post-media-malaise/ (accessed July 15, 2014).

Quaranta, Domenico. 2013. *Beyond New Media Art.* Link Editions. http://www.artandeducation.net/announcement/you-are-here-art-after-the-internet-edited-by-omar-kholeif/ (accessed July 15, 2014).

19

Artistic Visualization

Lev Manovich

Before the end of the 1990s, the use of data visualization was limited to particular scientific disciplines or financial pages of newspapers. It was not part of the vernacular visual culture. By the end of the 2000s, the situation had changed dramatically. For example, the Museum of Modern Art in New York (MoMA) presented a dynamic visualization of its collection on five screens in its lobby. MoMA also included a number of artistic visualizations in its large survey exhibition *Design and the Elastic Mind* (2008). The *New York Times* was regularly featuring custom visualizations both in its print and web editions created by the in-house *New York Times* interactive team. The Web was full of numerous sophisticated visualization projects created by artists, designers, scientists, and students. If one searches for certain types of public data, the first result returned by a Google search links to automatically created interactive graphs of the respective data. Dozens of free web-based visualization tools have become available. In short, three hundred years after William Playfair started the field by inventing the now classic visualization techniques (bar chart, pie chart, line chart), data visualization has finally entered the realms of both high and popular cultures.

This shift was acknowledged by the leading data visualization designers themselves:

> Information visualization is becoming more than a set of tools, technologies and techniques for large data sets. It is emerging as a medium in its own right, with a wide range of expressive potential. (Rodenbeck 2008)

> Visualization is ready to be a mass medium. (Viégas and Wattenberg 2010)

Artists played a key role in the popularization of the data visualization field in the 2000s, and created some of the most memorable visualizations of the decade. They also created a new visual programming environment—Processing (2001) by Ben Fry and Casey Reas—and built a large community around it. Through Processing

A Companion to Digital Art, First Edition. Edited by Christiane Paul.

many more art and design students learned programming and started to explore computer graphics, interactives, and visualization. Artists also set up and taught in hundreds of digital art programs around the world, thus preparing a new generation of people who could create images, animations, spaces, sounds, and all other media types (including visualizations) via programming.

The development of the data visualization field in the 2000s happened in parallel to another technological and social movement—the rise of Big Data, that is, massive data sets, which could not be easily understood by using the existing approaches that modern society had developed to analyze information. Among the key sources of such data was "social media," user-generated content and user activities on social networks such as Facebook, Instagram, Twitter, Google+, Weibo, etc. Because all leading social media networks made it easy for anybody with knowledge of programming to download their user data and content (using their APIs, which stands for Application Programming Interfaces), they also indirectly contributed to the popularization of data visualization. Getting, cleaning, and organizing a large data set can typically take a significant amount of time, but downloading social media data from the networks is relatively simple and fast. As a result, many memorable visualizations of large data sets in the 2000s featured data from Twitter, Flickr, and other then popular social media networks.

In this chapter I will not try to address every kind of aesthetic strategy developed by visualization artists, or to review all important projects created in that field. Instead I will focus on what I see as one of the most important and interesting developments in this area of digital art. I will discuss work by artists who challenged the most fundamental principles of the data visualization field as it has existed since the 18th century. Instead of continuing to represent data using points, lines, and other geometric primitives, they pioneered a different method which I call "media visualization": new visual representations derived from visual media objects (images, video, text). I will analyze well-known examples of artistic visualizations that use this approach: *Listening Post* (Ben Rubin and Mark Hansen, 2001), *Cinema Redux* (Brendan Dawes, 2004), and *The Preservation of Favoured Traces* (Ben Fry, 2009).

Along with examples from the classics of artistic data visualization, I will also use relevant ones from the projects created in my own research lab. Following the pioneering work of other artists discussed in this chapter, we developed software tools to visualize massive cultural data sets and applied them to a variety of data sets, ranging from 4535 covers of *Time* magazine to 2.3 million Instagram photos from thirteen global cities.

In order for us to understand how visualization artists went against the norms of the field, we first need to understand these conventions, which will be discussed in the following section.

Defining Data Visualization

What is data visualization? Despite the growing popularity of datavis (a common abbreviation for "data visualization"), it is not so easy to come up with a definition that would work for all the types of projects being created today and, at the same time, would clearly separate datavis from other related fields, such as scientific visualization and information design. So let us start with a provisional definition that we can modify later. Let us define data visualization as a mapping between discrete data and a visual representation. We can also use different concepts besides "representation," each bringing an additional meaning to the subject. For example, if we believe that a brain uses a number of distinct representational and cognitive modalities, we can define data visualization as a mapping from other cognitive modalities (such as mathematical and propositional) to an image modality.

My definition does not cover all aspects of data visualization—such as the distinctions between static, dynamic (i.e., animated), and interactive visualization (the latter, of course, being most important today). In fact, most definitions of datavis (or its synonym, information visualization) by computer science researchers equate it with the use of interactive computer-driven visual representations and interfaces. Here are examples of such definitions: "Information visualization (InfoVis) is the communication of abstract data through the use of interactive visual interfaces" (Keim et al. 2006); "Information visualization utilizes computer graphics and interaction to assist humans in solving problems" (Purchase et al. 2008).

Interactive graphic interfaces in general, and interactive visualization applications in particular, offer many new techniques for manipulating data elements—from the ability to change how files are shown on the desktop in modern operating systems to the multiple coordinated views available in some visualization software such as Mondrian by Martin Theus (2013). However, regardless of whether you are looking at a visualization printed on paper or a dynamic arrangement of graphic elements on your computer or smartphone screen—generated by using interactive software and changeable at any moment—the image you are working with in both cases is a result of mapping. So what is special about images produced by such mapping?

For some researchers, data visualization is distinct from scientific visualization in that the latter uses numerical data while the former uses non-numeric data such as text and networks of relations. For example, "In contrast to scientific visualization, information visualization typically deals with nonnumeric, nonspatial, and high-dimensional data" (Chen 2005). I am not sure that this distinction holds up in practice. Plenty of datavis projects use numbers as their primary data, but even when they focus on other data types, they still often use some numerical data along with them. For instance, a typical network visualization may use both the data about the structure of the network (which nodes are connected to each other) and the quantitative data about the strength of these connections (for example, how many messages are exchanged between members of a social network). As a concrete example of datavis that combines non-numerical and numerical data, consider the well-known project *History Flow* (2003) by Fernanda B. Viégas and Martin Wattenberg, which shows how a given Wikipedia page grows over time as different authors contribute to it. The contribution of each author is represented by a colored line. The width of the line changes over time reflecting the amount of text contributed by an author to the Wikipedia page. Another datavis classic, Aaron Koblin's *Flight Patterns* (2005), uses numerical data about the flight schedules and trajectories of all planes that fly over the United States to create an animated map that displays the pattern formed by their movement over a 24-hour period.

Rather than trying to separate data visualization and scientific visualization by using some a priori concept, one could instead enter each term in Google image search and compare the results. The majority of images returned by a search for "data visualization" are two-dimensional and use vector graphics—points, lines, curves, and other simple geometric shapes. The majority of images returned when searching for "scientific visualization" are three-dimensional; they use solid 3D shapes or volumes made from 3D points. The results returned by these searches suggest that the two fields indeed differ—not because they necessary use different types of data but because they privilege different visual techniques and technologies.

Scientific visualization and data visualization come from different cultures (science and design); their development corresponds to different areas of computer graphics technology. Data visualization developed in the 1980s along with the field of 3D computer graphics, which at that time required specialized graphics workstations. Information visualization developed in the 1990s along with the rise of desktop 2D graphics software and the adoption of PCs by designers. Its popularity accelerated in the 2000s, the two key factors being the easy availability of big data sets via APIs provided by major social network services since 2005 (as I already mentioned above), and the new high-level programming languages specifically designed for graphics (i.e., Processing[1]) and software libraries for visualization (i.e., Prefuse[2]).

Can we differentiate data visualization from information design? This is a trickier issue, but here is my way of distinguishing the two. Information design starts with data that already has a clear structure, and its goal is to visually express this structure. For example, the famous London tube map designed in 1931 by Harry Beck uses structured data: tube lines, tube stations, and their locations within London geography (Beck 1931). In contrast, the goal of data visualization is to discover the structure of a (typically large) data set. This structure is not known a priori; visualization is successful if it reveals it. A different way of expressing this is to say that information design works with information, while data visualization works with data. As always is the case with regard to actual cultural practices, it is easy to find examples that do not fit this distinction—but a majority do. Therefore I think that this distinction can be useful in allowing us to understand the practices of data visualization and information design as partially overlapping but ultimately different in terms of their functions.

Finally, what about the earlier practices of visually displaying quantitative information in the 19th and 20th century that are known to many people via the examples collected in the pioneering books by Edward Tufte (1983, 1990, 1997, and 2006)? Do they constitute datavis as we understand it today? As I already noted, most definitions provided by researchers working within computer science equate data visualization with the use of interactive computer graphics (a number of definitions of information visualization from the recent literature is available at InfoVis:Wiki 2013). Using software, we can visualize much larger data sets than previously was possible; create animated visualization; show how processes unfold in time; and, most importantly, manipulate visualizations interactively. These differences are very important, but for the purposes of this chapter, which is concerned with the visual language of visualization, they do not matter. The switch from pencils to computers did not affect the core idea of visualization—mapping some properties of data into a visual representation. Similarly, while the availability of computers led to the development of new visualization techniques (scatter plot matrix, treemaps, etc.), the basic visual language of datavis remained the same as it was in the 19th century—points, lines, rectangles, and other graphic primitives. Given this continuity, I will use the term "data visualization" (or "datavis") to refer to both earlier visual representations of data created manually and contemporary software-driven visualization.

Finally, how can we distinguish between regular data visualization and artistic visualization? There are certainly many ways to do this. I am going to suggest three complementary distinguishing features. Not every artistic visualization has to have all three—but in my opinion, the best ones do. First, in contrast to usual data visualization work done for clients, artistic visualizations are typically self-initiated. This allows the best visualization designers to experiment freely and to come up with solutions that don't use commonly accepted visualization techniques and therefore may also be more challenging for viewers to process. Second, the most outstanding work introduces fundamentally new visualization techniques, thus pushing the visualization field forward. (To draw a historical analogy, we can compare commercial visualization work to realist art of the 19th century, and artistic visualization to modernist art.) But the most important distinction is the third one. The best artistic visualizations do not simply reveal patterns and relationships in the data. Instead, through the choice of the data set and the use of particular (often novel) visualization techniques, they make statements about the world, history, societies, and human beings—just as artists do in other mediums.

Given the growing importance of "data" in modern societies in the 2000s and 2010s, it is appropriate to represent and comment on society through visualizations of data sets. Thus, artistic data visualizations are equivalents of portraits, landscapes, genre scenes, and cityscapes in traditional art. But instead of representing the world through its visible forms, they depict it through presentation of data sets.

Reduction and Space

In my opinion, the practice of data visualization, from its beginnings in the second part of the 18th century until today, relied on two key principles. The first principle is *reduction*. Datavis uses graphical primitives such as points, straight lines, curves, and simple geometric shapes to stand in for data objects and relations between them—regardless of whether these "objects" are people, their social relations, stock prices, incomes of nations, unemployment statistics, or anything else. By employing graphical primitives (or, to use the language of contemporary digital media, vector graphics), datavis is able to reveal patterns and structures in the data objects that these primitives represent. However, the price being paid for this power to reveal is extreme schematization. We throw away 99% of what is specific about each object to represent only 1%—in the hope of revealing patterns across this 1% of objects' characteristics.

Data visualization is not unique in relying on such extreme reduction of the world in order to gain new power over what is extracted from it. Datavis came into its own in the first part of the 19th century when, in the course of just a few decades, almost all graph types commonly found today in statistical and charting programs were invented (Friendly and Denis 2001). This development of the new techniques for visual reduction parallels the reductionist trajectory of modern science in the 19th century. Physics, chemistry, biology, linguistics, psychology, and sociology propose that both the natural and social world should be understood in terms of simple elements (molecules, atoms, phonemes, just noticeable sensory differences, etc.) and the rules of their interaction. This reductionism becomes the default "meta-paradigm" of modern science and continues to rule scientific research today. For instance, currently popular paradigms of complexity and artificial life focus our attention on how complex structures and behavior emerge out of interaction of simple elements.

Even more direct is the link between 19th-century datavis and the rise of social statistics. Philip Ball summarizes the beginnings of statistics in this way:

> In 1749 the German scholar Gottfried Achenwall suggested that since this "science" [the study of society by counting] dealt with the natural "states" of society, it should be called Statistik. John Sinclair, a Scottish Presbyterian minister, liked the term well enough to introduce it into the English language in his epic Statistical Account of Scotland, the first of the 21 volumes of which appeared in 1791. (Ball 2004, 64–65)

In the first part of the 19th century many scholars including Adolphe Quetelet, Florence Nightingale, Thomas Buckle, and Francis Galton used statistics to look for "laws of society." This inevitably involved summarization and reduction: calculating the totals and averages of the collected numbers about citizens' demographic characteristics, comparing the averages for different geographical regions, asking if they followed a bell-shaped normal distribution, and so on. It is therefore not surprising that many—if not most—graphical methods that are standard today were invented during this time for the purposes of representations of such summarized data. According to Friendly and Denis (2001), between 1800 and 1850, "In statistical graphics, all of the modern forms of data display were invented: bar and pie charts, histograms, line graphs and time-series plots, contour plots, and so forth."

Do all these different visualization techniques have something in common besides reduction? They all use *spatial variables*—position, size, shape, and, more recently, curvature of lines and movement—to represent key differences in the data and reveal the most important patterns and relations. After reduction this is the second core principle of datavis as it was practiced for three hundred years—from the very first line graphs (1711), bar charts (1786), and pie charts (1801) to their ubiquity today in all graphing software such as Excel, Numbers, Google Docs, and OpenOffice (historical data from Friendly and Denis 2001).

This principle can be rephrased as follows: datavis privileges spatial dimensions over other visual dimensions. In other words, we map the data properties in which we are most interested into topology and geometry. Other less important properties of the objects are represented through different visual dimensions—tones, shading patterns, colors, or transparency of the graphical elements.

As examples, consider two common graph types: a bar chart and a line graph. Both first appeared in William Playfair's *Commercial and Political Atlas* (published in 1786) and became commonplace in the early 19th century (Friendly and Denis 2001). A bar chart represents the differences between data objects via rectangles that have the same width but different heights. A line graph represents changes in the data values over time via changing height of the line.

Another common graph type—the scatter plot—similarly uses spatial variables (positions and distances between points) to make sense of the data. If some points form a cluster, this implies that the corresponding data objects have something in common; if you observe two distinct clusters this implies that the objects fall into two different classes.

Consider another example: network visualizations that today function as distinct symbols of "network society" (see Manuel Lima's authoritative gallery, visualcomplexity.com, which houses over seven hundred network visualization projects). Like bar charts and line graphs, network visualizations also privilege spatial dimensions: position, size, and shape. Their key addition is the use of straight or curved lines to show connections between data objects. For example, in *distellamap* (2005) Ben Fry connects pieces of code and data by lines to show the dynamics of the software execution in Atari 2600 games. In Marcos Weskamp's *FlickrGraph* (2005) the lines visualize the social relationships between users of Flickr. Of course, in addition to lines many other visual techniques can be used to show relations—see for instance a number of maps of science created by Katy Borner and her colleagues at the Information Visualization Lab at Indiana University (see Lima 2014 and InfoVisLab 2014).

I believe that the majority of data visualization practices from the second part of the 18th century to the present follow the same principle—reserving spatial arrangement (we can call it "layout") for the most important dimensions of the data, and using other visual variables for the remaining dimensions. This principle can be found in visualizations ranging from the famous dense graphic showing Napoleon's March on Moscow by Charles Joseph Minard (1869, discussed in Tufte and Finley 2002) (Figure 19.1) to the recent *The Evolution of The Origin of Species* by Stefanie Posavec and Greg McInerny (2009). Distances between elements and their positions, shape, size, line curvature, and other spatial variables code quantitative differences between objects and/or their relations (for instance, who is connected to whom in a social network).

Visualizations typically use colors, fill-in patterns, or different saturation levels to partition graphic elements into groups. In other words, these non-spatial variables function as group labels. For example, Google Trends[3] uses line graphs to compare search volumes for different words or phrases; each line is rendered in a different color. However, the same visualization could have simply used labels attached to the lines—without different colors. In this case, color ads readability but it does not add new information to the visualization per se.

The privileging of spatial over other visual dimensions was also true for the plastic arts in Europe between the 16th and 19th centuries. A painter commonly first worked out the composition for a new work in many sketches; then the composition was transferred to a canvas and shading was fully developed in monochrome. Only after that color was added. This practice seems to assume that the meaning and emotional impact of an image depends most of all on the spatial arrangements of its parts, as opposed to colors, textures and other visual parameters. In classical Asian "ink and wash painting," which first appeared in the 7th century in China and was later introduced to Korea and then Japan (14th century), color did not even appear. The painters used exclusively black ink exploring the contrasts between objects' contours, their spatial arrangements, and different types of brushstrokes.

It is possible to find data visualizations where color is the main dimension—for instance, a common traffic light, which "visualizes" the three possible behaviors of a car driver: stop, get ready, go. This example shows that, if we fix the spatial parameters of visualization, color can become the salient dimension. In other words, it is crucial that the three lights have exactly the same shape and size. Apparently, if all elements of the visualization have the same values with regard to spatial dimensions, our visual system can focus on the differences represented by colors, or other non-spatial variables.

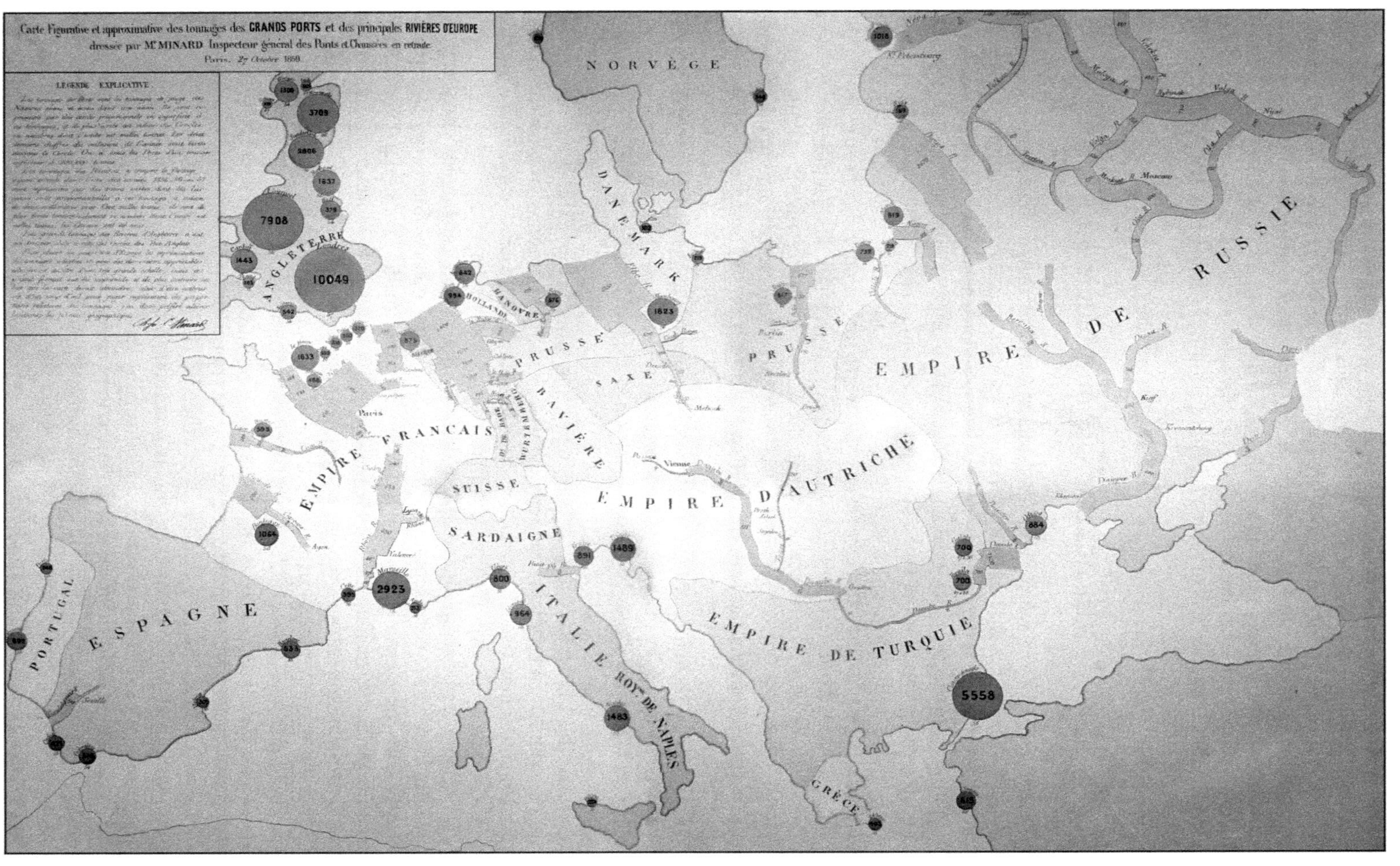

FIGURE 19.1 Charles Joseph Minard, *Map of the Tonnage of the Major Ports and Principal Rivers of Europe*, 1859. Map reproduced from Cartographia, https://cartographia.wordpress.com/2008/06/16/minards-map-of-port-and-river-tonnage/. Public domain.

The two key principles that I suggested—*data reduction* and *privileging of spatial variables*—do not account for all possible visualizations produced during the last three hundred years. However, they are sufficient to separate datavis (at least as it was commonly practiced until now) from other techniques and technologies for visual representation: maps, engraving, drawing, oil painting, photography, film, video, radar, MRI, infrared spectroscopy, etc. They give data its unique identity—the identity that remained remarkably consistent for almost three hundred years, that is, until the 1990s.

Visualization without Reduction

The meanings of the word "visualize" include "make visible" and "make a mental image." This implies that until we "visualize" something, this "something" does not have a visual form. It becomes an image through a process of visualization.

If we survey the practice of datavis from the 18th until the end of the 20th century, the idea that visualization takes non-visual data and maps it into a visual domain works quite well. However, it seems to no longer adequately describe certain new visualization techniques and artistic visualization projects developed since the middle of the 1990s. Although these techniques and projects are commonly discussed as "data visualization," it is possible that they actually represent something else—a fundamentally new development in the history of representational and epistemological technologies, or at least a new broad visualization method for which we don't yet have an adequate name.

Consider a technique called tag cloud (Wikipedia 2014). The technique was popularized by Flickr in 2005 and today can be found on numerous web sites and blogs. A tag cloud shows the most common words in a text in the font size corresponding to their frequency in the text. We can use a bar chart with text labels to represent the same information, which in fact may work better if the word frequencies are very similar. But if the frequencies fall within a larger range, we don't have to map the data into a new visual representation such as the bars. Instead, we can vary the size of the words themselves to represent their frequencies in the text.

The tag cloud exemplifies a broad method that I will call media visualization: creating new visual representations from actual visual media objects or their parts. Rather than representing text, images, video, or other media though new visual signs such as points or rectangles, media visualizations build new representations out of the original media. Images remain images; text remains text.

In view of our discussion of the data reduction principle, we can also call this method "direct visualization," or "visualization without reduction." In direct visualization, the data is reorganized into a new visual representation that preserves its original form. Usually, this does involve some data transformation such as changing data size. For instance, the text cloud reduces the size of text to a small number of most frequently used words. However, this is a reduction that is quantitative rather than qualitative. We don't substitute media objects by new objects (i.e., graphical primitives typically used in infovis), which only communicate selected properties of these objects (for instance, bars of different lengths representing word frequencies). My phrase "visualization without reduction" refers to the preservation of a much richer set of data objects' properties when visualizations are created directly from them.

Not all media visualization techniques, such as a tag cloud, originated in the 21st century. If we retroactively project this concept into history, we can find earlier techniques that use the same idea. For instance, the familiar book index can be understood as a form of media visualization technique. Looking at a book's index one can quickly see if particular concepts or names are given more importance in the book—they will have more entries; less important concepts will take up only a single line.

While both the book index and tag cloud exemplify a media visualization method, it is important to consider the differences between them. The older book index technique relied on the typesetting technology used for printing books. Since each typeface was only available in a limited number of sizes, the idea that you can precisely map the frequency of a particular word into its font size was counterintuitive—so it was not invented. In contrast, the tag cloud technique is a typical expression of what we can call "software thinking"—that is, the ideas that explore the fundamental capacities of modern software. The tag cloud explores the capacities of software to vary every parameter of a representation and to control it by using external data. The data can come from a scientific experiment, from a mathematical simulation, from the body of the person in an interactive installation, from calculating certain properties of the data, and so on. If we take these two capacities for granted, the idea to arbitrarily change the size of words based on certain information—such as their frequency in a text—is something we may expect to be "actualized" in the process of cultural evolution. (In fact, all contemporary interactive visualization techniques rely on the same two fundamental capacities.)

The rapid growth in the number and variety of visualization projects, software applications, and web services since the late 1990s was enabled by the advances in the computer graphics capacities of PCs including both hardware (processors, RAM, displays) and software (C and Java graphics libraries, Flash, Processing, Flex, Prefuse, etc.) These developments both popularized data visualization and also fundamentally changed its identity by foregrounding animation, interactivity, and more complex visualizations that represent connections between many more objects than were previously processed (to give an example, it took the open source data visualization software Mondrian 1.0, running on my 2009 Apple PowerBook laptop with a 2.8 GHz processor and 4 GB of RAM, approximately 7 seconds to render a scatter plot containing 1 million points). But along with these three highly visible trends, the same advances also made the "media visualization" approach possible—although it has not been given its own name so far.

Media Visualization: Examples

In this section I will discuss three well-known art projects that exemplify a "media visualization" approach: *Listening Post*, *Cinema Redux*, and *The Preservation of Favoured Traces*. *Cinema Redux* was created by interactive designer Brendan Dawes in 2004. Dawes wrote a program in Processing that sampled a film at the rate of one frame per second and scaled each frame to 8 x 6 pixels. The program then arranged these miniature frames in a rectangular grid with every row representing a single minute of the film. Although Dawes could have easily continued this process of sampling and remapping—for instance, representing each frame though its dominant color—he chose instead to use the actual scaled-down frames from the film. The resulting visualization represents a trade-off between the two possible extremes: preserving all the details of the original artifact and abstracting its structure completely. A higher degree of abstraction may make the patterns in cinematography and narrative more visible, but it also further removes the viewer from the experience of the film. Staying closer to the original artifact preserves the original detail and aesthetic experience, but may not reveal some of the patterns.

What is important in the context of our discussion is not Dawes's choice of particular parameters for *Cinema Redux* but this reinterpretation of the previous constant of visualization practice as a variable. Infovis designers would typically map data into new diagrammatic representations consisting of graphical primitives. This was the default practice. With computers, a designer can select any value on the "original data"/ abstract representation dimension. In other words, a designer can now choose to use graphical primitives, or the images in their original state, or any format in between. While the title of Dawes's project refers to the idea of reduction, it can be actually understood as expansion in the historical content of earlier datavis practice—that is, an expansion of typical graphical primitives (points, rectangles, etc.) into the actual data objects (film frames).

Before software, visualization usually involved the two-stage process of first counting or quantifying data, and then graphically representing the results. Software allows for direct manipulation of the media artifacts without quantifying them. As demonstrated by *Cinema Redux*, this manipulation can successfully make visible the relations between a large number of these artifacts. Of course such visualization without quantification is made possible by the a priori quantification required for turning any analog data into a digital representation. In other words, it is the "reduction" first performed by the digitization process that paradoxically now allows us to visualize the patterns across sets of analog artifacts without reducing them to graphical signs.

For another example of media visualization, let us turn to Ben Fry's *The Preservation of Favoured Traces* (2009). This web project is an interactive animation of the complete text of Darwin's *On the Origin of Species* (1859–1872). Fry uses different colors to show the changes made by Darwin in each of six editions of his famous book. As the animation plays, we see the evolution of the book text from edition to edition, with sentences and passages deleted, inserted and rewritten. In contrast to typical animated information visualizations that show some spatial structure constantly changing its shape and size in time to reflect changes in the data (for example, the changing structure of a social network over time), the rectangular shape containing the complete text of Darwin's book always stays the same in Fry's project—what changes is its content. This allows us to see how the pattern of additions and revisions to the book become more and more intricate over time, as the changes from all the editions accumulate.

At any moment in the animation we have access to the compete text of Darwin's book—as opposed to only a diagrammatic representation of the changes. At the same time, it can be argued that *The Preservation of Favoured Traces* does in fact involve some data reduction. Given the typical resolution of computer monitors and web bandwidth today, Fry was not able to actually show all the actual book text at the same time.[4] Instead sentences are rendered as tiny rectangles in different colors. However, when you mouse over any part of the image, a pop-up window shows the actual text. Because all the text of Darwin's book is easily accessible to the user in this way, I think that this project can be considered an example of media visualization.

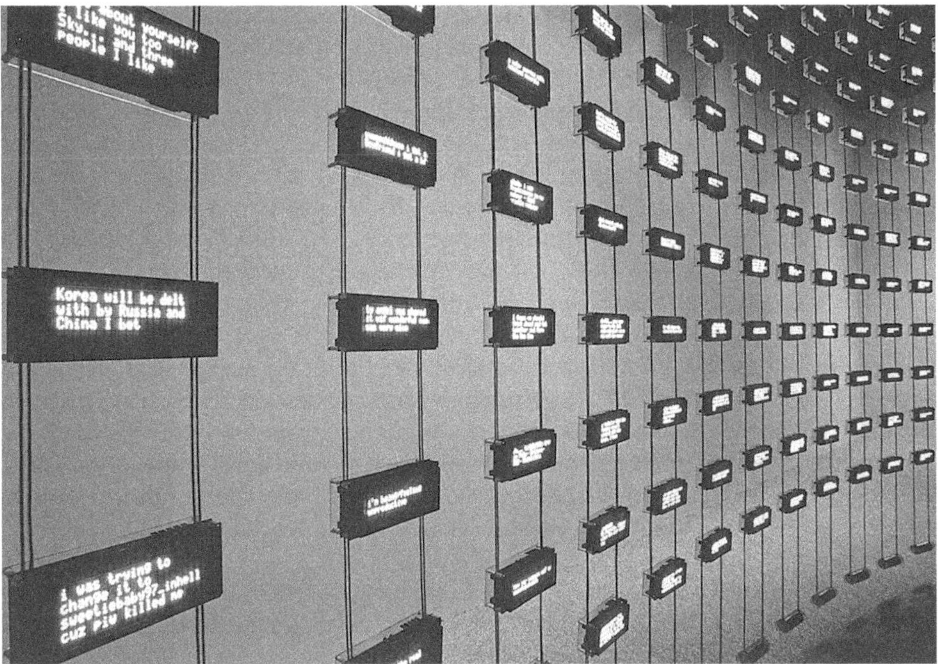

FIGURE 19.2 Ben Rubin and Mark Hansen, *Listening Post*, 2001. Installation shot, detail.

Let's add one more example—*Listening Post* by Ben Rubin and Mark Hansen (2001). Usually this work is considered to be a computer-driven installation rather than an example of datavis. *Listening Post* pulls text fragments from online chat rooms based on various parameters set by the artists in real time and streams them across a display wall made from a few hundred small LED screens in a six-act looping sequence (Figure 19.2). Each act uses its own distinct spatial layout to arrange the dynamically changing text fragments. For instance, in one act the phrases move across the wall in a wave-like pattern; in another act words appear and disappear in a checkerboard pattern. Each act also has its distinct sound environment driven by the parameters extracted from the text that is being animated on the display wall.

One could argue that *Listening Post* is not a visualization because the spatial patterns are pre-arranged by the artists and not driven by the data. This argument makes sense but I think it is important to keep in mind that, while layouts are pre-arranged, the data in these layouts is not; it is a result of the real-time data mining of the Web. While the text fragments are displayed in pre-defined layouts (wave, checkerboard, etc.), the overall result is also always unique because the content of these fragments is always different.

If the authors were to represent the text via abstract graphical elements, we would simply end up with the same abstract pattern in every repetition of an act, but because they show the actual text changing all the time, the patterns that emerge inside the same layout are always different. This is why I consider *Listening Post* to be a perfect representative of the media visualization category; the patterns it presents depend as much on the content of all text fragments appearing on the screen wall as on their pre-defined composition. We can find other examples of info projects that similarly stream data into pre-defined layouts. Manuel Lima identified what he calls a "syntax" of network visualizations, including commonly used layouts such as radial convergence, arc diagrams, radial centralized networks, and others (to see his taxonomy of network display methods, select "filter by method"; Lima 2014). The key difference between most of these network visualizations and *Listening Post* lies in the fact that the former often rely on existing visualization layout algorithms. Thus they implicitly accept the ideologies behind these layouts—in particular the tendency to represent a network as a highly symmetrical and/or circular structure. The authors of *Listening Post* wrote their own layout algorithms that allowed them to control the layouts' intended meanings. It is also important to note that they use six very different layouts that cycle over time. The meaning and aesthetic experience of this work—showing both the infinite diversity of the Web and, at the same time, the existence of many repeating patterns—to a significant extent derive from the temporal contrasts between these layouts. Eight years before Bruno Latour's argument that our ability to create "a provisional visualization which can be modified and reversed" allows us to think differently since any "whole" we can construct is just one of numerous others (Latour 2010), *Listening Post* beautifully staged this new epistemological paradigm enabled by interactive visualization.

The three influential projects I considered here demonstrate that, in order to highlight patterns in the data, we don't have to *reduce* it by representing data objects via abstract graphical elements. We also don't have to summarize the data as is commonly done in statistics and statistical graphics; think, for instance, of a histogram that divides data into a number of bins. This does not mean that, in order to qualify as a "media visualization," an image has to show 100% of the original data—every word in a text, every frame in a movie, and so on. Out of the three examples I just discussed, only *The Preservation of Favoured Traces* does this. Neither *Cinema Redux* nor *Listening Post* use all the available data; instead they *sample* it. The former project samples a feature film at the fixed rate of one frame per second; the latter project filters the online conversations using set criteria that change from act to act. What is crucial is that the elements of these visualizations are not the result of a remapping of the data into some new representation format; they are the original data objects selected from the complete data set. This strategy is related to the traditional rhetorical figure of synecdoche—in which a part is made to represent the whole or vice versa—specifically its particular case in which a specific class of object refers to a larger, more general class. (For example, in *Cinema Redux* one frame stands for a second of a film.)

While sampling is a powerful technique for revealing patterns in data, *The Preservation of Favoured Traces* demonstrates that it is also possible to reveal patterns while keeping 100% of the data. If you ever used a magic marker to highlight important passages of a printed text, you have already been employing this strategy. Although text highlighting normally is not thought of as visualization, we can see that in fact it is an example of a media visualization that does not rely on sampling.

Cinema Redux and *The Preservation of Favoured Traces* also break away from the second key principle of traditional visualization: the communication of meaning via new spatial arrangements of the elements. In both projects, the layout of elements is dictated by the original order of the data—shots in a film, sentences in a book. This is possible and also appropriate because the data that these projects visualize is not the typical data used in datavis. A film or a book are not just a collection of data objects, they are narratives made from these objects (i.e., the data has an assigned sequential order). Although it is certainly possible to create effective visualizations that remap a narrative sequence into a completely new spatial structure as *Listening Post* does—see also *Writing Without Words* (2008) by Stefanie Posavec and *The Shape of Song* (2001) by Martin Wattenberg—*Cinema Redux* and The *Preservation of Favoured Traces* demonstrate that preserving the original sequences also can be effective.

Preserving the original order of data is particularly appropriate for the visualization of cultural data sets that have a time dimension. We can call such data sets "cultural time series." Whether it is a feature film (*Cinema Redux*), a book (*The Preservation of Favoured Traces*), or a long Wikipedia article (*History Flow*), the relationships between the individual elements (film shots, the book's sentences) and also between larger parts of a work separated in time (film scenes, the book's paragraphs and chapters) are of primary importance to the work's evolution, meaning, and its experience by users and viewers. While we consciously or unconsciously notice many of these patterns during the watching and reading of or interaction with the work, the strategy of *projecting time into space*—meaning, laying out movie frames, book sentences, magazine pages in a single image—gives us new possibilities to study the work. Thus, *space* starts to play a crucial role in media visualization after all: it allows us to see *patterns between media elements that are normally separated by time.*

Let me finish this discussion with a few more examples of media visualizations created at my own lab, the Software Studies Initiative.[5] Inspired by the artistic projects that pioneered the media visualization approach, as well as by the resolution and real-time capabilities of interactive super-visualization systems such as HIPerSpace (35,840 x 8000 pixels = 286,720,000 pixels total; see Graphics, Visualization and Virtual Reality Laboratory 2010) developed at the California Institute for Telecommunication and Information Calit2 (www.calit2.net) where our lab is located, my group has been working on techniques and software to allow for interactive explorations of large sets of visual cultural data (see Software Studies Initiative 2014). Some of the visualizations we created use the same strategy as *Cinema Redux*—arranging a large set of images in a rectangular grid. However, the fact that we have access to a very high resolution display sometimes allows us to include 100% of data—as opposed to having to sample it. For example, in *Mapping Time* we created an image showing 4553 covers of every issue of *Time* magazine published between 1923 and 2009 (Manovich and Douglass 2009a). We also compared the use of images in the *Science* and *Popular Science* magazines by visualizing approximately 10,000 pages from each magazine during the first decades of their publication in the project *The Shape of Science* (Huber, Manovich, and Zepel 2010). Our most data-intensive media visualization *Manga Style Space* is 44,000 x 44,000 pixels; it shows 1,074,790 Manga pages organized by their stylistic properties (Manovich and Douglass 2010) (Figure 19.3).

Like *Cinema Redux, Mapping Time* and *The Shape of Science* make equal the values of spatial variables to reveal patterns in the content, colors, and compositions of the images. All images are displayed at the same size and arranged into a rectangular grid according to their original sequence. Essentially, these direct visualizations use only one dimension, with the sequence of images wrapped around into a number of rows to make it easier to see the patterns without having to visually scan a very long image. However, we can also turn such one-dimensional image timelines into 2D, with the second dimension communicating additional information. Consider the 2D timeline of *Time* covers we created in *Timeline* (Manovich and Douglass 2009b).

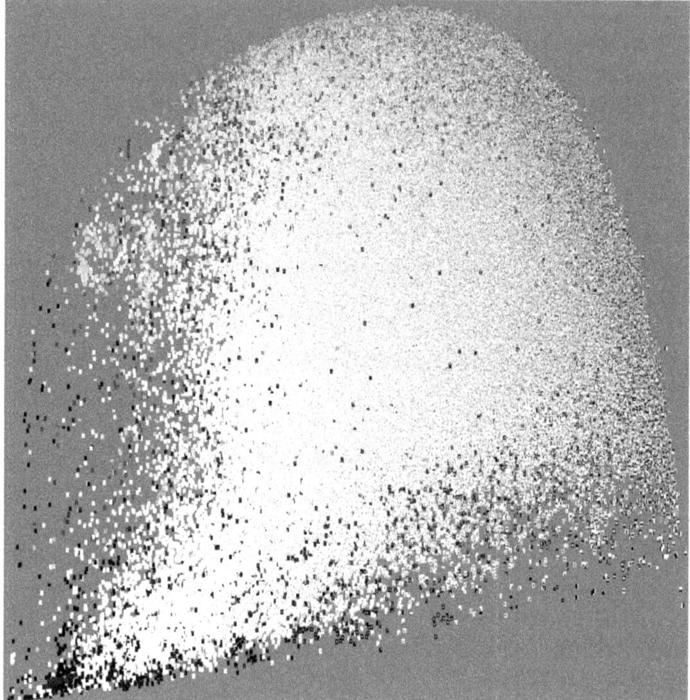

FIGURE 19.3 Jeremy Douglass and Lev Manovich, *Manga Style Space*, 2010. Visualization of 1 million manga pages. All manga pages are analyzed by software to measure selected visual properties. In the visualization, the pages are sorted by two of these properties: X-axis shows standard deviation of grayscale values; Y-axis corresponds to entropy, depicting the range from low detail/no texture/flat images to high detail/ texture/3D. We don't see any distinct clusters, but only continuous variation. This example suggests that our standard concept of "style" may not be appropriate for looking at particular characteristics of big cultural samples since "style" assumes presence of distinct characteristics, not continuous variation across a whole dimension.

The horizontal axis is used to position images in the original sequence: time runs from left to right, and every cover is arranged according to its publication date. The positions on the vertical axis represent new information—in this case, average saturation (the perceived intensity of colors) of every cover which we measured using image analysis software.

Such mapping is particularly useful for showing variations in the data over time. We can see how color saturation gradually increases until *Time*'s publication reaches its peak in 1968. The range of all values (i.e., variance) per year of publication also gradually increases, but it reaches its maximum value a few years earlier. It is perhaps not surprising to see that the intensity (or "aggressiveness") of mass media as exemplified by changes in the saturation and contrast of *Time* covers gradually rises up to the end of the 1960s. What is unexpected, however, is that since the beginning of the 21st century, this trend is reversed: the covers now have less contrast and less saturation.

The strategy used in this visualization is based on a familiar technique, the scatter graph. However, if a normal scatter graph reduces the data displaying each object as a point, we display the data in its original form. The result is a new graph type, which is literally made from images and can be appropriately called an "image graph."

Conclusion

In conclusion, I want to return to the key topic of this chapter—a move from traditional visualization that relies on extreme compression of the information to "visualization without reduction," which I defined as visualization that shows a much richer set of data objects' properties and/or all media objects directly. I see this move as a very positive one, because it allows one to think about data patterns and details without the dramatic reduction that was at the core of traditional visualization techniques. These 19th-century data reduction techniques (thematic map, bar plot, line graph, timeline, etc.) were the tools of a modern Panopticon society obsessed with classifying and controlling its subjects and resources. This does not mean that we can't use them today for comparisons between qualities, for understanding temporal or spatial trends, or in many other situations. (We still use arithmetic and logic developed two thousand years ago, and calculus developed in the 17th and 18th centuries.) What is crucial today is to understand that traditional data visualization techniques are no longer the only option for visually exploring data of networked cultures.

If we can visualize data with much less or no reduction, we can focus on individual variations rather than summaries. This would also allow us to think about the full range of diversity in the social and cultural phenomena. In contrast, the use of classical visualization techniques often hides this diversity; variations and outliers can get lost when everything is reduced to a few summary bars (for example, dividing a society into a few ethnic groups or two genders or a few income classes), or described by a simple statistical model.

As data sets are quickly increasing in size today, we have now entered the real race. Media visualization techniques such as sampling a larger set of frames from a feature file in *Cinema Redux* works well for one film or a handful of films. But imagine trying to visualize millions of YouTube videos! Even the largest among currently used displays, such as HIPerSpace, would not be able to show sampled frames from more than a few hundred videos at best. And if we try to show millions of videos, we would have to reduce each one to a single point—which would be no better than using traditional bar charts or line graphs to show main tendencies in the data.

As this example demonstrates, the dramatic growth in the size of the data sets since the second part of 2000s (that is, the rise of Big Data) challenged everything we learned about visualizing data. We need artists to invent new techniques to deal with the mega-scale of contemporary data at the level of individual variations, and engineers and computer scientists to create appropriate hardware and software to support these techniques.

How to deal with the new scale of information and at the same time represent its variability and diversity is a major new challenge for visualization artists, as well as the design community. To make a comparison with modernism again, modernist artists showed the visible reality we saw with our unmediated vision (landscape, a person, groups of objects, and so on)—while filtering it through various styles (impressionism, post-impressionism, cubism, expressionism, etc.). But now our key challenge is no longer how to "see differently" or "make it new"—instead we need to learn how to see at all, given the scale of the data our world generates.

Notes

1 http://www.processing.org (accessed January 15, 2015).
2 http://www.prefuse.org (accessed January 15, 2015).
3 http://www.google.com/trends.
4 I have created a few visualizations that show a whole book in a single image (see Software Studies Initiative 2009a and 2009b). To display the whole text of Tolstoy's *Anna Karenina* in the smallest font that can be read, I had to render a 14,000 × 6000 pixel image—well beyond the normal screen resolution today.
5 http://www.softwarestudies.com (accessed January 15, 2015).

References

Ball, Philip. 2004. *Critical Mass.* London: Arrow Books.

Beck, Harry. 1931. "London Underground Map." http://britton.disted.camosun.bc.ca/beck_map.jpg (accessed October 21, 2014).

Chen, Chaomei. 2005. "Top 10 Unsolved Information Visualization Problems." *IEEE Computer Graphics and Applications* 25(4): 12–16. doi: 10.1109/MCG.2005.91.

Dawes, Brendan. 2004. "Cinema Redux." http://brendandawes.com/projects/cinemaredux/ (accessed October 21, 2014).

Friendly, Michael, and Daniel J. Denis. 2001. "Milestones in the History of Thematic Cartography, Statistical Graphics, and Data Visualization." http://www.datavis.ca/milestones (accessed October 21, 2014).

Fry, Ben. 2005. "Distellamap." http://benfry.com/distellamap/ (accessed October 21, 2014).

Fry, Ben. 2009. "Preservation of Favoured Traces." http://benfry.com/traces/ (accessed October 21, 2014).

Graphics, Visualization and Virtual Reality Laboratory. 2010. "Research Projects: HIPerSpace." http://vis.ucsd.edu/mediawiki/index.php/Research_Projects:_HIPerSpace (accessed October 21, 2014).

Huber, William, Lev Manovich, and Tara Zepel. 2010. "The Shape of Science." http://www.flickr.com/photos/culturevis/sets/72157623862293839/ (accessed October 21, 2014).

InfoVisLab. 2014. "Research." http://ivl.cns.iu.edu/research/ (accessed October 21, 2014).

InfoVis:Wiki. 2013. "Information Visualization." http://www.infovis-wiki.net/index.php?title=Information_Visualization (accessed October 21, 2014).

Keim, Daniel A., Florian Mansmann, Jörn Schneidewind, and Hartmut Ziegler. 2006. "Challenges in Visual Data Analysis." *In Tenth International Conference on Information Visualization*, 9–16. London: IEE. doi: 10.1109/IV.2006.31.

Koblin, Aaron. 2005. "Flight Patterns." http://www.aaronkoblin.com/work/flightpatterns/ (accessed October 21, 2104).

Latour, Bruno. 2010. "Tarde's Idea of Quantification." In *The Social after Gabriel Tarde: Debates and Assessments*, edited by Mattei Candea, 145–162. London: Routledge.

Lima, Manuel. 2014. "Visual Complexity." http://www.visualcomplexity.com/vc/ (accessed October 21, 2014).

Manovich, Lev. 2002. "Data Visualization as New Abstraction and Anti-Sublime." http://manovich.net/index.php/projects/data-visualisation-as-new-abstraction-and-anti-sublime (accessed October 21, 2014).

Manovich, Lev, and Jeremy Douglass. 2009a. "Mapping Time." http://www.flickr.com/photos/culturevis/4038907270/in/set-72157624959121129/ (accessed October 21, 2014).

Manovich, Lev, and Jeremy Douglass. 2009b. "Timeline." http://www.flickr.com/photos/culturevis/3951496507/in/set-72157622525012841/ (accessed October 21, 2014).

Manovich, Lev, and Jeremy Douglass. 2010. "Manga Style Space." http://www.flickr.com/photos/culturevis/4497385883/in/set-72157624959121129/ (accessed October 21, 2014).

Marchand-Maillet, Stéphane, Eric Bruno, and Carol Peters. 2007. "*MultiMatch Project - D1.1.2* - State of the Art Image Collection Overviews and Browsing." http://puma.isti.cnr.it/linkdoc.php?icode=2007-EC-030&authority=cnr.isti&collection=cnr.isti&langver=en (accessed October 21, 2014).

Posavec, Stefanie. 2008. "Writing without Words." http://www.stefanieposavec.co.uk/-everything-in-between/#/writing-without-words/ (accessed October 21, 2014).

Posavec, Stefanie, and Greg McInerny. 2009. "The Evolution of *The Origin of Species.*" www.visualcomplexity.com/vc/project.cfm?id=696 (accessed October 21, 2014).

Purchase, Helen C., Natalia Andrienko, T.J. Jankun-Kelly, and Matthew Ward. 2008. "Theoretical Foundations of Information Visualization." In *Information Visualization: Human-Centered Issues and Perspectives. Lecture Notes in Computer Science No. 4950*, edited by Andreas Kerren, John T. Stasko, Jean-Daniel Fekete, and Chris North, 46–64. Berlin and Heidelberg: Springer. doi: 10.1007/978-3-540-70956-5_3.

Rodenbeck, Eric. 2008. "Information Visualization is a Medium." Keynote lecture delivered at Emerging Technology Conference, San Diego, California, March 3–6.

Rubin, Ben, and Mark Hansen. 2001. "Listening Post." http://ear-test.earstudio.com/?cat=5 (accessed October 21, 2014).

Software Studies Initiative. 2009a. "Anna Karenina. "https://www.flickr.com/photos/culturevis/sets/72157615900916808/ (accessed October 21, 2014).

Software Studies Initiative. 2009b. "Hamlet." https://www.flickr.com/photos/culturevis/sets/72157622994317650/ (accessed October 21, 2014).

Software Studies Initiative. 2014. "Cultural Analytics." http://lab.softwarestudies.com/p/cultural-analytics.html (accessed October 21, 2014).

Theus, Martin. 2013. "Mondrian." www.theusrus.de/Mondrian/ (accessed October 21, 2014).

Tufte, Edward. 1983. *The Visual Display of Quantitative Information.* Cheshire, CT: Graphics Press.

Tufte, Edward. 1990. *Envisioning Information.* Cheshire, CT: Graphics Press.

Tufte, Edward. 1997. *Visual Explanations: Images and Quantities, Evidence and Narrative.* Cheshire, CT: Graphics Press.

Tufte, Edward. 2006. *Beautiful Evidence.* Cheshire, CT: Graphics Press.

Tufte, Virginia, and Dawn Finley. 2002. "Minard's Data Sources for Napoleon's March." http://www.edwardtufte.com/tufte/minard (accessed October 21, 2014).

van Ham, Frank, Martin Wattenberg, and Fernanda B. Viégas. 2009. "Mapping Text with Phrase Nets." *IEEE Transactions on Visualization and Computer Graphics* 15(6): 1169–1176. doi: 10.1109/TVCG.2009.165.

Viégas Fernanda B., and Martin Wattenberg. 2003. "History Flow. "http://www.bewitched.com/historyflow.html (accessed October 21, 2014).

Viégas Fernanda B., and Martin Wattenberg. 2010. "Interview: Fernanda Viégas and Martin Wattenberg from Flowing Media." http://infosthetics.com/archives/2010/05/interview_fernanda_viegas_and_martin_wattenberg_from_flowing_media.html (accessed October 21, 2014).

Wattenberg, Martin. 2001. "The Shape of Song." http://www.turbulence.org/Works/song/ (accessed October 21, 2014).

Weskamp, Marcos. 2005. "Flickrgraph." http://www.visualcomplexity.com/vc/project_details.cfm?id=91&index=91&domain= (accessed October 21, 2014).

Wikipedia. 2014. "Tag Cloud." http://en.wikipedia.org/wiki/Tag_cloud (accessed October 21, 2014).

20

Critical Play
The Productive Paradox

Mary Flanagan

We live in a world filled with marvelous, dreadful, funny, exhilarating, monotonous, and curious games. On laptops, monitors, phones, and beyond, digital technology is enabling play to emerge in new and unexpected ways. Games exist for entertainment, for passing the time, for fun—and they are older than human written language. Created with rules and bound in a particular time, space, or context, games display some of the most fundamental aspects of human life: collaboration, competition, and strategy. Games are indeed a form of creative and artistic expression, just like filmmaking is an art form, for example. What happens when games emerge as something more than mere entertainment and take on themes that elevate them to involve larger human questions, as art typically does? Just as there are many different types of films—some being "art films" that pose critical questions of the medium—games too emerge as having an edgy art segment in their field of creation. This chapter concerns games like that, games that require a type of "criticality" to play.

Computer games are more popular than ever before and have become a major cultural medium across a wide demographic range. From apps played on mobile devices to "Triple A" games featuring realistic graphics and played on a console box, games have indeed solidly entered everyday life and are interwoven with financial, social, and personal meaning. Games have been recognized as art not only for their aesthetics but also for their potential as sites for commentary and critical perspectives. Like other digital art forms, game-based works have increasingly become provocative and introspective as well as playful. Much of digital art treads into the domain of the playful, with tongue-in-cheek critiques of surveillance, re-examinations of our relationships with technology, interventions in social networks, and more. Indeed, a lot of responsive digital art has playful or even game-like qualities. And like other forms of art, games reflect the culture of their creation. In my 2009 book *Critical Play*, I trace the concept of "Critical Play" through what could be called an "art history of games." Critical play, as a concept, seems to embody a deep contradiction. To be

A Companion to Digital Art, First Edition. Edited by Christiane Paul.

critical does not seem whimsical or playful: it implies *analysis*. To play implies a certain fantasy or whimsy that criticality most certainly lacks. In this essay I would like to make some propositions about critical play by showing how the pursuits of artists have contributed to creating critical play in digital arts practice. I will explore the work of several artists and the games *Unmanned* (2012), *Mainichi* (2012), *Every Day the Same Dream* (2009), *Waco Resurrection* (2004), *[perfect.city]* (2009), *PainStation* (2001), *Uncle Roy All Around You* (2003), *Brainball* (1999), *[giantJoystick]* (2006), and others to offer three propositions from a critical play perspective. Games can be the means for creative expression, the instruments for conceptual thinking, and the tools to help examine social issues. These propositions will uncover strengths and weaknesses of games as a medium for social change and revolutionary play.

As media theorist Marshall McLuhan once stated, "New technological environments are commonly cast in the molds of the preceding technology out of the sheer unawareness of their designers" (McLuhan 1972, 47). McLuhan thus suggests that we initially do not have many ways and methods to examine the implications of new technologies, and thereby can make the mistake of misunderstanding the benefits and dangers of what has emerged. Because games are a cultural medium, they carry embedded beliefs about the culture in which they are created within their representation systems and structures. This holds true whether the designers intended to embed these beliefs and values or not. It has therefore fallen to fields such as philosophy and art practice to ask the big questions. These, and a sense of "critical play," can be sources to draw from for the careful examination of games. Importantly, these questions arise from "networked politics"; critical games increasingly are easier to find out about, and the movement of indie game developers has become a strong and often critical community. Galvanized around festivals such as IndieCade, the cultural network of independent game developers dovetails with the culture of artists working in games. Indeed, crossover artists seamlessly operate in both networks.

The language of games is now very familiar due to the popularity of commercial video games. Artists disrupt this familiarity in interesting ways. Both the art world and the game world use the term "game art," but it can mean very different things. In the commercial game world, "game art" can mean the graphics that go into a commercial game. In the art world "game art" constitutes a genre of creative works that reference or use games for conceptual artistic ends.

Thinking "Critical Play"

What does it mean to play critically? When is a game critical, and when isn't it? Examining a dictionary entry for the key word "critical," one can find several useful directions for answering these questions[1] First of all, a game could just *be critical* in the literal sense—make disapproving comments, or reach a negative conclusion about something. A political game that might criticize a particular party might be said to be critical on this level.

Secondly, being critical might mean to analyze the merits and faults of a work such as a film, or a game, to scrutinize it in the sense of "critical" acclaim or critics' trashing of a new body of work. Yet there are many criteria and many critics to choose from, and looking at the acquisition of art games by art institutions such as New York's Museum of Modern Art (Antonelli 2012), we can see that certain games garner more critical acclaim in arts circles than others.

Thirdly, criticality might offer a detailed and scholarly analysis and commentary: a critical edition of a book would include extensive notes and likely a revisionist reading. The heart of the matter really is this: throughout millennia, games have been used for critical thinking—of course, a playful type of critical thinking. Take, for example, chess: it is a game that lays out a clear and equal battle on a checkered board. Both players have equal opportunities; both have equal access to information. Chess is said to help players think strategically and understand cause and effect through time. Moves later, players might regret an action, or see the flaws in their opponent's strategies. This is possible because of the fundamental affordances of games themselves. A well-crafted game will allow for trial and error, for experimentation, for thinking ahead, for failure. But *further than that*, game art might be critical if it examines the medium itself. How does making a game affect the subject, the voice, and the point? Does the game reflect on the creation of games themselves? Games that can be said to foster critical play likely tread in this territory. While chess is a critical thinking type of game, the work *Rethinking War Games: Three Player Chess* by Ruth Catlow (2003), which positions two royal sides against each other while the pawns in the middle, played by a third player, try to stop them, is a game that reflects on the representation of conflict, and on ways in which games reinforce binary conflicts and new game goals (in the case of three-player chess, the goal of the pawns to stop the conflict) to create reflective, critical play.

Definitions of critical, however, can express an increasing urgency in their use. Nuclear reactors "go critical" when they are about to reach a new state; diseases reach a critical point where turning back is not possible. The urgency of criticality is upon us. Thus, looking at the merits of play, creating new readings, offering detailed analyses, and creating situations in which new ways of making games emerge are of crucial importance to both art and culture at this juncture. For example, it is a critical time for examining playful techniques and games with regard to their increasing use in systems that employ "gamification"—what I like to call "the slavery of play"—in education, health care, the workplace, and other contexts. It also is a critical time for examining the use of game-like interfaces for war. These issues are pressing, and are so right now because their emergence has happened quietly, and out of the light of the everyday citizen. Artists step in—lest we disregard the purpose of art entirely—to see things in new ways and share these reflections with all.

A Concise History of "Critical Play"

Artists have been fascinated with games and playing with conventions for centuries, but the popularity of play across 20th-century art movements led to the increasing incorporation of themes of plan and games into artworks and into artists' processes. The Dada artists, operating in the period between World Wars I and II, were prone to absurd art that toyed with, and broke, previous "high art" conventions and also mocked nationalism and materialism. The movement was a reaction to the violence and destruction of World War I, which tore Europe apart with unprecedented violence. Instead of sculpting with clay or chiseling marble, Dada artists used found objects and everyday materials to express and transgress. Examples of Dada art include the found object sculptures and experimental writing of Elsa von Freytag-Loringhoven, paintings and collages using chance in their creation such as those by Hans (Jean) Arp, and quirky found object sculptures by Marcel Duchamp such as *Fountain*, the famous repurposed urinal exhibited in the New York City Armory art show of 1913. Before Dada, artists, according to Hans Arp, "attempted perfection; we wanted an object to be without flaw, so we cut the papers with a razor, pasted them down meticulously, but it buckled and was ruined … that is why we decided to tear prewrinkled paper, so that in the finished work of art imperfection would be an integral part, as if at birth death were built in" (Liberman 1960, 58).

Adhering to the rebellious nature of the Dada artists, the surrealism movement emerged in the late 1920s and 1930s. Surrealists were characterized by a fascination with the mind and often used playful methods, such as parlor games, to tap into unconscious processes that could then emerge as new insights within their work. An example would be the *Cadavre Exquis* (*Exquisite Corpse*) in which one person starts a drawing on unfolded paper, and others finish it by folding their own section, so no one artist sees the product of the whole group until the end. While they also wrote fiction and poetry, Surrealists are most famous for their paintings depicting dreams and nightmares—think of the work of Salvador Dali or Remedios Vara—and their self-perceptions, infused with unconscious hopes and fears, as embodied in the works of Leonora Carrington and Max Ernst. The processes involved in creating such works were often playful, such as the use of automatic writing and other social games for developing ideas.

After World War II moved masses of artists around the world, performance pieces that broke down the barriers between performer and audience, bringing people together in space and time, emerged as a core artistic approach. In Japan Gutai art emerged, and, in the United States and Europe, Fluxus became a new form of avant-garde expression. Fluxus artists opposed the idea of precious art and instead tried to turn the everyday into art. They used performance scores describing everyday acts, as in Alison Knowles's *Make a Salad* (1962) in which preparing a salad becomes a playful act of communal performance art. Commenting on her 2012 performance of the work under the High Line Park in New York City, Knowles stated, "The ingredients are indeterminate except that they're edible. I don't have anything funny in there. I don't put popcorn in or something" (Morais 2012). Why shouldn't making a salad be art? What can this type of work reveal about everyday life?

Fluxus artists used materials such as paper handouts and found objects for whimsical game boxes. The boxes offered unusual objects for play and created surprising, nonsensical combinations of materials and instructions to help players see the world in new ways. This is only a small sample of some of the 20th-century art practices that involved a critical use of play in the investigation of artistic concerns. The 20th century's rich tradition of strange games, its fascination with chess, and absurd, playful performances were instrumental in how we see art today and how we can approach electronic games from a critical play perspective. Through a critical play lens we might better understand the deep significance of artists' games such as *Every Day the Same Dream* or *Mainichi*—both discussed in the following sections, or propositions—which link players not to the "slavery of play" but rather to fundamental aspects of the human condition. The three propositions outlined in the following will reveal strengths and weaknesses of games as a medium for creative and revolutionary experience. If, as I argue in the first proposition set forth, that games always hold within them cultural beliefs, norms, and human values, then how are creative practitioners to tackle the thorny responsibility of creating games that not only reflect, but *revolutionize*, culture? How are games most effectively used in political and social change movements? Do games represent a different form of new media aesthetics?

Proposition 1: Critical Play Exposes and Examines Dominant Values

A critical play approach is built on the premise that games carry beliefs within their representation systems and mechanics. Games—like film, television, and other media—are created by those who live in culture and are surrounded by their own cultural imaginary, and are a cultural medium that carries embedded beliefs, whether intended or not. Artists home in on the questions raised by these conditions in their work; therefore, artists using games as a medium of expression manipulate elements common to games—representation systems and styles, rules of progress, codes of conduct, context of reception, winning and losing paradigms, ways of interacting in a game—and explore the material properties they entail, much like marble and chisel or pen and ink bring with them their own intended possibilities, limitations, and conventions. Criticality in play can be fostered in order to question an aspect of the game's "content," or an aspect of a play scenario's function, which might otherwise be considered assumed or necessary.

In the online game work *Unmanned* (2012), Molleindustria and Jim Munroe feature a storyline focused on a US soldier who participates in combat by piloting unmanned aerial vehicles, or UAVs. Often called "video game warfare," the practice of commanding UAEs, including drone planes, to attack suspected combatants has disparagingly been labeled a cowardly way to conduct war (Narcisse 2012). It is just that sense of distance, that sense of cowardice, which frames the reading of the central character of *Unmanned*. He is depicted in rough polygon graphics as an overly stereotypical, white, large military man whose day job is committing violence from afar (Figure 20.1). The pilot goes about his everyday tasks and players are engaged to help him with mundane activities, such as making sure he stays on the highway when driving, guiding his razor to shave, or playing military simulation video games with his son during "bonding time." In addition to assisting him "mechanically," players can enter into the character's thought processes in simple dialog trees, deciding if actions trouble him or if he will respond defensively with militaristic tropes of might and the shallow regrets that only those in power can proffer.

Yet it is not only the content of the game that gives this work a critical edge. First of all, the game is divided into a two-part screen to divide the attention of the player. This divide works very well to set up a dialogue between actions and consequences, between the political and the personal. The rough graphics, so unrealistic when compared to commercial games that depict war, stand in stark contrast to professional video game values and suggest that the experience might be more introspective in nature. Unlike many military games, this is a slow game, one in which not much happens except for the mundane, while the real toll of war in one distant place through remote commanding has a hollowing, sinister effect in the other "safe" place, as corresponding to the two viewing windows available to players of the game.

Thus *Unmanned* exemplifies critical play in form as well as content, asking players to think deeply about their decisions, the issue at hand, and the nature of games themselves. Criticality in *Unmanned* is fostered by the game's theme, its storyline, its setting, and narrative premise; its game mechanics, dialogue options, and interaction roles for the player; in its rules and reward structure, as well as in its music and aesthetics. The game is able to touch on social, cultural, political, and personal themes using the intricacies of a game system.

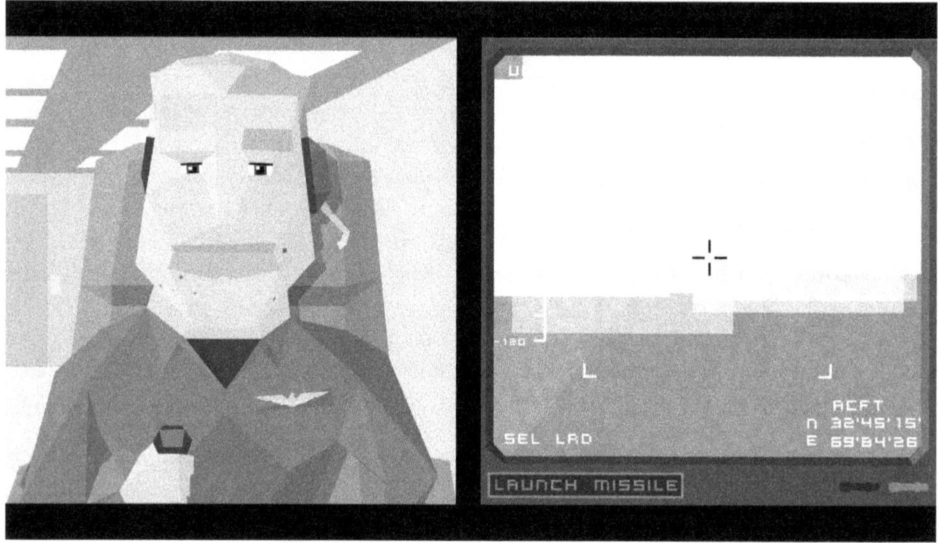

FIGURE 20.1 Molleindustria, *Unmanned*, 2012. Screenshot. Image courtesy of Paolo Pedercini.

In the downloadable game *Mainichi* (2012), artist Mattie Brice uses an old-style role playing game aesthetic to involve the player in a "day-in-the-life" game (Mainichi means "everyday" in Japanese). You help the game's protagonist—also named Mattie and looking like Mattie, with dark skin and dark hair—get ready to go out, go down the street, then meet up with one of her friends at a coffee house. You help her pick up two beverages at the virtual coffee shop, flirt with the barista, and gab with a friend. In chatting about the flirtation, the friend asks Mattie, "Does he know?" After the conversation, the day begins again, and the player can try alternatives such as not wearing makeup, or dressing casually.

If players are coming to the game without reading much about it, they will soon discern its subtext, revealed through time: players are to role-play in the shoes of Brice herself, who "wanted to communicate an experience that I couldn't do with words alone" (Brice 2012). While in the house, Mattie has an internal dialogue aimed at cheering herself up or thoughts on getting ready to go out. The internal dialogue is another element *Mainichi* shares with *Unmanned*: rarely do mainstream games let us enter into the player's hopes, fears, and internal mindset to this degree—especially when these thoughts also reflect on social norms.

It is entirely possible to play through the street scene, for example, with little interaction with other characters. Interacting with these other characters, though, can be disturbing, and the encounters add much to the impact of the work. We overhear a person on the street asking a friend if Mattie is a boy or a girl. A man approaches Mattie on the street and says, "What's up pretty? Hey, I want to talk to you," then reacts vehemently, exclaiming "You're a man!" When Mattie later chats with her friend over coffee, she confesses, "It's hard to feel happy sometimes." The game's options are limited, as are societal roles; the game sheds light on banal micro-aggressions, misunderstandings, and the daily, lived experience of difference.

Both *Unmanned* and *Mainichi* expose dominant cultural values and set up situations in which those values are conscientiously negotiated. Each of these game artworks offers players opportunities to form their own critical examinations of play.

Proposition 2: Critical Play Can Mean Toying with the Notion of Goals, Making Games with Problematic, Impossible, or Unusual Endings

The term "critical play" was a culmination of my interest in both computer games and my own work as an artist. I use play and game fundamentals in projects that range from software art, drawings, and installation, to sculpture (some of them specifically game-related), and are shown in more traditional art venues. I also run an experimental game design lab, Tiltfactor, which fosters the design of games for social impact. Important threads play out in any art, no matter what the form, and critical play is an idea that can help extend the definition of the "avant-garde" to game design. Like alternative theories of narrative texts, poetry, and film, critical play points to the ways in which some games ask much more of the viewer than others in terms of a critical dialogue and reflection. These are the games that engage with "radical" game design and involve players in new ways. Computer games are often seen as a new medium not necessarily aligned with older forms of play, but this is an oversight. Critical play readily manifests in older and current games designed by artists who intend their work to offer political or social critique in order to propose ways of understanding larger cultural issues.

In Molleindustria's *Every Day The Same Dream* (or EDTSD) (2009) players guide a worker through his morning routine and get him to his job at an office where he sits in an Orwellian-style, replicable cubicle. A precursor to *Unmanned*, EDTSD is a point-and-click game in which players can make few decisions and have few options. They take on the role of the worker starting their day in bed, waking up and getting dressed, kissing the spouse goodbye, getting in the car, driving to work, confronting the boss about their lateness, and going home. This pattern can be played repeatedly; every day is nearly the same "dream" from beginning to end. Whenever a player chooses a slightly different option in the routine, a new "dream" day begins. Are players working toward being a new person? This is what one of the few characters in the game—the lady in the elevator—suggests. Or is it a representation of the logic of capitalism that has created the most complex form of alienation, alienation of people from their work and from each other? Other characters include a homeless man, who takes players to a quiet spot, and a cow encountered in a field. These offbeat characters not only break the monotonous pace of the game's "bad dream" but also disrupt the expectations of those used to playing less introspective games.

While the game could do without the stereotypical 1950s gender roles as a means to suggest oppression—the protagonist's wife is already up early in the morning, cooking him breakfast—the lack of player choice or agency in conducting the virtual life effectively functions as a critique of the characters' lives and a postmodern condition in which labor is both separated from life experience and valued only in particularly abstract and absurd ways. The game is in many ways the antithesis of *The Sims*, the popular "dollhouse" game released in 2000. In EDTSD the home gradually empties, the acquisition of material becomes meaningless, and work is pointless. The work process within the game is an exploration of the bleakness and alienation of daily life in a world with empty, unconnected labor and long days.

Artists frequently strip games of their potential agency, their game-specific elements: no rules, no player actions, no risks, no rewards, no bonuses or deaths. A key feature of games is that they are bound by their own rule sets, and therefore invite regulation, supervision, and of course, subversion. To scholars such as Brian Sutton-Smith (1997), play is culturally associated, at least in part, with transgressive and subversive actions. Thus play itself could be seen as a type of subversion, one that looks at expectations and weaves in a social critique inherent to critical play. A good example of this approach might be the ultimate subversion of a game as offered in Cory Arcangel's *Super Mario Clouds* (2002): Arcangel removed all of the game-like elements from a Super Mario Brothers Nintendo cartridge, and stripped it to its barest, unplayable essence.

Much like abstract art in which every detail has been removed to get to the heart of image making, Arcangel's clouds roll by infinitely through an empty sky. *Super Mario Clouds*, like many other works of game art, demonstrates that artists' games are not always playable and that this unplayability is a very intentional decision. Unplayable games provide rule frameworks for thinking or, as Felix Guattari might say, "devices for producing subjectivity" (Guattari 1995). It is in this context that themes similar to those addressed in EDTSD can be found in my own work, but in the form of a video installation featuring an ongoing game scenario. *[perfect.city]* (2009) is a game-based exploration of the South Korean city of Songdo, a planned international metropolis developed by corporations, specifically Gale International, with a technological infrastructure by technology companies. Songdo is designed to be perfect: plans call for the elimination of social ills, care-free living, and happiness for all citizens—in fact, plans in the form of 3D building models were input into Google Earth before the city was even built. In my project I first explored this "virtual" city and then modeled what this "perfect city" might be like for people inhabiting it. To do this I took the models for the city, translated them into buildings in the popular computer game *The Sims 2*, and then populated this city with virtual inhabitants with their own personalities and characteristics. My virtual *[perfect.city]* became functional before New Songdo was actually built.

During the construction of the actual Songdo city atop a giant landfill south of Seoul, ubiquitous technology was considered a "feature" of the planned infrastructure. Since then, concerns about an all-knowing, "Big Brother style" technological infrastructure have increasingly been raised. As a corporate venture, public space in New Songdo will be privatized. What effect will this have on people's private lives? "We will build in all this functionality," answers Catherine Maras, Microsoft's Director of Worldwide E-Government who is involved in the Songdo project, "Really it's opt-in or opt-out. Whatever the citizens want to make their lives easier" (Duffin 2008).

[perfect.city] is shown as a two-channel video installation consisting of a large double-sided projection screen. One side of the screen alternates between live-action footage of the artist recreating the design process of the city, scrubbing backwards and forwards through time, mixed with a time-lapse recording of the planning and construction of the virtual city. This video component mimics a documentary-style look at "the making of" New Songdo. The opposite screen shows the slow motion city in action as developed in *The Sims 2*. The people inhabiting the environment are a population wandering aimlessly to and from virtual jobs, or sitting on park benches,

purposeless. All are well dressed; all are clean and tidy. They walk amid a bland and featureless urban streetscape. This future city is unattached to history, and the somnambulistic attributes of the pedestrians point to the weary, stale, and unprofitable experience of techno-utopianism. The featureless city streets depicted call into question the all too brief period and limited input from non-corporate entities devoted to planning the city.

[perfect.city] explores the use of technology in everyday settings and the ways in which it both reflects and creates phenomenological experiences. These experiences are interdependent, symbiotic, and create meaning in a mutual fashion. By embodying and depicting the role of "planner and developer" in *[perfect.city]*, I perform the process of creating utopic visions in which dreams pass into action and back into dreams. While these cycles are complex, the work deliberately minimizes the aesthetics of the video; I hack the city together from the banal position of my desk. The resulting video created from the process reveals the ambiguity of bleakness and beauty; this happens on the programming side, through the construction of boring behaviors, and in the image, derived from the real 3D models upon which such "utopia" was built.

Artists have been using play in subversive and disturbing ways, making impossible and grotesque objects or nonsensical game kits whose rules are enticingly unresolvable in the conventional sense of traditional games, where winners, losers, player roles, and game goals are clearly articulated. In *Waco: Resurrection* (2004) by the artist team C-Level, players must enter the mind of US Seventh-Day Adventist "Branch Davidian" cult leader David Koresh who has been resurrected in the game. Koresh became notorious not only for his cult activities but for the 51-day standoff with federal authorities at his compound in Waco, Texas, in 1993. The standoff culminated in a massive shootout, and left seventy-six people dead in a great fire. Koresh himself was killed. While engaging with the game, players wear the "head" of Koresh, a headset and mask of his face that has a voice-activated control mechanism and built-in speakers blasting messages of government agents, religious readings, and much battle noise to provide an immersive, chaotic experience for players (Figure 20.2).

By wearing the "head" of Koresh, players adopt his appearance and his subjective point of view. In the game, each player appears as Koresh—each character being identical but surrounded by a differently colored "aura." The mission is to stay alive as long as possible, as all players control their Koresh character to run, shot, jump, and hide. Players can also energize themselves by accessing one of the different types of Bibles falling from the sky; each contains a specific phrase that will provide special power. Players' utterance of the Bible phrase is picked up by the voice recognition hardware in the Koresh headset and raises their respective aura; as players compete with each other, they use their voice-activated controls to shout "messianic messages" in order to excel in the game. As they raise their aura, they gain more followers. The Koresh who collects the most converts until the time of death wins the game (Stern 2003).

It is significant that *Waco: Resurrection* was created on the 10th anniversary of the real-life events in Texas and functions as an intentional commentary on "holy wars." The work can be read as a critique of the US military invasion of the Middle East. The artists emphasize the documentary elements of the game and its attention to historic detail, but the work's real innovations are the ways in which players critically examine the cycle of religious leadership and belief and in which war is tied into the artists' critique. The game is networked in the sense that multiple players in one

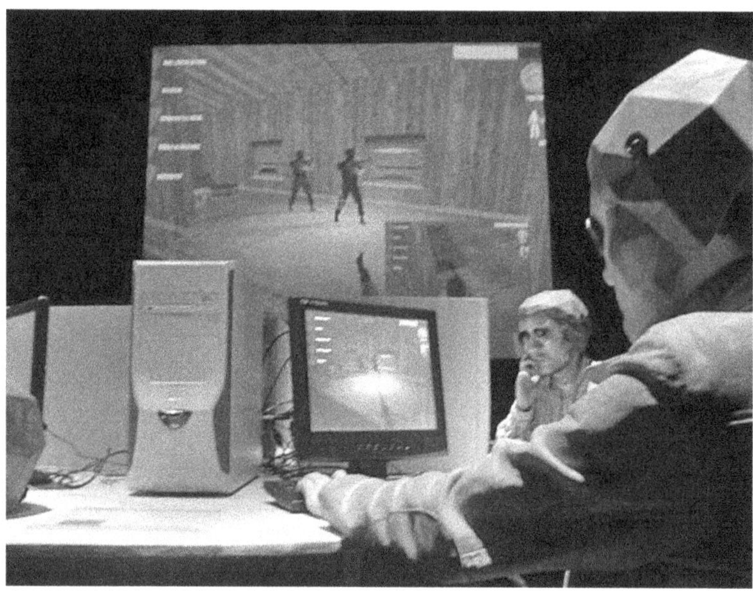

FIGURE 20.2 Eddo Stern, Peter Brinson, Brody Condon, Michael Wilson, Mark Allen, Jessica Hutchins (C-Level), *Waco Resurrection*, 2004. Installation shot. Image courtesy of Eddo Stern.

game world strive to gather followers, but it also alludes to the networks of power, radicalism, and violence inherent in both politics and religion. Although the game might look as if it glamorizes aggression, violence and narcissism in the game are treated very knowingly and critically. In both its gameplay and themes, *Waco Resurrection* is indeed a critical game. It is coincidental that it prophetically anticipates behavior, such as the gathering of "followers," that would become common practice on social networks a decade later.

Every Day the Same Dream, *Super Mario Clouds*, *[perfect.city]*, and *Waco Resurrection* each represent vastly different "genres" of digital gameplay, yet they all complicate the idea of game goals. Each of these critical games presents players with problematic, impossible, or unusual endings and thus helps them to not only reconsider each of the game situations presented but to also reflect on the meaning and strategies of games themselves.

Proposition 3: Criticality Can Lead to Extreme New Kinds of Play, and Make Familiar Types of Play Unfamiliar

People across every social category are exposed to games in some form on a daily basis, and as many as 97% of US youth play games, half of them for an hour or more daily (Lenhart et al. 2008). With the increasing accessibility of mobile technology (such as smartphones and tablets), these numbers only continue to rise. The use rates of electronic media and entertainment are particularly high among teenagers and young adults. On any given day, 30% of all kids aged 2–18 will play a video game; those who do spend an average of just over an hour playing (Rideout, Foehr, and

Roberts 2010). Games have been recognized as artworks not only for their aesthetics but also for their function as sites for commentary and critical perspectives. Like other digital art forms, game-based works have increasingly become provocative and introspective, as well as playful. And like other forms of art, games reflect the culture of their creation. Games can offer a range of interactions, but these often become predictable variations that reach wide audiences due to the mass production of game consoles and controllers. One novel take on game interactions is pursued in the artwork *PainStation* (2001) developed by Volker Morawe and Tilman Reiff, two Cologne-based media artists operating as the collective //////////fur////. The custom-made, two-player *PainStation* unit houses game controls and a monitor on which to play. Two people play the classic arcade game *Pong*, against each other, placing their hands on "Pain Execution Units" that offer feedback to them. Players place their hands across two electrodes: the heel of the palm on one, a fingertip on the other. In order to win *PainStation*, players will have to endure pain: if the player misses the ball, for example, the slip causes heat, lashes, or electric shocks depending on the Pain Inflictor Symbol indicator. Players have to endure heat and electric shocks to play. (In subsequent versions of the unit, an "I agree" consent button was implemented into the unit, and the whip that beats the players' hands could be exchanged for a variety of materials and adjustable pain levels.)

Regardless of the score achieved in the game, the first person to remove his or her hand from the pain device loses. Unlike other computer-mediated games that detach players from the embodied experience of play via small game controllers, *PainStation* brings the body back into play with a visceral vengeance. The game raises the stakes for the future of play. While it may feel like a whimsical, humorous introduction of embodiment back into game play, the unit can truly inflict harm, and this is precisely the tension that the work introduces. Players work together and receive the same punishment, creating a community of endurance and, if you are playing against a friend, empathy. But the work does "hurt," and for some people it isn't just a game but an endurance test or dangerous rite of passage. Thus the strange dichotomy between play and not-play moves center stage. This is play both familiar and unfamiliar, play that is dangerous and disturbing—*PainStation* allows players to be critical of the effects of games and the strange nature of embodiment while playing.

Another example of a game that reflects on game mechanics and strategies themselves is *Brainball* (1999), which critiques the fast-paced nature of computer games and the assumed concept of competition in a game. In *Brainball*, players compete to relax. Two people sit at a table, don electroencephalogram monitoring bands on their heads, and play to move a ball forward through brain activity. The players' brainwaves are shown on a screen so the public can watch. The brainwaves that move the ball forward are alpha and theta waves, which are generated by relaxing, and the more relaxed player will therefore score a goal over the opponent.

Since its creation by Magnus Jonsson at Sweden's Interactive Institute in 1999, *Brainball* has become a classic work that reverses gaming conventions and reveals new ways in which we might play. It has shown around the world and has been updated and released as an app. As *Brainball* shows, artists working with games build systems that ask questions and often focus the game mechanics on the very processes that make games playful, interesting, and fun. Whether working in analog or digital media, game artists transcend technologies and engage with rule systems that enable the discovery of key ideas. Game artists express themselves through rules, end states, game goals, actions in a game, game narratives, and other elements, employing a range of strategies for criticality.

A locative media art game that reflects upon ubiquitous technology, games, intimacy, and the connection between virtual and physical space is Blast Theory's *Uncle Roy All Around You* (2003), which launched at the Institute of Contemporary Arts in London. In URAAY, participants—divided into Street Players and Online Players—collaborate to find the character embodying "Uncle Roy" in a city within 60 minutes. Street Players find themselves wandering around the city with handheld devices and custom software showing the location of online players. They declare their position in the software on a map, and are given an online avatar so that Online Players can also see them. Online Players can then send private messages to the Street Players to help them find their way.

Directions from Uncle Roy lead Street Players to a specific office where they ring a buzzer and enter. Online Players enter a virtual office and are invited to join the Street Players by watching them in the office via web cam after answering a set of questions. They are confronted with the scenario, "Somewhere in the city there is a stranger who is also answering these questions. Are you willing to make a commitment to that person that you will be available for them if they have a crisis? The commitment will last for 12 months and, in return, they will commit to you for the same period." If Online Players agree, they have to enter their physical home address and can then "enter" the physical office (Blast Theory 2003). Street Players find a postcard in the office with the question, "When can you begin to trust a stranger?" and are asked to take it with them. Further commands lead the Street Player into the back of a limousine waiting outside the office, in which someone asks them the same questions the Online Player has answered including the one for a 12-month commitment to the other player. If Street Players agree, they are paired with an Online Player and mail the postcard to an Online Player's address while returning the game equipment to the kick-off point. In URAAY, players are asked to reflect on surveillance culture, the anonymity of networked connections, as well as the temporality of games by bringing these issues to the forefront during play. The game ultimately is exploring ethical questions; instead of establishing a simple, temporary networked interaction that can be disregarded, will players make a one-year commitment resulting from that interaction? What are the ethical boundaries of online surveillance and friendship?

As a final example of the third proposition for critical play, I would like to use my project *[giantJoystick]* (2006), an interactive sculpture consisting of an oversized game controller modeled after the Atari 2600 joystick. In this case, the change in scale occurring with *[giantJoystick]* creates new kinds of play: the joystick is so large that players need to collaborate in order to use it. In addition, the work makes familiar types of play unfamiliar: most game players know how to use a joystick very well, but when faced with one that is larger than one's body, they often must relearn how to engage. The shift in scale acts as a dynamic and subtle reminder of players' own embodiment and their connection to others through play.

In each of these very different types of works—*PainStation, Brainball, Uncle Roy All Around You*, and *[giantJoystick]*—criticality of mechanisms, strategies, and conventions creates new types of play. Players are "injured" by engaging with a mere computer game. They have to try to relax instead of summoning their competitive urges and "tensing up" to play. They are asked to trust others in the real world during and after playing together. They have to use their bodies and work together to play a game with which they might otherwise engage in an unconsciously instinctive way. In each of these situations, the player is being asked to rethink their play experience and find new meaning in the changes in interaction and experience that critical play provides.

The Future of Critical Play

Games are indeed their own unique art form, but not all games are critical. Indeed, there are many games, like many plays and films, that just wish to "be games." In this essay, however, there are benefits and strengths to playing critically, and creating critical games. Each of the propositions discussed in this essay suggest ways in which artists working with games can foster criticality. Proposition 1 reveals that artists' games nurture an environment where players can reflect upon dominant cultural values and see everyday assumptions in a new light. Proposition 2 upsets what players might know or experience as a game in the first place, shifting rules for play and impossible or unusual endings. Such repositioning of games might be novel or even shocking to those used to typical types of games, but gradually the definitions for games are expanding and shifting as the medium attracts an increasing number of eclectic makers and thinkers. Proposition 3 uncovers the ways in which a critical stance through play can lead to novel play forms. In a time where games have permeated the mainstream on an international level, criticality play forms a significant contribution to conceptual art. Given the pervasiveness of play and the successes of games as a commercial media form, a critical stance in play provides a fresh reading for what is considered to be a normal way of interacting in games. Indeed, new kinds of games can ask us to think in new ways. What are the big-picture implications for critical play? At its best, it can give us a lens through which we engage with the world, and not just the artworld, but the world of politics, the military, health care, education, and psychology. "What must be changed is the game itself, not the pieces," noted one of the key founders of surrealism, André Breton (1953, 76). Critical play may have emerged from the arts, but it need not stop within the arts. Such thinking is emerging among designers and gamers who are experiencing these ideas for the first time and responding through games. As we have seen, the critical games discussed here are emerging from social groups, indie gamers, activists, and youth asking questions with the medium of their time. Critical games provide avenues in which artists' social interventions can move beyond rhetoric and be effective in engaging with, and shaping solutions to, pressing social issues.

Note

1 The Oxford English Dictionary offers eight meanings for the adjective *critical*: (1) fault-finding; (2) exercising careful judgment and prone to punctuality or exactness; (3) occupied with the act of criticism, being related to criticism or critical theory; (4) the crisis or tipping point of a disease or disaster; (5) that which constitutes a crisis related to the issue, such as a critical path or involving fear or suspense on an uncertain grave issue; (6) crucial and decisive; (7) a point at which a condition passes over into another condition or a reactor maintains a chain reaction; and (8) that which is distinguished by slight or difficult to determine differences ("critical, adj." OED 2013).

References

Antonelli, Paola. 2012. "Video Games: 14 in the Collection, for Starters." *Inside/Out*: Museum of Modern Art (MoMA) blog, November 29. http://www.moma.org/explore/inside_out/2012/11/29/video-games-14-in-the-collection-for-starters/ (accessed November 14, 2013).

Blast Theory. 2003. "Uncle Roy All Around You Walkthrough." http://www.blasttheory.co.uk/projects/uncle-roy-all-around-you/ (accessed November 1, 2013).

Breton, Andre. 1953/1995. *La Cle des Champs*, translated by Michael Parmentier and Jacqueline d'Amboise. Lincoln: University of Nebraska Press.

Brice, Mattie. 2012. "Postpartum: Mainichi – How Personal Experience Became a Game." *BorderhouseBlog*, November 12. http://borderhouseblog.com/?p=9591 (accessed November 9, 2013).

"critical, adj." *OED Online*. September 2013. Oxford University Press. http://www.oed.com/view/Entry/44592?redirectedFrom=critical& (accessed November 14, 2013).

Duffin, Linda. 2008. "South Korea's Newest City Emerges." *BBC News*, June 30. http://news.bbc.co.uk/2/hi/7425192.stm (accessed November 2, 2013).

Guattari, Felix. 1995. *Chaosmosis: An Ethico-Aesthetic Paradigm*, translated by Paul Bains and Julian Pefanis. Bloomington: Indiana University Press.

Lenhart, Amanda, Joseph Kahne, Ellen Middaugh, Alexandra Macgill, Chris Evans, and Jessica Vitak. 2008. *Teens, Video Games and Civics*. Washington, DC: Pew Internet and American Life Project.

Liberman, Alexander. 1960. *The Artist in his Studio*. New York: Viking.

McLuhan, Marshall. 1972. *Take Today: The Executive as Dropout*. New York: Harcourt Brace Jovanovich.

Morais, Betsy. 2012. "Salad as Performance Art." *The New Yorker*, April 26. http://www.newyorker.com/online/blogs/culture/2012/04/salad-as-performance-art.html (accessed October 30, 2013).

Narcisse, Evan. 2012. "From the Makers of the Wikileaks Video Game, Here's One About Killing People With Unmanned Drones." *Kotaku.com*, February 2. http://kotaku.com/5885470/indie-game-unmanned-makes-you-a-creepily-depressedjingoistic-uav-drone-pilot/ (accessed June 1, 2013).

Rideout, Victoria J., Ulla G. Foehr, and Donald F. Roberts. 2010. *Generation M2: Media in the Lives of 8- to 18-Year-Olds*. The Henry J. Kaiser Family Foundation.

Stern, Eddo. 2003. "C-Level's Waco Resurrection Game Design Doc." Eddo Stern web site. http://eddostern.com/text/wacodesigndoc.pdf (accessed 12 September 2013).

Sutton-Smith, Brian. 1997. *The Ambiguity of Play*. Cambridge, MA: Harvard University Press.

Further Reading

Dali, Salvador. 1974. "The Conquest of the Irrational" (1936). In *Salvador Dali: A Panorama of His Art*, edited by A. Reynolds Morse. Cleveland: Salvador Dali Museum.

Fer, Briony. 1993. *Realism, Rationalism, Surrealism: Art Between the Wars*. New Haven, CT: Yale University Press.

Flanagan, Mary. 2009. *Critical Play*. Cambridge, MA: The MIT Press.

Gammel, Irene. 2003. *Elsa: Gender, Dada, and Everyday Modernity: A Cultural Biography.* Cambridge, MA: MIT Press.

Haslam, Malcolm. 1978. *The Real World of the Surrealists.* New York: Rizzoli.

Hendricks, Jon, ed. 1988. *FLUXUS CODEX.* New York: Harry N. Abrams.

Higgins, Hannah. 2002. *Fluxus Experience.* Berkeley: University of California Press.

Motherwell, Robert, and Jack D. Flam, eds. 1981. *The Dada Painters and Poets: An Anthology* Boston: G.K. Hall & Co.

Pearce, Celia. 2006. "Games AS Art: The Aesthetics of Play." *Visible Language* 40(1), Special Issue: Fluxus After Fluxus, 90–112.

Part IV

Digital Art and the Institution

21

Contemporary Art and New Media

Digital Divide or Hybrid Discourse?

Edward A. Shanken

Since the mid-1990s, new media art (NMA) has become an important force for economic and cultural development internationally, establishing its own major institutions.[1] Collaborative, transdisciplinary research at the intersections of art, science, and technology also has gained esteem and institutional support, with interdisciplinary PhD programs proliferating around the world. During the same period, mainstream contemporary art (MCA) experienced dramatic growth in its market and popularity, propelled by economic prosperity and the propagation of international museums, art fairs, and biennial exhibitions. This dynamic environment has nurtured tremendous creativity and invention by artists, curators, theorists, and pedagogues operating in both domains. Yet rarely does the mainstream artworld converge with the new media artworld. As a result, their discourses have become increasingly divergent.

MCA practice and writing are remarkably rich with ideas about the relationship between art and society. Indeed, they are frequently engaged with issues that pertain to global connectivity and sociability in digital, networked culture. Given the proliferation of computation and the Internet, it perhaps was inevitable that central discourses in MCA would employ, if not appropriate, key terms of digital culture, such as "interactivity," "participation," "programming," and "networks." But the use of these terms in MCA literature typically lacks a deep understanding of the scientific and technological mechanisms of new media, the critical discourses that theorize their implications, and the interdisciplinary artistic practices that are co-extensive with them. Similarly, mainstream discourses typically dismiss NMA on the basis of its technological form or immateriality, without fully appreciating its theoretical richness, or the conceptual parallels it shares with MCA.

New media not only offers expanded possibilities for art, but also valuable insights into the aesthetic applications and social implications of science and technology. At its

A Companion to Digital Art, First Edition. Edited by Christiane Paul.

best, it does so in a meta-critical way. In other words, it deploys technology in a manner that self-reflexively demonstrates how new media is deeply imbricated in modes of knowledge production, perception, and interaction, and is thus inextricable from corresponding epistemological and ontological transformations. To its detriment, NMA and its discourses sometimes display a weak understanding of art history and recent aesthetic and theoretical developments in MCA. Due to the nature of NMA practice and theory, as a matter of principle it often refuses to adopt the formal languages and material supports of MCA. These are just a couple of reasons why it frequently fails to resonate in those contexts.

The perennial debate about the relationship between electronic art and mainstream art has occupied artists, curators, and theorists for many decades. Questions of legitimacy and self-ghettoization—the dynamics of which are often in tension with each other—have been central to those debates. In seeking legitimacy, NMA has not only tried to place its practices within the theoretical and exhibition contexts of MCA but also has developed its own theoretical language and institutional contexts. The former attempts generally have been so fruitless and the latter so successful that an autonomous and isolated NMA artworld emerged. It has expanded rapidly and internationally since the mid-1990s, and has all the amenities found in MCA, except, of course, the market and legitimacy of MCA.

This scenario raises many questions that establish a fertile ground for discussion and debate. What are the central points of convergence and divergence between MCA and NMA? Is it possible to construct a hybrid discourse that offers nuanced insights into each, while laying a foundation for greater mixing between them? How have new means of production and dissemination altered the role of the artist, curator, and museum? What insights into the canon of art history and into emerging art and cultural forms might be gleaned from such a rapprochement?

Artworlds

The extraordinary pluralism that characterizes contemporary art does not conform to conventional historical narratives that suggest a linear development, if not progression, of art. The multifaceted nature of avant-garde practices emerging in the 1960s—from minimalism and conceptual art to happenings, Fluxus, and performance, to earth art, pop art, video, and art and technology—constitute a remarkable diversity of artistic exploration that was synchronous with the revolutionary youth culture of the time and the dramatic growth of the market for contemporary art. Although some of these tendencies either implicitly or explicitly shunned the art market/gallery system by refusing to produce objects that corresponded to the traditional forms of collectible commodities, the market found ways of selling either physical objects or ephemera related to many of these practices. The recent popularity and collectability of video art demonstrates MCA's ability and desire to commodify relatively ephemeral art forms for which there previously was no market.

The pluralism that emerged in the 1960s has multiplied over the last half century, fueled by brisk market growth for the work of living artists (to wit, the prices commanded by Gerhard Richter and Damien Hirst) in combination with globalization and the increasing professionalization of the field. Globalization has brought an influx of non-Western artists, theorists, investors, and institutions, contributing great cultural variation and aesthetic innovation while simultaneously growing the market. Artists have opportunistically selected and combined the conceptual and formal inventions of various precursors to contest conventional notions of style, originality, and materiality. They have responded to emerging cultural transformations by exploring theoretical questions, social issues, and formal concerns particular to contemporary exigencies and cultural milieus, expanding the materials, contexts, and conceptual frames of art in the process. Professionalization has resulted in a growing sector of artists who earn a living teaching at institutions of higher education and therefore have the freedom, resources, and intellectual imprimatur to pursue non-commercial work. This is the scenario in which the notion of artistic research has taken a significant stronghold, spawning a growing number of practice-based PhD programs, and in which interdisciplinary practices involving new media art and art–science collaborations, in particular, have flourished. As a result of these factors, there are a growing number of parallel artworlds. Each of these has its own generally agreed-upon aesthetic values and criteria for excellence, historical/theoretical narratives, and internal support structures.

Despite the critical recognition and museological acceptance of video, performance, installation, and other unconventional forms of artistic production, the contemporary art market—and especially the resale sector dominated by big auction houses—remains tightly tethered to more or less collectible objects, and the vast majority of works acquired are painted canvases and works on paper. It is no surprise that the flow of capital in the art market exerts tremendous influence on MCA discourses, through systemic interconnections between artists, galleries, journals, collectors, museums, biennials and art fairs, critics, and art schools. It is this particular contemporary art system that is known as "the artworld," both by its own denizens and by those whose work lies outside of it.

Throughout this upheaval, MCA has retained, if not amplified, its influence as the primary arbiter of artistic quality and value through its control of the market. Moreover, despite the artworld's proven ability to commodify artworks that are not conventional objects, it has not *yet* successfully expanded its market to include (or exploit) some of the key parallel artworlds, such as the discursive, socially engaged, and collaborative artworks theorized by the likes of Grant Kester (2004, 2012), Claire Bishop (2012a), and Tom Finkelpearl (2012) or the work of new media artists theorized by scholars, including the contributors to this volume. This begs the question of how relevant MCA remains in terms of addressing contemporary exigencies. To what extent does it function as a vital discursive field for theoretical debates that have relevance beyond satisfying the demands of a self-perpetuating elitist system that brokers prestige in exchange for capital?

This purposely provocative question is hardly new. The difference now is that parallel artworlds today have their own extensive, self-perpetuating institutional infrastructures that are far more highly developed and funded than the loose formation of artists' collectives and alternative spaces of the 1960s and 1970s. In other words, the MCA artworld in the 2000s and 2010s has much more serious competition than ever before. While it may retain authority regarding questions of market value, it has lost much of its authority with respect to a broader critical discourse because in that domain it is not the only (or most interesting) game in town. Indeed, as of this writing, the Google citation index of Lev Manovich's *The Language of New Media* (2001) exceeds that of all the works published throughout their careers by Rosalind Krauss, Hal Foster, and Nicholas Bourriaud combined!

Three decades ago, art critic John Perreault observed that "the art system—composed of dealers, collectors, investors, curators, and artists—could continue without any good art at all" (Heartney 2012). Noting that "many artists *use* digital technology," Claire Bishop's *Artforum* article "Digital Divide" (2012b) asked a provocative and insightful question: "how many really confront the question of what it means to think, see, and filter affect through the digital? How many *thematize* this, or reflect deeply on how we experience, and are altered by, the digitization of our existence?" Unfortunately, Bishop limited her discussion to "the mainstream art world" and dismissed the "sphere of 'new media' art" as a "specialized field of its own." As a result, she could only "count on one hand the works of art that do seem to undertake this task." When Bishop was called to task in print (Cornell and Droitcour 2013) for her exclusion of NMA, she rebutted that "new media or digital art" were "beyond the purview of my article and [...] my expertise" (2013). Could a contemporary art historian/critic be taken seriously if s/he stated that performance or video or installation lay beyond their expertise? Bishop's admission of ignorance, made without a hint of embarrassment, is a double-edged sword: even as she acknowledges the presence of NMA, she self-righteously condones an account of contemporary art that ignores it, thereby reifying the gap between MCA and NMA that she ostensibly seeks to address. Indeed, such omissions from critical discourse are ideologically charged. As passive-aggressive forms of rhetorical violence, they strip that which is excluded of its authority and authenticity, ensuring its subaltern status. Although Bishop deserves credit for raising the issue in a mainstream context and for serving as a lightning rod for the ensuing polemic, art criticism this shallow and ill-informed—if not willfully ignorant and hegemonic—is destined for obsolescence or ignominy as a straw man. It unwittingly demonstrates Perreault's contention that MCA can continue without any good art, or worse yet, in blissful ignorance of a whole area of artistic practice.

It must be recognized that the very notion of an "artworld" has been a problematic concept since Arthur Danto (1964) introduced the term. Sociologist Howard Becker challenged the notion of a univocal artworld, claiming that there were multiple artworlds. According to Becker, each of the many artworlds consists of a "network of people whose cooperative activity, organized via their joint knowledge of conventional means of doing things, produces the kind of art works that [particular] art world is noted for" (Becker 1982, x). That said, and despite great pluralism and internal friction, there is arguably a more or less coherent network in contemporary art that dominates the most prestigious and powerful institutions. This is not to propose a conspiracy theory but to observe a dynamic, functioning system.

Further, following Perreault, the mainstream contemporary artworld (MCA) does not need new media art (NMA); or at least it does not need NMA in order to justify its authority. Indeed, the domination of MCA is so absolute that the term "artworld" is synonymous with it. Despite the distinguished outcomes generated by the entwinement of art, science, and technology for hundreds of years and especially in the last century, MCA collectors, curators, and institutions struggle to recognize NMA as a valid, much less valuable, contribution to the history of art. As Magdalena Sawon, co-founder/co-director of Postmasters Gallery notes, NMA does not meet familiar expectations of what art should look like, feel like, and consist of based on "hundreds of years of painting and sculpture."[2] It is deemed uncollectible because, as Christie's contemporary art expert Amy Cappellazzo observes, "collectors get confused and concerned about things that plug in" (Thornton 2008, 21).

The operational logic of the MCA—its job, so to speak—demands that it continually absorb and be energized by artistic innovation, while maintaining and expanding its own firmly entrenched structures of power in museums, fairs, and biennials, art stars, collectors, galleries, auction houses, journals, canonical literature, and university departments. This is by no means a simple balancing act and each of these actors has a vested interest in minimizing volatility and reinforcing the status quo, while maximizing their own rewards in a highly competitive environment. Their power lies in their authoritative command of the history and current practices of MCA and in promoting consensus and confidence in the market that animates it. As such, their power, authority, financial investment, and influence are imperiled by perceived interlopers, such as NMA, which lie outside their expertise and which, in form and content, challenge many of MCA's foundations, including the structure of its commercial market. Witness, for example, the distress of the "big four" labels of the music recording industry over the incursion of new media into established channels of distribution. From this perspective, there are substantial reasons for the old guard to prevent the storming of the gates, or at least to bar the gates for as long as possible. Typical strategies include ignoring interlopers altogether or dismissing them on superficial grounds. NMA, if not ignored (e.g., Bishop), is typically dismissed on the basis of its technological materiality but without recognition or understanding of its conceptual dimensions and its numerous parallels with the concerns of MCA (Shanken 2001; Murray 2007). At the same time, Jack Burnham, who championed art and technology in the 1960s, was critical of the "chic superficiality that surrounded so many of the kinetic performances and 'light events'" and noted that, "there was … more than a little of the uptown discotheque" in much of such work (1975, 128–129). So it is not surprising that similar criticisms continue to be made by both NMA and MCA critics, though unfortunately the latter tend to throw out the wheat with the chaff. The uneasy relationship between art and technology and between MCA and NMA has a long and complex history. But the growing international stature of NMA and the seemingly irrepressible momentum it has gathered make MCA's ongoing denial of it increasingly untenable.

For its part, NMA has achieved a level of self-sustaining, autonomous independence from MCA that is perhaps unprecedented. Like MCA, NMA is marked by pluralism and internal frictions. Yet no other movement or tendency in the history of art since 1900 has developed such an extensive infrastructure, including its own museums, fairs, and biennials, journals, literature, and university departments that function independently but in parallel with MCA. In contrast to MCA, it (mostly) lacks galleries, collectors, and a secondary market. But new media art institutions and practitioners have found financial support from diverse corporate, governmental, educational, and not-for-profit sources that are local, regional, national, and transnational. The Ars Electronica Center, in Linz, Austria, built in 1996, completed a $40 million expansion in 2009. This may pale in comparison to the $429 million extension for the Tate Modern or the $720 million budget for the new downtown branch of the Whitney Museum. However, given that the population of Linz is under 200,000, $40 million represents a substantial and ongoing dedication of cultural resources to NMA. As suggested above, the number of scholarly citations for key works of MCA and NMA theory is also illuminating. Despite MCA's refusal to seriously reckon with NMA, NMA is, in a manner of speaking, an artworld force to be reckoned with.

Bridging the Gap: Implicit vs. Explicit Influence and Medium Injustice

In an effort to bridge the gap between the discourses of MCA and NMA, I convened a panel at Art Basel in June 2010 with Nicolas Bourriaud, Peter Weibel, and Michael Joaquin Grey, two curators who, respectively, represent MCA and NMA, and an artist whose career has moved very fluidly between both worlds.[3] One obvious indication of the gap was demonstrated by the simple fact that Weibel, arguably the most powerful individual in the NMA world, and Bourriaud, one of the most influential MCA curators, had never met before.[4] Citing the example of photography and Impressionism, Bourriaud argued that the influences of technological media on art are most insightfully and effectively presented *indirectly*, for example, in non-technological works. As he wrote in his renowned book, *Relational Aesthetics*, "The most fruitful thinking ... [explored] ... the possibilities offered by new tools, but without representing them as *techniques*. Degas and Monet thus produced a *photographic way of thinking* that went well beyond the shots of their contemporaries" (2002, 67). On this basis, he further asserted that "the main effects of the computer revolution are visible today among artists who do not use computers" (67). On one hand, the metaphorical implications of technologies have important effects on perception, consciousness, and the construction of knowledge. But on the other hand, this position exemplifies the historical, ongoing resistance of mainstream contemporary art to recognize and accept emerging media.

Photography, initially shunned as a bona fide form of fine art practice, became a central aspect of mainstream contemporary art practice a century later. This occurred not simply because photography was relatively unaccomplished compared to painting during the heyday of Impressionism (1874–1886), as Bourriaud suggests. Rather, the acceptance of photography was delayed primarily because of the rigid constrictions of the prevailing discourses of late 19th- and early 20th-century art, which were unable to see—literally and figuratively—beyond the mechanical procedures and chemical surfaces of the medium in order to recognize the valuable contributions it had to offer MCA of the time. Although the Museum of Modern Art in New York collected its first photograph in 1930 and launched the Department of Photography as an independent curatorial division in 1940, photography remained a poor relation in comparison to painting and sculpture for another half century. By the 1980s changes in the discourses of MCA, collector attitudes, and market conditions, and the practice of photography itself, resulted in the medium's warm embrace by MCA (though not as photography per se, but as art that happened to be a photograph). In the 2000s photography became highly collectible and expensive. Average auction prices rose in value 285% between 1994 and 2008, with works by contemporary artists Cindy Sherman and Andreas Gursky reaching auction highs of $2.1 million and $3.3 million respectively (West 2008). Video, equally shunned at the moment of its emergence in the 1960s and now the darling of MCA curators, reached a market peak of over $700,000 for a work by Bill Viola in 2000 (Horowitz, 2011).

Regarding the reception of the "new media" of the 19th century, John Tagg (1993) has noted that the more experimental aspects of photography were not well assimilated and the impact of the discourses of photography and contemporary art on each other was highly asymmetrical: the latter changed very little, while the former lost its edge in the process of fitting in. Ji-hoon Kim (2009) has further observed that despite the extraordinary assimilation of video by MCA, much experimental film and video, particularly the sort of material championed by Gene Youngblood in *Expanded Cinema* (1970) and its progeny, has been excluded from mainstream museum shows while being celebrated in exhibitions held in new media contexts. Inevitably, new media and the longer history of electronic art will be recognized by MCA as well, once a potential market for it is developed and promoted. A proactive theorization of the issues and stakes involved may play an important role in informing the ways in which that merger unfolds. Needless to say, many in the NMA community are wary of losing this critical edge in the seemingly inevitable process of assimilation.

Bourriaud's argument authorizes a particular history of photography aligned with a conventional history of art in which technological media remain absent from the canon. A history of art that accepts, if not valorizes, the explicit use of technological media, as in kinetic art and new media, will reconsider its precursors. In this scenario, one can imagine an alternative history of photography that celebrates the chronophotographic practices of Eadweard Muybridge, Etienne-Jules Marey, and Thomas Eakins concurrent with Impressionism. Such a revisionist history will recognize that such work consists not just of the images produced but of the complex and inextricable amalgam of theories, technologies, and techniques devised in order to explore perception. It will recognize, as well, the substantial transit of ideas between art and science (Marey was a successful scientist whose work influenced Muybridge, who conducted extensive research at University of Pennsylvania and collaborated with Eakins, both artists deeply concerned with biomechanics.) The important artistic, scientific, and hybrid art-science researches of these pioneers will be interpreted, moreover, as key monuments in and of themselves, not just as metaphorical inspirations for their contemporaries working with oil and canvas. It took decades, in fact, for these chronophotographic discoveries (to say nothing of the advent of cinema) to penetrate painters' and sculptors' studios. And when they did, they infected art with both implied and explicit motion and duration, as in the work of Duchamp, Gabo, Wilfred, Boccioni, and Moholy-Nagy in the 1910s and 1920s, subsequently influencing time-based art including NMA.

Bourriaud's comparison of photography during the Impressionist era with computers and computer networking since the mid-1990s is troubling for reasons related to historical incommensurabilities. The Eighth (and final) Impressionist Exhibition in 1886 predates the introduction of the Kodak #1 camera (1888), prior to which the practice of photography was limited to professionals and elite amateurs. By contrast, new media started becoming a widespread, popular phenomenon by the mid-1990s, with the advent of the Web (1993) occurring just four years prior to the appearance of an exhibition of net.art at Documenta X (1997) and five years prior to the original French publication of *Relational Aesthetics* in 1998 (the same year that e-mail became a Hollywood trope in *You've Got Mail*). Most importantly, since the 1880s, photography and its extensions in cinema and television radically altered visual culture, saturating it with images. The context of image production and consumption during the Impressionist era—and its impact on art—simply cannot be compared with how the image economy since the late 1990s has impacted art (to say nothing of how key artistic tendencies since the 1960s strategically shifted focus away from image-centric discourses.) This is especially true since the advent of Web 2.0 in the mid-2000s, when new media tools and corresponding behaviors transformed the landscape of cultural production and distribution: social media sites like Facebook, YouTube, and Twitter now compete with search engines like Google and Yahoo for popularity, "prosumer" is a marketing term, and critics debate whether the Internet is killing culture (Keen 2007) or enabling powerful new forms of creativity (Shirky 2008).

Bourriaud's position is, moreover, at odds with the actuality of what he curates and writes about. For if he genuinely embraces the so-called "post-medium condition" as he suggested at Art Basel, then the exclusionary prejudice against the use of technological media in and as art would not exist. The curator would not favor indirect influences of technology on art and his discussions and exhibitions of contemporary art would be blind to medium. But that is not the case. Peter Weibel astutely picked up on Bourriaud's distinction between direct and indirect influences and pointed out the hypocrisy of valuing the indirect influence of technology while scorning the direct use of technology as an artistic medium in its own right. Weibel accurately and provocatively labels this "media injustice." As Christiane Paul has noted, "Bourriaud's distinction would be an absolute oddity in terms of art history, theory, and practice; the most important reflections on video unfolded in the medium of video art itself (not in painting), which is true for almost every medium."[5] Indeed, the implicit/explicit dichotomy that Bourriaud constructs serves as a thinly veiled rhetorical device to elevate the former member of the pair—the lofty, theoretical ideal—at the expense of the latter – the quotidian, practical tool. This ontology, predicated on binary oppositions, must be challenged and its artifice and ideological aims deconstructed in order to recognize the inseparability of artists, artworks, tools, techniques, concepts, and concretions as actors in a network of signification. The gap between MCA and NMA cannot be bridged until such binary oppositions are expunged from discourse, rather than recapitulated in the positions taken by Bourriaud, Bishop, and other like-minded MCA curators and critics.

The Post-Medium Condition and Its Discontents

Far from embracing the "post-medium condition," Rosalind Krauss, who coined the term, considers it an alarming situation that must be resisted. Noting that Clement Greenberg saw the modernist avant-garde as the "singular defense against the corruption of taste by the spread of kitsch's 'simulacrum of genuine culture'" (2009, 141), Krauss argues that the artists she champions—Ed Ruscha, William Kentridge, Sophie Calle, Christian Marclay—are "hold-outs against the 'post-medium condition'" and "constitute the genuine avant-garde of our day in relation to which the post-medium practitioners are nothing but pretenders" (Krauss 2009, 142). In place of traditional media, declared dead by postmodernism, these artists, she claims, have adopted alternative forms of "technical supports." According to Krauss, Ruscha's technical support is the automobile, Kentridge's is animation, Calle's investigative journalism, and Marclay's synchronous sound. Such contentions, tenuous at best, limit the interpretation of highly complex works and practices to a single aspect—just as Greenberg did—obscuring the complex layering of ideas, media, and technical supports that converge in them.

For example, by constricting Kentridge's work to animation, Krauss misses the richness of the artist's accomplishment in joining drawing, animation, performance, and storytelling. Kentridge's direct, corporeal interaction with media demands recognition of the medium specificity and historical trajectories of the various practices he incorporates in his work, even as it embodies the post-medium condition's hybridization of media, which contests such specificity. Moreover, to focus on such formal concerns completely obscures the social and political conditions of apartheid under which the artist lived in South Africa, the critique of which is central to his work, to say nothing of the gut-wrenching pathos of Kentridge's existential reflections on the human condition.

Limiting a work of NMA to any single "technical support," be it Roy Ascott's engagement with planetary consciousness, Susan Kozel's exploration of embodiment and affect in projects such as *AffeXity: Passages and Tunnels* (2013) (Figure 21.1), or the Jogging's Tumbler-based investigation of image and object economies, has the advantage of avoiding the discussion of technological media. But it does the same violence to the subtleties of the specific media—and media ecologies—that the artists employ in, and as part of, their work. It is, moreover, blind to social, political, affective, and emotional qualities.

The artist Krauss singles out as the primary culprit of post-mediality is Joseph Kosuth, whose offense appears to be a post-Duchampian theory and practice that is not limited to medium-specific concerns but demands a broader questioning of the nature of art itself, as articulated in his influential three-part essay "Art After Philosophy" (1969). The best NMA arguably exploits precisely this opening up of artistic inquiry beyond a myopic fixation on medium or support, as heralded by

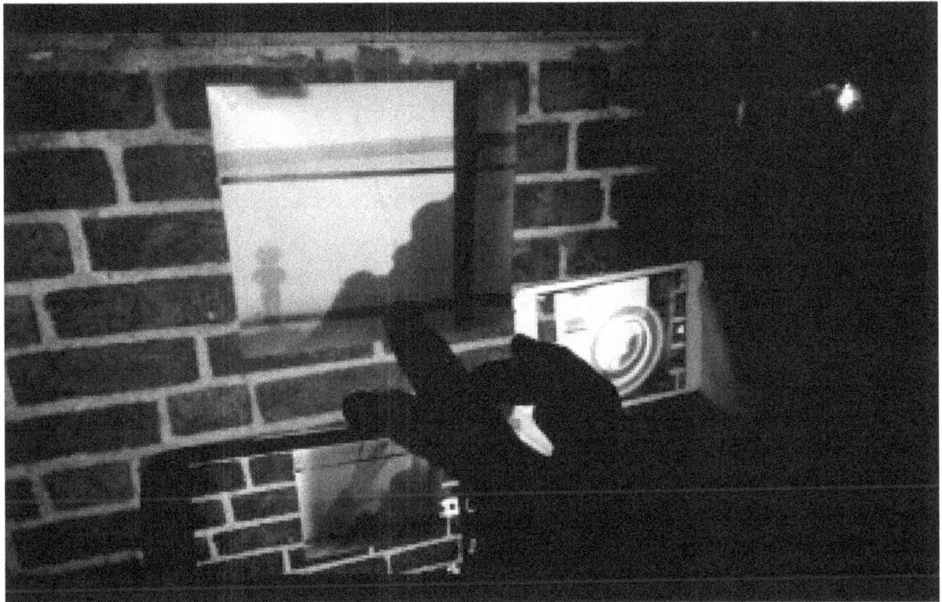

FIGURE 21.1 Susan Kozel, *AffeXity: Passages and Tunnels*, 2013. Re-new Digital Arts Festival, Nikolaj Kunsthal, Copenhagen, October 31, 2014. Susan Kozel (artistic direction and concept), Jeannette Ginslov (video, edit, and concept), Wubkje Kuindersma (dance), Camilla Ryd (images and interaction design), Jacek Smolicki (sound), Daniel Spikol (technical production), Oliver Starpov (dance). This project explores affect in urban spaces. Dance improvisation and screen dance techniques for video capture and editing are combined with augmented reality. Choreographies are suspended as hidden layers of media, discovered by joining physical space and smart devices.

Kosuth and others over four decades ago. The obsession with media in NMA is more of a problem for MCA critics than it is for new media critics; the latter apply a broad range of methods, including media theory, media archaeology, and science and technology studies to wrestle with the particularities of the various media employed, while also engaging with the profound meanings and affective experiences elicited by the best works. Not content to contribute to inbred modernist discourses (from which they have been excluded anyway on the basis of the superficial formal elements of their work), new media artists—like the artists engaged in nearly every successive avant-garde practice before them, from cubist collage to performance art—have used unconventional materials and techniques to question the nature of art itself, often challenging the object-oriented obsession of the MCA artworld and the dynamics of its market-driven demand for collectible widgets. In accord with Bishop's criteria, they seriously investigate "what it means to think, see, and filter affect through the digital [...] and [...] reflect deeply on how we experience, and are altered by, the digitization of our existence" (2012c, 334). Indeed, as our existence becomes increasingly digitized, the material emblems of cultural capital that MCA persists in peddling seem increasingly out of place, or at least increasingly in tension with, the actual flow of ideas, images, and artworks via computer networks and online distribution channels. This tension is, in fact, as Artie Vierkant (2010) argues, a central concern of so-called post-Internet artists (including Oliver Laric, Seth Price, and himself), for whom the artwork "lies equally in the version of the object one would encounter at a gallery or museum, the images and other representations disseminated through the Internet and print publications, bootleg images of the object or its representations, and variations on any of these as edited and recontextualized by any other author."

The gauntlet Krauss lays down to the post-medium "pretenders" might appear to apply to most new media (and post-Internet) artists. But this gauntlet does not really make sense in the context of NMA. The theories and technologies at the core of the historical development of new media tools, together with the artistic and social practices associated with their application, seem to occupy a hybrid stance, straddling medium specificity and a range of non-specific tendencies, including intermedia, multimedia, participation, and convergence.

On one hand, new media practices and discourses embrace medium specificity, paralleling structural film practices. For example, the early work of Steina and Woody Vasulka explores the intrinsic material qualities of video as an electronic medium, including the relationship between audio and video, feedback, and real-time registration. Similarly, theorist Hayles (2004) has argued for media-specific criticism; Fuller (2008), Manovich (2013), and others have developed the field of software studies and cultural analytics; Shanken (2007), Paul (2008), Quaranta (2011), Graham and Cook (2010), and others have argued for critical and curatorial methods specific to NMA; and other contemporary new media discourses talk about digitally born entities, digitally native objects, digital research methods, network cultures, and so on.

On the other hand, the foundational principle of digital computing theorized by Alan Turing conceives of the computer as a "universal machine," one that can emulate the specific functions of any other dedicated device. This concept is distinctly at odds with medium specificity. Technologist Alan Kay's conception and development of the Dynabook, a multimedia personal computer, which he theorized in the 1970s as a "metamedium" (1977), and the recent expansion of that concept (Manovich 2013), further distance new media practices and discourses from Greenbergian modernism.

Contra Krauss, this affirmation of what might be called "postmedia multiplicity" should be embraced as a strategic questioning of the nature of media in artistic, technological, and social contexts. In other words, NMA's refusal to uphold the specter of modernism is anything but a failure; rather, it signals success in pursuing, if not achieving, its own goals. In this regard its convergence with the more general evolution of MCA toward a post-medium condition establishes grounds for forging a rapprochement between the two ostensibly independent discourses.

Krauss's retrograde claim that certain artists' use of "technical supports" represents the "genuine avant-garde of our day" and her condemnation of post-medium practitioners as "pretenders" sets up an unnecessary binary opposition and an indefensible hierarchy of value. Like Bourriaud's opposition of the implicit and explicit effects of technology on artistic practice, Krauss's rhetorical crutch must be unhobbled and the system of values it serves to artificially prop up must be deconstructed. Perhaps one of the most useful contributions that NMA can make to MCA discourses is an understanding of the relationship between materials, tools, and techniques that embraces both medium specificity and the post-medium condition.

Further Provocations

Regarding Bourriaud's focus on implicit influences, it is worth exploring the idea that MCA that does not use new media may have something very valuable to add to the discourses of NMA. Along these lines, the curator suggests that,

> art creates an awareness about production methods and human relationships produced by the technologies of its day … [B]y shifting these, it makes them more visible, enabling us to see them right down to the consequences they have on day-to-day life. (Bourriaud 2002)

In other words, by appropriating the underlying logics of emerging technologies, taking them out of their native contexts and embedding them in more or less traditional artistic media, their effects can be brought into greater relief. Unplugged examples of NMA may offer potentially useful perspectives on how NMA can be more successfully presented in exhibition contexts and may also provide examples that demonstrate parallels between implicit and explicit approaches to science and technology, catalyzing the formation of a hybrid discourse that joins both.

One of the frequently noted shortcomings of NMA is that it does not satisfy the formal aesthetic conventions of MCA. In part this failure can be explained, if not excused, on the basis of the nature of the media and the theoretical commitments of the artists working with them. For example, in some cases it is difficult to justify displaying a work of net art in an art museum or gallery. Doing so is arguably antithetical to what some NMA practitioners and critics take to be one of the conceptual and formal strengths of certain net art and post-Internet art practices: creating work that need not be seen in any particular place, or in one particular form, much less on the high altar of traditional aesthetic values, but is designed to be seen, if not interacted with, reinterpreted, and recirculated, wherever there is a networked computer or mobile device—that is, literally *anywhere*. What happens to net art, and one's experience of it, when it is corralled into a traditional exhibition context? Is it still net art or has it become a strangely neutered doppelganger? Expanding on David Joselit's (2012) categories of "image fundamentalists" and "image neoliberals" (which fix art in originary cultural contexts or global financial markets, respectively), Brad Troemel (2013) has proposed the category of "image anarchists," which reflects a "generational indifference toward intellectual property, regarding it as a bureaucratically regulated construct [...] Image anarchism is the path that leads art to exist outside the context of art." This is perhaps what MCA fears most.

Citing Inke Arns, Quaranta (2011) asks, How can we "underline New Media Art's 'specific form of contemporaneity'" in a way that does not "violate th[e] taboos" of MCA? The direction that this line of questioning proposes must itself be questioned. Violating taboos has played an important role in the history of art. A peripheral discourse like NMA occupies a clear vantage from which to reveal and contest the status quo. This position is enabled not just by the explicit use of technological media but by challenging the museum and gallery—or any specific locale—as the privileged site of exhibition and reception. The proliferation and increasing mainstream acceptance of socially engaged art practices that take place outside of museum contexts demonstrates that such challenges are far from unique to NMA. However, if NMA lies down and accepts assimilation on terms set by MCA, then much of its critical value will have been usurped.

One must recall that, on the basis of conventional aesthetic criteria, Duchamp's *Fountain* (1917) was rejected by the organizers of the 1917 exhibition of the Society of Independent Artists. Just as the canonization of such readymades demanded an expanded conception of what constituted art, so the acceptance of NMA within mainstream discourses demands an expansion of aesthetic criteria. In comparison with these early conceptual interventions, Duchamp's kinetic, perceptual investigations, such as his *Rotary Glass Plates* (1920) and later *Rotoreliefs* (key monuments in the history of NMA) are considered relatively inconsequential in MCA discourses. These works use electronic media in order to interrogate duration, subjectivity, affect, and perception. In so doing, they also contest conventional aesthetic values and demand a reconfiguration of both art and the experience of viewing it. Indeed, just as NMA demands a rewriting of the history of photography, so it demands a reconsideration of Duchamp's kinetic, perceptual work as key monuments in the archaeology of time-based art.

The sort of deep challenges to the nature of art that Duchamp and Kosuth proposed, and that are posed by the best NMA, should be celebrated as a great strength. Yet, I am compelled to agree with curator Catherine David's assertion that "Much of what today's artists produce with New Media is very boring" (quoted in Quaranta 2011). To be fair, however, one must add that much of what today's artists produce without new media is at least equally boring. Indeed, only a very small fraction of mainstream artists actually succeed in gaining recognition and acceptance of their work within the discourses of MCA. So it is not the case that NMA simply fails the litmus test of MCA, for most MCA fails too.

Many works of art that employ the tools of new media and have gained mainstream acceptance generally are not acknowledged by MCA as works of NMA per se, just as the artists responsible for them often do not identify with the NMA artworld as their primary peer group. Electronic works by Duchamp and Moholy-Nagy from the 1920s, structural films and early video installations by Michael Snow, Anthony McCall, Bruce Nauman, and Dan Graham in the 1960s and 1970s, the use of computer-controlled electric light in the work of James Turrell, Jenny Holzer, and Olafur Eliasson, and the computer-manipulated video installations of Doug Aitken, Douglas Gordon, Christian Marclay, and Pipilotti Rist, spanning the 1980s–2000s, all comfortably fit within both NMA and MCA discourses. Hans Haacke's early technological and systems-oriented works, praised by Jack Burnham in the 1960s and later shunned by Buchloh (1988), have been reclaimed (Bijvoet 1997; Shanken 1998; Skrebowski 2008; Jones 2012), part of a larger reconsideration of "systems aesthetics" (Shanken 2009). The use of computers by Frank Stella, James Rosenquist, and Sol Lewitt in the design and fabrication process is well known but hushed in MCA discourses. Robert Rauschenberg, best known as a pop artist, was also a central figure in the group Experiments in Art and Technology (E.A.T.), which he co-founded in 1966. Although this aspect of Rauschenberg's career is downplayed in MCA discourses, the artist famously promoted acting "in the gap between art and life," which for him clearly included using technology as a valid art medium. Further, his collaborations with engineer Billy Klüver demonstrate a conviction to bridge the gap between art and technology, as in *Oracle* (1962–1965) and *Soundings* (1968).

In "Paragraphs on Conceptual Art" (1967) LeWitt's uneasy relationship with technology is revealed by the tension between his metaphorical claim that, "In conceptual art … [t]he idea becomes a machine that makes the art" and his warning that "New materials are one of the great afflictions of contemporary art." The ongoing prejudice against the explicit use of technological media by Bourriaud and others recapitulates this parochial and conflicted attitude. But there is much to be gained by recognizing and exploiting continuities between implicit and explicit uses of technology in art. Joining Lewitt with the practices of NMA, several of the conceptual artist's wall drawings of the 1970s were interpreted by computer code in Casey Reas's *Software Structures* (2004). Commissioned for the Whitney Museum's artport web site, Reas asked several programmers to code Lewitt's instructions in various programming languages. The outcomes yielded multiple forms, suggesting strong parallels between the analog interpretation of Lewitt's ideas by the assistants who executed the wall drawings in physical space and the digital interpretation of those same ideas by programmers in virtual space.

Notwithstanding these parallels, MCA audiences and critics have trouble seeing the everyday appliances and vernaculars of computing (operating systems, applications, web sites, keyboards, monitors, printers) as aesthetic objects (Murray 2007). Similar difficulties were faced by the visual banality of conceptual art, the ephemerality and objectlessness of performance art, and the remote contexts of earth art, yet these tendencies managed to overcome their hurdles, in part by the clever marketing of saleable objects by dealers, a practice that, in some cases, can be interpreted as antithetical to the conceptual underpinnings of the work. But even in cases where the production of art commodities might be logically consistent with NMA practice, few artists have succeeded in producing visual forms that warrant merit on the basis of MCA standards.

For the new media artist seeking to meet those standards, Jonas Lund's *The Fear of Missing Out* (2013) offers a novel approach. A computer algorithm sifts through a database of "top-ranking curators, works, galleries and artists," generating the title, materials, and instructions for the "ideal work to create at a given point in [the artist's] career, before she's thought of it herself" (Rao 2013). As in many conceptual and post-conceptual art practices, the actual objects are presumably less important than

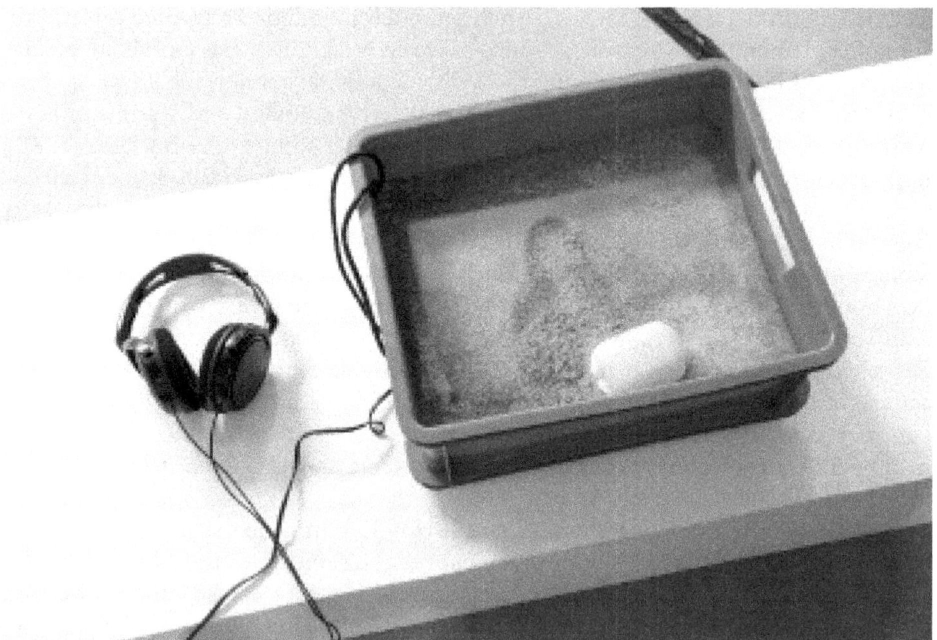

FIRURE 21.2 Jonas Lund, *Cheerfully Hats Sander Selfish*, 2013. Coconut soap, 7 minute 50 second video loop.

the underlying ideas but must nonetheless conform to MCA standards. Indeed, Lund observes he must "follow the instructions in a convincing way… [to] transform it into something viable" (Rao 2013). Here the idea includes an ironic meditation on (and mediation of) automated digital systems and Big Data, subjectively rendered aesthetic objects, and the MCA market. Figure 21.2 shows another of Lund's works, *Cheerfully Hats Sander Selfish* (2013).

We live in a global digital culture in which the materials and techniques of new media are widely available and accessible to a growing proportion of the population. Millions and millions of people around the world participate in social media, and have the ability to produce and share with millions and millions of other people their own texts, images, sound recordings, videos, GPS traces. In many ways early NMA works that enabled remote collaboration, interaction, and participation, such as Ascott's *La Plissure du Texte* (1983), can be seen as modeling social values and practices that subsequently emerged in tandem with the advent of Web 2.0 and participatory culture. A YouTube video like *Daft Hands* (2007) can delight and amaze over 50 million viewers, spawning its own subculture of celebrities, masterpieces, and remixers. If Lund's algorithm and database are any good and he open-sourced them, then in theory anyone with decent chops could make market-worthy MCA objects. In this context, what are the roles of the professional artist, curator, theorist, and critic? What do they have to offer that is special, that adds value and insight to this dynamic, collective, creative culture? Why care anymore about MCA or NMA, per se? What is at stake preserving these distinctions and in distinguishing such artistic practices from broader forms of popular cultural production and reception? Do such distinctions merely serve to protect MCA and NMA from interlopers by preserving a mythical status to their exclusive, lucrative and/or prestigious practices?

Bourriaud's (2002) parameters for evaluating an exhibition offer some insight into these difficult questions:

> … this "arena of exchange," must be judged on the basis of aesthetic criteria, in other words, by analyzing the coherence of this form, and then the symbolic value of the "world" it suggests to us, and of the image of human relations reflected by it […]. All representation […] refers to values that can be transposed into society. [spelling corrected]

This general statement defines "aesthetic criteria" in terms of formal coherence, "symbolic value," "human relations," and the modeling of social values. As these terms are neutral with respect to medium and context, they offer the sort of openness that would enable the confluence of various artworlds.

Specialized artistic practices offer poetic and metaphorical approaches to challenging issues, shifting values, and social relations. These approaches are substantively different from other disciplinary methods in terms of how they contest existing forms of knowledge and construct alternative modes of understanding. The approaches themselves are challenging due to the complex and often paradoxical layering of aesthetic concepts and materials. Like high-level research in science and other disciplines, the outcomes are often not comprehensible to laypeople who are unfamiliar with the field's specialized disciplinary languages and methods. As such, they are unlikely to be popular on YouTube. But YouTube popularity is no more valid as a criterion for judging such artistic research than it would be for judging scientific research. *Daft Hands* is an iconic manifestation of participatory culture and is highly successful in terms of the criteria of that culture, that is, YouTube popularity. For all of its appealing cleverness, virtuosity, and style, *Daft Hands* does not, as *La Plissure du Texte* did, create a working model of a possible future world, much less accurately anticipate some key features of that world (i.e., the world of participatory culture in which *Daft Hands* circulates). To use Bourriaud's aesthetic criteria, *Daft Hands* does not, as *La Plissure du Texte* did, imbue "symbolic value" to "the 'world' it suggests to us and of the image of human relations reflected by it."

Ultimately, art research sets itself apart from popular culture by elaborating visionary, symbolic, and metacritical practices that respond to cultural exigencies. In this respect, technological media may offer precisely the tools needed to reflect on the profound ways in which that very technology is deeply embedded in modes of knowledge production, perception, and interaction, and is thus inextricable from corresponding epistemological and ontological transformations. This metacritical method may offer artists the most advantageous opportunities to comment on and participate in the social transformations taking place in digital culture today, in order to, as Bourriaud implores, "inhabit the world in a better way" (2002, 11–12).

The $34.2 Million Question

In this spirit of imagining a better way to inhabit the world (and a better world to inhabit), I initiated a Facebook debate on May 10, 2013 that placed in tension two different sets of values: those of the commercial art market and those of telematic art. In my status update, I asked:

> What would the world be like if Roy Ascott's *La Plissure du Texte*, 1983 (or your favorite work of net.art or proto-net.art) sold at auction for $34.2 million instead of an abstract painting by Gerhard Richter? In what sort of world (and artworld) would that be possible?

Perhaps the most insightful response came from Caroline Seck Langill, who wrote, "And all that money would be distributed, like the artwork." This short, sharp prod shrewdly suggested an alternative economic model derived from Ascott's theory of "distributed authorship," whereby royalties from the resale of a telematic artwork would be shared among the project's geographically disparate participants.

And why not? There are cultural economies in which the creation and hording/multiplying of wealth for its own sake is not valued as highly as sharing, gifting, and ritual expending. Over half a century ago, Yves Klein's *Zones of Immaterial Pictorial Sensitivity* (1959) brilliantly challenged the MCA market by juxtaposing capitalist models of exchange with the incalculable value of art. The "authentic immaterial value" of the invisible work of art could be acquired only through an exchange of gold (half of which was thrown into the Seine by the artist), for which the collector attained a receipt of ownership, which had to be burned to achieve full immaterialization.

The basic conventions of the art market, for example, ease of exchange and signature, are not neutral qualities or formal characteristics. Rather, they embody deeply held ideological commitments, just as the basic conventions of Ascott's telematic art embody deeply held ideological commitments. So what are the implications if these worlds collide and MCA ends up valuing most highly (and putting its money where its mouth is) a work that challenges its traditional values? If, as Langill intimates, MCA were to embrace Ascott's *La Plissure* and its ideology of distributed authorship, it would be logically consistent for MCA actors to express those commitments by distributing the economic wealth generated by the sale of the work. What, after all, could generate more cultural capital in a gift economy than making a gift of the appreciation in value of an artwork that was a harbinger of participatory culture?

Acknowledgments

Portions of this essay were published as "Contemporary Art and New Media: Outline for Developing a Hybrid Discourse," in *ISEA2010 Proceedings*; "Alternative Nows and Thens To-Be," in *Alternative Now* (online festival reader), Wroslaw: WRO2011 Biennial of Media Arts, 2011; reprinted in *Repasando el Futuro* (English/Spanish) Barcelona: ArtFutura, 2011, 13–27; "Response to Domenico Quaranta's 'The Postmedia Perspective,'" *Rhizome.org*, January 26, 2011; and in "Edward Shanken on 'Is New Media Accepted in the Artworld?,'" *Artfagcity*, September 6, 2011.

Notes

1 These include the Ars Electronica Center and annual festival in Linz, Austria, The Center for Art and Media and the Media Museum in Karlsruhe, Germany, Eyebeam and Rhizome.org in New York, the FILE festival in São Paolo, and nomadic annual meetings such as the International Symposium on Electronic Art (ISEA) and the

International Conference on the Histories of Media, Art, Science, which have been hosted from Singapore to Istanbul.

2 Interview with the author, April 13, 2010. Postmasters Gallery is one of the few galleries in New York that does not draw distinctions between New Media and Contemporary Art, representing important artists associated with both artworlds.

3 Bourriaud, the MCA curator renowned for his theorization of "relational aesthetics," co-founded and co-directed the Palais de Tokyo in Paris, 1999–2005, and organized Altmodern, the fourth Tate Triennial in spring 2009. Weibel directed Ars Electronica from 1986 to 1999, when he became Chairman and CEO of the ZKM | Center for Art and Media, Karlsruhe, and served as Artistic Director of the Biennial of Seville (Biacs3) in 2008 and the Moscow Biennale in 2011. Grey received a Golden Nica award from Ars Electronica in 1994 and his work has entered the permanent collections of the Whitney Museum, MOMA, LA MOCA, Gemäldegalerie, and the Serpentine Gallery. Solo exhibitions include P.S. 1 MOMA, Barbara Gladstone Gallery, and Lisson Gallery.

4 A video recording of the event can be found on the Art Basel web site. See http://www.art.ch/go/id/mhv/.

5 Christiane Paul, personal correspondence with the author, November 12, 2013.

References

Becker, Howard. *Art Worlds*. Berkeley: University of California Press, 1982.

Bijvoet, Marga. 1997. *Art as Inquiry: Toward New Collaborations Between Art, Science, and Technology*. Bern: Peter Lang.

Bishop, Claire. 2012a. *Artificial Hells: Participatory Art and the Politics of Spectatorship*. London and Brooklyn: Verso, 2012.

Bishop, Claire. 2012b. "Digital Divide: Contemporary Art and New Media" *Artforum* (September): 434–441.

Bishop, Claire. 2013. Rejoinder to Cornell and Droitcour. *Artforum* (January): 38.

Bourriaud, Nicolas. 2002. *Relational Aesthetics*, translated by Simon Pleasance and Fronza Woods with Mathieu Copeland. Paris: Les presses du reel, c.1998 [French].

Buchloh, Benjamin. 1988. "Hans Haacke: Memory and Instrumental Reason." *Art in America* 76(2) (February): 97–108, 157–159.

Burnham, Jack. 1975. "Steps in the Formulation of Real-Time Political Art." In *Hans Haacke: Framing and Being Framed, 7 Works 1970–75*, edited by Kaspar Koenig. Halifax: The Press of the Nova Scotia College of Art and Design.

Cornell, Lauren, and Brian Droitcour. 2013. "Technical Difficulties." Reply to Claire Bishop, "Digital Divide," *Artforum* (January): 36, 38.

Danto, Arthur. 1964. "The Artworld." *The Journal of Philosophy* 61(19): 571–584. American Philosophical Association Eastern Division Sixty-First Annual Meeting, October 15, 1964.

Finkelpearl, Tom. *What We Made: Conversations on Art and Social Cooperation*. Durham, NC: Duke University Press, 2012.

Fuller, Matthew, ed. 2008. *Software Studies: A Lexicon*. Cambridge, MA: The MIT Press.

Graham, Beryl, and Sarah Cook. 2010. *Rethinking Curating: Art after New Media*. Cambridge, MA: The MIT Press.

Hayles, N. Katherine, 2004. "Print Is Flat, Code Is Deep: The Importance of Media-Specific Analysis." *Poetics Today* 25(1) (Spring): 67–90.

Heartney, Eleanor. 2012. "The Incredible Shrinking Art Critic." *Brooklyn Rail*, December 10, 2012. http://www.brooklynrail.org/2012/12/artseen/the-incredible-shrinking-art-critic (accessed October 28, 2014).

Horowitz, Noah. 2011. *Art of the Deal: Contemporary Art in a Global Financial Market.* Princeton, NJ: Princeton University Press.

Jones, Caroline. 2012. "Systems Symptoms: Jack Burnham's 'Systems Esthetics.'" *Artforum* 51(1) (September): 113–114, 116.

Joselit, David. 2012. *Art After.* Princeton, NJ: Princeton University Press.

Kay, Alan, and Adele Goldberg. 1977. "Personal Dynamic Media." *Computer* 10:3 (March): 31–41.

Keen, Andrew. 2007. *The Cult of the Amateur: How Today's Internet Is Killing Our Culture.* New York: Crown Business Publishing.

Kester, Grant. 2004. *Conversation Pieces: Community and Communication in Modern Art.* Berkeley, CA: University of California Press, 2004.

Kester, Grant. 2012. *The One and the Many: Contemporary Collaboration in a Global Context.* Durham, NC: Duke University Press, 2012.

Kim, Ji-Hoon. 2009. "The Postmedium Condition and the Explosion of Cinema." *Screen* 50(1): 114–123.

Kosuth, Joseph. 1969. "Art After Philosophy I, II, III." *Studio International* CLXXVIII (Oct., Nov., Dec.): 134–137; 160–161, 212–213.

Krauss, Rosalind. 2009. "The Guarantee of the Medium." In *Studies across Disciplines in the Humanities and Social Sciences 5*, edited by Tiina Arppe, Timo Kaitaro, and Kai Mikkonen, 139–145. Helsinki: Helsinki Collegium for Advanced Studies.

LeWitt, Sol. 1967. "Paragraphs on Conceptual Art." *Artforum* 5(10): 79–83.

Manovich, Lev. 2013. *Software Takes Command.* New York: Bloomsbury Academic.

Murray, Soraya. 2007. "New Media Anxiety: Art History and the Problem of Modern Technology." Doctoral dissertation, Cornell University.

Paul, Christiane, ed. 2008. *New Media in the White Cube and Beyond: Curatorial Models for Digital Art.* Berkeley, CA: University of California Press.

Quaranta, Domenico. 2011. "The Postmedia Perspective," *Rhizome*, January 12.

Rao, Mallika. 2013. "Controversial New Project Uses Algorithm to Predict Art." *Huffington Post*, November 5.

Shanken, Edward A. 1998. "The House That Jack Built: Jack Burnham's Concept of Software as a Metaphor for Art." *Leonardo Electronic Almanac* 6(10) (online). Abridged version reprinted in *Reframing Consciousness: Art and Consciousness in the Post-Biological Era*, edited by Roy Ascott, 156–160. Exeter: Intellect, 1999). Reprinted in English and Spanish in *a minima* 12 (2005): 140–151.

Shanken, Edward A. 2001. "Art in the Information Age: Technology and Conceptual Art." In *SIGGRAPH 2001 Electronic Art and Animation Catalog*, 8–15. New York: ACM SIGGRAPH. Expanded in *Leonardo* 35(4) (2002): 433–438.

Shanken, Edward A. 2007. "Historicizing Art and Technology: Forging a Method, Firing a Canon." In *Media Art Histories*, edited by Oliver Grau, 43–70. Cambridge, MA: The MIT Press.

Shanken, Edward A. 2009. "Reprogramming Systems Aesthetics: A Strategic Historiography." In *Proceedings of the Digital Arts and Culture Conference 2009*, edited by Simon Penny et al. Berkeley: University of California Press, 2009. Reprinted in *Relive: Media Art Histories*, edited by S. Cubitt and P. Thomas, 83–96. Cambridge: MIT Press, 2013; and in E. Shanken, *Systems*, Whitechapel/MIT, 2015, 123–129.

Shirkey, Clay. 2008. *Here Comes Everybody: The Power of Organizing Without Organizations.* New York: Penguin.

Skrebowski, Luke. 2008. "All Systems Go: Recovering Hans Haacke's Systems Art." *Grey Room* 30 (Winter): 54–83.

Tagg, John. 1993. *The Burden of Representation: Essays on Photographies and Histories.* Minneapolis, MN: University of Minnesota Press.

Thornton, Sarah. 2008. *Seven Days in the Art World.* London: Granta.

Troemel, Brad. 2013. "The Accidental Audience." *The New Inquiry*, March 14.

Vierkant, Artie. 2010. "The Image Object Post-Internet." http://jstchillin.org/artie/vierkant.html (accessed December 4, 2013).

West, Nina P. 2008. "The $900,000 Librarian." *Forbes.com*, October 1.

Youngblood, Gene. 1970. *Expanded Cinema.* New York: P. Dutton Co.

22

One of Us!
On the Coupling of New Media Art and Art Institutions

Richard Rinehart

New media art is marrying into the family of the artworld. Is she marrying for the family name? To plunder the estate? Or is she merely wife number seven in a weary harem? Before we get to these questions, it will be helpful to define one of our subjects, "new media art." For my purposes here, new media art denotes something that is clear at the center, but blurry at the edges. At the center of new media art lies art for which computation is essential and inextricable. This understanding usually denotes works that employ computation as idea and material and in production and presentation. The definition blurs at its borders where it overlaps with conceptual, performance, installation, social practice art and other art forms that became more prevalent after the 1960s. This blurring is not only acceptable; it is essential to understanding how the implications and challenges of new media art (including those covered below) ripple throughout the larger artworld. Are these boundaries stable? That question is exactly what I would like to investigate here. This essay will be less about how new media art developed in relation to other art practices—how it fits into the history of art—and more about ongoing shifts in the interface between new media art and the discipline of art history, the museum, and other institutions that make up the artworld. I am especially curious about the current state of that relationship and about some of the tractable implications for both sides.

By the mid-1990s, artists had already accumulated decades of experimenting with computational media, but this era marked the debut of the Internet to society at large (in the form of the World Wide Web), the start of the "dot com" economic bubble, and a concurrent explosion of artistic activity around new technologies unprecedented in scale and reach. But this excitement also created tensions. In the essay "Can Art History Digest Net Art?," art historian Julian Stallabrass writes about this era, "From its beginnings, Internet art has had an uneven and conflicted relationship with the established art world" (Stallabrass 2009, 165). In this era, the major museums, curators, and publications of the established artworld displayed a benign neglect toward

A Companion to Digital Art, First Edition. Edited by Christiane Paul.

new media art. But this neglect went two ways. One of the early projects of new media art was to use the global and increasingly popular reach of networked media to bypass these cultural "gatekeeper" institutions and much of this early activity was not posited as art per se, but either as political protest—often in the form of hacktivism—or creative engagement with network structures. These creators were as likely to cleave to the industry of new media as to the artworld, whether in a creative, monetary, or critical relationship—and sometimes all three. The historicity of this era explains, in part, the ideology and rhetoric that helped forge the developing relationship between new media art and the institution.

It should come as no surprise that communications emanating from Silicon Valley, in the form of hi-tech industry marketing and talks delivered by "visionary" CEOs, are typified by a certain amount of techno-positivist hyperbole. New media art, in particular Internet art or "net art," grew rapidly during the same time as the tech bubble (1995–2000) in an ideological and logistical embrace with hi-tech that continues today. Partly because of this, the discourse of new media art is conflated with that of the tech industry; in particular, both are inflected with a strong utopian impulse. This is not to say that everyone involved in the hi-tech industry or new media art participates in carnival barking. Many in the hi-tech industry are familiar with the Gartner Hype Cycle (Gartner 2009), a simple chart predicting that most hi-tech hyperbole goes through five stages: the technology trigger; the peak of inflated expectations; the trough of disillusionment; the slope of enlightenment; and the plateau of productivity. In the world of new media art, the Critical Art Ensemble published a paper entitled "Utopian Dreams—Net Realities" that attacked inflated utopian discourse as early as 1995, but did not disavow entirely the promise of new technologies for artists (Critical Art Ensemble 1995). However, despite occasional critiques, the utopian impulse has remained a defining characteristic of both discourses:

> "Everything is possible."
> Hewlett Packard (2002) corporate tagline
>
> [The digital revolution will bring] "... social changes so profound their only parallel is probably the discovery of fire."
> Louis Rosetto (1993), founding editor of *Wired* magazine
>
> "We are as gods and might as well get good at it."
> Stewart Brand (1968), founder of the Whole Earth Catalog, Long Now Foundation, and Global Business Network

As Mark Surman explains in his conference paper, "Wired Words: Utopia, Revolution, and the History of Electronic Highways,"

> Not surprisingly, the language of the wired world and the electronic highway reemerged in the early part of the 1990s. Magazine racks and TV screens filled up with news about the "new" highway. Headlines screamed "Welcome to the Highway of Hope" and "The Info Highway: Bringing a Revolution in Entertainment, News and Communication" (*Globe and Mail*, May 13, 1994, cover and *Time*, April 12, 1993, cover). Conferences were organized to talk about wired cities, and the most popular, profitable, new magazine of the era was just, well, *Wired*. [...] "Everything has changed in the Wired World: technology has reinvented how we live, work and play"

and "We are in the midst of sweeping technological changes that will affect our lives even more than the industrial revolution" (*Globe and Mail Information Highway* supplement, May 1995, cover, and *Futurescape*, p. C4). (Surman 1996)

The discourse of new media art often does not stray far from the mothership:

> The Museum of Contemporary Art, Shanghai proudly presents "Merging/Emerging-Art, Utopia and Virtual Reality" from the 8th of March. This new media art exhibition combines art with technology and delivers to the audience the creative power of a new era. [...] Merging/Emerging-Art, Utopia and Virtual Reality brings out a global perspective that transcends art movements, races and countries. [...] It transcends the boarders of art and music, to create a utopia of an all encompassing art, allowing the audience's imagination to run free. (MOCA Shanghai 2009)

In the hands of theoretician Nicholas Bourriaud the discourse can be more subtly intoned while retaining its utopian inflection:

> The modern political era, which came into being with the Enlightenment, was based on the desire to emancipate individuals and people. The advances of technologies and freedoms, the decline of ignorance, and improved working conditions were all billed to free humankind and help to usher in a better society. [...] It is evident that today's art is carrying on this fight, by coming up with perceptive, experimental, critical and participatory models, veering in the direction indicated by Enlightenment philosophers, Proudhon, Marx, the Dadaists and Mondrian. (Bourriaud 1998)

In addition to mirroring each other's utopian tone, hi-tech and new media art discourses also find several specific points of agreement. Stewart Brand once quipped, "Information wants to be free" (quoted in Clarke 2000), a sentiment that directly informs new media art's resistance to copyright and other throttles on creative re/use. Apple Computer's marketing for iMovie claims that buyers will "Make home movies look like Hollywood masterpieces" (Apple 2009). This notion of consumer-as-producer is a commercial variation on the Beuysian notion that everyone is an artist, an egalitarian idea that has been especially popular among some interactive and participatory new media artists. The hi-tech industry positions itself as existing outside mainstream industries—ahead of them, of course, necessitating a "new economy" and new stock market indicators. Bypassing the artworld's institutional filters and constraints and going directly to the people, Internet art claimed a similar maverick position for itself.

The hi-tech industry and new media art share more than a few high-level concepts. They are also conflated at operational and logistical levels, something that must be considered in the larger field of cultural production (Bourdieu 1993). First, and most obvious, is the fact that new media art makes use of technologies (and their implied practices) developed by the hi-tech sector. New media art also produces content that often shares its format and distribution mechanisms with hi-tech's commercial and entertainment content. This creates a direct and ongoing conversation between an art form and an industry that is emblematic of the relationship between art film and Hollywood, but has no analog in a gallery filled with oil paintings. Hi-tech and new media art also share bodies. Many new media artists have the requisite skills to land themselves jobs in this related industry from where they further conflate their work and artistic practice. Because of their hybrid existence and maverick status with regard to the artworld, these artists often organize and show their work not in art galleries, but at industry events like the long-standing SIGGRAPH conference, further mixing the relative discourses.

The utopic energy of new media art together with the promise of popular relevancy and private resources, as well as the sheer volume of creative work, produced a seductive pull that not even the mainstream artworld could resist forever. In the tech bubble years, the mainstream artworld itself caught tech fever and pursued an imagined generation of maverick millionaire donors. Museum directors who harkened to the information age were led by Maxwell Anderson, who rose from director of the Emory University Art Gallery to director of the Whitney Museum in this period. Lawrence Rinder, Curator of Contemporary Art under Anderson, wrote for the milestone 2000 Whitney new media art exhibition *Bitstreams*, "Nothing since the invention of photography has had a greater impact on artistic practice than the emergence of digital technologies" (Rinder 2001). But new media art's dalliance with the tech industry was not entirely forgiven and Rinder, reflecting on *Bitstreams* later, lamented how the "technophiles" of new media art perpetuate,

> an unfortunate silo-ing of a community of digerati; a parallel universe of digital practice, sort of like the parallel universe of ceramics practice or studio glass practice. There's nothing wrong with it, per se, but in its isolation, it develops in such a way that is not as ideally fertile as it might be if it were more open to discourse across disciplines. There is a real resistance, in that community, to sharing the goods, or the candy, or whatever. (Anderson 2009)

This was not the first, nor the last, time that the community of new media art would be characterized as a ghetto, an assertion that Jon Ippolito, New Media Professor at the University of Maine, turned on its head in a post to the CRUMB listserv:

> Here are some numbers from February 2003:
> Metropolitan Museum of Art (best-known brick-and-mortar museum)
> 2 million artworks
> 5 million visitors per year
> 5,000,000/2,000,000 = 2.5 visits per artwork
>
> Rhizome.org (best-known virtual museum)
> 600 artworks
> 4 million visitors per year
> 4,000,000/600 = 7,000 visits per artwork
>
> Remind me, which is the ghetto? (Ippolito 2012)

In these dynamics lay some of the complexities, cited via Stallabrass earlier, of the developing relationship between new media art and art institutions. One can almost see a troubled marriage represented in these exchanges, as accusations fly; which party is open and sharing of themselves, and with whom if not each other, and who is cast as the neglected partner versus the unrequited suitor? But, in addition to the mutual suspicion, there is true love and not a little lu$t. The year 2000–2001 was a pivotal year in this relationship. Two milestone new media exhibitions at major museums caught the nation's attention, but in a moment of unfortunate coitus interruptus, the dot com economic bubble burst along with many museums' dreams of new board blood and new money from the new economy.

Shifting now from the ideological or emotional aspects of this relationship, let us look at some of the specific mechanisms through which new media art and art institutions came to accommodate each other structurally. The depth of exchange—the give and take—in each functional area described below is telling.

With full respect to exhibitions of new media art presented around the world up to 2000 and their importance to art history, the moment for new media art exhibitions that signaled a sea change in the relationship between new media art and the artworld in the United States has to be when two major museums, the Whitney and SFMOMA (San Francisco Museum of Modern Art), opened major group exhibitions of new media art—*Bitstreams*, *Data Dynamics*, and *010101*—within three months of each other in 2001. Rising from the American coasts like two arms crossing swords in the air somewhere above the Midwest, these shows caught the attention of American mass media. Both museums downplayed the importance of the venues and the simultaneity of the two shows. "There have been, over the last five or ten years, many shows dealing with technology," said Whitney curator Larry Rinder, "The fact that SFMOMA and the Whitney are having shows at the same time isn't significant" (Spingarn-Koff 2001). But the modesty was moot. *New York Magazine* disagreed, noting that *Bitstreams* was a meeting of new media art and the artworld writ large, "Tech-savvy artists are painting with keyboards, sculpting with software, and avoiding natural light—it interferes with their plasma screens. Now they're being welcomed by the Whitney Museum. Can they bring the art world up to code?" (*New York Magazine* 2001), and on the cover of their April 2001 issue covering both exhibitions, *ArtNews* declared "Digital art comes of age!" (*ArtNews* 2001).

Behind the public glitz, new media artists and museums were negotiating the terms of such presentations. The Whitney was criticized for presenting several works of interactive Internet art included in the 2000 Whitney Biennial on a single projector, blurring the autonomy of each work and nullifying interactive elements (Mirapaul 2000). Benjamin Weil, curator of *010101*, included Internet art in that show, but would not allow it into the museum, requiring viewers to experience certain works on site and others online at home. While museums wrestled with how to best present various forms of new media art, some artists were experimenting with making the format of their art more gallery-friendly. Artists whose work had previously been limited to interactive web sites experienced through a standard browser or ad hoc configurations that could be installed for a festival began to make works that were meant to be displayed in durable hi-tech installations in gallery settings. Other artists, such as Shirley Shor, were taking the presentation strategies full circle. Shor, who had been creating ephemeral projection-based works with installation elements, such as *Landslide* (Shor, *Landslide*, 2013), for galleries, began making small-scale self-contained wall-hanging multimedia sculptures, such as *Urban Dream* (Shor, *Urban Dream*, 2013)—discrete objects that could be lifted off the gallery wall, taken home in the buyer's car, then hung and plugged in. This shift in technology, presentation strategy, and institutional context—and an increasing number of like examples—show that the new media art project of bypassing the institution is retained by select new media artists, but no longer characterizes that community in the way it once did. That is not to say that any such adjustments to the gallery, market, and institution on the artist's side are always compromises or "selling out"; after all, variability characterizes new media art. When museums currently present new media artists, as in the 2011 Whitney exhibition *Cory Arcangel: Pro Tools*, the discussion of technology seems perhaps a little less anxious and the issues around presentation a little less raw.

In the 2000s, the artworld also responded to new media art by creating new positions within the museum's org chart. At the larger institutions, these were dedicated, if not full-time, positions: Christiane Paul was named Adjunct Curator of New Media Arts at the Whitney and Steve Dietz Curator of New Media at the Walker Art Center. At smaller museums, the position might be hybrid. In some cases, entire organizations of new media and art were brought together as when Rhizome—perhaps *the* new media art organization—was brought under the umbrella of the New Museum.

After the initial wave of careers were forged within new media art and museums, and the institutions came to recognize that new media art might not be the intellectually impoverished ghetto it had been characterized as, many progenitors (several authors in this volume) moved on to second careers in academia. Mark Tribe, founding director of Rhizome, went to teach at Brown University and then the School of Visual Arts; Jon Ippolito, Associate Curator of Media Arts at the Guggenheim, became director of the Stillwater new media program at the University of Maine; Beryl Graham accepted a professorship at the University of Sunderland; and Christiane Paul curates at the Whitney and teaches at the New School. Again, sometimes entire institutions were transformed by the introduction of new academic programs and departments, as was the case when UC Berkeley launched the Berkeley Center for New Media.

The private sector within the artworld has been slower to respond to new media art, but is by no means absent. The New York galleries Postmasters and Bitforms and San Francisco's Catherine Clark Gallery were early experimenters with the commercial sale, copyright, and collecting of new media art. But the ways in which new media art challenges the art market remain the least developed of the mutual influences inventoried here.

The discourse unfolding through professional discursive vehicles like conferences, journals, and listservs demonstrates the greatest area of exchange between new media art and the artworld and reveals something of the nature of their intermingling. The perceived need and call for new media art to be "historicized" has come from both sides. The 2005 Media Art Histories conference brought together new media curators and artists with academic art historians to try to hammer out a deal in a kind of Malta-at-Banff. As with all discourse, some positions are taken at the level of language. "Post-Internet," for instance, describes art that may or may not be Internet-formatted but is Internet-aware in the sense that the Net is a social construct as much as a technology; a contemporary condition with implications for all art forms. But these reconciliations (those outlined above and others) between new media art and the mainstream artworld may come at the cost of a certain kind of erasure. Stallabrass draws parallels between the historicization of Internet art and that of photography:

> The recent apotheosis of photography in the museum offers a warning [for Internet art]: the art-historical texts that accompany, for example, Andreas Gursky's major show at the Museum of Modern Art in New York (2001), or Thomas Struth's show at the Metropolitan Museum (2003), certainly break photography out of its ghetto but at the cost of suppressing the history of photography, the comparisons being

with the grand tradition of painting. It was as if photography could only be validated by (doubtful) associations with the already sanctified tradition of Western art. (Stallabrass 2009, 167)

This warning rings true for new media art and, even at the level of style or taste-culture, it seems somehow uncool today to talk about new media art as a thing unto itself in the higher echelons of the artworld. New media art that was once openly referred to as a community of practice, a set of operations and behaviors, or (god forbid) a genre, has been discursively contained in an historic period (net.art), instrumentalized as a tool, or at best left as a passive subject to be operated upon by art history's methodologies. Of course, this assimilation has been largely consensual and has yielded as many benefits as consequences to both parties, but all results are worth recording including the potentially deleterious side-effects in our next arena of functional exchange: collecting and preserving new media art.

New media art *is* being collected by museums and private collectors, but not on the same scale that it is being exhibited and talked about. Why? The first answer is the obvious one: fear, fear of investing in a piece that may cease functioning in a couple of years (to say nothing of the unproven market value equation). It is far easier to live with new media art for the duration of a three-month exhibition than to ponder how one will leave it as a legacy for one's grandchildren. We will return to this concern momentarily, but let's move to a second reason: lack of evaluative criteria. The artworld is at the barest beginning of being able to speak about behaviors and interactivity in ways that are as rigorous and time-tested as are the criteria and formal language for traditional plastic forms. And if we cannot speak of it, how do we evaluate it? It is one thing to include a new media artwork in a temporary exhibition that may require a select few points of contextualization; it is another to make the permanent commitment of collecting in which the context must be the entire institution, every other work in the collection, and history itself. To include a new media artwork in an exhibition, it need merely be "interesting" or "relevant"; to include the work in the collection, it must be great—and few are willing to go there with new media art.

The Getty's Art & Architecture Thesaurus (AAT) offers one example of the distillation of formal language that is essential to evaluation and thus collecting. Terms in the AAT are selected and ranked in part by their ubiquity in the professional literature. Those terms are then used by collection managers to classify objects in the collection. So, the AAT encapsulates the whole process, from talking about the work to collecting it (or at least cataloging it). The AAT currently includes almost 250,000 terms and yet many terms that are widely used to describe new media art remain missing. A search for "net art" on the AAT web site yields nothing, and a search for "net.art" breaks the database (with an obvious irony). Despite the popularity of Bourriaud-ian theories in art history circles, not even "relational" appears in the AAT, and formal language for describing behaviors and interactions seems far off. Perhaps one consequence of the aforementioned discursive assimilation of new media art is that we may not bring the profane language of the tech industry into the professional tomes and will have to rely on canonical art terms to describe new media works (if it's good enough for "contemporary art," why shouldn't it work for new media art?)

Of course terminology is not the only arena for the evaluation of works being considered for a collection (with lack of the former providing a hindrance to the latter); we must also consider the work's place in history. Certain art-historical methodologies seem well suited to describing new media artwork; for instance the context-rich social art history exemplified by Janet Wolff or T.J. Clark (especially since much new media art is about reabsorbing social context into the work itself). Institutional critique or even an interdisciplinary history that included the histories of art, media, and technology would seem equally suitable lenses. Unfortunately, such methodologies are currently out of favor, passé among a new breed of radically conservative curators and directors who retro-enact even earlier methodologies that avoid the "clutter" of theoretical models (Benton 2005), methodologies such as connoisseurship (AAH 2013; CAA 2013), close readings of discrete works, and the search for beauty (Artlyst 2013; Pilger 2013). New media art proves problematic under these lights, and the curators emphasizing connoisseurship and beauty are exactly the ones least likely to consider different criteria for what they deem just another subset of contemporary art; another wife in the harem.

Of course these obstacles to collecting are not universal, and the historical imperative is so urgent that new media art is collected, on a modest scale, despite them. But once a new media artwork is collected, how is it preserved? More specifically, how does the partnership between new media art and art institutions help and hinder this operation? Would this child be better cared for in a single-parent home?

Many new media art preservation efforts leap quickly to solving the technical problems, and I cannot stress enough how important triage and digital forensics are; they are the action-oriented responses to an urgent situation and utterly appropriate. However, new media art will be well served if we simultaneously ask questions that may take longer to answer. There are questions of institutional suitability: are art museums the best places to collect and preserve new media art? The answer may seem obvious, but museums routinely make use of third-party collections storage and conservators. Are digital libraries better suited to preserving new media art either on behalf of museums or as final repositories? The questions raised by the Variable Media Initiative (Variable Media Initiative 2013) are not those that come up naturally in a mad rush to transfer endangered bitstreams from optical to magnetic media and yet they desperately need to be asked (and answered!). At some point, we need to have the equivalent of the Sistine Chapel restoration debates around new media artworks. Is rerouting dead links in the preservation of Douglas Davis's *The World's First Collaborative Sentence* (1994) through the Internet Archive's Way Back Machine (Ryzik 2013) the same as removing fig leaves and loincloths that had been painted on Michelangelo's nudes after the fact? Curators and artists need to weigh in on conservation issues like defining the boundary where a new media artwork (i.e., the conservator's commitment) ends and the environment (such as the network) begins.

Preservation creates a kind of Venturi chamber for new media art; if the life cycle of an artwork can be considered the flow in a pipe, then preservation is a constricted section of that pipe through which the contents change form. As discussed above, a given work of new media art may or may not be characterized as such when entering the collection; it may be characterized simply as another instance of contemporary art. The latter approach often results in a kind of "atomizing" of new media artworks, seeing each one as such a unique instance such that no cohesive strategy is possible and concluding that each one must be considered exclusively. Of course, museums (as opposed to libraries and archives) traditionally treat their collections at the item level, and item-level conservation is no exception. But item-level care does not preclude preservation strategies that address the problems of a class of works and yet allow for individual applications. This begs the question of what classification is acceptable for new media art. If the only answer allowed is "It's just contemporary art" then the special issues that new media art highlights are flattened into a broader set of concerns and new media art's technological materiality may be the only conservation issue deemed prominent enough to address. One way or another, this art that entered preservation's Venturi chamber as contemporary art will be transformed into new media art, but probably for the misleading fact of its materiality. New media art presents a range of challenges to preservation that are not just technical; they are also conceptual. Almost all of these concerns also apply to other forms of contemporary art (and thus, solutions should cross-pollinate), but new media art brings these issues into sharper focus and a more prominent position of urgency among the host of concerns.

For instance, preserving new media art requires that we find our way between two extreme views of materiality: the museological view that unique and original materiality is of utmost importance to preserving every work of art; and the technological view that all computational activity is enacted at many layers of abstraction from physical materiality, making the latter replaceable and unimportant (Turing 1950). If this is, in art-historical terms, a synchronic problem, its diachronic equivalent would be a better understanding of how changes in the technology and materiality of a new media artwork affect a hermeneutic reading of that work over time. For instance, if we upgrade the equipment of new media artworks to keep them functioning, do these new materials confuse historic readings of the work? This raises the related question of where historical authenticity lies—in materiality or in functionality (for works that "function" in more than symbolic ways). Documentation, a function that is concurrent with preservation, may need to function in new ways with regard to new media art. New media art is, in relation to traditional art forms, more media-independent but more context-dependent, making documentation necessary not only for an historic understanding of the work, but for its continued existence. This may seem obvious, but how you document and how you use the documentation is critical. In collecting performance art, museums have already made the collectively repeated mistake of acquiring documentation, props, and artifacts from performances, cataloging those as material artifacts and then eliding into presenting those artifacts as proxies for the performances or, worse, as the artwork itself (usually through careless use of another form of documentation, the wall label). Performance art challenged the museum, and new media art will challenge it even more, leaving traces that are invisible to the human eye on scales inaccessible to the human body and entailing a legion of environmental contingencies that are as fragile as a flicker of electricity.

Emerging from the Venturi chamber of preservation into the curatorial realm of future exhibitions, our artwork is transformed back into "contemporary art." But this journey is dissatisfying, not the crucible necessary to forge new media artworks into the evidence of history. Effective preservation requires that we treat these works as new media art going in and coming out because curatorial and conceptual questions (like those suggested above as well as others) affect preservation and vice versa. Our mutual agreement to assimilate new media art into conceptual art may have the unintended consequences of suppressing a sufficiently rigorous discussion around preservation—limiting it to bits and bytes—and of suppressing the need for institutional changes that may be necessary for a healthy marriage of these new works to the institution.

It is not only for preservation that new media art, per se, is important. New areas of intellectual inquiry open up when we focus on conceptual issues that are fundamental to this art but ancillary for others and that cohere into really interesting configurations only when these works are addressed in proximity to each other and at a certain distance from others. In order for it to speak its own history, we need to call new media art by its name.

Stallabrass concludes in his essay:

> It [Internet art] offers art history the prospect of a much deeper transformation than that effected by photography. Whether either Internet art or art history will survive such a development is an open question. (Stallabrass 2009, 178)

This is a question worth periodically revisiting, with regard to new media art and the institutions of the artworld in general. I am not arguing here that new media art be codified into staff titles, Dewey decimal classifications, or institutional structures (organizing curatorial and academic art departments by media seems at odds with current artistic practices anyway), but that we allow for Stallabrass's transformations to reveal institutional imperatives and opportunities and new avenues of scholarship.

Learning to speak the others' language is always a good basis for a relationship, and Rhizome's VocabWiki project (Conservation Online 2013) was a brave experiment in mapping AAT terms to new media art folksonomies. Art history expanded its linguistic toolkit centuries ago when it lifted formal terms from music (composition, harmony, tone, etc.). Perhaps it is time for another great expansion, this time from the realms of the technology industry and human–computer interface design.

Rigorous theoretical critical attention—exemplified by Institutional Critique—has been largely limited to art institutions' exhibitionary and discursive practices, perhaps because these are seen as the areas in which art is publicly debated and defined. The doors to the museum's vaults, however, hide a relatively inviolate collection of ideologies, agendas, and social stakes waiting to be revealed and refined—and new media art provides one way in.

Perhaps art history can learn to tolerate new media art's *ménage à trois* with the hi-tech industry, help new media art salvage and refine its utopian project, and gamely risk being swept up in the process. New media art seems faced with a dilemma: allow every utopian gesture to be read as a signifier for the hyperbolic discourse of the hi-tech industry—or distance itself with a radical break in which the most identifiable trope of hi-tech, utopianism, must be left behind if not denounced outright. Of course, this is a false dilemma, a binary trap of self/other or criticism/object where hi tech is cursorily vilified and utopia is transformed into an object of study instead of a site for mutual action. Not all utopian strategies need be overtly political, didactic, or even positive if nuanced readings are available. Even negative positions can help to intelligently edit a utopic vision (though exclusive use of dystopic parody leads to nothing but a mirror image of the status quo and that does not move forward the utopian project). Art history's "heterotopias"—à la Foucault (1967) and Jameson (2004)—also may not hold the solution. Heterotopia is too often conceived as a space without consequences. This is the pitfall of the white cube that new media art initially sought to escape, opting to be in, and of, the world instead. "Being of the world" in this sense means modeling ethical, intersubjective relationships with real people in the form of art audience participants. It means interacting with consequence as an aesthetic material. Informed tactics, such as using interactivity to model intersubjective spaces with audiences, allow new media art to take raw cultural impulses and convert them into critical actions that precipitate institutional transformations.

References

AAH (Association of Art Historians). 2013. "The Knowing Gaze: The Shifting Role of the Connoisseur and Connoisseurship in Art and Its Histories." Web site about conference panel. http://www.aah.org.uk/annual-conference/2013-conference/session17 (accessed November 25, 2013).

Anderson, Maxwell. "Lawrence Rinder: In Conversation." YouTube video: 18:45–19:20. Indianapolis Museum of Art. Recorded October 27, 2009. http://www.youtube.com/watch?v=Mnz_26Qo1T8 (accessed August 28, 2013).

Apple Computer. 2009. "iMovie" web site. Apple.com. http://www.apple.com/ilife/imovie/ (accessed October 30, 2009).

Artlyst. 2013. "Rob and Nick Carter Reengaging with Art of the Past." Web site about exhibition at Fine Art Society. http://www.artlyst.com/articles/rob-and-nick-carter-reengaging-with-art-of-the past (accessed November 25, 2013).

Art News. 2001. Cover. *ArtNews* 100(4) (April).

Benton, Thomas H. 2005. "Life After the Death of Theory." *Chronicle of Higher Education.* http://chronicle.com/article/Life-After-the-Death-of-Theory/44910 (accessed November 25, 2013).

Bodow, Steve. "The Whitney's Digital Sampler." Web site. Nymag.com. Published March 26, 2001. http://nymag.com/nymetro/arts/features/4507/ (accessed August 20, 2013).

Bourdieu, Pierre. 1993. "The Field of Cultural Production, or: The Economic World Reversed." *The Field of Cultural Production: Essays on Art and Literature.* New York: Columbia University Press.

Bourriaud, Nicolas. *Relational Aesthetics.* France: Les Presses du reel, 1998.

Brand, Stewart. 1968. Opening line. *Whole Earth Catalog* (Fall): 1.

Brand, Stewart. 2000. Quoted by Roger Clarke in "Information Wants to be Free" 2000. http://www.rogerclarke.com/II/IWtbF.html (accessed on November 30, 2009).

CAA (College Art Association). 2013. "The New Connoisseurship: A Conversation among Scholars, Curators, and Conservators." Program sessions. Web site about conference panel. http://conference.collegeart.org/2013/sessions/friday1430 (accessed November 25, 2013).

Conservation Online. "Lexical and Classification Resources." http://cool.conservation-us.org/lex/ (accessed November 25, 2013).

Critical Art Ensemble. 1995. "Utopian Dreams—Net Realities." Well.com. http://www.well.com/~hlr/texts/utopiancrit.html (accessed November 15, 2009).

Foucault, Michel. "Of Other Spaces (1967), Heterotopias." *Architecture / Mouvement / Continuite.* October 1984. http://foucault.info/documents/heteroTopia/foucault.heteroTopia.en.html (accessed November 25, 2013).

Gartner, Inc. "Understanding Hype Cycles." Gartner.com. http://www.gartner.com/pages/story.php.id.8795.s.8.jsp (accessed November 25, 2013).

Hewlett Packard. "HP Launches New Global Brand Advertising Campaign" 2002. HP.com. Web site press release. http://www.hp.com/hpinfo/newsroom/press/2002/021118a.html (accessed November 1, 2009).

Ippolito, Jon. 2012. "Ghetto Blasting." CRUMB email listserv. New-Media-Curating Archives web site. https://www.jiscmail.ac.uk/cgi-bin/webadmin?A2=new-media-curating;99b47a12.1207 (accessed August 28, 2014).

Jameson, Frederic. 2004. "The Politics of Utopia." *New Left Review* 25 (January–February).

Mirapaul, Matthew. 2000. "For Museums, Internet Art is a Tricky Fit." *New York Times*. Nytimes.com. Published March 30. http://www.nytimes.com/library/tech/00/03/cyber/artsatlarge/30artsatlarge.html (accessed August. 25, 2013).

MOCA Shanghai. 2009. "Exhibitions." MOCA Shanghai web site. http://www.mocashanghai.org/index.php?_function=exhibition&_subFunction=pastExhibition&exhibition_id=39&_view=detail (accessed November 25, 2014).

Pilger, Zoe. 2013. "Review: Instagram: Power of Beauty – Exhibition Fails to put the 'Art' in Smartphone." Review of exhibition at National Portrait Gallery. *Independent*, September 18. http://www.independent.co.uk/arts-entertainment/art/reviews/review-instagram-power-of-beauty--exhibition-fails-to-put-the-art-in-smartphone-8822583.html (accessed November 25, 2013).

Rinder, Lawrence. "Whitney ArtPort: Past Exhibitions" web site, Whitney Museum of American Art. Accessed August 29, 2013. http://whitney.org/www/artport/newSite/exhibitions/past-exhibitions.shtml

Rosetto, Louis. 1993. "Preface." *Wired* 1(1): 10.

Ryzik, Melena. 2013. "When Artworks Crash: Restorers Face Digital Test." *New York Times*. Nytimes.com. Published June 9. http://www.nytimes.com/2013/06/10/arts/design/whitney-saves-douglas-daviss-first-collaborative-sentence.html?pagewanted=all&_r=0; http://whitney.org/Exhibitions/Artport/DouglasDavis (accessed August 30, 201).

Shor, Shirley. *Landslide*. http://www.shirleyshor.com/Landslide (accessed November 25, 2013).

Shor, Shirley. *Urban Dream*. http://www.shirleyshor.com/Urban-Dream (accessed November 25, 2013).

Spingarn-Koff, Jason. 2001. "010101: Art for our Times." Web site. Wired.com. Published February 28, 2001. http://www.wired.com/culture/lifestyle/news/2001/02/41972 (accessed August 28, 2014).

Stallabrass, Julian. 2009. "Can Art History Digest Net Art?" In *Netpioneers 1.0: Contextualising Early Net-based Art*. Berlin: Sternberg Press.

Surman, Mark. 1996. "Wired Words: Utopia, Revolution, and the History of Electronic Highways." INET96 conference proceedings. http://www.isoc.org/inet96/proceedings/e2/e2_1.htm (accessed August 28, 2014).

Turing, Alan. 1950. "Computing Machinery and Intelligence." In *The Essential Turing*, edited by Jack Copeland, 446. Oxford: Clarendon Press.

Variable Media Initiative. "Variable Media Network." http://www.variablemedia.net (accessed November 25, 2013).

23

The Digital Arts In and Out of the Institution—Where to Now?

Sarah Cook with Aneta Krzemień Barkley

The digital media landscape we inhabit has been shifting for over fifty years. Cybernetics, virtuality, new media, the digital—call each grain of sand what you will. In this territory, artists and creative producers have continually sought to create not only new forms of art, but also new interdisciplinary initiatives for the presentation of their work, establishing a more stable ground for it to be experienced and appreciated. Media arts can take many forms—as the chapters in this book attest—from software to sculpture, installation to algorithmic instruction. In this chapter we focus on the challenges that the broader category of "new media art" has brought to its own presentation, including how it has been curated. Curating has usually been considered a primarily museological activity, but when it comes to new media art, we commonly understand curating as an engagement with myriad different aspects of the production, presentation, and reception of the work of art. As has been argued before,

> The modes of curating engendered by working with new media art can be more widely applied to any art that may be process oriented, time-based or live, networked or connected, conceptual or participative. (Cook and Graham 2010, 283)

This chapter briefly describes how this understanding has come about and discusses some of the ways in which the products and processes of these hybrid arts practices have been supported. By identifying some of the exhibition formats that have emerged over time, we are left with a *who, when, what, where, how, and why* of the curating of new media and digital arts, providing the structure for this chapter. While trying to highlight some recent examples, this chapter also gives an overview, which is inevitably patchy and subjective; after all, any method of curating adopted in response to the variety of work in the field of new media art might only be applicable to a single work of art in a single place at a single time. It is important to remember that although "new media art" is in an almost constant state of emergence because of its use of new

A Companion to Digital Art, First Edition. Edited by Christiane Paul.

technologies [...] the challenge of curating emerging art might be addressed by the passage of time" (Cook and Graham 2010, 284).

If the new media landscape has been forming for over fifty years, then the field of study of curatorial practice is even younger, fully emerging only in the last thirty years, well after the longer traditions of art history (or even museology). The rise of curatorial practice as a field of scholarship shares the same timeframe as that of the heady emergence of new media arts, linked to a wider understanding of and access to technologies of intercommunication. A raft of books published since the early 2000s has addressed "the curatorial"—almost all of them generally based on the commercial art world and the global biennial format, places from which new media art has been largely absent.[1] Thus it would appear that an ongoing critical examination of curatorial practice as it is manifested in specific contexts is still very much needed.

One key question to consider is how curating new media arts might be different from curating any other form of art, and whether the digitality of new media art is the reason why the art might need different curatorial treatment or has not sat as comfortably in particular established curatorial frameworks. Publications such as this one, and *Rethinking Curating* (Cook and Graham 2010), as well as the new-media-curating discussion list run through the CRUMB[2] web site, have sought to advance critical reflection about the processes that curatorial practice entails. Through CRUMB and other initiatives much work has been done to bring curators and producers working in the field of contemporary art into conversation with those working in the field of practice that addresses new media and the digital.

What?

> The art world has [problems] with multiple authorship, the aesthetics of activism, the exhibiting of process instead of product, and audience interaction. (Cook and Graham 2010, 290)

As other chapters in this book describe, there has been a longstanding divide between the worlds of contemporary art and new media art: contemporary art has been defending itself against occasional claims by new media art to be different or more cutting edge, and new media art has been lamenting that it shouldn't be ignored. One defensive assertion by contemporary art has been that many, if not all, contemporary artists use media as some part of their practice. The counter-criticism this draws from the media art side is that contemporary artists might use technology, but they do so in an unreflective way, without questioning where the technology comes from, how it functions, and what hidden discourses and limitations lie within its preformatted functionality and its quick and easily manifested results (Schindler and Broeckman 2011). In a lecture for the BBC, Turner Prize-winning artist Grayson Perry (whose practice is predominantly ceramics) demonstrated exactly this position, saying:

> I use digital. It's now the default option of many artists. We live in the 21st century. I use Photoshop. My tapestries are woven on a computer-controlled loom and I'm not alone in this now [...] technology is so amazingly quick and brilliant that it changes the way we look at art [...] So art now really follows, chases technology rather than leads it [...] technology in many ways is more cutting edge than art [...]

> [Art] can't compete in many ways with the kind of majesty of Google Earth or the kind of buzz and huge, humungous gossip of Twitter. (Perry 2013)

The point missed by Perry is that the practice of media artists involves a critique of technology as much as it contributes new forms of art to the landscape. Media artists continually redefine their artistic practices to highlight critical arguments surrounding media culture, arguments they see as lacking in "mainstream" visual artists' (or designers') use of media technology. Therefore projects that use material scraped from the Web might be stylistically commenting on the interface design of web sites, such as Sakrowski's *curatingYouTube*, a platform for a variety of projects based on and around the online video-sharing site that employ curating "as a technique of action, used as a means of orientation and to position itself in the web 2.0 phenomena by artistic strategies" (Sakrowski 2007).

Historically, the technologies from which new media art draws are strongly related to commercial "entertainment systems," or come from a larger military-industrial-academic complex. This adds another contextual frame for understanding new media's place in the landscape of the museological artworld and the fact that some early works of media art are found in media, science, or technology museums. New media artworks, perhaps more than other art forms, are rooted in contexts outside of the art museum or gallery.[3] As Christiane Paul has noted,

> While all art forms and the movements that sustain them are embedded in a larger cultural context, new media can never be understood from a strictly art historical perspective: the history of technology and media sciences plays an equally important role in the formation and reception of new media art practices. (Paul 2006)

Most media artists are not seeking to be in competition with the technology industries and its commercial products, just as some of them are ambivalent about being part of an artworld with its own commercial products. A large percentage of self-identifying "media artists" considers the visual arts context as elitist, hermetically closed, and market-oriented, and therefore not a desirable place to be. It has been argued that media artists largely do not want to belong to a commercial world where everything has to be streamlined to a commercial outlook (Jones 2005). They consider the media art field as a better place to be because it is more open, gives them greater possibilities of experimentation, and provides more scope for connecting to fields that are commonly not considered art, including political activism, media criticism, and media culture (Schindler and Broeckman 2011).

Given this view of the landscape, it is no wonder that it is difficult to perform the curatorial tasks of identifying, describing, and historicizing the type or genres of artwork emerging from the intersection of art and "creative technology." Many contributors to this book have done much to make this process easier for future investigators. Considering these conditions of production and reception, it comes as no surprise, then, that new media art is often described as process-oriented. Terms such as "collaboration," "participation," and "networking" are key descriptors of both the working method of the artist and the characteristic of the resulting media artwork.

Caitlin Jones has convincingly described how art is changed when the studio is the laptop, the network, and the Web (Jones 2010). This observation is just as relevant now as it might have been thirty or forty years ago when artists experimenting with video used TV editing suites as their studios. Technological developments change art practice by changing how art is made; this is a fact curators need to acknowledge and be aware of, as it necessarily has implications for how the work is shown, made accessible to audiences, and preserved for art history.

Media technologies are interactive or responsive. The digital is seemingly fleeting or ephemeral, but is accessed haptically, is tactile, instantaneous, live. Media are mutable and not static. They are variable, iterative, changing, morphing, and, above all, unstable.

Who?

> [Curators'] stated objections to new media art can be contradictory and may be borne [*sic*] of lack of awareness about the conceptual and practical issues that new media art presents. (Cook and Graham 2010, 285)

Given the variety of work that has emerged from this ever-changing field, telling a clear story of how museums and galleries have dealt with it has presented a number of obstacles. Firstly, as debates on curatorial practice are often driven by curators describing their own activities,[4] they usually focus on aims and intentions rather than a critical examination of outcomes. What remains is case-by-case reflection on the "best practice" of curating. In each case the lessons learned may reflect different stages in the curatorial process—from siting the work (which might have involved commissioning it in the first place) and engaging audiences and the press in its reception, to documenting its impacts or effects on the understanding of art in society.

Most of the recent critical writing on curating has reflected on art institutions and how emerging forms of art have challenged the institution. While new media and the digital continues to be an emerging form of art, it has not often been featured in this literature, which draws a thread from debates such as "new museology" (Vergo 1989; Stam 1993) through the "third wave of institutional critique" (Sheikh 2006; Raunig and Ray 2009) to what has been known as "new institutionalism" (Ekeberg 2003; Doherty 2004; Farquharson 2006; Möntman 2006), all of which are best explored elsewhere than in this chapter. To this list we can add the debates specifically addressing how changes to institutional curatorial practice have been brought about by new media. These debates can be summarized by noting that the changes in practice have been more readily accepted when the new media in question are a technological tool of education or interpretation (Gansallo in Cook 2001; Dewdney and Ride 2006) than when the digital is in fact the medium for the art shown in these institutions (Paul 2008; Quaranta 2010).

From this literature we have learned that there are potentially as many curatorial "modes," or ways of working, as there are curators (Cook and Graham 2010). Curating entails processes of creation and interpretation, or staging and historicizing. The more challenging the work of art is to its site, and the more demanding it is of its audience in terms of engagement and participation, the more frequently is the analogy drawn between the tasks of a curator and that of a producer. The practice of curating, it has been noted, has changed from one concerned primarily with selection, storytelling, or careful keeping of objects to one in which networking, advocacy, and commissioning are key roles (Gleadowe 2000). There has always been a certain amount of impresario in the figure of a curator.

When?

What changes with the introduction of new media and the digital into the field of art is not so much the curatorial task of selection or collection—though the scope of material available, and access to it, is considerably widened—but rather the timeline on which these processes take place. Within the digital medium, it is possible for the means of production of the work of art to be synchronous with its means of distribution. British artists Jon Thomson & Alison Craighead, for example, make artwork that sometimes uses live webcams available freely online. Their Internet-based project *Template Cinema* (2004) draws together video from camera feeds, soundtracks from streaming sources, and, in some cases, inter-titles from online message boards or chat rooms, to generate new short films every few minutes, which are projected into gallery space as well as available for watching online (Figure 23.1). While some aesthetic decisions about the framing of the work are written into the code of the work, the films are essentially authored live as visitors watch them. This requires a steady Internet connection for the piece to function, as well as an Internet populated with freely available webcams, presenting challenges to the collection of that work for permanent exhibition.

This type of "liveness" and contiguousness distinguishes new media art from other art forms that use the digital in production but not necessarily distribution—such as photography—though parallels can be drawn between new media and live performance such as theatre and music. But if the production—the making, the bringing into being—of the work takes place at the same time as the art audience's witnessing and appreciation of it (as in the case of generative art, for example), then the curator's role is changed, as is the artist's and the audience's, especially in cases where audience response is part of the work. All parties have the chance at involvement with artistic intention earlier in the timeline of the work's conception (a work may consider audience response as part of its conception and not be launched without it).

For instance, in projects that use mobile technologies—app-based artworks such as Jason Sweeney's *Stereopublic*, to name one example—users may be invited to contribute to a database that makes up the work during the project's lifetime; in this case by mapping locations in a city that are quiet and noise free, and uploading audio, video, photographic, and text-based contributions. In these works there may be a set timeframe during which they are "live" or they may exist indefinitely, available to be viewed and interacted with in public space. Works like these, as with much Internet-based art, could be said to exhibit themselves: they are launched by artists and exist without the obvious need for the curatorial framing that a museum or gallery provides in order to engage their publics who might encounter them while browsing online on their computers, or mobile phones, whether on the Web or in an app store.

As we can see, new media art practices, through their collaborative, participatory and networked guises, present substantial challenges to the institutional structure, never mind the physical walls, of the museum.[5] New media art can also be highly contextual—critically or playfully responsive to its context of presentation—changing its guise for its reception, such as for instance, web site-based works that noticeably redesign their pages for different screen sizes (from mobile devices to desktops), a technological feature exploited with glee in works by net artists JODI or Constant Dullaart. However, this dependence on context could be due to many different aspects of the work and not just one condition of its technological implementation.

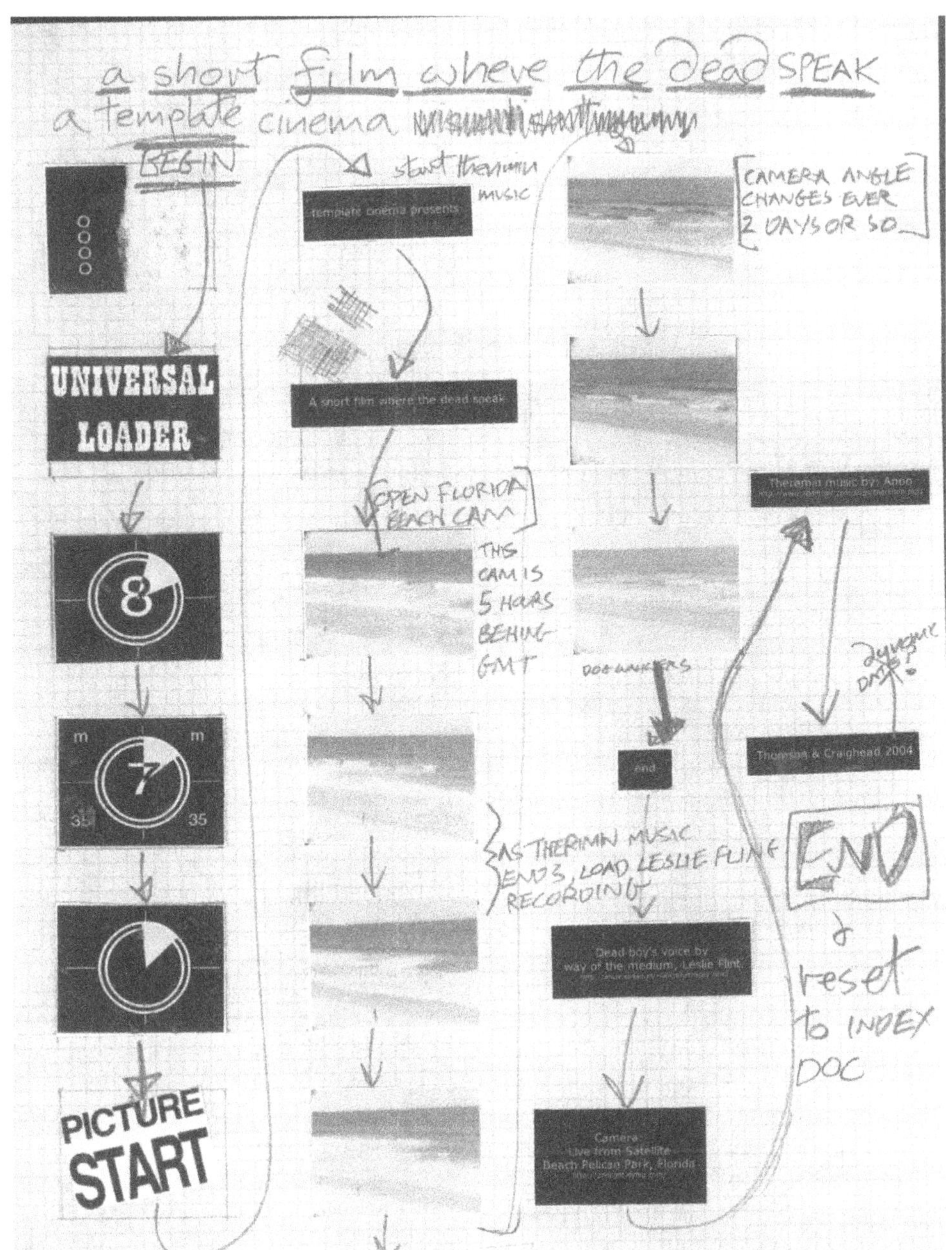

FIGURE 23.1 Thomson & Craighead, sketch for *Template Cinema*, 2004.

For instance, the work may challenge the notion of a single author, or a set timeframe of its exhibition, or the response required from viewers/users, as well as the ways in which projects are modified for presentation online versus presentation in a physical space. Consider, for example, the biological project *Pigs Bladder Football* (2011–) by John O'Shea, which marries the industry of synthetic biology and organ "growing" with debates around ethical meat products and the food industry, all through the

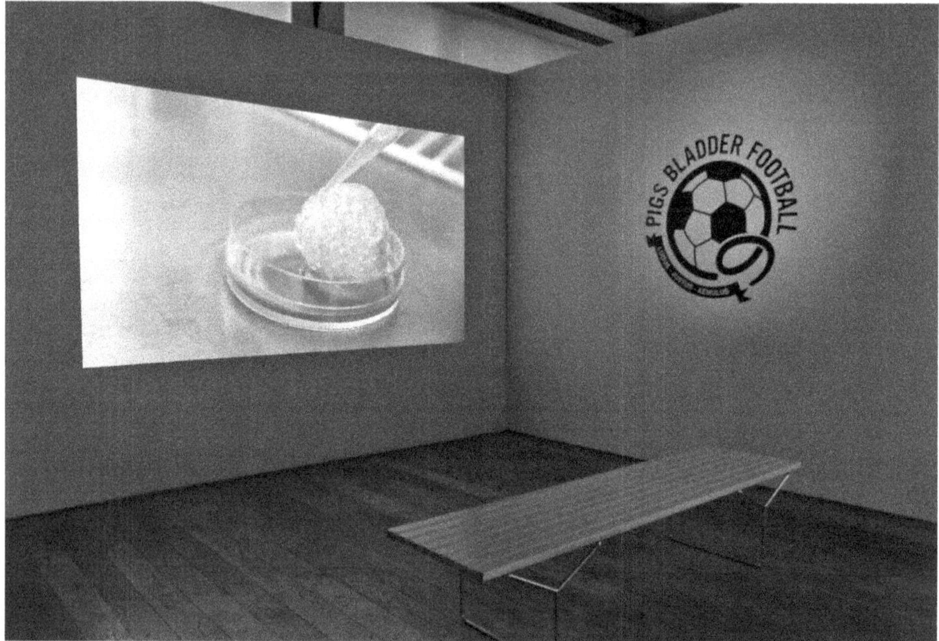

FIGURE 23.2 John O'Shea, *Pigs Bladder Football*, 2011– . Installation view (video). *Pigs Bladder Football* was originally commissioned by Abandon Normal Devices (UK) and was made possible through the Wellcome Trust Arts Award scheme and the collaboration of Professor John Hunt at University of Liverpool Clinical Engineering Unit.

appealing metaphor of sport. The iterative artwork is ongoing; it began with substantial research in a scientific laboratory in which the artist learned from a scientist how to grow synthetic spheres from bladders (in reference to the fact that footballs were previously made from animal bladders rather than plastics) (Figure 23.2). The work exists in documentary form, with prototype evidence for gallery presentation, but also in the form of participatory football games as performance events, and public engagement workshops aimed at making balls from offal and discussing the issues of food production, waste, and medical research.

Furthermore, new media art might undermine existing museum structures, such as the collection, by being seemingly reproducible rather than consisting of a unique single object. New media art's "liveness" and, in some cases, easy accessibility or participatory nature, "reorients the concept and arena of the exhibition" (Paul 2006) as the *raison d'etre* of the gallery.

At a professional development workshop hosted by the Harris Museum in Preston, UK, other issues concerning the disadvantages of the museum in addressing media art were discussed. A key problem identified was the creation of an appropriate historical narrative for digital arts in relation to existing art collections. Curators noted that one problem audiences might have with media art in the museum is the gap in the collection narrative—as much work dating back to the 1950s (such as site-specific, network- or systems-based work and other ephemeral forms) is "missing"—which then makes it difficult for audiences to make conceptual leaps between older and contemporary projects. Not all museums have the budgets or mandates to retrospectively collect, and there also is the problem of finding a display strategy for this missing work, which, perhaps due to its informational nature—which characterizes any networked or algorithmic or instruction-based art practice—is often buried in archives.

This situation begins to explain why new media art has struggled alongside long-standing presentation formats for art, which have historically been static. These formats have been safe, not "live." They have sought to preserve works in an immutable form, for generations to come to see and appreciate. Museums—those with collections or those without, such as Kunsthallen and galleries—have prioritized slow and steady, long-term exhibition formats and clear checklists of objects. These generalizations are not without their contradictory tales—of Roman sculptures cleaned rather than left with their faded paint, or of the inclusion of holograms or 3D fly-through of architectural monuments in blockbuster exhibitions, for instance. The traditional exhibition of art has been deeply disturbed by the introduction of the digital age, despite active curatorial attempts against that incursion. For the many museums that have experimented with handheld devices or flashy web sites, there are just as many that have completely ignored art made through the use of digital means (sometimes for the reasons mentioned above). Alongside those who create technology-led educational projects, artists too are using digital tools, but as their medium, to make really exciting and genuinely interesting work (politically, socially, and aesthetically).

As such, new media art engenders a new kind of museum—one "without walls" or one that is "ubiquitous" (Dietz et al. 2004). This new kind of museum has been described as "a parallel, distributed, living information space open to artistic interference—a space for exchange, collaborative creation, and presentation that is transparent and flexible" (Paul 2006). In the context of the earlier list of institutional critique, and new institutionalism, we find new media art as a key player in the debates about the future of museums.

What has made this historical trajectory interesting to witness in the recent overlap between the rise of an awareness of "the curatorial," and the maturation of new media art—which surfaces in blockbusters, itinerant exhibitions, the museum without collection, and the public-consultation/celebrity-endorsed rehang of the collection, on one side, and a complete upsetting of the notion of what art is, how it is made, who its authors are, how it should be attributed, and how it comes into being or engages its public, on the other—is that the more interesting responses have not always come from the traditional players in the art sector. The institutional organizations that have supported media arts have not always been recognizable as museums or galleries, public or commercial.

Where?

If we step aside from the "mainstream" visual art discourse, then one of the social contexts in which new media art has emerged is that of the media-specific infrastructure accessible to technically minded artists—servers, databases, and computer networks (peer to peer, open source). Developed in parallel with, or even against, the more commercially minded digital landscape, are grass-roots, ad-hoc, and temporary "autonomous zones," meet-ups, get-togethers, and file exchange initiatives.

The written art history of this media art activity, and its outputs in the form of net art, to name one example, is very much in development, and key case studies in this history would be artist-run servers such as *irational.org*, or those with attendant e-mail discussion lists about art, culture, and technology such as *The Thing*, *Rhizome*, *Faces*, *Sarai.net*, *Nettime*, *7-11*, and many others.[6] The artists who configured, administered, and populated these servers with their projects and documentation usually did not identify themselves as an artistic group, or movement, per se. But *irational.org*, in particular—through its affiliation with a shared domain name and its attendant filing system—appears to be a curated collection of socially engaged, industry-critiquing work dating back to the earliest point of social networking and the Web. In the context of technological development, at least in the UK, *irational.org* is related to other initiatives that have emerged out of London, such as *backspace*, *I/O/D*, or the artist-led network Furtherfield (who run the *net-behaviour* mailing list). Through a medialab space, then an informal exhibition space, and now a more publicly sited small gallery in a building in the middle of a London park, Furtherfield have championed art that critiques the current digital age. Funded by Arts Council England, in part a result of their educational roots as an open access media space, Furtherfield may be maturing into a good example of how to marry the curating of new media art exhibitions with lively critical discussion and online publishing.

On the sketchy map of the landscape of pioneers of new media art, one could place —alongside these networking, exchange-space projects—the not-for-profit educational organizations that, through attracting funding from research councils and thus amassing industry-level equipment, ensured the tools of making *and* the critical discourse around the digital and were accessible to artists in the early days. Centers such as Ars Electronica in Austria (the center was founded in 1996, the organization Ars Electronica in 1979), The Banff Centre's New Media Institute in Canada (active 1994–2007), and Eyebeam in New York (founded 1997, with their early e-mail list, Blast) all began with an agenda of ensuring art practice kept pace with commercial media industries such as television and filmmaking, and science and technology disciplines such as engineering, robotics, and software (Druckrey 1999). Artists were often the caged mice in these "labs"—getting to play with the tools but being evaluated on what they did with them, in case a commercial product or piece of valuable IP emerged. This model continues today.

Other kinds of laboratories based on creative technological production, with less of an explicit remit to support art, have also hosted artists for the same ends, and early examples of this practice have been well documented at commercial technology companies such as Xerox or Bell Telephones (Harris 1999; Century 2009). Much has been written about the culture of creativity in university labs such as those at MIT, and city councils have followed the scent of profitable blue-sky research at which artists are so good, supporting labs such as Kitchen Budapest or Medialab Prado in Madrid. An example of this type of environment is Inspace at the University of Edinburgh in Scotland, which for over four years was home to an at times office-based arts commissioning organization, New Media Scotland. Until early 2014, Inspace functioned as the university's own in-house, public-facing industry partner. To audiences attending Inspace's regular expanded-cinema film club (Atmosphere), festival-related exhibitions, or live new music and performance gigs, the fact that they were in a university research lab might not have been obvious. To the university's fundraisers trying to woo research partners from industry such as, for instance, the Disney

Corporation for animation technology or the aerospace industry for robotics, a space in which prototypes could be tested on an audience open to experimental experiences was a clincher in the deal.

University or city-funded medialabs are also incubators of new media and digital arts practices for philanthropic and social-inclusion or educational remits, not just for commercial gain. An example of the latter category is the Centro Multimedia in Mexico City, which is part of an enormous college complex, the Centro Nacional de las Artes, incorporating dance, music, and visual arts schools. While Centro Multimedia is known internationally for its cutting edge biennial festival of electronic arts (Transitio) and its international symposia, which bring key thinkers worldwide to Latin America, its lab spaces are production sites in part for government-funded art in the media industries.

Contexts

> Changing the interface to a new media artwork will always change the meaning of the piece; therefore, the challenges for display are not just practical ones. (Cook and Graham, 2010, 284)

As the above loosely sketched map suggests, there are numerous kinds of places where media arts have emerged, and the role of the curator within them is not always clear, with key figures acting as lab managers, producers, or research professors. It also is not always obvious how curators can best show the work that emerges from these incubators. Yet curators have always been willing to try, using their strengths in refining the works and artists' input to make projects presentable to a public (keeping in mind that the public is comprised of a number of different audiences with their own reasons, respectively, for being interested). As such, New Media Scotland has repeatedly programmed art events for the Edinburgh International Festival and the Edinburgh Science Festival, just as Medialab Prado takes its *interactivos¿* workshop and exhibition program to other cities and venues as part of its skill-sharing and networking remit. Outside of Mexico, Centro Multimedia might be best known for its Transitio Festival and it is similarly impossible to think of Ars Electronica without considering the international aspect of its annual conference and festival, which functions as a kind of professional trade show (perhaps because the branding and documentation of the festival tends to be stronger than that of the artworks emerging year-round from its labs).

The question of how to best show the work emerging from these initiatives is one that is difficult to answer, as each work might have its own particular characteristics conditioning how it is received by its audiences or users (and how it is documented). For instance, there has been a long debate about the value of showing net-based art in physical spaces, with key examples of exhibitions since the early 2000s demonstrating the pros and cons of that practice, including The Walker Art Center's *gallery 9*, the Tate's online commissions, the Whitney Museum's *artport* (2001–) and *2002 Whitney Biennial*, and the *Net_Condition* (1999–2000) exhibition at the ZKM with its net art browser interface, to name just a handful. No one successful model exists, and in 2013 a number of exhibitions revisited online collections of web-based work, or practices meant for distribution via a server, and tried to reinvigorate, restage, or even re-enact them for gallery presentation, such as the exhibition *SAVE AS* (2013) curated by Raitis Smits from the RIXC medialab in Riga, which featured works from the late 1990s by JODI, Heath Bunting, Evan Roth, and others, installed on retro-fitted old desktop computers sitting on temporary-looking wooden shelving storage units and keeping the aesthetic of the archive in line with the age of the works.[7] While space is almost always already "public" on the Web, curatorial decision making is called into question whenever works leave the "studio" spaces of their creation to be placed in public spaces of reception. This is even the case when both those spaces are online—an artist may post their work on their own server but it may change its meaning when it is recontextualized into a curated online exhibition alongside other works. Due to its technological infrastructure, new media art often makes it possible to scale works up or down (handheld on a portable screen or projected? Audio on headphones or loudspeakers?) and "turn on or off" features or aspects of the work to suit the space.

The scalability and modularity of works made by using media technology does invite careful consideration—when a work meant for a small screen and single viewing is projected its feel and the experience of viewing it are changed. Interactive works might require careful set-up in terms of the pacing of interaction (one at a time or an arrangement where many can "play"), and the creation of light and dark spaces for audiences to engage with each other or the work. Works processing live data may need fixed Internet connections and good quality computers and projectors, as well as some signage or explanation outlining the significance of the live-ness, or ever-changing quality of the work. Generative work might require technology for producing the work's output, such as printers, cutters, or milling machines, and exhibition strategies addressing how and when to display its iterative results. The lab-grown nature of work might also lead to problems with its reception, risking the possibility that it might be perceived as being solely about its gee-whiz-bang prototypical newness (as noted at the start of this chapter in reference to the generally held misapprehension that technology-driven art can't compete with commercial technology). Curators may want to take work "out of the lab" in order to emphasize aspects of its aesthetics, interaction, or meaning beyond how it was made. This change of interface—sometimes just a change of space in which the work is shown—will necessarily change the meaning of the work, and may run counter to its intention. This conceptual challenge is one that can't be solved by a simple formula but perhaps by following "best practice" examples.

Festivalism

> I call it Festival Art: environmental stuff that, existing only in exhibition, exalts curators over dealers and a hazily evoked public over dedicated art mavens. The [1999 Venice] Biennale's director, the veteran Swiss impresario Harald Szeemann might be said to have invented Festivalism [...] Installation art, of which the founding father was Marcel Duchamp, used to nurture a quasi-political hostility to "commodity capitalism." That's over. The battle line between non-sellable and sellable art has become a cordial abyss, with crowd-beguiling Festival Art, on one side, and, on the other, humanity's eternal commerce in objects of esteem. (Marketed art works are not commodities, incidentally; economically, they behave more like handmade money.) (Schjeldahl 1999)

Festivals have played a large role in how new media art has circulated, in part because they are regular (to keep up with new developments in the field), mobile (taking place in different cities related to a globally interconnected though sometimes placeless—because virtual or online—activity), yet also specialist events (gathering a critical mass of like-minded people otherwise "curatorial invisible" to the artworld) (Cook and Graham 2010). These new media art festivals have distinguished themselves in key programmatic ways from the artworld's more common format of the "Biennial," emphasizing skill sharing and professional development rather than trying to reinforce market concerns with the product of art. Many case studies could be written about how these festivals—Transmediale in Berlin; ISEA, which moves every year; 01SJ in San Jose; Images and ImagineNATIVE in Toronto; LA Freewaves in California; Impakt in the Netherlands; Sonar in Barcelona, FutureEverything in Manchester, NEoN in Dundee (Figure 23.3), to name only a handful—have shaped both the work exhibited at them, and the discourses around new media arts practice emerging from them. As Peter Schjeldahl's (perhaps now outdated) criticism notes, festivals engender forms of art that are non-saleable, "environmental," exist only for the time of the exhibition, and then return to being a pile of parts (hardware, software, the infrastructure of display or participation) again at the end. General trends can be observed in the development of these festivals, which started as subject-specialist events (focused on video, music, film, or video gaming), and expanded to encompass digital creativity more widely—as for instance in the case of the SXSW (South by Southwest) music and film festival, which from 2007 onwards included a strand on "Interactivity." What follows here are three brief analyses of festival examples that

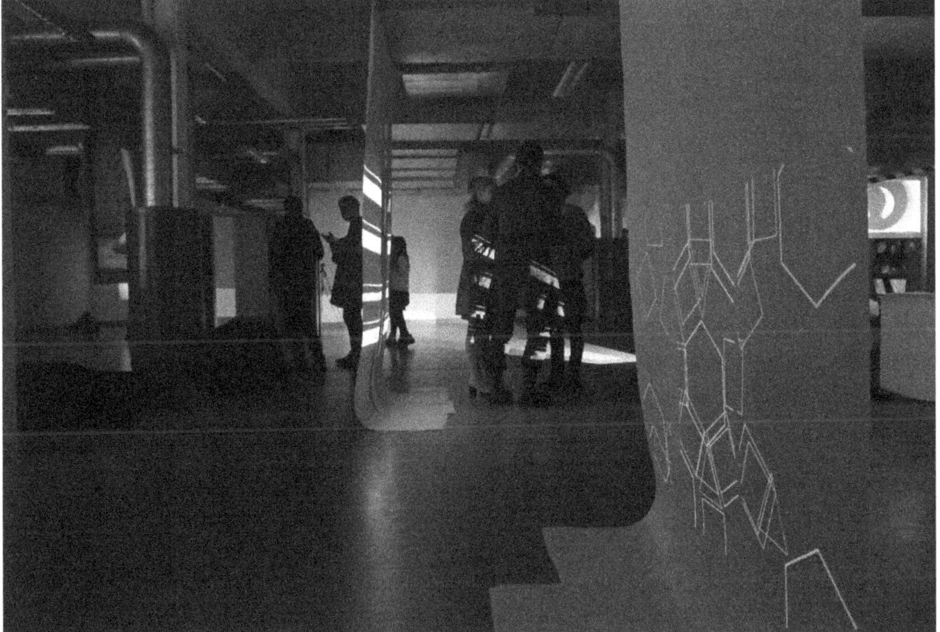

FIGURE 23.3 Installation view of NEoN Digital Arts Festival closing event (BYOB), Dundee, Scotland.

illustrate, on an anecdotal level, some of the differences between modes of curating and programming new media art.[8]

Due to its unique geographic positioning between the UK cities of Liverpool and Manchester, and the more rural environments of Cumbria and North Yorkshire, the AND (Abandon Normal Devices) Festival is located at institutions with gallery and cinema spaces (including FACT and Cornerhouse), and contributes to a gallery program at a number of institutions, while also organizing a variety of festival-specific events. The AND curatorial model is a cross between more traditional institutional curating and a commissioning agency—it is collaborative, with clear artistic vision and branding. Part of the AND Festival mission was to become a platform for creative initiatives in the region, strengthening collaboration between its cultural partners. The festival's curatorial process itself is also based on collaboration between curators from different institutions and partners. Working firmly within a curator-as-producer model, the festival does not have a main curator or an artistic director. The staff of AND are producers and managers who shape the program collaboratively with staff from partnering organizations.

This has meant that the festival has been able to stay focused on artistic risk taking and experimentation, with a keenly felt political slant. Its subtitle is "Festival of New Cinema and the Digital Culture," but it takes the abandonment of normality as its key calling. AND is also noted for its producers' and curators' endeavor to support long-term, process- and research-based work. John O'Shea's *Pigs Bladder Football*, mentioned above, was one of the works developed into exhibition form by AND. Among the reasons why they can do this is that they have been successful in attracting and nurturing a younger audience that is urban and familiar with the festival format in both cities (Liverpool and Manchester being just over 45 minutes' travel apart and hosts to numerous other arts festivals). Many events, such as workshops and screenings, take place during the day, with some of the most exciting live ones requiring advance booking and having limited capacity, which adds to the appeal of being out of the ordinary. The fact that Manchester is internationally renowned for festivals of experimental theater and performance—with participants as varied as Björk, Laurie Anderson, and Philip Glass—and the future-casting thinktank conference FutureEverything (formerly a music and sound festival called Futuresonic) means that another festival focused on the digital in a geographic location bursting with media industries is more readily accepted.

By contrast, the Transitio Festival of Electronic Arts and Video (emerging in 2003 out of a former film and video art festival) is a biennial key programming component of the Centro Multimedia in Mexico City, with funding from the government's cultural programming budget. In the alternate years, Centro Multimedia engages in an international conference on a topic of interest to the field of new media arts, such as biotechnology or open source software. The key components of the festival, devoted to a theme that is decided in advance, are a symposium, programming of exhibitions, screenings and performances, and a prize highlighting the work of young artists.

Transitio's mandate is that the Centro Multimedia, for each edition of the festival, must appoint a new artistic director who is responsible for the decision making in response to the chosen theme, as well as for the appointment of curators and curatorial projects, and the fee structure to be adopted. While guidance is given by the Centro Multimedia team—and generous use of other government-funded exhibition spaces around the city, such as Kunsthallen, small museums, and cultural centers, is offered—the director is encouraged to work within the format of what has worked well in previous editions, ensuring some continuity of the "look" and "feel" of the festival.

The fifth edition appointed an artistic director and curatorial team from outside Mexico for the first time, on the theme of "Biomediations"; I was one of the curators responsible. This international team may have worked to strengthen the reputation of the festival outside Mexico, but put additional pressure on the local organizers to negotiate venues, technology rentals, and installation details in response to artists' demands being issued at a distance. The emphasis on showing new installation work is greatly problematized by the format of a festival, which generally runs for fewer than ten days, as it is potentially cost-prohibitive to ship physical works of art and negotiate spaces for such a short exhibition timeframe. It takes time to build partnerships with venues in a city, or to convince an organization's board that the majority of the year's programming budget might be spent on such a short-lived event. Mexico City is a huge and densely populated city with considerable distances between the venues and varied local audiences (numbering in the many hundreds at opening events) for each of them. That said, the intense exchanges that can take place when artists and symposium speakers—including theorists, curators, and producers—are all physically present are worth the organizational anxieties.

The AV Festival in the Northeast of the UK, founded in 2002, can be said to be halfway between these two models. It has a full-time, year-round artistic director based in the region and has thus far only been able to hire production staff in the run-up to the main event. Despite, or perhaps because of, this small team, it hosts tightly curated exhibitions and commissioned works at partner institutions in the cities of Newcastle, Gateshead, Sunderland, and Middlesborough. Hardly anything but the AV Festival would link those venues, as some are collecting museums, others Kunsthallen or artist-run galleries, some science centers or libraries, and, of course, cinemas. This presents a challenge for branding and for journalistic research: Are all the works art? Can they all be given the same weight as finished projects rather than experimental prototypes? By developing relationships over the long term with its partners, the festival has moved from what started as a two-weekend, ten-day event in previous editions to a month-long season, in which different weekends might be programmed for target different audiences—one for live music, another for film, for instance—and the exhibitions can fit a museum's usual four- to six-week timetable. For the 2012 edition of the festival (themed: *As Slow As Possible*), one national newspaper sent three different journalists—a music critic, a film critic, and an art critic—to cover the events, each writing entirely separate reviews from within the discourse of their own disciplines.

How?

Festivals continue to be a good format for experiencing new media art because their short duration alleviates some of the challenges of its presentation—from the potential lack of robustness of the technology employed in the work to the strains of heavy audience interaction with that technology. However, the drawbacks of the "festivalism" of new media art are that it promotes "short-termism" in both the presentation and appreciation of the work, emphasizes newness in the work itself, and struggles to move new media art away from trendy topics to more considered historicization that presentation within a museum program might allow.

Additionally, the curatorial role in festivals and their temporary installations of art definitely shifts further toward that of producer. Producers are the ones who coordinate and facilitate the collaborative process. Since most of the work is done on a project-by-project basis, even if it has been proposed and conceptually framed by a curator, the process of delivery is taken over by the producers once the project has been "agreed" upon. Festivals and commissioning agencies usually focus on "delivery" rather than generating critical debate or producing knowledge around certain practices (Krzemień Barkley 2013), though there are exceptions to this, as in the three examples discussed.

The danger is that this leads to the weakening of the curatorial role, as well as the role of institutions, beyond facilitating the production of new work. It can be argued that institutional curating, by adopting models from festivals and commission agencies, loses sight of its other key roles—producing knowledge, instigating debate, presenting critical discourses, developing critical contexts in which to discuss emerging art, as well as historicizing the practices (Krzemień Barkley 2013).

In an earlier text I described three types of exhibitions that might respond to the challenges presented by new media art and still maintain some of these other aspects of curatorial work: the "exhibition as software program or data flow," such as a traveling exhibition that generates a network of gallery spaces (each "node" able to adapt and modify the content displaying different aspects and outcomes of each project); the "exhibition as trade show" (a short term, commercial-like presentation for projects requiring specialized technical support or the testing out of new projects); and the "exhibition as broadcast" (in which the audience rather than the artwork might be what is distributed, and events might take place simultaneously in different locations with the use of networked technologies). I also theorized models of curatorial practice, which accompanied the changing exhibition formats: the iterative, the modular, the distributed (Cook 2008). Exciting examples of works of new media art can be found in all these types of exhibitions and others besides.

Many of the curatorial "platforms" responding to new media art practices are themselves hybrids addressing the hybridity of the forms they serve. They also highlight distribution as much as exhibition. For example, *Kingdom of Piracy* (KOP) was both an online and sometimes physically sited workspace that was first launched in 2001, presented at Ars Electronica in 2002, FACT in 2003, and other places beyond that, with commissioned artworks and writing projects curated by Shu Lea Cheang, Armin Medosch, and Yukiko Shikata.[9] KOP encouraged remixing, released digital content freely, and questioned the proprietary structures of art making and exhibition. Another example is *or-bits.com*, a web-based curatorial platform curated by Marialaura Ghidini devoted to supporting practices and dialogues around artistic production, display, and distribution online.[10] In the *or-bits.com* project, thematically structured exhibitions of web-based artworks are complemented by projects in other formats such as radio streams, limited edition boxes of multiples, booksprints and publications, writing and mapping workshops, and exhibitions in physical gallery spaces.

Yet, despite the already long tradition of curatorial experimentation with presentation models of "emergent" and hybrid practices (especially digital media, and "socially engaged," collaborative and participatory practices),[11] gallery exhibition formats—even within institutions dedicated to presenting "new" practices—have proven to be inflexible, and remain largely conventional (Krzemień Barkley 2013). Some possible solutions, or ways to reinvigorate the formats for presenting and distributing new media art, which could be adapted to the more cautiously static museum or gallery settings, include the following.

Context-Specific/Context-Responsive/Context-Sensitive Curating

While art theory has long wrangled with the notion of the site-specific—in relation to sculpture and other work presented in public space—new media art, with its responsiveness to its context, aligns itself more closely with the notion of the "context-specific," indicating an expanded concept of site-specificity that understands site as dynamic, "constituted by social, economical and political processes" (Kwon 2004, 3). The idea of the "context-specific" draws from debates on public, socially engaged community art and place-based practices. New media art shares characteristics with many of these types of projects, and so the results of their critical analysis could be usefully applied to new media. The curatorial training program of de Appel inculcates its students in "context-responsive" practices, identifying its focus as "curating in the expanded field," which is investigated through "the polarity between freelance and institutional curating" (De Appel web site). Curator Maria Lind refers to this approach as "context-sensitive" curating (Lind 2013). Key questions to this approach to curating are raised by art theorist Claire Doherty:

> How can curators support artistic engagements with places which can be seen to be "constructed out of a particular constellation of social relations"? [...] How do such works coalesce to form a meaningful "exhibition" for the biennial visitor when the experience of place itself is an event in progress? [...] How do context-specific projects and artworks become meaningful outside the signifying context of the exhibition? (Doherty 2007)

This is exactly the challenge when the "constellation of social relations" is the network itself, such as the Web, or a technological platform whose development is in progress. An example might be *Anti-Data-Mining (ADM) VIII*, created by the artist group RBYN in 2011, which exists within the online stock market: it is a robot that trades based on algorithms, searching for patterns in order to predict other moves made by other software bots. *Anti-Data-Mining (ADM) VIII* is communicated via its own Twitter feed, and the "performance" (as the artists call it) stops when the project reaches bankruptcy (the bot is not designed to make money per se, and its initial kitty was the amount of the grant given to the artists to make the work).[12] Curating this long-term research project work into an exhibition about data flows, or markets, or software art, involves exhibiting documentation of its existence and progress via its web site, as the actual "place" of its workings is not publicly accessible.

Durational Approaches

Given the rapid pace of change in technology and the often lamentable emphasis on the newness of the work, the idea, or its production or distribution process, a retaliatory strategy to ensure considered attention to the work might be to slow down. Such a durational approach would involve working over long timeframes, in a cumulative way, developing relationships with specific groups intrinsic to the intention of the work or working method of the artist (for instance, working with the elderly, young people, or war veterans, who may be necessary participants in the creation or public manifestation of the work).[13] These types of projects are often initiated in response to initiatives across a given place—tied in with regeneration, educational engagement, or other local government agendas. One of the key problems with this model has been raised by artist and educator Dave Beech:

> Duration is problematic because it is presented as solution for art's social contradictions, whereas the only viable political solution must be to problematize time for art. If we are going to think politically about art, site, publics and time, we need to put the ideology of duration behind us. We have to stop keeping tabs on our own use of time. Let's think instead about delay, interruption, stages, flows, of instantaneous performances, lingering documents, of temporary objects and permanent moments, of repetition, echo and seriality and break with this binary opposition altogether. (Beech 2011, 325)

Dave Beech's statement nearly perfectly describes the project *Foghorn Requiem* (2013) by Lise Autogena and Joshua Portway, in collaboration with composer Orlando Gough, produced in the UK for the Festival of the Northeast.[14] The project involved the coordination of a new piece of artist-created software, customized foghorns mounted on over fifty different boats of all sizes (from international ferries and cruise ships to small lifeboats), an on-land foghorn at a lighthouse about to be decommissioned, three brass bands and their conductor, and a live audience of thousands for the one-off, outdoor concert. The customized horns were designed to sound in response to the software, which would calculate distance, direction, wind speed, climatic conditions, and the like. The "lingering document" is the audience's collective memory of the deafening but plaintiff wail of the last sounding of the Souter Lighthouse foghorn, which resonated long after the software failed to trigger the composition fully.

Since new media art offers the possibility of simultaneous production and reception—with generative processes, live streaming, design, or modulation on the fly—the challenge of breaking with time, without the work itself breaking down, is tricky. Some projects are essentially iterative—it takes time to manage and coordinate groups of people, document outcomes, develop prototypes, and then move on to the next stage—and this is a mammoth challenge to curatorial models of creation/exhibition. In New Media Scotland's InSpace in Edinburgh, for example, the response to this challenge was to capitalize on the flexibility of the space, and the hunger of their repeat audience, and create formats that enabled them to engage in both short-term turnaround projects, such as fortnightly events, as well as long-term projects, such as commissions, which could be revealed in stages as and when they were ready for public outing with more or less fanfare.

Collaborative Approaches

The most obvious challenge of new media art (and many other forms of socially engaged practices) is the fact that the creation and presentation of the work is so highly collaborative, with different people adopting different roles on conceptual, technical, and administrative levels. Projects are often defined collaboratively, within a team, and with communities, partners, and stakeholders. Collaborative curatorial approaches are lauded in tough economic climates (when it saves money to engage in co-commissioning, by combining resources, and seeking alternative sources of funding). In a museological context, collaborative ways of working can also overcome resistance to new media art, in that other members of the exhibition or collections team could rely on well-informed colleagues, whether in-house or adjunct, to explain the relevance of the work, for example when museums curate exhibitions across departments, as in the case of the exhibition *010101: Art in Technological Times* held at SFMoMA in 2001, which drew on expertise across art, design, architecture, film, and video, and had exhibitions in gallery space and online.[15]

However, collaborative approaches to the curating of new media art entail a danger of becoming too unfocused, as curators may be forced to work on a project-by-project basis because funds are not available for longer term planning, or because partnerships change as people move about on short-term contracts. Not all museums have been open to collaborating with curators-at-large or host adjunct positions to include this "specialism" in their program, and curators have often felt the precarity of outsourcing their skills. Starting in the early 2000s, a number of institutions of contemporary art lost their emerging art form curators due to a lack of appreciation of the ongoing value of such work on the part of institutional directors, as the uncertainty of what "going digital" meant and misconceptions about what such initiatives might cost swirled around their heads.[16]

The other consideration with regard to collaborative approaches is that there is the risk of the curatorial remit becoming too opportunistic—realizing projects because certain time-limited funding is available for them (such as medical, genetic, or scientific funding for projects that engage with biotechnology). This connects to the larger problem within the new media arena of works being curated because they are trendy, or "on trend" with themes playing out in wider technological culture.

Why?

In a *Guardian* interview, the CEO of FACT in Liverpool, Mike Stubbs, was asked to name one thing that is key to running a successful venue. He replied, "Continuing re-invention, knowing your audience, and enabling the most direct routes between the themes and messages explored by the artists and the public that will be coming to see their work" (Caines 2012).

Continual reinvention is the key challenge for curators in adapting their understanding of where, when, and how new media and digital arts are best received by audiences. As the above examples have shown, new media art has been at home in its self-created "digital commons," but in order to be in closer dialogue with contemporary art, design, scientific research, or technological development, it has had to imagine new kinds of museums. Are these currently observable formats of exhibition, presentation, and reception doomed (or best utilized) as short-term existences whilst the ground beneath their feet settles? Or do they presage possible futures for how the digital arts might create entirely new types of institutions which cause us to rethink the notion that art history resides solely in the museum? Given the rapid rate of change within the technological sphere, context-responsive curating might raise the prospect of "context-generative" curating of new media art (Krzemień Barkley 2013). The rhetoric of constant reinvention of the types of spaces, places, and contexts most suited to new media art—whether online, in print, via mobile devices, in public space, etc.—seems to be logically contradictory when the institution's own format is very clearly defined by its spaces (whether physical or virtual) and when it has a traditional approach to its main collecting activity or programming strands.

The sheer practicalities of working within certain exhibition formats strongly limit an institution's flexibility and suitability for presentation of technologically or conceptually more experimental and hybrid practices. Curatorial approaches and models of production emerging on the "peripheries" of institutional practice, such as collaboration and engagement programs, or even beyond the institutions, such as festivals, are not without their limitations, but seem to offer a greater potential for incubating new practices (Krzemień Barkley 2013).

Notes

1 This is a contentious claim based on a widely held assumption, as little scholarship is published on the place of media art in contemporary art biennials. One exception is Franco (2013), "The First Computer Art Show at the 1970 Venice Biennale. An Experiment or Product of the Bourgeois Culture?"
2 CRUMB, founded in 2000 at the University of Sunderland by Sarah Cook and Beryl Graham, is an online resource for curators of new media art. See http://www.crumbweb.org.
3 As Annette Schindler has noted (in a report about European media arts funding, which she produced with Andreas Broeckmann), the field of media arts has often held an ambivalent position toward visual and contemporary arts. In her analysis some media art "pioneers" (artists such as JODI, and Ubermorgen) are completely integrated into the mainstream visual art discourse (evidenced by their solo shows in European kunsthalles), while other artists regretfully have little access to the discourse, and continue to seek recognition from the mainstream (Schindler 2011).
4 See for instance: Obrist (2008); Hiller and Martin (2002).
5 However, as Christiane Paul has noted, "it would be misguided to assume that new media art intentionally engages in Institutional Critique as a field of artistic practice. Only in the case of Internet art, which exists in its own potentially global exhibition space and does not need an institution to be presented to the public, did Institutional Critique occasionally become an explicit focus of artistic explorations" (Paul 2006).
6 See the discussion on the CRUMB mailing list for October 2013 hosted by Charlotte Frost. http://www.crumbweb.org (accessed January 4, 2015).
7 Another recent experiment are the exhibitions of NETescopio (netescopio.meiac.es)—an online archive of net-based art developed by the Museo Extremeño e Iberoamericano de Arte Contemporáneo—curated by artist Gustavo Romano. In these restagings, called *Desmontajes, Re/apropiaciones e Intrusiones. Tácticas del Arte en la Red* (which took place at Laboratorio Arte Alameda and the Spanish Cultural Centre in Mexico City in 2013) some of the web-based works were re-performed by invited net artists in a live mash-up vj style. For video walk-through documentation see http://www.youtube.com/watch?v=qAj5D8v98ZU" \l "t=48"http://www.youtube.com/watch?v=qAj5D8v98ZU#t=48 (accessed January 4, 2015).

8 These examples were chosen due to the author's first-hand experience of curating exhibitions within them and witnessing, as an audience member, numerous editions of them.
9 Kingdom of Piracy: http://residence.aec.at/kop/ (accessed January 4, 2015).
10 Or-bits: http://or-bits.com/ (accessed January 4, 2015).
11 For the beginnings of a list, see http://archive.rhizome.org/artbase/56398/timeline.html (accessed January 4, 2015).
12 As the artists write, the bot is "designed to invest and speculate on the financial markets. Its decisions are taken with the help of an internal algorithmic intelligence system, and can be influenced by a wide range of external arbitrary parameters. The whole decision system allows the program to foresee the next moves in the markets, while it tries to identify and anticipate the relevant and effective patterns within the financial chaotic oscillations." See http://antidatamining.net/ (accessed January 4, 2015).
13 Thinking about the duration in the context of curatorial practice has been informed by the texts in O'Neill and Doherty (2011).
14 More information is available at http://foghornrequiem.org/ (accessed January 4, 2015).
15 See the report on *010101* by Beryl Graham (2002).
16 The then director of the ICA in London, Ekow Eshun, was lambasted by those in the live art and new media art field for claiming, in his notice canceling the program in October 2008, that the art form lacked "the depth and cultural urgency" to justify "continued and significant investment" (see comments and discussion at http://www.theguardian.com/stage/theatreblog/2008/oct/23/ica-live-arts-closure?commentpage=1 (accessed January 4, 2015). In 2012, the director of the National Gallery in London clearly stated his dislike of video, conceptual, and performance art, all of which are precursors to new media art practice (see http://www.theguardian.com/culture/charlottehigginsblog/2012/oct/15/nicholas-penny-video-art (accessed January 4, 2015).

References

Beech, Dave. 2011. "The Ideology of Duration in the Dematerialised Monument. Art, Sites, Public and Time." In *Locating the Producers. Durational Approaches to Public Art*, edited by Paul O'Neill and Claire Doherty, 312–325. Amsterdam: Valiz.

Caines, Matthew. 2012. "Arts Head: Mike Stubbs, Director, FACT." *Guardian*, September 25. http://www.theguardian.com/culture-professionals-network/culture-professionals-blog/2012/sep/25/mike-stubbs-fact-liverpool-interview?commentpage=1 (accessed June 25, 2013).

Century, Michael. 2009. "Encoding Motion in the Early Computer: Knowledge Transfers between Studio and Laboratory." In *Place Studies in Art, Media, Science and Technology* edited by Gunalan Nadarajan and Andreas Broeckmann, 29–45. Berlin: VdG.

Cook, Sarah. 2001. "An Interview with Matthew Gansallo." http://www.crumbweb.org/getInterviewDetail.php?id=1 (accessed January 4, 2015).

Cook, Sarah. 2008. "Immateriality and Its Discontents. An Overview of Main Models and Issues for Curating New Media." In *New Media in the White Cube and Beyond: Curatorial Models for Digital Art*, edited by Christiane Paul, 26–49. Berkeley, CA: University of California Press.

Cook, Sarah, and Beryl Graham. 2010. *Rethinking Curating: Art After New Media*. Cambridge, MA: The MIT Press.

Current debate (notes) at University of Central Lancashire in partnership with the Harris Museum, Preston, on May 24, 2011.

De Appel Curatorial Programme. Web site. "History of de Appel CP." http://www.deappel.nl/cp/p/1/ (accessed January 4, 2015).

Dewdney, Andrew, and Peter Ride. 2006. *The New Media Handbook*. Abingdon, UK. Routledge.

Dietz, Steve, Howard Besser, Ann Borda, and Kati Geber with Pierre Lévy. 2004. "Virtual Museum (of Canada): The Next Generation." http://besser.tsoa.nyu.edu/howard/Papers/vm_tng.doc (accessed January 15, 2015).

Doherty, Claire. 2004. "The Institution is Dead! Long Live the Institution! Contemporary Art and New Institutionalism." *Engage* 15. http://www.engage.org/seebook.aspx?id=697 (accessed January 15, 2013).

Doherty, Claire. 2007. "Curating Wrong Places ... Or Where Have All the Penguins Gone." In *Curating Subjects*, edited by Paul O'Neill. Amsterdam: De Appel. http://salonesdeartistas.com/wp-content/uploads/2011/09/claire-doherty-curating-wrong-places-2007.pdf (accessed January 20, 2013).

Druckrey, Timothy, with Ars Electronica, eds. 1999. *Ars Electronica: Facing the Future*. Cambridge, MA: The MIT Press.

Ekeberg, Jonas, ed. 2003. *New Institutionalism*, Verksted 1. Oslo: Office for Contemporary Art Norway.

Farquharson, Alex. 2006. "Bureaux de Change." *Frieze* 101. http://www.frieze.com/issue/article/bureaux_de_change/ (accessed January 4, 2015).

Franco, Francesca. 2013. "The First Computer Art Show at the 1970 Venice Biennale. An Experiment or Product of the Bourgeois Culture?" In *Relive Media Art Histories*, edited by Sean Cubitt and Paul Thomas. Cambridge, MA: The MIT Press.

Gleadowe, Teresa. 2000. "Curating in a Changing Climate." In *Curating in the 21st Century*, edited by Gavin Wade, 29–38. Wolverhampton, UK: New Art Gallery, Wallsall, and University of Wolverhampton.

Graham, Beryl. 2002. *Curating New Media Art: SFMOMA and 010101*. http://www.crumbweb.org/getCRUMBReports.php?&sublink=2 (accessed January 4, 2015).

Harris, Craig, ed. 1999. *Art and Innovation. The Xerox Parc Artist-in-Residence Program*. Cambridge, MA: The MIT Press.

Hiller, Susan, and Sarah Martin, eds. 2002. *The Producers: Contemporary Curators in Conversation* (5). B.Read/Eight. Gateshead, UK: BALTIC.

Jones, Caitlin. 2005. 'My Art World Is Bigger Than Your Art World." *The Believer* 3(10): 3–13.

Jones, Caitlin. 2010. "The Function of the Studio (when the studio is a laptop)." *Art Lies* 67.

Krzemień Barkley, Aneta. 2013. "Contemporary Models of Institutional and Curatorial Praxis: A Study of the Foundation for Art and Creative Technology (FACT)." PhD thesis draft. University of Liverpool.

Kwon, Miwon. 2004. *One Place After Another: Site Specific Art and Locational Identity*. Cambridge, MA: The MIT Press.

Lind, Maria. 2013. "About Working With and Around Tensa Kunsthall." Presentation at LJMU, Liverpool, March 27, 2013.

Möntman, Nina, ed. 2006. *Art and Its Institutions. Current Conflicts, Critique and Collaborations.* London: Black Dog Publishing.

Obrist, Hans Ulrich. 2008. *A Brief History of Curating.* Zurich: JRP.

O'Neill, Paul, and Claire Doherty, eds. 2011. *Locating the Producers: Durational Approaches to Public Art.* Amsterdam: Valiz.

Paul, Christiane. 2006. "New Media Art and Institutional Critique: Networks vs. Institutions." In *Institutional Critique and After: Soccas Symposium*, edited by John C. Welchman, Isabelle Graw, and Alexander Alberro. Zurich: JRP Ringier. http://intelligentagent.com/writing_samples/CP_New_Media_Art_IC.pdf.

Paul, Christiane, ed. 2008. *New Media in the White Cube and Beyond: Curatorial Models for Digital Art.* Berkeley, CA: University of California Press.

Perry, Grayson. 2013. "Nice Rebellion, Welcome In!" The BBC Reith Lecture: Playing to the Gallery, October 29. http://www.bbc.co.uk/programmes/b00729d9 (accessed January 4, 2015).

Quaranta, Domenico. 2010. *Media, New Media, Postmedia.* Milan: Postmedia Books.

Raunig, Gerald, and Gene Ray, eds. 2009. *Art and Contemporary Critical Practice: Reinventing Institutional Critique.* London: MayFlyBooks.

Sakrowski, Robert. 2007. CuratingYouTube. http://www.curatingyoutube.net/about/.

Schindler, Annette, and Andreas Broeckman. 2011. "Media Art Funding Survey." Notes from a talk held on May 3, 2011 at PNEK, Oslo, Norway. http://www.mikro.in-berlin.de/wiki/tiki-index.php?page=Media+Art+Funding+Survey (accessed January 4, 2015).

Schjeldahl, Peter. 1999. "The Art World: Festivalism." *The New Yorker*, July 5.

Sheikh, Simon. 2006. "Notes on Institutional Critique." *Eipcp webjournal.* http://eipcp.net/transversal/0106/sheikh/en (accessed March 15, 2013).

Stam, Deirdre, C. 1993. "The Informed Muse: The Implications of 'The New Museology' for Museum Practice." *Museum Management and Curatorship* 12(3): 267–283.

Vergo, Peter, ed.1989. *The New Museology.* London: Reaktion Books.

24

The Nuts and Bolts of Handling Digital Art

Ben Fino-Radin

Introduction

During the short timeframe in which there has been a discourse on the conservation of digital art, ethical, philosophic, economic, and institutional issues have been extensively discussed. It is surprisingly rare, though, to find detailed technical studies of actual on-the-ground, hands-on conservation of digital works of art, either as artwork-centric case studies, or as a general technical overview of day-to-day practices. This belies the fact that such conservation work is in fact being conducted in institutions collecting digital art. The problem is due partially to the fact that it is quite common for specialists to be temporarily contracted, from outside the conservation field, for assisting with the conservation of complex digital artworks. The technical knowledge and skills of such specialists, however, rarely penetrate the scholarly discourse of such practices, and thus, such discourse is rarely grounded in hard technical fact. A truly deep material understanding of digital art has yet to permeate the conservation field in the way it has in the older and more canonized mediums of analog video and film.

The intent of this chapter is to serve as a thorough introduction and guide to the fundamental goals, concepts, and theories of the conservation of digital works of art, and to then delve fully into a survey of tools, methods, and practices used in the day-to-day care of these works—drawing from fields such as digital preservation, digital forensics, retrocomputing, and video game preservation. To illustrate these concepts and practices, real-world examples from media conservation at New York's Museum of Modern Art (MoMA) will be employed. Examples are not provided in a purely case-study format, but rather as simple and practical examples to more fully illustrate a broader and holistic practice. This chapter should not be interpreted as a linear guide—the various phases of the conservation lifecycle of artworks presented here, in practice, can occur in virtually any order. Indeed, certain aspects covered in this

A Companion to Digital Art, First Edition. Edited by Christiane Paul.

chapter may never be applied to a work at all due to limitations of resources of time and funding. Such is the reality of conservation practice in the real world, where time, budgets, and people are finite.

Fundamental Concepts

The fundamental issue addressed by this chapter is the fact that any work of art that employs technology of any kind is inherently tied to a market that is opposed to long-term preservation and stability—obsolescence has come to be essential to the economics of technology. This problem of obsolescence and reliance on the market is certainly a prevalent force in the conservation of *all* contemporary art;[1] however, it is especially fundamental in media conservation. Obsolescence is an essential inherent vice that defines the unique responsibilities of a media conservator. The unique roles of conservation of technology-based art could be summarized as the following: mitigating obsolescence, navigating the minefield of variability, and protecting the integrity of the artwork. Pip Laurenson (2006) has formulated the following as the fundamental roles and responsibilities of contemporary conservation and media conservation:

- Conservation is the means by which the work-defining properties are documented, understood, and maintained.
- Conservation as a practice aims to preserve the identity of the work of art.
- Conservation aims to be able display the work in the future.
- Conservation enables different possible authentic installations of the work to be realized in the future.

Technologies and materials in consumer products age, stop working, and become difficult or impossible to replace. This problem will never end. That such products become part of artworks means conservators are fighting a battle that *cannot* be won by opposition to change and strict notions of authenticity, but rather finds success through elegantly coping with and managing acceptable degrees of change. This is best powered by deep understanding of the fundamental nature of these technologies and materials, their inherent vice, and their unique properties and characteristics.

Learning the Work—Initial Conservation Assessment and Interview

The responsibilities of conservation begin even before a work of any sort enters a collection. Conservators play an essential role in the pre-acquisition and acquisition process, helping curators to understand latent preservation risks inherent in a given work, what materials must actually be collected, and long-term costs. When dealing with digital art the very first phase of the acquisition process is an initial assessment of the work conducted either through direct interaction with and examination of the work itself, or research conducted solely through documentation of the work. This initial assessment by a conservator is critical. Were the collecting institution to rely solely on the artist's discretion to define what digital objects and constituent parts of the work were to be collected, in many cases, this material alone would be insufficient for long-term preservation. Often it may be the case that the artist's first impulse is to readily provide collectors and institutions with exhibition-ready materials. While best archival practices have permeated the analog video world—owing in part to the artist's reliance on production houses for the creation of master tapes—in the digital world, where the artist is no longer reliant on professionals for production and distribution, all bets are off. The purpose of the initial conservation assessment is to understand specific and broad technical features of the work: What is the work? Is it software? Is it web-based? Is it digital video? What tools did the artist use to create the work? What external dependencies are required to properly render the work for exhibition? Does the work require an Internet connection, and if so, what is it supporting? Asking such questions of the work forms an initial set of facts—or in many cases, unanswered questions—that can inform an initial pre-acquisition conversation between the artist and the collecting institution.

Once a basic and fundamental understanding of the artwork's material form has been reached, it is time to engage the artist in a series of questions, in order to further inform and guide the acquisition decision-making process. The desire of the institution, of course, is to acquire any and all materials and information required for the long-term stewardship of the artwork, regardless of what any future conservation strategy for the work at hand may be. After one has assessed the form and boundaries of the work, it is central to accomplishing this goal to learn exactly how the artist created the end result—understanding the production environment, tools, and decision-making process. Rather than requiring artists to meet a strict format policy based on what the institution deems may be an *archival* format, the intent in this phase of the acquisition is to understand what might constitute a *master* or *archival format* given the specific and particular production environment of the work at hand. The form this dialogue takes can vary greatly, depending to a very great extent on the time the conservator and artist have available. However, a surprising amount of ground can be covered through a brief e-mail exchange comprising a handful of very basic questions. There is no magic list of essential questions that covers all bases in all situations. Instead, questions should be tailored to the work, with the goal of first understanding the artist's process. The second goal should be to understand any recreation or reformatting of the work that has occurred prior to acquisition. It is often the case that by the time a work is being acquired by an institution, the artist has had to recreate, revisit, or produce new exhibition files for a given artwork. If this is the case, it is critical to understand the process used by the artist: what files serve as the "masters," what tools were used, what were their criteria for quality assurance, and what form the work took in any subsequent exhibition contexts.

This pre-acquisition dialogue is not to be mistaken for a formal artist's interview. An artist interview is a critical tool for delving deeper into specific conservation issues latent in the work, usually, post-acquisition. Much has been written on the methodology of artist's interviews (Beerkens 2012), and the interview is well established as a tool in contemporary conservation. It is in no way specific to the conservation of artworks that employ media or technology. In the mid-2000s, the Variable Media Network attempted to simplify and standardize the process of the artist's interview through the development of a questionnaire. This methodology, however, had severe inherent biases—namely its scripted question-based format, and its rather dichotomic framing of "storage, emulation, migration, and reinterpretation" as mutually exclusive strategies. Coming to realize these flaws, the Variable Media Questionnaire[2] eventually evolved away from being a static list of questions to be posed to artists, and into a more general tool for building custom questionnaires for any constituents. Despite the value that interviews with artists can offer, it is critical to integrate such documentation and evidence as simply one factor among many—not as factual guidance that should dictate the life of an artwork, but as qualitative evidence. Media conservators, of course, hold the perspective of the artist as crucial to the balance of factors that inform the understanding of an artwork, and are chiefly concerned with documenting this—however, the artist's interview should not put the artist in the position of making "life or death" decisions such as whether or not the artwork should be *discarded* in the event that a fundamental technology ceases to function. To pose such drastic scenarios to the artist in the cold format of a scripted questionnaire disregards and denies the sociological complexities involved in the very situation of the interview. Glenn Wharton and Fernando Domínguez Rubio write:

> As conservators of contemporary art expand their practice to include artist interviews, they have a lot to learn from allied professions with years of experience in qualitative research. Oral historians, anthropologists, and sociologists know the advantages but also the risks involved with the use of interview research [...] interviews are research tools with potentially problematic assumptions and unintended consequences. [...] The questions we ask, and the ones we don't, as well as how we ask them, shapes the kind of responses and information we obtain. It is for this reason that interviews are better understood as guided conversations. (Wharton and Rubio 2013)

Wharton and Rubio go on to discuss the interview situation as a scenario wherein the artists "stage" themselves—presenting an image and opinions, wittingly or not, that may not be consistent with the reality of the artwork. An interview is simply a recording of a specific snapshot of the artist's evolving self in a highly contextual and loaded situation. Considering the setting of the interview, the interviewer, and the context of the institution that is collecting the work, all information produced in an interview setting is in fact far from objective fact. To take such interview questions as the canonical guide for the future conservation treatment of the work would, somewhat ironically, accomplish the opposite of what the conservator sets out to do—the act would freeze the work in time, according to the parameters and variables that were present in the particular interview. A more effective use of artist's interview practice recognizes conservation's own subjectivity, and views the artist's interview as merely one factor, a very important one, in the media conservator's holistic consideration of the work rather than an immutable checklist of questions.

Collection and Capture

Regardless of the broader form of an artwork—be it a complex installation that includes digital video, an executable piece of software, or a single-channel digital video—all digital components of an artwork are generally delivered to collecting institutions on some sort of tangible carrier of digital information—a hard drive, thumb drive, or optical disc (such as a CD or DVD). It is today understood that such tangible media carriers are not acceptable forms of storage for long-term preservation, and that the digital objects they contain must be captured and migrated to a centralized form of digital storage that is properly monitored and maintained by IT professionals. This point of capture is a critical moment in that there are essential facts of provenance that must be documented: where the digital object originally came from, what process was undertaken to capture the digital objects, by whom they were captured, and when. The digital archives field has similar concerns, and in order to meet these needs has adopted many tools and methods originating in the field of "digital forensics":

> The same forensics software that indexes a criminal suspect's hard drive allows the archivist to prepare a comprehensive manifest of the electronic files a donor has turned over for accession; the same hardware that allows the forensics investigator to create an algorithmically authenticated "image" of a file system allows the archivist to ensure the integrity of digital content once captured from its source media; the same data-recovery procedures that allow the specialist to discover, recover, and present as trial evidence an "erased" file may allow a scholar to reconstruct a lost or inadvertently deleted version of an electronic manuscript—and do so with enough confidence to stake reputation and career. (Kirschenbaum, Ovenden, and Redwine 2010)

Tools that provide such detailed and standards-based documentation of the original carrier media and the process by which the digital objects were extracted are not only useful in preserving whole computer environments, but are helpful even when the tangible carrier is simply a delivery device with no inherent worth as a physical artifact. If the delivery device is from the artist, it may contain contextual evidence that would be of great interest and potential use to researchers interested in technical art history. By capturing detailed metadata about the original order of files, the file system(s) present on the original hard drive, information about its partition map, technical details of the artist's working environment are preserved—this information may prove invaluable in future conservation scenarios, just as an X-ray revealing the characteristics of a painting's canvas weave may provide critical evidence for identification or authentication.

There are ample free and open source tools for aiding in this acquisition process. A project led by the School of Information and Library Science at the University of North Carolina, Chapel Hill (SILS) and the Maryland Institute for Technology in the Humanities (MITH) called BitCurator has endeavored to gather the best free and open source digital forensics tools in one portable environment. This offers those working in digital archives, museum conservation, and generally any cultural heritage collection tasked with the acquisition of physical media carriers, a soup-to-nuts system for managing all phases of this process while employing standards-based metadata for the documentation of process and material. There are, however, some basic needs that can be met even in the absence of the adoption of a full suite of tools such as BitCurator. In the Museum of Modern Art's conservation department, we have developed a simple and basic tool[3] to act as a stopgap until a more developed digital forensics workflow is put into practice. This tool provides the basic assurance that files are transferred from the tangible media carrier to centralized storage flawlessly, ensuring bit-for-bit authenticity.

The following sections provide examples of some solutions for the capture of specific tangible media carrier types. These carriers have been divided into two sections: contemporary carriers that can easily be connected to contemporary acquisition workstations, and legacy media carriers that are more challenging to work with. For all examples of disk imaging and capture workflows a Lenovo X230 ThinkPad with two bootable operating systems—Ubuntu 12.04 LTS, and Windows 7 (64 bit)—was used.

Mountable Contemporary Materials: 3.5" High Density Floppy Disks

Why, you may ask, is a section covering contemporary media carriers leading off with something so antiquated as a floppy disk? While certainly not contemporary, these disks are quite commonly found in artists' personal archives if they were working with computers during the 1990s. Secondly, 3.5" floppy disks that are marked "High Density" can today be accessed very easily with contemporary USB floppy disk drives, which are at the time of writing both affordable and abundantly available. These drives, unfortunately, are only able to read 1.2 MB high density (HD) floppies, leaving 3.5" double-sided double-density (DSDD) disks, and 5.25" floppy disks out in the dark. Identifying the difference between HD and DSDD 3.5" floppy disks can be easily accomplished by counting the number of holes present in the two back corners of the disk (the side held when inserting a disk). HD floppies have two holes, while DSDD disks only have one. Identifying this difference is absolutely critical, as the two formats require completely different recovery strategies. The ability to mount 3.5" HD floppies natively on a host system is significant—it dictates an incredibly simple capture process. Furthermore—there is a fundamental best practice that must be followed when dealing with tangible media carriers in a conservation context, which the 3.5" floppy disk happens to offer as a feature of the format, and therefore serves as an introduction to the concept of write blocking.

Write blocking is the practice of employing some method of preventing one's acquisition workstation from in any way writing data to attached media for acquisition. Nearly all contemporary operating systems (Linux being the major exception) write hidden files and metadata to removable storage media the instant it is connected and accessed. If a conservator were to inadvertently write such data to a hard drive belonging to an artist, this would be a fundamental and undocumented compromise of the authenticity and provenance of the tangible media carrier, one that would certainly be the cause of questions in future contexts, such as, "What are these files from 2014 doing among these files that the artist made in 1994?" When mounting any sort of media in conservation, archival, or forensic settings, it is a best practice to implement some form of write blocking. This ensures that the artifact may be read, but not written to. In this, our first example of 3.5" high density floppy disks, the carrier itself possesses built-in write-blocking capabilities. If one were to inspect the underside of a 3.5" HD floppy, it can be observed that one of the two holes in its form factor has a small plastic switch that alternatively renders one of the holes open or closed. When this write-blocking tab is in the "open" position such that one can see through the hole, the disk is write-protected or "safe." If this tab is in the "closed" position, it is write-enabled. For our purposes, when handling floppy disks containing artists' materials we always want this switch to be in the write-protected position. Once this is ensured, one can insert the disk into an external USB drive, and begin the actual process of capturing the disk.

In order to accomplish the capture and documentation of tangible media carriers from the previously discussed perspective of low-level capture for purposes of archival provenance, and enabling future scholarship of technical art history, we produce what is called a "disk image," a recording of every bit read from the tangible media carrier. There are many tools for producing disk images, and many formats of disk images. We will begin with the most basic and oldest of tools and formats—producing "raw" disk images with the "dd" program. On Linux and Macintosh systems, the "dd" or "direct duplicate" program is a command line-based utility packaged as part of GNU coreutils.[4] To produce a disk image with dd, the most basic invocation possible is:

```
$ dd if = foo of = bar
```

where "foo" represents the path to the "device file" of the disk we seek to image, and "bar" represents the file path and name of the image we wish to create. A device file is essentially a directory or file in a Unix or Linux file system, which points to a peripheral device such as our external USB floppy drive. Let us apply this methodology to a specific use case. We have a 3.5" HD floppy disk with the words "Drawings 1994" written on its label. We know that it is a high-density floppy disk, as it has two holes in its form factor, in addition to having the "HD" logo stamped in one corner. We ensure that the write-blocking tab is set, but before we insert this disk into our external USB drive, we need to become familiar with what volumes and devices are already mounted on our host machine, so that once we insert the floppy disk, we can identify it as a new device listed among the previously identified devices. By typing the "mount" command into our Linux terminal, we are offered a listing of all currently mounted volumes (be they physical disks or disk images). This listing includes the device file, as well as the volume name, which will be useful in determining which device file has been assigned to the floppy disk drive. After inserting the floppy disk and invoking the "mount" command once more, we can see that there is a new line, listing a device file path of /dev/disk01s2 with a volume titled "Drawings 1994". This device file /dev/disk01s2 is precisely what we need to pass to our "dd" command as the "input file." However, before we proceed, we must unmount the attached volume. If we do not do this, dd will throw an error, reporting that the device is busy or in use. "Drawings 1994" can be unmounted by invoking "umount Drawings\ 1994." Note that the "\" character is employed to indicate to the terminal that there is a space in the volume name. Invoking the "mount" command once more, we now see that the entry for "Drawings 1994" is gone. Now, we can safely run our final dd command:

```
$ dd if = /dev/disk01s2 of = ~/ Drawings_1994
```

The above line specifies the input file as our previously discovered device file. The output file simply specifies what to name the output, and where to put it—and in our case we used the tilde (~) character as a shortcut for our user's home directory, and named the output as "Drawings_1994". While running, dd does not provide any output to the user. Upon completion we are offered a message that lists the number of bytes sent and received. This is instructive of how dd functions—its most basic function is the duplication of bytes. It is only our specific use of the device file as input that sets its role as the creation of a disk image. By default, dd reads and writes data in chunks of 526 bytes. This is perfectly acceptable for something so small in capacity as a floppy disk. For larger storage devices, however, a larger byte size may be specified with the "bs" option (i.e., bs=16M).

The above process can be seen as the most base-level strategy for the production of disk images. dd is a tried and true tool that has withstood the test of time—and as part of GNU coreutils it is by default available on standard Linux distributions, and Mac OS X. It is, however, extremely limited on several counts: firstly, the absence of user feedback presents a major usability problem. Second, dd does not provide any built-in, user auditable or human readable means for ensuring that the disk image is in fact a bit-for-bit representation of the source disk. While it can be assumed that dd employs some kind of error checking during the copy process, the user's inability to audit this, or to retain any record of this for later audits, leaves much to be desired. There are, however, several tools that do just that. Guymager is an open source application for Linux that allows users to produce disk images in raw (dd) format as well as two formats that are used in the world of digital forensics: Expert Witness Format, and Advanced Forensic Image format. The latter two formats allow one to include metadata about the original source media and imaging process. FTK Imager is another free tool that provides a graphical user interface for Windows users, and command line interface for Linux and Macintosh users.

Mountable Contemporary Materials: Hard Drives

In the mid-1980s, as personal computers began to include internal hard disk drives, two main connection interfaces would be used: Small Computer System Interface (SCSI) and Integrated Drive Electronics (IDE). A variation of the IDE connection standard is also referred to as Parallel AT Attachment (PATA). The significance of the personal computer's transition from complete reliance on removable storage media (the floppy disk) to the introduction of internal hard disk storage cannot be overstated. In his seminal text *Mechanisms: New Media and the Forensic Imagination,* Matthew Kirschenbaum writes,

> my work was suddenly somehow part of the computer itself, not shunted back out to peripheral media. The computer was no longer just a processing engine [...] but something more like an individualized entity, with its own unique memory. In a roomful of otherwise identical-looking terminals I could point to one in particular and say, "that's my computer." (Kirschenbaum 2008)

Unlike 3.5" HD floppy disks, hard drives provide no means of built-in write blocking capabilities. Not only does this introduce the need for a dedicated hardware write-blocking device to act as an intermediary between the drive and the capture workstation, but, as described above, these drives can employ one of a variety of physical interfaces, or connections—each connection standard requiring a different kind of write blocker. The Forensics Wiki[5] provides a good guide to various models of commercially available write blockers. An essential limitation, though, is that since these devices come from the law enforcement world, they are concerned with contemporary applications. Thus it is already increasingly difficult to find write blockers for hard drives with SCSI connections. After connecting a hard drive to a write blocker, connecting the write blocker to the workstation, and powering on all devices, the workflow for the production of disk images, or acquisition of files, is precisely the same as the workflow described above for 3.5" HD floppy disks.

Unmountable Media: 3.5" DD and 5.25" Disks

Unlike 3.5" HD floppy disks, and hard disk drives compatible with contemporary forensic bridges, 3.5" DSDD (double-sided double-density) disks, and all variety of 5.25" floppy disks, present a much more challenging process of capture. The methods suggested previously for the capture of the 3.5" HD floppy disks are only possible due to the ability to connect these devices to one's workstation using physical hardware that is currently compatible with contemporary computers. When working with 3.5" DSDD floppy disks, and 5.25" disks, we must employ much more advanced tools, due to the fact that the drives capable of reading these formats are not readily compatible with contemporary computers. 3.5" DSDD floppy disks are not readable by the type of USB 3.5" floppy drives that can still be found today, and in the case of 5.25" floppy disks there is essentially no form of ordinary contemporary consumer hardware for reading these disks. In both cases we must turn to vintage hardware that would have been originally used for reading and writing such media, and rely on an intermediary device that will allow us to connect it to our contemporary workstation. In some ways this quite parallels the digital capture of legacy analog videotape. Just as one must use a U-matic video cassette deck for the playback of U-matic tapes, one must use a 3.5" DSDD drive or 5.25" floppy drive, respectively, for the reading of such disks. We then must employ some means of allowing our contemporary capture workstation to interact with this device. The key in this case is called a "floppy controller." This is a small device that acts as an intermediary between the vintage floppy drive and the contemporary workstation. One such device is the Kryoflux, which provides a hardware device for controlling 3.5" DSDD and 5.25" drives, as well as software for the production of disk images. This device, created by the Software Preservation Society,[6] also allows for the creation of incredibly low-level disk images, which record not the bits as interpreted by the workstation, but rather a recording of the actual voltage fluctuations produced by the floppy drive's reading of the magnetic flux reversals present on the disk. This is recorded in a proprietary format, but is a useful artifact to retain in addition to a standard "sector level" (i.e., the voltages as interpreted into bits readable by a computer) disk image in a raw format. The Kryoflux web site offers a free download of the Kryoflux software, as well as a detailed manual.[7]

When a Disk Image is Overkill

In day-to-day operations of a collecting institution working with contemporary born-digital materials being delivered by artists, there are times when a disk image is overkill. For instance, if an artist purchases a small portable hard drive simply so that they can deliver four video files—and that is all that they place on this newly purchased hard drive—it could be argued that creating and retaining an image of this hard drive is privileging the carrier over the content. In such a case, is the lowest level capture possible of the ***disk drive*** itself what is worthy of preservation, or is a verifiably bit-perfect copy of the individual files contained on that drive what is of primary interest? If the artist happened to use a 1 TB hard drive, but the files only occupied 100 GB of storage, a raw disk image would in fact be 1 TB, retaining a recording of the empty space on disk. This is desirable, of course, when a bit-perfect digital surrogate of the hard disk is critical, such as in the case of a complex software-based artwork that is acquired with a dedicated computer, containing dependencies and a specific operating system; or in the case of an archive of artists' materials, where materials may not be cataloged at the file level and it is desirable to take the approach of a "more productless process," getting bit-perfect digital surrogates of the physical artifacts (disks). However, in our hypothetical scenario where the artist has simply purchased a brand-new hard drive, placed four files on it, and delivered it to the collecting institution, the disk image is arguably unnecessary. To retain a disk image in such cases would be akin to digitizing an hour-long digital betacam tape that only contained fifteen minutes of content. The materials of use and interest are the files themselves.

At the Museum of Modern Art we have devised a small tool for assisting in the acquisition of materials in cases where we want to simply extract specific files from a disk, but would also like to maintain the "original order" of these files, to have verifiable proof that they were copied from disk flawlessly, and in the end store the materials in a standards-based format that will allow us to ensure a seamless chain of custody. This tool, called pre-ingest.py, is written in Python, and can be found on GitHub.[8] What it actually does is relatively trivial, and in most cases it leverages other modules for accomplishing its work, but the end result is the assurance of a perfect chain of custody. Instructions on the tool's use can be found in its readme and help file, but here we will review its essential processes:

1 The user invokes the script, providing a source volume or directory, as well as a destination volume or directory. As this tool was developed for use at MoMA, there is a flag for including the MoMA accession number of the artwork for which the materials being transferred belong. The purpose of this act is to automatically (via means of our collections management system's API[9]) name the destination directory according to the following format: ArtistLastName_ArtistFirstName---Title_Of_Work---AcessionNumber---PersistentID.
2 Using the *hashlib* module, a list of sha512 checksums are produced of the files that were specified as the source volume or directory. This is a recursive process, meaning that any and all sub-directories are included at an infinite depth.
3 A directory is created at the specified destination, with the naming format described in step 1, and the files in the specified source are then copied to this directory, using *rsync* in a manner that preserves the original order of files, and all metadata inherent to the files, such as file permissions, and created, modified and last opened dates.
4 Upon completion of the *rsync* transfer, the destination directory is converted to what is called a "Bag"—a standard sometimes referred to as BagIt. "BagIt is a hierarchical file packaging format designed to support disk-based or network-based storage and transfer of arbitrary digital content."[10] The types of bags that this tool creates (using the python-bagit module) have four essential parts: (1) the payload—or the files that we transferred; (2) the manifest, which is a text file that lists all files contained in the payload, and a sha512 checksum for each; (3) a file called bagit.txt, which contains information about how the bag was created; and finally (4) the tag-manifest, which is a text file that is similar to the bag manifest,

except that it lists the metadata files (bag manifest, and bagit.txt), and checksums for them. The idea of the bagit standard is that with this structure and these files, one can check and validate the "fixity" of the payload—in other words, one can ensure that the files one is stewarding have not become corrupt, have not been altered, and are present and accounted for. That this metadata is stored in a flat-file format is important, as it ensures that this critical information travels with the files themselves, and does not live in some external document or application. In fact, the bagit standard was very much designed for interoperability, for easy sharing of materials between institutions. The standard has seen wide adoption in the digital preservation community, and more recently in museums of contemporary art stewarding digital collections.

5 The final action taken by the pre-ingest tool is validation. The script reads the bag manifest, and compares the checksums of the transferred files with the list (stored in memory) of checksums it created in step 1 of the files on the mounted source media. If any checksum does not match, this means that something has mangled one of the files, and the tool notifies the user.

Post-Capture Preparation for Long-term Storage

The capture process is only the first step in the lifecycle of stewarding digital artwork. Once this process is complete, there are further actions that must be taken on the digital objects, and institutional resources that must already be in place. First and foremost is storage infrastructure—the entire purpose of extracting these digital objects from their tangible media carriers is so that they can be stored in a centralized, managed, and monitored storage environment. There are three essential requirements for any preservation-oriented digital storage system: lots of copies, lots of locations, and the ability to manage the integrity of these copies. The generally accepted recommendation is that three copies of collections materials be maintained, each in a different geographic location (Phillips et al. 2013). There are numerous ways to achieve those basic three commandments of digital preservation storage, and the nature of exactly how any given institution meets these requirements will vary greatly from one institution to another. Factors such as the size of the institution, the storage capacity required for the digital collections, the anticipated growth rate of digital collection, and budget for IT infrastructure and staffing need to be taken into consideration.

The Matters in Media Art consortium, comprising MoMA, Tate, and SFMOMA, has worked to develop recommendations for digital collections storage that takes those varying factors into account,[11] providing three different tiers of solution. Ultimately, it is quite impossible to provide specific digital preservation storage recommendations without knowledge of all of the contextual parameters outlined above. For some institutions, cloud services will make sense—for instance, if the capacity needed for the collection is quite small, and if internal IT support is already taxed to the limit. Meanwhile, for a massive collection that requires ample storage capacity and happens to have robust IT support and existing storage infrastructure, including offsite locations, cloud storage would not make any sense as it would come at great cost, when, instead, existing in-house resources and expertise could be leveraged.

In addition to having geographically diverse data stores, the collections data must be monitored for integrity. In the world of enterprise grade storage systems, the storage appliances themselves conduct some measures of integrity checking, both for ensuring that data between online mirrored data stores is the same, and for ensuring the data within one site has not become corrupt. This also exists in the consumer realm: for example, a desktop RAID (Redundant Array of Independent/Inexpensive Disks) drive employs methods for knowing when a block of data has been corrupted, and must be restored from a redundantly stored block. This sort of integrity checking is not, however, sufficient for preservation purposes—the reason being that these checks occur at the *block*[12] level, which is beneath the file level (individual files are composed of many blocks). Therefore, these sorts of integrity checks that occur at the storage appliance are completely ignorant of the unit of information we care about in our use case—we are concerned with the integrity, safety, and authenticity of the *files*. As well, one cannot audit a typical storage appliance for a log of proof that, for example, a given digital video file is an authentic bit-for-bit copy of the file that was received at acquisition. To achieve this goal, we produce, store, and audit checksums at the file level. Previously the BagIt standard was introduced. This standard is a perfect example of one means by which file-level fixity metadata can be produced at acquisition, stored (in this case alongside the actual collections materials themselves), and checked periodically. There are ample tools for creating, managing, and checking the validity of Bags. Part of the convenience of the Bag format's design is that the fixity metadata for digital objects inherently travels with the objects—it is independent of whatever storage appliance the materials live on, and can travel with the digital objects even for loans between institutions. There are some cases though where one may wish to monitor file-level fixity on a set of materials that are not stored in the BagIt format, and it may be inconvenient to store the materials in Bags. Recently, New York-based consulting firm AVPreserve has released an open source tool for doing just that—easily maintaining and monitoring fixity of any digital materials, whether or not they are stored in the BagIt format.[13]

Beyond the File System: Digital Repositories

Most storage systems offer no more than a file system. This can be effective as a first step for many institutions implementing digital collections storage: simply maintaining a series of directories that are carefully organized, to which access is limited for collections security concerns, and which follows the best practices in terms of number of copies and geographic diversity. Often this is the first step for collecting institutions. There is, however, a next step that is absolutely critical for properly and effectively preserving and managing digital collections over the long term, and that is the implementation of a digital repository. The term "digital repository" carries different meaning in different contexts—in the academic library and archives world, "digital repository" can refer to a system that simply houses the publications of faculty and students. Generally speaking, though, in the digital preservation world, "digital repository" refers to a system which houses digital materials in a preservation-oriented system. Standards have been developed for the fundamental design model of digital preservation repositories,[14] as well as for assessing the overall merit of the design, implementation, and management of such repositories.[15] Within the context of collecting art institutions, the best metaphor is to think of a digital repository as the digital equivalent of art storage—a place where conditions are monitored and carefully controlled, access is tightly controlled and documented, the location of materials is carefully tracked, and any movement of collections materials in or out is robustly documented. This is precisely the purpose of a digital repository in the museum setting.

Historically speaking, such systems have long existed for digital libraries and archives,[16] yet up until recent efforts by the Museum of Modern Art no such system has been designed for the particular needs of institutions collecting digital art. After years of working to define the functional requirements and use cases of such a system, MoMA began developing the first digital repository for museum collections—known as the DRMC—in 2013. Early on, it was found that the open source digital preservation processing system Archivematica[17] fulfilled a great many of the DRMC's functional requirements. Archivematica is a microservices-based[18] system that processes digital objects according to the OAIS model, conducting tasks such as virus checking, filename sanitization, file format identification, characterization,[19] policy-based normalization,[20] and generates incredibly verbose standards-based metadata as a record of all of these activities. Archivematica then packages these digital objects and metadata in the BagIt format. These bags are called Archival Information Packages (AIP), a term from the OAIS model. Again, this fulfilled a great many of the DRMC's requirements, but the missing piece of the repository was a system that correlated AIPs with their respective artwork in MoMA's existing collections management system, as well as providing the ability to record the complex relationships between digital materials (i.e., x file requires y software for exhibition), managing fixity checks, and providing the capability to conduct essential collections management activities such as monitoring the growth of the collection and identifying trends and anomalies with respect to digital file formats and characteristics. MoMA worked with Artefactual Systems (the makers of Archivematica) to develop a new new system for managing digital repositories, and specifically accomplishing the aforementioned aspects of ongoing stewardship and preservation. This tool, called Binder, has been released as free and open-source software, and is available for download at github.com/artefactual/binder.

Intervention and Exhibition: Fundamental Treatment Concepts

At this point we have surveyed the absolutely critical, but rather rudimentary topics of pre-acquisition analysis, acquisition and capture procedure, storage solutions, checking and maintaining integrity, and digital repositories. These topics are less frequently discussed in conservation literature than the theoretical and conceptual aspects of time-based media conservation; however, they are absolutely critical in forming the foundation in support of conservation activities. This section will introduce, from a practical standpoint, the various concepts that inform treatment strategies employed in time-based media conservation.

Emulation

Chances are that you have used an emulator, whether you know it or not. Emulation is commonly used in commercial technology to mitigate obsolescence—for instance, the ability to play classic Nintendo Entertainment Systems on contemporary Nintendo gaming platforms. Simply put, an emulator is a piece of software that simulates the precise conditions and behaviors of a formerly hardware-based computer environment other than the one on which said software is running. In a sense, emulation can be thought of as "virtual reality" from the perspective of the software running inside of it. For example, if one runs a piece of software written for the Apple //e computer inside of an emulation of the Apple //e on a contemporary computer (even a Windows-based machine), the software has no idea that it is not actually running on an Apple //e. Emulation is an incredibly economical and effective strategy for the execution and exhibition of software-based works as one emulation can potentially provide access to many artworks (any that require the emulated environment), without any modification of the artwork's source materials. There is an important distinction to draw here between a true emulator, and what is, within the retrocomputing world, affectionately referred to as a "hackulator." Emulation means that the software of the emulator is designed to simulate the hardware of a specific machine and its peripherals—for instance, the Multiple Emulator Super System (MESS) offers a Macintosh IIci emulator, which simulates specifically the hardware of the Macintosh IIci. Hackulators, on the other hand, while they purport to be emulators—and are intended for the execution of obsolete software—are a mish-mash of various systems, implemented in a far less rigorous manner. The goal of a hackulator is simply to get the emulation close enough so that software that would have run on a range of similar systems will function in the hackulator. The Sheepshaver emulator is a good example of this. Sheepshaver is incredibly popular within the vintage Macintosh software community, and is a useful tool, but it is most certainly a hackulator. It is not designed to simulate the hardware of any specific Macintosh, but rather simulates a generic Power PC Macintosh processing architecture. The upside is that Sheepshaver is very easy to use, and quick to configure. Within the context of conservation, however, it can be said that true emulation is the only viable option. In order to rely on emulation as an access and display strategy in the museum setting for software-based artworks, one must be able to compare an emulation qualitatively with the artwork running on its original platform—so as to analyze the fidelity of the emulation to the properties, behavior, look, and feel of the original environment. If an emulator that one compares to an original environment is in fact a hackulator, the analysis is essentially useless, since the hackulator is not in fact attempting to simulate the precise properties of the machine to which one is comparing it.

Virtualization

Virtualization is similar to a hackulator in the sense that virtualization does not provide the emulation of a specific hardware model—this is not its purpose or intent. Virtualization is simply the act of simulating a generic processor platform for the execution of operating systems and software indented for that architecture. Virtualization occurs within the framework of a given virtualization platform—for instance, VirtualBox or VMware—and allows one to build a library of virtual machines that are managed by the platform, allowing one to save machine states, export disk images, and other such management tasks. Virtualization is today ubiquitous for web servers—rather than the days of having dedicated rack servers, today with only one rack appliance, a sysadmin can host numerous virtual servers, all with different purposes and software environments. This can be incredibly useful for the long-term preservation and access to artworks that are web-based, and require very specific server environments, as virtualization removes a device specific dependency that is not tenable over the long term. Such a solution was devised at SFMOMA for the treatment of Lynn Hershman Leeson's *Agent Ruby* (1999–2002). At the outset of the conservation treatment of this work, it had been running on a woefully vintage dedicated server, one that of course would not be sustainable in the long term. The solution that was devised was to create a virtual server on SFMOMA's existing infrastructure, and migrate the work's environment to this new contained virtualization.[21] Yet again, this act is in a sense analogous to the digitization of analog videotape, in that it is a process of taking an unstable physical asset, and producing a digital surrogate that if properly stewarded can be (completely in theory) maintained indefinitely.

Recreation, Reinterpretation, and Replacement

The most involved of all time-based media conservation strategies is the act of recreation or reinterpretation. This method entails rebuilding an artwork based on technical documentation, and qualitative documentation of the original. This sort of recreation is not always a herculean undertaking that requires complete recreation from the ground up—in some cases it could be replacement of one technical component with another (for example, control software for projectors and motors in an installation-based artwork), with fine tuning based on direct observation, study of documentation, and qualitative analysis. Such cases are certainly non-trivial in that they introduce the potential for drastic change in the look and feel of the work, and so must be engaged in with rigorous analysis of results, and weighing of acceptable levels of change. Such is the fundamentally unique nature of time-based media and digital artworks—their distinctively allographic nature (Goodman 1972; Laurenson 2006).

Intervention and Exhibition: The Magnavox Odyssey

In 2014, MoMA acquired the very first home gaming console[22]: the *Magnavox Odyssey* (1972). Its inventor, Ralph Baer, was unquestionably a visionary—not only inventing the very concept of a home gaming console, but also inventing the lightgun, which went on to become a ubiquitous accessory in both home and arcade gaming. The Magnavox Odyssey came with many different games in the form of what to the layperson would look much like cartridges. These cartridges would be inserted into the Odyssey to change games. Interestingly, though, these cartridges did not contain the games at all—they contained no software or logic. Rather, all game logic for the various games played on the Odyssey was present internally in the console. When inserted, the Odyssey's cartridges would complete a connection of a specific circuit in the Odyssey, setting the device to change to a specific game. Therefore, in the case of the Magnavox Odyssey, there is no software; no floppy disks, hard drives, or game cartridge ROMs to stabilize. While documentation of the Odyssey was delivered on a CD-R, requiring the capture workflows we have explored, there are no digital software materials present in the Odyssey itself that require stabilization.

While it does contain digital components, its logic and design can be completely documented through schematics. There is no source code. Nonetheless, the Odyssey presents immense challenges for display and exhibition in a way that allows museum visitors to play and interact with the system.

The Odyssey is entirely monochrome—black and white—and was intended to be played on consumer televisions of the late 1970s, which of course had cathode ray tubes monitors. When stepping back to observe the anatomy and mechanics of the various games available on the Odyssey, they appear to be incredibly similar due to the primitive graphics of the system. There are usually up to three points of light on screen: the two players and a ball of some kind—sometimes a stripe down the center of the screen. As a way of circumventing the limitations of this technology, and realizing a richer gaming experience, the Odyssey came with color overlays for each game. These overlays were printed on a type of acetate, and would adhere to the cathode ray tube monitor by way of static electricity. These overlays served to essentially set the scene for the game, for example, tennis (Figure 24.1) The interactive video elements produced by the Magnavox Odyssey console were so primitive that these overlays were needed to make one game more visually distinct from another—as well as indicating to the player the active areas of play.

Senior Curator of Architecture and Design Paola Antoinelli, who spearheaded MoMA's collection of video games as examples of interaction design, wanted to include the Magnavox Odyssey game *Tennis* in the 2014 exhibition *A Collection of Ideas.*[23] The exhibition was to be staged in the Architecture and Design department's third-floor gallery space devoted to rotating exhibitions of the permanent collection. It was in this gallery that MoMA exhibited the first group of video games collected,

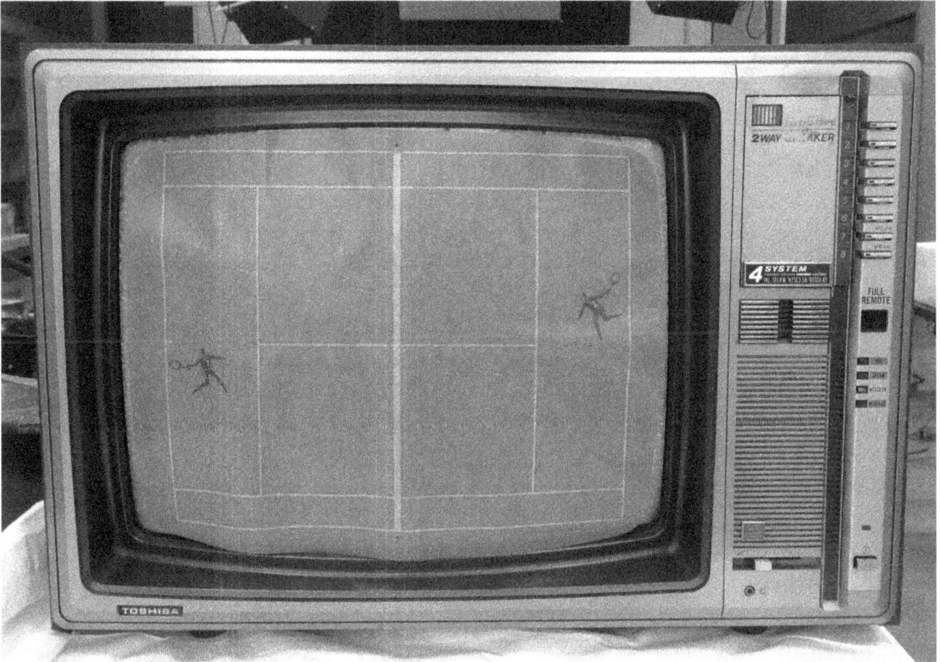

FIGURE 24.1 Overlay for Magnavox Odyssey *Tennis.* Photo courtesy of Ben Fino-Radin.

in the 2013 exhibition *Applied Design*. The general display strategy and visitor experience that Paola and her curatorial team designed for the video games was one that exhibited the games stripped of their original dedicated hardware. Instead of bulky arcade consoles, and in this case, the delicate vintage plastic controls of the Magnavox Odyssey, flat LCD screens were embedded in the wall, and custom shelves (devised by MoMA's exhibition design team, carpenter, and media conservators) were mounted below the screens to host the controls of the games. The aim was to limit the viewer's attention to the flow of interaction between the haptic experience of the controls, and on-screen graphics of the game. For this particular exhibition, there was a desire to steer away from a consideration of the arcade cabinet, or game console itself as a design object. This presented massive challenges to MoMA's media conservation team, who are responsible for ensuring that these collections are exhibited in an authentic manner respectful of the work's material and conceptual integrity—managing acceptable degrees of change.

The essential constraint in exhibiting the Magnavox Odyssey in this context was that we simply could not use the original vintage hardware—both due to curatorial intent and to the fact that interactive displays at MoMA see massive amounts of use, and would experience significant wear and tear. Any parts that might wear out or break due to heavy use had to be able to be replaced quickly. This alone ruled out the use of expensive and rare vintage components from a practicality standpoint. After consulting with the Odyssey's designer Ralph Baer, we found a potential solution that would involve a bit of smoke and mirrors, and careful design, to effectively simulate the properties of the Odyssey's look and feel. Mr. Baer produced, from time to time, contemporary replicas of his prototype for the Magnavox Odyssey—a device called the Brown Box. The Brown Box (named for the humble wooden box in which it was housed) offered all of the same games as the Odyssey, though rather than having cartridges for each game, the Brown Box simply offered a bank of switches that allowed the player to change games. We were able to test and access the Brown Box replica during a visit with Mr. Baer, and found that the interaction, game mechanics, and behavior of *Tennis* on the Brown Box was acceptably similar to *Tennis* on the Magnavox Odyssey. As the Brown Box replica was composed of contemporary components, it would be much more feasible to service during exhibition. Because of the Brown Box replica's fidelity to the Odyssey, as well as the ability to affordably and quickly replace parts, the clear solution was to employ the Brown Box replica as a stand-in for the Odyssey.

In order to maintain the curatorial vision of stripping away the accoutrements of vintage hardware, the decision was made to rehouse the Brown Box replica, and build new controller enclosures for it. Not only would this allow us to eliminate the faux-vintage wood grain of the Brown Box replica, thus keeping within the parameters of the exhibition's design, but this act would also allow us to reconfigure the physical layout of the controls to match the physical arrangement of the Odyssey's controls—thus framing the Brown Box replica not as a recreation of the Brown Box, but as a recreation of the Odyssey. Before engaging in the rehousing process, an assessment was made as to the reversibility of the process of complete rehousing—reversibility being a requirement of *any* conservation treatment. It was found that this would be entirely executable in a reversible manner.

Aside from the design and haptic experience of the Odyssey's controls, the most critical item of consideration was the on-screen experience of the tennis game.

As stated, the Odyssey's video output was completely black and white. The tennis game overlay, however, placed a green cast over the screen, as well as depicting the white lines of the tennis court, and two tennis players. It is undeniable that the Odyssey's overlays are a critical aspect of the device's aura and characteristics as a design object. While at-home players did not always use the overlays, to present this artifact to a public who is likely seeing the Odyssey for the first time without the overlays, would be to do a disservice to the subtle details of the very specific design of the Magnavox Odyssey's gaming experience. The Brown Box replica offers the ability to flip a switch that turns the black background of the game screen to a bright green color—and in fact many museums that have exhibited the Brown Box replica have chosen to display it with this option selected. As our mission here was not to exhibit the Brown Box replica, but rather to use the replica as a behind-the-scenes engine for the means of reproducing the experience of the Odyssey, the use of this feature was out of the question. Furthermore, use of the original overlays was not possible, since the brightness of the LCD panels used for the exhibition were significantly less than a CRT would have provided, and would not properly illuminate the overlay. Thus, MoMA created a reproduction of the overlay with a level of translucency appropriate for the brightness of the LCD. Finally, as the Odyssey would have been played on a 4:3 aspect ratio CRT, the wall-embedded LCD was masked at the left and right sides, so that it bore 4:3 proportions, without the blemish of black pillar-boxes visible on screen (Figure 24.2).

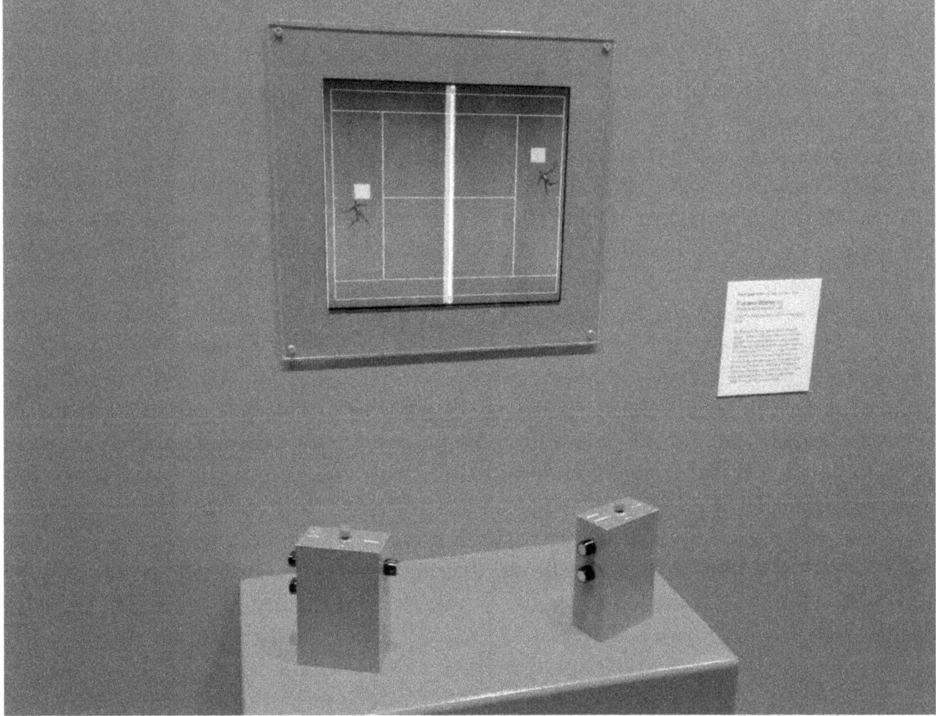

FIGURE 24.2 Installation shot of Magnavox Odyssey at MOMA, New York. Photo courtesy of Ben Fino-Radin.

The Magnavox Odyssey as exhibited at MoMA is but one example of the hybrid approach of technical expertise and media-archaeological historic knowledge that media conservators must offer when exhibiting such digital objects in the museum setting: a careful balance of servicing curatorial intent, the aura and significant properties of the original object, and the logistical realities of interactive exhibitions.

Documentation Practices

The solution for the display of the Magnavox Odyssey at MoMA we have just explored is *highly* specific, and was carried out with very particular technical knowledge. Were the Odyssey to be exhibited in fifty years' time, in the absence of any documentation of the process that was undertaken to come to this solution, it would prove an immense challenge. Not only would the staff who were present during the initial staging likely no longer be present, but it is possible that there would no longer be any functioning cathode ray tube monitors. Thus, there would no longer be a possibility of assessing the fidelity of recreations and emulations against the properties of the original gaming experience. It is critical to have sufficient documentation of the artwork materials in what has been identified as an ideal state. As previously discussed, any post-treatment instantiation of a work (i.e., emulation) must be qualitatively compared directly with the work in its original state. One can only conduct such assessment and side-by-side comparison as long as the vintage and dedicated hardware of the work still functions. It is for this reason that the visual documentation of such ideal states, involving original and dedicated hardware, is of the utmost importance. Relying on a CRT for studying the visual properties of a CRT will only be possible for so long. However, relying on demonstrably accurate photographic and video documentation is certainly sustainable.

Arguably the most challenging aspect of the long-term stewardship of time-based media art and digital art is that the work truly does not exist until it is installed. For this reason, documentation of exhibitions is central to the stewardship of these works. When an artwork—be it software-based, web-based, single-channel digital video, or variable installation with digital components—is exhibited, there are critical forms of documentation that must be gathered. At MoMA, the institution's Media Working Group—comprising all museum stakeholders that are involved in the lifecycle of digital works, from media conservation, AV, and IT to curatorial, registrar, and exhibitions—has devised policy and procedures for just this purpose. It is critical to gather any relevant documentation, and when possible interviews with stakeholders, as soon as possible after the staging of such an exhibition. This can include interviews and walkthroughs of the exhibition with the artist, artist's technicians, the curator, art handlers, and other technical support staff that are familiar with maintaining the work during exhibition. Floor plans, technical diagrams, and technical interviews can provide additional critical evidence for the future re-instantiation of the work. Decades can pass between a work's first and second exhibition at the same institution. Of course, during that passage of time experts in exhibiting the work will leave, or their memories will inevitably fade. As supplement to documenting one's own exhibition of works, it is also central to the long-term stewardship of the work to seek out documentation of the work as previously installed, staged, and exhibited by the artist and other institutions. A work with variable parameters may have been exhibited—or instantiated—several times before entering an institution's collection and coming under the stewardship of conservation. Such evidence is immensely useful, as it provides the conservator with documentation of alternate instantiations of the work.

Conclusion

We have reviewed many of the practical aspects—the nuts and bolts—of handling, storing, and caring for digital art: conversations with the artist prior to acquisition, capture of media, storage, digital repositories, intervention and treatment fundamentals, and documentation practices. This chapter marks a moment in time when the conservation field has begun to engage with the technical underpinnings of digital materials as employed by artists—truly a turning point in the field's evolution. This evolution has come decades after artists began working with digital materials, and many years after institutions began to collect such material. Considering the thousands of years of artistic production that preceded the emergence of contemporary conservation of art as we know it today (as an evidence-based, scientific, analytical, and inherently humanistic and sociological practice), the outlook is in fact rather positive when it comes to the ability of the conservation field to meet the challenges of stewarding digital materials. As collecting institutions with the capacity for deep material and technical research increasingly commit to the curation, collection, and stewardship of digital art, the future does certainly look bright.

Notes

1 See, for instance, "Icons in Plastic," a recent panel hosted by the Getty Research Institute on the conservation of plastics in cultural heritage collections. http://www.getty.edu/conservation/publications_resources/public_programs/icons_plastic.html (accessed January 15, 2015).
2 http://variablemediaquestionnaire.net/ (accessed January 15, 2015).
3 https://github.com/finoradin/pre-ingest
4 dd(1) manual page, 1994. Retrieved from Mac OS 10.9.3 distribution.
5 http://www.forensicswiki.org/wiki/Write_Blockers (accessed January 15, 2015).
6 http://www.softpres.org/ (accessed January 15, 2015).
7 http://www.kryoflux.com/ (accessed January 15, 2015).
8 https://github.com/finoradin/pre-ingest (accessed January 15, 2015).
9 https://github.com/smoore4moma/TmsApi (accessed January 15, 2015).
10 https://tools.ietf.org/html/draft-kunze-bagit-09 (accessed January 15, 2015).
11 http://www.tate.org.uk/about/projects/matters-media-art (accessed January 15, 2015).
12 http://en.wikipedia.org/wiki/Block_(data_storage) (accessed January 15, 2015).
13 https://github.com/avpreserve/fixity (accessed January 15, 2015).
14 http://www.iso.org/iso/catalogue_detail.htm?csnumber=57284 (accessed January 15, 2015).
15 http://www.iso.org/iso/home/store/catalogue_tc/catalogue_detail.htm?csnumber=56510 (accessed January 15, 2015).

16 http://fedorarepository.org/. http://projecthydra.org/. http://islandora.ca/ (accessed January 15, 2015).
17 https://www.archivematica.org/wiki/Main_Page (accessed January 15, 2015).
18 http://dx.doi.org/10.2218/ijdc.v5i1.151 (accessed January 15, 2015).
19 The process of automatically generating verbose technical information about the characteristics of a given digital object (i.e., format, dimensions, resolution, color space, character encoding, codec, and the like).
20 The process of converting copies of the digital object from their original file format to specified preservation and access-oriented file formats.
21 http://www.docam.ca/en/annual-summits/2010-summit/429-virtualizing-agent-ruby.html (accessed October 12, 2015).
22 http://www.pong-story.com/odyssey.htm (accessed January 15, 2015).
23 http://www.moma.org/visit/calendar/exhibitions/1461 (accessed January 15, 2015).

References

Beerkens, Lydia, ed. 2012. *The Artist Interview. For Conservation and Presentation of Contemporary Art. Guidelines and Practice.* Heijningen, Netherlands: Jap Sam Books.

Goodman, Nelson. 1972. *Languages of Art: An Approach to a Theory of Symbols.* Indianapolis, IN: Hackett Publishing.

Kirschenbaum, Matthew G. 2008. *Mechanisms: New Media and the Forensic Imagination.* Cambridge, MA: The MIT Press.

Kirschenbaum, Matthew G., Richard Ovenden, and Gabriela Redwine. 2010. *Digital Forensics and Born-Digital Content in Cultural Heritage Collections.* Washington, DC: Council on Library and Information Resources. http://www.clir.org/pubs/reports/pub149 (accessed September 15, 2014).

Laurenson, Pip. 2006. "Authenticity, Change and Loss in the Conservation of Time-Based Media Installations." *Tate Papers – Tate's Online Research Journal.* (Autumn) http://www.tate.org.uk/download/file/fid/7401 (accessed January 15, 2015).

Phillips, Megan, Jefferson Bailey, Andrea Goethals, and Trevor Owens. 2013. "The NDSA Levels of Digital Preservation: An Explanation and Uses." Washington, DC: Library of Congress, National Digital Stewardship Alliance. http://www.digitalpreservation.gov/ndsa/working_groups/documents/NDSA_Levels_Archiving_2013.pdf (accessed September 15, 2014).

Wharton, Glenn, and Fernando Domínguez Rubio. 2013. "Conservation Interviews: Problematic Assumptions and Unintended Consequences." INCAA Conservation Interviews. Posted May 23. http://incca-na.org/conservation-interviews/ (accessed January 15, 2015).

25

Trusting Amateurs with Our Future

Jon Ippolito

This essay focuses on unofficial preservation practices and why they are sometimes more effective than professional enterprises.[1] After challenging the prevailing expectations about durability as the touchstone of long-term cultural memory, this chapter looks at the rise of preservation by so-called amateurs in writing emulators and crowdsourcing the replication of 3D artifacts. It concludes with the challenges of such proliferative preservation to conventional notions of cultural heritage.

The Oldest Human Record

Take a look at Figure 25.1. Which of these is the oldest human record? The Rosetta Stone, the Cycladic idol, the *Megatherium*, or the Gudea Cylinders?

The Megatherium *Lives*

This is the oldest human record I have found: the story of the mapinguary, passed down from generation to generation among the Indians of the Brazilian rainforest. Twenty feet tall, as strong as a dozen gorillas, adorned with matted hair covering a bony carapace—the giant ground sloth made such an impression on the tribes of the Amazon that nearly every one has a word for this creature, which most call the mapinguary.

The native accounts are detailed enough that scientists have been able to identify their protagonist as the giant ground sloth, *Megatherium*. In fact, when a native of Peru's Machiguenga people matter-of-factly described seeing a mapinguary at the natural history museum in Lima, ethnobiologist Glenn Shepard was able to corroborate

A Companion to Digital Art, First Edition. Edited by Christiane Paul.

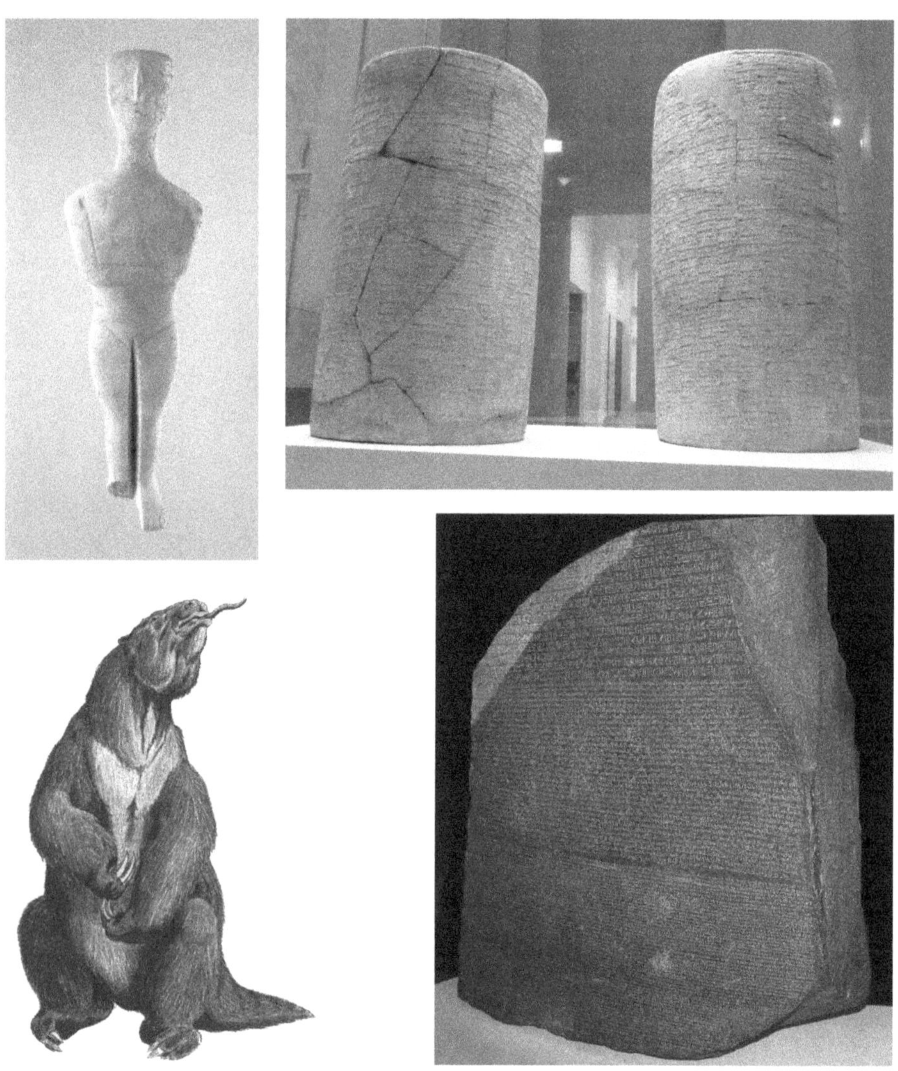

FIGURE 25.1 Clockwise from upper left: Female figure of the Dokathismata type (Getty Museum). Marble, from Cycaldes, Greece, 30.2 cm (11 7/8 in.). Digital image courtesy of the Getty's Open Content Program.
The Gudea Cylinders. Photo by Ramessos. (Public domain)
The Rosetta Stone. Photo copyright Hans Hillewaert. Some rights reserved (Creative Commons Attribution-Share Alike 4.0 International license.)
Artist's rendering of the Megatherium. Image by DiBgd. (Public domain)

the mapinguary's pedigree: the museum has a diorama with a model of the *Megatherium* (Rohter 2007).

How do I know these stories are older than the pyramids or Machu Picchu? Because the diorama in Lima depicted *prehistoric* mammals. The *Megatherium* is a creature that died out tens of thousands of years ago, yet survives in the stories of Indians of the Brazilian rainforest.

The legend of the mapinguary isn't just some stone tool or potshard from which we can infer a story about an experience long past. It is the story itself. Or rather, it is the persistence of key elements in the story, as retold over at least two thousand generations, that has kept alive accounts of human encounters with this prehistoric animal. Indigenous storytellers even "remember" features of the mapinguary that paleontologists cannot read from the bones: it had reddish fur, avoided water, and moved silently through the thick jungle. Their stories even tell us how the *Megatherium* smelled: the name mapinguary means "fetid beast."

Paleontologists have begun to accept other indigenous stories as genuine memories, including a giant, man-eating bird known to science as Haast's eagle, extinct for five hundred years but alive in Maori legend (*Slashdot* 2009).

What Are Professional Archivists To Make of This?

All of this is hard to understand from the perspective of museums and archives, which depend on the dedication of a staff of experts in a centralized institution to safeguard cultural memory. The proliferation of recorded media in the last century would seem to underscore the necessity of media specialists and climate-controlled warehouses to look after all those silver gelatin prints and reels of celluloid. Even performance theorists such as Peggy Phelan imply that performance cannot be stored.[2]

Perhaps not. But storage isn't the only mode of safeguarding culture, and in this age of rapid obsolescence, storage is turning out to be the least reliable of them.

During the conquest of South America, imperial centers in Spain and Portugal controlled indigenous populations by prohibiting performative practices such as dance and ritual in favor of archival practices such as writing. But while books can be burned and temples destroyed, stories such as the mapinguary survived even the conquistadors' deliberate attempt to obliterate them.

Relying on preservation vigilantes may sound unprofessional, but they served culture well for tens of thousands of years before priests and preparators came along. In the battle of the proprietary versus the prolific, the historic record may be debatable, but the prehistoric is not. Euro-ethnic preservationists fool themselves into thinking that stone tablets and figurines in museums are the oldest artifacts on record. But the oldest cultural knowledge survives not in durable formats, but in social ones.

I am going to make a radical claim: that the future of new media lurks in the Amazon rainforest. Well, not only in the Amazon, but really anywhere that so-called amateurs thrive, because it is only by their paradigm of proliferative preservation that we will keep the rich technological culture of the present alive. I have already suggested how well distributed memory works in indigenous practices. For the rest of this chapter, I will try to explain why it works equally well in digital practices, with particular attention to emulation and crowdsourcing, and the preservation paradigm known as variable media. I will end with some of the challenges to proliferative preservation, and the reasons I am confident we can overcome them. First, however, we need to accept the ascendance of the amateur.

The Amateurs Arrive

The rise of amateur producers has been one of the defining features of the turn of the millennium. Theorist Bernard Stiegler calls this class the *amatorat* (Stiegler 2011); hardware and software manufacturers call them *prosumers*; start-up founders and venture capitalists call the phenomenon Web 2.0. The introduction to the *Eternal September* exhibition curated by Valentina Tanni argues that "every system previously used to managing and controlling cultural production is now experiencing a deep crisis, which is also causing the inevitable collapse of all the related business models. The ultimate consequence of this scenario is also the most radical one: the questioning of 'professionalism'" (Tanni 2014).

Rather than ascribe this trend to the Internet, we can trace the dawn of the phenomenon to as far back as the mid-1960s. The legend of Nam June Paik picking up the first Sony Portapak to film the pope from a taxi in 1965 may be apocryphal (Sherman 2007), but there is no doubt that artists such as Frank Gillette, Ira Schneider, and Paik were among the earliest adopters of mobile camcorders. As Tanni reminds us, art critic Gene Youngblood foretold the death of the professional in the 1982 SIGGRAPH catalogue:

> A tool is "mature" insofar as it's easy to use, accessible to everyone, offering high quality at low cost and characterized by a pluralistic rather than singular practice, serving a multitude of values. Professionalism is an archaic model that's fading in the twilight of the Industrial Age. (Tanni 2014)

As of this writing, amateurs connected via social networks and mobile apps continue to disrupt professions from taxi driver to hotel owner, as evidenced by sharing economies such as Uber and Airbnb. While the jury may still be out on whether these platforms empower or enslave their unpaid contributors, academic studies (Benkler 2007) bear out what we already know from millions of Wikipedia articles and Facebook posts: amateurs can be remarkably effective at filling gaps previously occupied by paid middlemen.

The Amateurs Take Control

Notwithstanding what you read in a thesaurus, "non-specialist" is no longer a trustworthy synonym for amateur. To many, the word "amateur" may conjure up cat videos on YouTube or coffee shop reviews on Yelp; yet much of the Internet's unpaid labor force wields specialized knowledge or skill. Amateurs in the Internet age can just as easily be experts as laypersons, especially when it comes to expertise in a narrow specialty like Klingon grammar or *My Little Pony* episodes—or retro-computing forensics.[3]

To prove this point, Stiegler turns to amateur astronomers to represent his *amatorat*, since in recent years non-professionals have made notable contributions to our knowledge of the skies. NASA's "clickworkers" peruse photos of Mars to identify craters with an accuracy equal to or better than astrophysics grad students (Benkler 2007, 69). Armed with little more than an English degree and a backyard telescope, amateur David Levy discovered no less than nine comets—and eleven more once professionals let him play with their equipment (Levy 2004–).

One of the most extraordinary exploits of amateur stargazing—not to mention restoring a technological artifact—involved breathing new life into a crippled spacecraft. In 1978 NASA and the European Space Agency launched the satellite ISEE-3 into an orbit around the sun, after which it became the first spacecraft to visit a comet. Although ISEE-3 once again approached the Earth in 2014, it received no hero's welcome, for NASA had abandoned the satellite in 1997 and had neither the budget nor time to recover a connection based on outdated software protocols.

That gap of budget and time led Randall Monroe, creator of the XKCD comic, to suggest that amateur astronomers might be able to reverse-engineer the signal processor on their own and re-establish contact with the errant spacecraft. As if in response to Monroe's appeal to the crowd, on May 29, 2014, a team of unofficial astrophysicists sent one of the most astonishing tweets in the world of amateur science: @agentGav: We Are Now In Command of the ISEE-3 Spacecraft.

By July 2 the team announced they had successfully fired the thrusters for the first time since 1987. Digital conservators may take heart from the example of this unofficial team of space Samaritans, who crowdfunded time on dish antennae to reach across a million miles of emptiness and reanimate a 36-year-old software protocol. Suddenly saving a Flash-based work of Internet art doesn't sound so hard.

Outperforming the Professionals: Emulation

Citizen science aside, how can amateurs contribute to the preservation of human creativity? The most obvious example is emulation, the poster child for unofficial solutions to new media problems. Defined by RAND computer scientist Jeff Rothenberg as the ability of a new computer to impersonate an older one, emulation is a preservation practice that as of this writing is far more likely to be found in a teenager's bedroom than a conservator's lab. An emulator is a computer program that "fools" original code into assuming that it is running on the hardware for which it was designed, thus enabling software from an out-of-date computer like the Atari or Gameboy to run on a contemporary one like a Macintosh, Windows, or Linux PC. To be sure, a handful of professional institutions have experimented with emulation; a case study will show why they are falling behind in the race to save digital culture.

Professional Emulators: Falling Behind

Our best efforts to preserve the rich outpouring of the last few decades known as media art are being buried underneath an avalanche of obsolete floppy disks, restrictive End User License Agreements, and antisocial archival practices.[4] Even when aware of promising strategies such as emulation, museums and other cultural institutions are having trouble adapting to them.

Let me illustrate this by starting with one of the few triumphs of the artworld's preservation efforts: the renewal of Grahame Weinbren and Roberta Friedman's *Erl King* (1983–1985), one of the first examples of interactive video. Loosely based on stories by Goethe and Freud, this kiosk-based installation allows users to control the direction of a narrative by touching the screen to trigger seamless cinematic transitions. The original hardware included a 1982 Sony SMC-70 computer, three analog laserdisks, and a touchscreen; the software was a PASCAL program custom-written by the artists and their collaborators, which ran on the CP/M operating system, a precursor to DOS.

This piece was on its last legs when the Variable Media Network,[5] a partnership with the Guggenheim Museum and Daniel Langlois Foundation among others, chose it as a poster child for the exhibition *Seeing Double: Emulation in Theory and Practice* (2004).[6] When the original and emulated version were exhibited side by side, a survey of visitors concluded that the two were practically indistinguishable. The technique of emulation, whereby a newer computer impersonates an older one, enabled preservationists to salvage the source code and user experience of the *Erl King* while replacing its body with up-to-date guts.

The successful emulation of the *Erl King* was only possible because of a perfect storm consisting of talented technicians, an eager and forthcoming artist, access to the original software and hardware, and organizations willing to fund. It is hard to imagine spending two years and tens of thousands of dollars to recreate every interactive video installation from the 1980s, much less every endangered example of media art.

So our shining example of a successful emulation is shining all the brighter because it is pretty much standing alone, surrounded by less fortunate works that are all going dark.

Amateur Emulators: Going Strong

If we professionals are falling behind, who's keeping up? Super Mario Brothers, that's who. When it comes to preservation, the Olympians of new media art are getting their butts kicked by an Italian plumber.

While professional conservators have only managed to future-proof a tiny sliver of new media artworks created since 1980 in any systematic and extensible way, a global community of dispersed amateurs has safeguarded the lion's share of a different genre of early computational media: video games.

Take, for example, the FCEUX emulator, at the time of this writing the top-ranked emulator on the prominent site Emulator Zone for the enormously popular Nintendo Entertainment System (NES). FCEUX can trace its genealogy back to an early emulator called Family Computer Emulator, or FCE, so called because Nintendo released the NES in Asia as "Family Computer" (Figure 25.2). In the manner of many open source projects, no company controlled the source code for this emulator; instead the programmer, known by the name Bero, released his abashedly titled "dirty code" online for other gaming fans to tinker with and extend. One such fan, known as Xodnizel, released an improvement called FCE Ultra that became so popular in the early 2000s that it spawned a half-dozen "forks," or versions modified by other users. By the late 2000s, NES fans merged four of the forks to produce FCEUX, a cross-platform and cross-standard emulator released under the GPL open-source license.

I cannot think of a single instance of software created by the professional preservation community in this supple way, passed from hand to hand over decades, diverging, reconverging, and constantly improving without a single institution or copyright holder at the wheel.

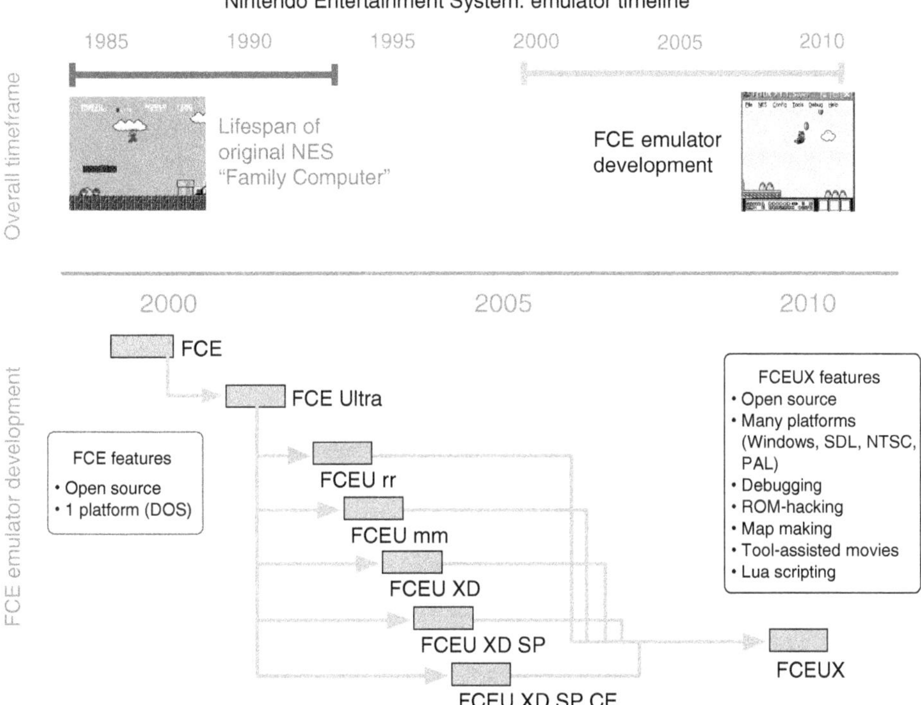

FIGURE 25.2 Development timeline of the Nintendo Entertainment System and the FCE family of emulators built for it. Courtesy of Jon Ippolito.

Learning from the Amateurs: Crowdsourcing

The amateur preservationists responsible for the FCE emulator stream are not laboring away in some government-funded think-tank or corporate software lab. They are banging out code in an Internet cafe, or in a university computer club, or in their underwear in the basement of their mother's house. But some clever organizations have realized that in proliferative preservation, the benefits of crowdsourcing can easily offset any range of quality of amateur contributions.

Photosynth (2008),[7] a project by Microsoft and the University of Washington, attaches the hundreds of amateur photographs tagged "Notre Dame" from the photo-sharing site Flickr to a pre-existing CAD model of Paris's Notre Dame cathedral, which otherwise would show just the geometry, without any visual texture. By automatically mapping each photo onto the correct vantage point and angle using a computer vision algorithm, Photosynth lets viewers explore a virtual Notre Dame at virtually any range of detail, from distant views of its skyline to detailed close-ups of its facade.

Rather than map crowdsourced images onto a shape, some applications perform the reverse reconstruction by deriving a shape from crowdsourced images of its surface. Like the replicators featured in *Star Trek*, 123D Catch (2009)[8] compiles multiple photos of a physical object taken with a smartphone into a virtual model that can be printed out using a 3D printer. It isn't hard to imagine an architectural historian using Photosynth to reconstruct, say, how Times Square has changed over the decades, or imagining a conservator using 123D Catch to preserve replicas of endangered three-dimensional objects, whether at risk of theft (such as the solid gold *Mask of Agamemnon*, 1500 BC) or of degradation (such as artist Matthew Barney's vaseline *DRILL TEAM* dumbbells, 1991). As hybrid examples of proliferative preservation, these applications employ software written by experts to collocate images taken by lay photographers.

Some forward-thinking museums have already begun to incorporate this kind of curatorial crowdsourcing. The San Francisco Museum of Asian Art invited the creators of 123D Catch to capture a handful of sculptures from their collection, and made all of the digital files freely available for anyone to download and even print using 3D printers (Hurst 2012). While the invited public could scan any sculpture that interested them, the curators selected five they believed to be of particular historical interest. All of the digital files from this "scanathon" were freely available for anyone to download and print on the online 3D object repository Thingiverse.

The Brooklyn Museum has gone further, and has enabled lay visitors to curate the collection themselves. Their 2008 exhibition *Click!* invited the public to submit photographs, which were evaluated by an online audience and finally displayed on the museum walls. The Brooklyn curators have been even more promiscuous with their collection data, creating an API that gives third parties the ability to curate their collection without permission. They have even allowed visitors to add metadata to collection records, so that the son of a Yoruba carver was able to discover his father's sculpture online and identify the maker's name, clan, and date of death.[9]

Challenges of Proliferative Preservation

Of course there are downsides to trusting amateur preservationists to do the job of professionals. I am going to focus on three of these concerns here: the loss of artistic integrity, the loss of material context, and the clash of amateur and professional cultures.

Loss of Artistic Integrity

The most common complaint is the loss of artistic integrity through deviation from a work's original intent. Here are three examples:

1 Art investors tried to cut up Picasso's *Trois Femmes* (1959) into one-inch squares to sell as "original Picassos" (Bird and Ponte 2006, 213, 278; Forrest 2008).
2 Ted Turner tried to make older movies more palatable to contemporary audiences by colorizing them or editing smoking scenes out of classic cartoons (Collins 1989).
3 George Lucas added updated special effects to the first three *Star Wars* movies of the 1970s, so they would stand up technically alongside the prequels from the 2000s, as well as seemingly minor alterations that changed important aspects of character development. Most infamously, Lucas added a blast effect behind the

head of actor Harrison Ford, to show that his character only shot the space villain Greedo in self-defense; in the eyes of hardcore *Star Wars* fans, this whitewashing of the formerly unsavory Han Solo diminished his return to grace at the end of the film, and they responded with a vigorous online campaign to protest that "Han Shot First."

These examples are all pretty clearly deviations from the spirit of the original, even when perpetrated by the original creator (as in the case of George Lucas). That said, there is only a problem if we assume the *either/or* logic of analog media: either you have the original Picasso or you have a bunch of fragments in its place; television shows either the black-and-white *Asphalt Jungle* or the colorized version.

Either/or versus both/and

But digital artifacts operate not by a logic of *either/or* but one of *both/and*. As most digital files can be cloned without loss, a preservator can migrate a work without affecting its original version. Conservators bent on rescuing an equine sculpture from Athens's smoggy skies might move it to the British Museum, but this has the unfortunate side effect of leaving a gaping hole in the Parthenon. Migrating an audio file from WAV to MP3 or Ogg Vorbis, by contrast, does not require removing the original file.

Removing analog artifacts can hurt the artifacts as well as the context. In the 1600s, Venetians keen on "rescuing" the chariot horses of Athena and Poseidon from the Turk-controlled Parthenon succeeded only in shattering them when the pulleys slipped. In the 1800s, Lord Elgin's ship carrying his first shipment of marbles sank off the island of Cythera.

If the effect of analog preserving is often fragmentation, the effect of digital preservation can be proliferation: the act of preserving becomes a palimpsest, writing new versions into the cultural niche formerly occupied only by a single version. The original lingers, but is joined in the same space by other renditions.

Take the case of museum artifacts 3D-printed by museumgoers who have photographed them. The same company that makes 123D Catch, Autodesk, also makes MeshMixer, software that makes it easy to tweak, warp, and otherwise remix 3D designs. One of the participants in the Asian Art Scanathon used MeshMixer to create an iPhone case based on a stone relief of *Kumbhakarna Battling the Monkeys*, and contemplated building an Arduino-powered LED lamp from his 3D model of an 13th-century *Seated Ganesha* sculpture. Phone cases and lamps hardly sound like the ideal vehicles for preserving Ramayana stone reliefs or elephant deities, but such proliferative preservation has been the norm rather than the exception for the tens of thousands of years that indigenous peoples kept culture alive through refashioning and retelling.[10]

In a recent example of 3D scanning as preservation, anthropologists at the Smithsonian were in talks with an Alaskan tribal leader who needed to pass on the ritual duties associated with an orca-shaped hat that had ended up in their collection. Unfortunately, the leader's health was failing too quickly to wait for the full repatriation process. So the museum arranged for a 3D replica of the killer-whale hat to be scanned from the original. The stand-in was milled, repainted by an artist, and sent to the tribe to be used in the ceremony. Since then, elders have brought in other hats to be scanned, and have danced with originals and duplicates in the same ceremony.

The Smithsonian reports hearing from some native communities that would prefer to use the replica and keep the original in a museum (*Anthropology* 2012; Waibel 2012).

In fact, most digital artists inadvertently generate multiple versions of their works in the very act of creating them, simply because that is how new media work. The single work *Apartment*, for example, first released by Martin Wattenberg, Marek Walczak, and Jonathan Feinberg in 2002, went through twenty-two variations in less than eighteen months.[11] Indeed, one of the main complaints that *Star Wars* fans have made about George Lucas is his attempt to squelch access to the original versions of the movies—a completely artificial erasure of history that isn't necessary given the *both/and* logic of digital video.

How then do preservationists accommodate the sometimes conflicting desires of creators and their audience? The opinions of artists as to how their work should be preserved form the kernel of the Variable Media Questionnaire,[12] a project begun at the Guggenheim in 1998 and currently maintained by the Forging the Future alliance, which tracks opinions about how artworks may change in the future when their current media expire. The Questionnaire asks creators to choose the most appropriate strategy for dealing with the inevitable slippage that results from translating to new mediums: storage (mothballing a PC), emulation (playing Pong on your laptop), migration (putting Super-8 on DVD), or reinterpretation (Hamlet in a chat room). It is not sociological survey, but an instrument for documenting the opinions of creators and others associated with a work as to how that work should be categorized, seen, and (if at all) recreated in the future. It is meant to be applied in a case-by-case fashion, one work at a time. This reflects a confidence that the ingenuity of artifact makers may supersede the ability of media experts to come up with a one-size-fits-all technical fix.

While the artist's own opinion formed the core of the first version of this questionnaire, subsequent versions were revised to gather feedback from many sources, from experts such as the artist's technicians or curators to members of the lay public, so as to leave a broader historical record as the basis for future decisions about the best way to preserve a work. This is essential for preserving the aging work of dead artists such as Eva Hesse; rather than choosing either storage, recommended by her estate, or emulation, favored by fellow artist Sol LeWitt, the Questionnaire offers both opinions and lets the future decide which is most appropriate.

Even living artists can benefit from crowdsourcing opinions about their work for future preservation. The project *Botaniq* (2011)[13] by media artist Gabriel Vanegas offers "diaries of an observer and interactor ... to be able to look at the work of art more than in its materiality, as an artifact that narrates stories of a cultural moment, an unique journey, particular and unrepeatable." *Botaniq* appears to aim for a pre-taxonomic form of documentation:

> The conquerors of America faced a similar problematics on having seen the impossibility of showing to Europe the new beautiful species that they were discovering since the trip by ship was very long, bringing only dissected bodies, without movement, smell, color or flavor. That is why the notations and the diaries of the members of the expeditions went from being just a documentation or a copy to become the reality itself.[14]

Of course, natural history textbooks are fond to point out the cultural biases exhibited by eyewitness "botanists," as in Hendrick Goltzius's 1598 drawing of a beached whale sporting an ear where its pectoral fin should be. What they seldom point out is that some witness accounts, such as Jan Saenredam's 1602 engraving of an anatomically correct whale, are better than others (Sears Goldman 2012). For her oral history of *The Giver of Names*, Lizzie Muller and collaborator Caitlin Jones interviewed artist David Rokeby but also random audience participants and museum attendants, whose reactions portray a side of the work that even the artist didn't anticipate (Muller 2008). With enough eyeballs, an accurate portrayal of the new species may emerge.

Loss of Material Context

Another common criticism leveled at emulation, migration, and other "variable media" preservation strategies is their detachment of a work from its original hardware; this detachment is all the more likely once you let amateurs in on the job of reinterpreting works in new media.

It is true that certain works, such as Nam June Paik's *TV Crown* (1965) or Cory Arcangel's *Hogan's Alley* (2002), resist translation into new mediums because their artistic meaning is bound up with a specific apparatus such as a cathode-ray tube or light gun. Some art historians and conservators would claim that this is true of the majority of cultural artifacts, leaving the variable media paradigm a viable strategy only for conceptual art and its descendants.

This subtle critique is important, but misguided. For the variable media paradigm claims not that an artwork is divorceable from its material substrate, but that it *already has many material substrates.* A single-channel video by Pipilotti Rist employs a new projector every time it travels to a new museum. The bricks purchased for a favela installed by Marjetica Potrc are different for a New York installation than for one in Johannesburg. Mark Morris's *Nutcracker* looks completely different from Mikhail Baryshnikov's, which looks different from George Balanchine's. A Java applet by John F. Simon, Jr. looks larger or smaller, brighter or duller, and runs faster or slower depending upon whether its viewer has a 1998 Powerbook or a 2008 MacBook.

With this multiplicity in mind, the variable media paradigm starts not from an assumption of universality but of differentiation. From this perspective, an artwork consists not of the Platonic essence to which every physical instance aspires, but the accumulation of attempts to achieve the artist's intent as rendered in different browsers, resolutions, durations, and publics.

The Clash of Cultures

The third concern sometimes raised about proliferative preservation is not about the work being preserved but about the folks doing the preserving. It's all very well to recognize that game fanatics have built an incredible stockpile of emulators to preserve their favorite pastime, but how do the diversions of a dispersed fanbase translate into preservation tactics that can be used immediately by professionals in libraries and conservation labs? Few of the genres collected by museums and archives command the rabid obsession that gamers devote to Mario or Minecraft. Museum conservators study resins and spectrometry, not ROMs and savefiles. And whereas the vast majority of games were designed for widespread commercial platforms from the Atari to the Xbox, many new media artworks are unorthodox assemblages of custom code, network connections, environmental inputs and outputs, and other non-standard elements.

Fortunately, those new media works that don't depend on hardware idiosyncrasies can avail themselves of "emulation as a service," a model that emerged in the early 2010s. Initiatives such as bwFLA,[15] JSMESS,[16] and the Olive project[17] offer screen-based works a new browser-based habitat that's easily accessible and in same cases doesn't require specialized software to install. Even if most emulators to date have been developed by game-loving geeks, the collateral benefit of chip-level emulation means that they inadvertently emulate non-gaming software as well. Visit the JSMESS emulation portal and you can run primordial accounting software for a Texas Instruments home computer alongside *E.T. the Extra-terrestrial* for the Atari game console; the JavaScript is agnostic as to whether the application is productive or frivolous. For its part, the bwFLA web site lists use cases that include reproducing scientific experiments, accessing historic digital documents, re-enacting business processes to understand past decisions, and enabling "crowd curation."[18] If these easy-to-access environments prevail, digital art may enjoy an afterlife in the cloud.

What about works created for esoteric platforms that aren't available via emulation as a service? Even if museums and archives may not have the technical chops to build emulators themselves, they can band together to choose an extinct but historically important platform that would benefit various constituencies and then fund the development of an emulator for that platform. As one example, artists Char Davies, Golan Levin, and Karl Sims made important work that depended on hardware by the now-defunct company Silicon Graphics, so writing an emulator for those machines could rescue an entire class of endangered art. Or museums could help influence the development of an emulator to improve access to an entire collection. After collaborating on the bwFLA emulation service, artist Dragan Espenschied took the post of digital conservator at the new media art platform Rhizome. He has since worked to integrate bwFLA directly into Rhizome's collection of software art, so that viewing and interacting with an obsolete work might be as easy playing a YouTube video.

Of course, few archives have a digital conservator on staff as of this writing, and not many conservators are as intimate as Espenschied with what's lurking beneath the hood of an emulation platform. So instead of trying to build a collaborator and emulator themselves, museums can crowdsource the problem by putting out calls for help from communities who get excited by working with art and creative culture. It isn't enough to start a random Kickstarter campaign, however. You need to research and build bridges to the communities you're targeting. Michael Dille, a member of the CMU Computer Club who helped resurrect the lost Andy Warhol Amiga artworks from the 1980s, says it is not enough for museums to ask for help on a blog read only by a close-knit community. Rather, an institution in need might seek out niche clubs online or in academia likely to have the requisite enthusiasm and free time, or announce a "fun little contest" with a small monetary bounty and the promise of some fame to resurrect their obscure artifact (Dille 2014).

These communities are already out there, waiting for an enterprising museum to collaborate with them. Calling itself "an active archive of computer art," the ReCode project invites volunteer programmers to reverse-engineer the images illustrated in the magazine *Computer Graphics and Art* published from 1976 to 1978, releasing them as Processing sketches released under the open MIT license.[19] The digital artists of Re-programmed Art, meanwhile, recreate with Arduinos and other contemporary technologies the sculptures and installations of Gruppo T, an Italian collective of artists that pioneered an algorithmic approach to artmaking in the 1960s.[20]

Beyond emulation, collecting institutions should also recognize other preservation problems they share with the gaming community, with an eye toward teaming up or repurposing each other's solutions. How, for example, can preservators recreate the full participatory experience of a work whose content came, and presumably should continue to come, from its audience? As soon as artists got their hands on HTML in the mid-1990s, they began making projects that open the door for other users to participate. Alexei Shulgin invited his fellow netizens to contribute screenshots of their desktops. Martin Wattenberg invited gallerygoers to sit at a kiosk and build apartments out of words. Mark Napier created a *Digital Landfill* as a repository for other people's cast-aside e-mails, images, and other unwanted bits.

While the gaming community hasn't solved the problem of archiving user-generated content, it suffers even more keenly from the problem. Second Life contains thousands of custom dwellings created by its users; Minecraft contains millions. Were a game conservator merely to archive and replay the source code for one of these games—either on the original hardware or running under emulation—it would do nothing to preserve the rich history of virtual architecture, costumes, and props invented by its former inhabitants.

Another example of a common preservation conundrum is how to represent the timeline of a work that has been remixed. Art in the Internet age has a tendency to mutate as it propagates through and beyond its intended community. Sometimes this is intentional, as when Olia Lialina invited other artists to transform her most famous work and added their remixes to her *Last Real Net Art Museum*. At other times the metamorphosis is unauthorized, as when a photograph of a Sandinista hurling a Molotov cocktail inspired a painting by Joy Garnett, which triggered a copyright suit filed by the original photographer, which in turn inspired hundreds of additional derivative images produced by Internet artists in protest. We might think of these third-party variations on an original work the way game modders think about the scores of third-party mods for a popular game like *Civilization*. While of questionable authenticity, in the traditional sense that they are not part of the original work's scope, mods like these are part of the social history of the work and in some cases become more important than the work itself.

While no one has yet found a silver bullet to archive the networks of remix culture in their full complexity, the gaming world has online forums like the Civilization Fanatics Center that nourish modding culture (Bell and Ippolito 2015), while some museum curators have explored version-tracking systems like CC-Mixter or The Pool.[21] Leaders from both domains should be comparing notes. A rare example of this is the consortium project Preserving Virtual Worlds, in which librarians from Stanford rubbed shoulders with computer scientists from Urbana-Champaign to interview influential game designers and imagine how to keep the most important video games and online environments from disappearing from history without a trace. The lessons learned from these game studies will benefit any parallel efforts to rescue other creative genres dependent on interactivity, participatory content, and remix.

Conclusion

I hope I have shown that some of the bugaboos of proliferative preservation seem a lot less scary once you realize that digital media are inherently multiple and variable. One bugaboo that won't be going away any time soon is the fact that proliferative preservation loosens the control of culture's traditional custodians over the future of the culture they are supposed to preserve.

Yet, as threatening as these amateurs may seem, the cultural elite would do well to find a way to live symbiotically with them, because the creativity and ingenuity they bring to the job of cultural perseverance can inject a much-needed vitality into the professional archive and its dusty shelves. As much as professional conservators might fear an army of amateurs, such "unreliable archivists" have kept their culture alive by retelling and rescripting while highbrow electronic artworks decay into inert assemblages of wire and plastic in their climate-controlled crates. The 21st century may never know the remarkable art created for the Sony SMC-70 or Silicon Graphics Onyx, but the future of the mapinguary and Mario is all but assured.

If the custodians of culture want to add artists such as Grahame Weinbren and Char Davies to that future, they will need to fund more than conservation labs and climate-controlled vaults. Artists' studios, online forums, and remote villages are where culture is birthed and resurrected by its indigenous producers. Permanent exhibitions nourish art less than temporary exhibitions, where works are upgraded and displayed before being routed to their next venue. Conservators need to understand strategies such as emulation, migration, and reinterpretation and make sure the artists they work with understand them, too. And museums need to allocate less of their budgets to renting storage space and more to funding the process of creating, and recreating, art.

Notes

1 This essay expands on ideas developed in my chapter "Unreliable Archivists" from the book *Re-Collection: Art, New Media, and Social Memory* (Rinehart and Ippolito 2014). An earlier version of this essay was given as a keynote at the Fifth National Symposium of the Brazilian Association of Cyberculture Researchers, Universidade Federal de Santa Catarina, Brazil, November 16, 2011. The author wishes to thank Yara Guasque, Jason Scott, Dragan Espenschied, and Christiane Paul for their help in shaping this essay.

2 Peggy Phelan writes that "performance cannot be saved, recorded, documented, or otherwise participate in the circulation of representations of representation" (quoted in Taylor 2003, 5).

3 Through his involvement with the Carnegie Mellon Computer Club, Michael Dille was instrumental in recovering Andy Warhol's digital art for the obsolete Amiga platform; he jokes that a reporter who wanted to talk to the kids who reconstructed the Warhols never addressed him Dr. Dille despite his graduate-level experience with digital forensics. Private correspondence with the author, May 13, 2014.

4 For a lugubrious litany of the obstacles facing today's preservators, see the "Death by Technology," "Death by Institution," and "Death by Law" chapters of *Re-collection: Art, New Media, and Social Memory* (Rinehart and Ippolito 2014).

5 http://variablemedia.net (accessed August 10, 2014).

6 *Seeing Double: Emulation in Theory and Practice*, Solomon R. Guggenheim Museum, New York, March 18–May 16, 2004. http://variablemedia.net/e/seeingdouble (accessed August 10, 2014).

7 http://photosynth.net/ (accessed August 10, 2014). For an excellent overview, see Blaise Aguera y Arcas, "How PhotoSynth Can Connect the World's Images" (2007).
8 http://www.123dapp.com/ (accessed August 10, 2014).
9 The crowdsourced information about provenance was visible at the following URL on May 18, 2012, but it has since been moved: http://www.brooklynmuseum.org/opencollection/objects/147096/Figure_of_a_Clergyman/right-tab/talk/.
10 See, for example, the discussion of the production of Malanggan cloth in Papua New Guinea in Joline Blais, "Indigenous Domain: Pilgrims, Permaculture, and Perl" (n/d).
11 See the appendix of "Death by Wall Label" (Ippolito 2008).
12 http://variablemediaquestionnaire.net (accessed August 10, 2014).
13 http://botaniq.org/ (accessed August 10, 2014).
14 http://botaniq.org/2010/09/17/theory-of-botaniq/ (accessed August 10, 2014).
15 bwFLA – Emulation as a Service. http://bw-fla.uni-freiburg.de (accessed October 3, 2014).
16 JSMESS – The JavaScript MESS. http://jsmess.textfiles.com (accessed October 3, 2014).
17 Olive Executable Archive. https://olivearchive.org (accessed October 3, 2014).
18 bwFLA – Emulation as a Service.. http://bw-fla.uni-freiburg.de (accessed October 3, 2014).
19 http://recodeproject.com (accessed October 4, 2014).
20 http://www.reprogrammed-art.cc (accessed October 4, 2014).
21 For a general description of this dynamic, see "The Open Museum" chapter in *Re-collection: Art, New Media, and Social Memory* (Ippolito and Rinehart 2014).

References

Aguera y Arcas, Blaise. 2007. "How PhotoSynth Can Connect the World's Images." *TED2007*, March. http://www.ted.com/talks/blaise_aguera_y_arcas_demos_photosynth (accessed August 10. 2014).

Anthropology: The Newsletter of The Department of Anthropology National Museum of Natural History. Spring 2012. http://anthropology.si.edu/outreach/anthropolog/Springanthropologa.pdf (accessed August 10, 2014).

Bell, John, and Jon Ippolito. 2015. "Diffused Museums: Networked, Augmented, and Self-Organized Collections." In *The International Handbooks of Museum Studies*, edited by Michelle Henning. Malden, MA: Wiley-Blackwell.

Benkler, Yochai. 2007. *The Wealth of Networks: How Social Production Transforms Markets and Freedom*. New Haven, CT: Yale University Press.

Bird, Robert C., and Lucille M. Ponte. 2006. "Protecting Moral Rights in the United States and the United Kingdom: Challenges and Opportunities under the U.K.'s New Performances Regulations." *Boston University International Law Journal* 24.

Blais, Joline. n/d. "Indigenous Domain: Pilgrims, Permaculture, and Perl." *ThoughtMesh*. http://thoughtmesh.net/publish/6.php (accessed October 3, 2014).

Collins, Glenn. 1989. "Tribute for a Dauntless Bette Davis." *The New York Times*, April 20. http://www.nytimes.com/1989/04/20/movies/tribute-for-a-dauntless-bette-davis-yes.htmlhttp://www.nytimes.com/1989/04/20/movies/tribute-for-a-dauntless-bette-davis-yes.html (accessed August 13, 2014).

Dille, Michael. 2014. Private correspondence with Jon Ippolito. May 13.

Forrest, Nicholas. 2008. "Picasso Gets the Chop!!" *Art Market Blog*, Sydney, April 17. http://www.artmarketblog.com/2008/04/17/picasso-gets-the-chop-artmarketblogcom/ (accessed November 2, 2013).

Hurst, Nathan. 2012. "3D-Print Your Own Ancient Art at Museum Scanathon." *Wired*, October 2. http://www.wired.com/2012/10/scanathon/ (accessed November 1, 2013).

Ippolito, Jon. 2008. Appendix to "Death by Wall Label." In *New Media in the White Cube and Beyond: Curatorial Models for Digital Art*, edited by Christiane Paul. Berkeley, CA: University of California Press.

Levy, David. 2004– . "About." Personal web site. http://jarnac.jarnac.org/aboutdavid.htm (accessed October 13, 2015).

Muller, Lizzie. 2008. "Towards an Oral History of New Media Art." Daniel Langlois Foundation for Art, Science, and Technology. http://www.fondation-langlois.org/html/e/page.php?NumPage=2101 (accessed August 10, 2014).

Rinehart, Richard, and Jon Ippolito. 2014. *Re-Collection: Art, New Media, and Social Memory.* Cambridge, MA: The MIT Press.

Rohter, Larry. 2007. "A Huge Amazon Monster Is Only a Myth. Or Is It?" *The New York Times*, July 8. http://www.nytimes.com/2007/07/08/world/americas/08amazon.html (accessed February 9, 2012).

Sears Goldman, Victoria. 2012. "Omen and Oracle: Dutch Images of Beached Whales." Posted August 22. http://www.victoriasearsgoldman.com/16th-17th-century-dutch-images-beached-whales (accessed August 10, 2014).

Sherman, Tom. 2007. "The Premature Birth of Video Art." *iDC* e-mail list, January 8. https://mailman.thing.net/pipermail/idc/2007-January/000949.html (accessed October 3, 2014).

Slashdot. 2009. "Maori Legend of Man-Eating Birds Is True." September 14. http://science.slashdot.org/story/09/09/14/1718211/Maori-Legend-of-Man-Eating-Birds-is-True (accessed February 9, 2012).

Stiegler, Bernard. 2011. "Le temps de l'amatorat." *Alliage* 69, October. Published online July 17, 2012. http://revel.unice.fr/alliage/index.html?id=3272 (accessed October 3, 2014).

Tanni, Valentina, curator. 2014. Curatorial statement. *Eternal September: The Rise of Amateur Culture.* Škuc Gallery, Ljubljana, September 2–26, 2014. http://www.aksioma.org/eternal.september (accessed October 3, 2014).

Taylor, Diana. 2003. *The Archive and the Repertoire: Performing Cultural Memory in the Americas.* Durham, NC: Duke University Press.

Waibel, Gunther. 2013. Presentation at Digital Curation Summit, Washington, DC, January 8. Organized by Johns Hopkins University, University of Arizona, and Simmons College.

26

Enabling the Future, or How to Survive FOREVER

Annet Dekker

> A wall covered with paper print outs, resembling an architectural drawing of the inside of an immense house. Some of its surroundings can be discerned: a beach, a yacht. Against a black background colourful bars show the contours of the different rooms. Each print also describes the specific space, from bathroom to kitchen, to attic. The early computer aesthetics are clearly visible in the typeface as well as the minimal and crude design of the drawing. On the other side of the wall is a large table with various screens: a 1980s television CRT monitor, a flat screen computer monitor and an iPad touchscreen. Two kids are trying to play the game, running backwards and forwards, they are finding their way through the game by comparing the images on the television monitor with the plan of the mansion on the other side of the wall.[1] (JODI, *Jet Set Willy FOREVER*, 2010, at the exhibition *Funware*, MU, Eindhoven, November 2010)

Around the turn of the millennium, artist duo JODI, Joan Heemskerk and Dirk Paesmans, started to revive the old computer game *Jet Set Willy* (1984) (Figure 26.1). The game had attracted their attention because it had been programmed in BASIC, one of the first computer languages designed to empower users of one of the initial personal home computers, the now obsolete ZX Spectrum, which was released in the UK in 1984. The popular video game *Jet Set Willy* was one of the earliest non-linear games, featuring branching storylines, from the 1980s. The protagonist of the game, the tired miner Willy, is ordered by his housekeeper to tidy up all the items left around his house after a huge party before being allowed to go to sleep. The player moves Willy through the immense villa complex, consisting of sixty rooms, a beach and a yacht, and tries to gather as many objects as possible in each of the spaces. Trying to reprogram the code with the help of an emulator—a software application accurately imitating hardware or software functions—proved to be more difficult then JODI had envisioned.[2] The keys of the original keyboard had multiple functions and in order to

A Companion to Digital Art, First Edition. Edited by Christiane Paul.

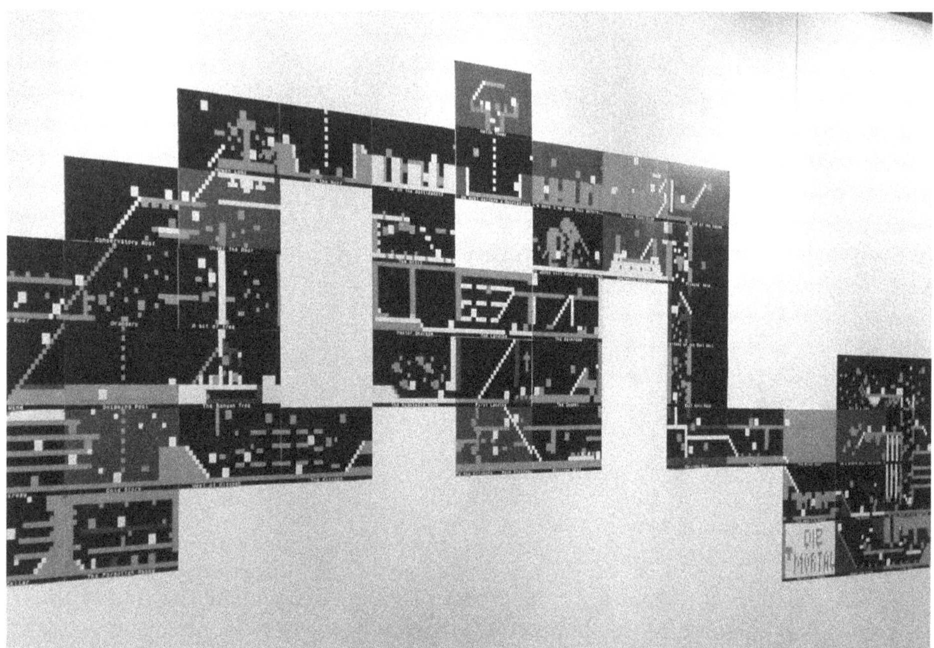

FIGURE 26.1 JODI, *Jet Set Willy FOREVER*, 2013. Floorplan of the game. Installation shot MU Eindhoven. Photo courtesy of Boudewijn Bollmann.

retype a command on a contemporary computer keyboard, even a simple "GOTO" statement (goto is a statement found in many computer programming languages that performs a one-way transfer of control to another line of code; at the level of machine code, a goto is a form of branch or jump statement) turned out to be a complicated issue, because all the easy short cuts were missing and one now needed to find the right key combination for each task. In the end, JODI gained control over the game by using the emulator to access the machine code—the binary or hexadecimal instructions to which a computer can respond directly—and, once inside, reconfigured the colors and sounds byte by byte. Their version was recorded on an audiocassette that could be played on the original ZX Spectrum. They lost some of the original hardware, the original audiotape from which the game played, but this didn't interfere with the experience of the user who could still play JODI's *Jet Set Willy ©1984* (2002) with the old keyboard since only the arrow-keys were needed to move Willy around in the game.

JODI are renowned for their subversive and, at first sight, often seemingly incomprehensible artworks, and, to make matters worse, their projects frequently vary from presentation to presentation. Not only do the artists present different variations of a work from venue to venue, they might suddenly, and without announcement, come in during an exhibition to change aspects of the work's presentation. Over the years *Jet Set Willy ©1984* has been exhibited in various ways. The first time it was shown on a table, with a 1980s television (CRT) monitor, the audiocassette with the tape, and the ZX Spectrum displayed on it. At other times JODI showed *Jet Set Willy Variations* (2002), a DVD containing multiple videos of modifications of the game, alongside the game itself. Almost ten years after the launch of the project, *Jet Set Willy ©1984* transformed into *Jet Set Willy FOREVER* (2010) when it was presented during the exhibition *Funware* at MU in Eindhoven. This time the artists decided to add documentation of the work as part of the presentation, thus making documentation part of the "final work." *Jet Set Willy FOREVER* included the game on a ZX Spectrum; the DVD; video documentation of the artists demonstrating how the game can be played during a previous presentation of the work; a set of written instructions on how to play the game, and sixty prints showing the interior of the game—a cross-section of the house. The organization of exhibitions always entails a discussion about the extent to which a work should speak for itself or whether additional explanation and documentation of the project's previous manifestations is needed. In the case of *Jet Set Willy*, documentation serves several purposes. It gives clues on how to install *Jet Set Willy* by showing on video what equipment is preferred and how to play the game. As such, the documentation could be seen as an informational document. However, JODI's approach to documentation material is different; they do not see the documentation of *Jet Set Willy FOREVER* as separate from the work or as merely educational and informational, but as integral element of the work itself. From an aesthetic perspective, the components of *Jet Set Willy FOREVER* declare the value of documentation as an aesthetic element of the work.

An emphasis on documentation is not uncommon when it comes to ephemeral artworks such as performance art, or dance and theatre pieces. In the case of artworks that contain or consist of components prone to become obsolete, documentation, for better or worse, often becomes a substitute for the project. Some conservators and curators find these scenarios frightening and consider the approach to "simply" change the presentation, or hardware, of an installation, or to show documentation instead of the work itself, utterly inappropriate. What implications do changes in the presentation format, or the exhibition of documentation, have for the conservation of an artwork? How will *Jet Set Willy FOREVER* survive in the future? More importantly, what can conservators and curators of contemporary art learn from JODI's practice of variability and use of documentation? Or, in more general terms, what is needed in order to enable digital artworks to survive FOREVER?

The first part of this chapter consists of a brief elaboration of the conservation practice in relation to digital art. In the second section a specific aspect of a conservation practice, the attempt to approach as close as possible the authentic state of an artwork, is analyzed in relation to digital art through an exploration of different artworks that exemplify specific challenges to the notion of authenticity.

Conservation Practice

Conservation is a relatively young field of theory and practice. One of the most debated issues in the field concerns the limits of restoration practices: how far can one go in making changes to the object, which guidelines need to be followed, and is the artwork or the artist's intent "leading" this effort? In other words, how can culturally significant artifacts such as works of art be preserved as close as possible to their "authentic" state or, if necessary, restored to that state by means of interventions? For a long time conservation research was focused on conserving the physical object with the help of scientific and technical research. With the introduction of (or return to) more unstable, ephemeral, and live art practices from the early 20th century onwards, conservation strategies changed. The conceptual, unstable, variable, or process-like character of many contemporary artworks challenged the conventional object-oriented approach of fine art conservation. Unlike traditional painting and sculpture, contemporary artworks often include ephemeral materials and technologies that quickly become obsolete. Furthermore, contemporary art forms such as digital art (but also conceptual art, much of installation and land art, performance art etc.) are not always made for eternity and inherently address the notion of change and variability within their own conceptual framework. The idea that a media object becomes obsolete even at the moment of its creation is not new. Consequently it seems logical to move away from a fixation on the conservation of the material or physical components of an artwork, as it would most likely turn out to be counterproductive. So how have conservators approached the conservation of digital art?

Important steps in developing methods for the conservation of time-based media have been made by several collaborative research projects, among them the Variable Media Network, Matters in Media Art, Inside Installations, and DOCAM.[3] There are three basic notions underlying the methodologies of these initiatives: enabling artist(s) participation as much as possible; flexibility; and openness (provenance and transparency). This way of thinking confirms the necessity to let go of traditional preservation methods that focus on the recreation of the work and to develop new ways of documenting obsolete artworks. In addition, it entices new approaches to the conservation of works of art. As Pip Laurenson suggests in her article "Authenticity, Change, and Loss in the Conservation of Time-Based Media Installations," the focus of conservation must move away from the purely material to include the original experience and contextual meaning of the artwork. In her exploration of a conceptual framework for the conservation of time-based media installations she concludes that,

> The reference "state" of an object has been replaced with the concept of the "identity" of the work, which describes everything that must be preserved in order to avoid the loss of something of value in the work of art. (Laurenson 2006)

In other words, as opposed to the traditional view taken in the conservation of fine arts, it is not necessarily material objects that are considered to be most valuable, but rather the intrinsic qualities of the artwork that provide the viewer with a certain experience. The value of a digital artwork does not necessarily reside strictly in the materiality of the medium itself but in a number of contributing elements that, together, establish the work's aesthetic qualities. What is interesting to note here is that, along with these more conceptual changes in understanding conservation, the Variable Media Initiative proposed new ways of dealing with the preservation of technical components of an artwork. Their approach seeks to offer choices ranging from the storage of a work and the acceptability of emulation or migration strategies to the artist's refusal of any modification to their work, which consequently will lead to its "death." What the Variable Media approach puts forth is the "idea of endurance by variability" or "permanence through change" (Depocas, Ippolito, and Jones 2003). According to Jon Ippolito (2003, 47–53) four possible strategies can be used, depending on the artist's approval, to make decisions about the conservation of a work:

1 *Storage*: Storage of the physical work (hardware, equipment, or archive digital files on disk). The disadvantage of storage is that the artwork will expire once ephemeral materials cease to function.

2 *Emulation*: Imitation of the original look of the piece by completely different means. Possible disadvantages are the financial costs that can be high and inconsistencies with the artist's intent.
3 *Migration*: Involves upgrading equipment and source material of the work. The major drawback is that the original appearance of the artwork will change in its new medium.
4 *Reinterpretation*: Reinterpretation of the work each time it is recreated. It is a dangerous technique, when not warranted by the artist, but it may be the only way to recreate performance, installation, or networked art designed to vary with context.

Following the initial research of the Variable Media Network the Guggenheim Museum, in partnership with the Daniel Langlois Foundation, organized the exhibition *Seeing Double* (2004) to test the promise of these experimental conservation treatments for new media artworks, among them JODI's *Jet Set Willy ©1984*. The exhibition presented a series of original artworks paired with their emulated or migrated versions. It offered a unique opportunity for both art experts and the public to directly compare both versions and decide for themselves whether the recreations captured the spirit of the originals. The exhibition generated insights into the workings and reinstallation of various works—all of them developed in consultation with the artists—but, beyond that, showed that there was a public interest in these previously "hidden" practices. This "behind-the-scenes" type of exhibition has become increasingly popular, and one can argue that the public's understanding and appreciation of the artworks increases when these issues are made accessible. This might ultimately lead to a new conservation paradigm where public interference with and questioning of conservation practices may lead to more inclusive approaches (Muller 2008; Roms 2008).[4] *Seeing Double* also brought to light challenges connected to the differences between works housed within a museum collection or outside of the institutional context when it comes to presentation and preservation. Reflecting on the exhibition, it can be argued that traditional preservation approaches conducted by museums are often insufficient when applied to digital work and more flexible models and interdisciplinary collaboration is needed to tackle digital conservation.

These are all relevant points that, when carefully considered, could lead to better conservation practices. At the same time, all of these approaches are still based on the idea of a "finished" artwork, thereby holding on to some of the traditional ways of dealing with objects and documents. As Laurenson puts it, the common understanding of an artwork (as the object of conservation) still is that of "a unique object," where the "notion of authenticity is based on physical integrity," which then guides decisions about the changes that can be made to the work (Laurenson 2006).[5] As stated before, the notion of art as a unique object poses several problems for the understanding of digital artworks. Despite the variable nature expressing itself in ever-changing constellations of elements that get exhibited—JODI's *Jet Set Willy FOREVER* being a prime example—authenticity can nevertheless still be identified and remains important when thinking about strategies for conserving digital art.

Authentic Alliances

Drafted by forty-five representatives from twenty-eight countries, *The Nara Document on Authenticity* (Larsen 1994) has become an important document on authenticity. According to its content, conservation of cultural heritage in all its forms and historical periods is rooted in the values attributed to the heritage. The ability to understand these values depends, in part, on the degree to which information sources about these values qualify as credible or truthful. Knowledge and understanding of these information sources and their meaning, in relation to original and subsequent characteristics of the cultural heritage, form a requisite basis for assessing all aspects of authenticity. This is the departure point for most conservators when thinking about the treatment of artworks. David Lowenthal (2008) stressed that authenticity will always be variable and—due to the insistence on the value of cultural and geographical differences in determining authenticity—will become even more challenging, if not contradictory to pursue.[6] In the same article Lowenthal also points to the devaluation of the notion and use of authenticity by referring to authenticity as a buzzword of the 21st century that has come to describe anything non-commercial. How legitimate indeed are the criteria used to validate something as authentic, or why should a Western perspective on heritage be the leading one? Although these are important questions that deserve answers, I would like to focus here on the ways in which artists are pushing the question of the relevance of authenticity. While recognizing the controversies surrounding the importance of authenticity, I would argue that it is still worthwhile to use the notion of authenticity for gaining a better understanding of an artwork's inherent qualities.

In line with Laurenson (2006) I argue for a practice that encourages thinking about "authentic instances," leaving intact the notion of authenticity but allowing for change and variability. This way of working rejects the freeze frame associated with traditional conservation and acknowledges the value of the communicative turn in preservation. Taking advantage of the "variable nature" of definitions of authenticity, I would like to argue for something more speculative and process driven: the notion of "authentic alliances." Alliance stems from the Old French word *aliance*—from *alier* (modern: *allier*); to *ally* in English—and is used to define "anything akin to another by structure, etc." (Webster's 1913). In his analysis of Proust, Gilles Deleuze describes several sets of "machines" that, through learning and process, produce collections of incomplete parts (fragments):

> A One and a Whole that would not be the principle but, on the contrary, the "effect" of the multiplicity and of its disconnected parts. One and Whole that would function as effect, effect of machines, instead of as principles. A communication that would not be posited in principle but would result from the operation of the machines and their detached parts, their noncommunicating fragments. (Deleuze 2000/1964, 163).

Following Deleuze, I would like to connect the concept of alliances to authenticity in order to stress the importance of seeing seemingly different parts as a whole. These alliances function as "effects" that show the deeper reality underlying a well-formed whole constructed from parts. From this perspective, I would like to emphasize the inherent intertwined structures through which digital art is created. This approach implies that artworks reveal themselves through fragments and that such fragments are likely to change over time, creating not a nicely narrated story of events amounting to a plot, but conjunctures that, through their gaps, attain meaning. Rather than taking the obvious viewpoint of an audience member who experiences the work, that is, the package or presentation of digital art, I want to place the focus elsewhere, bringing into view the invisible but governing principles that drive digital art. This understanding of authenticity not only opens a path leading to new directions for conservators, but also suggests ways for dealing with forms of (in)visible structures that exist all around. Moreover, I would like to stress the significance and promote the acknowledgment of dispersed networks through which knowledge and practices survive. Applied this way, the notion of "alliances" not only serves to identify the authenticity of digital art, but, as I will show, also manifests itself in the network of caretakers, or better a "community of concern," that is formed around certain digital artworks and the people who take care of or safeguard the work. A community of concern places emphasis on collective intelligence (Levy 1999), or the idea of a knowledge community (Jenkins 2006), in which everyone knows something, but no one knows everything. This shifts the emphasis of responsibility from caretaking to concern. A dispersed network of knowledge with a non-hierarchical structure places importance on localized knowledge, avoiding standardization and ensuring variability rather than creating a freeze state.[7] Such networks are not restricted to digital art, and can also be found in other practices. Geert Lovink and Ned Rossiter (2005), for example, put forward the concept of "org nets"—organized networks that should be seen in opposition to commercial social networking web sites. These network formations are based on people who come together for a common purpose by building strong ties among dispersed individuals, thereby bringing goal-driven organization to the Internet. This process of networking reaffirms the significance that the notion of authentic alliances can hold for digital art, as well as other art practices.

Through an exploration of different net artworks, in the following I will analyze authenticity in net art by identifying its "nominal" qualities that ensure that an artwork is properly named; defined simply as the identification of the object (material), authorship (author), and the origins (time).

An Example: mouchette.org

Mouchette.org (1997) is a project that started in the early days of the Internet and is still running. The project presents itself as the web site of a thirteen-year-old girl who tells stories about her life, while inviting others to participate and play in her worlds (Figure 26.2). Over the years the site has grown and more and more stories have been added, each occupying their own web space within the site. Next to orchestrating her online presence, Mouchette organized offline projects, from birthday parties to music CDs, postcards, and a Guerrilla Fanshop. Some of these are easy to trace, but others are more difficult to track, and even Martine Neddam, the artist behind the project, does not remember all the projects or performances that have become part of the Mouchette network. In order to keep track of new articles or projects, she has been regularly checking the referrer site for links to statistics of mouchette.org since 1998, but offline events, in particular, prove to be hard to trace, because of a lack of official "commissioning" contracts or exhibitions where all the Mouchette-related projects are exhibited together, a concrete "end date" for (components of) the project, or other parameters that usually determine an artwork. This type of a distributed network of projects and events exemplifies what Deleuze refers to as "a One and a Whole." Instead of departing from one form of the work and evolving into slight variations, as in Laurenson's "authentic instances," mouchette.org is a (still growing) ecology of different projects circling around the brand Mouchette. As such, it would make sense

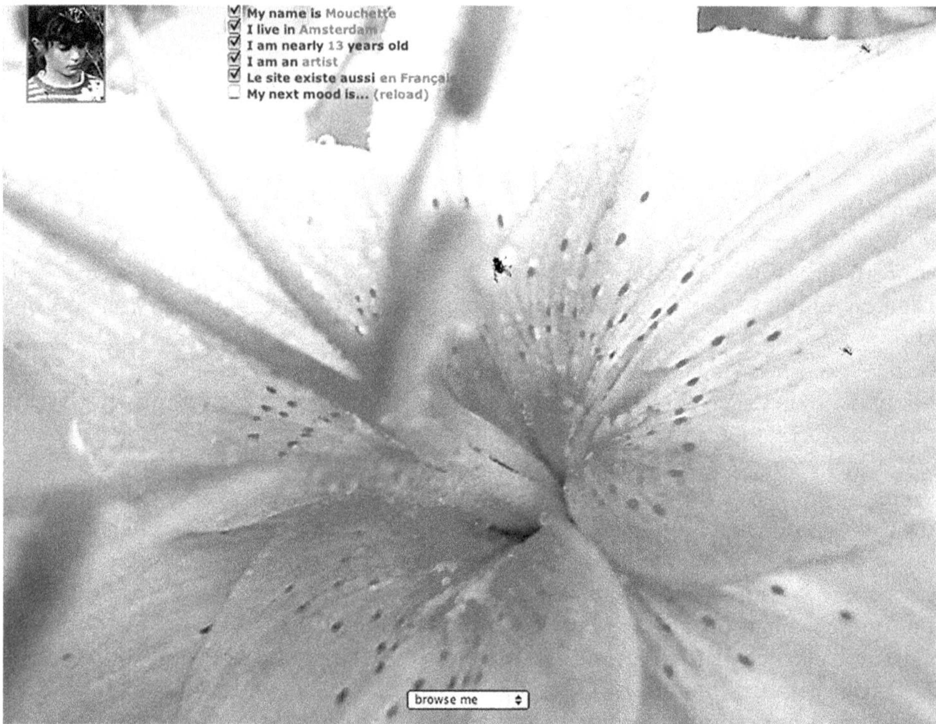

FIGURE 26.2 Mouchette.org, 1997. Screenshot.

to refer to mouchette.org as *authentic alliances*. This understanding gives prominence to a set of relationships and processes and moves away from the idea of the final, finished object.

Material

In order to determine material authenticity of an artwork, empirical observations concerning the materials, techniques, condition, and configuration are typically undertaken (Munoz Viñas 2005; Appelbaum 2007). This determination process for proof of authenticity is often undertaken with the help of technical tools. Until World War II several chemical methods of analysis were available to restore artworks, and since the 1940s analysis started to develop and use techniques that were based on physics. All these methods required that small samples were taken from the artwork, and often the techniques proved destructive. In the last decades the use of X-rays, lasers, and 3D visualization techniques proved to be less destructive and these techniques kept developing, being supplemented by synchroton radiation and multi-spectral digital cameras. Throughout the years, conservation has been divided into two camps: those stressing the importance of material conditions of an artwork, and those emphasizing the value of preserving the conceptual part of the artwork, meaning the cultural significance of the work that most commonly resides in the conceptual intent of the artist.[8] Instead of seeing these approaches as a binary opposition, I would like to focus on the intricate relation between the two, thereby once again affirming the validity of authentic alliances.

Digital artworks typically consist of a combination of software and hardware. Hardware refers to the physical components of the computer, such as the monitor, keyboard, wires, and data storage (hard drives, mouse, printers, graphic and sound cards, memory, motherboard, chips etc.). Software components are mostly hidden, not directly visible, their aesthetics shielding the programming and functionality beneath it. In more general terms, software consists of the instructions that are entered into the memory of the computer, and is referred to as "soft" because it is more malleable than the hardware (Petzold 2000). Although the distinction between software and code is often blurred in common parlance, understanding the difference between the terms often helps to identify authenticity. Software is the computer program that end users perceive and/or interact with, while code is what constructs that software; each software can consist of layers of code. Another useful distinction can be made between code and data; code refers to the instructions of the programming language themselves, and data is the source material that the code manipulates (Petzold 2000), for example, health or weather statistics. In other words, the physical computer's processor carries out the instructions of the written code.

Many digital artists emphasize the importance of writing their own code. The hand of the author/artist expresses itself in comments, particular styles of coding, or even silly jokes, that all influence the outcome of a project.[9] In their analysis of the role of code, Geoff Cox and Alex McLean propose that there is a need to understand "programming as a performative speech act" (Cox and McLean 2013, 38). In other words, they stress a specificity that can be interpreted as human-machine writing. This understanding of code underscores the distinction between the written code and its execution, while not seeing them as operating independently but as deeply intertwined, with one influencing the other—and, in the case of live coding, mutually influencing each other.[10] As Cox and McLean argue, "Saying words or running code or simply understanding how they work is not enough in itself. What is important is the relation to the consequences of that action" (Cox and McLean 2013, 38). There are many levels of interpreting, compiling, and linking that take place in the execution of written code which can be understood only in the context of the overall structure and processes of the computer. In this sense, the authenticity of a work has to be considered as the relation between the material and conceptual: in its writing and thus in its execution, code is conceptual and material at the same time. This is not to say that the conceptual and material are identical. Code as an entity is fixed and static, a language that is interpreted by the program that runs it. As Florian Cramer and Ulrike Gabriel suggest, "software is machine control code, it follows that digital media are, literally, written" (Cramer and Gabriel 2001). Moreover, software may be read and executed as a mental act, "as it was common before computers were invented" (Cramer 2002), and code therefore could exist without a computer. Just as any other interpretation, the meaning of code depends on context. Therefore a distinction needs to be made between the code and its execution.

German media theorist Friedrich Kittler was a strong advocate for "hardware over software." He argued that people are blinded by easy-to-use (commercial) software systems that prevent them from looking at the core of the material, the computer chip. In his seminal text "There is No Software" (1995), Kittler proposed a materialist concept that favors the Turing machine as a circuit-based computational machine, claiming that software would only conceal the actual working of the hardware. In other words, according to Kittler we are losing our insight into the logic of the machine. This deterministic view, however, is difficult to uphold since it does not recognize the programmer's sensitivity and mental process in the act of writing code, or the code as actor. Many programmers testify to their act of mentally visualizing the result of their code while writing, thereby executing code without actually using the physical machine (McWilliams 2009). The interchange between the machine and the programmer writing the code is certainly something that cannot be disputed, so it seems to make more sense to argue that the relationship between a programmer and a computer is a dialogue in which one does not necessarily supersede the other. Similar to the binary stance in conservation theory, Kittler's argument omits the correlation between what a work does and what it means—in other words, the importance of the "social space," the way in which material becomes meaningful only through an extended process, a prolonged active exchange. Moreover, such a process does not only occur in the execution of the work but also in the process of creating it. Especially among the free/libre open source software (FLOSS) developers, who engage in collaborative creative production, it is the social network that makes the material meaningful.

For many digital artworks, and especially net art projects, hardware is considered as less important than software, even though the aesthetics of the hardware on which the work is presented may have influenced the appearance of the project itself—from the use of colors to the size and resolution of the computer screen, all of which are important elements that (co)establish the aesthetics of artworks. Nevertheless hardware remains less important in the sense that audiences can experience net-based work on all kinds of equipment (from CRT monitors and laptop screens to smartphones and touch screens), and in very diverse environments (at home or the office, on a table, in bed, on the train, in the park, etc.). This is not to say that presentation of net art projects outside of their "natural habitat"—for example, in an exhibition—might not ideally require specific hardware, but in some cases a fixation on hardware issues draws the attention away from the concept of the work, turning it into an object, or even a material fetish. It therefore could be argued that authenticity in a digital artwork can foremost be traced by examining software, the programming and the code. At the same time, authenticity of code is not a standalone feature, or material, because of the strong relation between writing and execution, and vice versa. Once again it makes more sense to refer to *authentic alliances* that affirm the aesthetic intertwining of several actions.

Author

The second identifier of authenticity is authorship of the respective work. The questions surrounding what is real and what is fictional, what is tangible and what is virtual, are almost synonymous with the questions raised by the Internet as environment where people frequently take on different or adapted identities.[11] This makes it difficult to identify an author as "authentic," because anyone can assume a virtual identity; the author can be a group of people, as in the case of JODI; and authorship can also be dispersed among a group of people, as in the case of the web site mouchette.org. However, there are ways to at least find out who the owner of a web site is, for example by using the Internet service WhoIs. WhoIs is a free query and response protocol widely used for querying databases that store the registered users or assignees of an Internet resource, such as a domain name or an IP address. Everyone looking up mouchette.org / .net / .com over the years would have noticed that the contact changed. Whereas Martine Neddam, hosting with Dreamhost, used to be visible as administration contact and registrant, she changed her data to conceal her identity a few years ago.[12] Even in a case like this, however, payment of a fee will make the historical hosting information traceable. This can be achieved through Hosting History, a tool exclusive to DomainTools that allows you to view IP addresses, name servers, and registrars for a given domain name over time. If a domain name has changed its host or has been transferred to another registrar, the old value, the new value, and the date when the event occurred can be retrieved.[13] In other words, total anonymity on the Internet is not that easily achieved. However, it needs to be stressed that the owner of a domain name is not automatically also the author of the content of the web site.

Different stakeholders may pose a problem for conservators when it comes to determining authenticity, and artists are often creating ambiguities with regard to the status of authorship(s). Ambiguity is an often-found characteristic of digital artworks and, although it may not be easily found or traced in either the presentation or back-end of the work, it can be an extremely important element that, to a large extent, drives a work. To stick with the example of mouchette.org, this process becomes obvious when Mouchette talks about the function of questions in her work:

> I can offer the use of my soul, that digital soul of mine, to hundreds of Internet users, that twisted soul, full of surprises and unexpected connections, that soul in the shape of a labyrinth. […] I lost the exit of this maze, and now I'm locked up in a soul which is keeping my body in jail. Which password will set me free, which magic formula, which string of characters? I believe this magic formula will be a question. Which question? That's the question! Yes, I love questions! I also like to write stories in the form of questions. (Mouchette 2005, 206)

This strategy of "concealment," or at least not volunteering the whole story, and questioning instead of answering, is of course not confined to digital art and can be found in the practice of many artists from all disciplines; as artist Lynn Hershman puts it, the truth "is always apparent in the flaws, […] it's in the crack in the wall, not the replication of it" (Giannachi, Kaye, and Shanks 2012, 228). This process of concealment (in the broadest sense) is also what often makes it difficult to interview artists about their work. Not only might they genuinely not be aware of the importance of certain aspects of their work (that therefore remain hidden) or have ideas for its future, they also might very well know the answers, but decide not to give them.

The identity of artists/authors may not always directly reveal itself on the Internet. The aforementioned tools can be used to trace a person behind an identity, but there is no guarantee. There also remain other unresolved questions regarding authorship—some of them related to copyright—that can render traditional ideas of authenticity problematic. When a collector buys a networked digital artwork that relies on audience participation, for example, who will be able to claim their percentage of the purchase price: the artist(s), the audience who contributed parts of the work, or other parties in the network structure, such as a commercial platform that is used "for free" in the presentation or distribution of the piece? These are important issues that, at times, have prevented museums and private collectors from acquiring digital artworks. For quite some time now, the idea of single authorship has been contested in the broader field of contemporary art, and it has been argued that any project involving multiple people taking on various tasks in the creation process is multi-authored. Whereas, in contemporary arts, the person who developed the conceptual idea is often regarded as the author—even though others might have executed the work—the authorship of software(-based) artworks is less determined, especially in the case of generative software art, which, in whole or in part, is created by autonomous systems. Considering the function of algorithms adds another aspect to the notion of authorship, further complicating the determination of authenticity. In computer science an algorithm is generally understood as a set of rules that precisely defines a sequence of operations (Stone 1972, 4). This theoretical understanding of algorithms overlooks the functions it can fulfill for end users, understating the crucial role of algorithms when their cultural, political, and social values cannot and should not be underestimated (Goffey 2008). The Facebook game *Naked on Pluto* (2010) by Dave Griffiths, Aymeric Mansoux, and Marloes de Valk is exemplary in this context. The work is based on algorithms that operate bots in the game, self-executing processes and actions whose behaviors are triggered in a certain context. It is important to note that the bots in *Naked on Pluto* are personifications of algorithms used by Facebook and other social networks in order to feed on information about the user or give information to the user, often in less than transparent ways. The bots in *Naked on Pluto* are anthropomorphized; they prompt the user for responses and give continuous feedback on the game world. In other words, the bots generate the stories in the game based on the contexts in which they may find themselves (De Valk and Mansoux 2012). The bots therefore are not just mere aids, but actually have agency in creating the work. Florian Cramer has noted that conventional software companies try to stick to the idea that software functions mostly as a tool, an aid for the artist, thereby denying the larger function and authorship of algorithms. *Naked on Pluto*—as well as other digital artworks discussed by Cramer, such as Cornelia Sollfrank's *net.art generator* (1997)—reverse this idea by "redefining authorship as the artistic design of an algorithmic process" (Cramer 2005, 84). Cramer raises the question of who or what creates the work. One needs to ask, who is, or (better) are the author(s): the artists who developed the conceptual idea, the artists who programmed the bots, the users who play the game, or the program itself? In other words, the authenticity of the author(s) is not a fixed position anymore. Once again the notion of *authentic alliances* becomes useful, because it highlights that one author isn't more important than the other in the creation of a work, and that each single "author" can only function in relation to other "authors," so that their alliance makes the project function. In the case of most digital art, questions concerning ownership, authorship, and copyright may replace traditional questions regarding the materiality of an object. Moreover, concepts such as ownership and authorship themselves have to become the subject of critical discussion.

Time

The third identifier of authenticity relates to the dating of an artwork. As stated before, traditional conservation is based on the idea of a unique object and tries to freeze the "ideal state" of this object in time. Barbara Appelbaum has advocated for conservators to include non-material information in their research and practice, such as the respective value the object holds for its custodians or stakeholders. Reconstruction of such a "full" history of the object would lead to the ideal state of the object (2007,

171–236); as such, "an ideal state is defined by time, not by physical description" (2007, 176). It is difficult, if not impossible, to define an ideal state in the case of digital artworks since one of their characteristics is their continuous process. This is not to say that artists do not have a preferred temporal framework for the respective performance or presentation of a work. However, the latter says little about the work in all its facets and more about the experience of the work's presentation at a certain moment in time. This cannot be equated with identifying the intentions of the work and/or the artist. What is even more important is that such an ideal state tells more about (technical or conceptual) dictates of the present than intentions for the project in previous manifestations. In this context Miriam Clavir talks about the belief of museums in an "authentic moment," which by implication turns them into static entities:

> Freezing a culture's history at one moment in time in museum displays, the "ethnographic present" (as it has been termed in anthropology) creates an understanding of indigenous cultures' history as being important only within a constructed, fixed period in the past. (Clavir 2002, 32)

This attitude signals one of the biggest differences between museums and artists in the way they regard their legacy. Although this may not apply to all digital artists, many of them change the presentation of a work according to the respective space, finances, or context, adapting it each time it is presented (Ippolito 2008; Noël de Tilly 2009). Museum conservators and curators often point out that a presentation is always formed in time, through talks with the artist, until a final presentation is chosen (Dekker 2012a). Such a practice can be seen with JODI who are constantly adding to their work, and Martine Neddam who believes that the preservation of a work of art ideally becomes a new work (Dekker 2012b). Similarly, the artists behind *Naked on Pluto* put a lot of emphasis on the reuse of a game engine, which provides an interesting platform for making new works. It could be argued that, in the case of *Naked on Pluto*, the game engine is more of a tool than a conceptual part of the project, while Neddam's work uses the content of her projects to create new ones. However, *Naked on Pluto*'s creators see the game engine as both conceptual and artistic, and even the most crucial creative part of their work. The artworks discussed here may continue to develop indefinitely, by building on the existing work to create new variations. The artists are not seeing their projects as static, but as constantly developing. Such a variable approach is very difficult to accommodate within contemporary museum conservation practices, from challenges with regard to their registration—how to enter the work into standardized databases—to decisions on what exactly to conserve. Although it is possible in theory to create a database that can handle all of these data elements and relate them to each other in various ways in order to trace different histories and variations, the question remains whether it would be desirable to implement such an organization of data? Rather than promoting advanced databasing models, I would like to argue for extended knowledge derived from databases or documentation models by using them in different ways—not necessarily as "enforcers of truth," but as boundary objects for triggering a dialogue, or as resources that can function as departure points for creating new stories (Van Saaze and Dekker 2013).

It is important to acknowledge that digital artworks are never stable—since technical changes and updates continuously shape the work—and to see them as localized and specialized entities in time, both in the sense that they can be time-based and that their appearance may vary over time.[14] Conservator Hanna Hölling describes how small changes to artworks, especially media artworks, are frequently made in museum collections, particularly when artworks are taken out of the warehouse in order to be reinstalled in a different place (Hölling 2013, 199). However, these changes are different from the ones I am referring to in digital artworks where change is sometimes made at the expense of the current artwork. One implication of taking an approach of "localized knowledge" is the realization that conservation of digital artworks will always be based on case studies. It will make it hard to implement and pursue standardization. Knowledge dependent on time and context can become contradictory. When "local" solutions are crucial, what happens to the authority of a conservator, or a museum? In other words, whose voice(s) will be the leading ones in issues of conservation, or who controls knowledge? Knowledge may reside with the artists, the audiences, the programmer, the curator, and others. While this condition may balance out knowledge hierarchies,[15] it also calls for education and critical thinking about technical and social systems, as well as their function, possibilities, and limitations, in order to confront political and ethical challenges. In other words, it requires paying attention to elements that are not directly visible but still determining factors. Furthermore, this approach calls for changes within the institutions that are currently dealing with cultural heritage in order to enable them to take maximum advantage of new knowledge systems and collaborative ways of working.

Identifying Authentic Alliances and the Use of Documentation

Taking advantage of the "variable nature" of defining authenticity, I have argued to adopt the notion of *authentic alliances* to come to terms with the characteristics of net art. By using this concept I don't want to attempt to recover a past in order to better understand the present. By emphasizing "alliances" I want to uncover the core of net art which is not always immediately visible, and address its implications. Identifying authenticity by looking at the work, author, and date will not necessarily give a good understanding of authenticity, since some identifiers are more noticeably present than others. Moreover, such analyses would not do justice to the fluidity of the work. Net art is not a stable entity that can be examined by static means. What determines net art as authentic is found in relation to alliances. The notion of alliances offers a layered way of looking at artworks. This means that different elements of an artwork shouldn't be identified as singular entities, but they should be seen as one influencing the other. Net art is a process, where different properties of the work, authorship, and time are in alliance to each other. This doesn't mean that questions about material, author, and time are irrelevant, but there is a shift of focus to questions relating to ownership, authorship, and copyright. As I said before, these concepts should be further analyzed and discussed in the light of human and non-human (machinic) relations. Documentation is one way of doing that as it plays an important role in determining authenticity. As has been shown with regard to JODI's work, documentation is made and used in very different ways. In analyzing and comparing documentation methods used by museum conservators and artists I have identified three different, often parallel, stages of documentation that are most prominent in artists' practices (Dekker 2013). For the purpose of this text it suffices to say that documentation itself is a contested subject. Documentation as a presentation form, in the sense of capturing the "final" result or state of a work, can be seen as being unfaithful to the art form. The prospect of experiencing only a mediation of performance art or any live art event, even in written words, has disturbed many art scholars. Choreographer Peggy Phelan, for example, explicitly stated:

> Performance honors the idea that a limited number of people in a specific time/space frame can have an experience of value which leaves no visible trace afterward. Writing about it necessarily cancels the "tracelessness" inaugurated within this performative promise. (Phelan 1993, 149)[16]

Similarly, documentation created for the purpose of recreating a work in the future, such as artists' interviews, can create many problems, ranging from the challenge of interviewing artists in a way that allows for extracting, formulating, or even comprehending their intent, to pinning down often ambiguous practices in models and methods.[17]

Obviously, any form of documentation will be a substitute for an original experience, but are there ways of thinking about documentation other than evoking its absent object or event? Is it possible to arrive at an expanded understanding of documentation that helps to identify authentic alliances? Digital art most commonly does not consist of a single or even multiple definable objects; as live event, it manifests itself through relations and/or interaction. Becky Edmunds, a videographer specialized in dance who has been making video documentation for several live performance groups, tries to enjoy the gap between the live event and its documentation, by

> providing small pieces of information through which a viewer might be able to actively reconstruct an imagined version, myth or memory of what the event might have been. [...] my practice questions how much information is needed in order for a viewer to be able to construct a version in their own imagination from the "fragmentary, petrified vestige" that I can provide them with. My work points to all that has been omitted, as much as to that which I have decided to include. (Edmunds 2006)

Edmunds is not interested in providing the viewer with an "authentic" recording, a notation, but tries to capture the essence of the performance. This approach reveals a new way of thinking about documentation that reflects the form of the work or event while at the same time informing the work and serving as a way to preserve "tacit" knowledge:[18]

> If documentation can be viewed as a part of the live event, not as an after-thought, but as a valued aspect of the process, then the documentation of the performance or process can be as creative and as challenging as the live event. (Edmunds 2006)

Documentation here can be thought of as a form of dialogue, reflection, and response that can be used both as a tool in the creative process and as a document conveying knowledge.

Fiona Wilkie also understands documentation this way and proposes that watching documentation can disclose alternative dimensions of the work (Wilkie 2004). She considers the meaning of video documentation of Blast Theory's performance installation *Desert Rain* (2000) and compares it to participation in the installation itself.[19]

By understanding video documentation from a framework of site-specificity, she approaches the work through a discourse of spatial engagement, in which the work operates between different spaces and contexts—in the case of *Desert Rain*, real space (the physical installation) and virtual space (the online participants, as well as the context of the Gulf War on which the work reflects). When viewed in a new context, documentation will create different connotations, which, as Wilkie suggests, can add new layers to the work. As in JODI's *Jet Set Willy FOREVER*, the video documentation adds new layers of meaning to Blast Theory's performances, which could potentially deepen the conceptual ideas behind the work in new, and perhaps unforeseen, ways.

To briefly summarize, documentation of digital art constructs a situation in which diverse practices respond to a variety of needs and ideas surrounding artistic work. This process potentially allows documentation to develop as a critical space in its own right, a space in which the issues and concerns of the work are addressed through appropriate forms without necessarily becoming reproductions (Lycouris 2000). It is important to realize the meaning and value of documents and documentation, which is in the alliance of documentation as process, presentation, and preservation—in an understanding of the relations and contexts of the documented work. This alliance allows documentation to develop as a critical space in which the issues and concerns of the work are addressed. From this perspective, documentation can be seen as a mode of production as well as a mode of critical interpretation, which helps in overcoming the fragmented view inherent in traditional meanings of the term. I therefore argue for an extended concept of documentation that treats it not merely as a way of capturing (live) events, but as a form of dialogue, response, and reflection. This approach will lead to a better understanding of the artwork's authentic alliances and could potentially open up opportunities for creating new versions of a work, building, elaborating, and commenting on a previous state. As *Jet Set Willy* illustrates, documentation, when introduced into a presentation context, has the potential to deepen a work's conceptual idea, adding new layers to it and opening the potential for elaborating on the original version, thereby allowing it to survive FOREVER.

Acknowledgments

The research for this text was made possible with financial support from the Mondriaan Fund Mediation Grant. I would like to thank Matthew Fuller and the research group *New Strategies in the Conservation of Contemporary Art* for their feedback, and especially Angela Matyssek for her critical comments on this article.

Notes

1 Personal observation at the opening of the exhibition *Funware* at MU in Eindhoven, November 12, 2010.
2 See also the interview with JODI conducted for the exhibition and research project *Seeing Double* by the Variable Media Network in 2004. http://variablemedia.net/e/seeingdouble/ (accessed January 15 2014).
3 The variable media concept was developed in 1998 by Jon Ippolito. The Variable Media Network proposes an unconventional preservation strategy based on identifying

ways that creative works might outlast their original medium: http://www.variable media.net (accessed January 15 2014). Matters in Media Art was initiated in 2003 by a consortium of curators, conservators, registrars, and media technical managers from New Art Trust, MoMA, SFMOMA, and Tate, to provide guidelines for care of time-based media works of art (e.g., video, film, audio, and computer-based installations): http://www.tate.org.uk/about/projects/matters-media-art (accessed January 15 2014). Another consortium followed with a similar research: Inside Installations was a three-year research project (2004–2007) into the care and administration of installation art: http://www.inside-installations.org (accessed January 15 2014). The DOCAM Research Alliance was created by the *Daniel Langlois Foundation for Art, Science and Technology* (DLF) in 2005. It has brought together numerous partners from Canada and abroad who have joined the Alliance from both the academic sector and from a community of interest. Over the project's five-year mandate its main objective was to develop new methodologies and tools to address the issues of preserving and documenting digital art, technological and electronic artworks: http://www.docam.ca/ (accessed January 15 2014).

4 This might also be one of the reasons why more attention is paid to the implementation of oral histories in conservation today. Muller focuses on media art installation and argues that documenting audience experiences with new media art better explains and emphasizes the interaction, the system, and generative processes in new media art. Roms discusses primarily anecdotal evidence of engagement with performance; she focuses on Welsh performers with whom she organized public conversations, in particular. The latter also emphasizes that the appreciation of the authenticity of the past is more dependent on the observer's perception and not on what the observed communicates.

5 The theoretical debate surrounding authenticity was originally rooted in the need to distinguish forgeries and fakes from original artworks; see, among others, Dutton (1983) and an edited volume by Matyssek (2010) that addresses the issue of "the death of an artwork," or the conservation of the original in contemporary art. This debate is, of course, deeply connected to the economic value of artworks, a topic that, as interesting as it may be, will not be dealt with in this chapter. For more information on the historical formation of cultural capital related to the culture of copy, see, among others, Fyfe (2004).

6 By emphasizing that any culture can decide on its own heritage as described in the Nara Documentation (Larsen 1994), Lowenthal argues that every culture therefore is "entitled to do just as it chooses with its own heritage, which need not be shown to, let alone shared with, others" (2008).

7 The term "community of concern" was suggested during a meeting of the research group New Strategies in Contemporary Conservation (September 7, 2012). See also, for example, Van Saaze (2012) on the formations around the legacy of Robert Smithson's artworks.

8 This focus is maintained by most of the groups I listed, Variable Media Network, Matters in Media Art, and Inside Installations.

9 For more information, see Cox and McLean (2013) on the importance of the recognition of code as speech, and for linguistic analogies between code and natural languages. Drawing on Roland Barthes' *S/Z*, Cramer (2003) distinguishes between "readerly" and "writerly" texts, arguing that the command line encourages the reader to become an active producer by making the difference between the act of writing and the tool with which writing occurs.

10 For more information about live coding in connection to preservation, see Yuill (2008).
11 See, among others, Turkle (1995, 2009), whose research focuses on the psychology of human relationships with technology and on how people relate to computational objects, or Butler (1990) on the performative qualities of identity.
12 The last update on mouchette.org that I could trace in a WhoIs query was made in 2007 by Weiss (2009, 8.4.1.).
13 http://www.domaintools.com/research/hosting-history/?q=dreamhost.com (accessed January 15, 2014).
14 In the use of the term "localized" I am following Deleuze (2000/1964) who distinguishes the localized from the totalizing notion of standardization. Latour (1987) also has emphasized that universal knowledge is bound by localized time and space, and, moreover, that such specialized knowledge tends to move through sparsely populated networks before it affects other (external) alliances. See also Bowker and his thorough analysis of the importance of and need for local knowledge (2005, 201–221).
15 I'm not suggesting here that everyone will be equal—in most decision-making processes this will not be the case. What I'm emphasizing is that there are people with different kinds of knowledge around the table. To put it simply: everyone has a piece of a puzzle, and all together they complete the image; however, what the image will be is most often decided by those in charge.
16 A very similar but much older debate can be traced in music, in this case between analysis versus performance. See, for example, Nicolas Cook's statement, "the way we talk about music does not simply replicate it but rather affects the way we make it, not to mention what we make *of* it" (Cook 1999, 10).
17 Sloggett (1998) and Van de Wetering (1989) talk more explicitly about the shortcomings of interviews as a one-directional strategy for conservation. For more information about artist interviews see Beerkens et al. (2012). Jones (2007) mentions several challenges underlying documentation models, some of which are expanded upon by Dekker (2013).
18 The notion of tacit knowledge refers to the whole range of conceptual and sensory information, that is, all forms of knowledge that cannot be represented: knowledge that cannot be fully articulated, expressed in formulas, or described in documents (Polanyi 1966). The notion of tacit knowledge is not uncontested and often viewed as merely subjective. In conservation tacit knowledge refers to the artist's intent and the social and cultural context in which a work is presented or performed.
19 For more information about Blast Theory and *Desert Rain*, see http://blasttheory.co.uk/bt/work_desertrain.html (accessed January 15, 2014).

References

Appelbaum, Barbara. 2007. *Conservation Treatment Methodology*. Oxford: Butterworth-Heinemann.

Beerkens, Lydia, Paulien 't Hoen, IJsbrand Hummelen, Vivian van Saaze, Tatja Scholte, and Sanneke Stigter, eds. 2012. *The Artist Interview. For Conservation and Presentation of Contemporary Art. Guidelines and Practice.* Heijningen: Japsam Books.

Bowker, Geoffrey C. 2005. *Memory Practices in the Sciences.* Cambridge, MA: The MIT Press.

Butler, Judith. 1990. *Gender Trouble: Feminism and the Subversion of Identity.* New York and London: Routledge.

Clavir, Miriam. 2002. *Preserving What Is Valued: Museums, Conservation and First Nations.* Columbia: University of British Columbia Press.

Cook, Nicolas. 1999. "Words about Music, or Analysis versus Performance." In *Theory into Practice. Composition, Performance and the Listening Experience – Nicolas Cook, Peter Johnson, Hans Zender*, edited by Peter Dejans, 9–52. Leuven: Leuven University Press, Orpheus Institute.

Cox, Geoff, and Alex McLean. 2013. *Speaking Code: Coding as Aesthetic and Political Expression.* Cambridge, MA: The MIT Press.

Cramer, Florian. 2002. "Concepts, Notations, Software, Art." In *Software Art: Thoughts*, edited by Olga Goriunova and Alexei Shulgin. Moscow: read_me 1.2 media art festival.

Cramer, Florian. 2003. "Ten Theses about Software Art." http://cramer.pleintekst.nl/all/10_thesen_zur_softwarekunst/10_theses_about_software_art.pdf (accessed October 13, 2015).

Cramer, Florian. 2005. *Words Made Flesh: Code, Culture, Imagination.* Rotterdam: Piet Zwart Institute.

Cramer, Florian, and Ulrike Gabriel. 2001. "Software Art." http://cramer.pleintekst.nl/essays/software_art_and_writing/ (accessed September 27, 2014).

Dekker, Annet. 2012a. Private talks with curators/conservator at Van Abbemuseum, October 2012.

Dekker, Annet. 2012b. Personal e-mail correspondence with Martine Neddam, August 12, 2012.

Dekker, Annet. 2013. "Enjoying the Gap. Comparing Contemporary Documentation Strategies." In *Preserving and Exhibiting Media Art: Challenges and Perspectives*, edited by Cosetta Saba, Julia Noordegraaf, Barbara Le Maître, and Vinzenz Hediger, 149–169. Amsterdam: University of Amsterdam Press.

Deleuze, Gilles. 2000/1964. *Proust & Sings. The Complete Text.* London: The Athlone Press.

Depocas, Alain, Jon Ippolito, and Caitlin Jones, eds. 2003. *Permanence Through Change: The Variable Media Approach.* New York/Montreal: The Solomon R. Guggenheim Foundation/Daniel Langlois Foundation for Art, Science and Technology.

De Valk, Marloes, and Aymeric Mansoux. 2012. Personal interview. October 31, 2012.

Dutton, Denis, ed. 1983. *The Forger's Art: Forgery and the Philosophy of Art.* Berkley, CA: University of California Press.

Edmunds, Becky. 2006. "A Work of Art from A Work of Art." http://beckyedmunds.com/#/on-documentation/4531976852 (accessed September 27, 2014).

Fyfe, Gordon. 2004. "Reproductions, Cultural Capital and Museums: Aspects of the Culture of Copies." *Museum and Society* 2(1): 47–67.

Giannachi, Garbriella, Nick Kaye, and Michael Shanks. 2012. *Archaeologies of Presence: Art, Performance and the Persistence of Being.* New York and London: Routledge.

Goffey, Andrew. 2008. "Algorithm." In *Software Studies: A Lexicon*, edited by Matthew Fuller, 15–20. Cambridge, MA: The MIT Press.

Hölling, Hanna. 2013. "Re: Paik. On Time, Changeability and Identity in the Conservation of Nam June Paik's Multimedia Installations." PhD thesis, University of Amsterdam.

Ippolito, Jon. 2003. "Accommodating the Unpredictable: The Variable Media Questionnaire." In *Permanence Through Change: The Variable Media Approach*, edited by Alain Dépocas, Jon Ippolito, and Caitlin Jones, 47–53. New York/Montreal: The Solomon R. Guggenheim Foundation/Daniel Langlois Foundation for Art, Science and Technology.

Ippolito, Jon. 2008. "Death by Wall Label." In *New Media in the White Cube and Beyond. Curatorial Models for Digital Art*, edited by Christiane Paul, 106–132. Berkeley, CA: University of California Press.

Jenkins, Henry. 2006. *Convergence Culture: Where Old and New Media Collide*. New York: New York University Press.

Jones, Caitlin. 2007. "State of the Art (of Documentation): Three Case Studies for the Daniel Langlois Foundation's Ten Year Anniversary Exhibition." http://www.fondation-langlois.org/html/e/page.php?NumPage=1988 (accessed September 27, 2014).

Kittler, Friedrich A. 1995. "There is No Software." *CTheory*. A032, October 18. http://www.ctheory.net/articles.aspx?id=74 (accessed September 27, 2014).

Larsen, Knut Einar, ed. 1994. *Nara Conference on Authenticity. Proceedings*. Nara, Japan: International Council for Monuments and Sites (ICOMOS), UNESCO World Heritage Centre, ICCROM.

Latour, Bruno. 1987. *Science in Action: How to Follow Scientists and Engineers Through Society*. Milton Keynes, UK: Open University Press.

Laurenson, Pip. 2006. "Authenticity, Change and Loss in the Conservation of Time-Based Media Installations." *Tate Papers*, 6. http://www.tate.org.uk/research/publications/tate-papers/authenticity-change-and-loss-conservation-time-based-media (accessed September 27, 2014).

Levy, Pierre. 1999 (1994 in French). *Collective Intelligence: Mankind's Emerging World in Cyberspace*. Cambridge: Perseus Books.

Lovink, Geert, and Ned Rossiter. 2005. "Dawn of the Organised Networks." *The Fibreculture Journal* 5. http://five.fibreculturejournal.org/fcj-029-dawn-of-the-organised-networks/ (accessed September 27, 2014).

Lowenthal, David. 2008. "Authenticities Past and Present(1)." *CRM The Journal of Heritage Stewardship* 5(1). http://crmjournal.cr.nps.gov/02_viewpoint_sub.cfm?issue=Volume%205%20Number%201%20Winter%202008&page=1&seq=1 (accessed September 27, 2014).

Lycouris, Sophia. 2000. "The Documentation of Practice: Framing Trace." *Working Papers in Art and Design 1*. http://sitem.herts.ac.uk/artdes_research/papers/wpades/vol1/lycouris2.html (accessed September 27, 2014).

Matyssek, Angela, ed. 2010. *Wann Stribt ein Kunstwerk? Konservierung des Originalen in der Gegenwartkunst*. Munich: Verlag Silke Schreiber.

McWilliams, Chandler B. 2009. "The Other Software." *UC Irvine: Digital Arts and Culture 2009*. http://escholarship.org/uc/item/3vg159kn (accessed September 27, 2014).

Mouchette. 2005. "Rape, Murder and Suicide Are Easier When You Use a Keyboard Shortcut: Mouchette, an On-Line Virtual Character." By Mouchette with Manthos Santorineos, introduction by Toni Sant. *Leonardo Journal* 38(3): 202–206.

Muller, Lizzie. 2008. "Towards an Oral History of New Media Art." Montreal: Daniel Langlois Foundation. http://www.fondation-langlois.org/html/e/page.php?NumPage=2096 (accessed September 27, 2014).

Muñoz Viñas, Salvador. 2005. *Contemporary Theory of Conservation.* Oxford: Butterworth-Heinemann.

Noël de Tilly, Ariane. 2009. "Moving Images, Edited Artworks and Authenticity." In *Art, Conservation and Authenticities: Material, Concept, Context.* Proceedings of the International Conference held at the University of Glasgow, September 12–14, 2007, edited by Erma Hermens and Tina Fiske, 208–216. London: Archetype Publications.

Petzold, Charles. 2000. *Code: The Hidden Language of Computer Hardware and Software.* Redmond, WA: Microsoft Press.

Phelan, Peggy. 1993. *Unmarked: The Politics of Performance.* New York and London: Routledge.

Polanyi, Michael. 1966. *The Tacit Dimension.* London: Routledge.

Roms, Heike. 2008. *What's Welsh for Performance? An Oral History of Performance Art in Wales.* Cardiff: Samizdat Press.

Sloggett, R. 1998. "Beyond the Material: Idea, Concept, Process, and Their Function in the Conservation of the Conceptual Art of Mike Parr." *The American Institute for Conservation of Historic & Artistic Works* 37(3): 316–333.

Stone, Harold S. 1972. *Introduction to Computer Organization and Data Structures.* New York: McGraw-Hill.

Turkle, Sherry. 1995. *Life on the Screen: Identity in the Age of the Internet.* New York: Simon & Schuster.

Turkle, Sherry, ed. 2009. *Evocative Objects: Things We Think With.* Cambridge, MA: The MIT Press.

Van de Wetering, Ernst. 1999. "Conservation-Restoration Ethics and the Problem of Modern Art." In *Modern Art: Who Cares? An Interdisciplinary Research Project and an International Symposium on the Conservation of Modern and Contemporary Art*, edited by Ijsbrand Hummelen and Dionne Sillé, 247–249. Amsterdam: Foundation for the Conservation of Modern Art/Netherlands Institute of Cultural Heritage.

Van Saaze, Vivian. 2012. "The Ethics and Politics of Documentation. On Continuity and Change in the Work of Robert Smithson." In *Robert Smithson – Art in Continual Movement: A Contemporary Reading*, edited by Ingrid Commandeur and Trudy van Riemsdijk-Zandee, 63–84. Amsterdam: Alauda Publishers.

Van Saaze, Vivian, and Annet Dekker. 2013. "Surprising Usages of a Documentation Model: On the Notion of Boundary Objects and Beyond." *The International Journal of Performance Arts and Digital Media (IJPADM)* 9 (1): 99–114.

Webster's Revised Unabridged Dictionary. 1913. G. & C. Merriam.

Weiss, Matthias. 2009. Netzkunst. Ihre Systematisierung und Auslegung anhand von Einzelbeispielen. Weimar: VDG Verlag und Datenbank für Geisteswissenschaften.

Wilkie, Fiona. 2004. "Documenting Live and Mediated Performance—the Blast Theory Case Study." In *A Guide to Good Practice in Collaborative Working Methods and New Media Tools Creation (by and for artists and the cultural sector)*, edited by Lizbeth Goodman and Katherine Milton. Commissioned by AHDS Performing Arts. Kings College, London. http://www.ahds.ac.uk/creating/guides/new-media-tools/wilkie.htm (accessed October 13, 2015).

Yuill, Simon. 2008. "All Problems of Notation Will Be Solved by the Masses: Free Open Form Performance, Free/Libre Open Source Software, and Distributive Practice." In *FLOSS+Art*, edited by Aymeric Mansoux and Marloes de Valk, 64–91. Poitiers: GOTO10 and OpenMute.

Further Reading

Dutton, Denis. 2005. "Authenticity in Art." In *The Oxford Handbook of Aesthetics*, edited by Jerrold Levinson, 693–705. New York: Oxford University Press.

27

Exhibition Histories and Futures

The Importance of Participation and Audiences

Beryl Graham

> It is in the installation design of the first half of the twentieth century that the sources of such practices as viewer interactivity and site specificity, as well as multimedia, electronic and installation-based work, are to be found. (Staniszewski 1998, xxiii)

Why are histories of exhibitions, rather than histories of art, of particular importance for new media art? As Mary Anne Staniszewski pointed out in 1998, the history of exhibition installations is one particularly badly served by art histories, to the point of being culturally "repressed." She identifies several interconnected institutional methods and hierarchies that contribute to this historical void, among them a relegation of exhibition installation to low-status "design," and a tradition of installation photographs—if they are published at all—being stylishly uncluttered by audiences (1998, xxi, xxiii). This chapter aims to address histories of both new media art exhibitions and non-new media exhibitions, involving installation art and site-specific art, and placing a particular emphasis on interactive and participatory art.

As Staniszewski states, installation-based and site-specific artwork share some concerns with multimedia artworks, because the exhibition *is* the artwork rather than a display of the artwork—an interactive installation, for example, does not fully exist as an artwork unless it is exhibited, and interacted with by the audience. The fundamental interplay of space, time, and materiality is familiar to curators of installation art and media installations of various kinds, and needs careful consideration of artists' intent for the wider cultural context of the space (Reiss 1999; Frohne, Schieren, and Guiton 2005; Guiton 2005; Graham and Cook 2010; Mondloch 2010). Take, for example, Ryota Kuwakubo's artwork *The Tenth Sentiment* from 2011. An installation of a model train moving on its track through a landscape of mundane household objects in a darkened room is entirely animated by a small light on the front of the train,

A Companion to Digital Art, First Edition. Edited by Christiane Paul.

which casts beautiful and fleeting shadows across the walls. A mere catalog of the objects and media involved, or an installation shot, would do little to document the experience of the exhibit, or the behaviors of the audience: the domestic hush in the intimate darkness, the small pleasurable sighs at an unexpected light effect, or the sheer amount of time that people spend watching the repeated slow circuits around the room, and their awareness that other people are also staying to wonder. Staniszewski also identifies viewer interactivity as a key issue for exhibition histories; if audiences are missing from exhibition documentation, then all exhibitions appear to be static objects—the art-historical norm.

In art-historical terms, some of the first stumbling blocks for documentation concern basic nomenclatures: "new media art," a notoriously problematic term to start with, can cover a whole range of different media, systems, and means of distribution. As discussed in the book *Rethinking Curating* (Graham and Cook 2010), the "behaviors" of the work rather than the specific media used are often most useful for rethinking curatorial methods in terms of the particular systems and values of new media art. Steve Dietz identified three main characteristics of net art: connectivity, computability, and interactivity (Dietz 1999). Each behavior, when applied to new media art in general, can be related to different exhibition histories, ranging from installation and performance art to video. Connectivity, for example, might be a familiar feature to curators of live art or 1960s conceptual art including mail art, and presented similar issues with regard to what is documented about live events, and what might be collected in the form of scores or instructions. A particularly apt documentation photograph from the event *Reunion* in Toronto in 1968 shows Marcel Duchamp and John Cage playing chess in order to generate an audio composition by Cage, surrounded by cables that connect hardware to hardware, while Alexina "Teeny" Duchamp looks on with a handy bottle of wine to lubricate the social connections (Graham and Cook 2010, 91). When it comes to "computability," it is sometimes difficult for art historians to differentiate between the generative, evolving, and algorithmic nature of computer software and the instruction sets of conceptual art, but the art-historical emphasis on understanding materials and processes from gouache to bronze casting should offer useful tools for this differentiation. It is the third behavior of "interaction," however, that seems to present the most fundamental problems for documenting and historicizing exhibitions (Graham and Cook 2010, 91; Graham 2014c). In this chapter I am discussing exhibitions of new media that display these behaviors, rather than digital versions of analog media such as photography and video, which fit more smoothly into existing art-historical categories and exhibition models.

While the installation-based and interactive nature of some new media art makes its exhibition of particular importance, it is often a sum of several factors that makes exhibition histories crucial. There are interconnected threads between art practice, criticism, collection, exhibition, and future historicization that can easily be broken, and question both the basic tenets of what art historians might be looking at and the methods they use for research. If the systems and processes of new media art production and distribution are not understood by curators and critics, the exhibitions cannot be critically examined; if the behaviors of the media are not understood by curators, then they cannot be exhibited effectively; unexhibited works are rarely collected; collected works without effective documentation are difficult to properly re-exhibit; uncollected works have no provenance and cannot be not loaned; and artworks or exhibitions with little critical text, documentation, or provenance are highly unlikely to enter art history (assuming the search terms can be found in the first place). Although routes to collection and historicization are important for all "new" art forms, the links between documentation and other factors hence become particularly important for new media art because of the combinations of behaviors displayed by the art (Graham 2013, 2014a, 2014b, 2014c, 2015).

Staniszewski has suggested the re-examination of the taxonomies of art history in order to facilitate considering "installation as an aesthetic medium and historical category" (Staniszewski 1998, xxi). In 1968, curator Jack Burnham, in illuminating why new tools and methods might be necessary, stated that "my lack of success with the tools of art scholarship is in part responsible for this present book. Had the tools served their purpose, I might not have sought out others less respected" (Shanken 2007, 48). It has to be acknowledged that some of these tools appropriate for new media art might still be regarded as "less respected" by art historians more than forty years after Burnham's statement. As explored in this chapter, certain "behaviors," such as participation or interaction, might cause new media art to be placed with a firm hand in museum "education" departments, rather than in the collections, archives, or libraries from where the sheen of the historical canon might be glimpsed. If the documentation of exhibitions and behaviors falls not only outside of the museum but also into the heaving mass of the Internet and the hands of the viewers themselves, then the hierarchy of art-historical validation might truly struggle to include these tools, however useful they may be.

How then can a history of exhibitions inform curators about the challenges of exhibiting new media art? More specifically, how can histories of exhibitions dealing with interaction and participation inform the curation of new media art involving these behaviors? This chapter addresses these questions by exploring examples of past and recent exhibitions, and examining the kinds of documentation that are now available and understood through the lens of new media art and social systems.

New Media Systems—Databases, Taxonomies, and Methods

> Whilst most literary portrayals depict collectors of fine and decorative art, much more collecting is devoted to, well, "collectibles." The classification of Collectibles on eBay employs forty-five main headings—such as "Brewerania and Beer," "Disneyana" and "Militaria"—under which are arranged approximately 500 categories … (Altshuler 2009, 38)

New media technologies are used for selling things, collecting things, categorizing things, curating things, digitizing the analog, production, distribution, pornography, relational databases, collections management, art interpretation … and art. As curator Steve Dietz pointed out in 2005, one result of the fact that new media are used for both production and distribution is that new media artworks might be found in a library or archive, as well as in a collection (Dietz 2005). In the context of exhibition histories, an important characteristic of new media is that a databased archive might be an archive of documentation of art or exhibitions, such as *The Archive of Digital Art*,[1] or an archive/collection of art itself, where the art can be experienced *as* an exhibition, such as on the *Turbulence* web site, which features commissioned net art. In addition to the ability of new media databases to act as both exhibition and archive, there is the affordance that online databases can be participatory, which challenges ideas of who is doing the documenting, exhibiting, and collecting. It could be argued that Vimeo, blogs, Flickr, or the Internet itself are the largest, most connected and most participatory documentation archives of art. When it comes to online collections, both Rhizome's Artbase and runme.org feature open submission of works from artists and, as described in the following paragraphs, offer the possibility of self-tagging to form a folksonomy. All of these factors can challenge the existing categories and methods of art historians (Graham 2014b).

The ways in which modes of collecting new media art might differ from those of other art forms also concerns many interconnected factors. The issue of *what* exactly is collected addresses the factor of materiality—the artwork might comprise hardware or software, installation instructions and/or a set of written rules for what kinds of future software, data, or display might be suitable for its exhibition. This affects economic modes of collection, where artwork *is* being bought in custom material forms, which might be freely available on the Internet, such as the net art works by Vuk Ćosić sold as short-run limited editions at the Bryce Wolkowitz Gallery in 2006 (Graham and Cook 2010, 202). Modes of "editioning" adopted from the sale of prints and video art are being applied to accommodate the "versioned" nature of software, with version 2.3 succeeding version 2.2, and "beta" test versions. Economic modes that radically challenge notions of art authorship, such as Open Source, also are a rethinking of what might be collected, for example when an artist is paid for customizing software, or for providing educational support for an artwork rather than making a unique art object, as Felix Stalder suggests (2010). Private collectors are buying new media art, and seem prepared to consider different modes of collecting. Wolf Lieser, who has been running galleries that sell digital art since 1999, stresses the long-term approach to private collecting: "From the beginning I have approached my customers on the basis, that first of all: this is the future in art; second, forget about the old concepts of buying a painting and taking it home. Instead consider your acquisition a contribution to the artist, so he can work better and create better art" (CRUMB 2012). This thinking about the long-term effects of supporting artwork also is the basis for the commissioning of new work with the possibility of future acquisition for the collection of an institution. For new media art, there are some modes of commissioning and collecting that have been adapted to fit the "versioned" nature of software—for example, an artist might be commissioned to produce a work to "beta" phase as outlined above, and that beta phase might be collected, with the awareness that the work might be developed into future versions, whilst keeping the core title of the artwork. Curator Benjamin Weil has named the role of the curator in commissioning media works as that of "producer," in order to acknowledge the nature of the facilitating role over a long period of time to help produce a work for a particular museum space or collection. He has also suggested the model of collecting for only a limited number of years, so that new media works might enter collections with a little less institutional anxiety about conservation (CRUMB and CAS 2010). The fact that all of these issues are connected suggests possibilities for integrated modes of collection, exhibition, and audience participation, which could perhaps be applied to integrated modes of documentation and historicization for exhibitions (Graham 2014b).

Curators and artists familiar with the workings of online databases and tagging systems have also found possible solutions to the taxonomical problems outlined so far. Ironically, finding new media art in mainstream art databases or archives can be a problem in the first place, since many of them simply do not use terms such as "new media," "digital," or "electronic" at all, as outlined by Richard Rinehart in this book. Out of necessity, those working with new media art have not only developed their own taxonomies of behaviors, metamedia, or monomedia (Manovich 2013), but have also been open to alternative methods of "folksonomy"—taxonomies developed by many users rather than individuals or small groups of experts. The web site runme.org is a repository of software art and, because software art has very few established subcategories, keywords for its classification are developed by those who submit artworks and use the site. The most used keywords become more central to the database. The artwork *Naked on Pluto* (2012) by Aymeric Mansoux, Marloes de Valk, and Dave Griffiths, for example, falls into the self-assigned category of "social software" and is tagged with the keywords "social – lisp – Facebook – ascii – Twitter – propaganda – human – criticism – apocalyptic – surveillance – open_source – friendly – community – anachronistic – story – multiuser – free_software – capitalism – 1980s." This artist-led approach bodes well for future metadata that fits the artwork, and might also be used for creating taxonomies for the behaviors of exhibitions as well as new media art in general.

The use of the same media systems for both interpretation and creation of art can, however, lead to complications for the documentation of exhibitions. The 1985 exhibition *Les Immatériaux*, curated by François Lyotard for the Pompidou Centre, Paris, for example, is relatively well known in theoretical and curatorial terms, yet it is still difficult to get an impression of what the actual experience of the show might have been. Installation shots of gallery-goers wearing headphones, and computer screens and keyboards tucked away in dark corners exist, but considerable further research is needed to find out, for example, whether the headphones were artwork or interpretation, or how the online discussion actually functioned (Dernie 2006, 72–73; Gere 2006, 18; Graham and Cook 2010, 19). This confusion between educational and art technologies is a particular issue for new media. These kinds of installation details make a huge conceptual difference for those who seek to establish histories of different exhibition types and illustrate how the documentation of exhibitions could inform the future installation of the work. It is no coincidence that exhibitions of conceptual or immaterial work have become good historical case studies for examining the relationship between exhibition forms and their behaviors, which in turn can be read in terms of subsequent new media affordances. Artist and curator Lucy Lippard, for example, with her expertise in dealing with the immateriality of art objects, carefully conceived of the "catalogs" for her Numbers Shows 1969–1974 as a series of printed cards which could rearranged at will by the audience and reflected an equality of status between the artists in the exhibitions: "The catalogues existed as informational content that could be sorted and used freely; they applied a predigital model, pre-empting something of the CD-ROM or web-based archive" (Butler 2012, 25). Database and taxonomical systems can therefore be related to both the form and function of exhibitions, but the concern for the experience of the audience also requires consideration of social systems.

Behaviors—Live, Social, Participative

> The Utopian vision for archives is of a participative, more representative model, which not merely represents the perspective of those in authority but also minority groups and interests. (Breakell 2010, 10)

As Staniszewski points out, issues surrounding exhibition histories have an impact on not just one kind of art medium, but on all media that share characteristics of interaction, because the presentation communicates the work, and the audience is key. As Breakell has identified more recently, the issue of participation (closely connected to that of interaction) in systems of archiving and historicizing is firmly connected to representation, social systems, power, and control. If, as outlined in the previous section, the participatory nature of new media database systems raises the fundamental question of who archives and collects, then the process of historicizing participatory and interactive art exhibitions brings up related issues (Graham 2014c).

The history of conceptual art exhibitions has been useful in informing the exhibition of interactive and participatory work of all media: the 1970 exhibition *Information* at MOMA in New York, curated by Kynaston McShine, was notable for the way in which McShine responded to conceptual art not only through new curatorial tools and methods, but also through the integration of ideas of interaction and participation. Hans Haacke's work *MoMA Poll* (1970) in that show, for example, was founded on active participation by the audience, who voted on political questions, with their votes being visible to all, in clear plastic posting boxes. These types of interaction and installation traditionally were the responsibilities of different departments within a museum, but were now brought together via artistic practice, and McShine planned the exhibition installation in collaboration with MoMA's production manager. The installation included several beanbags as audience seating, eschewing hard modernist benches and opening up the possibility for audience members to choose where to put them, to interact with each other, or engage in solitary contemplation of artworks (Staniszewski 1998, 270). Audience comfort is of course not always the first thing on artists' minds. It may be the work's intent to discomfort or provoke. For *Information* (1970), Stig Broegger designed wooden platforms that were placed in the gallery, and around public spaces in New York and New Jersey, and the exhibition included photographs of people's reactions to these objects—using them or watching others use them. A photograph from the MoMA archive of Curatorial Exhibition Files shows a platform placed between a rather short-sighted viewer and an artwork on a wall, with a caption reading, "One of Broegger's Platforms Frustrates a Viewer, So He Leans, 1970" (Lauder 2010, 103). The nature of what is documented is of obvious importance here.

The recent fascination with the relational—dialog, participation, and interaction—in art has also informed the debate on exhibition histories, albeit with some apparent confusion about the terms "interaction," "participation," and "collaboration," and especially who might be relating to what (Graham and Cook 2010, 116–117). Nevertheless, this debate has led to a welcome growth in the number of curators writing about the processes of events and exhibitions in discursive space, among them practitioners such as Harrell Fletcher whose experience with participatory projects includes both online and offline systems that are themselves collaboratively curated, such as *Learning to Love You More* (2004–) with Miranda July (Sanchez 2007; Fletcher 2013). What new media can offer to this literature are clear and useful ways of understanding relationships between artists, artworks, and audiences or participants, which can take forms similar to Paul Baran's diagrams of centralized, decentralized, and distributed networks. His diagrams of nodes and connections map out the way in which networks function, with many-to-many networks such as the Internet being "distributed" (Graham and Cook 2010, 58; Graham 2010; Graham 2015). Many curators have been explicitly informed by these concepts, including the NODE.London network, which organized a "no curator" mode of new media art festival where art events across London were organized by small "nodes" of groups or individuals who made events happen locally, and coordinated themselves into a festival using shared open media tools and joint publicity. NODE.London are admirably open about their processes, and honest about the hierarchies at play even in decentralized models (Graham and Cook 2010, 261).

As Breakell outlines in the opening quote of this section, these participatory systems have deeply political ramifications for audiences' access to art, collections, and histories. As Friedrich Kittler stated in 1997, databased new media can easily create the desire that "Visitors too—they especially—should be given access not just to lovingly presorted information but to all available information" (1996, 73). This perspective naturally leads on to considerations of what an exhibition is, whether on- or offline, and how exhibition installations can match the nature of the art itself.

Exhibitions for Behaviors

> I think all of us are interested in diminishing the hierarchy between the archive and collection for obvious reasons, but those hierarchies still do affect conditions that mean the archive will probably be less accessible to some scholars than the collection—it is certainly not accessible to the public. So I just want to ensure that we engage with that piece somehow through our collection, and that it is really accessible and present in how we're constructing that history. (Comer in Graham 2012)

Art usually is exhibited before it is collected and, if the art is to have a future, it will hopefully be exhibited and then re-exhibited from a collection. Stuart Comer, Curator of Film at Tate Modern, echoes Steve Dietz's point from 2005 concerning the fact that new media art might be found in the library, the archive, or the collection of an arts organization. Museums, after all, can mean various things when they describe collections of items as "display collection," "study collection," "archive," or "library." Curators of live art, film, and video might face a similar situation, and documentation might offer various models for reinstalling historical works. Given the hierarchies of power and accessibility involved, how does the audience get to access that collection in the form of public display? In 2012, The Tanks, a new wing of the Tate Modern building in London, opened to the public. The Tanks opens straight from the main Turbine Hall and has a particular remit to show work from the Tate collections. The combination of curators tasked with programming the space is of particular interest, comprising Film and Video, Performance, and Education. In exhibitions of work such as Lis Rhodes's *Light Music* (1975), for example, it was important to maintain the participatory intent. Suzanne Lacey's 1987 performance *The Crystal Quilt*—which now exists in the form of a video, documentary, quilt, photographs, and sound piece—was not displayed simply as documentation or as a stand-alone artist's video, but was carefully reinstalled, with the sound installation being shown in one of the atmospheric oil storage tanks. As Stuart Comer says in the brochure for The Tanks program at Tate Modern, "They are not merely performance documentation that can be played back at whim, but rather rely on a specific set of instructions to reanimate both the existing film or video material and the actions that attend it" (Comer 2012, 42). It is interesting to trace how curators at Tate Modern have been informed by the archived documentation and first-hand experience of past exhibitions. The Robert Morris retrospective *Bodyspacemotionthings*, installed in 1971 and 2009 at Tate Modern, has been widely discussed in relation to participation, and for good reasons. Interestingly, the exhibition was instigated by live art and intermedia art curators as part of *The Long Weekend* (2009), perhaps because the areas of live and intermedia art have a pronounced interest in and respect for audience's participatory behaviors as an inherent characteristic of the art forms (Graham 2010).

Curators might be used to the process of conceptualizing exhibitions in general, but there are still more specific aspects to consider if an installation needs to facilitate interaction. New media artworks that are "installed" only online and are "site-specific" to the World Wide Web must also be carefully considered in terms of their interactive behaviors; since the Internet is inherently interactive, net artists are well used to these considerations. Here new media is calling into question, as it often does, what actually defines an exhibition. The artist Anthony Antonellis has been able to use this factor in wittily satirizing the ambivalent nature of making and curating new media art within the inherently participatory context of the Internet. His web site *put it on a pedestal.com*, for example, enables the user to drag and drop those most lowly of new media artifacts, animated GIFs, onto the equally cheesy artworld pedestal of their choice (Figure 27.1). He also set up the *Endangered GIF Preserve* to save hapless animated GIFs that have been nominated for deletion from Wikipedia. Each GIF is marked with the date of rescue and a link to its original Wiki habitat. Antonellis is showing full awareness of the ambivalent power of audiences to curate their own Internet exhibitions, the joy of deletion and broken links, and the equal compulsion to save and mend.

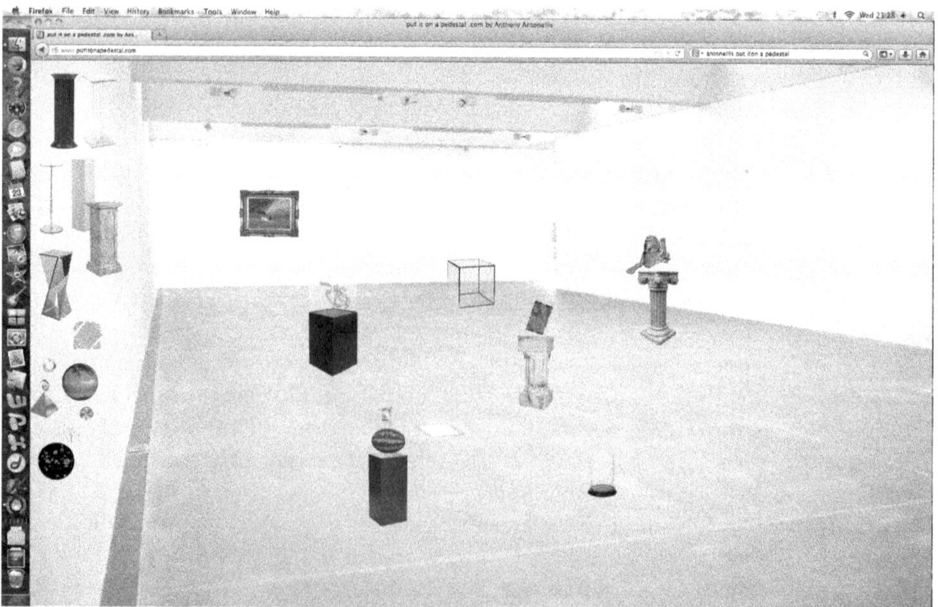

FIGURE 27.1 Screen shot from *put it on a pedestal.com*, Anthony Antonellis (2011). Reproduced by permission of Anthony Antonellis.

Interaction and participation are rather different systems from full collaborative co-production of exhibitions, but new media offers a very particular mode of "distributed" collaborative development—that of "open source" software. In this case many people contribute to creating the same product—the source code is available to all and written in such a way that the structure or "recipe" is open to other programmers/users for copying, improving, or adapting. The open source project Random Information Exchange (RIE) instigated by Dominic Smith in 2008, for example, invited members of the public to submit and exchange information on anything, from knitting and recipes to power generation. The project developed in the several "versions" characteristic of software production and existed both online and in various physical venues, with each physical installation, including a conference in Belfast and a gallery in New Zealand, fitted to the context and location. It is the artist who is in control of the exhibition installations in order to facilitate participation, and also in charge of the documentation of the work, in this case revealing the process and coding, in line with open source ethics. As Smith identified in his research, a key characteristic of the systems was the crediting of work, and in following as well as instigating exhibition ideas (Smith 2011; Graham 2014b).

Because of the history of new media—and its emphasis on process, social systems, and production methods—definitions of what might be "an exhibition" are a little more fluid, as are the boundaries between art and design. The question remains, however, how these diverse definitions of "exhibition" might be documented for future art historians.

Documenting Exhibitions ... and Audiences?

> [W]hat was wonderful to see was that we were learning through what people were posting online. We would see all kinds of documents come up either on Flickr or on YouTube and then say, "Wait a minute, what actually happened in the galleries?" (Frieling in Graham 2009)

If the documentation of exhibitions is what remains in the archives for future art historians, then it is of prime importance whether audiences are documented or documenting. For new media art, which is not yet well represented in collections, this issue is crucial. The artwork might be in a collection, but the exhibition itself is a temporary act. If documentation struggles to capture the artist's intent for the behavior of the artwork in an exhibition scenario, then it struggles even more to capture representative indications of the behaviors of audiences. If your exhibition encourages participation, then the simple factor of showing people in installation shots can at least indicate participatory intent. Carefully posed museum installation shots are one thing, but informal photos of the public in galleries is quite another. *The Art of Participation*, curated by Rudolf Frieling for SFMOMA in 2008, proved to be a learning experience for the institution. Previously, existing default restrictions on photography had been lifted, and the informal online documentation of this exhibition was considered to be not only a useful supplement to formal documentation, but also a way of feeding into documentation that might inform future "performances" of works from the collection (Frieling 2014).

Documentation, of course, is strongly related to issues of the conservation of artworks themselves, as Jon Ippolito points out: "Among the important questions for interactive behavior is whether traces of previous visitors should be erased or retained in future exhibitions of the work" (Ippolito 2003, 50). The restaging of the exhibition *When Attitudes Become Form: Bern 1969/Venice 2013* at the Prada Foundation in Venice in 2013 explicitly credits research at the Harald Szeemann collection and hundreds of photographs as facilitating the exhibition, indicating what kind of documentation might be most useful for building a history of exhibitions (Celant 2013). The 2010 book *Exhibiting the New Art: 'Op Losse Schroeven' and 'When Attitudes Become Form' 1969* provides a broad range of documentation, from formal and informal sources, covering process and product, enabling a comparison of documentation that might help to create a history of an exhibition and inform curators. The book includes floor plans, installation photographs by artists and curators, a chronology diary of curatorial process by Harald Szeemann, interviews with artists, and essays behind the scenes concerning marketing, sponsorship, and the press reception of the exhibitions (Rattemeyer et al. 2010). In this particular case, the approach to making histories of "new art" relates to conceptual art of the 1960s, but the methodologies would apply well to new media, or live art. What the collection of documents does not include, however, are any insights concerning the audiences themselves.

When audience studies in museum archives exist, they tend to be of the demographic kind most useful for the berating of arts organizations by funders and governments, so institutions might be reluctant to reveal them. As participation seems to be regarded a vaguely desirable aspect by politicians and funders, there is also the risk that documents such as press releases overstate the depth and scale of participation. Generally missing are documents that might help curators to understand how artwork behaviors might relate to audience behaviors, a set of relationships that is at the center of any participatory artwork. This is not, however, meant to advocate a "behaviorist," quantifiable approach to art: the research most useful to curators and artists might not concern conventional concepts of usability or comfort, but might explore different kinds of participation, such as the deliberate intent to frustrate demonstrated in Stig Broegger's platforms (Graham and Cook 2010, 182).

My own research in the 1990s sought both to establish methods of observation that would inform curators about solo and group interactions with art, and to integrate the existing tacit knowledge of artists into these interactions (Graham 1997). More recently, researcher and curator Lizzie Muller has conducted audience studies of interactive art that include documentation of complex audience experiences of interaction and recognize the importance of exploring the "experiential goals" of the artist. She worked with Caitlin Jones at the Daniel Langlois Foundation Centre for Research and Documentation to develop documentation of artworks by David Rokeby in ways intended to inform future artists and curators and to perhaps create an "oral history" of new media art (Jones and Muller 2008). As Rokeby's work is in many international art collections, this resource constitutes a large and deep independent body of documentation that may be beyond the means of individual institutions, but is accessible to any curator who might wish to re-exhibit the work in future contexts (Muller 2014). Muller's recent study of audience response to Anish Kapoor's sculptural work has been included in a public "living catalog" accompanying an exhibition of Kapoor's work at the Museum of Contemporary Art in Sydney. The catalog is available free as a download, and is added to during and after the exhibition; it points toward a future where the kinds of documentation supplementing collected works could also include records of audience experience (MCA 2013). Including the artist and the audience in the research process has been a key methodological shift toward taking participatory exhibitions seriously. When artists are engaged in studying audience behavior, they are able to integrate their own skills in working with space and time into their research. Rafael Lozano-Hemmer, for example, has made useful anecdotal observations on reactions to his participatory artworks in different countries and cultures, and ethnographic research on his public artwork *UnderScan* (2006–) yielded findings including interaction patterns that moved from observation to interaction and discussion between participants (Graham and Cook 2010, 183, 187). Online audience studies conducted by audiences themselves through crowdsourcing could complement formal research: the more audience members comment, tweet, and add their own oral histories, the more complex a picture of the audience might emerge for researchers. Artists, of course, have a practical interest in knowing how their audiences might behave, especially if their work is interactive. They also have a vested interest in ensuring that the documentation of their work is most useful for successful future exhibitions. If their work is informed by open source systems, as in the case of Dominic Smith's work, then the artists themselves can present excellent modes of documentation of their exhibitions.

The project *Invisible Airs* (2011) by YoHa, with assistance from Stephen Fortune, for example, was based on the expenditure database of Bristol City Council, which in theory at least was open to the public, according to the rhetoric of "open government." However, the data was extremely difficult to read and unlikely to reach any kind of public audience. "After attempting to read 20,000 comma-separated lines of apparently open-data, we understood that power revealed itself through boredom" (YoHa 2013). The artists decided to make interactive objects including a "riding machine"—a bicycle seat that pneumatically lurched the user up and down in response to higher or lower expenditure levels. The objects were placed in public places and dialogs with audience members were encouraged (Figure 27.2). A "Pneumatic Database Soiree" in the council chambers, which featured a lecture tracing the early formation of the database and its relation to power and governance and all five of the pneumatic machines, was also organized. Alistair Oldham independently produced a documentary of the project, which was informed by its processes of production, especially the workshops that took place as part of it. The web page of the project is explicitly aimed at cataloging resources that might be of use to others in investigating power, governance, and data, and presents plenty of documentation of audience use, including splendid photographs of the Lord Mayor of Bristol using the riding machine. The site also includes video of the pneumatic construction workshops and, in line with open source ethics, the code of both the original expenditure database, and the artists' software written for the works. In terms of taxonomies and critical vocabularies, the project clearly benefits from new media knowledge about audience, levels of interaction, and especially levels of openness—the site satirizes the rhetoric of "half-baked decentralized authority," which might gladden the heart of Paul Baran (YoHa 2013).

These examples illustrate that, when it comes to the documentation of exhibitions, both audiences and artists are actively working alongside the more traditional institutions, archivists, and historians. Whilst one kind of documentation does not replace the other, it can offer a triangulation of different kinds of documentation, which together might form a more complete picture of exhibitions. As has been pointed out

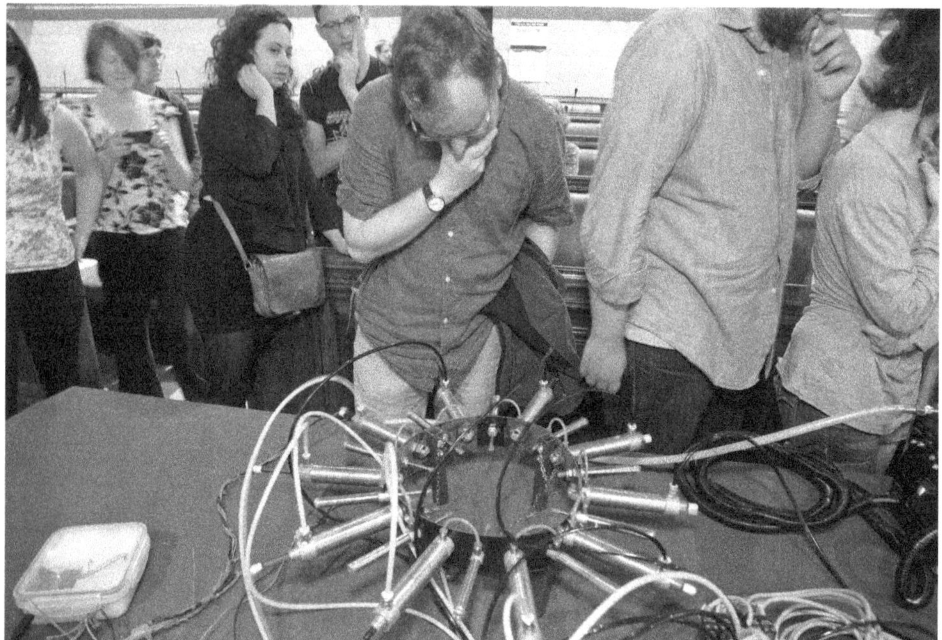

FIGURE 27.2 Viewers at *Invisible Airs* (2011) at Bristol City Council House. *Invisible Airs* was commissioned by The University of the West of England's Digital Cultures Research Centre (DCRC) in collaboration with the Bristol City Council's B-Open data project. Image reproduced by permission of Jamie Woodley, YoHa, Bristol City Council House.

by those including Jon Ippolito who further examines the roles of "amateurs" in this book, audiences are not only documenting but curating and taxonomizing (Graham and Cook 2010, 268; Graham 2013). Audiences are indeed so adept at surfing, tagging, and linking and using those links to "exhibit," that members of "surf clubs," such as Marisa Olson's *Nasty Nets*, create web-based work documenting and remixing their experiences online.[2] In these surf clubs there is little visible differentiation between artists, curators, geeks, or just regular web surfers. Surf clubs such as *Trail Blazers* include performative and competitive elements, offering opportunities to "show off your PRO surfing skills."[3] While this chapter does not cover this area in depth, the possibility for artist- and audience-created categories is one that potentially affects the new methods of art history discussed in the first section, with audiences not only providing documentation but also collectively identifying art "movements," a role that art historians have previously claimed for themselves.

Futures—Connected Modes of Documenting, Curating, and Historicizing?

> What emerges … is an emphasis on ways of being (referred to by Third Belgrade as "a strategy of behavior") and the qualities that institutions in the future ought to have; many of them suggesting generosity, active engagement and collaboration and

> a shift away from transactional or hierarchical relationships. The notion of an institution as a temporal as well as physical construct and how an institution might deal with the idea of time is also prevalent. (Ciric and Lai 2012, 21)

When contemporary art curators Biljana Ciric and Sally Lai asked artists and curators to consider what might be important for an *Institution for the Future*, Yoko Ono sagely advised: "Make sure the furniture is comfortable" (Ciric and Lai 2012, 15). This connection between philosophical strategies and the practicalities of exhibitions and audiences chimes with both Kynaston McShine's beanbags and the decentered or distributed network maps of new media. The key issue is that, without thorough histories of exhibitions, it will be difficult to judge factors of engagement or collaboration and hence inform future exhibitions and institutions. This chapter has given several examples of sources for different kinds of documentation, compiled by audiences or museums, which could be used for developing these histories. However, if these sources are to be brought together for intelligible histories, then theory and practice will need to be integrated, and the systems, methods, or modes of both art history and curating will need to understand each other. It could be argued that, since the same media are used for the creation of new media art itself and its documentation, archiving, and taxonomy, there already exists a shared system; however, there still are understandings to be resolved.

Within art institutions, the use of new media for archiving and for exhibition falls into different departments. Coming from a background in Museum Studies, Michelle Henning, however, suggests that "In my view, new media is most interesting for what it does to the hierarchies of knowledge in the museum, particularly in relation to the division between 'front and back regions' of the museum" (Henning 2010, 303). The divisions between medium-specific art forms, and between art and design, are challenged by the immateriality and medium-independent behaviors of various kinds of new media art, in particular by the behaviors of interactivity and participation. New media artist G.H. Hovagimyan also points out a possible overlap between archiving and exhibiting in the role of an individual curator:

> I would suggest that a curator especially a net art curator should become an instigator of a process that is open ended. To my mind this means setting up a loose structure that allows for maximum creativity and then inviting individuals to do something. You organize the material after the event occurs. In this way you are an archivist more than a curator. This is already somewhat of the default process on the web. What has not occurred is the next step which is the analysis and presentation of webmaterial in real life. That is the exciting part. (Hovagimyan 2007)

As Hovagimyan states, modes of collection are indissolubly linked to modes of display and, in the case of new media's particular behaviors, highlight a tension between the roles of collector, curator, and archivist along different points on a timeline. Modes of collection are strongly linked to the intent behind what is to be collected, by whom, and how. Individual artists and curators also need to make a choice in deciding how much of the exhibition-making process to make public. As Alexa Farber identifies, there is a growing demand for, and some response to, an idea of "openness" that works against curators' tendency to keep exhibition processes behind a velvet curtain until opening night, but fully aligns with new media ideologies of "open source" work processes (Farber 2007). Researchers at CRUMB[4] in the UK have long appreciated new media art curators' blogs, such as Barbara London's *Stir Fry* blog for MoMA, which caused some institutional concern in 1997. In 2011, however, Paola Antonelli's blog for the *Talk to Me* exhibition at the same museum was able to include useful details of the exhibition-making process, among them the discussion of works that were researched but ultimately not included in the exhibition, which would have been institutionally unthinkable a decade before. During an online discussion curator Amanda McDonald Crowley testified that is it useful for her to be able to "share the research I am doing on a particular topic that will lead to curatorial projects," using blogs, platforms such as scoop.it or delicio.us or any new media tool designed for sharing (MoMA 2011; Howard 2013; McDonald Crowley 2013).

There are an encouraging number of examples of institutions that are documenting processes, and developing modes of working that connect and integrate the network of issues surrounding the commissioning, collection, exhibition, and historicization of art. *Current: An Experiment in Collecting Digital Art*, for example, is a partnership between the Harris Museum and Art Gallery and folly in the UK that comprised an exhibition, acquisition, documented public debate, and audience considerations, presented as a practical case study in a wider research project. Lindsay Taylor of the Harris Museum and Art Gallery, Preston, maps the relationships that need to be established to both exhibit and collect new media art over a long period of time. In her case, the processes require a deep involvement of curators, exhibition organizers, collection committees, artists, and technicians. She found that a series of exhibitions and educational events helped to build both institutional and audience confidence in creating a collection of innovative work. The acquisition of work from a larger exhibition involved a panel of experts external to the museum and also the consideration of audience feedback on the exhibited work. The Museum decided to acquire *The distance travelled through our solar system this year and all the barrels of oil remaining* (2011) by Thomson & Craighead, and the artwork has since been exhibited again, which tested the efficacy of the documentation strategies, and has led to the commissioning of new artwork at the museum (Taylor 2014).

As Lindsay Taylor of the Harris Museum and Art Gallery pointed out, the basic problem that needed to be resolved in order to collect new media art was how to define the work on collection management systems that did not recognize the terminology related to it. These taxonomical issues are also slowly being addressed by differentiating between the critical vocabularies relating to digital, electronic, software, interactive, or participatory characteristics of new media art (Laurenson 2014; Smithsonian Institute 2013). There have been indications that museums' acquisition systems are capable of considering whole exhibitions if existing taxonomical structures can be adapted. When the Van Abbemuseum acquired a version of the exhibition *No Ghost Just a Shell*—instigated by artists Philippe Parreno and Pierre Huyghe and including work by other artists—the collection of an exhibition rather than an artwork presented problems because the database would only accept single artworks. This systemic problem was solved by creating special "work sets" in the collections management system that created a link between individual works, and by allowing the person entering the data to designate one inventory number to the project as a whole (Saaze 2013, 175).

If taxonomies, databases, and metadata can change, then perhaps the methods of art history also can. As discussed here, new media systems radically change notions of *who* historicizes, but can also have other effects. As outlined in the book *New Collecting* (2014), edited by Beryl Graham, underlying economic systems often fundamentally control which artworks are commissioned, exhibited, collected, and hence historicized, often putting any immaterial or new art form at a disadvantage. Lev Manovich suggests that the reason for the lack of a museum for cultural software in Silicon Valley is primarily an economic one: the companies there do not derive any profits from old software, and the software industry therefore does nothing to promote its history. This stands in contrast to art economics where at least some "new" art becomes a legitimate investment category, or to mainstream media economics where Hollywood continues to receive profits from old movies as it reissues them in new formats (Manovich 2013, 38). At the same time there is a growing number of examples showing that new media art, even immaterial software, is being collected, and that alternative economic modes, such as those suggested by Jonas Lund's web site *The Paintshop* (1212–), are viable. What the markets for new media art and contemporary art have in common is that the more famous the artist, the higher the price. The artist Jonas Lund satirized this golden rule in his participatory web site and exhibition *The Paintshop,* which allows people to use a digital painting tool in order to create a square painting that becomes part of a bigger patchwork of images. The paintings can be purchased as a digital print online, and the price of each painting is calculated using the Paintshop Rank™ algorithm and updated daily. The algorithm calculates the popularity of the painting by online hits, adds the "stature" of the artists as measured by the artfacts.net website, *et voilà*: an automated, participatory exhibition and gallery calculated on the basis of artistic fame (Lund 2012; Graham 2014b).

Writing and publishing also affects the basic framework of art history through the selection of works to be included in publications and the way in which the publications are conceived. The financial reality of academic publishing tends to mean that books like Staniszewski's, beautifully illustrated with installation shots from museum archives, are relatively rare. The book *Rethinking Curating* (Graham and Cook 2010) faced a particular challenge in both the textual and visual research on curatorial processes for new media art exhibitions, and a deliberate choice was made to research images of exhibition installations. In order to build the resources for a possible history of exhibitions that involve participation, it would seem valuable to document as many sources as possible and include visual installation material, as well as information about audience experience, in particular. The research for a report on the exhibition *010101* at SFMOMA in 2001 involved talking to gallery guards, press staff, docents, and IT providers, researching archives and talking to curators to reflect how the history of the exhibition was embodied through the whole organization and beyond (Graham 2002). The curators themselves often are the ones who see the need for case studies of exhibition processes, as the inclusion of case studies such as the one of the *Serious Games* exhibition, amongst others, in the book *New Media in the White Cube and Beyond* illustrates (Graham 2008).

The new media systems of participation and crowdsourced documentation previously described here have made a polyvocal approach to histories easier and perhaps have made it more likely to shape methods across art forms. A recent book on European Fluxus Festivals, for instance, fully acknowledges that all histories, especially those of process-based immaterial art, are based on "contradictory accounts," so that people are encouraged to send "artists' and eyewitnesses' statements" and join a electronic mailing list so that updates can be sent (Stegmann 2013). If art history publications are showing some changes in method, then the practice of curating new exhibitions—which offer the full potential of rethinking exhibition histories and futures—should creatively rise to the challenge of the relative lack of technology and digital media histories. The "media archeology" approach forged by those concerned with media histories has born fruit in the form of exhibitions such as Kristoffer Gansing's *The Art of the Overhead Festival* (2009), an open call for artworks using that most "unsexy and anonymous" medium, the overhead projector, that resulted in a lively resuscitation of a "dead medium" (Gansing 2013, 235).

Sarah Cook has curated a number of exhibitions that questioned the traditional chronological structure of art history, including *The Art Formerly Known as New Media*, co-curated with Steve Dietz for the Banff New Media Institute's (BNMI) 10th anniversary in 2005. The exhibition featured existing and newly commissioned works by artists who had been in residence or attended events at the BNMI in the past, thereby visually tracing the current influence of an institution and its approach upon artistic production. The show avoided the basic chronological approach to works produced at Banff, which might be expected of an anniversary show, by also exhibiting works that were created some years after the residency. This encouraged viewers to both consider possibilities for future artworks and reflect on the past. In 2011, Cook, with input from Jean Gagnon, curated the exhibition *Q.E.D. quod erat demonstrandum* in Liverpool as part of the AND festival and the Rewire MediaArtHistories conference. The exhibition combined more recent works, such as Sascha Pohflepp and Daisy Ginsberg's model of the weather forecast, with older ones. These older projects raised issues shared by live art—such as exhibiting documentation of the work instead of or in addition to the work itself. Norman White and Laura Kikauka's *Them Fuckin' Robots* (1988), for example, is an early networked robotic art piece for which the artists created a male and a female robot, respectively, without any consultation in advance of the live networked performance of the two robots' encounter. The 2011 exhibition of this work included video documentation of the performance, still images of White lying on a couch and his male robot lying on the floor in a domestic setting, and schematics and notebooks of the robots' production diagrams. Although the exhibition did not comprise a live performance, the selected documentation thereby gave a lively representation of both the product and processes of the artwork—the robots are no longer performing live, but the project is still kicking. Many media art exhibitions face a similar challenge in having to exhibit from archives. Extensive collections and archives, such as the one at the Nam June Paik Center in Seoul, have been curated very creatively in order to retain a sense of "animation" and futurity. The exhibitions include an area with documentation and objects from Paik's production workshop, the archive is nicely designed to be as welcoming as possible for the public, and relevant new art, amongst it highly experimental live projects by young artists, is regularly commissioned—with all these aspects working toward ensuring the future of the work in dynamic exhibited forms (Graham 2014b).

The inclusion of documentation and process-based archival materials alongside actual objects in exhibitions reflects not only the issues raised by live art, as previously described by Tate Modern's Stuart Comer, but also the ones brought up by new media, which relate to systems of documentation for art and design. The exhibition *Patent Pending* (2013), curated by Jaime Austin for Zero1 in San Jose, for example, was explicitly informed both by modifications to US patent law in 2013, which changed the system from a first-to-invent to a first-to-file one, and by plans to open a

US Patent and Trademark Office in Silicon Valley. Artworks included *Blow Up* by Scott Snibbe (patent no. US6923079), which records, amplifies, and projects human breath. When visitors blow into a rectangular array of twelve small impellers, they electronically control a large wall of twelve electric fans that magnify their breathing patterns. A keen awareness of the relationships between art, exhibitions, and systems of documentation typically is a particular strength of new media art curators. The interdisciplinary crossovers between art and design greatly broaden the toolkit of historians in a field where the art and design historians, respectively, are often educated separately, and the former might not conceive of searching for art in patent databases.

It is worth noting that Kristoffer Gansing, Sarah Cook, Dominic Smith, and I are all curators who have been explicitly informed by doctoral research on curatorial practice. This research has necessarily led the curators to question their own methods of practice and how they relate to new media behaviors and systems. This in turn has resulted in a critical examination of art-historical methods in relation to new media art. Each of the curators has drawn from different methods and systems: Gansing from Guattari's sociocultural and Foucault's politico-governance "transversal" approaches; Cook from media theory, such as the writings of Kittler, or histories of technology and experimentation; Smith from economic-participatory open source ethics; and I myself from theories of interaction and audience (Gansing 2013, 79; Cook 2004; Smith 2011; Graham 1997). This range of approaches points to benefits for long-term practice-led research and possible future methods that may come from outside of strictly art-historical territory.

Within art-historical practice itself, doctoral researchers are also applying methods in new ways to address new media behaviors, an example being Charlotte Frost's work on new media art histories, which entails methodologies in which the writing and research mirror the behaviors of new media art. In a discussion of net art histories that Frost hosted on the CRUMB mailing list in 2013 (Frost 2013a), contributors debated the dangers of anecdotal approaches, the archiving of bulletin boards, mailing lists, MUDs and MOOs, as well as materiality, anthropology, filtering, online art galleries mimicking the real-world layouts of gallery/museum spaces, and the critical differentiations between levels of crowdsourcing histories (Frost 2013a). The author James Elkins notably writes art books that involve degrees of crowdsourcing, resulting in print publications that are very well referenced from sources including Facebook. He matches these methods to subjects that are open-ended and have no single authority. Elkins differentiates between his use of a site such as Academia.edu—which is very active and focused, has lots of visitors and downloads, but no participatory community—and Facebook, which involves plenty of participation, and posts that might wander off topic. Elkins states that the openness of the system does not create a big problem for his writing: among 5000 people, there might be "many people whose opinions are wild in relation to academia, or in relation to the art market, or in relation to modernism or postmodernism—but less than 10 or so who are non-social, solipsistic, fanatical, fundamentalist, or otherwise unproductive." What worries him more are the 100 or so art historians who "have strong disciplinary allegiances, and they don't like to post, or be 'seen,' on unserious sites like Facebook" (Elkins in Frost 2013b). The CRUMB mailing list discussion also debated who, from which discipline, might be doing the curating, exhibiting, criticism, archiving, or historicizing, which reiterates the importance of interdisciplinary practice and methods, especially in educational institutions. As Charlie

Gere outlined in providing an example of a cross-media curriculum, "We start with the Wagnerian gesamtkunstwerk, and end with digital media realising Joseph Beuys' idea that 'Jeder [Mensch] ist ein Künstler' ('Everyone is an artist')" (Gere 2013). Since these two artists' ideas strongly relate to both artmaking and forms of exhibition, one could make an argument for rethinking all of the roles involved in the historicizing of exhibitions.

For art historians, tools such as cross-disciplinary research, distributed networks, and audience participation still might be "less respected," but they nevertheless are undeniably effective additions to their methodological toolkits. As program leader of a Master's in Curating, I am frequently called upon to rethink what kind of preparation future curators of all kinds of contemporary art might need; and the flexible methods informed by new media behaviors stand a good chance of meeting future challenges. If critical histories of participatory art are to be developed, then the writing of detailed exhibition histories that include audience roles is vital, and new media's understandings of participatory systems have much to offer to the future.

Notes

1 *The Archive of Digital Art*, formerly *The Database of Virtual Art*. https://www.digitalartarchive.at/ (accessed February 7, 2013).
2 http://archive.rhizome.org/artbase/53981/nastynets.com/ (accessed February 7, 2013).
3 http://nm.merz-akademie.de/trailblazers (accessed February 7, 2013).
4 CRUMB (Curatorial Resource for Upstart Media Bliss) is a resource for curators of new media, based at the University of Sunderland. http://www.crumbweb.org/ (accessed February 7, 2013).

References

Altshuler, Bruce. 2009. "Collection: Threads of Chance and Intention." In *A Manual: For the 21st Century Art Institution*, edited by Shamita Sharmacharja, 34–45. London: Wather Koenig.

Breakell, Sue. 2010. "For One and All: Participation and Exchange in the Archive." In *Revisualizing Visual Culture*, edited by Chris Bailey and Hazel Gardiner, 97–108. London: Ashgate.

Burnham, Jack. 1968. *Beyond Modern Sculpture*. London: Allen Lane/The Penguin Press.

Butler, Cornelia. 2012. "Women – Concept – Art: Lucy R. Lippard's Numbers Shows." In *From Conceptulism to Feminism: Lucy Lippard's Numbers Shows 1969–74*, Exhibition Histories series, edited by Cornelia Butler and other authors, 16–69. London: Afterall.

Celant, Germano, ed. 2013. *When Attitudes Become Form. Bern 1969/Venice 2013*. Milan: Progetto Prada Arte.

Ciric, Biljana, and Sally Lai, eds. 2012. *Institution for the Future*. Manchester: Chinese Arts Centre.

Comer, Stuart. 2012. "In Context: Projecting Memories of the Future." In *The Tanks Programme Notes*, edited by Charles Danby, 42–43. London: Tate.

CONT3XT.NET (Sabine Hochrieser, Michael Kargl, Franz Thalmair). 2007. "Visualising work.flows and (filtering)processes–." In *circulating contexts CURATING MEDIA/NET/ART*, edited by *CONT3XT.NET*, 54–59. Norderstedt: Books on Demand GmbH. Also available from: http://cont3xt.net/blog/?p=370.

Cook, Sarah. 2004. "The Search for a Third Way of Curating New Media Art: Balancing Content and Context In and Out of the Institution." PhD thesis, University of Sunderland.

CRUMB. 2008. *Documenting New Media Art Seminar*, March 5. http://www.crumbweb.org/getPresentation.php?presID=44 (accessed February 12, 2013).

CRUMB. 2012. *Collecting New Media Art Theme Jul 2012. CRUMB Discussion List Edits.* http://www.crumbweb.org/discussionArchive.php?&sublink=2 (accessed February 12, 2013).

CRUMB and CAS. 2010. *Commissioning and Collecting Variable Media Conference.* March 5, Newcastle, BALTIC. http://www.crumbweb.org/getSeminarDetail.php?id=14 (accessed February 12, 2013).

Dernie, David. 2006. *Exhibition Design.* London: Laurence King.

Dietz, Steve. 1999. "Why Have There Been No Great Net Artists?" *Through the Looking Glass: Critical Texts.* http://www.voyd.com/ttlg/textual/dietz.htm (accessed February 12, 2013).

Dietz, Steve. 2005. "Collecting New Media Art: Just Like Anything Else, Only Different." In *Collecting the New: Museums and Contemporary Art*, edited by Bruce Altshuler, 85–101. Princeton, NJ: Princeton University Press. http://www.yproductions.com/writing/archives/000764.html (accessed February 12, 2013).

Farber, Alexa. 2007. "Exposing Expo: Exhibition Entrepreneurship and Experimental Reflexivity in Late Modernity." In *Exhibition Experiments*, edited by Sharon Macdonald and Paul Basu, 219–239. London: Wiley-Blackwell.

Fletcher, Harrell. 2013. "Localizing the Traveling Exhibition." *The Exhibitionist* 7 (January): 60–64.

Frieling, Rudolf. 2014. "The Museum as Producer: Processing Art and Performing a Collection." In *New Collecting: Exhibiting and Audiences after New Media Art*, edited by Beryl Graham, 135–158. London: Ashgate.

Frohne, Ursula, Mona Schieren, and Jean-Francois Guiton, eds. 2005. *Present Continuous Past(s): Media Art. Strategies of Presentation, Mediation and Dissemination.* Vienna: Springer-Verlag.

Frost, Charlotte. 2013a. "[NEW-MEDIA-CURATING] October's theme: Art History Online, an introduction. October 1 2013 11:53:01 GMT+01:00." *New-Media-Curating Discussion List.* Available from http://www.jiscmail.ac.uk/lists/new-media-curating.html.

Frost, Charlotte. 2013b. "[NEW-MEDIA-CURATING] James Elkins on writing art history online. October 16 2013 23:27:04 GMT+01:00." *New-Media-Curating Discussion List.* http://www.jiscmail.ac.uk/lists/new-media-curating.html (accessed February 12, 2013).

Gere, Charlie. 2013. "Re: [NEW-MEDIA-CURATING] what's art history got to do with it? 10 October 2013 09:03:57." *New-Media-Curating Discussion List.* http://www.jiscmail.ac.uk/lists/new-media-curating.html (accessed February 12, 2013).

Gansing, Kristoffer. 2013. *Transversal Media Practices.* Published PhD thesis. Malmö: Malmö University. http://dspace.mah.se/bitstream/handle/2043/15246/Gansing%20KS%20muep_ny.pdf (accessed February 12, 2013).

Graham, Beryl. 1997. "A Study of Audience Relationships with Interactive Computer-Based Visual Artworks in Gallery Settings, through Observation, Art Practice, and Curation." PhD thesis, University of Sunderland. http://www.sunderland.ac.uk/~as0bgr/cv/sub/phd.htm (accessed February 7, 2013).

Graham, Beryl. 2002. "Curating New Media Art: SFMOMA and 010101." http://www.crumbweb.org/getCRUMBReports.php?&sublink=2 (accessed February 7, 2013).

Graham, Beryl. 2008. "Serious Games – Case Study." In *New Media in the White Cube and Beyond: Curatorial Models for Digital Art*, edited by Christiane Paul, 191–206. Berkeley, CA: University of California Press.

Graham, Beryl. 2009. "An Interview with Rudolf Frieling." *CRUMB*. http://www.crumbweb.org/getInterviewDetail.php?id=34 (accessed February 7, 2013).

Graham, Beryl. 2010. "What Kind of Participative System? Critical Vocabularies from New Media Art." In *The "Do-it-Yourself" Artwork: Participation from Fluxus to New Media*, edited by Anna Dezeuze, 281–305. Manchester: Manchester University Press.

Graham, Beryl. 2012. "Interview with Stuart Comer. Tate Tanks, and Collecting." *CRUMB*. http://www.crumbweb.org/getInterviewDetail.php?id=38 (accessed February 7, 2013).

Graham, Beryl. 2013. "Exhibition Histories and New Media Behaviours." *Journal of Curatorial Studies* 2(2): 242–262.

Graham, Beryl, ed. 2014a. *New Collecting: Exhibiting and Audiences after New Media Art*. London: Ashgate.

Graham, Beryl. 2014b. "Modes of Collecting." In *New Collecting: Exhibiting and Audiences after New Media Art*, edited by Beryl Graham, 29–55. London: Ashgate.

Graham, Beryl. 2014c. "Histories of Interaction and Participation: Critical Systems from New Media Art." In *Performativity in the Gallery: Staging Interactive Encounters*, edited by Outi Remes, Laura MacCulloch, and Marika Leino, 65–83. Oxford: Peter Lang.

Graham, Beryl. 2015. "Open and Closed Systems: New Media Art in Museums and Galleries." In *Museum Media: Handbook of Museum Studies Series*, edited by Michelle Henning, 449–472. London: Wiley-Blackwell.

Graham, Beryl, and Sarah Cook. 2010. *Rethinking Curating: Art After New Media*. Cambridge, MA: The MIT Press.

Henning, Michelle. 2010. "New Media." In *A Companion to Museum Studies*, edited by Sharon Macdonald, 302–318. Blackwell Companions in Cultural Studies. Chichester, UK: Wiley Blackwell.

Hovagimyan, G.H. 2007. "Processes of the List." *CONT3XT.NET*. Wed. June 13 15:08:06 CEST. http://cont3xt.net/blog/?p=370 (accessed February 7, 2013).

Howard, Lindsay. 2013. "The Way We Share: Transparency in Curatorial Practice." *New-Media-Curating Discussion List*. http://www.jiscmail.ac.uk/lists/new-media-curating.html (accessed March 8, 2013).

Ippolito, Jon. 2003. "Accommodating the Unpredictable: The Variable Media Questionnaire." In *Permanence Through Change: The Variable Media Approach*, edited by Alain Depocas, Jon Ippolito, and Caitlin Jones. New York: Guggenheim Museum. http://www.variablemedia.net/e/preserving/html/var_pub_index.html, pp. 47–54 (accessed February 7, 2013).

Jones, Caitlin, and Muller, Lizzie. 2008. "The Giver of Names: Documentary Collection." *Daniel Langlois Foundation, Centre for Research and Documentation*. http://www.fondation-langlois.org/html/e/page.php?Repere=200812&NumPage=2121 (accessed February 7, 2013).

Kittler, Friedrich. 1996. "Museums on the Digital Frontier." In *The End(s) of the Museum*, edited by John Hanhardt, 67–80. Barcelona: Fondacio Antoni Tapies.
Lauder, Adam. 2010. "Executive Fictions: Revisiting Information." MA thesis, Concordia University, Montreal. http://spectrum.library.concordia.ca/6900/1/Lauder_MA_F2010.pdf (accessed February 7, 2013).
Laurenson, Pip. 2014. "Old Media, New Media? Significant Difference and the Conservation of Software Based Art." In *New Collecting: Exhibiting and Audiences after New Media Art*, edited by Beryl Graham, 73–95. London: Ashgate.
Lund, Jonas. 2012. *The Paintshop*. http://thepaintshop.biz/ (accessed February 7, 2013).
Manovich, Lev. 2013. *Software Takes Command*. London: Bloomsbury Academic.
MCA, ed. 2013. *Anish Kapoor ePublication*. Sydney: MCA Publications. http://www.mca.com.au/apps/mca-publications/anish-kapoor-epublication/ (accessed February 7, 20130.
McDonald Crowley, Amanda. 2013. "Re: [NEW-MEDIA-CURATING] The Way We Share: Transparency in Curatorial Practice." *New-Media-Curating Discussion List*. http://www.jiscmail.ac.uk/lists/new-media-curating.html (accessed February 7, 2013).
MoMA. 2011. "Talk to Me | Our Process." http://wp.moma.org/talk_to_me/about/our-process/ (accessed February 12, 2013).
Mondloch, Kate. 2010. *Screens: Viewing Media Installation Art*. Minneapolis: University of Minnesota Press.
Muller, Lizzie. 2014. "Collecting Experience: The Multiple Incarnations of Very Nervous System." In *New Collecting: Exhibiting and Audiences after New Media Art*, edited by Beryl Graham, 183–202. London: Ashgate.
Rattemeyer, Christian, et al. 2010. *Exhibiting the New Art: "Op Losse Schroeven" and "When Attitudes Become Form" 1969*. London: Afterall.
Reiss, Julie H. 1999. *From Margin to Center: The Spaces of Installation Art*. Cambridge, MA: The MIT Press.
Saaze, van, Vivian. 2013. "Case Study: No Ghost Just a Shell by Pierre Huyghe, Philippe Parreno, and Many Others." In *Preserving and Exhibiting Media Art: Challenges and Perspectives, Framing Film 4*, edited by Vinzenz Hediger, Barbara Le Maitre, Julia Noordegraaf, and Cosetta Saba, 172–177. Chicago, IL: University of Chicago Press.
Sanchez, Marisa. 2007. "Tell Me Your Story: An Interview with Artist Harrell Fletcher." In *Searching for Art's New Publics*, edited by Jeni Walwin, 79–90. Bristol: Intellect.
Shanken, Edward A. 2007. "Historicizing Art and Technology: Forging a Method and Firing a Cannon." In *MediaArtHistories*, edited by Oliver Grau, 43–70. Cambridge, MA: The MIT Press.
Smith, Dominic. 2011. "Models of Open Source Production Compared to Participative Systems in New Media Art." PhD thesis, University of Sunderland, UK.
Smithsonian Institution Time-Based Media Art (TBMA) Working Group, interview by Crystal Sanchez. 2013. "Beryl Graham Interview." *Report on the Status and Need for Technical Standards in the care of Time-Based Media and Digital Art*. Washington DC: Smithsonian. http://www.si.edu/tbma/projects (accessed February 7, 2013).
Stalder, Felix. 2010. "Property, Possession and Free Goods Social Relationships as the Core of a New Economy of Immaterial Culture?" In *Owning Online Art – Selling And Collecting Netbased Artworks*, edited by Markus Schwander and Reinhard Storz, 75–88.

Basle: FHNW. http://www.ooart.ch/publikation/02.php?m=1&m2=2&lang=e (accessed February 7, 2013).

Staniszewski, Mary Anne. 1998. *The Power of Display: A History of Exhibition Installations at the Museum of Modern Art.* Cambridge, MA: The MIT Press.

Stegmann, Petra, ed. 2013. "The Lunatics Are on the Loose …" *European Fluxus Festivals 1962–1977.* Potsdam: Down with Art!

Taylor, Lindsay. 2014. "From Exhibition to Collection: Harris Museum and Art Gallery." In *New Collecting: Exhibiting and Audiences after New Media Art*, edited by Beryl Graham,111–134. London: Ashgate.

YoHa. 2013. *Invisible Airs | YoHa.* http://yoha.co.uk/invisible (accessed February 12, 2013).

Index

Figures are represented in italics

A Companion to Digital Art, First Edition. Edited by Christiane Paul.

Printed in the USA
CPSIA information can be obtained
at www.ICGtesting.com
LVHW081523181023
760988LV00002B/2